HANGŬL-

Simple Vowels	(v... si	
아 a (father)	애 ... (hat)	
야 ya (yard)	얘 yae (yam)	
어 ŏ (hut)	에 e (met)	
여 yŏ (yearn)	예 ye (yes)	
오 o (home)	외 oe (Köln)	와 wa (wan) 왜 wae (wag)
요 yo (yoke)		
우 u (do)	위 wi (wield)	워 wŏ (won) 웨 we (wet)
유 yu (you)		
으 ŭ (taken)	의 ŭi (taken + we)	
이 i (ink)		

The "o" written with each vowel is an unvoiced consonant which functions to indicate where an initial consonant maybe affixed to the vowel when writing a syllable. See the inside back cover for information on forming syllables.

STANDARD
ENGLISH-KOREAN
DICTIONARY

for Foreigners

Romanized

Edited by B. J. Jones

www.hollym.com

HOLLYM

Standard English-Korean Dictionary

First Published in 1982
Revised edition, 1985
Fourteenth printing, 2000
by Hollym International Corp.
18 Donald Place, Elizabeth, NJ 07208, U.S.A.
Phone: (908)353-1655   Fax: (908)353-0255
http://www.hollym.com

Published simultaneously in Korea
by Hollym Corporation; Publishers
13-13 Kwanchol-dong, Chongno-gu
Seoul 110-111, Korea
Phone: (02)735-7551~4   Fax: (02)730-5149, 8192
http://www.hollym.co.kr

ISBN: 0-930878-21-3
Library of Congress Catalog Card Number: 85-84204

Printed in Korea

Preface

There has been a growing demand, particularly among foreigners, of a new comprehensive English-Korean dictionary. It is our intention to meet this need for those who wish, as foreigners, to understand and speak Korean. The dictionary contains over 12,000 entry words more than any other English-Korean dictionary for foreigners in Korea. Special efforts were made to select more useful words and to take most commonly used meaning in English for the equivalent Korean word.

The McCune-Reischauer system, favored by many publishers, was adopted. Thus, Korean equivalents for selected English words were romanized in the context of McCune-Reischauer system, with a few exceptions to avoid the complexity of the system.

One of the most important features of this dictionary is the detailed and yet simplified explanation of words. English idioms and proverbs were used in illustrative sentences for those commonly used entries. The user will find that each entry word contains English synonyms with English pronunciation of Korean word.

The editor wishes to express a special appreciation to the people for their tireless assistance and suggestions which made this publication available to the public.

B. J. Jones

Korean Alphabet I

	ㄱ k(g)	ㄴ n	ㄷ t(d)	ㄹ r(l)	ㅁ m	ㅂ p(b)	ㅅ s(sh)
ㅏ a	가 k(g)a	나 na	다 t(d)a	라 r(l)a	마 ma	바 p(b)a	사 sa
ㅑ ya	갸 k(g)ya	냐 nya	댜 t(d)ya	랴 r(l)ya	먀 mya	뱌 p(b)ya	샤 sya
ㅓ ŏ	거 k(g)ŏ	너 nŏ	더 t(d)ŏ	러 r(l)ŏ	머 mŏ	버 p(b)ŏ	서 sŏ
ㅕ yŏ	겨 k(g)yŏ	녀 nyŏ	뎌 t(d)yŏ	려 r(l)yŏ	며 myŏ	벼 p(b)yŏ	셔 syŏ
ㅗ o	고 k(g)o	노 no	도 t(d)o	로 r(l)o	모 mo	보 p(b)o	소 so
ㅛ yo	교 k(g)yo	뇨 nyo	됴 t(d)yo	료 r(l)yo	묘 myo	뵤 p(b)yo	쇼 syo
ㅜ u	구 k(g)u	누 nu	두 t(d)u	루 r(l)u	무 mu	부 p(b)u	수 su
ㅠ yu	규 k(g)yu	뉴 nyu	듀 t(d)yu	류 r(l)yu	뮤 myu	뷰 p(b)yu	슈 syu
ㅡ ŭ	그 k(g)ŭ	느 nŭ	드 t(d)ŭ	르 r(l)ŭ	므 mŭ	브 p(b)ŭ	스 sŭ
ㅣ i	기 k(g)i	니 ni	디 t(d)i	리 r(l)i	미 mi	비 p(b)i	시 shi

Korean Alphabet II

ㅇ ng	ㅈ ch(j)	ㅊ ch'	ㅋ k'	ㅌ t'	ㅍ p'	ㅎ h
아 a	자 ch(j)a	차 ch'a	카 k'a	타 t'a	파 p'a	하 ha
야 ya	쟈 ch(j)ya	챠 ch'ya	캬 k'ya	탸 t'ya	퍄 p'ya	햐 hya
어 ŏ	저 ch(j)ŏ	처 ch'ŏ	커 k'ŏ	터 t'ŏ	퍼 p'ŏ	허 hŏ
여 yŏ	져 ch(j)yŏ	쳐 ch'yŏ	켜 k'yŏ	텨 t'yŏ	펴 p'yŏ	혀 hyŏ
오 o	조 ch(j)o	초 ch'o	코 k'o	토 t'o	포 p'o	호 ho
요 yo	죠 ch(j)yo	쵸 ch'yo	쿄 k'yo	툐 t'yo	표 p'yo	효 hyo
우 u	주 ch(j)u	추 ch'u	쿠 k'u	투 t'u	푸 p'u	후 hu
유 yu	쥬 ch(j)yu	츄 ch'yu	큐 k'yu	튜 t'yu	퓨 p'yu	휴 hyu
으 ŭ	즈 ch(j)ŭ	츠 ch'ŭ	크 k'ŭ	트 t'ŭ	프 p'ŭ	흐 hŭ
이 i	지 ch(j)i	치 ch'i	키 k'i	티 t'i	피 p'i	히 hi

The Korean Alphabet
and Their Sounds

(1) Vowels

1) Simple:

Korean Letter	Romanization	English sound
ㅏ 아	a	as *ah*
ㅓ 어	ŏ	as h*u*t
ㅗ 오	o	as *oh*
ㅜ 우	u	as d*o*
ㅡ 으	ŭ	as tak*e*n
ㅣ 이	i	as *i*nk
ㅐ 애	ae	as h*a*nd
ㅔ 에	e	as m*e*t
ㅚ 외	oe	as K*ö*ln

2) Compound:

Korean Letter	Romanization	English sound
ㅑ 야	ya	as *y*ard
ㅕ 여	yŏ	as *y*earn
ㅛ 요	yo	as *y*oke
ㅠ 유	yu	as *you*
ㅒ 애	yae	as *y*am
ㅖ 예	ye	as *y*es
ㅟ 위	wi	as *wi*eld
ㅢ 의	ŭi	as taken+*we*
ㅘ 와	wa	as *wa*n
ㅙ 왜	wae	as *wa*g
ㅝ 워	wo	as *wo*n
ㅞ 웨	we	as *we*t

(2) Consonants

1) Simple:

Korean Letter	Romanization	English sound
ㄱ	k (g)	as *k*ing or g*rocer
ㄴ	n	as *n*ame
ㄷ	t (d)	as *t*oy or *d*epend
ㄹ	r (l)	as *r*ain or *l*ily
ㅁ	m	as *m*other
ㅂ	p (b)	as *p*in or *b*ook
ㅅ	s (sh)	as *s*peech
ㅇ	ng	as *ah* or ki*ng*
ㅈ	ch (j)	as *J*ohn
ㅊ	ch'	as *ch*ur*ch*
ㅋ	k'	as *k*ite
ㅌ	t'	as *t*ank
ㅍ	p'	as *p*um*p*
ㅎ	h	as *h*igh

2) Double:

Korean Letter	Romanization	English sound
ㄲ	kk	as s*k*y or Ja*ck*
ㄸ	tt	as s*t*ay
ㅃ	pp	as s*p*y
ㅆ	ss	as e*ss*ential
ㅉ	tch	as *j*oy

A Comprehensive Chart for the Romanization of the Korean Language

I Consonants (Showing euphonic changes in consonant sequences within words.)

Final \ Initial	ㄱ ㅋ ㄲ ㄳ ㄺ — K	ㄴ — N	ㄷ — T	ㄹ (R) — (R)	ㅁ — M	ㅂ — P	ㅅ — S	ㅈ ㅊ — CH CH'	ㅋ — K'	ㅌ — T'	ㅍ — P'	ㅎ — H	ㄲ — KK	ㄸ — TT	ㅃ — PP	ㅆ ㅉ — SS TCH
ㄱ,ㅋ,ㄲ,ㄳ,ㄺ — K		ng-		ngn ng-	ng-							k'	kk			
ㄴ — N	n-g			ll												
ㄷ,ㅅ,ㅈ,ㅊ,ㅌ,ㅆ — N		(nn)					ns-	-ch'				t'		tt		ss tch
ㅎ — N-	-k'	n-	-t'	-l		-b	s-	-ch'								
ㄶ — N-		(nn)														
ㄹ (verb) ㄼ, ㄾ — L	-g	ll	-l			-b	(-p')									
ㄹ (noun) — L							ls-	ls- ch'				r-				
ㄼ, ㄽ — L							s-	-ch'				r-				
ㄻ — L		(nn) n-														
ㅁ, ㄻ (noun) — M			-d -n	-n		-b	ms-	-j								
ㅁ, ㄻ (verb) — M	-g		-d -n	-n		-b		-j								
ㅂ, ㅍ, ㄼ, ㅄ — P		m-			mn m-							p'			pp	
ㅇ — NG	-g		-d -n	-n		-b		-j								
ㅇ (+ㅅ) — NG				-n												
ㅎ —	t'	n- (nn) n-					s-	ch'						(tt)		(tch)

II Vowels

ㅏ	ㅑ	ㅓ	ㅕ	ㅗ	ㅛ	ㅜ	ㅠ	ㅡ	ㅣ	ㅘ	ㅝ	ㅐ	ㅔ	ㅚ	ㅟ	ㅢ	ㅙ	ㅞ	ㅒ	ㅖ
a	ya	ŏ	yŏ	o	yo	u	yu	ŭ	i	wa	wo	ae	e	oe	wi	ŭi	wae	we	yae	ye

Simplified Chart for the Romanization

	Final	ㄱ	ㄴ	ㄹ	ㅁ	ㅂ	ㅇ
Initial		K	N	L	M	P	NG
ㅇ		g	n	r	m	b	ng
ㄱ	K	kk	n-g(k)	lg(k)	mg(k)	pk	ngg(k)
ㄴ	N	ngn	nn	ll	mn	mn	ngn
ㄷ	T	kt	nd(t)	lt(d)	md(t)	pt	ngd(t)
ㄹ	(R)	ngn	ll	ll	mn	mn	ngn
ㅁ	M	ngm	nm	lm	mm	mm	ngm
ㅂ	P	kp	nb(p)	lb(p)	mb(p)	pp	ngb(p)
ㅅ	S	ks	ns	ls	ms	ps	ngs
ㅈ	CH	kch	nj(ch)	lj(ch)	mj(ch)	pch	ngj(ch)
ㅊ	CH'	kch'	nch'	lch'	mch'	pch'	ngch'
ㅋ	K'	kk'	nk'	lk'	mk'	pk'	ngk'
ㅌ	T'	kt'	nt'	lt'	mt'	pt'	ngt'
ㅍ	P'	kp'	np'	lp'	mp'	pp'	ngp'
ㅎ	H	k'	nh	rh	mh	p'	ngh

Guidelines for the Romanization of Korean

(1) Basic Principles for Transcription

1) Romanization is based on standard Korean pronunciation.
2) No symbols except Roman letters are used, so far as possible.
3) Romanization follows the principle of 'one letter (or set of letters) per phoneme.'

(2) Summary of the Transcription System

1) Vowels are transcribed as follows:

simple vowels ㅏ ㅓ ㅗ ㅜ ㅡ ㅣ ㅐ ㅔ ㅚ
                a ŏ o u ŭ i ae e oe

diphthongs ㅑ ㅕ ㅛ ㅠ ㅒ ㅖ ㅢ ㅘ ㅝ ㅙ ㅞ ㅟ
          ya yŏ yo yu yae ye ŭi wa wo wae we wi

[Note] Long vowels are not marked in transcription.

2) Consonants are transcribed as follows:

plosives (stops)	ㄱ	ㄲ	ㅋ
	k, g	kk	k'
	ㄷ	ㄸ	ㅌ
	t, d	tt	t'
	ㅂ	ㅃ	ㅍ
	p, b	pp	p'
affricates	ㅈ	ㅉ	ㅊ
	ch, j	tch	ch'
fricatives	ㅅ	ㅆ	ㅎ
	s, sh	ss	h

nasals	ㅁ	ㄴ	ㅇ
	m	n	ng

liquids	ㄹ
	r, l

[Note 1] ㄱ, ㄷ, ㅂ and ㅈ are transcribed respectively as *g*, *d*, *b* and *j*, between
vowels, or between ㄴ, ㄹ, ㅁ, or ㅇ
and a vowel; otherwise they are transcribed as *k, t, p,* and *ch.*

e.g. 가구 kagu 바둑 paduk 갈비 kalbi
제주 Cheju 담배 tambae 받침 patch'im

[Note 2] ㅅ is transcribed as *s* except in the case
of 시, when it is transcribed as *sh.*

e.g. 시루 shiru 신안 Shinan 신촌 Shinch'on
부산 Pusan 상표 sangp'yo 황소 hwangso

[Note 3] ㄹ is transcribed as *r* before a vowel,
and as *l* before a consonant or at the
end of a word: ㄹ ㄹ is transcribed as *ll.*

e.g. 사랑 sarang 물건 mulgŏn 발 pal
진달래 chindallae

(3) Special Provisions for Transcription

1) When Korean sound values change as in the
following cases, the results of those changes
are transcribed as follows:

1. The case of assimilation of adjacent consonants

e.g. 냇물 naenmul 부엌문 puŏngmun
낡는다 nangnŭnda 닫는다 tannŭnda
갔는다 kamnŭnda 진리 chilli
심리 shimni 압력 amnyŏk

　　　　독 립 tongnip
2. The case of the epenthetic ㄴ and ㄹ
　　e.g. 가랑잎 karangnip　낮 일 nannil
　　　　담 요 tamnyo　　홑이불 honnibul
　　　　풀 잎 p'ullip　　물 약 mullyak
3. The case of palatalization
　　e.g. 굳 이 kuji　　　해돋이 haedoji
　　　　같 이 kach'i
4. The case when ㄱ, ㄷ, ㅂ and ㅈ are adjacent
　　to ㅎ
　　e.g. 국 화 kuk'wa　　낳 다 nat'a
　　　　밟히다 palp'ida　　맞히다 mach'ida
〔Note〕 The tense (or glottalized) sounds, which
　　occur in cases when morphemes are
　　compounded as in the examples below,
　　are transcribed by voiceless consonants.
　　e.g. 장기 (長技) changki 사 건 sakŏn
　　　　냇 가 naetka　　작 두 chaktu
　　　　신 다 shinta　　산 불 sanpul
2) When there is a possibility of confusion in
pronunciation, or a need for segmentation, a
hyphen '-' may be used.
　　e.g. 연 구 yŏn-gu　　잔기 (殘期) chan-gi
　　　　물가에 mulka-e　종로에 Chongno-e
〔Note〕 In the transcription of personal names
　　and names of administrative units,
　　assimilated sound changes before or
　　after a hyphen are not transcribed.
　　e.g. 김복남 Kim Pok-nam
　　　　사북면 Sabuk-myŏn
3) The first letter is capitalized in proper names.
　　e.g. 인 천 Inch'ŏn　대 구 Taegu

세 종 Sejong

4) Personal names are written by family name first, followed by a space and then the given name. A hyphen will separate given names, except that non-Sino-Korean given names may be joined without a hyphen.

    e.g. 김정호 Kim Chŏng-ho
        남궁 동자 Namgung Tong-cha
        손 미희자 Son Mi-hŭi-cha
        정 마리아 Chŏng Maria

5) In spite of the Note to 2) above, administrative units such as 도, 시, 군, 구, 읍, 면, 리, 동 and 가 are transcribed respectively as *do*, *shi*, *gun*, *gu*, *ŭp*, *myŏn*, *ri*, *dong*, and *ga* and are preceded by a hyphen.

    e.g. 충청북도 Ch'ungch'ŏngbuk-do
        제 주 도 Chĕju-do
        의정부시 Ŭijŏngbu-shi
        파 주 군 P'aju-gun
        도 봉 구 Tobong-gu
        신 창 읍 Shinch'ang-ŭp
        주 내 면 Chunae-myŏn
        인 왕 리 Inwang-ri
        당 산 동 Tangsan-dong
        봉천 2동 Pongch'ŏn 2-dong
        종로 2 가 Chongno 2-ga
        퇴계로 5 가 T'oegyero 5-ga

[Note] Terms for administrative units such as 특별시, 직할시, 시, 군, 읍 and so on may be omitted.

    e.g. 부산직할시 Pusan   신창읍 Shinch'ang

6) Names of geographic features, cultural prop-

erties, and man-made structures may be written
without hyphens.

e.g. 남　산 Namsan
속리산 Songnisan
금　강 Kŭmgang
독　도 Tokto
해운대 Haeundae
경복궁 Kyŏngbokkung
도산서원 Tosansŏwon
불국사 Pulguksa
현충사 Hyŏnch'ungsa
독립문 Tongnimmun

[Note] Hyphens may be inserted in words of
five syllables or more.

e.g. 금동 미륵보살 반가상 Kŭmdong-mirŭk-
posal-pan-gasang

7) Some proper names, which cannot be abruptly
changed in view of international practices and
common longstanding transcriptions, may be
written as follows:

e.g. 서 울 Seoul　　　이순신 Yi Sun-shin
연 세 Yonsei　　　이 화 Ewha
이승만 Syngman Rhee

8) When they are difficult to print or to type-
write, the breve '˘' in ŏ, ŭ, yŏ, and ŭi, and
the apostrophe '’' in k', t', p', and ch', may
be omitted as long as there is no confusion in
meaning.

◄─◅ A ►─►

a *art.* not normally used in Korean.—*a book* ch'aek 책 /*a dog* kae 개 ; When *a* means each, it may be translated by *han* 한 or *il* 일 : ~ *week* il chu-il 일 주 일 ; (*a certain*) ŏ-ddŏn 어떤.

abacus *n.* chu-p'an 주판.

abalone *n.* chŏn-bok 전복.

abandon *v.* pŏ-ri-da 버리다, p'o-gi-ha-da 포기하다.

abate *v.* ① (*decrease*) ppae-da 빼다, kam-ha-da 감하 다. ② (*weaken*) yak-hae-ji-da 약해지다.

abbess *n.* yŏ-ja tae-su-do-wŏn-jang 여자 대수도원장.

abbey *n.* tae-su-do-wŏn 대수도원.

abbot *n.* tae-su-do-wŏn-jang 대수도원장.

abbreviate *v.* (*words*) saeng-ryak-ha-da 생략하다 ; (*shorten*) chu-ri-da 줄이다.

abbreviation *n.* saeng-ryak 생략, (*word*) yak-ŏ 약어.

abdicate *v.* mul-rŏ-na-da 물러나다 ; pŏ-ri-da 버리다.

abdomen *n.* pae 배, pok-bu 복부.

abduct *v.* yu-goe-ha-da 유괴하다.

abet *v.* sŏn-dong-ha-da 선동하다, ch'u-gi-da 추기다.

abhor *v.* mop-si si-rŏ-ha-da 몹시 싫어하다.

abide *v.* mŏ-mu-rŭ-da 머무르다 ; sal-da 살다. 「수완가」

ability *n.* nŭng-ryŏk 능력 : *a man of* ~ su-wan-ga

abject *adj.* ch'ŏn-bak-han 천박한, pi-ch'am-han 비참한.

able *adj.* hal su it-nŭn 할 수 있는, yu-nŭng-han 유능한.

abnormal *adj.* i-sang-han 이상한, pyŏn-ch'ik-ŭi 변칙의.

aboard *adv. & prep.* (*on board*) …ŭl t'a-go …을 타고.

abode *n.* chu-so 주소, kŏ-ch'ŏ 거처.

abolish *v.* p'ye-ji[ch'ŏl-p'ye]-ha-da 폐지[철폐]하다.

abolition *n.* p'ye-ji 폐지, ch'ŏl-p'ye 철폐.

A-bomb *n.* (*atomic bomb*) wŏn-ja-p'ok-t'an 원자폭탄.

abominable *adj.* chi-gŭt-ji-gŭt-han 지긋지긋한, chi-dok-han 지독한, chi-gyŏ-un 지겨운.

aboriginal *adj.* t'o-ch'ak-ŭi 토착의. —*n.* t'o-ch'ak-min 토착민.

abortion *n.* yu-san 유산(流産).

abound *v.* p'ung-bu-ha-da 풍부하다.

about *prep.* (*concerning*) …e tae-ha-yŏ …에 대하여. —*adv.* ① (*approximately*) yak 약. ② (*around*) chu-wi-e 주위에. 「wi-ŭi 위의.

above *prep.* …wi-e …위에. —*adv.* wi-ro 위로. —*adj.*

abridge *v.* (*shorten*) yo-yak-ha-da 요약하다.

abroad *adv.* hae-oe-e 해외에 ; nŏl-li 널리.

abrogate *v.* p'ye-ji-ha-da 폐지하다. 「뜻밖의.

abrupt *adj.* kap-jak-sŭ-rŏ-un 갑작스러운, ttŭt-ba-ggŭi

abscess *n.* pu-sŭ-rŏm 부스럼.

absence *n.* kyŏl-sŏk 결석, pu-jae 부재(不在).

absent *adj.* kyŏl-sŏk-han 결석한. —*v.* kyŏl-sŏk-ha-da 결석하다, kyŏl-gŭn-ha-da 결근하다.

absent-minded *adj.* mŏng-ha-go it-nŭn 멍하고 있는.

absolute *adj.* chŏl-dae-ŭi 절대의, chŏn-je-jŏk 전제적.

absolutely *adv.* chŏl-dae-ro 절대로.

absolution *n.* sa-myŏn 사면. 「면하다.

absolve *v.* yong-sŏ-ha-da 용서하다, sa-myŏn-ha-da 사

absorb *v.* hŭp-su-ha-da 흡수하다.

abstain *v.* chŏl-je-ha-da 절제하다, sam-ga-da 삼가다.

abstinence *n.* chŏl-je 절제 ; kŭm-ju 금주(禁酒).

abstract *adj.* ch'u-sang-jŏk-in 추상적인. —*n.* ch'u-sang 추상 ; (*summary*) chŏk-yo 적요(摘要).

absurd *adj.* (*unreasonable*) pul-hap-ri-han 불합리한 ; (*foolish*) ŏ-i-ŏp-nŭn 어이없는.

abundance *n.* p'ung-bu 풍부, yun-t'aek 윤택.

abundant *adj.* p'ung-bu-han 풍부한, man-ŭn 많은.

abuse *n.* (*of authority*) nam-yong 남용 ; (*verbal*) mo-yok 모욕. —*v.* (*revile*) mo-yok-ha-da 모욕하다 ; (*misuse*) nam-yong-ha-da 남용하다.

abusive *adj.* ip-jŏng sa-na-un 입정 사나운, yok-ha-nŭn 욕하는 : *use ~ language* yok-ŭl ha-da 욕을 하다.

acacia *n.* a-k'a-si-a 아카시아.

academy *n.* hak-sul-wŏn 학술원, a-k'a-de-mi 아카데미 ; (*school*) hak-wŏn 학원 ; (*society*) hak-hoe 학회.

accede *v.* tong-ŭi-ha-da 동의하다. 「가속(加速)하다.

accelerate *v.* ppa-rŭ-ge ha-da 빠르게 하다, ka-sok-ha-da

accent *n.* aek-sŏn-t'ŭ 액센트, kang-se 강세.

accept *v.* pat-a-dŭ-ri-da 받아들이다, pat-da 받다.

acceptable *adj.* su-rak-hal man-han 수락할 만한, ma-ŭm-e tŭ-nŭn 마음에 드는, man-jok-han 만족한.

access *n.* ① (*approach*) chŏp-gŭn 접근. ② (*admittance*) ch'u-rip 출입. ③ (*entrance*) ip-gu 입구.

accessary·accessory *n.* pu-sok-p'um 부속품, aek-se-sŏ-ri 액세서리. —*adj.* po-jo-jŏk-in 보조적인.

accessible *adj.* ka-gga-i-hal su it-nŭn 가까이할 수 있는.

accession *n.* (*reaching*) to-dal 도달 ; (*enthronement*) chŭk-wi 즉위 ; (*acquisition*) ch'wi-dŭk 취득.

accident *n.* ① (*unexpected event*) sa-go 사고. ② (*chance*) u-yŏn 우연 : *by ~* u-yŏn-hi 우연히.

accidental *adj.* u-yŏn-han 우연한, ttŭt-ba-ggwi 뜻밖의.

accidentally *adv.* u-yŏn-hi 우연히.

acclaim *v.* hwan-ho-ha-da 환호하다 ; oe-ch'i-da 외치다.

accommodate *v.* (*admit*) su-yong-ha-da 수용하다 ; (*adapt*) chŏk-ŭng-si-k'i-da 적응시키다. 「숙소.

accommodation *n.* chŏk-ŭng 적응 ; (*lodgings*) suk-so

accompaniment *n.* pu-su-mul 부수물 ; (*music*) pan-ju

반주. 「da 동반하다.

accompany v. ham-gge ka-da 함께 가다, tong-ban-ha-

accomplice n. kong-bŏm-ja 공범자.

accomplish v. i-ru-da 이루다, wan-sŏng-ha-da 완성하다.

accomplishment n. sŏng-ch'wi 성취, wan-sŏng 완성.

accord n. il-ch'i 일치. —v. il-ch'i-ha-da 일치하다.

according adv. ~ to ~e tta-ra ···에 따라.

accordingly adv. kŭ-rŏ-mŭ-ro 그러므로. 「코오디언.

accordion n. son-p'ung-gŭm 손풍금, a-k'o-o-di-ŏn 아

account v. kye-san-ha-da 계산하다 ; ···i-ra-go saeng-gak-ha-da ···이라고 생각하다. —n. kye-san 계산.

accountant n. hoe-gye-sa 회계사, kye-ri-sa 계리사.

accumulate v. ch'uk-jŏk-ha-da 축적하다.

accuracy n. (*correctness*) chŏng-hwak 정확, (*precision*) chŏng-mil-do 정밀도. 「정밀한.

accurate adj. chŏng-hwak-han 정확한, chŏng-mil-han

accusation n. ① (*indictment*) ko-bal 고발. ② (*blame*) pi-nan 비난, hil-ch'aek 힐책.

accuse v. ko-bal-ha-da 고발하다, pi-nan-ha-da 비난하다.

accustom v. ik-hi-da 익히다, sŭp-gwan-dŭ-ri-da 습관들

ace n. e-i-sŭ 에이스, u-su-sŏn-su 우수선수. 「이다.

ache v. a-p'ŭ-da 아프다. —n. a-p'ŭm 아픔.

achieve v. i-ru-da 이루다, tal-sŏng-ha-da 달성하다.

achievement n. ① sŏng-ch'wi 성취, tal-sŏng 달성. ② (*merit*) kong-jŏk 공적, ŏp-jŏk 업적.

acid adj. sin 신. —n. san 산(酸). 「ha-da 감사하다.

acknowledge v. ① in-jŏng-ha-da 인정하다. ② kam-sa-

acorn n. to-t'o-ri 도토리. 「알리다.

acquaint v. ···ŭl ch'in-hi al-da ···을 친히 알다, al-ri-da

acquaintance n. a-nŭn sa-i 아는 사이, ch'in-ji 친지.

acquiesce v. muk-in-ha-da 묵인하다.

acquire v. ŏt-da 얻다, sŭp-dŭk-ha-da 습득하다.

acquit v. ① mu-joe-ro ha-da 무죄로 하다, pang-myŏn-ha-da 방면(放免)하다. ② (*pay*) kap-da 갚다.

acre n. e·i·k'ŏ 에이커 ; (*pl.*) non-bat 논밭.

acrid adj. mae-un 매운, (*bitter*) ssŭn 쓴.

acrobat n. kok-ye-sa 곡예사, kwang-dae 광대.

across prep. & adv. kŏn-nŏ-sŏ 건너서.

act v. haeng-ha-da 행하다. —n. (*deed*) haeng-wi 행위 ; (*law*) pŏp-ryŏng 법령, cho-rye 조례 ; (*scene*) mak 막.

acting adj. ① chak-yong-ha-nŭn 작용하는. ② (*substitute*) tae-ri-ŭi 대리의 : *the ~ chairman* ŭi-jang sŏ-ri 의장 서리(署理).

action n. ① haeng-dong 행동, haeng-wi 행위. ② (*play*) yŏn-gi 연기(演技).

active adj. ① hwal-dong-jŏk-in 활동적인, hwal-bal-han 활발한. ② chŏk-gŭk-jŏk-in 적극적인.

activity n. hwal-dong 활동, hwal-yak 활약.

actor n. nam(-bae)-u 남(배)우.

actress n. yŏ(-bae)-u 여(배)우.   「현행의.

actual adj. sil-je-ŭi 실제의 ; (*present*) hyŏn-haeng-ŭi

acute adj. nal-k'a-ro-un 날카로운, mo-jin 모진.

adapt v. (*fit*) chŏk-ŭng-si-k'i-da 적응시키다.

add v. tŏ-ha-da 더하다.

addict v. ppa-ji-ge ha-da 빠지게 하다.

addition n. pu-ga 부가(附加) ; tŏt-sem 덧셈.   「가세.

additional adj. ch'u-ga-ŭi 추가의 : *~ tax* pu-ga-se 부

address v. (*speak to*) yŏn-sŏl-ha-da 연설하다 ; (*letter*) chu-so sŏng-myŏng-ŭl ssŭ-da 주소 성명을 쓰다. —n. ① chu-so 주소. ② (*speech*) yŏn-sŏl 연설.

addressee n. su-sin-in 수신인, pat-nŭn-i 받는이.

adequate adj. ŏ-ul-ri-nŭn 어울리는, chŏk-dang-han 적당한 ; (*sufficient*) ch'ung-bun-han 충분한.

adhere v. tŭl-rŏ-but-da 들러붙다 ; ko-su-ha-da 고수하다.

adhesion *n.* pu-ch'ak 부착, ko-ch'ak 고착.

adhesive plaster pan-ch'ang-go 반창고.

adjacent *adj.* pu-gŭn-ŭi 부근의, in-jŏp-han 인접한.

adjective *n.* hyŏng-yong-sa 형용사.

adjoin *v.* chŏp-ha-da 접하다, in-jŏp-ha-da 인접하다.

adjourn *v.* (*put off*) yŏn-gi-ha-da 연기하다 ; (*recess*) hyu-hoe-ha-da 휴회하다. 「조정하다.

adjust *v.* chŏng-don-ha-da 정돈하다 ; cho-jŏng-ha-da

adjutant *n.* pu-gwan 부관.

adjutant general ko-gŭp pu-gwan 고급 부관.

administer *v.* (*superintend*) kam-dok-ha-da 감독하다, (*manage*) kwal-li-ha-da 관리하다.

administration *n.* ① haeng-jŏng 행정, t'ong-ch'i 통치. ② (*management*) kwal-li 관리, kyŏng-yŏng 경영.

administrator *n.* haeng-jŏng-gwan 행정관.

admirable *adj.* kam-t'an-hal man-han 감탄할 만한, hul-ryung-han 훌륭한, chang-han 장한.

admiral *n.* hae-gun-dae-jang 해군대장 ; che-dok 제독.

admiration *n.* kam-t'an 감탄, ch'ing-ch'an 칭찬.

admire *v.* kam-t'an-ha-da 감탄하다 ; (*praise*) ch'ing-ch'an-ha-da 칭찬하다.

admission *n.* ① (*school*) ip-hak 입학, (*theater etc.*) ip-jang 입장. ② (*fee*) ip-hak-gŭm 입학금.

admit *v.* ① (*let in*) tŭ-ri-da 들이다. ② (*recognize*) in-jŏng-ha-da 인정하다. ③ (*concede*) yang-bo-ha-da

admittance *n.* ip-jang(-hŏ-ga) 입장(허가). 「양보하다.

admonish *v.* t'a-i-rŭ-da 타이르다, kwŏn-go-ha-da 권고

admonition *n.* ch'ung-go 충고, kyŏng-go 경고. 「하다.

ado *n.* (*fuss*) so-dong 소동 ; (*trouble*) su-go 수고.

adolescence *n.* ch'ŏng-nyŏn-gi 청년기.

adopt *v.* (*accept*) ch'ae-yong[ch'ae-t'aek]-ha-da 채용〔채택〕하다 ; (*a son*) yang-ja-ro sam-da 양자로 삼다.

adopted son yang-ja 양자.

adoration *n.* chon-gyŏng 존경, sung-bae 숭배. 「하다.

adore *v.* sung-bae-ha-da 숭배하다, hŭm-mo-ha-da 흠모

adorn *v.* kku-mi-da 꾸미다, chang-sik-ha-da 장식하다.

adrift *adv.* p'yo-ryu-ha-yŏ 표류하여.

adroit *adj.* som-ssi-it-nŭn 솜씨있는, ki-min-han 기민한.

adulation *n.* a-ch'ŏm 아첨, a-yang 아양.

adult *n.* ŏ-rŭn 어른, sŏng-in 성인 : ~ *education* sŏng-in-gyo-yuk 성인교육. 「질을 저하시키다.

adulterate *v.* (*debase*) p'um-jil-ŭl chŏ-ha-si-k'i-da 품

adultery *n.* kan-t'ong 간통, kan-ŭm 간음.

advance *v.* (*move forward*) chŏn-jin-ha-da 전진하다 ; (*propose*) chu-jang-ha-da 주장하다 ; (*promote*) sŭng-jin-si-k'i-da 승진시키다. 「wi 전위(前衛).

advanced *adj.* chin-bo-han 진보한 : *an* ~ *guard* chŏn-

advantage *n.* i-ik 이익, yu-ri 유리(有利).

advantageous *adj.* yu-ri-han 유리한.

Adventism *n.* ye-su chae-rim-sŏl 예수 재림설.

adventure *n.* mo-hŏm 모험, mo-hŏm-dam 모험담.

adventurer *n.* mo-hŏm-ga 모험가, t'u-gi-sa 투기사.

adverb *n.* pu-sa 부사(副詞).

adversary *n.* (*enemy*) wŏn-su 원수, chŏk 적 ; (*opponent*) sang-dae 상대.

adverse *adj.* ① (*opposed*) pan-dae-ŭi 반대의. ② (*unfortunate*) pu-run-han 불운한 ; (*unfavorable*) pul-ri-han 불리한. ③ (*confronting*) tae-ŭng-ha-nŭn 대응

adversity *n.* yŏk-gyŏng 역경 ; ko-nan 고난. 「하는.

advertise *v.* kwang-go-ha-da 광고하다.

advertisement *n.* kwang-go 광고, kong-si 공시.

advice *n.* ch'ung-go 충고 ; (*information*) al-rim 알림.

advisable *adj.* ① kwŏn-hal man-han 권할 만한. ② (*wise*) hyŏn-myŏng-han 현명한.

advise v. ch'ung-go-ha-da 충고하다.

adviser n. cho-ŏn-ja 조언자, ko-mun 고문(顧問): *a legal* ～ pŏp-ryul ko-mun 법률 고문.

advocate v. ch'ang-do-ha-da 창도하다. —n.(*upholder*) ch'ang-do-ja 창도자; (*pleader*) pyŏl-lon-ja 변론자.

adz(e) n. son-do-ggi 손도끼, kka-ggwi 까뀌.

aerial adj. ① kong-gi-ŭi 공기의, ki-ch'e-ŭi 기체의.② kong-jung-ŭi 공중의: ～ *attack* kong-sŭp 공습.

aeroplane n. (*Brit.*) pi-haeng-gi 비행기.

afar adv. mŏl-ri 멀리, a-dŭk-hi 아득히.

affable adj. sang-nyang-han 상냥한.

affair n. (*business*) il 일; (*event*) sa-gŏn 사건.

affect v. yŏng-hyang-ŭl chu-da 영향을 주다.

affectation n. kku-mi-nŭn t'ae-do 꾸미는 태도, (*false show*) hŏ-sik 허식.

affection n. ① (*love*) ae-jŏng 애정. ② kam-jŏng 감정. ③ (*disease*) chil-byŏng 질병.

affectionate adj. ta-jŏng-han 다정한.

affectionately adv. chŏng-dap-ge 정답게. 「하다.

affirm v. hwak-ŏn-ha-da 확언하다, tan-jŏng-ha-da 단정

affix v. ch'ŏm-bu-ha-da 첨부하다, pu-ch'i-da 붙이다.

afflict v. koe-rop-hi-da 괴롭히다, kol-ri-da 곯리다.

affliction n. (*suffering*) ko-t'ong 고통; (*calamity*) chae-nan 재난. 「chu-da 주다.

afford v. …hal yŏ-yu-ga it-da …할 여유가 있다;(*give*)

affront n. (*open insult*) mo-yok 모욕. —v. mo-yok-ha-da 모욕하다, yok-bo-i-da 욕보이다.

afire adv. pul-t'a-go 불타고, hŭng-bun-ha-yŏ 흥분하여: *set* ～ t'a-o-rŭ-ge ha-da 타오르게 하다.

aflame adj. & adv. pul-t'a-ol-ra 불타올라.

afloat adj. ttŏ-it-nŭn 떠있는. —adv. sŏn[ham]-sang-e 선[함]상에; hae-sang-e 해상에.

afraid *adj.* mu-sŏ-wŏ-ha-nŭn 무서워하
는, u-ryŏ-ha-nŭn 우려하는.

A-frame *n.* chi-ge 지게.

after *adv.* (*behind*) twi-e 뒤에 ; (*time*)
hu-e 후에. — *prep.* ···ŭi twi-e ···의
twi-e. ㄴ뒤에.

afternoon *n.* o-hu 오후.

afterward(s) *adv.* hu-e 후에.

again *adv.* ta-si 다시, tto 또.

[chi-ge]

against *prep.* ···e pan(-dae)-ha-yŏ ···에 반(대)하여.

age *n.* ① (*years*) na-i 나이, yŏn-ryŏng 연령 : *middle
~* chung-nyŏn 중년. ② (*period*) yŏn-dae 연대(年代) :
the Atomic A~ wŏn-ja-ryŏk-si-dae 원자력시대.

aged *adj.* na-i-mŏk-ŭn 나이먹은, nŭl-gŭn 늙은.

agency *n.* ① tae-ri(-jŏm) 대리(점) : *a general ~*
ch'ong-dae-ri-jŏm 총대리점. ② (*of government*) ki-
gwan 기관. ㄴ협의 사항.

agenda *n.* ŭi-sa il-jŏng 의사 일정, hyŏp-ŭi sa-hang

agent *n.* tae-ri-in 대리인 : *secret ~* mil-jŏng 밀정.

aggravate *v.* ak-hwa-si-k'i-da 악화시키다.

aggregate *adj.* (*collective*) chip-hap-jŏk-in 집합적인 ;
(*total*) ch'ong-gye-ŭi 총계의.

aggression *n.* kong-gyŏk 공격 ; ch'im-ryak 침략.

aggressive *adj.* ch'im-ryak-jŏk 침략적. ㄴ하다.

aggrieve *v.* koe-rop-hi-da 괴롭히다, hak-dae-ha-da 학대

agile *adj.* (*deft*) min-ch'ŏp-han 민첩한 ; (*nimble*)
yŏng-ri-han 영리한. ㄴ뒤흔들다.

agitate *v.* sŏn-dong-ha-da 선동하다 ; twi-hŭn-dŭl-da

ago *adv.* (chi-gŭm-bu-t'ŏ) ··· chŏn-e (지금부터) ··· 전
에 : *ten years ~* sip-nyŏn chŏn 10년 전.

agony *n.* ko-min 고민, ko-t'ong 고통.

agrarian *adj.* t'o-ji-ŭi 토지의, nong-ŏp-ŭi 농업의.

agree *v.* tong-ŭi-ha-da 동의하다, ŭng-ha-da 응하다.

agreeable *adj.* ma-ŭm-e tŭ-nŭn 마음에 드는, (*willing*) k'wae-hi ŭng-ha-nŭn 쾌히 응하는.

agreement *n.* (*treaty*) hyŏp-yak 협약 ; (*assent*) tong-ŭi 동의 ; (*concord*) il-ch'i 일치. 「의.

agricultural *adj.* nong-ŏp-ŭi 농업의, nong-hak-ŭi 농학

agriculture *n.* nong-ŏp 농업 ; nong-hak 농학.

ague *n.* ① hak-jil 학질. ② o-han 오한(惡寒).

ahead *adv.* chŏn-bang-e 전방(前方)에, ap-jang-sŏ-sŏ 앞장서서. 「ryŏk 조력.

aid *v.* top-da 돕다, wŏn-jo-ha-da 원조하다. —*n.* cho-

aid-de-camp *n.* chŏn-sok pu-gwan 전속 부관.

ail *v.* koe-rop-hi-da 괴롭히다 ; pyŏng-dŭl-da 병들다.

ailment *n.* (*illness*) pyŏng 병.

aim *v.* kyŏ-nu-da 겨누다. —*n.* mok-jŏk 목적.

aimless *adj.* mok-jŏk-ŏp-nŭn 목적없는.

air *n.* ① (*atmosphere*) kong-gi 공기. ② (*open space*) kong-jung 공중. ③ (*manner*) t'ae-do 태도.

air base kong-gun ki-ji 공군 기지.

air conditioning naeng-nan-bang 냉난방.

airplane *n.* pi-haeng-gi 비행기.

airport *n.* kong-hang 공항(空港).

air pressure ki-ap 기압.

aisle *n.* (chwa-sŏk sa-i-ŭi) t'ong-ro (좌석 사이의) 통로.

akin *adj.* (*of kin*) tong-jok-ŭi 동족의 ; (*resembling*) yu-sa-han 유사한. 「민활하게.

alacrity *n.* min-hwal 민활 : *with* ∼ min-hwal-ha-ge

alarm *v.* (*frighten*) kkam-jjak nol-ra-ge ha-da 깜짝 놀라게 하다 ; (*warn*) wi-gŭp-ham-ŭl al-ri-da 위급함 을 알리다. —*n.* nol-ram 놀람, kyŏng-bo 경보.

alarm clock cha-myŏng-jong 자명종.

alarming *adj.* nol-ra-un 놀라운, wi-gŭp-han 위급한.

alas *int.* a-i-go 아이고, a-a 아아, sŭl-p'ŭ-da 슬프다.

album *n.* ael-bŏm 앨범, sa-jin-ch'ŏp 사진첩, u-p'yo-ch'ŏp 우표첩.

alcohol *n.* al-k'o-ol 알코올.

alcoholism *n.* al-k'o-ol chung-dok 알코올 중독.

alder *n.* o-ri-na-mu 오리나무. 「주.

ale *n.* maek-ju 맥주 : *bottled* ~ pyŏng-maek-ju 병맥

alehouse *n.* maek-ju-jip 맥주집, pi-ŏ ho-ol 비어 호올.

alert *adj.* chu-ŭi-gi-p'ŭn 주의깊은 ; chae-bba-rŭn 재빠른.

algebra *n.* tae-su-hak 대수학(代數學).

alibi *n.* al-ri-ba-i 알리바이.

alien *n.* oe-guk-in 외국인. —*adj.* oe-guk-in-ŭi 외국인의.

alienate *v.* mŏl-ri-ha-da 멀리하다, tta-dol-ri-da 따돌리다.

alight *v.* ① nae-ri-da 내리다, ha-ch'a-ha-da 하차하다.
② (*settle*) nae-ryŏ-an-da 내려앉다.

alike *adj.* (*like each other*) kkok tal-mŭn 꼭 닮은.
—*adv.* (*similarly*) pi-sŭt-ha-ge 비슷하게.

alive *adj.* ① (*living*) sa-ra-it-nŭn 살아있는. ② (*active*)
hwal-bal-han 활발한.

all *adj.* mo-dŭn 모든. —*n.* chŏn-bu 전부. —*adv.*
(*completely*) chŏn-hyŏ 전혀, t'ong-t'ŭ-rŏ 통틀어.

allege *v.* (*assert*) chu-jang-ha-da 주장하다 ; (*declare*)
sil-lip-ha-da 신립(申立)하다.

alleged *adj.* chu-jang-doen 주장된 ; i-rŭn-ba 이른바.

allegiance *n.* ch'ung-sŏng 충성, ch'ung-sil 충실.

alley *n.* (*path*) o-sol-gil 오솔길, (*back street*) twit-gol-mok 뒷골목.

alliance *n.* ① yŏn-hap 연합. ② tong-maeng-guk 동맹국.

alligator *n.* ak-ŏ 악어.

all-important *adj.* a-ju chung-yo-han 아주 중요한.

allot *v.* ① (*assign*) hal-dang-ha-da 할당하다, pun-bae-ha-da 분배하다. ② chi-jŏng-ha-da 지정하다.

allow *v.* (*permit*) hŏ-rak-ha-da 허락하다, (*grant*) chi-gŭp-ha-da 지급하다.

allowance n. ① (*share allotted*) il-jŏng-ryang 일정량. ② (*compensation*) su-dang 수당.

allude v. ŏn-gŭp-ha-da 언급하다, am-si-ha-da 암시하다.

allure v. kkoe-da 꾀다, yu-hok-ha-da 유혹하다. —*n.* mae-hok 매혹, (*charm*) ae-gyo 애교.

allusion n. am-si 암시, ŏn-gŭp 언급.

ally n. tong-maeng-guk 동맹국. —*v.* tong-maeng-ha-da 동맹하다, che-hyu-ha-da 제휴하다.

almanac n. tal-ryŏk 달력 ; yŏn-gam 연감.

almighty adj. chŏn-nŭng-ŭi 전능의 ; tae-dan-han 대단한. —*n.* (*God*) chŏn-nŭng-ŭi sin 전능의 신.

almost adv. kŏ-ŭi 거의, tae-ch'e-ro 대체로. 「함.

alms n. ŭi-yŏn-gŭm 의연금 : ~ box cha-sŏn-ham 자선

aloft adv. wi-ro 위로 ; (*high up*) no-p'i 높이.

aloha int. an-nyŏng! 안녕 !

alone adj. hol-ro-ŭi 홀로의. —*adv.* hol-ro 홀로.

along prep. & adv. tta-ra-sŏ 따라서.

aloud adv. k'un so-ri-ro 큰 소리로, so-ri-no-p'i 소리높

alphabet n. al-p'a-bet 알파벳. 「이.

alphabetically adv. al-p'a-bet sun-ŭ-ro 알파벳 순으로.

alpine adj. no-p'ŭn san-ŭi 높은 산의 ; (*A*~) al-p'ŭ-sŭ san-ŭi 알프스 산의 : an ~ club san-ak-hoe 산악회.

alpinist n. tŭng-san-ga 등산가.

already adv. pŏl-ssŏ 벌써, i-mi 이미.

also adv. yŏk-si 역시, ma-ch'an-ga-ji-ro 마찬가지로.

altar n. che-dan 제단(祭壇).

alter v. pyŏn-gyŏng-ha-da 변경하다, pa-ggu-da 바꾸다.

alteration n. pyŏn-gyŏng 변경, kae-jo 개조.

alternate v. kyo-dae〔kyo-ch'e〕-ha-da 교대〔교체〕하다.

alternation n. kyo-dae 교대, kyo-ch'e 교체.

alternative n. yang-ja-t'aek-il 양자택일.

although conj. pi-rok …il-ji-ra-do 비록 …일지라도.

altitude *n.* no-p'i 높이, ko-do 고도 ; hae-bal 해발.

altogether *adv.* (*entirely*) chŏn-hyŏ 전혀, (*in all*) t'ong-t'ŭ-rŏ 통틀어 ; (*on the whole*) tae-ch'e-ro 대체로.

aluminium *n.* al-ru-mi-nyum 알루미늄.

alumnus *n.* cho-rŏp-saeng 졸업생, tong-ch'ang-saeng 동창생 ; ~ *association* tong-ch'ang-hoe 동창회.

always *adv.* hang-sang 항상, ŏn-je-na 언제나. 「하다.

amalgamate *v.* hap-dong[hap-byŏng]-ha-da 합동[합병]

amass *v.* ① (*pile up*) ssa-t'a 쌓다, (*accumulate*) ch'uk-jŏk-ha-da 축적하다. ② (*collect*) su-jip-ha-da 수 「집하다.

amateur *n.* a-ma-t'yu-ŏ 아마튜어.

amaze *v.* nol-ra-ge ha-da 놀라게 하다.

amazement *n.* nol-ra-um 놀라움, kyŏng-ak 경악.

amazing *adj.* nol-ra-un 놀라운, koeng-jang-han 굉장한.

ambassador *n.* tae-sa 대사(大使).

amber *n.* ho-bak 호박. 「an-ŭn 분명치 않은.

ambiguous *adj.* ae-mae-han 애매한, pun-myŏng-ch'i

ambition *n.* (*strong desire*) ya-mang 야망, ung-ji 웅지, p'o-bu 포부.

ambitious *adj.* ya-sim-jŏk-in 야심적인 : *Boys, be* ~ ! So-nyŏn-dŭl-i-yŏ tae-mang-ŭl ka-jyŏ-ra! 소년들이여, 대망을 가져라 ! 「앰뷸런스.

ambulance *n.* ku-gŭp-ch'a 구급차, aem-byul-rŏn-sŭ

ambush *n.* cham-bok 잠복, pok-byong 복병. —*v.* mae-bok-ha-da 매복(埋伏)하다.

amen *int.* a-men 아멘.

amend *v.* ko-ch'i-da 고치다, su-jŏng-ha-da 수정하다.

amendment *n.* su-jŏng 수정, kyo-jŏng 교정.

amends *n.* pae-sang 배상, pŏl-ch'ung 벌충.

America *n.* mi-guk 미국, a-me-ri-k'a 아메리카.

American *adj.* mi-guk-ŭi 미국의. —*n.* ① (*person*) mi-guk-in 미국인. ② (*language*) mi-guk-ŏ 미국어.

amiable *adj.* (*lovable*) kwi-yŏm-sŏng-it-nŭn 귀염성있는, sa-rang-sŭ-rŏ-un 사랑스러운.

amicable *adj.* u-ho-jŏk-in 우호적인, on-hwa-han 온화한.

amid(st) *prep.* ···ŭi ka-un-de ···의 가운데.

ammonia *n.* am-mo-ni-a 암모니아.

ammunition *n.* t'an-yak 탄약, kun-su-p'um 군수품.

amnesty *n.* t'ŭk-sa 특사(特赦), tae-sa 대사(大赦): *general* ~ il-ban sa-myŏn 일반 사면.

among(st) *prep.* ka-un-de 가운데. 「반한.

amorous *adj.* ho-saek-ŭi 호색의 ; (*enamoured*) pan-han

amour *n.* chŏng-sa 정사(情事), mil-t'ong 밀통.

amount *n.* (*altogether*) ch'ong-gye 총계 ; (*quantity*) aek-su 액수, yang 양(量). —*v.* i-rŭ-da 이르다, toe-da

ample *adj.* ch'ung-bun-han 충분한. 「되다.

amplifier *n.* aem-p'ŭ 앰프, hwak-sŏng-gi 확성기.

amplify *v.* hwak-dae-ha-da 확대하다 ; (*more details*) sang-se-hi sŏl-myŏng-ha-da 상세히 설명하다.

amputate *v.* chŏl-dan-ha-da 절단하다, chal-ra-nae-da

amputation *n.* chŏl-dan 절단. 「잘라내다.

amulet *n.* pu-jŏk 부적(符籍), aek-mak-i 액막이.

amuse *v.* chae-mi-na-ge ha-da 재미나게 하다.

amusement *n.* (*enjoyment*) hŭng 흥 ; (*entertainment*) o-rak 오락. 「거운.

amusing *adj.* chae-mi-it-nŭn 재미있는, chŭl-gŏ-un 즐

an *art.* not normally used in Korean. —(*one*) han 한, (*a certain*) ŏ-ddŏn 어떤.

anachronism *n.* si-dae ch'ak-o 시대 착오.

an(a)emia *n.* pin-hyŏl-jŭng 빈혈증.

analogy *n.* (*similarity*) yu-sa 유사, yu-ch'u 유추.

analyse·analyze *v.* pun-hae〔pun-sŏk〕-ha-da 분해〔분석〕

analysis *n.* pun-hae 분해, pun-sŏk 분석. 「하다.

anarchism *n.* mu-jŏng-bu-ju-ŭi 무정부주의.

anarchist *n.* mu-jŏng-bu-ju-ŭi-ja 무정부주의자.

anarchy *n.* mu-jŏng-bu 무정부.

anatomy *n.* hae-bu 해부, hae-bu-hak 해부학.

ancestor *n.* sŏn-jo 선조(先祖), cho-sang 조상.

ancestral *adj.* sŏn-jo-ŭi 선조의, cho-sang-ŭi 조상의.

ancestry *n.* cho-sang 조상 ; (*family descent*) ka-gye 가계(家系), mun-bŏl 문벌.

anchor *n.* tat 닻. —*v.* ta-ch'ul nae-ri-da 닻을 내리다; chŏng-bak-ha-da 정박하다.

anchorage *n.* chŏng-bak 정박, chŏng-bak-ji 정박지.

ancient *adj.* o-rae-doen 오래된, yet-nal-ŭi 옛날의.

and *conj.* (*between noun and noun*) …wa …와, (*everywhere else*) tto 또, kŭ-ri-go 그리고.

anecdote *n.* il-hwa 일화(逸話), ki-dam 기담(奇談).

anesthesia *n.* ma-ch'wi 마취, mu-gam-gak 무감각.

anesthetic *n.* ma-ch'wi-je 마취제.

anew *adv.* sae-ro 새로, ta-si han-bŏn 다시 한번.

angel *n.* ch'ŏn-sa 천사.　　　　　　　　　「하다.

anger *n.* no-yŏ-um 노여움. —*v.* no-ha-ge ha-da 노하게

angle *n.* ① (*corner*) mo-t'ung-i 모퉁이. ② kak-do 각도. ③ (*fishhook*) nak-si 낚시. —*v.* ① (*fish*) nak-si-jil-ha-da 낚시질하다. ② kkoe-ŏ-nae-da 꾀어내다.

angler *n.* nak-sit-gun 낚싯군.

Anglican Church sŏng-gong-hoe 성공회(聖公會).

Anglo-American *adj.* yŏng-mi-ŭi 영미의.

Anglo-American *adj.* yŏng-mi-ŭi 영미의, no-han 노한.

angry *adj.* sŏng-nan 성난, no-han 노한.

anguish *n.* sim-han ko-t'ong 심한 고통, pi-t'ong 비통.

animal *n.* tong-mul 동물, chim-sŭng 짐승.

animate *v.* ① saeng-myŏng-ŭl pu-rŏ-nŏ-t'a 생명을 불어넣다. ② (*inspire*) ko-mu-ha-da 고무하다.

animism *n.* mul-hwal-ron 물활론(物活論).

animosity *n.* wŏn-han 원한, chŭng-o-sim 증오심.

ankle *n.* pal-mok 발목 : ~ *bone* pok-sa-bbyŏ 복사뼈.

annals *n.* yŏn-dae-p'yo 연대표, yŏn-bo 연보.

annex *v.* (*add*) pu-ga[ch'ŏm-ga]-ha-da 부가〔첨가〕하다.
—*n.* ① (*affix*) pu-rok 부록. ② (*subsidiary building*)
pyŏl-gwan 별관.

annexation *n.* hap-byŏng 합병, pu-ga 부가.

annihilate *v.* chŏn-myŏl-si-k'i-da 전멸시키다 ; (*annul*)
p'ye-gi-ha-da 폐기하다.

anniversary *n.* ki-nyŏm-il 기념일, ki-il 기일(忌日).

announce *v.* ① (*give notice of*) al-ri-da 알리다.
② (*publish*) pal-p'yo-ha-da 발표하다.

announcer *n.* ŏ-na-un-sŏ 어나운서.

annoy *v.* koe-rop-hi-da 괴롭히다, sok-t'ae-u-da 속태우다.

annoyance *n.* koe-rop-him 괴롭힘.

annual *adj.* hae-ma-da 해마다 : ~ *income* yŏn-su 연수
(年收)/~ *rings* yŏl-lyun 연륜.

another *adj.* ① tto ha-na-ŭi 또 하나의. ② (*different*)
ta-rŭn 다른. —*n.* (*one more thing or person*) tto
ha-na 또 하나, tto han sa-ram 또 한 사람.

answer *v.* tae-dap-ha-da 대답하다. —*n.* tae-dap 대답.

ant *n.* kae-mi 개미.

antagonism *n.* chŏk-dae 적대, tae-rip 대립.

antagonist *n.* (*opponent*) pan-dae-ja 반대자, kyŏng-
jaeng-ja 경쟁자, chŏk-su 적수.

antarctic *adj.* nam-gŭk-ui 남극의. —*n.* nam-gŭk 남극.

antecedent *adj.* ap-sŏn 앞선 ; sŏn-haeng-ha-nŭn 선행
하는. —*n.* (*ancestry*) cho-sang 조상.

anthem *n.* sŏng-ga 성가 : *national* ~ kuk-ga 국가.

anthology *n.* (*collection of poems*) myong-si-sŏn 명
시선(名詩選) ; sŏn-jip 선집, mun-jip 문집.

anthropology *n.* il-lyu-hak 인류학.

anti-aircraft *adj.* tae-gong-ŭi 대공(對空)의, pang-

gong-ŭi 방공(防空)의.   「하다.
anticipate v. ye-gi-ha-da 예기하다, ye-sang-ha-da 예상
anticipation n. ye-gi 예기, ki-dae 기대.
anti-Communism n. pan-gong 반공(反共).
antidote n. hae-dok-je 해독제, che-hae-mul 제해물.
antipathy n. pan-gam 반감 ; hyŏm-o 혐오.
antique adj. ko-dae-ŭi 고대의 ; (*old-fashioned*) ku-sik-
ŭi 구식의. —n. kol-dong-p'um 골동품.
antiquity n. (*old times*) ko-dae 고대(古代) ; (*relics*)
ko-dae yu-mul 고대 유물.
antiseptic n. pang-bu-je 방부제.
antler n. nok-yong 녹용, ka-ji-jin ppul 가지진 뿔.
anus n. hang-mun 항문(肛門).
anxiety n. ① (*uneasiness*) kŭn-sim 근심, kŏk-jŏng 걱
정. ② (*eager desire*) yŏl-mang 열망.「nŭn 갈망하는.
anxious adj. kŏk-jŏng-doe-nŭn 걱정되는 ; kal-mang-ha-
anxiously adv. yŏm-ryŏ-sŭ-rŏ-un tŭ-si 염려스러운 듯이.
any adj. ŏ-ddŏn 어떤, mu-sŭn 무슨.
anybody pron. nu-gun-ga 누군가, a-mu-do 아무도.
anyhow adv. a-mu-t'ŭn 아뭏든, chwa-u-gan 좌우간.
anyone pron. nu-gu-dŭn-ji 누구든지, a-mu-do 아무도,
nu-gun-ga 누군가.   「do 아무것도.
anything pron. mu-ŏ-si-dŭn-ji 무엇이든지, a-mu-gŏt-
anyway adv. ŏ-jjaet-dŭn 어쨌든, ha-yŏ-t'ŭn 하여튼.
anywhere adv. ŏ-di-dŭn-ji 어디든지.
anywise adv. a-mu-rae-do 아무래도, kyŏl-k'o 결코.
apart adv. ttŏ-rŏ-jyŏ-sŏ 떨어져서, tta-ro-dda-ro 따로따
로 : *live* ~ tta-ro sal-da 따로 살다.   「방.
apartment n. ① a-p'a-a-t'ŭ 아파아트. ② (*room*) pang
ape n. wŏn-sung-i 원숭이.
apiece adv. kak-gak 각각, tta-ro-dda-ro 따로따로.
apologize v. (*excuse*) sa-gwa-ha-da 사과하다, (*ex-*

plain) pyŏn-myŏng-ha-da 변명하다.

apology *n.* sa-gwa 사과, pyŏn-myŏng 변명.

apoplexy *n.* chol-do 졸도(卒倒) : *cerebral* ~ noe-il-hyŏl [뇌일혈.

apostle *n.* sa-do 사도(使徒).

apostrophe *n.* ŏ-p'o-sŭ-t'ŭ-rŏ-p'i 어포스트러피.

apothecary *n.* yak-jong-sang 약종상.

appal(l) *v.* (*terrify*) sŏm-ddŭk-ha-ge ha-da 섬뜩하게 하다 ; (*dismay*) tang-hwang-k'e ha-da 당황케 하다.

appalling *adj.* so-rŭm-ggi-ch'i-nŭn 소름끼치는.

apparatus *n.* ki-gu 기구, chang-ch'i 장치.

apparent *adj.* myŏng-baek-han 명백한. [외견상.

apparently *adv.* myŏng-baek-hi 명백히 ; oe-gyŏn-sang

apparition *n.* (*ghost*) yu-ryŏng 유령.

appeal *v.* ho-so-ha-da 호소하다, ae-wŏn-ha-da 애원하다 ; (*law*) sang-go-ha-da 상고하다. —*n.* ① ho-so 호소. ② (*attraction*) mae-ryŏk 매력. [다.

appear *v.* na-t'a-na-da 나타나다, …ro po-i-da …로 보이다

appearance *n.* ① ch'ul-hyŏn 출현. ② oe-gwan 외관.

appease *v.* tal-rae-da 달래다, wi-ro-ha-da 위로하다.

appendicitis *n.* maeng-jang-yŏm 맹장염.

appendix *n.* pu-rok 부록, ch'u-ga 추가. [망.

appetite *n.* ① sik-yok 식욕. ② (*craving*) kal-mang 갈

applause *n.* pak-su kal-ch'ae 박수 갈채, ch'an-yang 찬양, ch'ing-ch'an 칭찬.

apple *n.* sa-gwa 사과, nŭng-gŭm 능금.

appliance *n.* (*apparatus*) ki-gu 기구, sŏl-bi 설비.

applicant *n.* chi-wŏn-ja 지원자, ŭng-mo-ja 응모자.

application *n.* sin-ch'ŏng 신청, chi-wŏn 지원.

applied *adj.* chŏk-yong-doe-nŭn 적용되는, ŭng-yong-ŭi 응용의 : ~ *chemistry* ŭng-yong-hwa-hak 응용화학.

apply *v.* ① chŏk-yong-ha-da 적용하다. ② (*make application*) sin-ch'ŏng-ha-da 신청하다.

appoint v. ① (*nominate*)chi-myŏng〔im-myŏng〕-ha-da 지명〔임명〕하다. ② (*fix*) chi-jŏng-ha-da 지정하다.

appointed adj. ① chi-jŏng-doen 지정된, yak-sok-han 약속한. ② (*equipped*) sŏl-bi-doen 설비된.

appointment n. ① (*nomination*) im-myŏng 임명;(*designation*) chi-jŏng 지정. ② (*promise*) yak-sok 약속.

appraise v. kap-sŭl mae-gi-da 값을 매기다.

appreciable adj. p'yŏng-ga-hal su it-nŭn 평가할 수 있는 ; (*noticeable*) a-ra-bol su it-nŭn 알아볼 수 있는.

appreciate v. ① (*enjoy*) kam-sang-ha-da 감상하다; (*assess*) p'yŏng-ga-ha-da 평가하다. ② (*feel grateful for*) kam-sa-ha-da 감사하다.

appreciation n. ① kam-sang 감상. ② kam-sa 감사.

apprehend v. ① (*arrest*) ch'e-p'o-ha-da 체포하다. ② (*understand*) i-hae-ha-da 이해하다. ③ (*fear*) u-ryŏ-ha-da 우려하다. 「p'o 체포.

apprehension n. ① i-hae 이해. ② pu-ran 불안. ③ ch'e-

apprehensive adj. ① (*anxious*) u-ryŏ-ha-nŭn 우려하는. ② (*intelligent*) yŏng-ri-han 영리한.

apprentice n. to-je 도제(徒弟), kyŏn-sŭp-saeng 견습생, (*novice*) ch'o-sim-ja 초심자.

approach v. ka-gga-i ka-da 가까이 가다, chŏp-gŭn-ha-da 접근하다. —n. chŏp-gŭn 접근.

appropriate adj. chŏk-dang-han 적당한. —v. ch'ung-dang-ha-da 충당하다.

approval n. sŭng-in 승인, (*sanction*) in-ga 인가.

approve v. sŭng-in-ha-da 승인하다.

approximately adv. (*almost*) tae-gang 대강, kŏ-ŭi 거 「의.

apricot n. sal-gu 살구.

April n. sa-wŏl 사월.

apron n. ap-ch'i-ma 앞치마, e-i-p'ŭ-rŏn 에이프런.

apt adj.(*inclined*)…ha-gi swi-un …하기 쉬운;(*suitable*)

chŏk-dang-han 적당한.

aquarium *n.* su-jok-gwan 수족관, yang-ŏ-jang 양어장.

arabesque *adj.* (*decoration*) tang-ch'o-mu-nŭi-ŭi 당초
(唐草)무늬의 ; (*fanciful*) koe-sang-han 괴상한.

arable land kyŏng-jak-ji 경작지.

arbitrary *adj.* im-ŭi-ŭi 임의의, tok-dan-jŏk-in 독단적인.

arbitrate *v.* chung-jae-ha-da 중재하다.

arbor *n.* su-mok 수목 : *A~ Day* sik-mok-il 식목일.

arc *n.* ho 호(孤), kung-hyŏng 궁형(弓形).

arch *n.* a-a-ch'i 아아치.

archaeology *n.* ko-go-hak 고고학(考古學).

archbishop *n.* tae-ju-gyo 대주교, tae-sa-gyo 대사교.

archery *n.* kung-sul 궁술, kung-do 궁도(弓道).

architect *n.* kŏn-ch'uk-ga 건축가.

architecture *n.* kŏn-ch'uk(-sul) 건축(술). 「북극.

arctic *adj.* puk-gŭk-ŭi 북극의. —*n.* (*the A~*) puk-gŭk

ardent *adj.* yŏl-ryŏl-han 열렬한. 「지구.

area *n.* ① (*space*) myŏn-jŏk 면적. ② (*district*) chi-gu

argue *v.* (*discuss*) non-ha-da 논하다, non-jaeng-ha-da
논쟁하다 ; (*contend*) chu-jang-ha-da 주장하다.

argument *n.* non-jaeng 논쟁 ; (*reason*) non-jŭng 논증.

arise *v.* i-rŏ-na-da 일어나다, pal-saeng-ha-da 발생하다.

aristocrat *n.* kwi-jok 귀족, kwi-jok-jŏk-in sa-ram 귀
족적인 사람;kwi-jok-jŏng-ch'i-ju-ŭi-ja 귀족정치주의자.

arithmetic *n.* san-su 산수.

arm *n.* ① p'al 팔. ② pyŏng-gi 병기, mu-gi 무기. —*v.*
mu-jang-ha-da 무장하다.

armament *n.* chang-bi 장비, mu-gi 무기, kun-bi 군비.

armchair *n.* al-lak-ŭi-ja 안락의자.

armed *adj.* mu-jang-han 무장한.

armistice *n.* hyu-jŏn 휴전 ; chŏng-jŏn 정전.

armo(u)r *n.* kap-ot 갑옷, kap-ju 갑주.

armo(u)red vehicle chang-gap-ch'a 장갑차.

army *n.* yuk-gun 육군.   ⌜jjŭm 쯤.

around *adv. & prep.* tul-re-e 둘레에 ; (*about*) yak 약,

arouse *v.* kak-sŏng-ha-da 각성하다, kkae-u-da 깨우다 ; (*excite*) pun-gi-si-k'i-da 분기시키다.

arrange *v.* ① (*put in order*) chŏng-don-ha-da 정돈하 다. ② (*make ready for*) chun-bi-ha-da 준비하다.

arrangement *n.* ① chŏng-don 정돈. ② (*preparation*) chun-bi 준비. ③ (*agreement*) t'a-hyŏp 타협.

array *n.* ① (*dress up*) kku-mi-da 꾸미다. ② (*place in order*) chŏng-ryŏl-si-k'i-da 정렬시키다.

arrest *v.* ch'e-p'o-ha-da 체포하다. —*n.* ch'e-p'o 체포.

arrival *n.* to-ch'ak 도착, to-dal 도달.

arrive *v.* to-ch'ak-ha-da 도착하다, to-dal-ha-da 도달하

arrogance *n.* o-man 오만, kŏ-man 거만.   ⌞다.

arrow *n.* hwa-sal 화살.

arsenal *n.* pyŏng-gi-go 병기고.

art *n.* ye-sul 예술, mi-sul 미술 ; (*craft*) ki-sul 기 술. —*v.* (~ *up*) ki-gyo-rŭl pu-ri-da 기교를 부리다.

artery *n.* tong-maek 동맥.

artful *adj.* (*ingenious*) kyo-myo-han 교묘한 ; (*sly*) kyo-hwal-han 교활한.

article *n.* ① (*newspaper*) ki-sa 기사. ② (*things*) mul-p'um 물품. ③ (*provision*) cho-hang 조항.

artificial *adj.* in-gong-jŏk 인공적, mo-jo-ŭi 모조의.

artillery *n.* ① tae-p'o 대포. ② (*branch of service*) p'o-byŏng 포병 : ~ *fire* p'o-hwa 포화(砲火).

artisan *n.* (*mechanic*) chik-gong 직공 ; (*handicrafts-man*) ki-gong 기공(技工).

artist *n.* ye-sul-ga 예술가, hwa-ga 화가(畫家).

as *adv.* …wa kat-ge …와 같게, …ka-t'ŭl man-k'ŭm …같을 만큼. —*conj.* …man-k'ŭm …만큼, …chŏng-do

···정도. —*prep.* ···ch'ŏ-rŏm 처럼, ···wa ka-ch'i ···와 같이, ···ro-sŏ ···로서. —*rel. pron.* ···wa ka-t'ŭn ···와 같은, ···ha-nŭn pa-ŭi ···하는 바의.

as far as (*and including*) kka-ji-nŭn 까지는, (ha-nŭn) han-e-sŏ-nŭn (하는) 한에서는.

as much as ···man-k'ŭm ···만큼.

ascend *v.* (*rise*) ol-ra-ga-da 올라가다, (*climb*) tŭng-ban-ha-da 등반하다 ; (*promote*) sŭng-jin-ha-da 승진 하다 : ~ *a mountain* tŭng-san-ha-da 등산하다.

ascent *n.* sang-sŭng 상승 ; (*advancement*) sŭng-jin 승 진 ; (*upward slope*) o-rŭ-mak-gil 오르막길.

ascertain *v.* hwak-in-ha-da 확인하다, a-ra-nae-da 알아 ⌊내다.

ascetic *n.* kŭm-yok-ju-ŭi-ja 금욕주의자.

ascribe *v.* ···t'a-sŭ-ro ha-da ···탓으로 하다.

ash *n.* chae 재 ; (*pl.*) (*remains*) yu-gol 유골.

ashamed *adj.* pu-ggŭ-rŏ-un 부끄러운, su-jŭp-ŏ-ha-nŭn

ashore *adv.* hae-byŏn-e 해변에. ⌊수줍어하는.

ash tray chae-ddŏ-ri 재떨이.

Asia *n.* a-si-a 아시아:*Southeast* ~ tong-nam-a 동남아.

aside *adv.* ① kyŏ-t'ŭ-ro 곁으로. ② (*apart*) pyŏl-do-ro 별도로. ③ (*except for*) ···ŭl che-ha-go ···을 제하고.

ask *v.* ch'ŏng-ha-da 청하다 ; (*inquire*) mut-da 묻다.

asleep *adv.* cham-dŭ-rŏ 잠들어.

asparagus *n.* a-sŭ-p'a-ra-gŏ-sŭ 아스파라거스.

aspect *n.* ① (*look*) yŏng-mo 용모. ② (*appearance*) mo-yang 모양. ③ (*phase*) kuk-myŏn 국면.

asphalt *n.* a-sŭ-p'al-t'ŭ 아스팔트. ⌈동경하다.

aspire *v.* yŏl-mang-ha-da 열망하다, tong-gyŏng-ha-da

ass *n.* ① (*donkey*) na-gwi 나귀. ② (*stupid*) pa-bo 바보. ③ (*arse*) ŏng-dŏng-i 엉덩이.

assail *v.* ① kong-gyŏk-ha-da 공격하다, sŭp-gyŏk-ha-da 습격하다. ② ta-gga-se-u-da 닦아세우다.

assassin *n.* am-sal-ja 암살자, cha-gaek 자객.

assassinate *v.* am-sal-ha-da 암살하다.

assassination *n.* am-sal 암살.

assault *n.* tol-gyŏk 돌격 ; sŭp-gyŏk 습격.

assemble *v.* mo-i-da 모이다, mo-ŭ-da 모으다.

assembly *n.* chip-hoe 집회, ŭi-hoe 의회(議會).

assent *n.* tong-ŭi 동의. —*v.* tong-ŭi-ha-da 동의하다.

assert *v.* tan-ŏn-ha-da 단언하다 ; (*maintain*) chu-jang-
ha-da 주장하다. 「ha-da 부과하다.

assess *v.* p'yŏng-ga-ha-da 평가하다 ; (*impose*) pu-gwa-

assets *n.* cha-san 자산, chae-san 재산.

assign *v.* (*allot*) hal-dang-ha-da 할당하다 ; (*appoint*)
chi-myŏng-ha-da 지명하다.

assimilate *v.* (*absorb*) tong-hwa-ha-da 동화하다 ; (*make
like*) kat-ge ha-da 같게 하다.

assist *v.* top-da 돕다, kŏ-dŭl-da 거들다.

assistance *n.* cho-ryŏk 조력, wŏn-jo 원조.

assistant *n.* cho-su 조수, po-jo-ja 보조자.

associate *v.* ① (*keep company*) kyo-je-ha-da 교제하
다. ② (*combine*) yŏn-hap-ha-da 연합하다. —*n.* tong-
ryo 동료 ; tong-ŏp-ja 동업자.

association *n.* ① (*connection*) yŏn-hap 연합. ② (*society*) hyŏp-hoe 협회. ③ (*companionship*) kyo-je 교제.

assort *v.* (*classify*) pul-lyu-ha-da 분류하다 ; (*group*)
jjak-ŭl mat-ch'u-da 짝을 맞추다. 「래다.

assuage *v.* wan-hwa-si-k'i-da 완화시키다, tal-rae-da 달

assume *v.* ttŏ-mat-da 떠맡다 ; (*pretend*) ka-jang-ha-
da 가장하다, (*presume*) ka-jŏng-ha-da 가정(假定)하다.

assumption *n.* ① ŏk-ch'ŭk 억측. ② hoeng-ryŏng 횡령.

assurance *n.* po-jŭng 보증 ; hwak-sin 확신.

assure *v.* po-jŭng-ha-da 보증하다, hwak-sil-ha-ge ha-da

asthma *n.* ch'ŏn-sik 천식(喘息). 「확실하게 하다.

astonish v. nol·ra·ge ha·da 놀라게 하다.

astonishment n. nol·ra·um 놀라움, kyŏng·ak 경악.

astound v. kkam·jjak nol·ra·ge ha·da 깜짝 놀라게 하다.

astray adj. & adv. (off the right way) kil·ŭl il·k'o 길을 잃고 : go ~ he·mae·da 헤매다.

astrology n. chŏm·sŏng·hak 점성학(占星學).

astronomer n. ch'ŏn·mun·hak·ja 천문학자.

astronomy n. ch'ŏn·mun·hak 천문학.   「ŭn 약은.

astute adj. (keen) ki·min·han 기민한 ; (crafty) yak-

asunder adv. san·san·i hŭ·t'ŏ·jyŏ 산산이 흩어져.

asylum n. su·yong·so 수용소 ; yang·yuk·wŏn 양육원 : lunatic ~ chŏng·sin·byong·wŏn 정신병원.

at prep. …e …에, …e·sŏ …에서, …ŭ·ro …으로, …chung·e …중에, …ŭl …을.

atheism n. mu·sil·lon 무신론, mu·sin·ang 무신앙.

athlete n. un·dong·ga 운동가, kyŏng·gi·ja 경기자.

athletics n. un·dong kyŏng·gi 운동 경기.

Atlantic n. tae·sŏ·yang 대서양.

atlas n. ① chi·do·ch'aek 지도책. ② to·hae 도해(圖解).

atmosphere n. ① (air) tae·gi 대기(大氣). ② (environment) pun·wi·gi 분위기, hwan·gyŏng 환경.

atom n. wŏn·ja 원자, a·t'om 아톰.

atomic adj. wŏn·ja·ŭi 원자의 : ~ energy won·ja·ryŏk 원자력 / ~ bomb wŏn·ja·p'ok·t'an 원자폭탄 / ~ pile wŏn·ja·ro 원자로(爐).

atrocity n. p'o·hak 포학, hyung·ak 흉악.

attach v. pu·ch'i·da 붙이다, ch'ŏm·bu·ha·da 첨부하다.

attaché n. tae·sa〔kong·sa〕·gwan·wŏn 대사〔공사〕관원.

attachment n. ① pu·ch'ak 부착. ② pu·sok·p'um 부속품. ③ (affection) ae·ch'ak 애착.   「공격.

attack v. kong·gyŏk·ha·da 공격하다. —n. kong·gyŏk

attain v. (gain) …ŭl tal·sŏng·ha·da …을 달성하다.

attainment *n.* tal-sŏng 달성, to-dal 도달.

attempt *v.* si-do-ha-da 시도하다. —*n.* ki-do 기도(企圖).

attend *v.* ① (*be present at*) ch'ul-sŏk-ha-da 출석하다.
② (*wait upon*) mo-si-da 모시다.

attendance *n.* ① ch'ul-sŏk 출석. ② si-jung 시중.

attendant *n.* su-haeng-wŏn 수행원.

attention *n.* chu-ŭi 주의 : *A~! Ch'a-ryŏ* 차려 !

attentive *adj.* cho-sim-sŏng-it-nŭn 조심성있는.

attest *v.* chŭng-myŏng-ha-da 증명하다 ; (*put on oath*)
maeng-se-si-k'i-da 맹세시키다.

attic *n.* ta-rak-bang 다락방, ko-mi-da-rak 고미다락.

attitude *n.* t'ae-do 태도, cha-se 자세.

attorney *n.* ① (*deputy*) tae-ri-in 대리인. ② (*lawyer*)
pyŏn-ho-sa 변호사.

attorney general kŏm-ch'al-ch'ong-jang 검찰총장.

attract *v.* kkŭl-da 끌다, yu-in-ha-da 유인하다 ; (*entice*)
mae-hok-ha-da 매혹하다.

attraction *n.* il-lyŏk 인력(引力), mae-ryŏk 매력.

attribute *v.* ⋯ŭi t'a-su-ro ha-da ⋯의 탓으로 하다.
—*n.* (*property*) sok-sŏng 속성.

auction *n.* & *v.* kyŏng-mae(-ha-da) 경매(하다).

audacity *n.* (*boldness*) tae-dam-mu-ssang 대담무쌍 ;
(*impudence*) an-ha-mu-in 안하무인.

audible *adj.* tŭl-ri-nŭn 들리는.

audience *n.* ch'ŏng-jung 청중.

audit *v.* hoe-gye-gam-sa-ha-da 회계감사하다. —*n.* ①
hoe-gye-gam-sa 회계감사. ② kyŏl-san 결산.

auditor *n.* kam-sa(-yŏk) 감사(역).

auditorium *n.* ch'ŏng-jung-sŏk 청중석 ; (*hall*) kang-
「dang 강당」

auditory *adj.* kwi-ŭi 귀의, ch'ŏng-gak-ŭi 청각의.

augment *v.* chŭng-ga-ha-da 증가하다, nŭl-da 늘다.

August *n.* p'al-wŏl 팔월.

aunt *n.* suk-mo 숙모, a-ju-mŏ-ni 아주머니.

aural *adj.* kwi-ŭi 귀의, ch'ŏng-gak-ŭi 청각의.

auspice *n.* ① (*omen*) chŏn-jo 전조, kil-jo 길조. ② (*patronage*) hu-wŏn 후원.

austere *adj.* ① (*stern*) ŏm-gyŏk-han 엄격한. ② (*simple*) tam-baek-han 담백한. ③ (*sour*) sin 신.

authentic *adj.* (*trustworthy*) mit-ŭl man-han 믿을 만한 ; (*genuine*) chin-jja-ŭi 진짜의.

author *n.* chŏ-ja 저자, chak-ga 작가.

authorities *n.* tang-guk 당국, kwan-hŏn 관헌.

authority *n.* kwŏn-wi 권위, kwŏn-han 권한.

authorized *adj.* in-ga-rŭl pat-ŭn 인가를 받은, kong-in-doen 공인된. [doen 공인된

autobiography *n.* cha-sŏ-jŏn 자서전.

automatically *adv.* cha-dong-jŏk-ŭ-ro 자동적으로.

automobile *n.* cha-dong-ch'a 자동차.

autumn *n.* ka-ŭl 가을.

avail *v.* ssŭl-mo-it-da 쓸모있다, yu-yong-ha-da 유용하다.

available *adj.* i-yong-hal su it-nŭn 이용할 수 있는.

avalanche *n.* sa-t'ae 사태, swae-do 쇄도.

avarice *n.* hŏ-yok 허욕, t'am-yok 탐욕. 「원수를 갚다.

avenge *v.* pok-su-ha-da 복수하다, wŏn-su-rŭl kap-da

avenue *n.* ka-ro-su-gil 가로수길 ; tae-ro 대로.

average *n.* p'yŏng-gyun 평균. —*adj.* p'yŏng-gyun-ŭi

avert *v.* pi-k'i-da 비키다, p'i-ha-da 피하다. [평균의.

aviation *n.* pi-haeng 비행, hang-gong 항공.

aviator *n.* pi-haeng-sa 비행사, pi-haeng-ga 비행가.

avoid *v.* p'i-ha-da 피하다, hoe-p'i-ha-da 회피하다.

avow *v.* (*declare openly*) kong-ŏn-ha-da 공언하다 ; (*confess*)cha-baek-ha-da 자백하다.

await *v.* …ŭl ki-da-ri-da …을 기다리다.

awake *v.* cham-ŭl kkae-da 잠을 깨다. —*adj.* kkae-ŏ-it-nŭn 깨어있는.

award *n.* sang-p'um 상품(賞品). —*v.* (*adjudge*) su-yŏ-ha-da 수여하다, sang-ŭl chu-da 상을 주다.

aware *adj.* al-go-sŏ 알고서 ; kkae-dat-go 깨닫고 : *be ~ of* …ŭl al-go it-da …을 알고 있다.
                                                              ⌜멀리.
away *adv.* (*off*) ttŏ-rŏ-jyŏ-sŏ 떨어져서 ; (*far*) mŏl-ri

awe *n.* tu-ryŏ-um 두려움.   ⌜시한.

awful *adj.* tu-ryŏ-un 두려운, mu-si-mu-si-han 무시무

awhile *adv.* cham-ggan 잠깐, cham-si 잠시.

awkward *adj.* (*embarrassing*) kŏ-buk-han 거북한; (*clumsy*) sŏ-t'u-rŭn 서투른, kkol-sa-na-un 꼴사나운.
                                                              ⌜자르다.
awl *n.* song-got 송곳.

ax(e) *n.* to-ggi 도끼. —*v.* to-kki-ro cha-rŭ-da 도끼로

axis *n.* kul-dae 굴대, ch'uk 축(軸).

axle *n.* kul-dae 굴대, ch'a-ch'uk 차축(車軸).

azalea *n.* chin-dal-rae 진달래, ch'ŏl-jjuk 철쭉.

⊰ B ⊱

---

babe *n.* kat-nan-a-gi 갓난아기 ; p'ut-na-gi 풋나기.

baby *n.* a-gi 아기 ;yu-a 유아 ; (*girl friend*)ae-in 애인.

bachelor *n.* ① ch'ong-gak 총각, tok-sin nam-ja 독신 남자. ② (*university graduate*) hak-sa 학사.

back *n.* (*of body*) tŭng 등 ; twi 뒤. —*adj. & adv.* twi-ŭi 뒤의, twi-ro 뒤로.—*v.* hu-t'oe-ha-da 후퇴하다.

backbone *n.* ch'ŏk-ch'u 척추, tŭng-bbyŏ 등뼈.

background *n.* pae-gyŏng 배경, i-myŏn 이면.

backward(s) *adv.* twi-ro 뒤로, kŏ-ggu-ro 거꾸로. —*adj.* twi-jjok-ŭi 뒤쪽의, (*late*) twi-jin 뒤진.

bacon *n.* pe-i-k'ŏn 베이컨.

bacteria *n.* se-gyun 세균, pak-t'e-ri-a 박테리아.

bad *adj.* na-bbŭn 나쁜, (*severe*) sim-han 심한.

badge *n.* hwi-jang 휘장, pae-ji 배지.

badger *n.* o·so·ri 오소리.

badly *adv.* (*wrongly*) na·bbŭ·ge 나쁘게 ; (*very much*) tae·dan·hi 대단히, mae·u 매우.

baffle *v.* (*frustrate*) chwa·jŏl·si·k'i·da 좌절시키다.

bag *n.* cha·ru 자루, ka·bang 가방, paek 백.

baggage *n.* su·ha·mul 수하물.

baggage check su·ha·mul·p'yo 수하물표.

baggage room su·ha·mul ch'wi·gŭp·so 수하물 취급소.

bail *n.* po·sŏk 보석 ; po·sŏk·gŭm 보석금. —*v.* po·sŏk·ŭl hŏ·ga·ha·da 보석을 허가하다. 「꿰다.

bait *n.* mi·ggi 미끼. —*v.* mi·ggi·ro kkoe·da 미끼로

bake *v.* kup·da 굽다, t'ae·u·da 태우다.

baker *n.* ppang kup·nŭn sa·ram 빵 굽는 사람.

bakery *n.* ppang·jip 빵집, che·bbang·so 제빵소.

balance *n.* ① (*equality*) kyun·hyŏng 균형. ② (*scales*) chŏ·ul 저울. —*v.* (*settle*) kyŏl·san·ha·da 결산하다.

balcony *n.* pal·k'o·ni 발코니, no·dae 노대(露臺).

bald *adj.* tae·mŏ·ri·ŭi 대머리의, pŏ·sŏ·jin 벗어진.

bale *n.* kku·rŏ·mi 꾸러미, (*pl.*) hwa·mul 화물.

baleful *adj.* hae·ro·un 해로운, ka·yŏp·sŭn 가엾은.

ball *n.* ① kong 공, po·ol 보올. ② (*social dancing*) mu·do·hoe 무도회.

ballad *n.* min·yo 민요, pal·ra·a·dŭ 발라아드.

ballet *n.* pal·re 발레, pal·re·dan 발레단.

balloon *n.* ki·gu 기구(氣球), p'ung·sŏn 풍선.

ballot *n. & v.* t'u·p'yo(·ha·da) 투표(하다).

ballroom *n.* mu·do·jang 무도장, taen·sŭ·ho·ol 댄스호올.

balm *n.* hyang·yu 향유, (*pleasant smell*) pang·hyang 방향(芳香). 「sun 죽순.

bamboo *n.* tae 대(竹), ch'am·dae 참대 : ~ *shoots* chŭk·

ban *v.* kŭm·ji·ha·da 금지하다. —*n.* kŭm·ji 금지 ; (*of religion*) p'a·mun 파문(破門).

banana *n.* pa-na-na 바나나.

band *n.* ① (*sash*) tti 띠. ② (*group*) tte 폐, mu-ri 무리. ③ (*music*) ak-dae 악대. —*v.* kkŭn-ŭ-ro muk-da 끈으로 묶다, (*unite*) tan-gyŏl-ha-da 단결하다.

bandage *n.* pung-dae 붕대. —*v.* pung-dae-ro kam-da 붕대로 감다. 「san-jŏk 산적.

bandit *n.* ① (*ruffian*) ak-dang 악당. ② (*brigand*)

bang *n.* t'ang ha-nŭn so-ri 탕 하는 소리; p'o-sŏng 포성. —*v.* t'ang so-ri na-da 탕 소리 나다.

banish *v.* ch'u-bang-ha-da 추방하다, nae-jjot-da 내쫓다.

banishment *n.* ch'u-bang 추방, yu-hyŏng 유형.

bank *n.* ① ŭn-haeng 은행. ② (*of river*) tuk 둑, che-bang 제방.

bankbook *n.* ŭn-haeng-t'ong-jang 은행통장.

banker *n.* ŭn-haeng-ga 은행가, ŭn-haeng-ŏp-ja 은행업자.

bank note chi-p'ye 지폐, ŭn-haeng-gwŏn 은행권.

bankruptcy *n.* p'a-san 파산, to-san 도산.

banner *n.* (*flag*) ki 기(旗), (*colors*) kun-gi 군기.

banquet *n.* yŏn-hoe 연회, hyang-yŏn 향연.

baptism *n.* se-rye 세례, yŏng-se 영세.

Baptist *n.* ch'im-rye-gyo-do 침례교도.

baptize *v.* se-rye-rŭl pe-p'ul-da 세례를 베풀다.

bar *n.* ① (*stick*) mong-dung-i 몽둥이. ② (*for drinks*) pa-a 바아, sul-jip 술집. —*v.* ka-ro-mak-da 가로막다.

barbarian *n.* ya-man-in 야만인. —*adj.* ya-man-sŭ-rŏn 야만스런, mi-gae-in-ŭi 미개인의. 「개한.

barbarous *adj.* ya-man-jŏk-in 야만적인, mi-gae-han 미

barber *n.* i-bal-sa 이발사:~'s shop i-bal-gwan 이발관.

barbed wire ka-si-ch'ŏl-sa-jul 가시철사줄, chŏl-jo-

bare *adj.* pŏl-gŏ-bŏ-sŭn 벌거벗은. ⌊mang 철조망.

barefoot *adj. & adv.* maen-bal-ŭi[ro] 맨발의[로].

barely *adv.* kyŏ-u 겨우, kan-sin-hi 간신히.

bargain *n.* (*transaction*) hŭng-jŏng 흥정, (*cheap purchase*) ssan mul-gŏn 싼 물건 : ~ *sale* yŏm-ga-p'an-mae 염가판매. —*v.* hŭng-jŏng-ha-da 흥정하다.

barge *n.* kŏ-rut-bae 거룻배, chim-bae 짐배.

bark *v.* (*bay*) chit-da 짖다. —*n.* (*wood*) na-mu kkŏp-jil 나무 껍질, su-p'i 수피.

barley *n.* po-ri 보리 : ~ *tea* po-ri-ch'a 보리차.

barn *n.* hŏt-gan 헛간, kwang 광.

barometer *n.* ki-ap-gye 기압계, ch'ŏng-u-gye 청우계, pa-ro-mi-t'ŏ 바로미터 ; chi-p'yo 지표.

baron *n.* nam-jak 남작(男爵). 「바라크.

barracks *n.* mak-sa 막사, pyŏng-yŏng 병영, pa-ra-k'ŭ

barrage *n.* t'an-mak 탄막, yŏn-sok an-t'a 연속 안타.

barrel *n.* ① wŏn-t'ong 원통, t'ong 통. ② han pae-rŏl 한 배럴. ③ (*of gun*) ch'ong-sin 총신, p'o-sin 포신.

barren *adj.* (*unproductive*) pul-mo-ŭi 불모의 ; (*sterile*) im-sin mot-ha-nŭn 임신 못하는.

barricade *n.* t'ong-haeng ch'a-dan-mul 통행 차단물.

barrier *n.* ul-t'a-ri 울타리, pang-ch'aek 방책 ; (*obstacle*) chang-hae 장해. 「다).

barter *n* & *v.* mul-mul-gyo-hwan(-ha-da) 물물교환(하

base *n.* ① ki-ch'o 기초. ② (*of operations*) ki-ji 기지 (基地). —*adj.* (*mean*) ch'ŏn-han 천한.

baseball *n.* ya-gu 야구, ya-gu-gong 야구공.

baseless *adj.* kŭn-gŏ-ŏp-nŭn 근거없는.

basement *n.* chi-ha-sil 지하실 ; ch'oe-ha-bu 최하부.

bashful *adj.* (*shy*) pu-ggŭ-rŏ-wŏ-ha-nŭn 부끄러워하는, su-jup-ŏ-ha-nŭn 수줍어하는.

basic *adj.* ki-bon-jŏk 기본적, ki-ch'o-jŏk 기초적.

basin *n.* ① (*for washing*) se-su tae-ya 세수 대야. ② (*bowl*) tae-jŏp 대접. ③ pun-ji 분지(盆地).

basis *n.* ki-ch'o 기초 ; (*army*) ki-ji 기지.

bask v. (*in the sun*) jjoe-da 쬐다.

basket n. pa-gu-ni 바구니, kwang-ju-ri 광주리.

basketball n. nong-gu 농구.   「저음(부).

bass n. ① (*fish*) nong-ŏ 농어. ② (*sound*) chŏ-ŭm(-bu)

bastard n. (*illegitimate child*) sa-saeng-a 사생아 ; sŏ-ja 서자(庶子) ; (*chap*)kae-ja-sik 개자식.

baste v. ① (*clothes*) si-ch'i-da 시치다. ② (*meat*) ki-rŭm-ŭl pa-rŭ-da 기름을 바르다.   「jwi 박쥐.

bat n. ① pae-t'ŭ 배트, t'a-bong 타봉. ② (*animal*) pak-

bath n. mok-yok 목욕.

bathe v. mok-yok-ha-da 목욕하다 ; tam-gŭ-da 담그다.

bathing n. mok-yok 목욕, su-yŏng 수영.

bathrobe n. hwa-jang-bok 화장복.

bathroom n. mok-yok-sil 목욕실, hwa-jang-sil 화장실.

baton n. chi-hwi-bong 지휘봉 ; pa-t'ong 바통.

battalion n. tae-dae 대대(大隊).

batter v. tu-dŭl-gi-da 두들기다.

battery n. ① (*electric*) chŏn-ji 전지. ② (*artillery*) p'o-byŏng-jung-dae 포병중대. ③ (*law*) ku-t'a 구타.

battle n. (*fight*) ssa-um 싸움, chŏn-t'u 전투. —v. ssa-u-da 싸우다, pun-t'u-ha-da 분투하다.

battlefield n. ssa-um-t'ŏ 싸움터, chŏn-jaeng-t'ŏ 전쟁터.

battle line chŏn-sŏn 전선.

battlement n. hyung-byŏk 흉벽(胸壁).

battleship n. chŏn-t'u-ham 전투함, chŏn-ham 전함.

bawdy adj. ŭm-t'ang-han 음탕한, oe-sŏl-sŭ-rŏn 외설스런.

bawl v. ko-ham-ch'i-da 고함치다, oe-ch'i-da 외치다.

bay n. ① (*gulf*) man 만(灣). ② (*fix*) kung-ji 궁지. ③ (*bark*) chit-nŭn so-ri 짖는 소리.

bayonet n. ch'ong-gŏm 총검. —v. ch'ong-gŏm-ŭ-ro jji-rŭ-da 총검으로 찌르다.

baza(a)r n. ① sang-jŏm-ga 상점가. ② (*fancy fair*)

pa-ja 바자, cha-sŏn-si 자선시(慈善市).

be *v.* ① (*existence*) it-da 있다. ② (*predicative*) i-da 이다. ③ (*honorific*) kye-si-da 계시다.

beach *n.* hae-byŏn 해변, mul-ga 물가, pa-dat-ga 바닷가.

beacon *n.* (*signal fire*) hwaet-bul 횃불, pong-hwa 봉화.

bead *n.* yŏm-ju-al 염주알, ku-sŭl 구슬 ; (*pl.*) yŏm-ju 염주.

beak *n.* (*bill*) chu-dung-i 주둥이, pu-ri 부리.

beam *n.* ① (*wood*) tae-dŭl-bo 대들보, to-ri 도리. ② (*of light*) kwang-sŏn 광선.   [yŏm-ju]

beaming *adj.* ① (*radiant*) pit-na-nŭn 빛나는. ② (*benign*) on-hwa-han 온화한.

bean *n.* k'ong 콩 : *soy ~s* tae-du 대두(大豆)/*~ sprouts* k'ong-na-mul 콩나물.

bear *n.* kom 곰. —*v.* ① (*endure*) kyŏn-di-da 견디다. ② (*yield*) maet-da 맺다. ③ (*a child*) na-t'a 낳다. ④ (*carry*) na-rŭ-da 나르다.   「러기.

beard *n.* ① su-yŏm 수염. ② (*awn*) kkŏ-ggŭ-rŏ-gi 꺼끄러기.

bearer *n.* un-ban-in 운반인 ; chi-ch'am-in 지참인, so-ji-ja 소지자.

bearing *n.* ① t'ae-do 태도. ② (*direction*) pang-wi 방위. ③ (*relationship*) kwan-gye 관계.

beast *n.* chim-sŭng 짐승, ya-su 야수.

beat *v.* ① (*hit*) ttae-ri-da 때리다. ② (*defeat*) chi-u-da 지우다. —*n.* (*of music*) pak-ja 박자.

beater *n.* ① ch'i-nŭn sa-ram 치는 사람. ② (*chaser*) mo-rit-gun 몰잇군. ③ t'a-bong 타봉.

beau *n.* ① (*dandy*) mŏt-jang-i 멋장이. ② (*male lover*) chŏng-bu 정부(情夫).

beautiful *adj.* a-rŭm-da-un 아름다운.

beautify *v.* a-rŭm-dap-ge ha-da 아름답게 하다.

beauty *n.* ① a-rŭm-da-um 아름다움, mi 미(美). ② mi-in 미인 : ～ *contest* mi-in tae-hoe 미인 대회.

beauty parlor mi-jang-wŏn 미장원.

because *conj.* …i-gi ttae-mun-e …이기 때문에, wae-nya-ha-myŏn 왜냐하면.

beckon *v.* ① son-ji-sŭ-ro pu-rŭ-da 손짓으로 부르다. ② (*lure*) yu-hok-ha-da 유혹하다.   「어울리다.

become *v.* ① …i toe-da …이 되다. ② (*suit*) ŏ-ul-ri-da

becoming *adj.* (*suitable*) ŏ-ul-ri-nŭn 어울리는.

bed *n.* ch'im-dae 침대 ; hwa-dan 화단.

bedbug *n.* pin-dae 빈대.

bedclothes *n.* ch'im-gu 침구, kŭm-ch'im 금침.

bedding *n.* ① (*bedclothes and mattress*) ch'im-gu-ryu 침구류. ② (*foundation*) t'o-dae 토대.

bedridden *adj.* nu-wŏ-man it-nŭn 누워만 있는.

bedroom *n.* ch'im-sil 침실, ch'im-bang 침방.

bedstead *n.* ch'im-dae-t'ŭl 침대틀.

bee *n.* kkul-bŏl 꿀벌 : *a queen* ～ yŏ-wang-bŏl 여왕벌.

beech *n.* nŏ-do-bam-na-mu 너도밤나무.

beef *n.* soe-go-gi 쇠고기, ko-gi 고기.

beefsteak *n.* pi-i-p'ŭ-sŭ-t'e-i-k'ŭ 비이프스테이크.

beehive *n.* (kkul-)pŏl-jip (꿀)벌집, pŏl-t'ong 벌통.

beer *n.* maek-ju 맥주 : ～ *hall* pi-ŏ ho-ol 비어 호올.

beet *n.* sa-t'ang-mu-u 사탕무우, kŭn-dae 근대.

beetle *n.* ttak-jŏng-bŏl-re 딱정벌레.

befall *v.* …ŭi sin-sang-e tak-ch'i-da …의 신상에 닥치다.

before *adv.* a-p'e 앞에, mŏn-jŏ 먼저. —*prep.*(*time*) chŏn-e 전에, pŏl-ssŏ 벌써 ;(*place*) a-p'e 앞에. —*conj.* …ha-gi chŏn-e …하기 전에.

beforehand *adv.* mi-ri 미리, sa-jŏn-e 사전에.

befriend v. tol·bwa·ju·da 돌봐주다 ; ···ŭi p'yŏn·ŭl tŭl·da ···의 편을 들다.

beg v. ① ku·gŏl·ha·da 구걸하다. ② (*beseech*) ch'ŏng·ha·da 청하다, kan·ch'ŏng·ha·da 간청하다.

beget v. (*procreate*) na·t'a 낳다 ; (*cause*) saeng·gi·ge ha·da 생기게 하다, ch'o·rae·ha·da 초래하다.

beggar n. kŏ·ji 거지, pi·rŏng·baeng·i 비렁뱅이.

begin v. si·jak·ha·da 시작하다, kae·si·ha·da 개시하다.

beginner n. ① (*novice*) ch'o·bo·ja 초보자. ② (*originator*) ch'ang·si·ja 창시자.

beginning n. si·jak 시작, si·ch'o 시초, pal·dan 발단.

beguile v. ① (*cheat*) sok·i·da 속이다. ② (*pass time*) ·sim·sim·p'u·ri·ha·da 심심풀이하다.

behalf n. (*interest*) i·ik 이익 : in[on] ~ of ···ŭl tae·sin·ha·yŏ ···을 대신하여 ; ···ŭl wi·ha·yŏ ···을 위하여.

behave v. ① ch'ŏ·sin·ha·da 처신하다, haeng·dong·ha·da 행동하다. ② (*work*) ki·dong·ha·da 기동하다.

behavior n. ch'ŏ·sin 처신, haeng·wi 행위.

behead v. mok·ŭl pe·da 목을 베다.

behind adv. twi·e 뒤에. —prep. ···ŭi twi·e ···의 뒤에.

behold v. po·da 보다. —int. po·ra 보라.

being n. ① (*existence*) sil·jae 실재(實在). ② (*human life*) in·saeng 인생. ③ (*essence*) pon·jil 본질.

belch v. t'ŭ·rim·ha·da 트림하다. —n. t'ŭ·rim 트림.

belief n. ① (*conviction*) hwak·sin 확신. ② (*trust*) sin·yong 신용. ③ (*faith*) mit·ŭm 믿음, sin·ang 신앙.

believe v. mit·da 믿다 ; saeng·gak·ha·da 생각하다.

bell n. chong 종, pel 벨.

bellow v. (*roar*) ul·bu·jit·da 울부짖다.

bellows n. p'ul·mu 풀무.

belly n. pae 배, pok·bu 복부.

belong v. sok·ha·da 속하다.

beloved *adj.* ka-jang sa-rang-ha-nŭn 가장 사랑하는, kwi-yŏ-un 귀여운. —*n.* (*darling*) ae-in 애인.

below *adv.* a-rae-e 아래에, mi-t'e 밑에.

belt *n.* ① hyŏk-dae 혁대, pel-t'ŭ 벨트. ② (*area*) chi-dae 지대 : *green* ~ nok-ji-dae 녹지대.

bench *n.* kin kŏl-sang 긴 걸상, pen-ch'i 벤치.

bend *v.* ku-bu-ri-da 구부리다, (*twist*) hwi-da 휘다.

beneath *adv. & prep.* a-rae-jjok-e 아래쪽에, …ŭi pa-ro a-rae-e …의 바로 아래에.

benediction *n.* ch'uk-bok 축복, ŭn-ch'ong 은총.

benefactor *n.* ŭn-in 은인 ; hu-wŏn-ja 후원자.

beneficial *adj.* yu-ik-han 유익한, i-ro-un 이로운.

benefit *n.* ① (*profit*) i-ik 이익. ② (*favor*) hye-t'aek 혜택. —*v.* …e-ge i-rop-da …에게 이롭다.

benevolence *n.* cha-sŏn 자선, pak-ae 박애.

benevolent *adj.* in-ja-han 인자한, cha-ae-ro-un 자애로운.

benign *adj.* in-ja-han 인자한, on-hwa-han 온화한.

benumb *v.* (*make numb*) ma-bi-si-k'i-da 마비시키다.

bequeath *v.* (*leave behind*) yu-jŭng-ha-da 유증(遺贈)하다, nam-gi-da 남기다.

bequest *n.* yu-san 유산 ; yu-mul 유물.

bereave *v.* il-k'e ha-da 잃게 하다, ppae-at-da 빼앗다.

berry *n.* chang-gwa 장과(漿果), ttal-gi 딸기.

berth *n.* ① (*ship or train*) ch'im-dae 침대. ② (*lodging*) suk-so 숙소.

beseech *v.* t'an-wŏn-ha-da 탄원하다, kan-ch'ŏng-ha-da 간청하다.

beset *v.* ① (*surround*) p'o-wi-ha-da 포위하다. ② (*attack*) sŭp-gyŏk-ha-da 습격하다.

beside *prep.* …yŏp'e …옆에, kyŏt'e 곁에.

besides *prep.* (*otherwise*) kŭ-ba-gge 그밖에 ; (*moreover*) tŏ-u-gi 더우기, ke-da-ga 게다가.

besiege *v.* ① p'o-wi-ha-da 포위하다. ② (*crowd around*) mil-ryŏ-o-da 밀려오다, swae-do-ha-da 쇄도하다.

best *adj.* ka-jang cho-ŭn 가장 좋은. —*adv.* ka-jang chal 가장 잘. —*n.* ch'oe-sŏn 최선, ch'oe-sang 최상.

bestow *v.* ① (*confer*) chu-da 주다, su-yŏ-ha-da 수여하다. ② (*place*) no-t'a 놓다.

bet *n.* nae-gi 내기. —*v.* (ton-ul) kŏl-da (돈을) 걸다.

betray *v.* ① pae-ban-ha-da 배반하다. ② chŏ-bŏ-ri-da 저버리다. ③ (*reveal*) nu-sŏl-ha-da 누설하다.

betroth *v.* yak-hon-ha-da 약혼하다.

better *adj.* tŏ-uk cho-ŭn 더욱 좋은. —*adv.* tŏ-uk cho-k'e 더욱 좋게. —*n.* po-da na-ŭn kŏt 보다 나은 것.

bettor *n.* nae-gi-ha-nŭn sa-ram 내기하는 사람.

between *prep.* …sa-i-e …사이에. —*adv.* sa-i-e 사이에.

beverage *n.* (*drink*) ŭm-ryo 음료, ma-sil kŏt 마실 것.

bewail *v.* (*lament*) sul-p'ŭm-e cham-gi-da 슬픔에 잠기다, pi-t'an-ha-da 비탄하다.

beware *v.* cho-sim[chu-ŭi]-ha-da 조심〔주의〕하다 : *B~* ~ *of the dog!* Kae cho-sim! 개 조심!

bewilder *v.* ŏ-ri-dung-jŏl-ha-ge ha-da 어리둥절하게 하다. tang-hwang-k'e ha-da 당황케 하다.

beyond *prep.* …ŭi chŏ-jjok-e …의 저쪽에, (*past*) …ŭl nŏm-ŏ-sŏ …을 넘어서. —*adv.* chŏ-jjok-e 저쪽에.

bias *n.* sa-sŏn 사선 ; ch'i-u-ch'im 치우침, p'yŏn-gyŏn

bib *n.* t'ŏk-ba-ji 턱받이.   〔편견.

Bible *n.* sŏng-gyŏng 성경, sŏng-sŏ 성서.

bicycle *n.* cha-jŏn-gŏ 자전거.

bid *v.* ① (*price*) kap-sŭl mae-gi-da 값을 매기다, ip-ch'al-ha-da 입찰하다. ② (*command*) myŏng-ryŏng-ha-da 명령하다. —*n.* (*tender*) ip-ch'al 입찰.

biennial *adj.* i-nyŏn-ma-da-ŭi 2년마다의.

bier *n.* ① sang-yŏ 상여. ② (*corpse*) si-ch'e 시체.

big *adj.* ① k'ŭn 큰 ; chung-yo-han 중요한. ② kwa-
bigot *n.* ko-jip-jang-i 고집장이.　　⌊jang-han 과장한.
bill *n.* ① kye-san-sŏ 계산서. ② (*of bank*) ŏ-ŭm 어음.
　③ (*deed*) chŭng-sŏ 증서 : ~ *of lading* sŏn-ha chŭng-
　gwŏn 선하 증권. ④ (*animal's*) pu-ri 부리.
billiards *n.* tang-gu 당구 : ~ *table* tang-gu-dae 당구대.
billion *n.* ① (*a thousand millions*) sip-ŏk 10억. ②
　(*a million millions*) il-jo 1조(兆).
billow *n.* & *v.* k'ŭn p'a-do(-ga il-da) 큰 파도(가 일다).
bimonthly *adj.* tu tal-ma-da-ŭi 두 달마다의, kyŏk-
　wŏl-ŭi 격월의.
bind *v.* muk-da 묶다, ku-sok-ha-da 구속하다.
binoculars *n.* ssang-an-gyŏng 쌍안경.
biography *n.* chŏn-gi 전기(傳記), il-dae-gi 일대기.
biology *n.* saeng-mul-hak 생물학.
bipartisan *adj.* ch'o-dang-p'a-jŏk 초당파적 : ~ *diplo-
　macy* ch'o-dang-p'a-jŏk oe-gyo 초당파적 외교.
birch *n.* cha-jak-na-mu 자작나무.
bird *n.* sae 새, nal-jim-sŭng 날짐승. ⌈t'ae-saeng 태생.
birth *n.* ch'ul-san 출산, t'an-saeng 탄생 ; (*descent*)
birthday *n.* saeng-il 생일 : *a* ~ *present* saeng-il-sŏn-
birthplace *n.* ch'ul-saeng-ji 출생지.　　⌊mul 생일선물.
birthright *n.* t'a-go-nan kwŏl-li 타고난 권리.
biscuit *n.* pi-sŭ-k'it 비스킷.
bishop *n.* sŭng-jŏng 승정 ; chu-gyo 주교 ; sa-gyo 사교.
bit *n.* (*small piece*) chak-ŭn cho-gak 작은 조각 ;
　(*small quantity*) cho-gŭm 조금, yak-gan 약간.
bite *v.* ① (*sting*) mul-da 물다. ② (*corrode*) pu-sik-
　ha-da 부식하다. —*n.* mul-gi 물기.
bitter *adj.* ① ssŭn 쓴. ② (*harsh*) chi-dok-han 지독한.
bitterly *adv.* mop-si 몹시, sim-ha-ge 심하게.
black *adj.* kŏm-ŭn 검은. —*v.* kka-ma-k'e ha-da 까맣

게 하다. —*n.* hŭk-saek 흑색.

blackboard *n.* ch'il-p'an 칠판, hŭk-p'an 흑판.

blacken *v.* kka-ma-k'e ha-da 까맣게 하다.

black market am-si-jang 암시장.

blacksmith *n.* tae-jang-jang-i 대장장이, ch'ŏl-gong 철 공 : *a* ~'s *shop* tae-jang-gan 대장간.

bladder *n.* pang-gwang 방광(膀胱).

blade *n.* ① (*of knife*) k'al-nal 칼날, (*sword*) k'al 칼. ② (*of grass*) p'ul-ip 풀잎.

blame *v.* pi-nan-ha-da 비난하다. —*n.* pi-nan 비난.

blameless *adj.* hŭm-ŏp-nŭn 흠없는.

blanch *v.* pa-rae-da 바래다, p'yo-baek-ha-da 표백하 다 ; ch'ang-baek-hae-ji-da 창백해지다.

blank *n.* paek-ji 백지. —*adj.* paek-ji-ŭi 백지의, kong-baek-ŭi 공백의.

blanket *n.* tam-yo 담요.

blaspheme *v.* (*curse and swear*) (sin-ŭl) mo-dok-ha-da (신을) 모독하다.

blast *v.* (*blow up*) p'ok-p'a-ha-da 폭파하다. —*n.* tol-p'ung 돌풍, p'ok-p'a 폭파.

blaze *n.* pul-ggot 불꽃. —*v.* t'a-o-rŭ-da 타오르다.

bleach *v.* (*make white*) p'yo-baek-ha-da 표백하다.

bleak *adj.* (*cold*) ssa-nŭl-han 싸늘한 ; (*desolate*) hwang-p'ye-han 황폐한, ssŭl-ssŭl-han 쓸쓸한.

bleat *v.* (*sheep, goat etc.*) mae-ae-mae-ae ul-da 매애 매애 울다. —*n.* u-rŭm-so-ri 울음소리.

bleed *v.* p'i-rŭl hŭl-ri-da 피를 흘리다.

blend *v.* twi-sŏk-da 뒤섞다, hon-hap-ha-da 혼합하다.

bless *v.* ch'uk-bok-ha-da 축복하다, ŭn-ch'ong-ŭl pil-da 은총을 빌다 ; ch'an-mi-ha-da 찬미하다.

blessing *n.* (*benediction*) ch'uk-bok 축복, (*devine favor*) ch'ŏn-hye 천혜(天惠).

blind *adj.* nun-mŏn 눈먼, chang-nim-ŭi 장님의.

blindman *n.* chang-nim 장님, so-gyŏng 소경.

blindness *n.* sil-myŏng 실명 ; maeng-mok 맹목.

blink *v.* nun-ŭl kkam-bak-gŏ-ri-da 눈을 깜박거리다.

bliss *n.* (*great enjoyment*) ta-si-ŏp-nŭn chŭl-gŏ-um 다
시없는 즐거움 ; chi-bok 지복(至福).　　　「집이 생기다.

blister *n.* mul-jip 물집. —*v.* mul-jip-i saeng-gi-da 물

bloc *n.* tan 단, kwŏn 권(圈), pŭl-rok 블록.

block *n.* ① (*of wood*) na-mu-t'o-mak 나무토막;(*lump*)
tŏng-ŏ-ri 덩어리. ② (*area*) ku-hoek 구획. —*v.* (*obstruct*) mak-da 막다, (*check*) pang-hae-ha-da 방해하

blockade *n.* pong-swae 봉쇄, tu-jŏl 두절.　　　「다.

blockhead *n.* mŏng-ch'ŏng-i 멍청이, pa-bo 바보.

blood *n.* p'i 피 ; (*lineage*) hyŏl-t'ong 혈통.

blood vessel hyŏl-gwan 혈관.

bloody *adj.* (*bleeding*) p'i-na-nŭn 피나는 ; (*with much
bloodshed*) p'i-t'u-sŏng-i-ŭi 피투성이의.　　「영하다.

bloom *v.* kko-ch'i p'i-da 꽃이 피다, pŏn-yŏng-ha-da 번

blossom *n.* kkot 꽃, kae-hwa 개화(開花).

blot *n.* ŏl-ruk 얼룩, o-jŏm 오점(汚點), kyŏl-jŏm 결점.
—*v.* (*stain*) ŏl-ruk-ji-ge ha-da 얼룩지게 하다.

blotter *n.* ap-ji 압지(押紙).

blouse *n.* pŭl-ra-u-sŭ 블라우스, chak-ŏp-bok 작업복.

blow *v.* pul-da 불다 ; (*explode*) p'ok-bal-ha-da 폭발하다.
—*n.* (*knock*) t'a-gyŏk 타격.

blue *adj.* p'u-rŭn 푸른 ; (*dismal*) ch'im-ul-han 침울한.

bluebell *n.* to-ra-ji 도라지.

blueprint *n.* ch'ŏng-sa-jin 청사진, kye-hoek 계획.

bluff *n.* ① (*cliff*) chŏl-byŏk 절벽, pyŏ-rang 벼랑. ②
(*bravado*) hŏ-se 허세.　　　　　　「실수를 하다.

blunder *n.* k'ŭn sil-su 큰 실수. —*v.* sil-su-rŭl ha-da

blunt *adj.* (*dull*) mu-din 무딘 ; mu-dduk-dduk-han 무
뚝뚝한 ; (*outspoken*) sol-jik-han 솔직한.

bluntly adv. t'ung-myŏng-sŭ-rŏp-ge 퉁명스럽게.

blur v. hŭ-ri-ge ha-da 흐리게 하다 ; ŏl-ruk-ji-ge ha-da 얼룩지게 하다. —n. (blot) ŏl-ruk 얼룩.

blush v. (be shamed) na-ch'ŭl pul-k'i-da 낯을 붉히다, ppal-gae-ji-da 빨개지다. —n. (rosy glow) hong-jo 홍조, pul-gŭ-re-ham 불그레함.

bluster v. kŏ-se-ge mo-ra-ch'i-da 거세게 몰아치다.

boar n. su-t'wae-ji 수퇘지 : wild ~ met-dwae-ji 멧돼지.

board n. ① (thin plank) p'an-ja 판자. ② (committee) wi-wŏn-hoe 위원회 : ~ of directors i-sa-hoe 이사회. —v. ① (embark on) ol-ra-t'a-da 올라타다. ② (lodge) ha-suk-ha-da 하숙하다.

boarder n. ha-suk-in 하숙인, ki-suk-saeng 기숙생.

boardinghouse n. ha-suk-jip 하숙집.

boast v. cha-rang-ha-da 자랑하다, ttŏ-bŏl-ri-da 떠벌리다. —n. cha-rang 자랑 ; hŏ-p'ung 허풍.

boastful adj. cha-rang-ha-nŭn 자랑하는.

boat n. chak-ŭn ki-sŏn 작은 기선, po-u-t'ŭ 보우트.

boatman n. paet-sa-gong 뱃사공. 「sil-p'ae 실패.

bobbin n. ① (sewing machine) puk 북. ② (spool)

bodily adj. sin-ch'e[yuk-ch'e]-ŭi 신체[육체]의. —adv. (as a whole) song-du-ri-jjae 송두리째.

body n. ① yuk-ch'e 육체 ; (corpse) si-ch'e 시체. ② (group) tan-ch'e 단체. ③ (letter) pon-mun 본문.

bodyguard n. ho-wi-byŏng 호위병, kyŏng-ho-in 경호인.

bog n. su-rŏng 수렁, nŭp 늪.

bogus adj. ka-jja-ŭi 가짜의, wi-jo-ŭi 위조의.

boil v. ① (liquid) kkŭl-t'a 끓다. ② (solids) sam-da 삶다. —n. (tumor) chong-gi 종기, pu-sŭ-rŏm 부스럼.

boiler n. po-il-rŏ 보일러.

boisterous adj. kŏ-ch'in 거친, nan-p'ok-han 난폭한.

bold adj. tae-dam-han 대담한.

bolt *n.* ① (*dart*) hwa-sal 화살. ② (*of a gate*) pit-jang 빗장. ③ (*lightning*) pŏn-gaet-bul 번갯불.

bomb *n.* p'ok-t'an 폭탄 : *hydrogen* ~ su-so p'ok-t'an 수소 폭탄/*incendiary* ~ so-i-t'an 소이탄. —*v.* p'ok-gyŏk-ha-da 폭격하다.

bonanza *n.* no-da-ji 노다지 ; (*run of luck*) ttŭt-ba-ggŭi haeng-un 뜻밖의 행운.

bond *n.* ① (*tie*) kyŏl-sok 결속. ② (*fetters*) sok-bak 속박. ③ (*finance*) chŭng-gwŏn 증권.

bondage *n.* no-ye-ŭi sin-se 노예의 신세 ; kul-jong 굴종.

bone *n.* ppyŏ 뼈, kol-gyŏk 골격.

bonfire *n.* mo-dak-bul 모닥불, hwa-t'ot-bul 화톳불.

bonnet *n.* po-nit 보닛.

bonus *n.* po-u-nŏ-sŭ 보우너스, sang-yŏ-gŭm 상여금 ; pae-dang-gŭm 배당금.

book *n.* ch'aek 책. —*v.* (*record*) ki-ip-ha-da 기입하다.

bookcase *n.* ch'aek-jang 책장, ch'aek-ggo-ji 책꽂이.

bookkeeping *n.* pu-gi 부기(簿記).

booklet *n.* so-ch'aek-ja 소책자, p'am-p'ŭl-ret 팜플렛.

bookstore *n.* sŏ-jŏm 서점, ch'aek-bang 책방.

boom *n.* (*in market value*) pyŏ-rak kyŏng-gi 벼락 경기 ; kŭp-dŭng 급등. 「을 올리다.

boost *v.* mi-rŏ-ol-ri-da 밀어올리다, kap-sŭl ol-ri-da 값

boot *n.* chang-hwa 장화, pan-jang-hwa 반(半)장화.

bootblack *n.* ku-du-da-ggi 구두닦기.

booth *n.* ① p'an-ja-jip 판자집. ② (*stand*) no-jŏm 노점 : *telephone* ~ kong-jung chŏn-hwa 공중 전화.

booty *n.* chŏl-li-p'um 전리품, no-hoek-mul 노획물.

boracic acid pung-san 붕산.

border *n.* ① ka-jang-ja-ri 가장자리, t'e-du-ri 테두리. ② kyŏng-gye 경계. —*v.* (*adjoin*) chŏp-ha-da 접하다.

bore *v.* ① (*annoy*) sil-jŭng-na-ge ha-da 싫증나게 하다,

② (*drill*) ku-mŏng ttul-t'a 구멍 뚫다.

born *adj.* t'a-go-nan 타고난, ch'ŏn-sŏng-ŭi 천성의.

borrow *v.* pil-ri-da 빌리다, ch'a-yong-ha-da 차용하다.

bosom *n.* ka-sŭm 가슴. —*adj.* (*cherished*) ka-sŭm-e kan-jik-han 가슴에 간직한: *a ~ friend* ch'in-u 친우.

boss *n.* tu-mok 두목, chu-in 주인, po-sŭ 보스. —*v.* (*control*) t'ong-sol-ha-da 통솔하다.

botanical garden sik-mul-wŏn 식물원.

botany *n.* sik-mul-hak 식물학.

both *adj.* yang-jjok-ŭi 양쪽의. —*pron.* tul ta 둘 다. —*adv.* …do …do …도 …도.

bother *v.* (*annoy*) kwi-ch'an-k'e ha-da 귀찮게 하다: ~ *about* kŏk-jŏng-ha-da 걱정하다. 「병마개 뽑이.

bottle *n.* pyŏng 병 : *a ~ opener* pyŏng-ma-gae ppop-i

bottom *n.* mit-ba-dak 밑바닥 ; ki-ch'o 기초.

bottomless *adj.* mit-ba-dak-i ŏp-nŭn 밑바닥이 없는.

bough *n.* k'ŭn ka-ji 큰 가지.

boulder *n.* tung-gŭn tol 둥근 돌, p'yo-sŏk 표석.

bounce *v.* t'wi-da 튀다, ttwi-ŏ-o-rŭ-da 뛰어오르다.

bound *v.* (*leap*) t'wi-da 튀다. —*n.* kyŏng-gye 경계, pŏm-wi 범위. —*adj.* mu-ggin 묶인.

boundary *n.* kyŏng-gye 경계, pŏm-wi 범위.

boundless *adj.* han-i ŏp-nŭn 한이 없는.

bountiful *adj.* (*generous*) kwan-dae-han 관대한.

bouquet *n.* kkot-da-bal 꽃다발 ; hyang-gi 향기.

bow *n.* ① (*archery*) hwal 활. ② (*of the head*) chŏl 절. —*v.* (*for saluta-tion*) chŏl-ha-da 절하다.

bowels *n.* nae-jang 내장.

bower *n.* (*arbor*) chŏng-ja 정자(亭子); ch'o-so 처소.

bowl *n.* sa-bal 사발, kong-gi 공기.

[chŏng-ja]

box *n.* sang-ja 상자 ; (*theater*) t'ŭk-byŏl-sŏk 특별석 ;
(*witness box*) chŭng-in-sŏk 증인석.

boxer *n.* kwŏn-t'u-sŏn-su 권투선수, pok-sŏ 복서.

boxing *n.* kwŏn-t'u 권투, pok-sing 복싱.

box office mae-p'yo-so 매표소.

boy *n.* ① so-nyŏn 소년, nam-ja a-i 남자 아이. ② a-dŭl
아들, nam-ja 남자. ③ (*young servant*) kŭp-sa 급사.

boycott *n.* pul-mae tong-maeng 불매 동맹, po-i-k'ot

boyhood *n.* so-nyŏn-gi 소년기. ⌐보이콧.

boy scouts so-nyŏn-dan 소년단.

brace *v.* (*support*) pŏ-t'i-da 버티다. —*n.* pŏ-t'im-dae
버팀대, chi-ju 지주 ; mel-bbang 멜빵.

bracelet *n.* p'al-jji 팔찌. ⌐괄호.

bracket *n.* ① kka-ch'i-bal 까치발. ② (*marks*) kwal-ho

brackish *adj.* (*salty*) jjap-jjal-han 짭짤한.

brag *v.* cha-rang-ha-da 자랑하다 ; (*boast of*) ppom-
nae-da 뽐내다. —*n.* cha-rang 자랑, hŏ-p'ung 허풍.

braggart *n.* (*boaster*) hŏ-p'ŭng-sŏn-i 허풍선이.

braid *v.* tta-t'a 땋다. —*n.* kkon kkŭn 꼰 끈.

brain *n.* noe 뇌, tu-noe 두뇌 ; chi-ryŏk 지력.

brainwash *n.* & *v.* se-noe(-ha-da) 세뇌(하다).

brake *n.* che-dong-gi 제동기, pŭ-re-i-k'ŭ 브레이크.

bramble *n.* ka-si-dŏm-bul 가시덤불, tŭl-jang-mi 들장미.

bran *n.* kyŏ 겨, mil-gi-ul 밀기울.

branch *n.* ① (*of tree*) ka-ji 가지. ② (*office*) chi-jŏm
지점. —*v.* kal-ra-ji-da 갈라지다.

brand *n.* ① (*trademark*) sang-p'yo 상표. ② (*stigma*)
nak-in 낙인, o-myŏng 오명(汚名).

brandy *n.* pŭ-raen-di 브랜디. ⌐ŭi 신품의.

brand-new *adj.* a-ju sae-ro-un 아주 새로운, sin-p'um-

brass *n.* not-soe 놋쇠. ⌐dŭ 브라스밴드.

brass band ch'wi-ju-ak-dan 취주악단, pŭ-ra-sŭ-baen-

brave *adj.* yong-gam-han 용감한. —*v.* yong-gam-ha-ge mat-sŏ-da 용감하게 맞서다.

bravery *n.* yong-gam 용감, yong-maeng 용맹.

brawl *n. & v.* mal-da-t'um(-ha-da) 말다툼(하다).

bray *n.* (*donkey*) u-rŭm-so-ri 울음소리.

brazier *n.* ① hwa-ro 화로. ② not-gat-jang-i 놋갓장이.

breach *n.* kkae-ddŭ-rim 깨뜨림, wi-ban 위반 ; pul-hwa 불화(不和) : *a ~ of contract* kye-yak-wi-ban 계약위반.

bread *n.* ppang 빵, sik-bbang 식빵.

breadth *n.* p'ok 폭, na-bi 나비.

break *v.* ① pu-su-da 부수다 ; jjo-gae-da 쪼개다. ② wi-ban-ha-da 위반하다. ③ chung-ji-ha-da 중지하다. —*n.* ① (*rupture*) p'a-goe 파괴. ② (*gap*) kal-ra-jin t'ŭm 갈라진 틈. ③ (*pause*) chung-dan 중단.

breakdown *n.* ① ko-jang 고장. ② p'a-son 파손. ③ pung-goe 붕괴.

breakfast *n.* cho-ban 조반.

breakwater *n.* pang-p'a-je 방파제.

breast *n.* ka-sŭm 가슴 ; (*woman*) yu-bang 유방, chŏt 젖.

breastwork *n.* hyung-byŏk 흉벽.

breath *n.* sum 숨, ho-hŭp 호흡.

breathe *v.* sum-swi-da 숨쉬다, ho-hŭp-ha-da 호흡하다.

breathless *adj.* sum-ga-bbŭn 숨가쁜.

breeches *n.* jjal-bŭn yang-bok-ba-ji 짧은 양복바지.

breed *v.* ① (*keep cattle*) ki-rŭ-da 기르다. ② (*propagate*) pŏn-sik-ha-da 번식하다. —*n.* chong-jok 종족.

breeze *n.* san-dŭl-ba-ram 산들바람, mi-p'ung 미풍.

brethren *n.* ① tong-p'o 동포, ② tong-ŏp-ja 동업자.

brevity *n.* kan-gyŏl 간결, kal-lyak 간략.

brew *v.* yang-jo-ha-da 양조하다, pit-da 빚다.

brewery *n.* yang-jo-jang 양조장.

bribe *n.* noe-mul 뇌물. —*v.* noe-mul-ŭl chu-da 뇌물을 주다.

bribery *n.* chŭng-hoe 증회, su-hoe 수회.

brick *n.* pyŏk-dol 벽돌.

brickyard *n.* pyŏk-dol kong-jang 벽돌 공장.

bride *n.* sin-bu 신부(新婦), sae-saek-si 새색시.

bridegroom *n.* sil-lang 신랑.

bridesmaid *n.* sin-bu tŭl-rŏ-ri 신부 들러리.

bridesman *n.* sil-lang tŭl-rŏ-ri 신랑 들러리.

bridge *n.* ta-ri 다리, kyo-ryang 교량.

bridgehead *n.* kyo-du-bo 교두보. 「ku-sok 구속.

bridle *n.* mal-gul-re 말굴레, ko-bbi 고삐 ; (*restraint*)

brief *adj.* kan-dan-han 간단한, kan-gyŏl-han 간결한.

brier *n.* jjil-re 찔레, (*wild rose*) tŭl-jang-mi 들장미.

brigade *n.* yŏ-dan 여단(旅團) ; tae 대(隊).

brigadier general yuk-gun-jun-jang 육군준장.

bright *adj.* pit-na-nŭn 빛나는, mal-gŭn 맑은 ; k'wae-hwal-han 쾌활한 ; ch'ong-myŏng-han 총명한.

brighten *v.* pit-na-ge ha-da 빛나게 하다 ; chŭl-gŏp-ge ha-da 즐겁게 하다. 「룽한.

brilliant *adj.* ch'al-lan-han 찬란한, hul-ryung-han 훌

brim *n.* ka-jang-ja-ri 가장자리, (*projecting rim*) t'e 테.

brimful *adj.* nŏm-ch'il tŭt-han 넘칠 듯한.

brine *n.* jjan-mul 짠물, kan-mul 간물.

bring *v.* (*of things*) ka-jyŏ-o-da 가져오다, (*of person*) te-ryŏ-o-da 데려오다 ; ch'o-rae-ha-da 초래하다.

brink *n.* ① ka-jang-ja-ri 가장자리. ② mul-ga 물가.

brisk *adj.* hwal-bal-han 활발한; sang-k'wae-han 상쾌한.

briskly *adv.* hwal-bal-ha-ge 활발하게. 「(剛毛).

bristle *n.* ppŏt-bbŏt-han t'ŏl 뻣뻣한 털, kang-mo 강모

Britain *n.* tae-yŏng-je-guk 대영제국, yŏng-guk 영국.

brittle *adj.* ① kkae-ji-gi swi-un 깨지기 쉬운. ② (*transitory*) hŏ-mang-han 허망한.

broad *adj.* nŏl-bŭn 넓은, kwan-dae-han 관대한 ; (*plain*) myŏng-baek-han 명백한.

broadcast *v.* ① pang-song-ha-da 방송하다. ② (*spread*) yu-p'o-ha-da 유포하다. —*n.* pang-song 방송.

broadcasting station pang-song-guk 방송국.

brocade *n.* su-no-ŭn pi-dan 수놓은 비단.

brochure *n.* so-ch'aek-ja 소책자, p'am-p'ŭl-ret 팜플렛.

broil *v.* (*grill*) kup-da 굽다. —*n.* ① (*roast meat*) pul-go-gi 불고기. ② ssa-um 싸움.

broken *adj.* ① pu-sŏ-jin 부서진. ② (*weakened*) nak-sim-han 낙심한: *a* ~ *heart* si-ryŏn 실연.

broker *n.* chung-gae-in 중개인, pŭ-ro-u-k'ŏ 브로우커.

bronchia *n.* ki-gwan-ji 기관지(氣管支).

bronchitis *n.* ki-gwan-ji-yŏm 기관지염. 「ŭi 청동의.

bronze *n.* ch'ŏng-dong 청동(靑銅). —*adj.* ch'ŏng-dong-

brooch *n.* pŭ-ro-u-ch'i 브로우치.

brood *n.* han-bae sae-ggi 한배 새끼. —*v.* (*meditate deeply*) kom-gom-i saeng-gak-ha-da 곰곰이 생각하다.

brook *n.* si-nae 시내, sil-gae-ch'ŏn 실개천.

broom *n.* pi 비. —*v.* (*sweep*) ssŭl-da 쓸다, ch'ŏng-so-ha-da 청소하다.

broth *n.* (*thin soup*) ko-git-guk 고깃국.

brothel *n.* mae-ŭm-gul 매음굴, kal-bo-jip 갈보집.

brother *n.* hyŏng-je 형제: *elder* ~ (*for men*) hyŏng-nim 형님; (*for women*) o-bba 오빠/ *younger* ~ tong-saeng 동생, a-u 아우.

brother-in-law *n.* (*husband's elder brother*) a-ju-bŏ-ni 아주버니; (*husband's younger brother*) si-dong-saeng 시동생; (*wife's brother*) ch'ŏ-nam 처남; (*sister's husband*) mae-bu 매부.

brow *n.* (*forehead*) i-ma 이마; (*eye*) nun-ssŏp 눈썹.

brown *n.* & *adj.* kal-saek(-ŭi) 갈색(의), ko-dong-saek (-ŭi) 고동색(의). 「da 상처를 내다.

bruise *n.* t'a-bak-sang 타박상. —*v.* sang-ch'ŏ-rŭl nae-

brush n. ① sol 솔, pŭ-rŏ-si 브러시. ② (for painting, writing) put 붓. —v. sol-jil-ha-da 솔질하다.

brutal adj. ya-su-jŏk-in 야수적인 ; (cruel) chan-in-han 잔인한, ya-bi-han 야비한.

brutality n. chan-in 잔인, mu-ja-bi 무자비.

brute n. ① (beast) chim-sŭng 짐승 ; ch'uk-saeng 축생. ② (cruel person) pi-in-gan 비인간.

bubble n. kŏ-p'um 거품 : ki-p'o 기포.

bubonic plague hŭk-sa-byŏng 흑사병, p'e-sŭ-t'ŭ 페스트.

buck n. ① su-sa-sŭm 수사슴. ② (dollar) tal-rŏ 달러(弗).

bucket n. yang-dong-i 양동이, pŏ-k'it 버킷.

buckle n. mul-rim-soe 물림쇠, hyŏk-dae-soe 혁대쇠, pŏ-k'ŭl 버클.

buckwheat n. me-mil 메밀.

bud n. pong-o-ri 봉오리, ssak 싹.

Buddha n. pu-ch'ŏ 부처.

Buddhism n. pul-gyo 불교.

Buddhist n. pul-gyo-do 불교도, pul-gyo sin-ja 불교 신자.

Buddhist scripture pul-gyŏng 불경

Buddhist temple chŏl 절.

[pu-ch'ŏ]

buddy n. (mate) tong-ryo 동료, jjak-p'ae 짝패.

budget n. ye-san 예산, ye-san-an 예산안.

buffer n. wan-ch'ung-gi 완충기.

bug n. pŏl-re 벌레 ; (bedbug) pin-dae 빈대.

bugle n. na-p'al 나팔, kak-jŏk 각적(角笛).

build v. se-u-da 세우다, kŏn-sŏl-ha-da 건설하다.

building n. kŏn-mul 건물, pil-ding 빌딩. 「전구.

bulb n. ① ku-gŭn 구근(球根). ② (electric) chŏn-gu

bulge n. pu-p'um 부품. —v. pu-p'ul-da 부풀다.

bulk n. (volume) yong-jŏk 용적, (size) k'ŭ-gi 크기,

(*cargo*) paet-jim 뱃짐.

bulky *adj*. pu-p'i-ga k'ŭn 부피가 큰.

bull *n*. hwang-so 황소 ; (*animal*) su-k'ŏt 수컷. 「위협하다.

bulldoze *v*. kang-haeng-ha-da 강행하다, wi-hyŏp-ha-da

bullet *n*. ch'ong-al 총알, t'an-hwan 탄환.

bulletin *n*. kong-bo 공보(公報), hoe-bo 회보 : *a ~ board* ke-si-p'an 게시판.

bullfrog *n*. sik-yong kae-gu-ri 식용 개구리.

bully *n*. kol-mok-dae-jang 골목대장 ; kkang-p'ae 깡패.

bump *v*. pu-dit-ch'i-da 부딪치다. —*n*. ① ch'ung-dol 충돌. ② (*swelling*) hok 혹. 「da-bal 꽃다발.

bunch *n*. song-i 송이, ta-bal 다발 : *a ~ of flower* kkot-

bundle *n*. ta-bal 다발, kku-rŏ-mi 꾸러미. 「대.

buoy *n*. pu-p'yo 부표(浮標), ku-myŏng-bu-dae 구명부

buoyant *adj*. ① chal ttŭ-nŭn 잘 뜨는. ② (*merry*) k'wae-hwal-han 쾌활한, hwal-gi-it-nŭn 활기있는.

burden *n*. mu-gŏ-un chim 무거운 짐, pu-dam 부담.

burdensome *adj*. pu-dam-i toe-nŭn 부담이 되는, kwi-ch'an-ŭn 귀찮은, sŏng-ga-sin 성가신.

bureau *n*. ① (*dresser*) ot-jang 옷장. ② (*office*) kuk 국(局), an-nae-so 안내소 : *an employment ~* chik-ŏp so-gae-so 직업 소개소.

burglar *n*. kang-do 강도, pam-do-duk 밤도둑.

burial *n*. mae-jang 매장(埋葬).

burn *v*. pul-t'a-da 불타다, hwa-sang-ŭl ip-da 화상을 입다, kŭ-ŭl-da 그을다. —*n*. hwa-sang 화상(火傷).

burnish *v*. ① (*polish*) tak-da 닦다. ② (*become bright*) pit-na-da 빛나다. —*n*. yun 윤, kwang-t'aek 광택.

burrow *n*. kul 굴. —*v*. kul-ŭl p'a-da 굴을 파다.

burst *v*. t'ŏ-ji-da 터지다 ; pyŏ-ran-gan na-t'a-na-da 별안간 나타나다. —*n*. p'ok-bal 폭발.

bury *v*. p'a-mut-da 파묻다, mae-jang-ha-da 매장하다.

bus *n.* pŏ-sŭ 버스.

bush *n.* su-p'ul 수풀, tŏm-bul 덤불. 「sa-ŏp 사업.

business *n.* chik-ŏp 직업 ; ŏp-mu 업무 ; chang-sa 장사;

bust *n.* ① pan-sin-sang 반신상(半身像), hyung-sang 흉상. ② (*failure*) sil-p'ae 실패. 「큰 소동.

bustle *v.* pŏp-sŏk-dae-da 법석대다. —*n.* k'ŭn so-dong

busy *adj.* pa-bbŭn 바쁜, pŏn-ch'ang-han 번창한.

but *conj.* kŭ-rŏ-na 그러나. —*prep.* …oe-e-nŭn …외에 는. —*adv.* ta-man 다만, tan-ji 단지 「점.

butcher *n.* p'u-ju(-han) 푸주(한) ; chŏng-yuk-jŏm 정육

butler *n.* chip-sa 집사, ch'ŏng-ji-gi 청지기.

butter *n.* bŏ-t'ŏ 버터. 「泳).

butterfly *n.* na-bi 나비 : ~ *stroke* chŏp-yŏng 접영(蝶

button *n.* tan-ch'u 단추. —*v.* tan-ch'u-rŭl ch'ae-u-da [tal-da] 단추를 채우다[달다].

buttonhole *n.* tan-ch'u ku-mŏng 단추 구멍.

buy *v.* sa-da 사다, ku-ip-ha-da 구입하다. —*n.* mae-ip

buyer *n.* sa-nŭn sa-ram 사는 사람, pa-i-ŏ 바이어.「매입.

buzz *v.* (*bees*) wing-wing so-ri-nae-da 윙윙 소리내다. —*n.* wing-wing-gŏ-ri-nŭn so-ri 윙윙거리는 소리 ; (*humming*) so-ŭm 소음.

by *adv.* kyŏ-t'e 곁에. —*prep.* ① …yŏ-p'e …옆에. ② (*by means of*) … ŭi-ha-yŏ …에 의하여. ③ (*before*) kka-ji-e-nŭn 까지에는.

by-product *n.* pu-san-mul 부산물. 「관자.

bystander *n.* ku-gyŏng-gun 구경군 ; pang-gwan-ja 방

bystreet *n.* twit-gol-mok 뒷골목, twit-gil 뒷길.

—◄❖ **C** ❖►—

cab *n.* ① t'aek-si 택시. ② ma-ch'a 마차.

cabbage *n.* yang-bae-ch'u 양배추, k'ae-bi-ji 캐비지.

cabin *n.* ① (*hut*) o-du-mak-jip 오두막집. ② (*ship*) sŏn-sil 선실. ③ (*signal ~*) sin-ho-so 신호소.

cabinet *n. & adj.* ① chang 장(欌). ② (*governmental*) nae-gak(ŭi) 내각(의) : *a C~ minister* kak-ryo 각료.

cable *n.* (*rope*) kul-gŭn pat-jul 굵은 밧줄, k'e-i-bŭl 케이블 ; (*underwater*) hae-jŏ chŏn-sŏn 해저 전선.

cable car k'e-i-bŭl k'a-a 케이블 카아.

cablegram *n.* hae-oe-jŏn-bo 해외전보, oe-jŏn 외전.

cadence *n.* un-yul 운율(韻律), ŏk-yang 억양.

cadet *n.* sa-gwan saeng-do 사관 생도, sa-gwan[kan-bu] hu-bo-saeng 사관[간부] 후보생.

cage *n.* ① (*bird*) sae-jang 새장. ② kam-ok 감옥.

cake *n.* ① kwa-ja 과자, k'e-i-k'ŭ 케이크. ② (*solid mass*) tŏng-ŏ-ri 덩어리.

calamity *n.* chae-nan 재난, pul-haeng 불행.

calculate *v.* ① kye-san-ha-da 계산하다, ye-sang-ha-da 예상하다. ② (*rely*) ki-dae-ha-da 기대하다.

calculation *n.* kye-san 계산 ; (*forecast*) ye-sang 예상.

calendar *n.* tal-ryŏk 달력, k'ael-rin-dŏ 캘린더.

calf *n.* ① song-a-ji 송아지. ② (*leg*) chong-a-ri 종아리.

calico *n.* ok-yang-mok 옥양목.

call *v.* ① pu-rŭ-da 부르다. ② (*visit*) pang-mun-ha-da 방문하다. ③ (*telephone*) chŏn-hwa-rŭl kŏl-da 전화를 걸다. —*n.* (*visit*) pang-mun 방문.

calling *n.* ① so-jip 소집. ② (*occupation*) chik-ŏp 직업.

calm *adj.* ko-yo-han 고요한, on-hwa-han 온화한.

camel *n.* nak-t'a 낙타.

camera *n.* sa-jin-gi 사진기, k'a-me-ra 카메라.

camp *n.* ya-yŏng 야영. —*v.* ya-yŏng-ha-da 야영하다.

campaign *n.* ① chŏn-jaeng 전쟁. ② chŏng-ch'i-un-dong 정치운동 : *an election ~* sŏn-gŏ-un-dong 선거운동.

camping *n.* ya-yŏng 야영, k'aem-p'u saeng-hwal 캠

프 생활, ch'ŏn-mak saeng-hwal 천막 생활. 「퍼스.
campus *n.* hak-gyo ku-nae 학교 구내, k'aem-p'ŏ-sŭ 캠
can *n.* kkang-t'ong 깡통. —*aux. v.* …hal su it-da …할
수 있다, (*may*) ha-yŏ-do cho-t'a 하여도 좋다.
Canadian *n.* k'ae-na-da-sa-ram 캐나다사람. —*adj.*
k'ae-na-da-ŭi 캐나다의.
canal *n.* ① un-ha 운하. ② to-gwan 도관(導管).
canary *n.* k'a-na-ri-a 카나리아.
cancel *v.* ch'wi-so-ha-da 취소하다, mal-sal-ha-da 말살
하다. —*n.* mal-sal 말살, p'ye-gi 폐기.
cancellation *n.* ch'wi-so 취소, mal-sal 말살.
cancer *n.* ① am 암 : ~ *of the lung* p'ye-am 폐암/~
of the stomach wi-am 위암/*uterine* ~ cha-gung-am
자궁암. ② (*C*~) ha-ji-sŏn 하지선(夏至線).
candid *adj.* sol-jik-han 솔직한, chŏng-jik-han 정직한.
candidate *n.* hu-bo-ja 후보자 ; chi-wŏn-ja 지원자.
candle *n.* ① yang-ch'o 양초. ② ch'ok-gwang 촉광.
candlelight *n.* ch'ot-bul 촛불.
candlestick *n.* ch'ot-dae 촛대.
cando(u)r *n.* sol-jik 솔직, chŏng-jik 정직.
candy *n.* sa-t'ang 사탕, k'aen-di 캔디.
cane *n.* ① chi-p'ang-i 지팡이, tan-jang 단장. ② (*stem*)
chul-gi 줄기 : *sugar* ~ sa-t'ang-su-su 사탕수수.
canned goods t'ong-jo-rim che-p'um 통조림 제품.
cannibal *n.* sik-in-jong 식인종.
cannon *n.* tae-p'o 대포, ki-gwan-p'o 기관포.
cannon ball (*shell*) p'o-t'an 포탄.
cannot *v.* …hal su ŏp-da …할 수 없다. 「중한.
canny *adj.* pin-t'ŭm-ŏp-nŭn 빈틈없는, sin-jung-han 신
canoe *n.* t'ong-na-mu-bae 통나무배, k'a-nu-u 카누우.
canopy *n.* tŏp-gae 덮개, ch'ŏn-gae 천개(天蓋) ; k'ae-
nŏ-p'i 캐너피.

canvas *n.* hwa-p'o 화포(畫布), k'aen-bŏ-sŭ 캔버스.

canvass *v.* ① (*examine thoroughly*) se-mil-hi cho-sa-ha-da 세밀히 조사하다. ② (*election*) yu-se-ha-da 유세하다. —*n.* sŏn-gŏ-un-dong 선거운동, yu-se 유세.

cap *n.* (*no brim*) mo-ja 모자 ; ttu-ggŏng 뚜껑.

capable *adj.* …hal su it-nŭn …할 수 있는.

capacity *n.* ① (*cubic content*) yong-jŏk 용적. ② (*ability*) chae-nŭng 재능. ③ (*function*) cha-gyŏk 자격.

cape *n.* ① ŏ-ggae mang-t'o 어깨 망토, k'e-i-p'ŭ 케이프. ② (*headland*) kot 곶(岬).

capital *adj.* chu-yo-han 주요한. —*n.* ① (*city*) su-do 수도. ② (*money*) cha-bon 자본. ③ (*letter*) tae-mun-ja 대문자.

capitalism *n.* cha-bon-ju-ŭi 자본주의.

capitalist *n.* cha-bon-ga 자본가 ; cha-bon-ju-ŭi-ja 자본주의자.

capitol *n.* kuk-hoe ŭi-sa-dang 국회 의사당.

capsule *n.* k'aep-syul 캡슐 ; kko-t'u-ri 꼬투리.

captain *n.* (*army*) tae-wi 대위 ; (*navy*) tae-ryŏng 대령 ; (*of warship*) ham-jang 함장 ; (*of merchant ship*) sŏn-jang 선장 ; (*of sport*) chu-jang 주장.

caption *n.* (*heading*) p'yo-je 표제 ; (*cinema*) cha-mak 자막(字幕). 「mu-ggin 묶인.

captive *n.* p'o-ro 포로. —*adj.* sa-ro-jap-hin 사로잡힌,

capture *n.* (*seizure*) p'o-hoek 포획, saeng-p'o 생포. —*v.* (*catch*) chap-da 잡다.

car *n.* ch'a 차, cha-dong-ch'a 자동차 ; chŏn-ch'a 전차.

caravan *n.* tae-sang 대상(隊商).

carbolic acid sŏk-t'an-san 석탄산.

carbon *n.* t'an-so 탄소 : ~ *paper* k'a-a-bon-ji 카아본지.

carburetor *n.* ki-hwa-gi 기화기(氣化器), k'a-a-byu-re-t'ŏ 카아뷰레터.

carcase·carcass *n.* (*animal*) si-ch'e 시체.

card *n.* ① k'a-a-dŭ 카아드. ② (*playing*) t'ŭ-rŏm-p'ŭ

트럼프. ③ (*calling*) myŏng-ham 명함.

cardboard *n.* ma-bun-ji 마분지.

cardinal *adj.* ① (*fundamental*) ki-bon-jŏk-in 기본적인. ② (*bright red*) sae-bbal-gan 새빨간.

care *v.* kŏk-jŏng-ha-da 걱정하다. —*n.* ① (*anxiety*) kŏk-jŏng 걱정. ② cho-sim 조심 : *take* ~ chu-ŭi-ha-da 주의하다. 「ŏp 직업.

career *n.* ① kyŏng-ryŏk 경력. ② (*occupation*) chik-

carefree *adj.* kŏk-jŏng-ŏp-nŭn 걱정없는, (*easy*) t'ae-p'yŏng-su-rŏn 태평스런. 「소중히 하는.

careful *adj.* chu-ŭi-gi-p'ŭn 주의깊은, so-jung-hi ha-nŭn

carefully *adv.* cho-sim-su-rŏp-ge 조심스럽게.

careless *adj.* cho-sim-sŏng-ŏp-nŭn 조심성없는, kyŏng-sol-han 경솔한. 「ge 경솔하게.

carelessly *adv.* so-hol-ha-ge 소홀하게, kyŏng-sol-ha-

carelessness *n.* pu-ju-ŭi 부주의, mu-gwan-sim 무관심.

caress *n. & v.* ae-mu(-ha-da) 애무(하다).

caretaker *n.* kwal-li-in 관리인 ; mun-ji-gi 문지기.

carfare *n.* kyo-t'ong-bi 교통비, pŏ-su-yo-gŭm 버스요금.

cargo *n.* hwa-mul 화물, paet-jim 뱃짐.

carnival *n.* ch'uk-je 축제(祝祭), k'a-a-ni-bal 카아니발.

carol *n.* ch'uk-ha-ŭi no-rae 축하의 노래 : *Christmas* ~ k'ŭ-ri-su-ma-su ch'uk-ga 크리스마스 축가(祝歌).

carp *n.* ing-ŏ 잉어 : *the silver* ~ pung-ŏ 붕어.

carpenter *n.* mok-su 목수, mok-gong 목공(木工).

carpet *n.* yang-t'an-ja 양탄자, yung-dan 융단.

carriage *n.* ① (*transport*) un-ban 운반 ; (*coach*) ma-ch'a 마차. ② (*bearing*) t'ae-do 태도.

carrier *n.* ① un-ban-in 운반인 ; (*mail*) u-ch'e-bu 우체부 ; (*A-frame*) chi-get-gun 지겟군. ② (*germ* ~) po-gyun-ja 보균자. ③ (*aircraft* ~) hang-gong-mo-ham

carrot *n.* tang-gŭn 당근. 「항공모함.

carry *v.* ① (*take*) na-rŭ-da 나르다, un-ban-ha-da 운반
하다 ; (*on the head*) i-da 이다 ; (*on the back*) chi-da
지다 ; (*in the arms*) an-da 안다 ; (*on the shoulder*)
me-da 메다 ; (*in the hand*) tŭl-da 들다 ; (*in the
belt*) ch'a-da 차다. ② hyu-dae-ha-da 휴대하다.

cart *n.* ch'a 차 ; chim-ma-ch'a 짐마차.

cartoon *n.* p'ung-ja-man-hwa 풍자만화.

cartridge *n.* t'an-yak-t'ong 탄약통, yak-p'o 약포.

carve *v.* cho-gak-ha-da 조각하다, sae-gi-da 새기다.

carver *n.* cho-gak-ga 조각가.

carving *n.* cho-gak 조각, cho-gak-sul 조각술.

case *n.* ① (*box*) sang-ja 상자. ② (*condition*) kyŏng-u
경우. ③ (*affair*) sa-gŏn 사건. ④ (*patient*) hwan-ja

casement *n.* yŏ-da-ji ch'ang-mun 여닫이 창문. 「환자.

cash *n.* hyŏn-gŭm 현금, hyŏn-ch'al 현찰. —*v.* (*exchange*) hyŏn-gŭm-ŭ-ro pa-ggu-da 현금으로 바꾸다.

cashier *n.* ch'ul-nap-gye 출납계, hoe-gye-wŏn 회계원.

cask *n.* t'ong 통 : *a wine* ~ sul-t'ong 술통.

casket *n.* chak-ŭn sang-ja 작은 상자 ; (*coffin*) kwan 관.

cast *v.* ① (*throw*) tŏn-ji-da 던지다. ② (*found*) chu-
jo-ha-da 주조하다. —*n.* ① (*mold*) chu-hyŏng 주형
(鑄型). ② (*of play*) pae-yŏk 배역. 「jŏn 궁전.

castle *n.* ① sŏng 성(城), sŏng-gwak 성곽. ② kung-

castor oil a-ju-gga-ri ki-rŭm 아주까리 기름, p'i-ma-ja-
yu 피마자유.

casual *adj.* u-yŏn-han 우연한, ttŭt-ba-ggŭi 뜻밖의.

cat *n.* ① ko-yang-i 고양이. ② (*guy*) nom 놈.

catalog(ue) *n.* mok-rok 목록, k'a-t'al-ro-gŭ 카탈로그.

catastrophe *n.* ① (*a great misfortune*) k'ŭn chae-nan
큰 재난. ② (*drama*) tae-dan-wŏn 대단원.

catch ① (*seize*) chap-da 잡다. ② (*overtake*) ch'u-
wŏl-ha-da 추월하다. ③ (*be attacked*) kam-yŏm-ha-

da 감염하다. ④ (*arrest*) chu-ŭi-rŭl kkŭl-da 주의를 끌
다. ⑤ (*understand*) i-hae-ha-da 이해하다.
category *n.* pŏm-ju 범주, k'ae-t'i-go-ri 캐티고리.
caterpillar *n.* p'ul-sswae-gi 풀쐐기, mo-ch'ung 모충.
cathedral *n.* tae-sŏng-dang 대성당.
Catholic *adj.* (*Roman*) ch'ŏn-ju-gyo-ŭi 천주교의. —*n.*
ch'ŏn-ju-gyo-do 천주교도, ku-gyo-do 구교도.
cattle *n.* so 소 ; (*livestock*) ka-ch'uk 가축.
cause *v.* i-rŭk'i-da 일으키다. —*n.* ① (*reason*) wŏn-in
원인 ; (*motive*) tong-gi 동기. ② tae-ŭi 대의(大義).
caution *n.* ① cho-sim 조심. ② (*warning*) kyŏng-go
경고. ③ (*surety*) tam-bo 담보.
cautious *adj.* cho-sim-sŏng-it-nŭn 조심성있는.
cavalier *n.* ki-sa 기사(騎士), ki-ma-byŏng 기마병.
cavalry *n.* ki-byŏng 기병, ki-byŏng-dae 기병대.
cave *n.* kul 굴, tong-gul 동굴, tong-hyŏl 동혈.
cavity *n.* ku-mŏng 구멍 ; kong-dong 공동(空洞).
cease *v.* kŭ-ch'i-da 그치다, kŭ-man-du-da 그만두다.
ceasefire *n.* hyu-jŏn 휴전 : the ~ line hyu-jŏn-sŏn 휴전선.
ceaseless *adj.* kkŭn-im-ŏp-nŭn 끊임없는.
cedar *n.* hi-mal-ra-ya sam-mok 히말라야 삼목(杉木).
ceiling *n.* ① ch'ŏn-jang 천장. ② kkok-dae-gi 꼭대기.
celadon *n.* (*porcelain*) ch'ŏng-ja 청자(靑瓷).
celebrate *v.* ch'uk-ha-ha-da 축하하다.
celebrated *adj.* i-rŭm-no-p'ŭn 이름높은, yu-myŏng-
han 유명한, chŏ-myŏng-han 저명한.
celebration *n.* ch'uk-ha 축하, che-jŏn 제전.
celebrity *n.* ① (*famous person*) myŏng-sa 명사, yu-
myŏng-in 유명인. ② (*fame*) myŏng-sŏng 명성.
celery *n.* sel-rŏ-ri 셀러리.
cell *n.* ① (*small room*) chak-ŭn tok-bang 작은 독방.
② (*hermit*) am-ja 암자. ③ (*prison*) kam-bang

감방. ④ (*biol.*) se-p'o 세포.

cellar *n.* chi-ha-sil 지하실 ; um 움.

cement *n.* si-men-t'ŭ 시멘트, yang-hoe 양회.

cemetery *n.* kong-dong-myo-ji 공동묘지.

censure *n.* pi-nan 비난, kyŏn-ch'aek 견책. —*v.* pi-nan-ha-da 비난하다, na-mu-ra-da 나무라다.

census *n.* kuk-se-jo-sa 국세조사, sen-sŏ-sŭ 센서스.

cent *n.* sen-t'ŭ 센트.

centenary *adj.* paek-nyŏn-ŭi 100년의. —*n.* paek-nyŏn-gan 100년간, paek-nyŏn-je 100년제(祭).

center *n.* chung-sim 중심, sen-t'ŏ 센터.

centigrade *adj.* paek-bun-do-ŭi 백분도의 : ~ *thermometer* sŏp-ssi on-do-gye 섭씨 온도계.

centiped(e) *n.* chi-ne 지네.

central *adj.* chung-ang-ŭi 중앙의, chung-sim-ŭi 중심의.

century *n.* se-gi 세기, paek-nyŏn 100년.

cereals *n.* kok-sik 곡식, kok-mul 곡물.

ceremony *n.* ye-sik 예식, ŭi-sik 의식(儀式) : *a marriage* ~ kyŏl-hon-sik 결혼식.

certain *adj.* (*sure*) hwak-sil-han 확실한 ; (*one, some*) ŏ-ddŏn 어떤 ; (*fixed*) il-jŏng-han 일정한.

certainly *adv.* ① hwak-sil-hi 확실히. ② (*exclamation*) kŭ-rŏ-k'o-mal-go 그렇고말고.

certificate *n.* chŭng-myŏng-sŏ 증명서. 「ha-da 보증하다.

certify *v.* ① chŭng-myŏng-ha-da 증명하다. ② po-jŭng-

chain *n.* soe-sa-sŭl 쇠사슬 ; (*a long line*) yŏn-sok 연속.

chair *n.* ŭi-ja 의자, kŏl-sang 걸상 ; ŭi-jang 의장.

chairman *n.* ŭi-jang 의장, hoe-jang 회장.

chalk *n.* pun-p'il 분필, ch'o-o-k'ŭ 초오크.

challenge *n.* to-jŏn 도전. —*v.* to-jŏn-ha-da 도전하다.

chamber ① (*room*) pang 방. ② (*assembly hall*) hoe-ŭi-so 회의소 : ~ *music* sil-nae-ak 실내악.

champion *n.* chŏn-sa 전사(戰士) ; (*winner*) u-sŭng-ja 우승자, (*player*) ch'aem-p'i-ŏn 챔피언.

chance *n.* (*opportunity*) ki-hoe 기회, ch'a-an-sŭ 차안스.

change *n.* ① pyŏn-gyŏng 변경. ② (*money*) chan-don 잔돈, kŏ-sŭ-rŭm-don 거스름돈. —*v.* pyŏn-ha-da 변하다, pa-ggu-da 바꾸다.

changeable *adj.* pyŏn-ha-gi swi-un 변하기 쉬운.

channel *n.* ① hae-hyŏp 해협, su-ro 수로. ② kyŏng-ro 경로. ③ (*radio, TV*) ch'ae-nŏl 채널. 「ha-da 노래하다.

chant *n.* no-rae 노래 ; sŏng-ga 성가. —*v.* (*sing*) no-rae-

chaos *n.* hon-don 혼돈, mu-jil-sŏ 무질서.

chap *n.* (*fellow*) nyŏ-sŏk 녀석, nom 놈 : *a good* ~ cho-ŭn nyŏ-sŏk 좋은 녀석.

chapel *n.* ye-bae-dang 예배당, (*service*) ye-bae 예배.

chaperon(e) *n.* sya-p'ŭ-rong 샤프롱.

chapter *n.* ① (*book*) chang 장(章). ② (*local divisions*) chi-bu 지부, pun-hoe 분회.

character *n.* ① sŏng-jil 성질 ; in-gyŏk 인격. ② myŏng-sŏng 명성. ③ (*letter*) kŭl-ja 글자.

charcoal *n.* sut 숯, mok-t'an 목탄.

charge *n.* ① ch'aek-im 책임. ② (*price demanded*) pu-dam 부담, yo-gŭm 요금. ③ (*accusation*) pi-nan 비난, ko-bal 고발. —*v.* (*attack*) chin-gyŏk-ha-da 진격하다.

chariot *n.* chŏn-ch'a 전차(戰車) ; ma-ch'a 마차.

charitable *adj.* in-ja-han 인자한, cha-bi-ro-un 자비로운.

charity *n.* cha-bi-sim 자비심, cha-ae 자애, sa-rang 사랑.

charm *v.* mae-hok-ha-da 매혹하다. —*n.* mae-ryŏk 매력.

charming *adj.* mae-ryŏk-jŏk-in 매력적인.

chart *n.* to-p'yo 도표, ch'a-a-t'ŭ 차아트 ; hae-do 해도 (海圖). 「hŏ-ga-jang 허가장.

charter *n.* ① hŏn-jang 헌장. ② t'ŭk-hŏ-jang 특허장,

chase *v.* twi-rŭl jjot-da 뒤를 쫓다. —*n.* ch'u-gyŏk 추격.

chaste *adj.* sun-gyŏl-han 순결한 ; ko-sang-han 고상한.

chat *n. & v.* chap-dam(-ha-da) 잡담(하다).

chatter *v.* chae-jal-jae-jal chi-ggŏ-ri-da 재잘재잘 지껄이 다. —*n.* chi-ggŏ-ri-nŭn so-ri 지껄이는 소리.

chauffeur *n.* un-jŏn ki-sa 운전 기사, un-jŏn-su 운전수.

cheap *adj.* ssan 싼, kap-ssan 값싼.

cheat *v.* sok-i-da 속이다 ; sok-yŏ ppae-at-da 속여 빼앗다.

check *v.* (*prevent*) chŏ-ji-ha-da 저지하다, (*control*) ŏk-je-ha-da 억제하다 ; (*collate*) tae-jo-ha-da 대조하다, ch'e-k'ŭ-ha-da 체크하다. —*n.* ① pang-hae 방해. ② chŏm-gŏm 점검, ch'e-k'ŭ 체크. ③ (*bank*) su-p'yo 수표.

checkbook *n.* su-p'yo-jang 수표장.

checkerboard *n.* chang-gi-p'an 장기판.

checkers *n.* sŏ-yang-jang-gi 서양장기.

cheek *n.* ppyam 뺨, pol 볼.

cheer *n.* ki-bun 기분, k'wae-hwal 쾌활 ; (*applause*) kal-ch'ae 갈채. —*v.* ① (*comfort*) ki-bbŭ-ge ha-da 기쁘게 하다. ② (*animate*) ki-un-ŭl tot-gu-da 기운을 돋구다 : *C~ up!* Ki-un-ŭl nae-ra! 기운을 내라 !

cheerful *adj.* ki-bun-jo-ŭn 기분좋은 ; k'wae-hwal-han 쾌활한.

cheese *n.* ch'i-i-jŭ 치이즈.

chemical *adj.* hwa-hak-ŭi 화학의. —*n.* hwa-hak-je-p'um 화학제품, yak-p'um 약품.

chemise *n.* sok-ch'i-ma 속치마, si-mi-i-jŭ 시미이즈.

chemist *n.* hwa-hak-ja 화학자 ; (*Brit.*) yak-je-sa 약제사.

chemistry *n.* hwa-hak 화학.

cheque *n.* su-p'yo 수표.

cherish *v.* so-jung-hi ha-da 소중히 하다 ; (*foster*) ma-ŭm-e p'um-da 마음에 품다.

cherry *n.* pŏ-jji 버찌 ; (*blossom*) pŏt-ggot 벚꽃 ; (*tree*) pŏt-na-mu 벚나무. —*adj.* chin-bun-hong-ŭi 진분홍의.

chess *n.* sŏ-yang-jang-gi 서양장기, ch'e-sŭ 체스.

chest *n.* ① (*breast*) ka-sŭm 가슴. ② (*box*) kwe 궤, sang-ja 상자. ③ (*funds*) cha-gŭm 자금.

chestnut *n.* pam 밤(栗), pam-na-mu 밤나무.

chew *v.* ssip-da 씹다.

chewing gum kkŏm 껌.

chick *n.* ① pyŏng-a-ri 병아리. ② (*child*) ŏ-rin-a-i 어
chicken *n.* tak 닭, tak-go-gi 닭고기.   ⌐린아이.

chicken sexer pyŏng-a-ri kam-byŏl-sa 병아리 감별사.

chief *adj.* chu-yo-han 주요한, ŭ-ddŭm-ga-nŭn 으뜸가는.
  —*n.* u-du-mŏ-ri 우두머리, chang 장(長).

chiffonier *n.* yang-bok-jang 양복장.

child *n.* a-i 아이, ŏ-rin-i 어린이, a-dong 아동.

childhood *n.* ŏ-rin si-jŏl 어린 시절, yu-nyŏn-gi 유년기.

chill *n.* naeng-gi 냉기(冷氣) ; (*cold fit*) o-han 오한.

chime *v.* chong-ŭl ul-ri-da 종을 울리다. —*n.* (*bell*)
  chong 종, ch'a-im 차임.

chimney *n.* kul-dduk 굴뚝, yŏn-t'ong 연통.

chin *n.* t'ŏk 턱, t'ŏk-ggŭt 턱끝.

China *n.* chung-guk 중국 : *Red* ~ chung-gong 중공.

china *n.* (*porcelain*) to-ja-gi 도자기, cha-gi 자기.

Chinese *adj.* chung-guk-ŭi 중국의, chung-guk-sik-ŭi
  중국식의 ; (*Communist*) chung-gong-ŭi 중공의. —*n.*
  (*people*) chung-guk-sa-ram 중국사람, chung-guk-
  in 중국인 : (*language*) chung-guk-ŏ 중국어.

chip *n.* t'o-mak 토막, na-mut-jo-gak 나뭇조각. —*v.*
  chal-ge ssŏl-da 잘게 썰다, kkak-da 깎다.

chirp *v.* jjaek-jjaek ul-da 짹짹 울다. —*n.* jjaek-jjaek-
  ha-nŭn u-rŭm-so-ri 짹짹하는 울음소리.

chisel *n.* kkŭl 끌, chŏng 정.   ⌐의협심.

chivalry *n.* ki-sa-do 기사도 ; (*gallantry*) ŭi-hyŏp-sim

chlorine *n.* yŏm-so 염소(鹽素).

chocolate *n.* ch'o-k'ŏl-rit 초컬릿.

choice *n.* sŏn-t'aek 선택, ko-rŭn kŏt 고른 것.

choir *n.* hap-ch'ang-dae 합창대, sŏng-ga-dae 성가대.

choke *v.* sum-mak-hi-ge ha-da 숨막히게 하다 ; ŏk-nu-
rŭ-da 억누르다. —*n.* chil-sik 질식.

cholera *n.* ho-yŏl-ja 호열자, k'ol-re-ra 콜레라.

choose *v.* ① sŏn-t'aek-ha-da 선택하다 ; (*elect*) sŏn-
ch'ul-ha-da 선출하다. ② (*want*) wŏn-ha-da 원하다.

chop *v.* (*cut*) cha-rŭ-da 자르다.
—*n.* chŏl-dan 절단.

chopsticks *n.* chŏt-ga-rak 젓가락.

chorus *n.* hap-ch'ang 합창.

Christ *n.* kŭ-ri-sŭ-do 그리스도.

Christian *n.* ki-dok-gyo-in〔sin-ja〕
기독교인〔신자〕.

[chŏt-ga-rak]

Christianity *n.* ki-dok-gyo 기독교.   「리스마스.

Christmas *n.* sŏng-t'an-jŏl 성탄절, k'ŭ-ri-sŭ-ma-sŭ 크

chronic *adj.* man-sŏng-ŭi 만성의, ko-jil-ŭi 고질의, (*habitual*) sang-sŭp-jŏk-in 상습적인.   「기록.

chronicle *n.* ① yŏn-dae-gi 연대기. ② (*record*) ki-rok

chrysanthemum *n.* kuk-hwa 국화.

chuckle *n.* kkil-ggil u-sŭm 낄낄 웃음. —*v.* kkil-ggil
ut-da 낄낄 웃다, hon-ja ut-da 혼자 웃다.

chum *n.* tan-jjak 단짝, ch'in-gu 친구.

church *n.* kyo-hoe 교회, ye-bae-dang 예배당.

cicada *n.* mae-mi 매미.

cider *n.* sa-i-da 사이다 ; sa-gwa-sul 사과술.

cigar *n.* yo-song-yŏn 여송연, si-ga-a 시가아.

cigaret(te) *n.* kwŏl-ryŏn 궐련, tam-bae 담배.

cinder *n.* sŏk-t'an chae 석탄 재, ttŭn sut 뜬 숯.

cinema *n.* yŏng-hwa-gwan 영화관, yŏng-hwa 영화.

circle *n.* ① (*round*) wŏn-hyŏng 원형. ② (*group*)
chip-dan 집단 ; …kye …계(界). ③ (*range*) pŏm-wi

범위. —v. hoe·jŏn·ha·da 회전하다.

circuit n. (round) sun·hoe 순회 ; (circumference) chu·wi 주위 ; (electric) hoe·ro 회로.

circular adj. wŏn·hyŏng·ŭi 원형의, tung·gŭn 둥근; sun·hwan·ha·nŭn 순환하는. —n. hoe·ram·jang 회람장.

circulate v. sun·hwan·ha·da 순환하다, tol·ri·da 돌리다.

circulation n. sun·hwan 순환, yu·t'ong 유통.

circumference n. wŏn·dul·re 원둘레 ; chu·wi 주위.

circumstance n. sa·jŏng 사정 ; hwan·gyŏng 환경.

circus n. kok·ma·dan 곡마단, sŏ·ŏ·k'ŏ·sŭ 서어커스.

cistern n. mul·t'ong 물통, mul·t'aeng·k'ŭ 물탱크.

citadel n. sŏng 성(城) ; pon·gŏ·ji 본거지.

citation n. ① (quotation) in·yong 인용. ② (testimonial) p'yo·ch'ang·jang 표창장.   「하다.

cite v. in·yong·ha·da 인용하다 ; p'yo·ch'ang·ha·da 표창

citizen n. si·min 시민, kong·min 공민.   「민권.

citizenship n. si·min·gwŏn 시민권, kong·min·gwŏn 공

city n. to·si 도시, si 시(市).

civic adj. si·min·ŭi 시민의, kong·min·ŭi 공민의.

civil adj. ① min·gan·ŭi 민간의. ② (polite) chŏng·jung·han 정중한. ③ (law) min·sa·ŭi 민사의.

civilian n. min·gan·in 민간인, mun·gwan 문관.

civilization n. mun·myŏng 문명, kae·hwa 개화.

civilize v. mun·myŏng·hwa·ha·da 문명화하다, (enlighten) kae·hwa·si·k'i·da 개화시키다.

claim n. yo·gu 요구. —v. ① (insist) chu·jang·ha·da 주장하다. ② (demand) yo·gu·ha·da 요구하다.

clam n. mu·myŏng·jo·gae 무명조개, tae·hap 대합.

clamber v. ki·ŏ·o·rŭ·da 기어오르다. —n. ki·ŏ·o·rŭ·gi 기어오르기, tŭng·ban 등반.

clamo(u)r n. oe·ch'i·nŭn so·ri 외치는 소리. —v. ttŏ·dŭl·

clan n. ① ssi·jok 씨족. ② tang·p'a 당파. ⌊da 떠들다.

clap *n.* pak-su 박수. —*v.* (*hands*) pak-su·ha·da 박수
하다 ; ka·byŏp·ge ch'i·da 가볍게 치다.

clarinet *n.* k'ŭl·la·ri·net 클라리넷.   「sŏng 투명성.

clarity *n.* (*clearness*) myŏng·k'wae 명쾌 ; t'u·myŏng-

clash *v.* ch'ung·dol·ha·da 충돌하다, pu·dit·ch'i·da 부딪
치다. —*n.* pu·dit·ch'i·nŭn so·ri 부딪치는 소리, ch'ung-
dol 충돌, (*discord*) al·ryŏk 알력.   「포옹하다.

clasp *v.* kkwak put·jap·da 꽉 붙잡다 ; p'o·ong·ha·da

class *n.* ① kye·gŭp 계급. ② (*school*) pan 반.

classic *adj.* ① ko·jŏn·ŭi 고전의. ② il·ryu·ŭi 일류의.
—*n.* ko·jŏn chak·p'um 고전 작품.

classification *n.* pul·lyu 분류, chong·byŏl 종별.

classify *v.* pul·lyu·ha·da 분류하다.

classmate *n.* tong·gŭp·saeng 동급생, tong·ch'ang·saeng

classroom *n.* kyo·sil 교실.   「동창생.

clatter *n.* tŏl·gŏ·dŏk·gŏ·ri·nŭn so·ri 덜거덕거리는 소리.
—*v.* wak·ja·gŭ·rŭ ttŏ·dŭl·da 와자그르 떠들다.

clause *n.* ① (*provision*) cho·hang 조항. ② (*sentence*)
chŏl 절. ③ (*music*) ak·gu 악구(樂句).

claw *n.* pal·t'op 발톱 ; chip·ge·bal 집게발.

clay *n.* chin·hŭk 진흙, ch'al·hŭk 찰흙.

clean *adj.* kkae·ggŭt·han 깨끗한. —*v.* kkae·ggŭ·si
ha·da 깨끗이 하다, tak·da 닦다.

cleaner *n.* ① ch'ŏng·so·bu 청소부. ② so·je·gi 소제기.

cleaning *n.* ch'ŏng·sŏ 청소 ; k'ŭl·li·i·ning 클리이닝.

cleanse *v.* ① (*clean*) kkae·ggŭ·si ha·da 깨끗이 하다.
② (*purge*) so·dok·ha·da 소독하다.

clear *adj.* mal·gŭn 맑은. —*v.* mal·ge ha·da 맑게 하다.

clearance sale chae·go chŏng·ri 재고 정리.

clearly *adv.* pal·ge 밝게, pun·myŏng·hi 분명히.

cleave *v.* ① (*split*) jjo·gae·da 쪼개다, tte·ŏ·no·t'a 떼
어놓다. ② (*stick*) tal·ra·but·da 달라붙다.

clench *v.* kkwak choe-da 꽉 죄다.

clergyman *n.* mok-sa 목사, sŏng-jik-ja 성직자.

clerk *n.* sa-mu-wŏn 사무원, chŏm-wŏn 점원.

clever *adj.* yŏng-ri-han 영리한, hyŏn-myŏng-han 현명

cleverness *n.* yŏng-ri-ham 영리함.   ㄴ한.

client *n.* ① so-song ŭi-roe-in 소송 의뢰인. ② tan-gol
son-nim 단골 손님, ko-gaek 고객.

cliff *n.* nang-ddŏ-rŏ-ji 낭떠러지, chŏl-byŏk 절벽.

climate *n.* ki-hu 기후, p'ung-t'o 풍토.

climax *n.* chŏl-jŏng 절정, k'ŭl-ra-i-maek-sŭ 클라이맥스.

climb *n.* ki-ŏ-o-rŭ-da 기어오르다. —*n.* tŭng-ban 등반.

cling *v.* tal-ra-but-da 달라붙다, mil-ch'ak-ha-da 밀착하

clinic *n.* chil-lyo-so 진료소, pyŏng-wŏn 병원.   ㄴ다.

clip *n.* k'ŭl-rip 클립. —*v.* (*cut*) ka-wi-ro cha-rŭ-da
가위로 자르다 ; (*grip*) kkwak chwi-da 꽉 쥐다.

cloak *n.* oe-t'u 외투, mang-t'o 망토.

clock *n.* kwae-jong-si-gye 패종시계.

clog *n.* ① chang-ae-mul 장애물. ② na-mak-sin 나막신.

cloister *n.* ① hoe-rang 회랑. ② (*monastery*) su-do-
wŏn 수도원, sŭng-wŏn 승원(僧院).

close *v.* (*shut*) tat-da 닫다 ; (*finish*) ma-ch'i-da 마치
다. —*adv.* ka-gga-i 가까이. —*adj.* (*near*) ka-gga-
un 가까운 ; (*intimate*) ch'in-han 친한.

closely *adv.* (*nearly*) ka-ggap-ge 가깝게 ; (*strictly*)
ŏm-mil-hi 엄밀히 ; (*tightly*) tan-dan-hi 단단히.

closet *n.* ① sa-sil 사실(私室). ② pyŏk-jang 벽장. ③

clot *n.* ŏng-gin tŏng-ŏ-ri 엉긴 덩어리. ㄴpyŏn-so 변소.

cloth *n.* ch'ŏn 천, ot-gam 옷감.

clothe *v.* (*dress*) o-sŭl ip-da 옷을 입다.

clothes *n.* ot 옷 ; (*bedclothes*) ch'im-gu 침구.

clothing *n.* (*collective*) ŭi-ryu 의류, ŭi-bok 의복.

cloud *n.* ① ku-rŭm 구름. ② (*flock*) tte 떼.

cloudless *adj.* ku-rŭm-ŏp-nŭn 구름없는.

cloudy *adj.* ku-rŭm-ggin 구름낀, hŭ-rin 흐린.

clover *n.* k'ŭl-ro-u-bŏ 클로우버.

clown *n.* ① (*jester*) ik-sal-gun 익살군, kwang-dae 광대. ② (*rustic*) si-gol-ddŭ-gi 시골뜨기.

club *n.* ① (*heavy stick*) kon-bong 곤봉. ② (*association*) k'ŭl-rŏp 클럽, tong-ho-hoe 동호회.

clue *n.* sil-ma-ri 실마리, tan-sŏ 단서.

clump *n.* ① (*thicket*) su-p'ul 수풀, tŏm-bul 덤불. ② (*lump*) tŏng-ŏ-ri 덩어리.

clumsy *adj.* (*unskilful*) sŏ-t'u-rŭn 서투른, ŏ-saek-han 어색한, (*tactless*) ŏl-bba-jin 얼빠진.

cluster *n.* song-i 송이 ; (*crowd*) mu-ri 무리, tt'e 떼. —*v.* (*round*) tte-rŭl ji-ŏ mo-i-da 떼를 지어 모이다.

coach *v.* chi-do-ha-da 지도하다, k'o-u-ch'i-ha-da 코우치하다. —*n.* ① tae-hyŏng-ma-ch'a 대형마차 ; (*railway*) kaek-ch'a 객차. ② (*athletic*) k'o-u-ch'i 코우치.

coal *n.* sŏk-t'an 석탄 : ~ *field* t'an-jŏn 탄전(炭田).

coalition *n.* yŏn-hap 연합, hap-dong 합동.

coal mine t'an-gwang 탄광, t'an-gaeng 탄갱(炭坑).

coarse *adj.* kŏ-ch'in 거친, hŏ-rŭm-han 허름한.

coast *n.* hae-an 해안, yŏn-an 연안(沿岸).

coat *n.* ut-ot 웃옷, sang-ŭi 상의, oe-t'u 외투.

cobbler *n.* ku-du 구두 ; (*shoemaker*) ku-du su-ri-gong 구두 수리공, sin-gi-ryo chang-su 신기료 장수.

cobweb *n.* kŏ-mi-jul 거미줄, kŏ-mi-jip 거미집.   「꼭지.

cock *n.* ① su-t'ak 수탉 ; su-k'ŏt 수컷. ② (*tap*) kkok-ji

coconut *n.* ya-ja yŏl-mae 야자 열매, k'o-k'o-nŏt 코코넛.

cocoon *n.* (*silkworm*) ko-ch'i 고치.

cod *n.* (*codfish*) tae-gu 대구.

code *n.* ① pŏp-jŏn 법전(法典). ② (*rules*) kwal-lye 관례, kyu-yak 규약. ③ (*cipher*) am-ho 암호.

cod-liver oil kan-yu 간유.　　　　　　「학의) 여학생.
co-ed *n.* (nam-nyo kong-hak-ŭi) yŏ-hak-saeng (남녀 공
coeducation *n.* nam-nyŏ kong-hak 남녀 공학.
coerce *v.* kang-yo-ha-da 강요하다, wi-ap-ha-da 위압하다.
coffee *n.* k'o-o-p'i 코오피.
coffin *n.* kwan 관(棺), nŏl 널.　　　　　　「il 코일.
coil *v.* tul-tul kam-da 둘둘 감다. —*n.* sa-ri 사리 ; k'o-
coin *n.* ton 돈, hwa-p'ye 화폐 ; *copper* ~ tong-jŏn 동전.
coincide *v.* il-ch'i-ha-da 일치하다, pu-hap-ha-da 부합하
coincidence *n.* il-ch'i 일치, pu-hap 부합.　　　「다.
coke *n.* k'o-u-k'ŭ-sŭ 코우크스, hae-t'an 해탄(骸炭).
cold *adj.* ch'an 찬, ch'a-ga-un 차가운 : *be* ~ ch'up-da
　ch'up-da 춥다 ; (*of hands and feet*) si-ri-da 시리다. —*n.* kam-
　gi 감기 : *catch* ~ kam-gi tŭl-da 감기 들다.　　「하다.
collapse *v.* mu-nŏ-ji-da 무너지다 ; soe-t'oe-ha-da 쇠퇴
collar *n.* k'al-ra 칼라, kit 깃.
colleague *n.* tong-ryo 동료, tong-ŏp-ja 동업자.
collect *v.* mo-ŭ-da 모으다, su-jip-ha-da 수집하다.
collection *n.* su-jip 수집, su-jip-p'um 수집품.
collective security (*of U.N.*) chip-dan an-jŏn-bo-jang
　집단 안전보장.
college *n.* tan-gwa-dae-hak 단과대학.　　　　「딧치다.
collide *v.* ch'ung-dol-ha-da 충돌하다, pu-dit-ch'i-da 부
collision *n.* ch'ung-dol 충돌, sang-ch'ung 상충.
colloquial *adj.* ku-ŏ(-ch'e)-ŭi 구어(체)의.
colonel *n.* yuk-gun-dae-ryŏng 육군대령.
colonist *n.* sik-min-ji kae-ch'ŏk-ja 식민지 개척자 ; hae-
　oe i-ju-min 해외 이주민.　　　　　　　　　「집단.
colony *n.* ① sik-min-ji 식민지. ② (*group*) chip-dan
colossal *adj.* kŏ-dae-han 거대한, pang-dae-han 방대한.
colo(u)r *n.* ① pit-ggal 빛깔, k'ŏl-rŏ 컬러. ② (*pl.*)
　kun-gi 군기(軍旗). —*v.* saek-ch'il-ha-da 색칠하다.

colt *n.* mang-a-ji 망아지 ; p'ut-na-gi 풋나기.

column *n.* ① (*pillar*) ki-dung 기둥. ② (*of newspaper*) nan 난(欄). ③ (*mil.*) chong-dae 종대(縱隊).

comb *n.* pit 빗. —*v.* pit-da 빗다.

combat *n.* (*fight*) chŏn-t'u 전투 ; (*struggle*) t'u-jaeng 투쟁. —*v.* kyŏk-t'u-ha-da 격투하다.

combination *n.* ① kyŏl-hap 결합, jja-mat-ch'u-gi 짜맞추기. ② k'om-bi-ne-i-syŏn 콤비네이션. 「합하다.

combine *v.* kyŏl-hap-ha-da 결합하다, yŏn-hap-ha-da 연

come *v.* ① o-da 오다. ② (*happen*) i-rŏ-na-da 일어나다. ③ (*be caused by*) yu-rae-ha-da 유래하다. ④ (*become*) …i toe-da …이 되다. ⑤ (*amount to*) …e tal-ha-da …에 달하다. 「디언.

comedian *n.* hŭi-gŭk pae-u 희극 배우, k'o-mi-di-ŏn 코미

comedy *n.* hŭi-gŭk 희극, k'o-mi-di 코미디.

comet *n.* hye-sŏng 혜성, sal-byŏl 살별.

comfort *n.* (*consolation*) wi-an 위안 ; (*ease*) al-lak 안락, —*v.* (*console*) wi-ro-ha-da 위로하다.

comfortable *adj.* p'yŏn-an-han 편안한, al-lak-han 안락한, ki-bun-jo-ŭn 기분좋은. 「배우.

comic *adj.* hŭi-gŭk-ŭi 희극의. —*n.* hŭi-gŭk pae-u 희극

command *n.* myŏng-ryŏng 명령. —*v.* myŏng-ryŏng-ha-da 명령하다 ; chi-hwi-ha-da 지휘하다.

commander *n.* ① chi-hwi-gwan 지휘관, sa-ryŏng-gwan 사령관. ② (*navy*) chung-ryŏng 중령 : ~ *in chief* ch'ong-sa-ryŏng-gwan 총사령관.

commandment *n.* kye-myŏng 계명, kye-yul 계율.

commemorate *v.* ki-nyŏm-ha-da 기념하다 ; (*celebrate*) kyŏng-ch'uk-ha-da 경축하다. 「da 개시하다.

commence *v.* (*start*) si-jak-ha-da 시작하다, kae-si-ha-

commencement *n.* cho-rŏp-sik 졸업식.

commend *v.* ① ch'u-ch'ŏn-ha-da 추천하다. ② (*praise*)

compose *v.* ku-sŏng-ha-da 구성하다, mat-ch'u-ŏ jja-da 맞추어 짜다 ; (*music*) chak-gok-ha-da 작곡하다.

composer *n.* chak-gok-ga 작곡가.

composition *n.* ① ku-sŏng 구성. ② (*written*) chakmun 작문. ③ (*music*) chak-gok 작곡.

composure *n.* (*calmness*) ch'im-ch'ak 침착, naengjŏng 냉정 ; (*self-control*) cha-je 자제.

compound *v.* hon-hap-ha-da 혼합하다. —*adj.* hap-sŏngŭi 합성의. —*n.* hon-hap-mul 혼합물.

comprehend *v.* ① al-da 알다, i-hae-ha-da 이해하다. ② p'o-ham-ha-da 포함하다, nae-p'o-ha-da 내포하다.

compress *v.* ap-ch'uk-ha-da 압축하다.

compromise *n.* & *v.* t'a-hyŏp(-ha-da) 타협(하다).

compulsion *n.* kang-je 강제, kang-yo 강요.

compulsory *adj.* kang-je-jŏk-in 강제적인 ; ŭi-mu-jŏk-in 의무적인, p'il-su-ŭi 필수의.

compute *n.* ① (*reckon*) sem-ha-da 셈하다. ② (*estimate*) ch'u-jŏng-ha-da 추정하다.

computer *n.* kye-san-gi 계산기, k'ŏm-p'yu-t'ŏ 컴퓨터 : *an electronic* ~ chŏn-ja kye-san-gi 전자 계산기.

comrade *n.* pŏt 벗, tong-ji 동지.

conceal *v.* kam-ch'u-da 감추다, sum-gi-da 숨기다.

concede *v.* yang-bo-ha-da 양보하다.   「(奇想).

conceit *n.* cha-bu-sim 자부심 ; (*fancy*) ki-sang 기상

conceive *v.* ① (*imagine*) sang-sang-ha-da 상상하다. ② (*child*) a-gi-rŭl pae-da 아기를 배다.

concentrate *v.* chip-jung-ha-da 집중하다.

concern *n.* ① (*relation*) kwan-gye 관계. ② (*anxiety*) kŭn-sim 근심. —*v.* (*relate to*) kwan-gye-ha-da 관계하다, kwan-sim-ŭl kat-da 관심을 갖다.

concerning *prep.* …e kwan-ha-yŏ …에 관하여.

concert *n.* ŭm-ak-hoe 음악회, k'on-sŏ-ŏ-t'ŭ 콘서어트.

concession *n.* (*yielding*) yang-bo 양보.

conciliate *v.* tal-rae-da 달래다, mu-ma-ha-da 무마하다.

concise *adj.* kan-gyŏl-han 간결한.

conclude *v.* ① …ŭi kyŏl-mal-ŭl chit-da …의 결말을 짓다. ② (*settle*) ch'e-gyŏl-ha-da 체결하다. 「체결.

conclusion *n.* ① chong-gyŏl 종결. ② (*treaty*) ch'e-gyŏl

conclusive *adj.* kyŏl-jŏng-jŏk-in 결정적인, kyŏl-ron-jŏk-in 결론적인, chong-guk-ŭi 종국의.

concord *n.* ① (*agreement*) il-ch'i 일치, hwa-hap 화합. ② (*treaty*) hyŏp-jŏng 협정.

concrete *adj.* ku-ch'e-jŏk-in 구체적인. —*n.* k'on-k'ŭ-ri-i-t'ŭ 콘크리이트. —*v.* kut-hi-da 굳히다.

concubine *n.* ch'ŏp 첩, so-ga 소가(小家).

concussion *n.* ① chin-dong 진동. ② noe-jin-t'ang 뇌진탕.

condemn *v.* ① (*blame*) pi-nan-ha-da 비난하다. ② (*sentence*) sŏn-go-ha-da 선고하다.

condense *v.* ap-ch'uk-si-k'i-da 압축시키다.

condescend *v.* kong-son-hi tae-ha-da 공손히 대하다.

condition *n.* ① (*state*) sang-t'ae 상태. ② (*in contracts*) cho-gŏn 조건. ③ (*rank*) sin-bun 신분. 「da 문상하다.

condole *v.* cho-wi-ha-da 조위(吊慰)하다, mun-sang-ha-

conduct *n.* haeng-wi 행위. —*v.* (*direct*) chi-hwi-ha-da 지휘하다 ; (*lead*) in-do-ha-da 인도하다.

conductor *n.* ① chi-hwi-ja 지휘자. ② ch'a-jang 차장.

cone *n.* wŏn-bbul 원뿔, wŏn-ch'u 원추. 「상의하다.

confer *v.* ① chu-da 주다. ② (*consult*) sang-ŭi-ha-da

confess *v.* cha-baek-ha-da 자백하다, ko-baek-ha-da 고백하다 ; (*recognize*) cha-in-ha-da 자인하다.

confession *n.* ko-baek 고백, cha-baek 자백.

confide *v.* ① (*put trust*) sin-yong-ha-da 신용하다. ② (*share secret*) pi-mil-ŭl t'ŏ-rŏ-no-t'a 비밀을 털어놓다.

confidence *n.* (*trust*) sin-yong 신용 ; (*assurance*) cha-sin 자신, hwak-sin 확신.

confine *v.* han-jŏng-ha-da 한정하다 ; ka-du-da 가두다.

confirm *v.* ① (*verify*) hwak-jŭng-ha-da 확증하다. ② (*fortify*) kong-go-hi ha-da 공고히 하다. 「하다.

confiscate *v.* mol-su-ha-da 몰수하다, ap-su-ha-da 압수

conflagration *n.* k'ŭn-bul 큰불, tae-hwa 대화(大火).

conflict *n.* t'u-jaeng 투쟁, ch'ung-dol 충돌. —*v.* ta-t'u-da 다투다, ch'ung-dol-ha-da 충돌하다.

conform *v.* il-ch'i-si-k'i-da 일치시키다 ; tta-rŭ-da 따르다.

confound *v.* (*confuse*) hon-dong-ha-da 혼동하다 ; (*perplex*) tang-hwang-k'e ha-da 당황케 하다.

confront *v.* …ŭi ma-jŭn-p'yŏn-e it-da …의 맞은편에 있다, chik-myŏn-ha-da 직면하다.

confuse *v.* hol-lan-si-k'i-da 혼란시키다 ; hon-dong-ha-da 혼동하다, ŏ-ji-rŏp-hi-da 어지럽히다.

confusion *n.* hol-lan 혼란, tang-hwang 당황.

congratulate *v.* ch'uk-ha-ha-da 축하하다.

congratulation *n.* ch'uk-ha 축하 ; ch'uk-sa 축사.

congress *n.* (*meeting*) hoe-ŭi 회의, tae-hoe 대회 ; (*national assembly*) kuk-hoe 국회. 「민의원.

congressman *n.* kuk-hoe-ŭi-wŏn 국회의원, min-ŭi-wŏn

conjunction *n.* ① kyŏl-hap 결합. ② chŏp-sok-sa 접속사.

connect *v.* yŏn-gyŏl-ha-da 연결하다, it-da 잇다.

connection *n.* ① yŏn-gyŏl 연결. ② kwan-gye 관계. ③ (*relative*) yŏn-jul 연줄, yŏn-go 연고.

connotation *n.* ham-ch'uk-sŏng 함축성.

conquer *v.* chŏng-bok-ha-da 정복하다, sŭng-ri-ha-da 승

conqueror *n.* chŏng-bok-ja 정복자. 「리하다.

conquest *n.* chŏng-bok 정복, hoek-dŭk 획득.

conscience *n.* yang-sim 양심, to-ŭi-sim 도의심.

conscientious *adj.* yang-sim-jŏk-in 양심적인.

conscious *adj.* chi-gak-i it-nŭn 지각이 있는, ŭi-sik-jŏk-in 의식적인.

consciousness n. ŭi-sik 의식, cha-gak 자각.

conscript n. ching-jip-byong 징집병. —v. (*draft*) ching-bal-ha-da 징발하다, ching-jip-ha-da 징집하다.

consecrate v. pa-ch'i-da 바치다, pong-hŏn-ha-da 봉헌하다.

consent v. sŭng-nak-ha-da 승낙하다, tong-ŭi-ha-da 동의하다. —n. sŭng-nak 승낙 ; tong-ŭi 동의.

consequence n. kyŏl-gwa 결과 ; chung-yo-sŏng 중요성.

conserve v. po-jon-ha-da 보존하다. 「하다.

consider v. suk-go-ha-da 숙고하다, pae-ryŏ-ha-da 배려

considerable adj. sang-dang-han 상당한.

consign v. wi-t'ak-ha-da 위탁하다, mat-gi-da 맡기다.

consist v. ① …ŭ-ro i-ru-ŏ-ji-da …으로 이루어지다. ② …e it-da …에 있다. ③ yang-rip-ha-da 양립하다.

console v. wi-ro-ha-da 위로하다. 「하는.

consonant n. cha-ŭm 자음. —adj. il-ch'i-ha-nŭn 일치

conspicuous adj. nun-e chal ttŭi-nŭn 눈에 잘 띄는 ; chŏ-myŏng-han 저명한, hyŏn-jŏ-han 현저한.

consort n. pae-u-ja 배우자 ; tong-ryo 동료.

conspirator n. kong-mo-ja 공모자, ŭm-mo-ja 음모자.

conspire v. (*plot*) kong-mo-ha-da 공모하다.

constable n. kyŏng-gwan 경관, sun-gyŏng 순경.

constant adj. ① (*same*) han-gyŏl-ga-t'ŭn 한결같은. ② (*continuous*) pu-dan-han 부단한.

constellation n. sŏng-jwa 성좌, pyŏl-ja-ri 별자리.

constituent n. ① sŏng-bun 성분. ② sŏn-gŏ-in 선거인.

constitute v. ① (*compose*) ku-sŏng-ha-da 구성하다. ② (*enact*) che-jŏng-ha-da 제정하다. ③ (*set up*) sŏl-rip-ha-da 설립하다.

constitution n. ① sŏl-rip 설립. ② (*law*) hŏn-bŏp 헌법. ③ (*composition*) ku-sŏng 구성. 「하다.

construct v. kŏn-sŏl-ha-da 건설하다, kŏn-jo-ha-da 건조

construction *n.* ① ku·jo 구조. ② kŏn·sŏl 건설. ③ (*syntax*) ku·mun 구문. 「sŏng·ŭi 구성의.
constructive *adj.* ① kŏn·sŏl·jŏk·in 건설적인. ② ku-
consul *n.* yŏng·sa 영사(領事).
consulate *n.* yŏng·sa·gwan 영사관.
consult *v.* ① sang·ŭi·ha·da 상의하다. ② chin·ch'al·ŭl pat·da 진찰을 받다. ③ (*refer to*) ch'am·go·ha·da 참
consume *v.* so·bi·ha·da 소비하다. 「고하다.
consumption *n.* ① so·bi 소비. ② (*tuberculosis*) p'ye· gyŏl·haek 폐결핵, p'ye·byŏng 폐병.
contact *n.* chŏp·ch'ok 접촉, kyo·je 교제.
contagion *n.* chŏn·yŏm(·byŏng) 전염(병).
contagious *adj.* chŏn·yŏm·sŏng·ŭi 전염성의. 「있다.
contain *v.* p'o·ham·ha·da 포함하다, tam·go it·da 담고
contaminate *v.* tŏ·rŏp·hi·da 더럽히다, o·yŏm·si·k'i·da 오염시키다 ; t'a·rak·si·k'i·da 타락시키다.
contemplate *v.* ① sim·sa·suk·go·ha·da 심사숙고하다. ② (*look at*) ŭng·si·ha·da 응시하다.
contemporary *adj.* ka·t'ŭn si·dae·ŭi 같은 시대의, tang-
contempt *n.* kyŏng·myŏl 경멸. 「dae·ŭi 당대의.
contend *v.* ① (*struggle*) ta·t'u·da 다투다, kyŏ·ru·da 겨루다. ② (*insist*) chu·jang·ha·da 주장하다.
content *adj.* (*satisfied*) man·jok·han 만족한. —*n.* ① man·jok 만족. ② nae·yong 내용.
contentment *n.* man·jok 만족.
contest *n.* non·jaeng 논쟁, ta·t'um 다툼. —*v.* ta·t'u· da 다투다, kyŏ·ru·da 겨루다. 「ryuk 아시아 대륙.
continent *n.* tae·ryuk 대륙 : *the ～ of Asia* a·si·a tae-
continue *v.* kye·sok[yŏn·sok]·ha·da 계속[연속]하다.
continuous *adj.* kye·sok·jŏk·in 계속적인.
contraband *n.* mil·su 밀수, (*smuggled goods*) mil· su·p'um 밀수품. —*adj.* kŭm·ji·doen 금지된.

contract *n.& v.* kye-yak(-ha-da) 계약(하다).

contradict *v.* pan-bak-ha-da 반박하다, mo-sun-doe-da
contrary *adj.* pan-dae-ŭi 반대의. └모순되다.

contrast *n.* tae-jo 대조, tae-bi 대비(對比).

contribute *v.* ① (*money etc.*) ki-bu-ha-da 기부하다 ;
  (*conduce*) kong-hŏn-ha-da 공헌하다. ② (*write for*)
  ki-go-ha-da 기고하다. ┌기고.

contribution *n.* ① ki-bu 기부 ; kong-hŏn 공헌. ② ki-go

contrive *v.* ① (*invent*) ko-an-ha-da 고안하다. ② (*man-age*) yong-k'e hae-ch'i-u-da 용케 해치우다.

control *v.* chi-bae-ha-da 지배하다 ; (*hold in check*)
  ŏk-je-ha-da 억제하다. —*n.* t'ong-je 통제.

controversy *n.* non-jaeng 논쟁, t'o-ron 토론.

convenience *n.* p'yŏn-ŭi 편의, pyŏl-li 편리.

convenient *adj.* p'yŏl-li-han 편리한.

convent *n.* su-nyŏ-wŏn 수녀원, su-do-wŏn 수도원.

convention *n.* ① (*custom*) in-sŭp 인습, kwal-lye 관
  례. ② (*session*) hoe-ŭi 회의, chip-hoe 집회.

conversation *n.* hoe-hwa 회화, tam-hwa 담화.

convert *v.* ① chŏn-hwan-ha-da 전환하다. ② (*religion*)
  kae-jong-si-k'i-da 개종(改宗)시키다.

convey *v.* na-rŭ-da 나르다, chŏn-dal-ha-da 전달하다.

convict *v.* yu-joe-ro p'an-gyŏl-ha-da 유죄로 판결하다.
  —*n.* choe-in 죄인, choe-su 죄수.

convince *v.* hwak-sin-ŭl ka-ji-ge ha-da 확신을 가지게
  하다 ; nap-dŭk-si-k'i-da 납득시키다. ┌송하다.

convoy *n.* ho-song-dae 호송대. —*v.* ho-song-ha-da 호

cook *v.* yo-ri-ha-da 요리하다. —*n.* yo-ri-sa 요리사.

cool *adj.* sŏ-nŭl-han 서늘한 ; naeng-jŏng-han 냉정한.
  —*v.* sik-hi-da 식히다.

coop *n.* tung-u-ri 둥우리, tak-jang 닭장.

co(-)operate *v.* hyŏp-dong-ha-da 협동하다, hyŏp-ryŏk-ha-da 협력하다.

cope v. ① tae-hang-ha-da 대항하다, mat-sŏ-da 맞서다.
② tae-ch'ŏ-ha-da 대처하다. 「동판.

copper n. ku-ri 구리, tong-동(銅) : ～ *plate* tong-p'an

copy v. pe-ggi-da 베끼다. —n. sa-bon 사본 ; (*book*)

coral n. san-ho 산호. 〔kwŏn 권 ; ch'o-go 초고.

cord n. ① (*thick string*) kul-gŭn kkŭn 굵은 끈. ②
(*small rope*) ka-nŭn pat-jul 가는 밧줄.

cordial adj. chin-sim-e-sŏ u-rŏ-na-nŭn 진심에서 우러
나는. —n. kang-sim-je 강심제.

core n. sok 속, haek-sim 핵심(核心), kol-ja 골자.

cork n. k'o-rŭ-k'ŭ 코르크. 「옥수수.

corn n. (*Am.*) kok-sik 곡식, kok-mul 곡물 ; ok-su-su

corner n. ① mo-t'ung-i 모퉁이, k'o-o-nŏ 코오너. ②
(*angle*) kak 각. ③ (*commerce*) mae-jŏm 매점.

coronation n. tae-gwan-sik 대관식, chŭk-wi-sik 즉위식.

corporal n. ha-sa 하사(下士), sang-byŏng 상병.

corporation n. pŏp-in 법인, yu-han-hoe-sa 유한회사.

corps n. kun-dan 군단, pyŏng-dan 병단.

corpse n. si-ch'e 시체, song-jang 송장.

correct adj. pa-rŭn 바른. —v. ko-ch'i-da 고치다.

correspond v. il-ch'i-ha-da 일치하다, pu-hap-ha-da 부
합하다 : ～ *with* t'ong-sin-ha-da 통신하다.

correspondence n. ① (*agreement*) il-ch'i 일치, sang-
ŭng 상응. ② (*communication*) t'ong-sin 통신.

corridor n. pok-do 복도, hoe-rang 회랑.

corrupt adj. (*rotten*) ssŏk-ŭn 썩은. —v. ssŏk-da 썩
다 ; (*become debased*) t'a-rak-ha-da 타락하다.

cosmetic adj. (*beautifying*) mi-yong-ŭi 미용의, hwa-
jang-yong-ŭi 화장용의. —n. hwa-jang-p'um 화장품.

cosmopolitan adj. se-gye-jŏk-in 세계적인. —n. se-gye-
in 세계인, se-gye-ju-ŭi-ja 세계주의자.

cost *v.* ① kap-na-ga-da 값나가다. ② (*require*) tŭl-da 들다, yo-ha-da 요하다. ③ hŭi-saeng-si-k'i-da 희생시키다. —*n.* (*expense*) pi-yong 비용, (*price*) kap 값.

costly *adj.* kap-bi-ssan 값비싼, ho-hwa-ro-un 호화로운.

costume *n.* pok-jang 복장, ŭi-sang 의상.

cosy *adj.* a-nŭk-han 아늑한, a-dam-han 아담한.

cot *n.* kan-i ch'im-dae 간이 침대 ; u-ri 우리.

cottage *n.* o-du-mak-jip 오두막집, nong-ga 농가.

cotton *n.* ① som 솜. ② (*cloth*) mu-myŏng 무명.

couch *n.* ch'im-sang 침상, kin ŭi-ja 긴 의자.

cough *n.* ki-ch'im 기침. —*v.* ki-ch'im-ha-da 기침하다.

council *n.* p'yŏng-ŭi-hoe 평의회, hyŏp-ŭi-hoe 협의회.

counsel *n.* (*consultation*) ŭi-non 의논 ; (*advice*) 'kwŏn-go 권고. —*v.* cho-ŏn-ha-da 조언하다, kwŏn-ha-da 권하다 ; hyŏp-ŭi-ha-da 협의하다.

count *v.* se-da 세다, kye-san-ha-da 계산하다 : ~ *for much* chung-yo-ha-da 중요하다. —*n.* kye-san 계산.

counter *n.* kye-san-gi 계산기, kye-san-dae 계산대. —*adj.* (*opposite*) pan-dae-ŭi 반대의, yŏk-ŭi 역(逆)의.

counteract *v.* pang-hae-ha-da 방해하다.

counterfeit *adj.* ka-jja-ŭi 가짜의. —*n.* ka-jja 가짜, mo-jo-p'um 모조품, wi-jo-p'um 위조품.

countess *n.* paek-jak pu-in 백작 부인.

country *n.* ① si-gol 시골, kyo-oe 교외. ② chi-bang 지방, chi-yŏk 지역. ③ (*nation*) na-ra 나라, kuk-ga 국가.

county *n.* kun 군(郡), (*Brit.*) chu 주(州).

couple *n.* han ssang 한 쌍, pu-bu 부부.

coupon *n.* k'u-u-p'on 쿠우폰, kyŏng-p'um-gwŏn 경품권.

courage *n.* yong-gi 용기, pae-jjang 배짱.

course *n.* ① (*route*) chil-lo 진로, k'o-o-sŭ 코오스. ② (*of study*) kang-jwa 강좌, kwa-jŏng 과정.

court *n.* ① (*law*) chae-p'an-so 재판소. ② k'o-o-t'ŭ 코

오트 : *a tennis* ~ t'e-ni-sŭ k'o-o-t'ŭ 테니스 코오트.

courtesy *n.* ye-jŏl 예절 ; chŏng-jung 정중 ; ho-ŭi 호의.

courthouse *n.* ① pŏp-wŏn 법원. ② kun-ch'ŏng 군청.

court-martial *n.* kun-bŏp-hoe-ŭi 군법회의.

courtship *n.* (*wooing*) ku-hon 구혼, ku-ae 구애(求愛).

courtyard *n.* an-ddŭl 안뜰, ap-ma-dang 앞마당.

cousin *n.* sa-ch'on 사촌, chong-hyŏng-je 종형제.

cover *v.* ① tŏp-da 덮다. ② (*hide*) kam-ch'u-da 감추다.
③ (*extend over*) chŏn-myŏn-e kŏl-ch'i-da 전면에 걸
치다 ; p'o-ham-ha-da 포함하다. —*n.* tŏp-gae 덮개.

coverlet *n.* tŏp-gae 덮개, i-bul 이불.

covet *v.* mop-si t'am-nae-da 몹시 탐내다.

cow *n.* am-so 암소 : ~ *boy* mok-dong 목동.

coward *n.* kŏp-jang-i 겁장이. —*adj.* kŏp-man-ŭn 겁많은.

cower *v.* um-ch'ŭ-ri-da 움츠리다 ; chil-ri-da 질리다.

crab *n.* ① ke 게. ② (*winch*) win-ch'i 윈치.

crack *n.* ① t'ŭm 틈, kŭm 금. ② (*shot*) pal-sa 발사.
—*v.* (*break*) jjo-gae-da 쪼개다, kkae-ji-da 깨지다.

cracker *n.* ① (*firecracker*)p'ok-juk 폭죽.② p'a-swae-
gi 파쇄기. ③ (*biscuit*) k'ŭ-rae-k'ŏ 크래커.

cradle *n.* ① yo-ram 요람(搖籃). ② pal-sang-ji 발상지.

craft *n.* ① (*skill*) ki-gyo 기교, son-jae-ju 손재주 ;
(*cunning*) sul-ch'aek 술책. ② kong-ye 공예.

craftsman *n.* ki-nŭng-gong 기능공, chang-in 장인.

crafty *adj.* kan-sa-han 간사한. 「기중기.

crane *n.* ① (*bird*) hak 학. ② (*machine*) ki-jung-gi

crash *n.* ① to-san 도산. ② ch'ung-dol 충돌. —*v.* wa-
rŭ-rŭ mu-nŏ-ji-da 와르르 무너지다.

crate *n.* kwe-jjak 궤짝, tae-ba-gu-ni 대바구니.

crave *v.* kan-ch'ŏng-ha-da 간청하다, kal-mang-ha-da
갈망하다. 「ri-da 느릿느릿 달리다.

crawl *v.* ki-da 기다, (*move slowly*) nŭ-rit-nŭ-rit tal-

crayon *n.* k'ŭ-re-yong 크레용.

crazy *adj.* (*insane*) mi-ch'in 미친 ; (*madly eager*) yŏl-gwang-ha-nŭn 열광하는.

creak *v.* ppi-gŏk-gŏ-ri-da 삐걱거리다.

cream *n.* k'ŭ-ri-im 크리임, yu-ji 유지.

crease *n.* chu-rŭm 주름, chŏp-ŭn kŭm 접은 금. 「하다.

create *v.* ch'ang-jo-ha-da 창조하다 ; sŏl-rip-ha-da 설립

creative *adj.* ch'ang-jo-jŏk-in 창조적인. 「조물주.

creator *n.* ch'ang-jo-ja 창조자, (*the C~*) cho-mul-ju

creature *n.* ① (*anything created*) ch'ang-jo-mul 창조물. ② (*living being*) saeng-mul 생물. ③ (*domestic animal*) ka-ch'uk 가축. ④ (*human being*) in-gan 인

credentials *n.* sin-im-jang 신임장. 「간.

credible *adj.* sin-yong-hal su it-nŭn 신용할 수 있는.

credit *n.* ① ch'ae-gwŏn 채권. ② (*belief*) sin-yong 신용. ③ (*honor*) myŏng-ye 명예.

creditable *adj.* ch'ing-ch'an-hal man-han 칭찬할 만한.

credulous *adj.* swip-sa-ri mit-nŭn 쉽사리 믿는, chal sok-nŭn 잘 속는.

creed *n.* sin-jo 신조 ; (*principle*) chu-ŭi 주의(主義).

creek *n.* sil-gae-ch'ŏn 실개천, k'ŭ-ri-i-k'ŭ 크리이크.

creel *n.* tong-bal 통발, mul-go-gi pa-gu-ni 물고기 바구

creep *v.* ki-da 기다, p'o-bok-ha-da 포복하다. 「니.

cremate *v.* hwa-jang-ha-da 화장(火葬)하다.

crepe *n.* k'ŭ-re-i-p'ŭ 크레이프.

crescent *n.* ch'o-sŭng-dal 초승달, sin-wŏl 신월(新月).

crest *n.* ① (*comb*) pyŏt 볏, to-ga-mŏ-ri 도가머리. ② (*head*) kkok-dae-gi 꼭대기, chŏng-sang 정상.

crevice *n.* kal-ra-jin t'ŭm 갈라진 틈, kŭm 금.

crew *n.* ① sŭng-mu-wŏn 승무원. ② p'ae-gŏ-ri 패거리.

cricket *n.* ① (*insect*) kwi-ddu-ra-mi 귀뚜라미. ② (*game*) k'ŭ-ri-k'et 크리켓.

crime *n.* choe 죄, pŏm-joe 범죄.

criminal *adj.* pŏm-joe-ŭi 범죄의, hyŏng-sa-sang-ŭi 형사상의. —*n.* choe-in 죄인. 「새빨간.

crimson *n.* chin-hong-saek 진홍색. —*adj.* sae-bbal-gan

cripple *n.* chŏl-rŭm-ba-ri 절름발이, pul-gu-ja 불구자.

crisis *n.* wi-gi 위기 ; (*decisive moment*) chung-dae-si-guk 중대시국, (*turning point*) kal-rim-gil 갈림길.

crisp *adj.* ① pa-sak-ba-sak-ha-nŭn 바삭바삭하는, kop-sŭl-gop-sŭl-han 곱슬곱슬한. ② sang-k'wae-han 상쾌한.

criterion *n.* p'yo-jun 표준, ki-jun 기준.

critic *n.* pi-p'yŏng-ga 비평가, kam-jŏng-ga 감정가 : *an art* ~ mi-sul p'yŏng-ron-ga 미술 평론가.

critical *adj.* ① pi-p'yŏng-jŏk-in 비평적인. ② chung-dae-han 중대한. ③ wi-gŭp-han 위급한. 「난하다.

criticize *v.* pi-p'yŏng-ha-da 비평하다 ; pi-nan-ha-da 비

croak *v.* kae-gol-gae-gol ul-da 개골개골 울다, t'u-dŏl-

crocodile *n.* ak-ŏ 악어. ⌊dae-da 투덜대다.

crony *n.* (*chum*) yet-bŏt 옛벗, ch'in-gu 친구.

crooked *adj.* ku-bu-rŏ-jin 구부러진, pi-ddu-rŏ-jin 비뚤어진 ; (*deformed*) ki-hyŏng-ŭi 기형의.

crop *n. & v.* su-hwak(-ha-da) 수확(하다).

cross *n.* sip-ja-ga 십자가. —*v.* kŏn-nŏ-da 건너다 ; (*intersect*) kyo-ch'a-ha-da 교차하다. 「mok 건널목.

crossing *n.* hoeng-dan 횡단 ; kyo-ch'a 교차 ; kŏn-nŏl-

crossroad *n.* ne-gŏ-ri 네거리, sip-ja-ro 십자로.

crouch *v.* (*bend down*) ung-k'ŭ-ri-da 응크리다.

crow *n.* kka-ma-gwi 까마귀. —*v.* (*cock*) ul-da 울다.

crowd *n.* ① kun-jung 군중. ② (*throng*) hon-jap 혼잡. —*v.* (*swarm*) pum-bi-da 붐비다.

crown *n.* ① wang-gwan 왕관. ② (*top*) kkok-dae-gi 꼭대기. —*v.* kwan-ŭl ssŭi-u-da 관을 씌우다.

crude *adj.* ka-gong-ha-ji an-ŭn 가공하지 않은 ; it-nŭn

kŭ-dae-ro-ŭi 있는 그대로의 ; mi-suk-han 미숙한.

cruel *adj.* chan-in-han 잔인한 ; mu-jŏng-han 무정한.

cruelty *n.* chan-in-sŏng 잔인성, mu-ja-bi 무자비.

cruise *v.* (*sail*) sun-hang-ha-da 순항하다.

cruiser *n.* sun-yang-ham 순양함(巡洋艦).

crumb *n.* ① ppang pu-sŭ-rŏ-gi 빵 부스러기, ppang ka-ru 빵 가루. ② (*bit*) so-ryang 소량.

crumble *v.* ① pu-sŭ-rŏ-ddŭ-ri-da 부스러뜨리다, pu-su-da 부수다. ② (*perish*) mang-ha-da 망하다.

crumple *v.* ku-gyŏ-ji-da 구겨지다, ku-gi-da 구기다.

crunch *v.* u-du-duk kkae-mul-da 우두둑 깨물다.

crusade *n.* sip-ja-gun 십자군, sŏng-jŏn 성전(聖戰).

crush *v.* nul-rŏ pu-sŭ-rŏ-ddŭ-ri-da 눌러 부스러뜨리다, jji-gŭ-rŏ-ddŭ-ri-da 찌그러뜨리다.

crust *n.* ① ppang kkŏp-jil 빵 껍질. ② (*hardened surface*) kut-ŏ-jin p'yo-myŏn 굳어진 표면.

crutch *n.* ① mok-bal 목발. ② (*prop*) pŏ-t'im 버팀.

cry *v.* ul-da 울다 ; (*shout*) so-ri chi-rŭ-da 소리 지르다. —*n.* u-rŭm-so-ri 울음소리 ; pu-rŭ-ji-jŭm 부르짖음.

crying *adj.* ① u-nŭn 우는, ul-bu-jit-nŭn 울부짖는. ② (*urgent*) kin-gŭp-han 긴급한.

crystal *n.* ① su-jŏng 수정(水晶), k'ŭ-ri-sŭ-t'al 크리스탈. ② kyŏl-jŏng-ch'e 결정체. —*adj.* t'u-myŏng-han 투명한.

cube *n.* ip-bang 입방, ip-bang-ch'e 입방체.

cubism *n.* ip-ch'e-p'a 입체파, k'yu-bi-jŭm 큐비즘.

cuckoo *n.* ppŏ-gguk-sae 뻐꾹새, ppŏ-ggu-gi 뻐꾸기.

cucumber *n.* o-i 오이 : *as cool as a ~* naeng-jŏng-han 냉정한, t'ae-yŏn-ja-yak-han 태연자약한.

cuff *n.* so-maet-bu-ri 소맷부리, k'ŏ-p'ŭ-sŭ 커프스.

culprit *n.* hyŏng-sa p'i-go-in 형사 피고인, choe-in 죄인.

cultivate *v.* ① kyŏng-jak-ha-da 경작하다 ; ki-rŭ-da 기르다. ② kyo-hwa-ha-da 교화(教化)하다.

cultivation n. ① (*tilling*) kyŏng-jak 경작, chae-bae 재배. ② yang-sŏng 양성. 「yang 교양.

culture n. ① mun-hwa 문화. ② (*refinement*) kyo-

cunning adj. kyo-hwal-han 교활한, kan-sa-han 간사한.

cup n. chan 잔, k'ŏp 컵 ; sang-bae 상배(賞杯).

cupboard n. ch'an-jang 찬장.

cure n. (*remedy*) ch'i-ryo 치료, ch'i-yu 치유. —v. (*heal*) ko-ch'i-da 고치다, nat-da 낫다. 「간 통행금지.

curfew n. so-dŭng 소등, ya-gan t'ong-haeng-gŭm-ji 야

curio n. kol-dong-p'um 골동품, mi-sul-p'um 미술품 : ~ *dealer* kol-dong-p'um-sang 골동품상.

curiosity n. ① ho-gi-sim 호기심. ② (*rare thing*) chin-gi-han mul-gŏn 진기한 물건.

curious adj. ho-gi-sim-e ch'an 호기심에 찬 ; (*eccentric*) koe-sang-han 괴상한, chin-gi-han 진기한.

curl n. kop-sŭl-mŏ-ri 곱슬머리. —v. kop-sŭl-gop-sŭl-ha-ge ha-da 곱슬곱슬하게 하다, k'ŏ-ŏl-ha-da 커얼하다.

curly adj. kop-sŭl-gop-sŭl-han 곱슬곱슬한.

currant n. kŏn-p'o-do 건포도.

current n. ① hŭ-rŭm 흐름, p'ung-jo 풍조. ② (*electricity*) chŏl-lyu 전류. —adj. ① yu-t'ong-doe-nŭn 유통되는. ② (*present*) hyŏn-jae-ŭi 현재의.

curriculum n. kyo-gwa-gwa-jŏng 교과과정, k'ŏ-ri-k'yul-rŏm 커리큘럼 : ~ *vitae* i-ryŏk-sŏ 이력서.

curse n. & v. chŏ-ju(-ha-da) 저주(하다).

curtain n. k'ŏ-ŏ-t'ŭn 커어튼, chang-mak 장막.

curve n. kok-sŏn 곡선. —v.(*bend*) ku-bu-ri-da 구부리다.

cushion n. pang-sŏk 방석, k'u-syŏn 쿠션.

custody n. ① (*safe keeping*) po-gwan 보관, kwal-li 관리. ② (*detention*) ku-sok 구속, kam-gŭm 감금.

custom n. ① sŭp-gwan 습관, kwal-lye 관례. ② (*import duties*) kwan-se 관세(關稅).

customer *n.* ko-gaek 고객, tan-gol-son-nim 단골손님.

customhouse *n.* se-gwan 세관.

cut *v.* ① pe-da 베다, kkŭn-t'a 끊다, sak-gam-ha-da 삭
감하다 ; (*carve*) sae-gi-da 새기다. ② (*absent from*)
kyŏl-sŏk-ha-da 결석하다. —*n.* (*gash*) sang-ch'ŏ 상처.

cute *adj.* ① kwi-yŏ-un 귀여운. ② (*shrewd*) ki-min-
han 기민한, pin-t'ŭm-ŏp-nŭn 빈틈없는.

cutlery *n.* k'al-bu-ch'i 칼붙이, k'al che-jo-ŏp 칼 제조업.

cycle *n.* ① chu-gi 주기. ② (*bicycle*) cha-jŏn-gŏ 자전거.
③ (*electricity*) chu-p'a 주파(周波), sa-i-k'ŭl 사이클.

cynical *adj.* pi-ggo-nŭn 비꼬는, naeng-so-jŏk-in 냉소
적인.

~~❧~~ D ~~❧~~

daffodil *n.* su-sŏn-hwa 수선화(水仙花).

dagger *n.* tan-do 단도, tan-gŏm 단검, pi-su 비수.

dahlia *n.* ta-al-ri-a 다알리아.

daily *adj.* mae-il-ŭi 매일의, il-sang-ui 일상의. —*adv.*
nal-ma-da 날마다. —*n.* il-gan-sin-mun 일간신문.

dainty *adj.* (*delicious*) ma-sit-nŭn 맛있는 ; (*elegant*)
u-a-han 우아한. —*n.* (*delicacy*) chin-mi 진미.

dairy *n.* nak-nong-jang 낙농장, nak-nong-ŏp 낙농업 :
~ *products* yu-je-p'um 유제품.

daisy *n.* sil-guk-hwa 실국화, te-i-ji 데이지.

dale *n.* chak-ŭn kol-jja-gi 작은 골짜기, kye-gok 계곡.

dam *n.* taem 댐, tuk 둑. —*v.* (*block up*) mak-da 막다.

damage *n.* son-hae 손해, son-hae-bae-sang 손해배상.
—*v.* son-hae-rŭl ip-hi-da 손해를 입히다.

dame *n.* kwi-bu-in 귀부인, suk-nyŏ 숙녀.

damn *v.* chŏ-ju-ha-da 저주하다, hok-p'yŏng-ha-da 혹
평하다 : *D~ it!* Chen-jang 젠장 !

damp *adj.* ch'uk-ch'uk-han 축축한, p'ul-i chuk-ŭn 풀이 죽은. —*n.* sŭp-gi 습기, (*fog*) an-gae 안개.

dance *n.* ch'um 춤, mu-yong 무용, mu-do-hoe 무도회. —*v.* ch'um-ŭl ch'u-da 춤을 추다.

dancer *n.* mu-yong-ga 무용가, taen-sŏ 댄서.

dandelion *n.* min-dŭl-re 민들레.

dandy *n.* mŏt-jang-i 멋장이. —*adj.* mŏ-sit-nŭn 멋있는.

danger *n.* (*risk*) wi-hŏm 위험 ; (*menace*) wi-hyŏp 위협, wi-hŏm-mul 위험물.   「로운.

dangerous *adj.* wi-hŏm-han 위험한, wi-t'ae-ro-un 위태

dangle *v.* mae-dal-da 매달다, pu-t'ŏ-da-ni-da 붙어다니다.

dare *v.* kam-hi …ha-da 감히 …하다.

daring *adj.* tae-dam-han 대담한, yong-gam-han 용감한.

dark *adj.* ŏ-du-un 어두운, (*dismal*) ŭm-ch'im-han 음침한. —*n.* ŏ-dum 어둠, am-hŭk 암흑.

darken *v.* ŏ-du-wŏ-ji-da 어두워지다.

darkness *n.* ŏ-dum 어둠 ; (*ignorance*) mu-ji 무지.

darling *adj.* sa-rang-ha-nŭn 사랑하는. —*n.* kwi-yŏ-un sa-ram 귀여운 사람 : *my* ~ yae-ya 애야 ; yŏ-bo 여보, tang-sin 당신.

darn *v.* kkwe-mae-da 꿰매다. —*n.* kip-gi 깁기.

dart *n.* tol-jin 돌진. —*v.* tol-jin-ha-da 돌진하다 ; (*go rapidly*) na-ra-ga-da 날아가다.

dash *v.* (*fling away*) nae-dŏn-ji-da 내던지다 ; (*rush against*) tol-jin-ha-da 돌진하다. —*n.* tol-jin 돌진.

data *n.* ① cha-ryo 자료, te-i-t'ŏ 데이터. ② chŏng-bo 정보 ; chi-sik 지식. ③ (*notes*) pi-mang-rok 비망록.

date *n.* ① nal-jja 날짜. ② te-i-t'ŭ 데이트 ; man-nal yak-sok 만날 약속. —*v.* …e-sŏ pi-rot-doe-da …에서

daughter *n.* ttal 딸.   [비롯되다.

daughter-in-law *n.* myŏ-nŭ-ri 며느리, ŭi-but-ddal 의

daunt *v.* wi-hyŏp-ha-da 위협하다.   [붓딸.

dawn *n.* sae-byŏk 새벽. —*v.* nal-i sae-da 날이 새다.

day *n.* ① nal 날, ha-ru 하루. ② (*daytime*) nat 낮. ③ (*epoch*) si-dae 시대.

daybreak *n.* sae-byŏk 새벽, tong-t'ŭl-nyŏk 동틀녘.

daylight *n.* haet-bit 햇빛 ; (*daytime*) chu-gan 주간.

daze *v.* nun-bu-si-ge ha-da 눈부시게 하다 ; mŏng-ha-ge ha-da 멍하게 하다. —*n.* hyŏn-hok 현혹.

dazzle *v.* nun-i pu-si-da 눈이 부시다, hyŏn-hok-si-k'i-da 현혹시키다. —*n.* nun-bu-sin pit 눈부신 빛.

dead *adj.* chuk-ŭn 죽은 ; hwal-bal-ch'i mot-han 활발치 못한 : *a* ~ *season* han-san-han ch'ŏl 한산한 철.

deadly *adj.* ch'i-myŏng-jŏk-in 치명적인. 「리의.

deaf *adj.* kwi-mŏk-ŭn 귀먹은, kwi-mŏ-gŏ-ri-ŭi 귀머거

deal *v.* ① ta-ru-da 다루다. ② (*trade*) kŏ-rae-ha-da 거래 하다. ③ (*deliver*) chu-da 주다. —*n.* (*treatment*) ch'wi-gŭp 취급 ; (*amount*) pul-lyang 분량.

dealer *n.* sang-in 상인, chang-su 장수. 「학장.

dean *n.* ① pu-gam-dok 부감독. ② (*college*) hak-jang

dear *adj.* ① ch'in-ae-ha-nŭn 친애하는. ② (*expensive*) pi-ssan 비싼. —*n.* ae-in 애인. —*int.* ŏ-mŏ-na 어머나.

death *n.* chuk-ŭm 죽음, sa-mang 사망.

debase *v.* (*depreciate*) ttŏ-rŏ-ddŭ-ri-da 떨어드리다 ; (*degrade*) ch'ŏn-ha-ge man-dŭl-da 천하게 만들다.

debate *v.* t'o-ron-ha-da 토론하다. —*n.* t'o-ron 토론, non-jaeng 논쟁. 「hye 은혜.

debt *n.* ① pit 빚, pu-ch'ae 부채. ② (*obligation*) ŭn-

debut *n.* ch'ŏt-mu-dae 첫무대, te-bwi 데뷔.

decade *n.* sip-nyŏn-gan 10년간 : *the first* ~ ch'oe-ch'o-ŭi sip-nyŏn-gan 최초의 10년간.

decay *n.* ① pu-p'ae 부패. ② (*decline*) soe-t'oe 쇠퇴. —*v.* ssŏk-da 썩다 ; soe-t'oe-ha-da 쇠퇴하다.

decease *v.* chuk-da 죽다. —*n.* sa-mang 사망.

deceit *n.* ki-man 기만, sa-gi 사기. 「다.

deceive *v.* sok-i-da 속이다 ; hyŏn-hok-si-k'i-da 현혹시키

December *n.* sip-i-wŏl 12월, sŏt-dal 섣달.

decent *adj.* chŏm-jan-ŭn 점잖은, ye-ŭi-ba-rŭn 예의바른 ; (*fair*) sang-dang-han 상당한.

deception *n.* ki-man 기만, sa-gi 사기, sok-im-su 속임수.

decide *v.* kyŏl-jŏng-ha-da 결정하다. 「결.

decision *n.* kyŏl-jŏng 결정, (*judgment*) p'an-gyŏl 판

decisive *adj.* kyŏl-jŏng-jŏk-in 결정적인.

deck *n.* kap-p'an 갑판. —*v.* (*adorn*) kku-mi-da 꾸미다.

declaration *n.* sŏn-ŏn 선언, kong-p'yo 공표.

declare *v.* sŏn-ŏn-ha-da 선언하다, tan-ŏn-ha-da 단언하다.

decline *v.* (*bend down*) ki-ul(-i)-da 기울(이)다, soe-t'oe-ha-da 쇠퇴하다 ;(*refuse*) kŏ-jŏl-ha-da 거절하다. —*n.* kyŏng-sa 경사, soe-t'oe 쇠퇴.

decorate *v.* kku-mi-da 꾸미다. 「훈장.

decoration *n.* ① chang-sik 장식. ② (*medal*) hun-jang

decorum *n.* (*etiquette*) ye-jŏl 예절, (*pl.*) ye-bŏp 예법 ; (*decency*) tan-jŏng 단정.

decoy *n.* (*bait*) mi-ggi 미끼, (*lure*) yu-in-mul 유인물.

decrease *v.* chul-da 줄다, kam-so-ha-da 감소하다. —*n.* kam-so 감소, ch'uk-so 축소.

decree *n.* pŏp-ryŏng 법령, p'o-go-ryŏng 포고령.

dedicate *v.* pa-ch'i-da 바치다, hŏn-nap-ha-da 헌납하다 ; (*give up*) nae-dŏn-ji-da 내던지다.

deduct *v.* ppae-da 빼다, kong-je-ha-da 공제하다.

deed *n.* ① haeng-wi 행위. ② kong-jŏk 공적. 「하다.

deem *v.* saeng-gak-ha-da 생각하다, kan-ju-ha-da 간주

deep *adj.* ki-p'ŭn 깊은, sim-wŏn-han 심원한.

deer *n.* sa-sŭm 사슴. 「chi-u-da 지우다.

defeat *n.* p'ae-bae 패배. —*v.* ch'yŏ-bu-su-da 쳐부수다 ;

defect *n.* kyŏl-jŏm 결점, kyŏl-ham 결함.

defence·defense *n.* pang-wi 방위, su-bi 수비.

defenceless *adj.* pang-bi-ŏp-nŭn 방비없는, mu-bang-bi-ŭi 무방비의. 「하다.

defend *v.* pang-ŏ-ha-da 방어하다, pyŏn-ho-ha-da 변호

defendant *n.* p'i-go 피고. 「보하다.

defer *v.* ① yŏn-gi-ha-da 연기하다. ② yang-bo-ha-da 양

defiance *n.* to-jŏn 도전, kong-gong-yŏn-han pan-hang 공공연한 반항; (*disregard*) mu-si 무시.

deficient *adj.* pu-jok-han 부족한, mo-ja-ra-nŭn 모자라는.

defile *v.* tŏ-rŏp-hi-da 더럽히다; mo-dok-ha-da 모독하다.

define *v.* chŏng-ŭi-rŭl nae-ri-da 정의를 내리다.

definite *adj.* myŏng-hwak-han 명확한, il-jŏng-han 일정한; han-jŏng-doen 한정된. 「syŏn 디플레이션.

deflation *n.* t'ong-hwa su-ch'uk 통화 수축, ti-p'ŭl-re-i-

deformity *n.* pul-gu 불구, ki-hyŏng 기형.

deft *adj.* som-ssi-jo-ŭn 솜씨좋은, (*skillful*) nŭng-suk-han 능숙한, nŭng-ran-han 능란한.

defy *v.* to-jŏn-ha-da 도전하다; kŏ-bu-ha-da 거부하다.

degeneration *n.* t'a-rak 타락, t'oe-bo 퇴보.

degrade *v.* kyŏk-ha-ha-da 격하하다, kang-dŭng-ha-da 강등하다; (*debase*) t'a-rak-si-k'i-da 타락시키다.

degree *n.* ① (*extent*) to 도(度), chŏng-do 정도. ② (*school*) hak-wi 학위. ③ (*rank*) tŭng-gŭp 등급.

deity *n.* sin 신(神), sang-je 상제(上帝).

delay *v.* yŏn-gi-si-k'i-da 연기시키다; kku-mul-gŏ-ri-da 꾸물거리다. —*n.* chi-ch'e 지체, yŏn-gi 연기.

delegate *n.* tae-p'yo 대표. —*v.* tae-p'yo-ro nae-se-u-da 대표로 내세우다, (*commit*) wi-im-ha-da 위임하다.

deliberate *v.* sin-jung-hi saeng-gak-ha-da 신중히 생각하다. —*adj.* sin-jung-han 신중한. 「의로.

deliberately *adv.* sin-jung-ha-ge 신중하게, ko-ŭi-ro 고

delicate *adj.* chŏng-gyo-han 정교한; (*slender*) ka-nyal-p'ŭn 가냘픈 ; (*sensitive*) min-gam-han 민감한.

delicious *adj.* ma-sit-nŭn 맛있는.

delight *v.* chŭl-gŏp-ge ha-da 즐겁게 하다. —*n.* ki-bbŭm 기쁨, hwan-hŭi 환희. 「bbŭn 기쁜.

delightful *adj.* (mae-u) chŭl-gŏ-un (매우) 즐거운, ki-

deliver *v.* ① (*relieve*) ku-hae-nae-da 구해내다. ② (*distribute*) pae-dal-ha-da 배달하다. ③ (*utter*) chin-sul-ha-da 진술하다. ④ (*toss*) tŏn-ji-da 던지다.

deliverance *n.* ① ku-jo 구조. ② sŏk-bang 석방.

delivery *n.* ① (*letter*) pae-dal 배달. ② (*childbirth*) ch'ul-san 출산.

delta *n.* sam-gak-ju 삼각주(三角洲), tel-t'ŏ 델터.

delude *v.* sok-i-da 속이다, hyŏn-hok-ha-da 현혹하다.

delusion *n.* ki-man 기만, ch'ak-gak 착각.

demand *n. & v.* yo-gu(-ha-da) 요구(하다). 「민주정체.

democracy *n.* min-ju-ju-ŭi 민주주의, min-ju-jŏng-ch'e

democratic *adj.* min-ju-jŏng-ch'e-ŭi 민주정체의, min-ju-jŏk-in 민주적인, tae-jung-jŏk-in 대중적인.

demon *n.* ak-ma 악마, to-ggae-bi 도깨비.

demonstrate *v.* ip-jŭng-ha-da 입증하다, si-ryŏn-ha-da 실연(實演)하다, si-wi-ha-da 시위하다.

demonstration *n.* (*proof*) chŭng-myŏng 증명 ; (*mass meeting*) si-wi-un-dong 시위운동, te-mo 데모.

den *n.* kul 굴, u-ri 우리, so-gul 소굴.

denomination *n.* ① (*title*) myŏng-ch'ing 명칭. ② (*kind*) chong-ryu 종류. ③ (*units*) tan-wi 단위. ④ (*religious sect*) chong-p'a 종파.

denote *v.* p'yo-si-ha-da 표시하다, na-t'a-nae-da 나타내다.

denounce *v.* (*blame*) pi-nan-ha-da 비난하다, ko-bal-ha-da 고발하다 ; (*repudiate*) p'ye-gi-ha-da 폐기하다.

dense *adj.* mil-jip-han 밀집한, cho-mil-han 조밀한 ; chi-t'ŭn 짙은 : *a ~ forest* mil-rim 밀림.

dentist *n.* ch'i-gwa-ŭi-sa 치과의사.

deny *v.* pu-in-ha-da 부인하다, kŏ-jŏl-ha-da 거절하다.

depart *v.* ttŏ-na-da 떠나다, ch'ul-bal-ha-da 출발하다; (*pass away*) se-sang-ŭl tt'ŏ-na-da 세상을 떠나다.

department *n.* pu-mun 부문; (*suffix*) …pu …부, …kuk …국(局), …kwa …과.

department store paek-hwa-jŏm 백화점.

departure *n.* ch'ul-bal 출발, ttŏ-nam 떠남.

depend *v.* ŭi-ji-ha-da 의지하다, ŭi-jon-ha-da 의존하다.

dependent *n.* pu-yang ka-jok 부양 가족, sik-gaek 식객.

depict *v.* (*portray*) kŭ-ryŏ-nae-da 그려내다, myo-sa-ha-da 묘사하다, (*describe*) sŏ-sul-ha-da 서술하다.

deplore *v.* sŭl-p'ŏ-ha-da 슬퍼하다, ae-do-ha-da 애도하다.

deposit *n.* (*in a bank*) ye-gŭm 예금; (*sediment*) ang-gŭm 앙금, jji-ggi 찌끼. —*v.* ye-gŭm〔kong-t'ak〕-ha-da 예금〔공탁〕하다.

deprave *v.* t'a-rak-si-k'i-da 타락시키다, ak-hwa-si-k'i-da 악화시키다.

depress *v.* ① ŏk-ap-ha-da 억압하다. ② pul-gyŏng-gi-ro man-dŭl-da 불경기로 만들다.

depression *n.* ① (*commercial*) pul-gyŏng-gi 불경기. ② (*mental*) nak-sim 낙심, u-ul 우울.

deprive *v.* ppae-at-da 빼앗다, pak-t'al-ha-da 박탈하다.

depth *n.* ki-p'i 깊이, ki-p'ŭn kot 깊은 곳.

deputy *n.* tae-ri(-in) 대리(인), sŏ-ri 서리(署理). —*adj.* tae-ri-ŭi 대리의, pu-ŭi 부(副)의.

deride *v.* pi-ut-da 비웃다, cho-rong-ha-da 조롱하다.

derive *v.* i-ggŭ-rŏ-nae-da 이끌어내다.

descend *v.* ① nae-ryŏ-o-da 내려오다, pi-t'al-ji-da 비탈지다. ② chŏn-ha-yŏ-ji-da 전하여지다.

descendant *n.* cha-son 자손, hu-ye 후예.

descent *n.* ① (*coming down*) kang-ha 강하. ② (*lineage*) ka-gye 가계(家系), hyŏl-t'ong 혈통.

describe v. ① sŏ-sul-ha-da 서술하다, myo-sa-ha-da 묘사하다. ② (trace) kŭ-ri-da 그리다.

description n. sŏ-sul 서술, sŏl-myŏng-sŏ 설명서.

desert n. sa-mak 사막. —adj. pul-mo-ŭi 불모의. —v. (forsake) pŏ-ri-da 버리다 ; t'al-ch'ul-ha-da 탈출하다.

deserter n. to-mang-ja 도망자, to-mang-byŏng 도망병.

deserve v. …hal ka-ch'i-ga it-da …할 가치가 있다, …ŭl pat-ŭl ka-ch'i-ga it-da …을 받을 가치가 있다.

design n. sŏl-gye 설계, ku-sang 구상 ; ŭi-do 의도. —v. sŏl-gye-ha-da 설계하다, ti-ja-in-ha-da 디자인하다.

designate v. chi-jŏng[chi-myŏng]-ha-da 지정〔지명〕하다, im-myŏng-ha-da 임명하다.　　　　　　　「rŏn 소망스런.

desirable adj. pa-ram-jik-han 바람직한, so-mang-sŭ-

desire n. yok-mang 욕망, so-mang 소망, yo-gu 요구. —v. pa-ra-da 바라다, yo-mang-ha-da 요망하다.

desk n. ch'aek-sang 책상.

despair n. chŏl-mang 절망. —v. chŏl-mang-ha-da 절망하다, tan-nyŏm-ha-da 단념하다.

desperate adj. chŏl-mang-jŏk-in 절망적인, p'il-sa-jŏk-in 필사적인, cha-p'o-ja-gi-ŭi 자포자기의.

despise v. myŏl-si-ha-da 멸시하다, kkal-bo-da 깔보다.

despite prep. …e-do pul-gu-ha-go …에도 불구하고.

despond v. sil-mang-ha-da 실망하다, nak-sim-ha-da 낙심하다, ki-ga chuk-da 기가 죽다.

despot n. chŏn-je-gun-ju 전제군주, (tyrant) p'ok-gun 폭군.

dessert n. ti-jŏ-ŏ-t'ŭ 디저어트.

destination n. mok-jŏk-ji 목적지 ; ye-jŏng 예정.

destitute adj. ka-nan-han 가난한, kung-p'ip-han 궁핍한 : a ~ family kŭk-bin ka-jŏk 극빈 가족.

destroy v. p'a-goe-ha-da 파괴하다, mu-nŏ-ddŭ-ri-da 무너뜨리다 ; (kill) chuk-i-da 죽이다.　　　　　　「축함.

destroyer n. ① p'a-goe-ja 파괴자. ② ku-ch'uk-ham 구

destruction *n.* p'a-goe 파괴, p'a-myŏl 파멸.

detach *v.* (*seperate*) tte-ŏ-nae-da 떼어내다, pul-li-ha-da 분리하다 ; (*dispatch*) p'a-gyŏn-ha-da 파견하다.

detail *v.* ① sang-se-hi mal-ha-da 상세히 말하다. ② t'ŭk-p'a-ha-da 특파하다. —*n.* se-bu 세부(細部).

detain *v.* (*hold in custody*) ku-ryu-ha-da 구류하다 ; (*keep waiting*) ki-da-ri-ge ha-da 기다리게 하다.

detect *v.* a-ra-nae-da 알아내다, t'am-ji-ha-da 탐지하다.

detective *n.* t'am-jŏng 탐정 ; hyŏng-sa 형사.

determination *n.* kyŏl-sim 결심.   「da 결심하다.

determine *v.* kyŏl-jŏng-ha-da 결정하다, kyŏl-sim-ha-

detest *v.* mop-si mi-wŏ-ha-da 몹시 미워하다.

devastate *v.* yu-rin-ha-da 유린하다, hwang-p'ye-k'e ha-da 황폐케 하다.

develop *v.* ① pal-dal-ha-da 발달하다. ② (*photo*) hyŏn-sang-ha-da 현상하다.   「*to*) hyŏn-sang 현상.

development *n.* ① pal-dal 발달, kae-bal 개발. ② (*pho-*

deviate *v.* pit-na-ga-da 빗나가다, pŏ-sŏ-na-da 벗어나다.

device *n.* (*scheme*) ko-an 고안, (*apparatus*) chang-ch'i 장치 ; kung-ri 궁리 ; ŭi-jang 의장(意匠), kye-ch'aek

devil *n.* ak-ma 악마, kwi-sin 귀신.   「계책.

devise *v.* ko-an-ha-da 고안하다, kung-ri-ha-da 궁리하다.

devote *v.* pa-ch'i-da 바치다 ; mat-gi-da 맡기다.

devotion *n.* hŏn-sin 헌신 ; (*piety*) sin-sim 신심.

devour *v.* ① (*eat hungrily*) ke-gŏl-sŭ-re mŏk-da 게걸 스레 먹다. ② t'am-dok-ha-da 탐독하다.

dew *n.* i-sŭl 이슬, pang-ul 방울.

dexterous *adj.* son-jae-ju-it-nŭn 손재주있는.

diagram *n.* (*figure*) to-p'yo 도표, to-hyŏng 도형, to-sik 도식 ; (*drawing*) chak-do 작도.   「다이얼.

dial *n.* hae-si-gye 해시계, p'yo-si-p'an 표시판, ta-i-ŏl

dialect *n.* sa-t'u-ri 사투리 ; kwan-yong-ŏ 관용어.

dialog(ue) *n.* tae·hwa 대화, mun·dap 문답.

diameter *n.* chi·rŭm 지름, chik·gyŏng 직경. 「아몬드.

diamond *n.* kŭm·gang·sŏk 금강석, ta·i·a·mon·dŭ 다이

diaper *n.* ① ma·rŭm·mo·ggol mu·nŭi 마름모꼴 무늬.
② (*breechcloth*) ki·jŏ·gwi 기저귀.   「다.

diarrhoea *n.* sŏl·sa 설사 : *have* ~ sŏl·sa·ha·da 설사하

diary *n.* il·gi 일기, il·ji 일지.

dice *n.* chu·sa·wi 주사위, chu·sa·wi no·ri 주사위 놀이.

dictate *v.* ① pat·a·ssŭ·da 받아쓰다. ② (*order*) myŏng·
ryŏng·ha·da 명령하다.   「ryŏng 명령.

dictation *n.* pat·a·ssŭ·gi 받아쓰기 ; (*command*) myŏng·

dictator *n.* tok·jae·ja 독재자, chi·ryŏng·ja 지령자.

dictatorship *n.* tok·jae 독재, tok·jae·gwŏn 독재권.

dictionary *n.* sa·jŏn 사전(辭典), cha·jŏn 자전.

die *v.* chuk·da 죽다. —*n.* chu·sa·wi 주사위.

diet *n.* ① kuk·hoe 국회. ② (*food*) ŭm·sik·mul 음식물.

differ *v.* ta·rŭ·da 다르다, t'ŭl·ri·da 틀리다.

difference *n.* ch'a·i 차이 ; (*discord*) pul·hwa 불화.

different *adj.* ta·rŭn 다른, sang·i·han 상이한.

difficult *adj.* ŏ·ryŏ·un 어려운, kka·da·ro·un 까다로운.

difficulty *n.* ŏ·ryŏ·um 어려움, kol·lan 곤란.

diffident *adj.* cha·sin·ŏp·nŭn 자신없는, su·jup·ŭn 수줍은.

diffuse *v.* (*scatter*) ppu·ri·da 뿌리다, po·gŭp·ha·da 보
급하다. —*adj.* san·man·han 산만한.   「하다.

dig *v.* p'a·da 파다, k'ae·da 캐다 ; t'am·gu·ha·da 탐구

digest *v.* ① so·hwa·ha·da 소화하다. ② (*simplify*) yo·
yak·ha·da 요약하다. —*n.* ① so·hwa 소화. ② kae·yo

digestion *n.* so·hwa 소화 ; tong·hwa 동화(同化). 「개요.

digger *n.* ① kwang·bu 광부. ② kong·bu pŏl·re 공부 벌레.

dignity *n.* wi·ŏm 위엄, wi·p'ung 위풍 ; (*high position*)
ko·wi 고위, ko·gwan 고관.

dike·dyke *n.* to·rang 도랑, tuk 둑 ; che·bang 제방.

diligence *n.* pu·ji·rŏn·ham 부지런함, kŭn·myŏn 근면.

diligent *adj.* pu·ji·rŏn·han 부지런한, kŭn·myŏn·han 근면한, kong·bu·ha·nŭn 공부하는. 「다.

dilute *v.* mul·gge ha·da 묽게 하다, hŭi·sŏk·ha·da 희석하

dim *adj.* ŏ·dum·ch'im·ch'im·han 어둠침침한 ; hŭi·mi·han 희미한. 「jŏk 면적, yong·jŏk 용적.

dimension *n.* ① ch'i·su 치수 ; ch'a·wŏn 차원. ② myŏn-

diminish *v.* chu·ri·da 줄이다, tŏl·da 덜다. 「결.

dimple *n.* ① po·jo·gae 보조개. ② chan·mul·gyŏl 잔물

din *n.* si·ggŭ·rŏ·un so·ri 시끄러운 소리, so·ŭm 소음.

dine *v.* chŏng·ch'an·ŭl tŭl·da 정찬을 들다, chŏ·nyŏk sik·sa·rŭl ha·da 저녁 식사를 하다.

dining *n.* sik·sa 식사 : ~ *car* sik·dang·ch'a 식당차/ ~ *room* sik·dang 식당/~ *table* sik·t'ak 식탁.

dinner *n.* chŏng·ch'an 정찬, man·ch'an 만찬 : *a* ~ *party* man·ch'an·hoe 만찬회, o·ch'an·hoe 오찬회.

dip *v.* chŏk·si·da 적시다, tam·gŭ·da 담그다.

diphtheria *n.* ti·p'ŭ·t'e·ri·a 디프테리아.

diploma *n.* myŏn·hŏ·jang 면허장 ; cho·rŏp·jang 졸업장.

diplomacy *n.* oe·gyo 외교, oe·gyo·sul 외교술.

diplomat *n.* oe·gyo·gwan 외교관, oe·gyo·ga 외교가.

dipper *n.* kuk·ja 국자, chu·gŏk 주걱. 「처참한.

dire *adj.* mu·si·mu·si·han 무시무시한, ch'o·ch'am·han

direct *adv.* (*immediate*) chik·jŏp·jŏk·in 직접적인 ; (*frank*) sol·jik·han 솔직한 ; (*straight*) ttok·ba·rŭn 똑바른. —*v.* (*order*) chi·si·ha·da 지시하다, myŏng·ryŏng·ha·da 명령하다 ; chi·do·ha·da 지도하다.

direction *n.* ① pang·hyang 방향. ② (*instruction*) chi·si·sŏ 지시서 ; sa·yong·bŏp 사용법.

directly *adv.* chik·jŏp 직접, chŭk·si 즉시.

director *n.* ① chi·do·ja 지도자. ② (*manager*) chung·yŏk 중역 ; chi·bae·in 지배인. ③ (*cinema*) kam·dok 감독.

directory *n.* in-myŏng-rok 인명록, (*telephone*) chŏn-hwa pŏn-ho-bu 전화 번호부.

dirt *n.* ssŭ-re-gi 쓰레기 ; chin-hŭk 진흙 ; o-mul 오물.

dirty *adj.* (*unclean*) tŏ-rŏ-un 더러운, (*base*) ch'ŏn-han 천한, sang-sŭ-rŏ-un 상스러운.

disable *v.* pul-gu-ro man-dŭl-da 불구로 만들다.

disadvantage *n.* pul-ri 불리, son-hae 손해.

disagree *v.* (*differ*) ŭi-gyŏn-i ta-rŭ-da 의견이 다르다 ; (*unsuitable*) chŏk-hap-ha-ji an-t'a 적합하지 않다.

disagreeable *adj.* pul-k'wae-han 불쾌한, si-rŭn 싫은.

disappear *v.* sa-ra-ji-da 사라지다, so-myŏl-ha-da 소멸

disappearance *n.* so-sil 소실, sil-jong 실종.   ⌊하다.

disappoint *v.* sil-mang-k'e ha-da 실망케 하다, chŏ-bŏ-ri-da 저버리다, chwa-jŏl-si-k'i-da 좌절시키다.

disappointment *n.* sil-mang 실망, nak-sim 낙심.

disapproval *n.* pul-ch'an-sŏng 불찬성, pu-dong-ŭi 부동의(不同意), pul-man 불만.

disapprove *v.* ① ch'an-sŏng-ha-ji an-t'a 찬성하지 않다. ② (*condemn*) pi-nan-ha-da 비난하다.

disarm *v.* ① kun-bi-ch'uk-so-ha-da 군비축소하다. ② mu-jang-ŭl hae-je-ha-da 무장을 해제하다.

disaster *n.* chae-nan 재난, pul-haeng 불행.   ⌈한.

disastrous *adj.* chae-nan-ŭi 재난의 ; pi-ch'am-han 비참

disbelieve *v.* mit-ji an-t'a 믿지 않다.

discern *v.* ① sik-byŏl[pun-byŏl]-ha-da 식별[분별]하다, pun-gan-ha-da 분간하다. ② in-sik-ha-da 인식하다.

discharge *v.* (*electricity*) pang-jŏn-ha-da 방전하다 ; (*from army*) che-dae-ha-da 제대하다 ; (*dismiss*) hae-go-ha-da 해고하다. —*n.* (*shoot*) pal-sa 발사, (*release*) hae-je 해제 ; (*performance*) su-haeng 수행.

disciple *n.* che-ja 제자, mun-ha-saeng 문하생.

discipline *n.* hul-lyŏn 훈련 ; (*public morals*) p'ung-gi 풍기. —v. (train) hul·lyŏn·ha·da 훈련하다 ; (reprimand) ching·gye·ha·da 징계하다.

disclose v. p'ok·ro·ha·da 폭로하다, tŭl·ch'u·ŏ·nae·da 들추어내다 ; ch'ŏn·myŏng·ha·da 천명하다.

discomfort n. pul·k'wae 불쾌, pu·ran 불안. 「케 하다.

disconcert v. (embarrass) tang·hwang·k'e ha·da 당황

discontent n. pul·man 불만, pul·p'yŏng 불평.

discontented adj. pul·man·sŭ·rŏ·un 불만스러운. 「치다.

discontinue v. chung·ji·ha·da 중지하다, kŭ·ch'i·da 그

discord n. ① pu·ril·ch'i 불일치. ② pul·hyŏp·hwa·ŭm 불협화음. —v. il·ch'i·ha·ji an·t'a 일치하지 않다 ; sa·i·ga na·bbŭ·da 사이가 나쁘다.

discount n. & v. ha·rin(·ha·da) 할인(하다).

discourage v. sil·mang·k'e ha·da 실망케 하다 ; (thwart) pang·hae·ha·da 방해하다. 「하다.

discourse n. tam·hwa 담화. —v. i·ya·gi·ha·da 이야기

discourtesy n. sil·rye 실례, (rude act) mu·rye 무례.

discourteous adj. pŏ·rŭt·ŏp·nŭn 버릇없는.

discover v. ① pal·gyŏn·ha·da 발견하다. ② kkae·dat·

discovery n. pal·gyŏn 발견. 「da 깨닫다.

discreet adj. sa·ryŏ·gi·p'ŭn 사려깊은, yong·ŭi·ju·do·han 용의주도한, sin·jung·han 신중한.

discretion n. sa·ryŏ pun·byŏl 사려 분별, sik·byŏl 식별.

discriminate v. sik·byŏl·ha·da 식별하다 ; ch'a·byŏl·ha·da 차별하다. —adj. ch'a·byŏl·jŏk·in 차별적인.

discrimination n. ch'a·byŏl 차별 ; ku·byŏl 구별.

discuss v. ŭi·non·ha·da 의논하다, t'o·ron·ha·da 토론하

discussion n. ŭi·non 의논, t'o·ŭi 토의. 「다.

disdain v. myŏl·si·ha·da 멸시하다. —n. myŏl·si 멸시.

disease n. pyŏng 병, chil·hwan 질환.

disgrace v. mang·sin·si·k'i·da 망신시키다. —n. pul·myŏng·ye 불명예, ch'i·yok 치욕.

disgraceful *adj*. su-ch'i-sŭ-rŏ-un 수치스러운.

disguise *v*. pyŏn-jang-ha-da 변장하다, ka-jang-ha-da 가장하다. —*n*. pyŏn-jang 변장, ka-myŏn 가면.

disgust *n*. sil-jŭng 싫증, hyŏm-o 혐오.

dish *n*. ① chŏp-si 접시. ② yo-ri 요리.

dishonest *adj*. chŏng-jik-ha-ji mot-han 정직하지 못한.

dishonesty *n*. pu-jŏng-jik 부정직, pul-sŏng-sil 불성실.

dishonor *n*. pul-myŏng-ye 불명예, ch'i-yok 치욕. —*v*. ch'ang-p'i-rŭl chu-da 창피를 주다.

disillusion *n*. hwan-myŏl 환멸, kak-sŏng 각성. —*v*. hwan-sang-e-sŏ kkae-ŏ-na-da 환상에서 깨어나다.

disinterested *adj*. (*unselfish*) sa-sim-i ŏp-nŭn 사심이 없는; (*impartial*) kong-p'yŏng-han 공평한.

disk *n*. wŏn-ban 원반, re-k'o-o-dŭ 레코오드.

dislike *n*. si-rŭm 싫음, hyŏm-o 혐오. —*v*. si-rŏ-ha-da 싫어하다, mi-wŏ-ha-da 미워하다.

disloyal *adj*. ch'ung-sŏng-sŭ-rŏp-ji mot-han 충성스럽지 못한, pul-sŏng-sil-han 불성실한.

dismal *adj*. (*gloomy*) ŭm-ch'im-han 음침한, u-ul-han 우울한; mu-si-mu-si-han 무시무시한.

dismay *n*. tang-hwang 당황; (*fear*) nol-ram 놀람. —*v*. tang-hwang-k'e ha-da 당황케 하다.

dismiss *v*. ① (*send away*) mul-rŏ-na-ge ha-da 물러나게 하다, hae-go-ha-da 해고하다. ② (*disband*) hae-san-si-k'i-da 해산시키다. ③ (*reject*) ki-gak-ha-da 기각하다.

dismount *v*. nae-ri-da 내리다, ha-ch'a-ha-da 하차하다.

disobedience *n*. pul-bok-jong 불복종, wi-ban 위반.

disobedient *adj*. sun-jong-ha-ji an-nŭn 순종하지 않는, mal-ŭl tŭt-ji an-nŭn 말을 듣지 않는.

disobey *v*. mal-ŭl tŭt-ji an-t'a 말을 듣지 않다, sun-jong-ch'i an-t'a 순종치 않다, ŏ-gi-da 어기다.

disorder *n*. nan-jap 난잡, mu-jil-sŏ 무질서. —*v*. ŏ-ji-rŏp·hi·da 어지럽히다.

dispatch *n.* kŭp·song 급송, kŭp·p'a 급파 ; (*express delivery*) sok·dal·u·p'yŏn 속달우편. —*v.* p'a·gyŏn·ha·da 파견하다 ; (*goods*) pal·song·ha·da 발송하다.

dispel *v.* jjo·ch'a·bŏ·ri·da 쫓아버리다, ŏp·sae·da 없애다.

dispense *v.* ① (*distribute*) na·nwŏ·ju·da 나눠주다. ② (*do without*) ŏp·si kyŏn·di·da 없이 견디다. ③ (*put up*) cho·je·ha·da 조제하다. 「하다.

disperse *v.* hŭt·t'ŏ·ji·da 흩어지다, hae·san·ha·da 해산

displace *n.* ① pa·ggu·ŏ no·t'a 바꾸어 놓다. ② (*remove from office*) hae·im·ha·da 해임하다.

display *n.* chin·yŏl 진열. —*v.* na·t'a·nae·da 나타내다.

disposal *n.* ch'ŏ·bun 처분, ch'ŏ·ch'i 처치.

dispose *v.* ① (*arrange*) pae·ch'i·ha·da 배치하다. ② (*deal with*) ch'ŏ·ri·ha·da 처리하다.

disposition *n.* ① ki·jil 기질. ② ch'ŏ·ri 처리.

dispute *n.* mal·da·t'um 말다툼, non·jaeng 논쟁. —*v.* mal·da·t'um·ha·da 말다툼하다.

disregard *v.* mu·si·ha·da 무시하다. —*n.* mu·si 무시.

disrespect *n.* mu·rye 무례, sil·rye 실례. 「다.

dissatisfy *v.* pul·man·ŭl p'um·ge ha·da 불만을 품게 하

dissect *v.* ka·rŭ·da 가르다, hae·bu·ha·da 해부하다.

dissipate *v.* hŭt·ddŭ·ri·da 흩드리다, il·so·ha·da 일소하

dissipated *adj.* pang·t'ang·han 방탕한. 「다.

dissolution *n.* hae·san 해산 ; so·myŏl 소멸.

dissolve *v.* ① nok·da 녹다. ② hae·san·ha·da 해산하다.

dissuade *v.* t'a·il·rŏ kŭ·man·du·ge ha·da 타일러 그만 두게 하다, tan·nyŏm·si·k'i·da 단념시키다.

distance *n.* kŏ·ri 거리, kan·gyŏk 간격.

distant *adj.* ① (*space*) mŏl·ri·it·nŭn 멀리있는. ② (*time*) o·raen 오랜. ③ (*relationship*) ch'on·su·ga mŏn 촌수가 먼. ④ (*not familiar*) sŏ·rŭm·han 서름한.

distaste *n.* si·rŭm 싫음, hyŏm·o 혐오.

distil(l) *v.* chŭng·ryu·ha·da 증류하다, ppum·da 뿜다.

distinct *adj.* ① myŏng·baek·han 명백한, sŏn·myŏng-han 선명한. ② (*seperate*) pyŏl·gae·ŭi 별개의. 「한.

distinctive *adj.* ku·byŏl·i pun·myŏng·han 구별이 분명

distinctly *adv.* pun·myŏng·hi 분명히, (*definitely*) ttok-ddok·ha·ge 똑똑하게, myŏng·baek·ha·ge 명백하게.

distinguish *v.* ku·byŏl·ha·da 구별하다. 「저한.

distinguished *adj.* i·rŭm·nan 이름난 ; hyŏn·jŏ·han 현

distort *v.* ① twi·t'ŭl·da 뒤틀다, jji·gu·rŏ·ddŭ·ri·da 찌그러뜨리다. ② kok·hae·ha·da 곡해하다.

distract *v.* hŭt·ddŭ·ri·da 흩뜨리다.

distress *n.* kŭn·sim 근심, ko·t'ong 고통 ; kon·gung 곤궁. —*v.* koe·rop·hi·da 괴롭히다, sŭl·p'ŭ·ge ha·da 슬프게 하다.

distribute *v.* na·nu·ŏ·ju·da 나누어주다.

distribution *n.* pun·bae 분배, pae·gŭp 배급.

district *n.* ① ku·yŏk 구역. ② (*region*) chi·bang 지방.

distrust *n.* pul·sin 불신. —*v.* mit·ji an·t'a 믿지 않다.

disturb *v.* ŏ·ji·rŏp·ge ha·da 어지럽게 하다, kyo·ran-ha·da 교란하다 ; pang·hae·ha·da 방해하다.

ditch *n.* to·rang 도랑, kae·ch'ŏn 개천.

dive *n.* cham·su 잠수. —*v.* mul·e ttwi·ŏ·dŭl·da 물에 뛰어들다, cham·su·ha·da 잠수하다.

diverse *adj.* (*different*) ta·rŭn 다른 ; (*varied*) ta·yang-han 다양한, ka·ji·gak·saek·ŭi 가지각색의.

divert *v.* ① (*turn aside*) chŏn·hwan·ha·da 전환하다. ② (*entertain*) ki·bun·ŭl p'ul·da 기분을 풀다.

divide *v.* na·nu·da 나누다, pul·li·ha·da 분리하다.

divine *adj.* sin·ŭi 신의 ; (*holy*) sin·sŏng·han 신성한. —*v.* (*foretell*) ye·ŏn·ha·da 예언하다.

division *n.* ① pun·hal 분할. ② (*boundary*) kyŏng·gye 경계. ③(*portion*) ku·hoek 구획. ④(*mil.*) sa·dan 사단.

divorce *n.* i-hon 이혼. —*v.* i-hon-ha-da 이혼하다.

dizzy *adj.* ŏ-ji-rŏ-un 어지러운, hyŏn-gi-jŭng na-nŭn 현기증 나는. —*v.* ŏ-ji-rŏp-ge ha-da 어지럽게 하다.

do *v.* ① (*act*) ha-da 하다. ② (*confer*) chu-da 주다. ③ (*make*) man-dŭl-da 만들다. ④ (*finish*) kkŭt-nae-da 끝내다. ⑤ (*enough*) ch'ung-bun-ha-da 충분하다.

docile *adj.* ka-rŭ-ch'i-gi swi-un 가르치기 쉬운, ta-ru-gi swi-un 다루기 쉬운, yu-sun-han 유순한.

dock *n.* ① (*artificial basin*) tok 독, sŏn-gŏ 선거(船渠), pu-du 부두. ② (*law*) p'i-go-sŏk 피고석.

dockyard *n.* cho-sŏn-so 조선소(造船所).

doctor *n.* ① ŭi-sa 의사. ② (*degree*) pak-sa 박사. —*v.* ch'i-ryo-ha-da 치료하다.

doctrine *n.* kyo-ri 교리 ; chu-ŭi 주의(主義) ; kyo-hun 교훈.

document *n.* mun-sŏ 문서, chŭng-sŏ 증서.

dodge *v.* sal-jjak p'i-ha-da 살짝 피하다.

doe *n.* ① am-no-ru 암노루. ② am-k'ŏt 암컷.

dog *n.* kae 개 : *a dirty* ~ tŏ-rŏ-un nyŏ-sŏk 더러운 녀석.

doleful *adj.* (*sad*) sŭl-p'ŭn 슬픈, u-ul-han 우울한.

doll *n.* ① in-hyŏng 인형. ② (*silly girl*) kkok-duk-gak-si 꼭둑각시.

dollar *n.* tal-rŏ 달러, pul 불(弗).

dolmen *n.* ko-in-dol 고인돌, tol-men 돌멘.

domain *n.* yŏng-t'o 영토, so-yu-ji 소유지 ; pun-ya 분야.

dome *n.* tŭng-gŭn chi-bung 둥근 지붕, (*vault*) tŭng-gŭn ch'ŏn-jang 둥근 천장.

domestic *adj.* ① (*household*) ka-jŏng-ŭi 가정의. ② (*national*) kuk-nae-ŭi 국내의. —*n.* ha-in 하인(下人).

domicile *n.* chu-so 주소, pon-jŏk-ji 본적지.

dominate *v.* (*rule*) chi-bae-ha-da 지배하다, (*rise above*) u-dduk sot-da 우뚝 솟다.

dominion *n.* chu-gwŏn 주권, t'ong-ch'i-gwŏn 통치권.

donate v. chŭng-yŏ-ha-da 증여하다, ki-jŭng-ha-da 기증하다, ki-bu-ha-da 기부하다.

donkey n. ① tang-na-gwi 당나귀. ② pa-bo 바보.

doom n. ①(*fate*)un-myŏng 운명, p'a-myŏl 파멸. ②(*sentence*) sŏn-go 선고. —v. un-myŏng-jit-da 운명짓다.

door n. mun 문, ch'u-rip-gu 출입구, to-ŏ 도어: ~ *keeper* mun-ji-gi 문지기, su-wi 수위/~ *knob* son-jap-i 손잡이 / *out of* ~s chip pa-gge-sŏ 집 밖에서.

doorbell n. ch'o-in-jong 초인종.

doorway n. tae-mun-gan 대문간, ch'u-rip-gu 출입구.

dormitory n. ki-suk-sa 기숙사, hap-suk-so 합숙소.

dose n. (*medicine*) il-hoe-bun 1회분 ; pok-yong-ryang 복용량. —v. t'u-yak-ha-da 투약(投藥)하다.

dot n. chŏm 점. —v. chŏm-ŭl jjik-da 점을 찍다.

dote v. ① mang-ryŏng-dŭl-da 망령들다, no-mang-ha-da 노망하다. ② sa-rang-e ppa-ji-da 사랑에 빠지다.

double adj. tu kop-ŭi 두 곱의. —v. pae-ro-ha-da 배로 하다. —n. kop 곱, pae 배(倍). 「의심하다.

doubt n. ŭi-sim 의심, ŭi-hok 의혹. —v. ŭi-sim-ha-da

doubtful adj. ŭi-sim-sŭ-rŏ-un 의심스러운. 「hi 확실히.

doubtless adj. ŭi-sim-ŏp-nŭn 의심없는. —adv. hwak-sil-

dough n. mil-ga-ru pan-juk 밀가루 반죽.

dove n. ① (*pigeon*) pi-dul-gi 비둘기. ② (*Holy Spirit*) sŏng-ryŏng 성령. 「mi-t'e 밑에.

down adv. & adj. a-rae-ro(-ŭi) 아래로(의). —prep.

downcast v. p'ul-i chuk-ŭn 풀이 죽은.

downstairs n. a-rae-ch'ŭng 아래층, ha-ch'ung 하층.

downtown n. to-sim-ji 도심지, pŏn-hwa-ga 번화가, (*business part of a city*) sang-ga 상가.

downward adv. a-rae-jjok-ŭ-ro 아래쪽으로.

downy adj. som-t'ŏl-ga-t'ŭn 솜털같은, p'ok-sin-p'ok-sin-han 폭신폭신한.

dowry *n.* (*bride*) chi-ch'am-gŭm 지참금.

doze *v.* chol-da 졸다, sŏn-jam-ja-da 선잠자다.

dozen *n.* yŏl-du-gae 12개, ta-sŭ 다스, t'a 타(打).

draft·draught *n.* ① (*rough copy*) ch'o-an 초안. ② (*conscription*) ching-byŏng 징병. ③ (*bank*) hwan-ŏ-ŭm 환어음. ④ t'ong-p'ung 통풍. —*v.* ① ki-ch'o-ha-da 기초(起草)하다. ② ching-jip-ha-da 징집하다.

drag *v.* kkŭl-da 끌다, kkŭ-rŏ-dang-gi-da 끌어당기다.

dragnet *n.* ① ye-in-mang 예인망. ② su-sa-mang 수사망.

dragon *n.* yong 용.

dragonfly *n.* cham-ja-ri 잠자리.

drain *n.* pae-su 배수(排水). —*v.* ① mul-ŭl ppae-da 물을 빼다 ; jjuk tŭ-ri-k'i-da 쭉 들이키다.

drake *n.* (*male duck*) su-o-ri 수오리. 「sa-gŭk 사극.

drama *n.* kŭk 극, tŭ-ra-ma 드라마 : *the historical* ~

dramatic *adj.* yŏn-gŭk-ŭi 연극의, kŭk-jŏk-in 극적인.

drape *n.* p'o-jang 포장, hwi-jang 휘장. —*v.* tŏp-da 덮다.

drapery *n.* (*textile fabrics*) p'i-ryuk 피륙, ot-gam 옷감.

drastic *adj.* maeng-ryŏl-han 맹렬한, ch'ŏl-jŏ-han 철저한.

draw *v.* ① (*pull*) kkŭl-da 끌다. ② (*pictures*) kŭ-ri-da 그리다. ③ (*inhale*) sum-ŭl swi-da 숨을 쉬다. 「애.

drawback *n.* kyŏl-jŏm 결점 ; (*hindrance*) chang-ae 장

drawer *n.* ① sŏ-rap 서랍. ② (*pl.*) p'aen-ch'ŭ 팬츠.

drawing *n.* che-do 제도(製圖), kŭ-rim 그림.

drawing room ŭng-jŏp-sil 응접실.

dread *n.* tu-ryŏ-um 두려움, kong-p'o 공포. —*v.* mu-sŏ-wŏ-ha-da 무서워하다, tu-ryŏ-wŏ-ha-da 두려워하다.

dreadful *adj.* mu-sŏ-un 무서운, tu-ryŏ-un 두려운.

dream *n.* kkum 꿈 ; kong-sang 공상. —*v.* kkum-ŭl kku-da 꿈을 꾸다, mong-sang-ha-da 몽상하다.

dreary *adj.* ssŭl-ssŭl-han 쓸쓸한, hwang-ryang-han 황량한 ; (*dull*) chi-ru-han 지루한.

dredger *n.* (*persons*) chun-sŏl in-bu 준설 인부 ; (*ships*) chun-sŏl-sŏn 준설선, ye-mang-ŏ-sŏn 예망어선.

dreg *n.* jji-ggŏ-gi 찌꺼기, ang-gŭm 앙금.

drench *v.* mul-e tam-gŭ-da 물에 담그다, hŭm-bbŏk chŏk-si-da 흠뻑 적시다. —*n.* mul-yak 물약.

dress *n.* ot 옷, ŭi-bok 의복. —*v.* ① (*put on*) ip-da 입다. ② (*adorn*) kku-mi-da 꾸미다, son-jil-ha-da 손질하다.

dresser *n.* ① ot ip-hi-nŭn sa-ram 옷 입히는 사람. ② (*dandy*) mŏt-jang-i 멋장이. ③ (*dressing table*) kyŏng-dae 경대, hwa-jang-dae 화장대.

drift *v.* p'yo-ryu-ha-da 표류하다, ttŏ-dol-da 떠돌다.

drill *n.* ① song-got 송곳. ② (*practice*) yŏn-sŭp 연습. —*v.* ① (*hole*) ku-mŏng-ŭl ttŭl-t'a 구멍을 뚫다. ② (*training*) hul-lyŏn-si-k'i-da 훈련시키다.

drink *v.* ma-si-da 마시다. —*n.* ŭm-ryo 음료.

drip *n.* (*of liquid*) pang-ul 방울. —*v.* (*from a height*) ttŏ-rŏ-ji-da 떨어지다.

drive *v.* mol-da 몰다, (*car*) un-jŏn-ha-da 운전하다. —*n.* ① tŭ-ra-i-bŭ 드라이브. ② (*path*) ch'a-do 차도. ③ (*campaign*) un-dong 운동.

driver *n.* un-jŏn-su 운전수 ; mal-mo-rit-gun 말몰잇군.

drizzle *n.* i-sŭl-bi 이슬비, ka-rang-bi 가랑비, po-sŭl-bi 보슬비. —*v.* i-sŭl-bi-ga nae-ri-da 이슬비가 내리다.

droop *v.* a-rae-ro ch'ŏ-ji-da 아래로 처지다, su-gŭ-rŏ-ji-da 수그러지다 ; (*flower*) si-dŭl-da 시들다.

drop *n.* pang-ul 방울, mul-bang-ul 물방울. —*v.* ttok-ddok ttŏ-rŏ-ji-da 똑똑 떨어지다.

drought *n.* (*dry weather*) ka-mum 가뭄, han-bal 한발.

drown *v.* mul-e ppa-ji-da 물에 빠지다.

drowsy *adj.* chol-li-nŭn 졸리는, cho-rŭm-i o-nŭn 졸음이 오는, na-rŭn-han 나른한.

drug *n.* yak 약, yak-p'um 약품. —*v.* yak-ŭl mŏk-i-da

약을 먹이다.　　　　　　　　　　　　　「mak 고막.

drum *n.* ① puk 북, tŭ-rŏm 드럼. ② (*eardrum*) ko-

drummer *n.* ko-su 고수(鼓手), tŭ-rŏ-mŏ 드러머.

drunkard *n.* chu-jŏng-gun 주정군, sul-go-rae 술고래.

dry *v.* mal-ri-da 말리다. —*adj.* ma-rŭn 마른, kŏn-jo-
han 건조한.

dual *adj.* i-jung-ŭi 이중의, i-wŏn-jŏk-in 이원적인 : ～
personality i-jung-in-gyŏk 이중인격.　　　　「수상한.

dubious *adj.* ŭi-sim-sŭ-rŏ-un 의심스러운, su-sang-han

duck *n.* o-ri 오리 : *the domestic* ～ chip-o-ri 집오리.

due *adj.* man-gi-ga toen 만기가 된 ; chi-dang-han 지당
한 ; to-ch'ak ye-jŏng-in 도착 예정인. —*adv.* pa-ro 바로.

duel *n.* kyŏl-t'u 결투, si-hap 시합. —*v.* kyŏl-t'u-ha-da

duet *n.* i-jung-ch'ang 이중창, i-jung-ju 이중주. 「결투하다.

duke *n.* kong-jak 공작(公爵).

dull *adj.* tun-han 둔한, mu-din 무딘.

duly *adv.* ① chŏng-dang-ha-ge 정당하게. ② che-si-
gan-e 제시간에. ③ sun-sŏ-dae-ro 순서대로. 「하는.

dumb *adj.* pŏng-ŏ-ri-ŭi 벙어리의, mal mot-ha-nŭn 말 못

dumbbell *n.* a-ryŏng 아령(啞鈴).

dunce *n.* chŏ-nŭng-a 저능아, mŏng-ch'ŏng-i 멍청이.

dung *n.* ttong 똥 ; (*manure*) kŏ-rŭm 거름.

dungeon *n.* ① (*underground prison*) chi-ha kam-
ok 지하 감옥. ② (*donjon*) a-sŏng 아성(牙城).

duplicate *n.* sa-bon 사본 ; pok-sa 복사. —*v.* i-jung-ŭ-ro
ha-da 이중으로 하다 ; pok-sa-ha-da 복사하다.

duration *n.* chi-sok 지속 ; ki-gan 기간.

during *prep.* …ha-nŭn tong-an …하는 동안.

dusk *n.* ttang-gŏ-mi 땅거미, hwang-hon 황혼.

dust *n.* mŏn-ji 먼지. —*v.* mŏn-ji-rŭl ttŏl-da 먼지를 떨다.

dustbin *n.* ssŭ-re-gi-t'ong 쓰레기통.

duster *n.* ch'ong-ch'ae 총채, mŏn-ji-ddŏ-ri 먼지떨이.

dusty *adj.* mŏn-ji t'u-sŏng-i-ŭi 먼지 투성이의.

dutiful *adj.* ŭi-mu-gam-i kang-han 의무감이 강한, pon-bun-ŭl chi-k'i-nŭn 본분(本分)을 지키는.

duty *n.* ① ŭi-mu 의무. ② (*tax*) se-gŭm 세금.

dwarf *n.* nan-jang-i 난장이. —*adj.* wae-so-han 왜소한, chak-ŭn 작은. —*v.* chak-ge ha-da 작게 하다.

dwell *v.* ① sal-da 살다. ② mŏ-mu-rŭ-da 머무르다.

dwindle *v.* ① (chŏm-jŏm) chak-a-ji-da (점점) 작아지다, chul-da 줄다. ② (*waste away*) ya-wi-da 야위다.

dye *v.* mul-dŭ-ri-da 물들이다. —*n.* mul-gam 물감.

dynasty *n.* wang-jo 왕조.

dysentery *n.* i-jil 이질, sŏl-sa-byŏng 설사병.

—◄ **E** ►—

each *adj.* kak-gak-ŭi 각각의, kak-ja-ŭi 각자의. —*pron.* kak-ja 각자, che-gak-gi 제각기.

eager *adj.* yŏl-jung-ha-nŭn 열중하는, yŏl-sim-in 열심인.

eagerly *adv.* yŏl-sim-hi 열심히, kan-jŏl-hi 간절히.

eagerness *n.* yŏl-sim 열심, kal-mang 갈망.

eagle *n.* tok-su-ri 독수리 ; (*emblem*) tok-su-ri-p'yo 독수리표.

ear *n.* ① kwi 귀. ② (*corn, etc.*) i-sak 이삭.

early *adj.* i-rŭn 이른. —*adv.* il-jji-gi 일찌기.

earn *v.* (*by labor*) pŏl-da 벌다 ; (*obtain*) ŏt-da 얻다 ; (*deserve*) pat-ŭl man-ha-da 받을 만하다.

earnest *adj.* chin-ji-han 진지한, yŏl-sim-in 열심인. —*n.* chin-ji-ham 진지함, chin-sim 진심.

earnestly *adv.* yŏl-sim-hi 열심히, chin-ji-ha-ge 진지하게, chin-sim-ŭ-ro 진심으로.

earnings *n.* so-dŭk 소득, (*wage*) im-gŭm 임금.

earphone *n.* su-sin-gi 수신기, su-hwa-gi 수화기.

earring *n.* kwi-go-ri 귀고리, i-ŏ-ring 이어링.

earth *n.* ① (*globe*) chi-gu 지구. ② (*ground*) tae-ji 대
지 ; (*soil*) hŭk 흙. ③ (*this world*) i se-sang 이 세상.
earthen *adj.* hŭl-gŭ-ro man-dŭn 흙으로 만든.
earthenware *n.* chil-gŭ-rŭt 질그릇, t'o-gi 토기(土器).
earthly *adj.* i se-sang-ŭi 이 세상의, sok-se-ŭi 속세의.
earthquake *n.* chi-jin 지진.   ⌜pi-yŏl-han 비열한.
earthworm *n.* ① chi-rŏng-i 지렁이. ② (*mean person*)
ease *n.* ① al-lak 안락 , p'yŏn-an 편안. ② an-sim 안심.
   —*v.* ① (*make comfortable*) p'yŏn-ha-ge ha-da 편하
게 하다. ② (*make easy*) an-sim-si-k'i-da 안심시키다.
easily *adv.* swip-ge 쉽게, yong-i-ha-ge 용이하게.
east *n.* tong-jjok 동쪽.   —*adv.* tong-jjok-ŭ-ro 동쪽으로:
   Far E~ kŭk-dong 극동/*E~ Asia* tong-a-si-a 동아
Easter *n.* pu-hwal-jŏl 부활절.   ⌞시아.
eastern *adj.* tong-jjok-ŭi 동쪽의, tong-bang-ŭi 동방의.
eastward *adj.* tong-jjok-ŭ-ro-ŭi 동쪽으로의.
easy *adj.* swi-un 쉬운 ; p'yŏn-han 편한 ; nŏ-gŭ-rŏ-un
   너그러운.   —*adv.* su-wŏl-ha-ge 수월하게.
easy chair al-lak-ŭi-ja 안락의자.
eat *v.* ① mŏk-da 먹다, (*honorific*) chap-su-si-da 잡수
   시다. ② (*gnaw*) ch'im-sik-ha-da 침식하다, pu-sik-ha-
   da 부식하다.
eaves *n.* ch'ŏ-ma 처마, ch'aeng 챙.
ebb *n.* (*reflux of tide*) ssŏl-mul
   썰물, kan-jo 간조(干潮). —*v.* ppi-
   da 삐다 ; soe-t'oe-ha-da 쇠퇴하다.
ebony *n.* hŭk-dan 흑단(黑檀).   [ch'ŏ-ma]
eccentric *adj.* pyŏl-nan 별난, koe-sang-han 괴상한.
   —*n.* koe-jja 괴짜, ki-in 기인(奇人).
echo *n.* me-a-ri 메아리, pan-hyang 반향.   —*v.* me-a-
   ri-ch'i-da 메아리치다.
eclipse *n.* (*solar*) il-sik 일식 ; (*lunar*) wŏl-sik 월식 ;

(*total*) kae-gi-sik 개기식(皆既蝕).   「학의.
economic *adj.* kyŏng-je-ŭi 경제의, kyŏng-je-hak-ŭi 경제
economical *adj.* kyŏng-je-jŏk-in 경제적인 ; (*thrifty*)
 검소한, chŏl-yak-ha-nŭn 절약하는.
economics *n.* kyŏng-je-hak 경제학.   「ga 검약가.
economist *n.* ① kyŏng-je-hak-ja 경제학자. ② kŏm-yak-
economize *v.* kyŏng-je-jŏk-ŭ-ro ssŭ-da 경제적으로 쓰다,
 chŏl-yak-ha-da 절약하다.
economy *n.* kyŏng-je 경제, (*frugality*) chŏl-yak 절약.
ecstasy *n.* hwang-hol-gyŏng 황홀경, kwang-hŭi 광희
 (狂喜), mu-han-han ki-bbŭm 무한한 기쁨.
eddy *n.* so-yong-do-ri 소용돌이, hoe-o-ri 회오리.
edge *n.* ① ka-jang-ja-ri 가장자리. ② (*blade*) nal 날.
 —*v.* nal-ŭl se-u-da 날을 세우다, kal-da 갈다.
edible *adj.* mŏk-ŭl su it-nŭn 먹을 수 있는, sik-yong-
 ŭi 식용의. —*n.* sik-ryo-p'um 식료품.
edict *n.* ch'ik-ryŏng 칙령, (*decree*) p'o-go 포고.
edifice *n.* kŏn-mul 건물, tae-jŏ-t'aek 대저택.   「다.
edify *v.* kyo-hwa-ha-da 교화하다, kye-bal-ha-da 계발하
edit *v.* p'yŏn-jip[p'yŏn-ch'an]-ha-da 편집〔편찬〕하다.
editor *n.* p'yŏn-jip-ja 편집자.
editorial *n.* sa-sŏl 사설, non-sŏl 논설. —*adj.* p'yŏn-jip
 (-ja)-ŭi 편집(자)의.   「훈련하다.
educate *v.* kyo-yuk-ha-da 교육하다, hul-lyŏn-ha-da
education *n.* kyo-yuk 교육, hun-yuk 훈육, to-ya 도야.
eel *n.* paem-jang-ŏ 뱀장어.
efface *v.* chi-u-da 지우다, mal-sal-ha-da 말살하다.
effect *n.* kyŏl-gwa 결과 ; yŏng-hyang 영향. —*v.* i-rŭ-
 k'i-da 일으키다, tal-sŏng-ha-da 달성하다.   「적인.
effective *adj.* yu-hyo-han 유효한, hyo-gwa-jŏk-in 효과
efficacy *n.* hyo-ryŏk 효력, hyo-nŭng 효능.
efficiency *n.* nŭng-ryul 능률, hyo-yul 효율.

effort *n.* no-ryŏk 노력, no-go 노고, su-go 수고.

egg *n.* al 알, (*of hen*) tal-gyal 달걀, kye-ran 계란.

eggplant *n.* (*vegetable*) ka-ji 가지.

egoism *n.* i-gi-ju-ŭi 이기주의, cha-gi pon-wi 자기 본위.

egotism *n.* ① cha-gi chung-sim 자기 중심. ② cha-man

Egypt *n.* i-jip-t'ŭ 이집트.   「자만.

eight *n.* yŏ-dŏl 여덟, p'al 8.

eighteen *n.* yŏl-yŏ-dŏl 열여덟, sip-p'al 18.

eighty *n.* yŏ-dŭn 여든, p'al-sip 80.

either *pron. & adj.* ŏ-nŭ han-jjok 어느 한쪽. —*adv.*
  & conj. ⋯gŏ-na ⋯gŏ-na ⋯거나 ⋯거나.

ejaculate *v.* kap-ja-gi so-ri chi-rŭ-da 갑자기 소리 지르다.

eject *v.* ① ch'u-bang-ha-da 추방하다, myŏn-jik-si-k'i-
  da 면직시키다. ② (*emit*) ppum-ŏ-nae-da 뿜어내다.

elaborate *adj.* chŏng-sŏng-dŭ-rin 정성들인 ; chŏng-
  gyo-han 정교한. —*v.* chŏng-gyo-ha-ge man-dŭl-da
  정교하게 만들다, ta-dŭm-da 다듬다.

elapse *v.* (*pass away*) kyŏng-gwa-ha-da 경과하다.

elastic *n.* ko-mu-ggŭn 고무끈. —*adj.* t'al-lyŏk-sŏng-
  it-nŭn 탄력성있는, sin-ch'uk-sŏng-it-nŭn 신축성있는.

elate *v.* ki-un-ŭl puk-do-du-da 기운을 북돋우다, ŭi-gi-
  yang-yang-ha-ge ha-da 의기양양하게 하다.

elbow *n.* p'al-ggum-ch'i 팔꿈치. —*v.* p'al-ggum-ch'i-ro
  ttŏ-mil-da 팔꿈치로 떠밀다.

elder *adj.* (*older*) son-wi-ŭi 손위의, yŏn-jang-ŭi 연장
  의. —*n.* yŏn-jang-ja 연장자, sŏn-bae 선배.

elder brother (*male's*) hyŏng-nim 형님 ; (*female's*)
  o-bba 오빠.

elderly *adj.* ① na-i-ga chi-gŭt-han 나이가 지긋한, ch'o-
  ro-ŭi 초로(初老)의. ② ku-sik-ŭi 구식의.   「언니.

elder sister (*male's*) nu-nim 누님 ; (*female's*) ŏn-ni

eldest daughter k'ŭn-ddal 큰딸, chang-nyŏ 장녀.

eldest son k'ŭn-a-dŭl 큰아들, chang-nam 장남.

elect *v.* (*choose*) ppop-da 뽑다, sŏn-gŏ-ha-da 선거하다.
　—*adj.* tang-sŏn-doen 당선된. 　　　　　「총선거.

election *n.* sŏn-gŏ 선거 : *a general ~* ch'ong-sŏn-gŏ

electric *adj.* chŏn-gi-ŭi 전기의 : *~ bulb* chŏn-gu 전구/
　~ current chŏl-lyu 전류/ *~ fan* sŏn-p'ung-gi 선풍
　기/ *~ heater* chŏn-yŏl-gi 전열기/ *~ light* chŏn-dŭng
　전등/*~ power house* pal-jŏn-so 발전소.

electrician *n.* chŏn-gi ki-sa 전기 기사.

electricity *n.* chŏn-gi 전기, chŏn-gi-hak 전기학.

electron *n.* chŏn-ja 전자(電子), el-rek-t'ŭ-ron 엘렉트론.

elegant *adj.* u-a-han 우아한, ko-sang-han 고상한.

elegy *n.* pi-ga 비가, ae-ga 애가(哀歌).

element *n.* yo-so 요소, wŏn-so 원소, sŏng-bun 성분.

elementary *adj.* ki-bon-jŏk-in 기본적인, ch'o-bo-ŭi 초보

elementary school kuk-min-hak-gyo 국민학교. 　「의.

elephant *n.* k'o-ggi-ri 코끼리.

elevate *v.* ① ol-ri-da 올리다 ; sŭng-jin-si-k'i-da 승진시
　키다. ② (*excite*) ko-mu-ha-da 고무하다. 　　「이터.

elevator *n.* sŭng-gang-gi 승강기, el-ri-be-i-t'ŏ 엘리베

eleven *n.* yŏl-ha-na 열하나, sip-il 11. 　　　「이 있는.

eligible *adj.* p'i-sŏn-gŏ cha-gyŏk-i it-nŭn 피선거 자격

eliminate *v.* ① che-gŏ-ha-da 제거하다, sak-je-ha-da 삭
　제하다. ② (*ignore*) mu-si-ha-da 무시하다.

elite *n.* el-ri-t'ŭ 엘리트, chŏng-su 정수(精粹).

elm *n.* nŭ-rŭp-na-mu 느릅나무.

eloquent *adj.* mal chal-ha-nŭn 말 잘하는, ung-byŏn-
　jŏk-in 웅변적인, sŏl-dŭk-ryŏk-it-nŭn 설득력있는.

else *adv.* kŭ-ba-gge 그밖에 : *or ~* kŭ-rŏ-ch'i an-ŭ-myŏn
　그렇지 않으면. 　　　　　　　「u-e 다른 경우에.

elsewhere *adv.* ta-rŭn kŏ-se 다른 곳에 ; ta-rŭn kyŏng-

embankment *n.* che-bang 제방, tuk 둑.

embark v. ① (*board*) pae·rŭl t'a·da 배를 타다. ② (*start*) ch'ul·bal·ha·da 출발하다.

embarrass v. nan·ch'ŏ·ha·ge ha·da 난처하게 하다, hol·lan·k'e ha·da 혼란케 하다 ; pang·hae·ha·da 방해하다.

embassy n. tae·sa·gwan 대사관.

embellish v. (*decorate*) a·rŭm·dap·ge ha·da 아름답게 하다 ; chang·sik·ha·da 장식하다.

emblem n. (*symbol*) sang·jing 상징 ; (*type*) chŏn·hyŏng 전형 ; (*mark*) p'yo·ji 표지. 「da 구현하다.

embody v. ku·ch'e·hwa·ha·da 구체화하다, ku·hyŏn·ha-

embrace n. p'o·ong 포옹. —v. kkyŏ·an·da 껴안다.

embroider v. su·no·t'a 수놓다, yun·saek·ha·da 윤색하다.

embroidery n. su 수(繡), cha·su 자수.

embryo n. ① t'ae·a 태아. ② pae·a 배아(胚芽).

emerald n. e·mŏ·ral·dŭ 에머랄드, ch'wi·ok 취옥.

emerge v. na·t'a·na·da 나타나다 ; pŏ·sŏ·na·da 벗어나다.

emergency n. pi·sang·sa·t'ae 비상사태, kin·gŭp·sa·t'ae 긴급사태, wi·gi 위기.

emigrant n. i·ju·min 이주민. —adj. i·min·ŭi 이민의.

emigrate v. i·min·ha·da 이민하다, i·ju·ha·da 이주하다.

eminence n. ① (*high position*) ko·wi 고위. ② (*superiority*) t'ak·wŏl 탁월. ③ (*lofty place*) ko·ji 고지.

eminent adj. ① chŏ·myŏng·han 저명한 ; t'ak·wŏl·han 탁월한. ② (*prominent*) t'wi·ŏ·na·on 튀어나온.

emotion n. chŏng·sŏ 정서 ; kam·dong 감동 ; kam·jŏng 감정.

emperor n. hwang·je 황제, che·wang 제왕. 「감정.

emphasize v. kang·jo·ha·da 강조하다, yŏk·sŏl·ha·da 역설하다.

empire n. che·guk 제국, che·jŏng 제정(帝政).

employ v. ch'ae·yong·ha·da 채용하다 ; (*use*) sa·yong·ha·da 사용하다. —n. ko·yong 고용 ; kŭn·mu 근무.

employe(e) n. ko·yong·in 고용인, chong·ŏp·wŏn 종업원.

employer *n.* ko-yong-ju 고용주, chu-in 주인.

employment *n.* ko-yong 고용, chik-ŏp 직업.

empress *n.* hwang-hu 황후, wang-bi 왕비.

empty *adj.* pin 빈 ; hŏt-doen 헛된. —*v.* pi-u-da 비우다.

emulate *v.* ① kyŏ-ru-da 겨루다, kyŏng-jaeng-ha-da 경쟁하다. ② …wa tong-gyŏk-i-da …와 동격이다.

enable *v.* …hal su it-ge ha-da …할 수 있게 하다.

enact *v.* ① (*decree*) che-jŏng-ha-da 제정하다, kyu-jŏng-ha-da 규정하다. ② (*act*) sang-yŏn-ha-da 상연하다.

enamel *n.* e-na-mel 에나멜. —*v.* e-na-mel-ŭl ip-hi-da 에나멜을 입히다.   「hok-ha-da 매혹하다.

enchant *v.* hwang-hol-ha-ge ha-da 황홀하게 하다, mae-

encircle *v.* tul-rŏ-ssa-da 둘러싸다.   「워싸다.

enclose *v.* pong-hae nŏ-t'a 봉해 넣다, e-wŏ-ssa-da 에

encompass *v.* tul-rŏ-ssa-da 둘러싸다.

encore *int.* ang-k'o-o-rŭ 앙코오르.   「닥치다.

encounter *v.* ma-ju-ch'i-da 마주치다, pu-dak-ch'i-da 부

encourage *v.* yong-gi-rŭl chu-da 용기를 주다 ; chang-ryŏ-ha-da 장려하다 ; cho-jang-ha-da 조장하다.

encouragement *n.* chang-ryŏ 장려, kyŏk-ryŏ 격려.

encroach *v.* ch'im-ip-ha-da 침입하다, ch'im-hae-ha-da

encyclopaedia *n.* paek-gwa-sa-jŏn 백과사전. ㄴ침해하다.

end *n.* kkŭt 끝 ; (*purpose*) mok-jŏk 목적 ; (*close*) kyŏl-mal 결말. —*v.* kkŭt-nae-da 끝내다.

endanger *v.* wi-t'ae-rop-ge ha-da 위태롭게 하다.

endear *v.* ae-jŏng-ŭl nŭ-ggi-ge ha-da 애정을 느끼게 하다.

endeavo(u)r *n.* (*effort*) no-ryŏk 노력 ; si-do 시도. —*v.* no-ryŏk-ha-da 노력하다 ; si-do-ha-da 시도하다.

ending *n.* (*termination*) kyŏl-mal 결말, ma-ji-mak 마지막 ; (*death*) chuk-ŭm 죽음.

endless *adj.* kkŭt-ŏp-nŭn 끝없는, mu-han-han 무한한.

endorse *v.* ① i-sŏ-ha-da 이서(裏書)하다. ② po-jŭng-ha-da 보증하다. ③ chi-ji-ha-da 지지하다.

endow v. (*give*) chu-da 주다, pu-yŏ-ha-da 부여하다, ki-bu-ha-da 기부하다. 「내(력).

endurance n. ch'am-ŭl-sŏng 참을성, in-nae(-ryŏk) 인

endure v. kyŏn-di-da 견디다, chi-t'aeng-ha-da 지탱하다.

enemy n. chŏk 적, chŏk-gun 적군, chŏk-guk 적국.

energy n. him 힘, e-nŏ-ji 에너지.

enforce v. ① sil-si-ha-da 실시하다, si-haeng-ha-da 시행하다. ② (*impose*) kang-yo-ha-da 강요하다.

engage v. ① chong-sa-ha-da 종사하다. ② yak-sok-ha-da 약속하다. ③ (*betroth*) yak-hon-ha-da 약혼하다.

engagement n. ① yak-hon 약혼. ② yak-sok 약속.

engine n. ki-gwan 기관, pal-dong-gi 발동기.

engineer n. ki-sa 기사, kong-hak-ja 공학자(工學者).

England n. yŏng-guk 영국, ing-gŭl-raen-dŭ 잉글랜드.

English n. & adj. (*language*) yŏng-ŏ(-ui) 영어(의).

Englishman n. yŏng-guk-sa-ram 영국사람.

engrave v. cho-gak-ha-da 조각하다, sae-gi-da 새기다.

engross v. ① (*fill one's mind*) yŏl-jung-k'e ha-da 열중케 하다. ② (*monopolize*) tok-jŏm-ha-da 독점하다.

enhance v. no-p'i-da 높이다, ang-yang-ha-da 앙양하다.

enjoin v. pu-gwa-ha-da 부과하다 ; myŏng-ha-da 명하다.

enjoy v. chŭl-gi-da 즐기다, (*possess*) nu-ri-da 누리다.

enjoyment n. hyang-rak 향락, hyang-yu 향유(享有).

enlarge v. k'ŭ-ge ha-da 크게 하다, hwak-dae〔chŭng-dae〕-ha-da 확대〔증대〕하다. 「교화하다.

enlighten v. kye-mong-ha-da 계몽하다, kyo-hwa-ha-da

enlist v. ① (*in army*) ŭng-mo-ha-da 응모하다, ip-dae-ha-da 입대하다. ② to-um-ŭl pat-da 도움을 받다.

enmity n. chŭng-o 증오, chŏk-ŭi 적의(敵意).

enormous adj. kŏ-dae-han 거대한, mak-dae-han 막대한 : ~ *profits* mak-dae-han i-ik 막대한 이익.

enough *adj.* ch'ung-bun-han 충분한. —*adv.* nŏk-nŏk-ha-ge 넉넉하게. —*n.* ch'ung-bun-ham 충분함.

enrage *v.* kyŏk-bun-si-k'i-da 격분시키다, no-ha-ge ha-da 노하게 하다.

enrich *v.* pu-yu-ha-ge ha-da 부유하게 하다.

enrol(l) *v.* ① tŭng-rok-ha-da 등록하다, pyŏng-jŏk-e ol-ri-da 병적에 올리다. ② (*in school*) ip-hak-si-k'i-da 입학시키다.

ensign *n.* ① (*badge*) ki-jang 기장. ② (*flag*) ki 기.

ensure *v.* ① (*protect*) po-ho-ha-da 보호하다. ② (*make certain of*) hwak-sil-ha-ge ha-da 확실하게 하다. ③ (*guarantee*) po-jŭng-ha-da 보증하다.

entangle *v.* ŏl-k'i-ge ha-da 얽히게 하다, nan-ch'ŏ-ha-ge ha-da 난처하게 하다.

enter *v.* ① (*go into*) tŭ-rŏ-ga-da 들어가다 ; (*start*) si-jak-ha-da 시작하다. ② (*join*) ka-ip-ha-da 가입하다. ③ (*record*) ki-ip-ha-da 기입하다.

enterprise *n.* sa-ŏp 사업, ki-ŏp 기업, ki-hoek 기획.

entertain *v.* ① (*amuse*) hŭng-gyŏp-ge ha-da 흥겹게 하다. ② (*hospitality*) hwan-dae-ha-da 환대하다. ③ (*harbor*) ma-ŭm-e p'um-da 마음에 품다.

entertainment *n.* chŏp-dae 접대, hwan-dae 환대.

enthusiasm *n.* yŏl-gwang 열광, yŏl-sim 열심.

enthusiastic *adj.* yŏl-gwang-jŏk-in 열광적인.

entice *v.* yu-hok-ha-da 유혹하다, kkoe-da 꾀다.

entire *adj.* chŏn-ch'e-ŭi 전체의, wan-jŏn-han 완전한.

entirely *adv.* wan-jŏn-hi 완전히, chŏn-hyŏ 전혀.

entitle *v.* cha-gyŏk-ŭl chu-da 자격을 주다, myŏng-ch'ing-ŭl pu-ch'i-da 명칭을 붙이다.

entrails *n.* nae-jang 내장, ch'ang-ja 창자.

entrance *n.* ① ip-jang 입장(入場), ip-hoe 입회. ② (*door*) ip-gu 입구 : ~ *fee* ip-jang-ryo 입장료.

entreat *v.* kan-ch'ŏng-ha-da 간청하다.

entrust *v.* wi-im-ha-da 위임하다, mat-gi-da 맡기다.

enumerate *v.* se-da 세다 ; yŏl-gŏ-ha-da 열거하다.

envelop *v.* ssa-da 싸다, pong-ha-da 봉하다.

envelope *n.* pong-t'u 봉투, (*wrapper*) ssa-gae 싸개.

envious *adj.* pu-rŏ-wŏ-ha-nŭn 부러워하는, sae-am-ha-nŭn 새암하는 ; chil-t'u-sim-i kang-han 질투심이 강한.

environment *n.* hwan-gyŏng 환경.

envy *n.* chil-t'u 질투, si-gi 시기, sŏn-mang 선망. —*v.* pu-rŏ-wŏ-ha-da 부러워하다.

epidemic *n.* yu-haeng-byŏng 유행병, chŏn-yŏm-byŏng 전염병. —*adj.* yu-haeng-sŏng-ŭi 유행성의.

Episcopalian Church kam-dok-gyo-hoe 감독교회.

episode *n.* sap-hwa 삽화, e-p'i-so-u-dŭ 에피소우드.

epitaph *n.* pi-mun 비문, pi-myŏng 비명(碑銘).

epoch *n.* (*new era*) sin-gi-wŏn 신기원, sin-si-dae 신시대 ; (*age*) si-dae 시대.

epoch-making *adj.* hoek-gi-jŏk-in 획기적인.

equal *adj.* ka-t'ŭn 같은, tong-dŭng-han 동등한.

equality *n.* p'yŏng-dŭng 평등, kyun-dŭng 균등. 「하게.

equally *adv.* ttok-ga-ch'i 똑같이, kyun-dŭng-ha-ge 균등

equation *n.* pang-jŏng-sik 방정식, tŭng-sik 등식.

equator *n.* chŏk-do 적도. 「춘(추)분.

equinox *n.* the vernal〔autumnal〕 ~ ch'un〔ch'u〕-bun

equip *v.* chun-bi-ha-da 준비하다, kat-ch'u-da 갖추다.

equipment *n.* sŏl-bi 설비, chang-gu 장구(裝具).

equivalent *adj.* tong-dŭng-han 동등한.

era *n.* ki-wŏn 기원(紀元), yŏn-dae 연대, si-dae 시대.

erase *v.* chi-u-da 지우다, sak-je-ha-da 삭제하다.

eraser *n.* chi-u-gae 지우개, ko-mu-ji-u-gae 고무지우개.

erect *adj.* kot-ŭn 곧은. —*v.* se-u-da 세우다.

err *v.* kŭ-rŭ-ch'i-da 그르치다, t'ŭl-ri-da 틀리다.

errand *n.* sim-bu-rŭm 심부름 ; (*mission*) sa-myŏng 사명 ; (*business*) pol-il 볼일, yong-gŏn 용건.

error *n.* chal-mot 잘못, (*fault*) e-rŏ 에러.

erupt *v.* t'ŏ-jyŏ na-o-da 터져 나오다, p'ok-bal-ha-da 폭발하다, pun-ch'ul-ha-da 분출하다.

eruption *n.* ① p'ok-bal 폭발. ② (*volcano*) pun-hwa 분화(噴火). ③ (*rash*) pal-jin 발진(發疹).

escape *n. & v.* to-mang(-ga-da) 도망(가다).

escort *v.* ho-song-ha-da 호송하다, ho-wi-ha-da 호위하다.

especial *adj.* t'ŭk-byŏl-han 특별한, t'ŭk-su-han 특수한.

espionage *n.* kan-ch'ŏp (haeng-wi) 간첩 (행위).

espouse *v.* (*take a wife*) chang-ga-dŭl-da 장가들다.

essay *n.* non-mun 논문, su-p'il 수필.

essence *n.* ① pon-jil 본질, chin-su 진수 : *the ~ of happiness* haeng-bok-ŭi pon-jil 행복의 본질. ② (*extract*) ek-sŭ 엑스. 「주요점.

essential *adj.* pon-jil-jŏk-in 본질적인. —*n.* chu-yo-jŏm

establish *v.* ① (*found*) sŏl-rip-ha-da 설립하다. ② (*constitute*) che-jŏng-ha-da 제정하다. ③ (*prove*) hwak-jŭng-ha-da 확증하다.

establishment *n.* ① sŏl-rip 설립, hwak-rip 확립. ② (*system*) che-do 제도. ③ si-sŏl 시설.

estate *n.* ① (*land*) t'o-ji 토지 ; (*property*) chae-san 재산. ② (*rank*) sin-bun 신분, chi-wi 지위.

esteem *n.* chon-jung 존중, chon-gyŏng 존경. —*v.* ① chon-gyŏng-ha-da 존경하다. ② (*consider*) kan-ju-ha-da 간주하다, yŏ-gi-da 여기다.

estimate *v.* p'yŏng-ga-ha-da 평가하다. —*n.* (*of cost*) kyŏn-jŏk 견적(見積) : *a written ~* kyŏn-jŏk-sŏ 견적서.

estrange *v.* (*turn away*) sa-i-rŭl na-bbŭ-ge ha-da 사이를 나쁘게 하다, i-gan-ha-da 이간하다.

et cetera ki-t'a tŭng-dŭng 기타 등등, tta-wi 따위.

eternal *adj.* yŏng-wŏn-han 영원한, pul-hu-ŭi 불후의.

eternity *n.* yŏng-wŏn 영원, mu-gung 무궁.

ethics *n.* yul-li-(hak) 윤리(학).

Ethiopia *n.* i-di-o-p'i-a 이디오피아.

etiquette *n.* ye-ŭi pŏm-jŏl 예의 범절, e-t'i-k'et 에티켓.

etymology *n.* ŏ-wŏn 어원(語源), ŏ-wŏn-hak 어원학.

Europe *n.* yu-rŏp 유럽, ku-ju 구주. 「유럽사람.

European *adj.* yu-rŏp-ŭi 유럽의. —*n.* yu-rŏp-sa-ram

evacuation *n.* ch'ŏl-gŏ 철거, myŏng-do 명도.

evade *v.* p'i-ha-da 피하다, t'al-ch'ul-ha-da 탈출하다.

evangelist *n.* pok-ŭm chŏn-do-ja 복음 전도자.

evaporate *v.* ① chŭng-bal-ha-da 증발하다, so-san-ha-da 소산(消散)하다. ② t'al-su-ha-da 탈수하다.

eve *n.* chŏn-ya 전야, chŏn-nal-bam 전날밤 : *Christmas* ~ k'ŭ-ri-sŭ-ma-sŭ chŏn-ya 크리스마스 전야.

even *adj.* (*level*) p'yŏng-p'yŏng-han 평평한. —*adv.* pi-rok 비록, …cho-ch'a-do …조차도.

evening *n.* chŏ-nyŏk 저녁, hae-jil-nyŏk 해질녁.

event *n.* ① sa-gŏn 사건. ② (*outcome*) sŏng-gwa 성과. ③ (*in sport*) kyŏng-gi chong-mok 경기 종목.

eventually *adv.* kyŏl-guk 결국, ma-ch'im-nae 마침내.

ever *adv.* ① yŏ-t'ae-ggŏt 여태껏, il-jji-gi 일찌기. ② (*always*) ŏn-je-na 언제나.

everlasting *adj.* kkŭt-ŏp-nŭn 끝없는, yŏng-wŏn-han 영원한. —*n.* yŏng-gu 영구, yŏng-wŏn 영원.

evermore *adv.* hang-sang 항상, yŏng-wŏn-hi 영원히.

every *adj.* mo-dŭn 모든, (*all possible*) on-gat 온갖 ; mae… 매…, …ma-da …마다 : ~ *day* mae-il 매일/ ~ *four day* na-hŭl-jjae-ma-da 나흘째마다.

everybody *pron.* nu-gu-na 누구나, che-gak-gi 제각기.

everyday *adj.* nal-ma-da-ŭi 날마다의, mae-il-ŭi 매일의.

everyone *pron.* nu-gu-na 누구나, kak-ja 각자.

everything *pron.* ① mu-ŏ-si-dŭn-ji 무엇이든지, man-sa 만사. ② ka-jang chung-yo-han kŏt 가장 중요한 것.

everywhere *adv.* ŏ-di-dŭn-ji 어디든지, to-ch'ŏ-e 도처에.

evidence *n.* chŭng-gŏ 증거, (*pl.*) ching-hu 징후.

evident *adj.* myŏng-baek-han 명백한, pun-myŏng-han 분명한, tt'u-ryŏt-han 뚜렷한.

evil *adj.* na-bbŭn 나쁜, sa-ak-han 사악한, pul-gil-han 불길한. —*n.* ak 악, chae-hae 재해. 「기시키다.

evoke *v.* pul-rŏ-nae-da 불러내다, hwan-gi-si-k'i-da 환

evolution *n.* chin-hwa 진화(進化), chŏn-gae 전개.

evolve *v.* ① chŏn-gae-ha-da 전개하다. ② chin-hwa-ha-da 진화하다. ③ (*give off*) pang-ch'ul-ha-da 방출하다.

exact *adj.* chŏng-hwak-han 정확한, chŏng-mil-han 정밀한 ; ŏm-gyŏk-han 엄격한. 「si 틀림없이.

exactly *adv.* chŏng-hwak-ha-ge 정확하게, t'ul-rim-ŏp-

exaggerate *v.* kwa-jang-ha-da 과장하다.

exalt *v.* ① (*raise high*) no-p'i-da 높이다. ② sŭng-jin-si-k'i-da 승진시키다. ③ ch'ing-ch'an-ha-da 칭찬하다.

examination *n.* ① si-hŏm 시험, kŏm-sa 검사. ② kŏm-t'o 검토. ③ sin-mun 신문.

examine *v.* ① si-hŏm-ha-da 시험하다, sim-sa-ha-da 심사하다. ② kŏm-t'o-ha-da 검토하다, cho-sa-ha-da 조사

example *n.* po-gi 보기, sil-rye 실례, mo-bŏm 모범. 「하다.

exasperate *v.* yak-o-rŭ-ge ha-da 약오르게 하다, hwa-na-ge ha-da 화나게 하다.

excavate *v.* (*dig*) p'a-da 파다, pal-gul-ha-da 발굴하다.

exceed *v.* nŏm-da 넘다, nŭng-ga-ha-da 능가하다.

exceedingly *adv.* chi-gŭk-hi 지극히, mop-si 몹시.

excel *v.* (po-da) nat-da (보다) 낫다, nŭng-ga-ha-da 능가하다, t'ak-wŏl-ha-da 탁월하다.

excellent *adj.* u-su-han 우수한, hul-ryung-han 훌륭한.

except *prep.* …ŭl che-oe-ha-go …을 제외하고. —*v.*

che-oe-ha-da 제외하다.

exception n. ye-oe 예외, che-oe 제외.

exceptional adj. ye-oe-jŏk-in 예외적인, tŭ-mun 드문.

excess n. ch'o-gwa 초과, kwa-da 과다 ; yŏ-bun 여분.

exchange n. & v. kyo-hwan(-ha-da) 교환(하다).

excite v. cha-gŭk-ha-da 자극하다, i-rŭ-k'i-da 일으키다.

excitement n. hŭng-bun 흥분, cha-gŭk 자극.

exclaim v. (cry out) oe-ch'i-da 외치다.

exclamation n. ① oe-ch'im 외침. ② kam-t'an 감탄.

exclude v. nae-jjot-da 내쫓다, pae-ch'ŏk-ha-da 배척하다.

excursion n. so-p'ung 소풍, yu-ram 유람.

excuse n. ku-sil 구실, p'ing-gye 핑계. —v. ① yong-sŏ-ha-da 용서하다. ② pyŏn-myŏng-ha-da 변명하다.

execute v. ① (carry out) sil-haeng-ha-da 실행하다. ② (punish) ch'ŏ-hyŏng-ha-da 처형하다.

execution n. ① (performance) su-haeng 수행. ② (punishment) sa-hyŏng chip-haeng 사형 집행.

executioner n. ① su-haeng-ja 수행자. ② (hangman) sa-hyŏng chip-haeng-ja 사형 집행자.

executive adj. haeng-jŏng-jŏk-in 행정적인. —n. haeng-jŏng-gwan 행정관 ; kan-bu yŏk-wŏn 간부 역원.

exercise n. un-dong 운동 ; yŏn-sŭp 연습. —v. un-dong-ha-da 운동하다 ; yŏn-sŭp-ha-da 연습하다.

exert v. him-ŭl nae-da 힘을 내다 ; (put forth) pal-hwi-ha-da 발휘하다 ; hwi-du-rŭ-da 휘두르다.

exertion n. no-ryŏk 노력, pun-bal 분발.

exhaust v. ① ssŏ-bŏ-ri-da 써버리다, t'ang-jin-ha-da 탕진하다. ② (tire out) chi-ch'i-ge ha-da 지치게 하다.

exhaustion n. so-mo 소모 ; p'i-ro 피로.

exhibit v. chŏn-si-ha-da 전시하다, chŏl-lam-ha-da 전람하다. —n. ch'ul-p'um 출품. 「회.

exhibition n. chŏl-lam-hoe 전람회, pak-ram-hoe 박람

exile *n.* ① ch'u-bang 추방. ② (*person*) mang-myŏng-ja 망명자. —*v.* ch'u-bang-ha-da 추방하다.

exist *v.* chon-jae-ha-da 존재하다, sa-ra-it-da 살아있다.

existence *n.* chon-jae 존재, sil-jae 실재.「da 퇴장하다.

exit *n.* ch'ul-gu 출구 ; t'oe-jang 퇴장. —*v.* t'oe-jang-ha-

expand *v.* p'ŏ-ji-da 퍼지다, hwak-jang-ha-da 확장하다, p'aeng-ch'ang-ha-da 팽창하다.

expect *v.* ki-dae-ha-da 기대하다, ye-gi-ha-da 예기하다.

expectation *n.* ki-dae 기대, ye-sang 예상.

expedient *adj.* p'yŏl-li-han 편리한 ; chŏk-dang-han 적당한. —*n.* pang-p'yŏn 방편.

expedition *n.* wŏn-jŏng 원정 ; t'am-hŏm 탐험.

expel *v.* ① ch'u-bang-ha-da 추방하다. ② (*from school*) t'oe-hak-si-k'i-da 퇴학시키다.

expense *n.* pi-yong 비용 ; (*expenditure*) chi-ch'ul 지출.

expensive *adj.* kap-bi-ssan 값비싼.

experience *n.* kyŏng-hŏm 경험, ch'e-hŏm 체험. —*v.* kyŏng-hŏm[ch'e-hŏm]-ha-da 경험[체험]하다.

experiment *n. & v.* sil-hŏm(-ha-da) 실험(하다).

expert *adj.* ik-suk-han 익숙한, no-ryŏn-han 노련한. —*n.* chŏn-mun-ga 전문가, myŏng-su 명수.

expire *v.* ① sum-ŭl nae-swi-da 숨을 내쉬다. ② (*terminate*) man-gi-ga toe-da 만기가 되다. ③ (*die out*) so-myŏl-ha-da 소멸하다, chuk-da 죽다.

explain *v.* sŏl-myŏng-ha-da 설명하다, pal-k'i-da 밝히다.

explanation *n.* sŏl-myŏng 설명, hae-sŏl 해설.

explicit *adj.* (*clear*) myŏng-baek-han 명백한, (*outspoken*) sum-gim-ŏp-nŭn 숨김없는. 「하다.

explode *v.* p'ok-bal-ha-da 폭발하다, p'a-yŏl-ha-da 파열

exploit *n.* kong-jŏk 공적, kong-hun 공훈. —*v.* ① i-yong-ha-da 이용하다. ② (*cultivate*) kae-bal-ha-da 개발하다. ③ (*extract*) ch'ak-ch'wi-ha-da 착취하다.

exploration *n.* t'am-hŏm 탐험, tap-sa 답사.

explore *v.* t'am-hŏm-ha-da 탐험하다 ; (*search into*) t'am-gu-ha-da 탐구하다, cho-sa-ha-da 조사하다.

explorer *n.* t'am-hŏm-ga 탐험가, t'am-gu-ja 탐구자.

explosion *n.* p'ok-bal 폭발, p'a-yŏl 파열. 「수출품.

export *v.* su-ch'ul-ha-da 수출하다. —*n.* su-ch'ul-p'um

expose *v.* no-ch'ul-ha-da 노출하다, tŭ-rŏ-nae-da 드러

exposure *n.* no-ch'ul 노출, p'ok-ro 폭로. 「내다.

express *v.* p'yo-hyŏn-ha-da 표현하다, na-t'a-nae-da 나타내다. —*adj.* t'ŭk-byŏl-han 특별한. —*n.* ① kŭp-haeng-yŏl-ch'a 급행열차. ② sok-dal 속달.

expression *n.* ① p'yo-hyŏn 표현. ② p'yo-jŏng 표정.

exquisite *adj.* chŏng-gyo-han 정교한, sŏm-se-han 섬세한 ; (*sharp*) nal-k'a-ro-un 날카로운.

extend *v.* nŭ-ri-da 늘이다, hwak-jang-ha-da 확장하다 ; (*reach*) ···e i-rŭ-da ···에 이르다.

extensive *adj.* nŏl-bŭn 넓은, tae-gyu-mo-ŭi 대규모의.

extent *n.* nŏl-bi 넓이, p'ŏm-wi 범위 ; chŏng-do 정도.

exterior *adj.* pa-gga-t'ŭi 바깥의, oe-gwan-sang-ŭi 외관상의. —*n.* oe-bu 외부, oe-mo 외모.

exterminate *v.* chŏn-myŏl-si-k'i-da 전멸시키다.

external *adj.* ① oe-bu-ŭi 외부의. ② hyŏng-sik-jŏk-in 형식적인. —*n.* oe-bu 외부, oe-mo 외모.

extinguish *v.* kkŭ-da 끄다 ; so-myŏl-si-k'i-da 소멸시키다.

extol(l) *v.* kyŏk-ch'an-ha-da 격찬하다.

extra *adj.* yŏ-bun-ŭi 여분의. —*n.* ① (*newspaper*) ho-oe 호외. ② ek-sŭ-t'ŭ-rŏ 엑스트러.

extract *v.* ppop-da 뽑다, pal-ch'we-ha-da 발췌하다. —*n.* ch'u-ch'ul-mul 추출물, (*excerpt*) pal-ch'we 발췌.

extraordinary *adj.* ① pi-sang-han 비상한, (*uncommon*) pi-bŏm-han 비범한, ŏm-ch'ŏng-nan 엄청난. ② (*additional*) im-si-ŭi 임시의.

extravagant *adj.* sa-ch'i-sŭ-rŏn 사치스런 ; t'ŏ-mu-ni-ŏp-nŭn 터무니없는, ŏm-ch'ŏng-nan 엄청난.

extreme *adj.* kŭk-tan-jŏk-in 극단적인 ; kwa-gyŏk-han 과격한 ; ch'oe-jong-ŭi 최종의. —*n.* kŭk-tan 극단.

eye *n.* nun 눈 : *artificial* ~ ŭi-an 의안(義眼).

eyebrow *n.* nun-ssŏp 눈썹 : ~ *pencil* nun-ssŏp ku-ri-gae 눈썹 그리개.

eyelash *n.* sok-nun-ssŏp 속눈썹.

eyelid *n.* nun-ggŏp-p'ul 눈꺼풀.

eyesight *n.* si-ryŏk 시력 ; si-gye 시계(視界).

—≪ **F** ≫—

fable *n.* u-hwa 우화(寓話).

fabric *n.* ① (*texture*) chik-mul 직물. ② (*building*) kŏn-mul 건물. ③ (*structure*) ku-jo 구조.

face *n.* ① ŏl-gul 얼굴. ② (*surface*) p'yo-myŏn 표면. —*v.* …e chik-myŏn-ha-da …에 직면하다.

facility *n.* ① yong-i-ham 용이함. ② (*skill*) chae-gan 재간. ③ (*convenience*) p'yŏn-ŭi 편의. ④ sŏl-bi 설비.

fact *n.* sa-sil 사실, sil-je 실제, chin-sang 진상.

faction *n.* tang-p'a(-sim) 당파(심), pun-jaeng 분쟁.

factor *n.* yo-so 요소, yo-in 요인, wŏn-dong-ryŏk 원동력.

factory *n.* kong-jang 공장, che-jak-so 제작소.

faculty *n.* ① chae-nŭng 재능. ② (*college*) hak-bu 학부.

fade *v.* si-dŭl-da 시들다, pa-rae-da 바래다.

fail *v.* sil-p'ae-ha-da 실패하다 ; pu-jok-ha-da 부족하다.

failure *n.* sil-p'ae 실패 ; nak-je 낙제.

faint *adj.* ① hŭi-mi-han 희미한 ; ka-nyal-p'ŭn 가냘픈. ② hyŏn-gi-jŭng-i na-nŭn 현기증이 나는. —*v.* ① hŭi-mi-hae-ji-da 희미해지다. ② ki-jŏl-ha-da 기절하다.

fair *adj.* ① a-rŭm-da-un 아름다운. ② (*just*) kong-p'yŏng-han 공평한. —*n.* si-jang 시장(市場) ; (*exhibi-*

tion) kong·jin·hoe 공진회.

fairly *adv.* ① kong·jŏng·ha·ge 공정하게. ② (*pretty*) sang·dang·hi 상당히, kkwae 꽤.

fairy *n.* yo·jŏng 요정. —*adj.* yo·jŏng·ŭi 요정의.

faith *n.* sin·ang 신앙, sin·nyŏm 신념, ch'ung·sil 충실.

faithful *adj.* ch'ung·sil·han 충실한, sil·loe·hal su it·nŭn 신뢰할 수 있는, mit·ŭm·i kut·ŭn 믿음이 굳은.

faithless *adj.* sin·ŭi·ga ŏp·nŭn 신의가 없는, pul·sil·han 불실한.

falcon *n.* song·gol·mae 송골매.

fall *v.* ttŏ·rŏ·ji·da 떨어지다. —*n.* ① ch'u·rak 추락. ② (*autumn*) ka·ŭl 가을. ③ (*pl.*) p'ok·p'o 폭포.

false *adj.* (*untrue*) kŏ·ji·sŭi 거짓의, (*wrong*) ku·rŭt·doen 그릇된, (*unfaithful*) pul·sŏng·sil·han 불성실한.

falsehood *n.* kŏ·jit·mal 거짓말, hŏ·wi 허위.

falter *v.* ① (*stumble*) pi·t'ŭl·gŏ·ri·da 비틀거리다. ② (*stammer*) mal·ŭl tŏ·dŭm·da 말을 더듬다.

fame *n.* myŏng·sŏng 명성, se·p'yŏng 세평.

famed *adj.* i·rŭm·nan 이름난, yu·myŏng·han 유명한.

familiar *adj.* ch'in·han 친한 ; chal al·go it·nŭn 잘 알고 있는 ; hŭn·han 흔한.

family *n.* ka·jok 가족, ka·jŏng 가정.

famine *n.* ki·gŭn 기근, ki·a 기아.

famous *adj.* yu·myŏng·han 유명한.

fan *n.* pu·ch'ae 부채, p'aen 팬. —*v.* pu·ch'ae·jil·ha·da 부채질하다 ; sŏn·dong·ha·da 선동하다.

fancy *n.* kong·sang 공상 ; pyŏn·dŏk 변덕. —*v.* kong·sang·ha·da 공상하다.

[pu·ch'ae]

fantastic *adj.* kong·sang·jŏk·in 공상적인, (*capricious*) pyŏn·dŏk·sŭ·rŏ·un 변덕스러운, pyŏl·nan 별난.

far *adj.* mŏn 먼 ; yo·wŏn·han 요원한. —*adv.* mŏl·ri 멀리 : ~ *away* mŏl·ri·e 멀리에.

farce *n.* so-gŭk 소극(笑劇), ik-sal 익살.

fare *n.* ① (*carriage*) un-im 운임, yo-gŭm 요금. ② (*passenger*) sŭng-gaek 승객. ③ (*food*) um-sik-mul 음식물 : *good* ~ sŏng-ch'an 성찬.

farewell *int.* an-nyŏng 안녕. —*n.* chak-byŏl 작별.

farm *n.* ① nong-jang 농장. ② yang-sik-jang 양식장. —*v.* kyŏng-jak-ha-da 경작하다.

farmer *n.* nong-bu 농부, nong-min 농민. 「머슴.

farm hand nong-jang no-dong-ja 농장 노동자, mŏ-sŭm

farmhouse *n.* nong-ga 농가. 「농경.

farming *n.* nong-ŏp 농업, nong-sa 농사, nong-gyŏng

farmyard *n.* nong-ga-ŭi ma-dang 농가의 마당.

far-reaching *adj.* kwang-bŏm-wi-han 광범위한, mŏl-ri-gga-ji mi-ch'i-nŭn 멀리까지 미치는.

far-sighted *adj.* ① wŏn-si-ŭi 원시(遠視)의. ② (*far-seeing*) sŏn-gyŏn-ji-myŏng-i it-nŭn 선견지명이 있는.

farther *adj.* tŏ mŏn 더 먼. —*adv.* tŏ mŏl-ri 더 멀리.

fascinate *v.* mae-hok-ha-da 매혹하다, hwang-hol-k'e ha-da 황홀케 하다, noe-swae-ha-da 뇌쇄하다.

fashion *n.* ① yu-haeng 유행. ② (*mode*) pang-sik 방식 ; hyŏng 형. —*v.* hyŏng-sŏng-ha-da 형성하다.

fashionable *adj.* yu-haeng-e mat-nŭn 유행에 맞는.

fast *adj.* ppa-rŭn 빠른 ; tan-dan-han 단단한 ; pul-byŏn-ŭi 불변의. —*adv.* (*tight*) tan-dan-hi 단단히. —*n.* tan-sik 단식. —*v.* tan-sik-ha-da 단식하다.

fasten *v.* tong-yŏ-mae-da 동여매다, cham-gŭ-da 잠그다.

fastidious *adj.* kka-da-ro-un 까다로운.

fasting *n.* tan-sik 단식. —*adj.* tan-sik-ŭi 단식의 : *a* ~ *cure* tan-sik yo-bŏp 단식 요법.

fat *adj.* sal-jjin 살찐 ; (*fertile*) pi-ok-han 비옥한. —*n.* kut-gi-rŭm 굳기름, chi-bang 지방. 「명적인.

fatal *adj.* un-myŏng-ŭi 운명의, ch'i-myŏng-jŏk-in 치

fate *n.* ① un-myŏng 운명 ; ak-un 악운. ② chuk-ŭm 죽음.

father *n.* ① a-bŏ-ji 아버지, pu-ch'in 부친. ② (*founder*) si-jo 시조. ③ (*priest*) sin-bu 신부.

father-in-law ① (*man's*) chang-in 장인. ② (*woman's*) si-a-bŏ-ji 시아버지. ③ (*stepfather*) kye-bu 계부.

fathom *n.* kil 길 (6 *feet*). —*v.* ki-p'i-rŭl chae-da 깊이를 재다, he-a-ri-da 헤아리다.

fatigue *n.* p'i-gon 피곤, p'i-ro 피로, no-go 노고(勞苦).

fault *n.* ① (*defect*) hŭm 흠, kyŏl-jŏm 결점. ② (*mistake*) kwa-o 과오, sil-su 실수. ③ (*sin*) choe 죄.

faultless *adj.* hŭm-ŏp-nŭn 흠없는, wan-jŏn-han 완전한.

favo(u)r *n.* ho-ŭi 호의, ch'ong-ae 총애 ; pu-t'ak 부탁. —*v.* ch'an-sŏng-ha-da 찬성하다 ; ch'in-jŏl-hi tae-ha-da 친절히 대하다, top-da 돕다.

favo(u)rite *adj.* ma-ŭm-e tŭ-nŭn 마음에 드는, a-ju cho-a-ha-nŭn 아주 좋아하는. —*n.* (*thing*) ma-ŭm-e tŭ-nŭn kŏt 마음에 드는 것 ; (*person*) ch'ong-a 총아.

fawn *n.* sae-ggi sa-sŭm 새끼 사슴.

fear *n.* kong-p'o 공포, kŏk-jŏng 걱정. —*v.* tu-ryŏ-wŏ-ha-da 두려워하다, kŏk-jŏng-ha-da 걱정하다.

feast *n.* ① ch'uk-je 축제, ch'uk-je-il 축제일. ② hyang-yŏn 향연, chan-ch'i 잔치. —*v.* (*regale*) sŏng-ch'an-ŭl tae-jŏp-ha-da 성찬을 대접하다. 「gi 표기」

feat *n.* kong-jŏk 공적(功績) ; (*surprising trick*) myo-

feather *n.* (*plume*) kit 깃, kit-t'ŏl 깃털.

feature *n.* ① (*characteristic*) t'ŭk-jing 특징. ② (*appearance*) yong-mo 용모. ③ (*scoop*) t'ŭk-jong-gi-sa 특종기사 ; in-gi p'ŭ-ro 인기 프로.

February *n.* i-wŏl 2월. 「yŏn-bang-ŭi 연방의.

federal *adj.* ① yŏn-hap-ui 연합의. ② (*F~*) (*Am.*)

fee *n.* yo-gŭm 요금 : *an admission ~* ip-jang-ryo 입장료 / *school ~s* su-ŏp-ryo 수업료.

feeble *adj.* yak-han 약한, ka-nyal-p'ŭn 가냘픈.

feed *v.* ① mŏk-i-da 먹이다; ki-rŭ-da 기르다. ②(*supply*) kong-gŭp-ha-da 공급하다. —*n.* ① (*for fowl*) mo-i 모이. ② (*for cattle, horses*) kkol 꼴, yŏ-mul 여물. ③ (*for dogs, cats*) pap 밥.

feel *v.* ① man-jyŏ po-da 만져 보다. ② (*with senses*) nŭ-ggi-da 느끼다. —*n.* nŭ-ggim 느낌. 「감정.

feeling *n.* nŭ-ggim 느낌, kam-gak 감각, (*pl.*) kam-jŏng 감정

feign *v.* ① ka-jang-ha-da 가장(假裝)하다, …in ch'e-ha-da …인 체하다. ② (*forge*) wi-jo-ha-da 위조하다.

fellow *n.* ① ch'in-gu 친구, tong-ryo 동료; nom 놈, nyŏ-sŏk 녀석. ② (*man*) nam-ja 남자, sa-na-i 사나이.

female *n.* yŏ-sŏng 여성, yŏ-ja 여자. —*adj.* ① (*used as animals*) am-k'ŏ-sŭi 암컷의. ② (*people*) yŏ-sŏng-ŭi 여성의 : ~ *dress* pu-in-bok 부인복.

fence *n.* ① (*hedge*) ul-t'a-ri 울타리, (*wall*) tam 담. ② (*fencing*) kŏm-sul 검술. 「효소.

ferment *v.* pal-hyo-ha-da 발효(醱酵)하다. —*n.* hyo-so

fern *n.* yang-ch'i-ryu 양치류, ko-sa-ri 고사리.

ferocious *adj.* ① hyung-ak-han 흉악한, chan-in-han 잔인한. ② sim-han 심한, mo-jin 모진.

ferry *n.* na-rut-bae 나룻배, na-ru-t'ŏ 나루터. —*v.* pae-ro kŏn-nŏ-da 배로 건너다.

ferryboat *n.* na-rut-bae 나룻배, yŏl-lak-sŏn 연락선.

ferryman *n.* na-rut-bae sa-gong 나룻배 사공.

fertile *adj.* ① (*productive*) ki-rŭm-jin 기름진, pi-ok-han 비옥한. ② (*prolific*) ta-san-ŭi 다산의.

fertilizer *n.* (*manure*) kŏ-rŭm 거름, pi-ryo 비료.

fervo(u)r *n.* yŏl-ryŏl 열렬, yŏl-jŏng 열정.

festival *n.* ch'uk-je(-il) 축제(일), chan-ch'i 잔치.

fetch *v.* ① ka-sŏ ka-jyŏ[te-ri-go]-o-da 가서 가져[데리고]오다. ② (*take out*) kkŏ-nae-da 꺼내다.

fetter *n.* ch'a-ggo 차꼬, chok-swae 족쇄. —*v.* ch'a-ggo-rŭl ch'ae-u-da 차꼬를 채우다, sok-bak-ha-da 속박하다.

feudal *adj.* yŏng-ji-ŭi 영지의, pong-gŏn-jŏk-in 봉건적인 : *the ~ system* pong-gŏn-je-do 봉건제도.

fever *n.* ko-yŏl 고열, yŏl-byŏng 열병 ; yŏl-gwang 열광.

few *adj.* so-su-ŭi 소수의, kŏ-ŭi ŏp-nŭn 거의 없는. —*n.* so-su 소수, tu-sŏ-nŏt 두서넛.

fiance *n.* (*male*) yak-hon-ja 약혼자.

fiber·fibre *n.* sŏm-yu 섬유, sŏm-yu-jil 섬유질.

fickle *adj.* (*changeable*) pyŏn-dŏk-sŭ-rŏ-un 변덕스러운, pyŏn-ha-gi swi-un 변하기 쉬운.   「sŏl 소설.

fiction *n.* ① (*invention*) hŏ-gu 허구. ② (*novel*) so-

fiddle *n.* che-gŭm 제금, (*violin*) pa-i-ol-rin 바이올린.

fidelity *n.* ch'ung-sil 충실, ch'ung-sŏng 충성.

field *n.* ① tŭl 들. ② (*scope*) pun-ya 분야.

field hospital ya-jŏn pyŏng-wŏn 야전 병원.

field marshal yuk-gun wŏn-su 육군 원수.   「(狂).

fiend *n.* (*devil*) ak-ma 악마, ma-gwi 마귀, kwang 광

fierce *adj.* sa-na-un 사나운, chi-dok-han 지독한.

fiery *adj.* pul-ga-t'ŭn 불같은, yŏl-ryŏl-han 열렬한 : *~ heat* jji-nŭn-dŭt-han tŏ-wi 찌는듯한 더위.

fifteen *n.* yŏl-da-sŏt 열다섯, sip-o 15.

fifty *n.* swin 쉰, o-sip 50. —*adj.* man-ŭn 많은.

fig *n.* mu-hwa-gwa 무화과.

fight *v.* ssa-u-da 싸우다. —*n.* ① ssa-um 싸움, kyŏk-t'u 격투. ② (*contest*) sŭng-bu 승부.

figure *n.* ① (*form*) hyŏng-sang 형상, mo-yang 모양. ② (*appearance*) oe-no 외모, oe-gwan 외관. ③ (*design*) to-hae 도해, kŭ-rim 그림. ④ (*numeral*) sut-ja 숫자. —*v.* kŭ-ri-da 그리다.   「men-t'ŭ 필라멘트.

filament *n.* ① sŏm-yu-ŭi han ol 섬유의 한 올. ② p'il-la-

file *v.* ① (*papers*) ch'ŏl-ha-da 철하다. ② (*send in*)

che-ch'ul-ha-da 제출하다. —*n.* ① (*tool*) chul 줄. ② (*for papers*) sŏ-ryu-ch'ŏl 서류철. ③ (*mil.*) tae-yŏl 대열.

filial *adj.* cha-sik-ŭ-ro-sŏ-ŭi 자식으로서의, hyo-sŏng-sŭ-rŏ-un 효성스러운 : ~ *piety* hyo-do 효도.

filibuster *n.* ŭi-sa pang-hae-ja 의사(議事) 방해자.

fill *v.* ch'ae-u-da 채우다, me-u-da 메우다. —*n.* ch'ung-bun 충분 ; (*satiety*) p'o-sik 포식.

film *n.* yŏl-bŭn mak 엷은 막 ; p'il-rŭm 필름.

filter *v.* kŏ-rŭ-da 거르다. —*n.* yŏ-gwa-gi 여과기.

filth *n.* ① ssŭ-re-gi 쓰레기, o-mul 오물 ; pun-nyŏ 분뇨. ② (*nasty language*) ŭm-dam-p'ae-sŏl 음담패설.

filthy *adj.* pul-gyŏl-han 불결한, ch'u-jap-han 추잡한.

fin *n.* chi-nŭ-rŏ-mi 지느러미. 「정적인.

final *adj.* ma-ji-mak-ŭi 마지막의, kyŏl-jŏng-jŏk-in 결

finally *adv.* ch'oe-hu-ro 최후로, ma-ch'im-nae 마침내.

finance *n.* ① chae-jŏng 재정, (*science*) chae-jŏng-hak 재정학. ② (*pl.*) (*funds*) chae-wŏn 재원.

find *v.* ① pal-gyŏn-hae-nae-da 발견해내다. ② (*something lost*) ch'at-da 찾다. ③ (*learn*) al-da 알다.

fine *adj.* ① hul-ryung-han 훌륭한, u-su-han 우수한. ② (*very thin*) ka-nŭ-da-ran 가느다란. ③ (*handsome*) a-rŭm-da-un 아름다운. —*n.* pŏl-gŭm 벌금.

finger *n.* son-ga-rak 손가락 : *the ring* ~ mu-myŏng-ji

fingernail *n.* son-t'op 손톱. 「무명지.

fingerprint *n.* chi-mun 지문(指紋).

finish *v.* kkŭt-nae-da 끝내다, wan-sŏng-ha-da 완성하다. —*n.* kkŭt 끝, chong-gyŏl 종결, ma-mu-ri 마무리.

fir *n.* chŏn-na-mu 전나무.

fire *n.* pul 불, (*conflagration*) hwa-jae 화재. —*v.* ① (*set on fire*) pul no-t'a 불 놓다. ② (*a gun*) sso-da 쏘다. ③ (*from job*) hae-go-ha-da 해고하다.

fire alarm hwa-jae kyŏng-bo-gi 화재 경보기.

fire bomb so-i-t'an 소이탄.

fire brigade so-bang-dae 소방대.

firecracker n. p'ok-juk 폭죽, ttak-ch'ong 딱총.

fire engine so-hwa p'ŏm-p'u 소화 펌프.

fire escape pi-sang-gu 비상구, so-bang sa-da-ri 소방 사

fire exit pi-sang-gu 비상구. ⌐다리.

fire extinguisher so-hwa-gi 소화기(消火器).

firefly n. kae-ddong-bŏl-re 개똥벌레.

fireman n. ① so-bang-su 소방수. ② hwa-bu 화부.

fireplace n. nal-lo 난로, pyŏk-nal-lo 벽난로.

firewood n. chang-jak 장작, ttael-na-mu 뗄나무.

firm n. sang-sa 상사, hoe-sa 회사. —adj. kyŏn-go-han 견고한, an-jŏng-doen 안정됨.

first adj. ch'ŏt-jjae-ŭi 첫째의, che-il-ŭi 제일의. —adv. ch'ŏt-jjae-ro 첫째로. —n. ch'ŏt-jjae 첫째, che-il 제일.

fiscal adj. kuk-go-ŭi 국고의 ; chae-jŏng-sang-ŭi 재정 상의 : a ~ stamp su-ip-in-ji 수입인지.

fish n. mul-go-gi 물고기, saeng-sŏn 생선. —v. nak-da 낚다, ko-gi-rŭl chap-da 고기를 잡다.

fisherman n. ŏ-bu 어부 ; (angler) nak-sit-gun 낚싯군.

fishery n. ŏ-ŏp 어업, su-san-ŏp 수산업.

fishing n. ko-gi-jap-i 고기잡이, ŏ-ŏp 어업 : ~ boat ŏ-sŏn 어선/~ line nak-sit-jul 낚싯줄/~ rod nak-sit-dae 낚싯대/~ village ŏ-ch'on 어촌. ⌐으로 치다.

fist n. chu-mŏk 주먹. —v. chu-mŏk-ŭ-ro ch'i-da 주먹

fit adj. chŏk-dang-han 적당한, al-ma-jŭn 알맞은 ; ŏ-ul-ri-nŭn 어울리는. —v. al-mat-da 알맞다, mat-ch'u-da 맞추다. —n. (convulsion) pal-jak 발작.

five n. ta-sŏt 다섯, o 5. ⌐da 수리하다.

fix v. ko-jŏng-si-k'i-da 고정시키다 ; (repair) su-ri-ha-

flag n. ki 기 : national ~ kuk-gi 국기(國旗).

flowerpot *n.* hwa-bun 화분.

flu *n.* (*influenza*) yu-haeng-sŏng kam-gi 유행성 감기.

fluctuate *v.* pyŏn-dong-ha-da 변동하다, p'a-dong-ha- ⌊da 파동하다.

fluent *adj.* yu-ch'ang-han 유창한.

fluid *n.* aek-ch'e 액체, yu-dong-ch'e 유동체. —*adj.* (*liquid*) yu-dong-sŏng-ŭi 유동성의. 「하는.

fluorescent *adj.* hyŏng-gwang-ŭl pal-ha-nŭn 형광을 발

flush *v.* ① ssi-sŏ-nae-ri-da 씻어내리다. ② (*be red*) pul-gŏ-ji-da 붉어지다. —*n.* ① (*rush of water*) pae-su 배수(排水). ② (*blush*) hong-jo 홍조(紅潮).

flute *n.* p'i-ri 피리, p'ŭl-ru-u-t'ŭ 플루우트.

flutter *v.* nal-gae-ch'i-da 날개치다. —*n.* ① p'ŏ-dŏk-gŏ-rim 퍼덕거림. ② (*stir*) tae-so-dong 대소동.

fly *n.* ① (*insect*) p'a-ri 파리. ② (*flight*) pi-haeng 비행. —*v.* ① (*bird*) nal-da 날다. ② (*kite*) nal-ri-da 날리다. ③ (*run away*) ta-ra-na-da 달아나다.

flypaper *n.* p'a-ri-yak chong-i 파리약 종이. 「일다.

foam *n.* kŏ-p'um 거품. —*v.* kŏ-p'um-i il-da 거품이

focus *n.* ch'o-jŏm 초점, p'o-u-k'ŏ-sŭ 포우커스.

fodder *n.* kkol 꼴, ma-ch'o 마초, sa-ryo 사료(飼料).

foe *n.* wŏn-su 원수, (*enemy*) chŏk 적.

fog *n.* an-gae 안개, yŏn-mu 연무(煙霧).

foil *n.* (*thin sheet of metal*) pak 박(箔): *gold* ~ kŭm-bak 금박/*silver* ~ ŭn-bak 은박.

fold *n.* chu-rŭm 주름. —*v.* chŏp-da 접다.

foliage *n.* (*mu-sŏng-han*) na-mut-ip (무성한) 나뭇잎.

folk *n.* (*people*) sa-ram-dŭl 사람들, (*pl.*) ka-jok 가족.

follow *v.* tta-ra-ga-da 따라가다, tta-rŭ-da 따르다; (*pursue*) ch'u-gu-ha-da 추구하다. 「수행원.

follower *n.* pu-ha 부하, (*attendant*) su-haeng-wŏn

folly *n.* ŏ-ri-sŏk-ŭm 어리석음, (*stupidity*) u-mae 우매.

fond *adj.* cho-a-ha-nŭn 좋아하는, chŏng-da-un 정다운.

food *n.* ŭm-sik 음식 : ~ *stuff* sik-ryang 식량, sik-ryo-p'um 식료품. 「da 속이다.

fool *n.* pa-bo 바보, mŏng-ch'ŏng-i 멍청이. —*v.* sok-i-

foolish *adj.* ŏ-ri-sŏk-ŭn 어리석은.

foot *n.* ① (*of the body*) pal 발. ② (*bottom*) mit 밑. ③ (*measure*) p'i-i-t'ŭ 피이트. ④ (*infantry*) po-byŏng 보병.

football *n.* ch'uk-gu 축구, p'ut-bo-ol 풋보올 ; ch'uk-gu-gong 축구공. 「ba-ri 삼발이.

footman *n.* ① chong-bok 종복 ; ma-bu 마부. ② sam-

footpath *n.* o-sol-gil 오솔길, po-do 보도, in-do 인도.

footprint *n.* pal-ja-ch'wi 발자취, pal-ja-guk 발자국.

footstep *n.* kŏ-rŭm-gŏ-ri 걸음걸이, pal-so-ri 발소리.

fop *n.* maep-si-gun 맵시군, mŏt-jang-i 멋장이.

for *prep.* …ŭl wi-ha-yŏ …을 위하여 ; (*on account of*) ttae-mun-e 때문에 ; …tong-an …동안.

forbear *v.* (*bear with*) ch'am-go kyŏn-di-da 참고 견디다 ; (*refrain*) sam-ga-da 삼가다.

forbid *v.* kŭm-ha-da 금하다 ; pang-hae-ha-da 방해하다.

force *n.* ① him 힘. ② (*pl.*) (*troops*) kun-dae 군대. (*effect*) hyŏ-ryŏk 효력. —*v.* ŏk-ji-ro …ha-ge ha-da 억지로 …하게 하다, kang-yo-ha-da 강요하다.

forceps *n.* chok-jip-ge 족집게, p'in-set 핀셋.

forcibly *adv.* kang-je-ro 강제로. 「걸어 건너다.

ford *n.* (*shallows*) yŏ-ul 여울. —*v.* kŏ-rŏ kŏn-nŏ-da

fore *n.* ap-bu-bun 앞부분, chŏn-myŏn 전면.

forecast *v.* ye-ch'ŭk-ha-da 예측하다, ye-bo-ha-da 예보하다. —*n.* (*anticipation*) ye-sang 예상 ; ye-bo 예보.

forefather *n.* cho-sang 조상, sŏn-jo 선조.

forefinger *n.* chip-ge-son-ga-rak 집게손가락.

forehead *n.* ① i-ma 이마. ② (*front part*) ap-jjok 앞쪽.

foreign *adj.* oe-guk-ŭi 외국의, oe-rae-ŭi 외래의.

foreigner *n.* oe-guk-in 외국인, oe-in 외인.

foreleg *n.* (*of animals*) ap-da-ri 앞다리.

foreman *n.* sip-jang 십장, kam-dok 감독.

foremost *adj.* maen mŏn-jŏ-ŭi 맨 먼저의 ; il-ryu-ŭi 일류의 ; chu-yo-han 주요한. —*adv.* maen mŏn-jŏ 맨 먼저.

forenoon *n.* o-jŏn 오전, a-ch'im-na-jŏl 아침나절.

forerunner *n.* sŏn-gu-ja 선구자, chŏn-ju-ja 전주자.

foresee *v.* mi-ri al-da 미리 알다, ye-gyŏn-ha-da 예견하다.

forest *n.* sup 숲, sam-rim 삼림.

foretell *v.* ye-ŏn-ha-da 예언하다, ye-go-ha-da 예고하다.

forever *adv.* yŏng-gu-hi 영구히, yŏng-wŏn-hi 영원히. —*n.* yŏng-wŏn 영원, (*eternity*) yŏng-gŏp 영겁.

foreword *n.* mŏ-ri-mal 머리말, sŏ-mun 서문.

forfeit *n.* (*fine*) pŏl-gŭm 벌금, kwa-ryo 과료. —*v.* sang-sil-ha-da 상실하다 ; mol-su-dang-ha-da 몰수당하다.

forge *n.* tae-jang-gan 대장간. —*v.* ① (*steel*) pyŏ-ri-da 벼리다. ② (*counterfeit*) wi-jo-ha-da 위조하다.

forgery *n.* wi-jo 위조 ; pyŏn-jo 변조.

forget *v.* i-jŏ-bŏ-ri-da 잊어버리다, mang-gak-ha-da 망각하다.

forgetful *adj.* chal i-jŏ-bŏ-ri-nŭn 잘 잊어버리는.

forgive *v.* ① yong-sŏ-ha-da 용서하다. ② (*remit*) myŏn-je-ha-da 면제하다, t'ang-gam-ha-da 탕감하다.

fork *n.* ① p'o-o-k'ŭ 포오크. ② kal-k'wi 갈퀴, soe-sŭ-rang 쇠스랑. —*v.* pun-gi-ha-da 분기하다.

forlorn *adj.* pŏ-rim-bat-ŭn 버림받은, (*desolate*) ko-dok-han 고독한, ssŭl-ssŭl-han 쓸쓸한.

form *n.* ① (*shape*) mo-yang 모양, hyŏng-t'ae 형태, (*appearance*) oe-gwan 외관. ② (*blank*) sŏ-sik 서식. —*v.* hyŏng-t'ae-rŭl i-ru-da 형태를 이루다.

formal *adj.* chŏng-sik-ŭi 정식의 ; (*in form*) hyŏng-sik-jŏk-in 형식적인.

formation *n.* ① ku-sŏng 구성, cho-jik 조직. ② (*army*) p'yŏn-dae 편대.

former *adj.* (*previous*) a-p'ŭi 앞의 ; yet-nal-ŭi 옛날의,

i-jŏn-ŭi 이전의. —*n.* (*the* ∼) chŏn-ja 전자.

formidable *adj.* mu-sŏ-un 무서운 ; kam-dang-ha-gi ŏ-ryŏ-un 감당하기 어려운.　　　　　　　　　　「처방.

formula *n.* ① kong-sik 공식. ② (*recipe*) ch'ŏ-bang

fornicate *v.* kan-ŭm-ha-da 간음하다, sa-t'ong-ha-da 사통하다.　　　　　　　　　　　　　　　「da 포기하다.

forsake *v.* chŏ-bŏ-ri-da 저버리다, (*give up*) p'o-gi-ha-

fort *n.* yo-sae 요새(要塞), sŏng-ch'ae 성채.

forth *adv.* ① a-p'u-ro 앞으로, (*onward*) chŏn-bang-ŭ-ro 전방으로. ② (*abroad*) pa-ggŭ-ro 밖으로.

forthcoming *adj.* ta-ga-o-nŭn 다가오는, i-bŏn-ŭi 이번의.

fortification *n.* ① pang-bi 방비. ② (*pl.*) (*defensive works*) pang-ŏ-gong-sa 방어공사. ③ kang-hwa 강화.

fortified area yo-sae chi-dae 요새 지대.

fortify *v.* ① yo-sae-hwa-ha-da 요새화하다, kang-hwa-ha-da 강화하다. ② twit-bat-ch'im-ha-da 뒷받침하다.

fortnight *n.* i-ju-il-gan 2주일간, po-rŭm 보름.

fortress *n.* yo-sae 요새, (*stronghold*) sŏng-ch'ae 성채.

fortunate *adj.* haeng-un-ŭi 행운의, un-jo-ŭn 운좋은, chae-su-ga cho-ŭn 재수가 좋은.

fortune *n.* ① (*chance*) un 운, un-su 운수, haeng-un 행운. ② (*wealth*) chae-san 재산, pu 부(富).

forty *n.* ma-hŭn 마흔, sa-sip 40.

forward *adj.* a-p'ŭi 앞의. —*adv.* a-p'u-ro 앞으로. —*v.* ch'ok-jin-ha-da 촉진하다 ; chŏn-song-ha-da 전송하다.

fossil *n.* hwa-sŏk 화석. —*adj.* ① hwa-sŏk-ŭi 화석의. ② (*antiquated*) ku-sik-ŭi 구식의.

foster *v.* ① (*rear*) ki-rŭ-da 기르다, tol-bo-da 돌보다. ② (*cherish*) so-jung-hi ha-da 소중히 하다.

foul *adj.* ① tŏ-rŏ-un 더러운, pul-gyŏl-han 불결한. ② ŭm-t'ang-han 음탕한. —*n.* kyu-ch'ik wi-ban 규칙 위반.

found *v.* ① (*establish*) ch'ang-sŏl-ha-da 창설하다. ②

(*lay the base of*) se-u-da 기초를 세우다.

foundation *n.* ① (*base*) ki-ch'o 기초. ② (*establishing*) kŏn-sŏl 건설. ③ (*endowment*) chae-dan 재단(財團).

founder *n.* ch'ang-rip-ja 창립자.

foundry *n.* ① chu-jo 주조(鑄造). ② chu-mul kong-jang 주물 공장.

fountain *n.* pun-su 분수, (*spring*) saem 샘.

fountain pen man-nyŏn-p'il 만년필.

four *n.* net 넷, sa 4 : *Form ~s!* Sa-yŏl-ro 4열로!

fourteen *n.* yŏl-net 열넷, sip-sa 14.

fowl *n.* ① tak 닭. ② (*poultry*) ka-gŭm 가금.

fox *n.* yŏ-u 여우 ; (*sly person*) kyo-hwal-han in-gan 교활한 인간 : *a silver ~* ŭn yŏ-u 은 여우.

fraction *n.* ① (*scrap*) p'a-p'yŏn 파편(破片), chak-ŭn cho-gak 작은 조각. ② (*math.*) pun-su 분수(分數).

fragile *adj.* pu-sŏ-ji-gi swi-un 부서지기 쉬운 ; hŏ-yak-han 허약한.

fragment *n.* ① kkae-jin cho-gak 깨진 조각, p'a-p'yŏn 파편. ② tan-jang 단장(斷章).

fragrance *n.* hyang-gi 향기 ; pang-hyang 방향.

frail *adj.* yak-han 약한, mu-rŭn 무른.

frame *n.* ① ku-jo 구조 ; ppyŏ-dae 뼈대, p'ŭ-re-im 프레임. ② (*mood*) ki-bun 기분. —*v.* (*shape*) hyŏng-sŏng-ha-da 형성하다 ; ko-an-ha-da 고안하다.

framework *n.* ① (*skeleton*) ppyŏ-dae 뼈대, kol-gyŏk 골격. ② (*system*) ch'e-gye 체계, ch'e-je 체제.

frank *adj.* sol-jik-han 솔직한 ; sum-gim-ŏp-nŭn 숨김 없는.

frantic *adj.* mi-ch'in-dŭt-han 미친듯한.

fraternal *adj.* hyŏng-je-ŭi 형제의, ch'in-han 친한.

fraud *n.* sa-gi 사기, hyŏp-jap 협잡, sa-git-gun 사깃군.

freak *n.* ki-hyŏng 기형, pyŏn-jong 변종.

freckle *n.* chu-gŭn-ggae 주근깨, (*stain*) ŏl-ruk 얼룩.

free *adj.* cha-yu-ŭi 자유의 ; (*without payment*) muryo-ŭi 무료의. —*v.* hae-bang-ha-da 해방하다.

freedom *n.* cha-yu 자유, cha-ju 자주(自主). 「다.

freeze *v.* ① ŏl-da 얼다. ② tong-gyŏl-si-k'i-da 동결시키

freight *n.* ① hwa-mul 화물. ② (*charges*) un-im 운임.

freight car hwa-mul-ch'a 화물차.

frequent *adj.* pin-bŏn-han 빈번한, (*habitual*) sang-sŭp-jŏk-in 상습적인. —*v.* cha-ju ka-da 자주 가다.

fresh *adj.* sin-sŏn-han 신선한, sing-sing-han 싱싱한.

freshman *n.* sin-ip-saeng 신입생, il-nyŏn-saeng 1년생.

fret *v.* ae-t'ae-u-da 애태우다, (*become irritated*) cho-ba-sim-ha-da 조바심하다. —*n.* ch'o-jo 초조.

friction *n.* (*rubbing*) ma-ch'al 마찰 ; al-ryŏk 알력.

Friday *n.* kŭm-yo-il 금요일.

friend *n.* ch'in-gu 친구, tong-mu 동무, pŏt 벗.

friendly *adj.* ch'in-han 친한, u-ho-jŏk-in 우호적인.

friendship *n.* u-jŏng 우정, u-ae 우애, ch'in-gyo 친교.

fright *n.* nol-ram 놀람, kong-p'o 공포.

frighten *n.* kkam-jjak nol-ra-ge ha-da 깜짝 놀라게 하다.

frigid *adj.* mop-si ch'u-un 몹시 추운, (*chilling*) ssal-ssal-han 쌀쌀한 ; (*formal*) ttak-ddak-han 딱딱한.

fringe *n.* ① (*tuft*) sul 술, ka-du-ri chang-sik 가두리 장식. ② (*border*) ka-jang-ja-ri 가장자리.

frivolous *adj.* kyŏng-sol-han 경솔한, (*silly*) pa-bo-ga-t'ŭn 바보같은, (*trivial*) si-si-han 시시한.

frog *n.* kae-gu-ri 개구리.

from *prep.* …ro-bu-t'ŏ …로부터, …e-sŏ …에서.

front *n.* ① ap 앞, (*forward part*) chŏng-myŏn 정면, ap-myŏn 앞면. ② (*fighting*) il-sŏn 일선.

frontier *n.* kuk-gyŏng 국경, pyŏn-gyŏng 변경.

frost *n.* sŏ-ri 서리. —*v.* sŏ-ri-ga nae-ri-da 서리가 내리다 ; (*freeze*) ŏl-ge ha-da 얼게 하다. 「sang 우거지상.

frown *v.* jji-p'u-ri-da 찌푸리다. —*n.* (*scowl*) u-gŏ-ji-

frozen *adj.* ŏn 언, (*congealed*) naeng-dong-han 냉동한.

frugal *adj.* kŏm-so-han 검소한, al-ddŭl-han 알뜰한 : *a ~ meal* kŏm-so-han sik-sa 검소한 식사.

fruit *n.* kwa-il 과일, kwa-sil 과실 ; (*plant products*) san-mul 산물 : *~ shop* kwa-il ka-ge 과일 가게.

frustration *n.* ① chwa-jŏl 좌절, sil-p'ae 실패 ; mu-hyo 무효. ② (*psych.*) yok-gu-bul-man 욕구불만.

fry *v.* ki-rŭm-e t'wi-gi-da 기름에 튀기다, p'ŭ-ra-i-ha-da 프라이하다. —*n.* t'wi-gim-yo-ri 튀김요리.

frying pan p'ŭ-ra-i nam-bi 프라이 남비, p'ŭ-ra-i-p'aen 프라이팬.

fuel *n.* yŏl-lyo 연료, chang-jak 장작, sin-t'an 신탄(薪「炭).

fugitive *adj.* ta-ra-na-nŭn 달아나는, mang-myŏng-ŭi 망명의. —*n.* to-mang-ja 도망자, mang-myŏng-ja 망명자.

fulfil *v.* ① su-haeng-ha-da 이행하다 ; kkŭt-nae-da 끝내다. ② (*satisfy*) ch'ung-jok-si-k'i-da 충족시키다.

full *adj.* ka-dŭk-ch'an 가득찬, ch'ung-bun-han 충분한. —*adv.* ka-dŭk-hi 가득히. —*n.* chŏn-bu 전부.

full moon po-rŭm-dal 보름달, man-wŏl 만월.

fume *n.* ① (*vapor*) yŏn-gi 연기, an-gae 안개, (*incense*) hyang-gi 향기. ② (*anger*) no-gi 노기.

fun *n.* chang-nan 장난, nong-dam 농담, chae-mi 재미.

function *n.* ki-nŭng 기능, chik-nŭng 직능, yŏk-hal 역할. —*v.* (*work*) chak-yong-ha-da 작용하다.

fund *n.* cha-gŭm 자금, (*pl.*) chae-wŏn 재원.

fundamental *adj.* ki-bon-jŏk-in 기본적인, kŭn-wŏn-jŏk-in 근원적인. —*n.* ki-bon 기본, ki-ch'o 기초.

funeral *n.* chang-rye-sik 장례식. —*adj.* chang-rye-ŭi 장례의.

fungus *n.* kyul-lyu 균류(菌類), pŏ-sŏt 버섯.

funnel *n.* ① (*boat*) yŏn-t'ong 연통. ② (*pouring*) kkal-ddae-gi 깔때기. ③ t'ong-p'ung-t'ong 통풍통.

funny *adj.* ① (*comical*) ik-sal-ma-jŭn 익살맞은, chae-mi-it-nŭn 재미있는. ② (*queer*) koe-sang-han 괴상한, ki-myo-han 기묘한. 「소설가.

funnyman *n.* kwang-dae 광대 ; hae-hak so-sŏl-ga 해학

fur *n.* mo-p'i 모피. 「da 닦다.

furbish *v.* (*polish*) kwang-ŭl nae-da 광을 내다, tak-

furious *adj.* kyŏk-bun-han 격분한, maeng-ryŏl-han 맹

furl *v.* (*roll*) mal-da 말다, (*fold*) chŏp-da 접다.「렬한.

furlough *n.* (*mil.*) hyu-ga 휴가. 「광로.

furnace *n.* hwa-ro 화로 ; (*smelter*) yong-gwang-ro 용

furnish *v.* ① (*supply*) kong-gŭp-ha-da 공급하다, tae-ju-da 대주다. ② (*equip*) pi-ch'i-ha-da 비치하다.

furnishings *n.* ka-gu-ryu 가구류, se-gan 세간.

furniture *n.* ka-gu 가구, se-gan 세간, pi-p'um 비품.

furrow *n.* ko-rang 고랑 ; (*wrinkle*) chu-rŭm 주름.

furry *adj.* mo-p'i-ro tŏp'in 모피로 덮인, mo-p'i-ro man-dŭn 모피로 만든.

further *adj.* kŭ wi-ŭi 그 위의, kŭ i-sang-ŭi 그 이상의.
—*adv.* kŭ wi-e 그 위에, ke-da-ga 게다가.

furthermore *adv.* tŏ-gun-da-na 더군다나. 「한.

furtive *adj.* mol-rae-ha-nŭn 몰래하는, ŭn-mil-han 은밀

fury *n.* ① kyŏk-jŏng 격정, kyŏk-bun 격분. ② maeng-ryŏl 맹렬, (*violence*) kwang-p'o 광포.

fuse *n.* ① (*electric*) p'yu-jŭ 퓨즈. ② (*ordnance*) sin-gwan 신관(信管), to-hwa-sŏn 도화선. —*v.* (*melt*) nok-i-da 녹이다, (*blend*) yung-hwa-ha-da 융화하다.

fusion *n.* ① yong-hae 용해. ② hap-dong 합동.

fuss *n.* ya-dan-bŏp-sŏk 야단법석, so-dong 소동. —*v.* ttŏ-dŭl-da 떠들다, an-dal-bok-dal-ha-da 안달복달하다.

futile *adj.* so-yong-ŏp-nŭn 소용없는, mu-ik-han 무익한 : *a* ～ *attempt* hŏt-doen si-do 헛된 시도.

future *n.* chang-rae 장래, mi-rae 미래. —*adj.* mi-rae-ŭi 미래의 ; nae-se-ŭi 내세의.

G

gabble v. chi-ggŏ-ri-da 지껄이다, chong-al-gŏ-ri-da 종알거리다. —n. chae-jal-gŏ-rim 재잘거림. 「부속품.

gadget n. chang-ch'i 장치 ; (*accessory*) pu-sok-p'um

gaiety n. myŏng-rang 명랑, yu-k'wae 유쾌.

gaily adv. k'wae-hwal-ha-ge 쾌활하게. 「이득.

gain v. ŏt-da 얻다, (*win*) i-gi-da 이기다. —n. i-dŭk

gait n. kŏ-rŭm-gŏ-ri 걸음걸이, po-jo 보조(步調).

gale n. kang-p'ung 강풍, chil-p'ung 질풍.

gallant adj. ① yong-gam-han 용감한, ssik-ssik-han 씩씩한. ② ch'in-jŏl-han 친절한. —n. mŏt-jang-i 멋쟁이.

gallery n. ① hwa-rang 화랑(畵廊). ② (*corridor*) pok-do 복도. ③ (*theater*) kwal-lam-sŏk 관람석.

gallon n. kal-ron 갈론(＝3.785 l).

gallop n. chil-ju 질주. —v. chil-ju-ha-da 질주하다.

gallows n. kyo-su-dae 교수대, kyo-su-hyŏng 교수형.

galvanized iron ham-sŏk 함석.

gamble n. & v. to-bak(-ha-da) 도박(하다). 「사냥감.

game n. ① yu-hŭi 유희, o-rak 오락. ② sa-nyang-gam

gang n. (*a group*) han p'ae 한 패 ; kaeng 갱.

gangster n. kaeng 갱, ak-dang 악당.

gap n. (*opening*) t'ŭm 틈, (*interval*) kan-gyŏk 간격.

gape v. ip-ŭl k'ŭ-ge pŏl-ri-da 입을 크게 벌리다, (*yawn*) ha-p'um-ha-da 하품하다.

garage n. ch'a-go 차고 ; kyŏk-nap-go 격납고.

garbage n. ssŭ-re-gi 쓰레기, jji-ggŏ-gi 찌꺼기.

garden n. ① ttŭl 뜰, chŏng-wŏn 정원. ② (*pl.*) yu-wŏn-ji 유원지.

gardener n. chŏng-wŏn-sa 정원사.

gargle v. yang-ch'i-jil-ha-da 양치질하다.

garland *n.* hwa-hwan 화환, hwa-gwan 화관.

garlic *n.* ma-nŭl 마늘.

garment *n.* kin ot 긴 옷, (*pl.*) ŭi-bok 의복, ŭi-sang 의상.

garnet *n.* sŏk-ryu-sŏk 석류석(石榴石).　「mul 장식물.

garnish *v.* chang-sik-ha-da 장식하다. —*n.* chang-sik-

garrison *n.* su-bi-dae 수비대, chu-dun-gun 주둔군.

garret *n.* ta-rak-bang 다락방, ko-mi-da-rak-bang 고미

garter *n.* yang-mal tae-nim 양말 대님.　　　└다락방.

gas *n.* ga-sŭ 가스:*natural* ~ ch'ŏn-yŏn-ga-sŭ 천연가스.

gasoline *n.* hwi-bal-yu 휘발유, ka-sol-rin 가솔린.

gasp *v.* ① hŏl-ddŏk-gŏ-ri-da 헐떡거리다. ② (*desire*)
kal-mang-ha-da 갈망하다.　　　　　　　　　「궤양.

gastric *adj.* wi-ŭi 위(胃)의 : ~*ulcer* wi-gwe-yang 위

gate *n.* mun 문, (*portal*) ch'u-rip-mun 출입문.

gather *v.* ① mo-ŭ-da 모으다, mo-i-da 모이다. ② (*creas-ing*) chu-rŭm-ŭl chap-da 주름을 잡다.

gathering *n.* mo-im 모임, hoe-hap 회합 ; su-jip 수집.

gaudy *adj.* ya-han 야한, hwa-ryŏ-han 화려한.

ga(u)ge *n.* kye-gi 계기(計器), ke-i-ji 게이지, p'yo-jun-ch'i-su 표준치수.　　　　　　　　　　　「시무시한.

gaunt *adj.* yŏ-win 여윈 ; (*grim*) mu-si-mu-si-han 무

gauze *n.* yal-bŭn ch'ŏn 얇은 천, ka-a-je 가아제.

gay *adj.* k'wae-hwal-han 쾌활한;(*showy*) ya-han 야한.

gaze *v.* ŭng-si-ha-da 응시하다, chi-k'yŏ-bo-da 지켜보
다. —*n.* (*steady look*) ŭng-si 응시, chu-si 주시.

gear *n.* t'op-ni-ba-k'wi 톱니바퀴, chang-ch'i 장치, ki-

gelatin(e) *n.* a-gyo 아교, chel-ra-t'in 젤라틴. └gu 기구.

gem *n.* po-sŏk 보석, ok 옥 ; il-p'um 일품(逸品).

gender *n.* sŏng 성(性), (*sex*) sŏng-byŏl 성별. 「bo 족보.

genealogy *n.* ① ka-gye 가계, hyŏl-t'ong 혈통. ② chok-

general *n.* chang-gun 장군. —*adj.* il-ban-jŏk-in 일반
적인, chŏn-ban-jŏk-in 전반적인.

general election ch'ong-sŏn-gŏ 총선거.

generate *v.* ① na-t'a 낳다 ; pal-saeng-ha-da 발생하다. ② (*electricity*) pal-jŏn-ha-da 발전하다.

generation *n.* ① il-dae 일대(一代), se-dae 세대 ; tong-si-dae-ŭi sa-ram-dŭl 동시대의 사람들. ② pal-saeng 발생.

generator *n.* pal-jŏn-gi 발전기, pal-saeng-gi 발생기.

generosity *n.* kwan-yong 관용, a-ryang 아량.

generous *adj.* ① kwan-dae-han 관대한, nŏ-gŭ-rŏ-un 너그러운. ② (*unsparing*) a-ggim-ŏp-nŭn 아낌없는.

genial *adj.* on-hwa-han 온화한, ch'in-jŏl-han 친절한.

genius *n.* ch'ŏn-jae 천재 ; ch'ŏn-sŏng 천성 ; t'ŭk-jing 특징.

genteel *adj.* p'um-wi-it-nŭn 품위있는, u-a-han 우아한.

gentle *adj.* on-hwa-han 온화한, chŏm-jan-ŭn 점잖은.

gentleman *n.* sin-sa 신사.

gentlewoman *n.* suk-nyŏ 숙녀, kwi-bu-in 귀부인.

gently *adj.* sang-nyang-ha-ge 상냥하게, chŏm-jan-k'e 점잖게 ; (*quietly*) cho-yong-ha-ge 조용하게. 「류 사회.

gentry *n.* sin-sa kye-gŭp 신사 계급, sang-ryu sa-hoe 상류.

genuine *adj.* chin-jŏng-han 진정한, chin-jja-ŭi 진짜의.

geography *n.* chi-ri-hak 지리학, chi-ji 지지(地誌) ; chi-

geology *n.* chi-jil-hak 지질학. 「se 지세(地勢).

geometry *n.* ki-ha-hak 기하학.

geophysics *n.* chi-gu-mul-ri-hak 지구물리학.

germ *n.* ① (*microbe*) pyŏng-gyun 병균, se-gyun 세균. ② (*origin*) kŭn-wŏn 근원, ki-wŏn 기원.

German *adj.* tok-il-ŭi 독일의. —*n.* (*people*) tok-il-sa-ram 독일사람 ; (*language*) tok-i-rŏ 독일어.

Germany *n.* to-i-ch'i 도이치, tok-il 독일. 「(發芽)하다.

germinate *v.* ssak-i t'ŭ-da 싹이 트다, pa-ra-ha-da 발아

gesture *n.* mom-jit 몸짓, che-sŭ-ch'ŏ 제스처.

get *v.* (*acquire*) ŏt-da 얻다 ; (*arrive*) i-rŭ-da 이르다 ; (*induce*) ha-ge ha-da 하게 하다 ; (*become*) …i toe-da …이 되다 : ～ *up* i-rŏ-na-da 일어나다. 「시한.

ghastly *adj.* mu-sŏ-un 무서운, mu-si-mu-si-han 무시무

ghost *n.* yu-ryŏng 유령, mang-ryŏng 망령, kwi-sin 귀

giant *n.* kŏ-in 거인. —*adj.* kŏ-dae-han 거대한. 「신.

giddy *adj.* ŏ-ji-rŏ-un 어지러운, ŏ-jil-ŏ-jil-han 어질어질한.

gift *n.* sŏn-mul 선물 ; (*natural ability*) ch'ŏn-bu-ŭi
chae-nŭng 천부의 재능.

gifted *adj.* chae-nŭng-i it-nŭn 재능이 있는. 「한.

gigantic *adj.* kŏ-in-ga-t'ŭn 거인같은, kŏ-dae-han 거대

giggle *v.* k'il-k'il ut-da 킬킬 웃다.

gild *v.* kŭm-bak-ŭl ip-hi-da 금박을 입히다, to-gŭm-ha-

gills *n.* (*fish*) a-ga-mi 아가미. 「da 도금하다.

ginger *n.* sae-ang 새앙, saeng-gang 생강 : ～ *group*
kŭp-jin-p'a 급진파. 「ha-ge 신중하게.

gingerly *adj.* sin-jung-han 신중한. —*adv.* sin-jung-

gingko·ginkgo *n.* ŭn-haeng-na-mu 은행나무.

ginseng *n.* in-sam 인삼 : *a Korean* ～ ko-ryŏ in-sam

gipsy·gypsy *n.* chip-si 집시. 「고려 인삼.

giraffe *n.* ki-rin 기린, chi-ra-p'ŭ 지라프.

gird *v.* (*encircle*) tu-rŭ-da 두르다, chol-ra-mae-da 졸라
매다 ; (*equip*) kŏl-ch'i-da 걸치다, ch'a-da 차다

girdle *n.* tti 띠, hŏ-ri-tti 허리띠. —*v.* tu-rŭ-da 두르다.

girl *n.* so-nyŏ 소녀, kye-jip-a-i 계집아이, ae-in 애인.

girlhood *n.* so-nyŏ si-jŏl 소녀 시절 ; so-nyŏ-dŭl 소녀들.

give *v.* chu-da 주다, pe-p'ul-da 베풀다 ; (*hold*) yŏl-da
열다 ; (*entrust*) mat-gi-da 맡기다 : ～ *up* p'o-gi-ha-da
포기하다, tan-nyŏm-ha-da 단념하다. 「자.

giver *adj.* chu-nŭn sa-ram 주는 사람, ki-jŭng-ja 기증

glacier *n.* ping-ha 빙하.

glad *adj.* ki-bbŭn 기쁜, chŭl-gŏ-un 즐거운.

gladden *v.* ki-bbŭ-ge ha-da 기쁘게 하다.

gladness *n.* ki-bbŭm 기쁨, chŭl-gŏ-um 즐거움.

glamo(u)r *n.* ma-ryŏk 마력, mae-ryŏk 매력 : *a ~ girl* mae-hok-jŏk-in yŏ-ja 매혹적인 여자.

glance *v.* hil-ggŭt-bo-da 힐끗보다. —*n.* hil-ggŭt-bo-gi 힐끗보기, (*meaning look*) nun-jit 눈짓.

gland *n.* sŏn 선(腺): *lymphatic ~s* im-p'a-sŏn 임파선.

glare *v.* (*light*) nun-i pu-si-da 눈이 부시다 ; (*stare fiercely*) no-ryŏ-bo-da 노려보다. —*n.* nun-bu-sin pit 눈부신 빛, (*fierce stare*) sso-a-bo-gi 쏘아보기.

glass *n.* ① yu-ri 유리 ; k'ŏp 컵. ② (*drinking*) sul 술, ŭm-ju 음주. ③ (*spectacles*) an-gyŏng 안경.

glassware *n.* yu-ri kŭ-rŭt 유리 그릇.

glazed *adj.* yun-t'aek-na-nŭn 윤택나는, kwang-t'aek-it-nun 광택있는, mae-ggŭn-mae-ggŭn-han 매끈매끈한.

gleam *n.* pit-nam 빛남 ; ŏ-ryŏm-p'ut-han pit 어렴풋한 빛, mi-gwang 미광. —*v.* pŏn-jjŏk-i-da 번쩍이다.

glean *v.* ① i-sak-ŭl chup-da 이삭을 줍다. ② su-jip-ha- da 수집하다.

glee *n.* ki-bbŭm 기쁨, hwan-hŭi 환희.

glen *n.* kol-jja-gi 골짜기, chop-ŭn kye-gok 좁은 계곡.

glide *v.* mi-ggŭ-rŏ-ji-da 미끄러지다, hwal-ju-ha-da 활주하다. —*n.* hwal-ju 활주.

glim *n.* tŭng-bul 등불, ch'ot-bul 촛불, pul-bit 불빛.

glimmer *v.* ka-mul-ga-mul pi-ch'i-da 가물가물 비치다, kkam-bak-i-da 깜박이다. —*n.* hŭ-rit-han pit 흐릿한 빛.

glimpse *n.* hil-ggŭt-bo-gi 힐끗보기, il-byŏl 일별.

glisten *v.* pan-jjak-i-da 반짝이다, pit-na-da 빛나다.

glitter *v.* pan-jjak-ban-jjak pit-na-da 반짝반짝 빛나다.

globe *n.* kong 공 ; (*the earth*) chi-gu 지구.

gloom *n.* ŏ-dum 어둠 ; u-ul 우울. —*v.* o-du-wŏ-ji-da 어두워지다.

gloomy *adj.* ŏ-du-un 어두운, ch'im-ul-han 침울한.

glorify *v.* ch'an-mi-ha-da 찬미하다. yŏng-gwang-ŭl pe-p'ul-da 영광을 베풀다.

glorious *adj.* yŏng-gwang-sŭ-rŏ-un 영광스러운.

glory *n.* yŏng-gwang 영광, yŏng-ye 영예 ; yŏng-hwa 영화(榮華), yung-sŏng 융성, nun-bu-sim 눈부심.

gloss *n.* kwang-t'aek 광택 ; (*specious show*) hŏ-sik 허식 ; (*comment*) chu-hae 주해(註解).

glossary *n.* so-sa-jŏn 소사전, yong-ŏ p'u-ri 용어 풀이.

glove *n.* chang-gap 장갑, kŭl-lŏ-bŭ 글러브.

glow *v.* ppal-ga-k'e ta-ra-o-rŭ-da 빨갛게 달아오르다. —*n.* paek-yŏl 백열, hong-jo 홍조. 「아교로 붙이다.

glue *n.* a-kyo 아교, p'ul 풀. —*v.* a-gyo-ro pu-ch'i-da

gnat *n.* mo-gi 모기, kak-da-gwi 각다귀.

gnaw *v.* mu-rŏ kkŭn-t'a 물어 끊다 ; ssol-da 쏠다.

go *v.* ① (*proceed*) ka-da 가다. ② (*work*) um-jik-i-da 움직이다. ③ (*elapse*) chi-na-ga-da 지나가다.

goal *n.* kyŏl-sŭng-jŏm 결승점, mok-p'yo 목표, mok-jŏk-

goat *n.* yŏm-so 염소. 「ji 목적지.

gobble *v.* ke-gŏl-sŭ-rŏp-ge mŏk-da 게걸스럽게 먹다.

go-between *n.* chung-gae-in 중개인, chung-mae-ja 중 매자 ; (*pander*) ttu-jang-i 뚜장이.

goblin *n.* yo-gwi 요귀, ma-gwi 마귀, ak-gwi 악귀.

god *n.* sin 신(神), (*G~*) ha-nŭ-nim 하느님.

goddess *n.* yŏ-sin 여신. 「존엄한.

godlike *adj.* sin-gwa ka-t'ŭn 신과 같은, chon-ŏm-han

godliness *n.* kyŏng-gŏn 경건, kyŏng-sin 경신(敬神).

gold *n.* kŭm 금, (*coin*) kŭm-hwa 금 화 ; (*color*) kŭm-bit 금빛.

golden *adj.* ① kŭm-bi-ch'ŭi 금빛의. ② (*precious*) kwi-jung-han 귀중 한. ③ yung-sŏng-han 융성한.

goldfish *n.* kŭm-bung-ŏ 금붕어.

golf *n.* kol-p'ŭ 골프.

gong *n.* ching 징, pa-ra 바라.

[ching]

good n. ch'ak-ham 착함. —*adj.* cho-ŭn 좋은, (*kind*) ch'in-jŏl-han 친절한 ; (*skilled*) nŭng-suk-han 능숙한.

good-by(e) n. chak-byŏl in-sa 작별 인사. —*int.* an-nyŏng-hi ka-sip-si-o 안녕히 가십시오, an-nyŏng-hi kye-sip-si-o 안녕히 계십시오.

goodness n. ch'ak-ham 착함, mi-dŏk 미덕 ; (*kindness*) ch'in-jŏl 친절 ; (*excellence*) u-ryang 우량.

goods n. mul-p'um 물품, sang-p'um 상품.

goose n. kŏ-wi 거위 : *wild* ~ ki-rŏ-gi 기러기.

gorgeous *adj.* ch'al-lan-han 찬란한, hwa-ryŏ-han 화려한 ; hul-lyung-han 훌륭한.

gosh *int.* ŏ-ma 어마, a-i-go 아이고, chŏ-rŏn 저런.

gospel n. pok-ŭm 복음.

gossip n. chap-dam 잡담, twit-gong-ron 뒷공론, ko-sip 고십 : *the* ~ *column* ko-sip-ran 고십란(欄).

gourd n. ho-ri-byŏng-bak 호리병박, cho-rong-bak 조롱박 : *the sponge* ~ su-se-mi-oe 수세미외.

gourmet n. sik-do-rak 식도락, mi-sik-ga 미식가.

govern v. ① chi-bae-ha-da 지배하다, ta-sŭ-ri-da 다스리다. ② (*determine*) kyŏl-jŏng-ha-da 결정하다.

government n. chŏng-bu 정부. chŏng-ch'i 정치.

governor n. t'ong-ch'i-ja 통치자, chi-sa 지사. 「스.

gown n. kin kŏt-ot 긴 겉옷, ka-un 가운, tu-re-sŭ 드레

grab v. um-k'yŏ-jap-da 움켜잡다, put-jap-da 붙잡다.

grace n. ① ŭn-ch'ong 은총, ho-ŭi 호의. ② (*elegance*) ki-p'um 기품, u-a 우아. ③ (*prayer*) ki-do 기도.

graceful *adj.* u-a-han 우아한, chŏm-jan-ŭn 점잖은.

gracious *adj.* (*merciful*) in-ja-han 인자한, cha-bi-ro-un 자비로운, (*courteous*) chŏng-jung-han 정중한.

grade n. (*degree*) tŭng-gŭp 등급, p'yŏng-jŏm 평점 ; (*form*) hak-gŭp 학급. —*v.* (*mark*) tŭng-gŭp-ŭl mae-gi-da 등급을 매기다.

gradual *adj.* chŏm-ch'a-jŏk-in 점차적인.

graduate *n.* cho-rŏp-saeng 졸업생. —*v.* cho-rŏp-ha-da 졸업하다, hak-wi-rŭl su-yŏ-ha-da 학위를 수여하다.

graduation *n.* cho-rŏp(-sik) 졸업(식).

graft *v.* chŏp-bu-ch'i-da 접붙이다. —*n.* chŏp-mok 접목.

grain *n.* ① kok-mul 곡물, nat-al 낟알. ② al-gaeng-i 알갱이. ③ kŭk-so-ryang 극소량. ④ (*temper*) ki-jil 기질.

grammar *n.* mun-bŏp 문법, ŏ-bŏp 어법.

grammatical *adj.* mun-bŏp(-sang)-ŭi 문법(상)의.

gramophone *n.* ch'uk-ŭm-gi 축음기. 「곡창.

granary *n.* kok-mul ch'ang-go 곡물 창고, kok-ch'ang

grand *adj.* ung-dae-han 웅대한, (*majestic*) tang-dang-han 당당한 ; ho-hwa-ro-un 호화로운.

grandchild *n.* son-ja 손자, son-nyŏ 손녀.

granddaughter *n.* son-nyŏ 손녀, son-ja-ddal 손자딸.

grandfather *n.* ha-ra-bŏ-ji 할아버지, cho-bu 조부.

grandmother *n.* hal-mŏ-ni 할머니, cho-mo 조모.

grandson *n.* son-ja 손자.

grandstand *n.* t'ŭk-byŏl kwal-lam-sŏk 특별 관람석.

granite *n.* hwa-gang-sŏk 화강석, ssuk-dol 쑥돌.

grant *v.* ① (*give*) chu-da 주다, su-yŏ-ha-da 수여하다. ② (*admit*) si-in-ha-da 시인하다, hŏ-ga-ha-da 허가하다.

grape *n.* p'o-do 포도 : ~ *sugar* p'o-do-dang 포도당.

grapevine *n.* p'o-do-dŏng-gul 포도덩굴.

grapple *v.* kkwak put-jap-da 꽉 붙잡다 ; (*fight*) kyŏk-t'u-ha-da 격투하다. —*n.* kyŏk-t'u 격투.

grasp *v.* ① kkwak chwi-da 꽉 쥐다. ② (*understand*) i-hae-ha-da 이해하다. —*n.* ① p'o-ch'ak 포착. ② (*power*) kwŏl-lyŏk 권력. ③ (*understanding*) i-hae

grasping *adj.* yok-sim-i man-ŭn 욕심이 많은. 「이해.

grass *n.* ① p'ul 풀, mok-ch'o 목초. ② (*meadow*) mok-jang 목장. ③ (*sod*) chan-di 잔디.

grasshopper *n.* me-ddu-gi 메뚜기, yŏ-ch'i 여치.

grassy *adj.* p'ul-i u-gŏ-jin 풀이 우거진, pul-ŭi 풀의.

grate *v.* mun-ji-rŭ-da 문지르다, kal-da 갈다.

grateful *adj.* ko-map-ge yŏ-gi-nŭn 고맙게 여기는 : *a ~ letter* kam-sa-ŭi p'yŏn-ji 감사의 편지. 「기쁘게 하다.」

gratify *v.* man-jok-si-k'i-da 만족시키다, ki-bbŭ-ge ha-da

gratitude *n.* kam-sa 감사, sa-ŭi 사의(謝意).

grave *n.* mu-dŏm 무덤, myo 묘. —*adj.* (*critical*) chung-dae-han 중대한, chang-jung-han 장중한.

gravel *n.* cha-gal 자갈. 「yŏ 정색하여.」

gravely *adv.* ŏm-suk-ha-ge 엄숙하게, chŏng-saek-ha-

gravestone *n.* myo-bi 묘비, pi-sŏk 비석.

graveyard *n.* myo-ji 묘지. 「yong 인력 작용.」

gravitation *n.* chung-ryŏk 중력(重力), il-lyŏk chak-

gravity *n.* ① chung-ryŏk 중력. ② il-lyŏk 인력 ; (*weight*) chung-ryang 중량.

gravy *n.* ko-gi kuk-mul 고기 국물.

graze *n.* (*cattle*) p'ul-ŭl ttŭt-ŏ-mŏk-da 풀을 뜯어먹다.

grease *v.* ki-rŭm 기름, chi-bang 지방, kŭ-ri-i-sŭ 그리 이스. —*v.* ki-rŭm-ŭl ch'i-da 기름을 치다.

great *adj.* k'ŭn 큰, wi-dae-han 위대한 ; (*numerous*) man-ŭn 많은 ; (*important*) chung-dae-han 중대한.

great-grandchild *n.* chŭng-son-ja 증손자.

great-grandfather *n.* chŭng-jo-bu 증조부.

great-grandmother *n.* chŭng-jo-mo 증조모. 「게.」

greatly *adv.* tae-dan-hi 대단히, mae-u 매우, k'ŭ-ge 크

greatness *n.* wi-dae-ham 위대함, kŏ-dae-ham 거대함.

greed *n.* yok-sim 욕심, t'am-yok 탐욕. 「nŭn 갈망하는.」

greedy *adj.* yok-sim-man-ŭn 욕심많은, kal-mang-ha-

green *adj.* ① ch'o-rok-saek-ŭi 초록색의, nok-saek-ŭi 녹색의. ② (*unripe*) sŏl-ik-ŭn 설익은. —*n.* ① ch'o-rok 초록, nok-saek 녹색. ② (*vegetables*) ch'ae-so 채소.

greenhorn *n.* p'ut-na-gi 풋나기, ch'o-sim-ja 초심자.

greenhouse *n.* on-sil 온실. 「da 영접하다.

greet *v.* in-sa-ha-da 인사하다, (*receive*) yŏng-jŏp-ha-

greeting *n.* in-sa 인사, (*pl.*) in-sa-jang 인사장.

grey·gray *n.* hoe-saek 회색. —*adj.* hoe-saek-ŭi 회
색의 ; (*dull*) u-jung-ch'ung-han 우중충한.

grief *n.* sŭl-p'ŭm 슬픔, pi-t'ong 비통, ko-noe 고뇌.

grieve *v.* sŏ-rŏ-wŏ-ha-da 서러워하다.

grill *n.* ① sŏk-soe 석쇠. ② ku-un ko-gi 구운 고기.

grim *adj.* ŏm-han 엄한, mu-sŏ-un 무서운.

grimace *n.* jji-p'u-rin ŏl-gul 찌푸린 얼굴. —*v.* ŏl-gul-
ŭl jji-p'u-ri-da 얼굴을 찌푸리다. 「히다.

grime *n.* ttae 때, mŏn-ji 먼지. —*v.* tŏ-rŏp-hi-da 더럽

grimly *adv.* ŏm-gyŏk-ha-ge 엄격하게.

grin *v.* sing-gŭt ut-da 싱긋 웃다.

grind *v.* ppa-t'a 빻다, kal-da 갈다.

grindstone *n.* maet-dol 맷돌.

grip *v.* kkwak put-jap-da 꽉 붙잡다.
—*n.* p'a-ak 파악, i-hae 이해.

groan *n.* sin-ŭm-so-ri 신음소리. —*v.*
sin-ŭm-ha-da 신음하다.

[maet-dol]

grocer *n.* sik-ryo-p'um chang-su 식료품 장수.

groceries *n.* sik-ryo-p'um 식료품, sik-p'um-jŏm 식품점.

groom *n.* ① sil-lang 신랑. ② (*footman*) ma-bu 마부.

grope *v.* son-ŭ-ro tŏ-dŭm-da 손으로 더듬다.

gross *adj.* (*big*) k'ŭn 큰 ; (*total*) ch'ong-gye-ŭi 총계의.

grotesque *adj.* koe-sang-han 괴상한, u-sŭ-un 우스운.

ground *n.* ttang 땅 ; (*play*) un-dong-jang 운동장.

ground floor il-ch'ŭng 일층.

group *n.* mu-ri 무리, chip-dan 집단. —*v.* ① tte-rŭl
chit-da 떼를 짓다. ② (*classify*) pul-lyu-ha-da 분류하
「다.

grove *n.* chak-ŭn sup 작은 숲, su-p'ul 수풀.

grow *v.* cha-ra-da 자라다 ; (*cultivate*) chae-bae-ha-da 재배하다 ; (*become*) ha-ge toe-da 하게 되다.

growl *v.* ŭ-rŭ-rŏng-gŏ-ri-da 으르렁거리다, t'u-dŏl-gŏ-ri-da 투덜거리다. —*n.* ŭ-rŭ-rŏng-gŏ-ri-nŭn so-ri 으르렁 거리는 소리. 「sŏng-in 성인.

grown-up *adj.* sŏng-jang-han 성장한. —*n.* ŏ-rŭn 어른,

growth *n.* ① sŏng-jang 성장, pal-jŏn 발전. ② (*cultivation*) chae-bae 재배. ③ chong-yang 종양(腫瘍).

grub *n.* yu-ch'ung 유충, kum-beng-i 굼벵이.

grudge *n.* wŏn-han 원한, ak-ŭi 악의. —*v.* ha-go sip-ji an-t'a 하고 싶지 않다, a-gga-wa-ha-da 아까와하다.

gruel *n.* (mul-gŭn) chuk (묽은) 죽. 「불평하다.

grumble *v.* t'u-dŏl-dae-da 투덜대다, pul-p'yŏng-ha-da

grunt *v.* kkul-ggul-gŏ-ri-da 꿀꿀거리다 ; p'u-nyŏm-ha-da 푸념하다. —*n.* pul-p'yŏng 불평.

guarantee *v.* po-jŭng-ha-da 보증하다. —*n.* po-jŭng 보증.

guarantor *n.* po-jŭng-in 보증인, tam-bo-in 담보인.

guard *n.* p'a-su-gun 파수군. su-wi 수위 ; (*conductor*) ch'a-jang 차장. —*v.* p'a-su-bo-da 파수보다, pang-wi-ha-da 방위하다. 「인.

guardian *n.* po-ho-ja 보호자 ; (*legal*) hu-gyŏn-in 후견

guess *v.* ch'u-ch'ŭk-ha-da 추측하다, (*Am.*) (*think*) saeng-gak-ha-da 생각하다. —*n.* ch'u-ch'ŭk 추측.

guest *n.* son-nim 손님, nae-bin 내빈, kaek 객(客).

guide *n.* an-nae-ja 안내자, ka-i-dŭ 가이드, p'yŏl-lam 편람. —*v.* an-nae-ha-da 안내하다, in-do-ha-da 인도하

guidebook *n.* yŏ-haeng an-nae-sŏ 여행 안내서. 「다.

g(u)ild *n.* kil-dŭ 길드, tong-ŏp cho-hap 동업 조합.

guilt *n.* choe 죄, yu-joe 유죄, pŏm-joe-haeng-wi 범죄

guilty *adj.* yu-joe-ŭi 유죄의, choe-it-nŭn 죄있는. 「행위.

guise *n.* (*appearance*) kŏt-bo-gi 겉보기, oe-gwan 외관 ; (*disguise*) ka-jang 가장, pyŏn-jang 변장.

gulf *n.* man 만(灣). —*v.* sam-k'i-da 삼키다.

gull *n.* kal-mae-gi 갈매기 ; (*dupe*) ŏl-gan-i 얼간이, sa-git-gun 사깃군. —*v.* sok-i-da 속이다.

gum *n.* ① ko-mu-p'ul 고무풀, ko'mu 고무 : ~*boots* ko-mu-sin 고무신. ② (*of the mouth*) it-mom 잇몸 ; (*o the eye*) nun-ggop 눈꼽. ③(*chewing* ~) kkŏm 껌.

gun *n.* ch'ong 총 : *air* ~ kong-gi-ch'ong 공기총/*squirt* ~ mul-ch'ong 물총.

gunner *n.* p'o-su 포수, ch'ong-sa-nyang-gun 총사냥군.

gunpowder *n.* hwa-yak 화약.

gush *v.* ssot-a-jyŏ na-o-da 쏟아져 나오다, nae-bbum-da 내뿜다. —*n.* so-sa-na-om 솟아나옴, pun-ch'ul 분출.

gust *n.* tol-p'ung 돌풍, chil-p'ung 질풍 ; (*outburst*) kyŏk-bal 격발, tol-bal 돌발. 「ha-su-do 하수도.

gutter *n.* ① (*groove*) hom-t'ong 홈통. ② (*ditch*)

guttural *adj.* mok-gu-mŏng-ŭi 목구멍의, mok-gu-mŏng so-ri-ŭi 목구멍 소리의.

gymnasium *n.* ch'e-yuk-gwan 체육관.

gymnastics *n.* ch'e-jo 체조, ch'e-yuk 체육.

gyroscope *n.* hoe-jŏn-ŭi 회전의(回轉儀), cha-i-ro-sŭ-k'o-u-p'ŭ 자이로스코우프.

---◄ **H** ►---

habit *n.* pŏ-rŭt 버릇, sŭp-gwan 습관, sŭp-sŏng 습성.

habitable *adj.* sŭp-gwan-jŏk-in 습관적인 ; sang-sŭp-jŏk-in 상습적인 ; (*usual*) p'yŏng-so-ŭi 평소의.

hack *v.* cha-rŭ-da 자르다, nan-do-jil-ha-da 난도질하다.

haggard *adj.* yŏ-win 여윈, su-ch'ŏk-han 수척한.

hail *n.* ssa-rak-nun 싸락눈. —*v.* ① ssa-rak-nun-i nae-ri-da 싸락눈이 내리다. ② (*call*) pu-rŭ-da 부르다.

hair *n.* t'ŏl 털, mŏ-ri-t'ŏl 머리털, tu-bal 두발.

hairbrush *n.* mŏ-ri-sol 머리솔.

hairdresser *n.* i-bal-sa 이발사, mi-yong-sa 미용사.

hale *adj.* kŏn-jang-han 건장한, t'ŭn-t'ŭn-han 튼튼한.

half *n. & adj.* pan 반, chŏl-ban(-ŭi) 절반(의).

half brother pae-da-rŭn hyŏng-je 배다른 형제, ŭi-but hyŏng-je 의붓 형제.   「han 미지근한.

half-hearted *adj.* yŏ-rŭi-ŏp-nŭn 열의없는, mi-ji-gŭn-

half holiday pan-gong-il 반공일, pan-hyu-il 반휴일.

half-mast *n.* pan-gi-ŭi wi-ch'i 반기(半旗)의 위치 : *a flag at* ~ pan-gi 반기, cho-gi 조기(吊旗).

half-moon *n.* pan-dal 반달.   「cha-mae 의붓 자매.

half sister pae-da-rŭn cha-mae 배다른 자매, ŭi-but

halfway *adj. & adv.* chung-do-ŭi[-e-sŏ] 중도의[에서].

half-wit *n.* (*fool*) pan-p'yŏn 반편, ŏl-gan-i 얼간이.

hall *n.* (*auditorium*) kang-dang 강당 ; (*corridor*) pok-do 복도, t'ong-ro 통로 : *city* ~ si-ch'ŏng 시청/ *music* ~ ŭm-ak-dang 음악당.

hallo(a) *int.* yŏ-bo 여보, i-rŏn 이런.

hallow *v.* (*make holy*) sin-sŏng-ha-ge ha-da 신성하게 하다, sin-e-ge pa-ch'i-da 신에게 바치다.

halo *n.* tal[hae]-mu-ri 달[해]무리, hu-gwang 후광.

halt *v.* (*army*) chu-dun-ha-da 주둔하다 ; (*stop*) mŏm-ch'u-da 멈추다. —*n.* chŏng-ji 정지 : *Company,* ~! Chung-dae sŏ 중대 서 !

halve *v.* i-dŭng-bun-ha-da 이등분하다, pan-ssik na-nu-

ham *n.* haem 햄.   ⌊da 반씩 나누다.

hamlet *n.* chak-ŭn ma-ŭl 작은 마을, ch'ol-lak 촌락.

hammer *n.* mang-ch'i 망치, hae-mŏ 해머. —*v.* mang-ch'i-jil-ha-da 망치질하다.   「하다.

hamper *n.* chok-swae 족쇄. —*v.* pang-hae-ha-da 방해

hand *n.* ① (*of the body*) son 손. ② (*laborer*) il-son 일손, (*skill*) som-ssi 솜씨. ③ (*timepiece*) si-gye-ba-nŭl 시계바늘. —v. kŏn-ne-ju-da 건네주다.

handbag n. son-ga-bang 손가방, haen-dŭ-baek 핸드백.

handbook n. p'yŏl-lam 편람, an-nae-sŏ 안내서.

handcart n. chim-su-re 짐수레, son-su-re 손수레.

handcuff n. su-gap 수갑, soe-go-rang 쇠고랑.

handful n. han chum 한 줌 ; so-su 소수, so-ryang 소량: *a ~ of children* so-su-ŭi a-i-dŭl 소수의 아이들.

handicap n. pul-ri-han cho-gŏn 불리한 조건, chang-ae 장애, haen-di-k'aep 핸디캡.

handicraft n. su-ye 수예, su-se-gong 수세공(手細工).

handily adv. p'yŏl-li-ha-ge 편리하게, kyo-myo-ha-ge 교묘하게.

handkerchief n. son-su-gŏn 손수건.

handle n. son-jap-i 손잡이, haen-dŭl 핸들. —v. cho-jong-ha-da 조종하다, ta-ru-da 다루다 ; mae-mae-ha-da 매매하다.

handshake n. ak-su 악수.

handsome adj. chal saeng-gin 잘 생긴, tang-dang-han 당당한 ; (*generous*) a-ryang-it-nŭn 아량있는.

handy adj. p'yŏl-li-han 편리한, kan-p'yŏn-han 간편한.

hang v. kŏl-da 걸다, mae-dal-da 매달다 ; (*remain in suspense*) mang-sŏ-ri-da 망설이다.

hangar n. kyŏk-nap-go 격납고, ch'a-go 차고.

Hangul n. (*Korean*) han-gŭl 한글.

hanker v. kal-mang[yŏl-mang]-ha-da 갈망[열망]하다.

happen v. i-rŏ-na-da 일어나다, saeng-gi-da 생기다, u-yŏn-hi …ha-da 우연히 …하다.

happiness n. haeng-bok 행복, haeng-un 행운.

happy adj. haeng-bok-han 행복한, ki-bbŭn 기쁜 ; (*lucky*) ta-haeng-han 다행한. 「ha-da 침공하다.

harass v. koe-rop-hi-da 괴롭히다 ; (*raid*) ch'im-gong-

harbo(u)r n. hang-gu 항구, (*refuge*) p'i-nan-ch'ŏ 피난처. —v. sum-gi-da 숨기다.

hard adj. (*solid*) tan-dan-han 단단한 ; (*difficult*) ŏ-ryŏ-un 어려운. —*adv.* (*earnestly*) yŏl-sim-hi 열심히.

hardly *adv.* kŏ-ŭi ···a-ni-da 거의 ···아니다.

hardship *n.* ko-ch'o 고초, ko-nan 고난, hak-dae 학대.

hardware *n.* ch'ŏl-mul 철물, ha-a-dŭ-we-ŏ 하아드웨어.

hardworking *adj.* kŭn-myŏn-han 근면한.

hardy *adj.* t'ŭn-t'ŭn-han 튼튼한, nae-gu-ryŏk-i it-nŭn 내구력이 있는 ; (*daring*) tae-dam-han 대담한.

hare *n.* t'o-ggi 토끼, san-t'o-ggi 산토끼.

hark *v.* tŭt-da 듣다, kwi-rŭl ki-u-ri-da 귀를 기울이다.

harlot *n.* mae-ch'un-bu 매춘부, ch'ang-bu 창부.

harm *n.* hae 해, son-hae 손해, son-sang 손상. —*v.* hae-ch'i-da 해치다, son-sang-ha-da 손상하다.

harmony *n.* cho-hwa 조화 ; (*music*) hwa-sŏng 화성.

harness *n.* (*horse equipment*) ma-gu 마구.

harp *n.* ha-a-p'ŭ 하아프 ; (*Korean*) kŏ-mun-go 거문고.

harrow *n.* ① ssŏ-re 써레, —*v.* ssŏ-re-jil-ha-da 써레질하다. ② (*torment*) mot-sal-ge kul-da 못살게 굴다.

harsh *adj.* kŏ-ch'in 거친 ; ka-hok-han 가혹한 ; (*discordant*) kwi-e kŏ-sŭl-ri-nŭn 귀에 거슬리는.

harshly *adv.* kŏ-ch'il-ge 거칠게, ŏm-ha-ge 엄하게.

hart *n.* (*stag*) su-sa-sŭm 수사슴.

harvest *n.* su-hwak 수확 ; (*result*) kyŏl-gwa 결과 : *good* ~ p'ung-nyŏn 풍년/*poor* ~ hyung-nyŏn 흉년.

haste *n.* sŏ-du-rŭm 서두름, kyŏng-sol 경솔.

hasten *v.* sŏ-du-rŭ-da 서두르다, (*speed up*) mo-ra-se-u-da 몰아세우다, chae-ch'ok-ha-da 재촉하다.

hastily *adv.* pa-bbi 바삐, cho-gŭp-hi 조급히.

hasty *adj.* kŭp-han 급한, sŏng-gŭp-han 성급한.

hat *n.* mo-ja 모자 : *My* ~! Ŏ-mŏ-na! 어머나 !

hatch *n.* ① (*ships*) sŭng-gang-gu 승강구. ② (*incubation*) pu-hwa 부화. —*v.* pu-hwa-ha-da 부화하다 ; (*contrive*) ko-an-ha-da 고안하다.

hatchet *n.* son-do-ggi 손도끼.

hate *v.* mi-wǒ-ha-da 미워하다, si-rǒ-ha-da 싫어하다.

hateful *adj.* mi-un 미운, chi-gyǒ-un 지겨운.

hatred *n.* mi-um 미움, chŭng-o 증오, hyǒm-o 혐오.

haughty *adj.* kyo-man-han 교만한, o-man-han 오만한:
  a ~ *air* o-man-han t'ae-do 오만한 태도.

haul *v.* chap-a-ggŭl-da 잡아끌다, kkŭ-rǒ-dang-gi-da

haunch *n.* ǒng-dǒng-i 엉덩이.   ⌐끌어당기다.

haunt *v.* cha-ju tŭ-na-dŭl-da 자주 드나들다, tal-ra-but-
  da 달라붙다. —*n.* cha-ju ta-ni-nŭn kot 자주 다니는 곳.

have *v.* (*possess*) ka-ji-da 가지다 ; (*eat*) mŏk-da 먹다 ;
  (*drink*) ma-si-da 마시다 ; (*obtain*) ŏt-da 얻다 ;(*wear*)
  ip-da 입다.

haven *n.* hang-gu 항구 ; (*shelter*) p'i-nan-ch'ǒ 피난처.

havoc *n.* p'a-goe 파괴, hwang-p'ye 황폐.

hawk *n.* mae 매(鷹).

hay *n.* kǒn-ch'o 건초, kkol 꼴.   「건초더미.

haystack *n.* kǒn-ch'o ka-ri 건초 가리, kǒn-ch'o-dǒ-mi

hazard *n.* wi-hǒm 위험, mo-hǒm 모험, (*chance*) un
  운. —*v.* mo-hǒm-ŭl ha-da 모험을 하다.

haze *n.* a-ji-raeng-i 아지랭이, an-gae 안개.

hazel *n.* kae-am(-na-mu) 개암(나무) ; (*light brown*)
  tam-gal-saek 담갈색.   「ssi 흐린 날씨.

hazy *adj.* an-gae kkin 안개 낀 : ~ *weather* hŭ-rin nal-

H-bomb *n.* su-so-p'ok-t'an 수소폭탄, su-so-t'an 수소탄.

he *pron.* kŭ-nŭn[-ga] 그는[가], chǒ-sa-ram-ŭn[-i] 저
  사람은[이]. —*n.* nam-ja 남자, su-k'ŏt 수컷.

head *n.* mǒ-ri 머리, (*intellect*) tu-noe 두뇌, chi-ryŏk
  지력 ; (*chief*) su-ryǒng 수령, chang 장(長).

headache *n.* tu-t'ong 두통, tu-t'ong-gǒ-ri 두통거리.

headlight *n.* he-dŭ-ra-i-t'ŭ 헤드라이트, chang-dŭng 장

headline *n.* p'yo-je 표제, che-mok 제목.   ⌐등(橙燈).

headlong *adv.* kŏ·ggu·ro 거꾸로, kon·du·bak·i·ro 곤두 박이로 ; (*rashly*) mu·t'ŏk·dae·go 무턱대고.

head office pon·jŏm 본점, pon·sa 본사. 「화기.

headphone *n.* mŏ·ri·e kŏ·nŭn su·hwa·gi 머리에 거는 수

headquarters *n.* pon·bu 본부, sa·ryŏng·bu 사령부: *general* ~ ch'ong·sa·ryŏng·bu 총사령부.

headstrong *adj.* wan·go·han 완고한, ko·jip sen 고집 센.

heal *v.* ① (*cure*) ko·ch'i·da 고치다. ② (*appease*) hwa·hae·si·k'i·da 화해시키다, mu·ma·ha·da 무마하다.

health *n.* ① kŏn·gang 건강. ② wi·saeng 위생. 「한.

healthy *adj.* kŏn·gang·han 건강한, t'ŭn·t'ŭn·han 튼튼

heap *n.* ① tŏ·mi 더미, mu·dŏ·gi 무더기. ② (*a lot*) ta·ryang 다량, ta·su 다수. —*v.* ssa·a·ol·ri·da 쌓아올리다.

hear *v.* tŭt·da 듣다 ; (*law*) sim·mun·ha·da 심문하다.

hearer *n.* ch'ŏng·ch'wi·ja 청취자, pang·ch'ŏng·in 방청

hearing *n.* tŭt·gi 듣기, ch'ŏng·ch'wi 청취. 「인.

hearse *n.* yŏng·gu·ch'a 영구차 ; kwan 관.

heart *n.* sim·jang 심장, (*mind*) ma·ŭm 마음.

heartbroken *adj.* ae·ggŭn·nŭn 애끊는, pi·t'an·e cham·gin 비탄에 잠긴. 「불평.

heartburn *n.* ① ka·sŭm·a·ri 가슴앓이. ② pul·p'yŏng

heart disease sim·jang·byŏng 심장병.

heart failure sim·jang·ma·bi 심장마비.

hearth *n.* nal·lo 난로 ; (*fireside*) no·byŏn 노변.

heartily *adv.* chin·sim·ŭ·ro 진심으로, mae·u 매우.

heartless *adj.* ① mu·jŏng·han 무정한, mo·rin·jŏng·han 몰인정한. ② yong·gi·ga ŏp·nŭn 용기가 없는.

hearty *adj.* ① ma·ŭm·e·sŏ u·rŏ·nan 마음에서 우러난 ; ch'in·jŏl·han 친절한. ② (*robust*) ki·un·ch'an 기운찬.

heat *n.* ① yŏl 열(熱) ; on·do 온도. ② (*anger*) kyŏk·no 격노. ③ (*zeal*) yŏl·sim 열심. —*v.* te·u·da 데우다, ttŭ·gŏp·ge ha·da 뜨겁게 하다.

heater *n.* nan·bang·jang·ch'i 난방장치, hi·i·t'ŏ 히이터.

heath *n.* hi·i·dŭ 히이드 ; (*wilderness*) hwang·ya 황야.

heathen *adj.* (*pagan*) i·gyo(·do)·ŭi 이교(도)의. —*n.* i·gyo·do 이교도, i·bang·in 이방인.

heave *v.* ① (*lift*) tŭ·rŏ·ol·ri·da 들어올리다. ② (*throw*) tŏn·ji·da 던지다. ③ (*pull*) chap·a·ggŭl·da 잡아끌다.

heaven *n.* ha·nŭl 하늘, ch'ŏn·guk 천국.

heavenly *adj.* ha·nŭl·ŭi 하늘의, ch'ŏl·lae·ŭi 천래의 ; (*holy*) sin·sŏng·han 신성한, kŏ·ruk·han 거룩한.

heavily *adv.* mu·gŏp·ge 무겁게 ; sim·ha·ge 심하게.

heavy *adj.* mu·gŏ·un 무거운 ; (*violent*) maeng·ryŏl·han 맹렬한 : *a ~ rain* p'ok·u 폭우. 「장벽.

hedge *n.* san·ul·t'a·ri 산울타리 ; (*barrier*) chang·byŏk

heed *v.* chu·ŭi·ha·da 주의하다, cho·sim·ha·da 조심하다.

heedful *adj.* cho·sim·sŏng·it·nŭn 조심성있는, chu·ŭi·gi·p'ŭn 주의깊은, cho·sim·ha·nŭn 조심하는.

heel *n.* twi·ggum·ch'i 뒤꿈치, kup 굽, twi·ch'uk 뒤축.

heifer *n.* am·song·a·ji 암송아지.

height *n.* ① no·p'i 높이 ; (*stature*) k'i 키. ② ko·ji 고지.

heighten *v.* no·p'i·da 높이다.

heir *n.* sang·sok·in 상속인, hu·gye·ja 후계자. 「동산.

heirloom *n.* ka·bo 가보, sang·jŏn tong·san 상전(相傳)

heiress *n.* yŏ·ja sang·sok·in 여자 상속인, yŏ·ja hu·gye-

helicopter *n.* hel·ri·k'op·t'ŏ 헬리콥터. 「ja 여자 후계자.

hell *n.* chi·ok 지옥, chŏ·sŭng 저승, hwang·ch'ŏn 황천.

hello *int.* (*telephone*) yŏ·bo·se·yo 여보세요 ; (*greeting*) an·nyŏng·ha·sip·ni·gga 안녕하십니까.

helm *n.* (*of ship*) k'i (배의) 키, cho·t'a·gi 조타기. —*v.* k'i·rŭl cho·jong·ha·da 키를 조종하다.

helmet *n.* ch'ŏl·mo 철모, t'u·gu 투구, hel·met 헬멧.

help *n.* to·um 도움, (*remedy*) ku·je·ch'aek 구제책. —*v.* top·da 돕다, to·wa·ju·da 도와주다.

helper *n*. top-nŭn sa-ram 돕는 사람, cho-ryŏk-ja 조력자.

helpful *adj*. to-um-i toe-nŭn 도움이 되는, (*useful*) yu-yong-han 유용한, p'yŏl-li-han 편리한.

helpless *adj*. ŏ-jji-hal su ŏp-nŭn 어찌할 수 없는.

hem *n*. (*cloth*) ka-jang-ja-ri 가장자리, ot-dan 옷단.

hemisphere *n*. pan-gu 반구(半球).

hemp *n*. sam 삼, tae-ma 대마.

hen *n*. am-t'ak 암탉, (*fowl*) am-k'ŏt 암컷.

hence *adv*. (*from now*) i-je-bu-t'ŏ 이제부터, yŏ-gi-sŏ-bu-t'ŏ 여기서부터 ; (*therefore*) kŭ-rŏ-mŭ-ro 그러므로.

henchman *n*. ① ch'u-jong-ja 추종자. ② hu-wŏn-ja 후원

hencoop *n*. tak-jang 닭장, tung-u-ri 둥우리.   ⌊자.

henhouse *n*. tak-jang 닭장.

her *pron*. kŭ yŏ-ja-ŭi〔rŭl, e-ge〕그 여자의〔를, 에게〕.

herald *n*. chŏn-dal-ja 전달자 ; (*harbinger*) sŏn-gu-ja 선구자. —*v*. (*announce*) al-ri-da 알리다.

herb *n*. ch'o-bon 초본(草本) : *a medicinal* ~ yak-ch'o 약초/*a poisonous* ~ tok-ch'o 독초.

herd *n*. ① chim-sŭng-ŭi tte 짐승의 떼. ② (*mob*) kun-jung 군중. ③ (*rabble*) ha-ch'ŭng-min 하층민.

herdsman *n*. mok-dong 목동, mok-ja 목자(牧者).

here *adv*. yŏ-gi-e 여기에, i-go-se 이곳에.

hereafter *adv*. chi-gŭm-bu-t'ŏ 지금부터, kŭm-hu 금후.

heredity *n*. yu-jŏn 유전.

heresy *n*. i-gyo 이교, i-dan 이단 ; i-ron 이론(異論).

heritage *n*. sang-sok chae-san 상속 재산, yu-san 유산.

hermit *n*. ŭn-dun-ja 은둔자(隱遁者), ŭn-ja 은자. 「공.

hero *n*. ① yŏng-ung 영웅. ② (*story*) chu-in-gong 주인

heroic *adj*. yŏng-ung-jŏk-in 영웅적인, yong-gam-han 용감한

heroine *n*. yŏ-jang-bu 여장부, yŏ-gŏl 여걸. ⌊용감한.

heron *n*. wae-ga-ri 왜가리.

herring *n*. ch'ŏng-ŏ 청어.

hers *pron.* kŭ yŏ-ja-ŭi kŏt 그 여자의 것.

herself *pron.* kŭ yŏ-ja cha-sin 그 여자 자신.

hesitate *v.* chu-jŏ-ha-da 주저하다, mang-sŏ-ri-da 망설
이다, kyŏl-dan-ŭl mot nae-ri-da 결단을 못 내리다.

hew *v.* (*cut*) pe-da 베다, (*chop*) jjik-da 찍다, ssŏl-da
hey *int.* i-bwa 이봐, ŏ-i 어이 ; ya-a 야아. ⌐썰다.

hiccough·hiccup *n.* ttal-gguk-jil 딸꾹질.

hide *v.* kam-ch'u-da 감추다, sum-da 숨다. —*n.* ka-
juk 가죽, p'i-hyŏk 피혁.

hideous *adj.* mu-si-mu-si-han 무시무시한, mip-sal-sŭ-
rŏ-un 밉살스러운.

high *adj.* no-p'ŭn 높은 ; ko-gŭp-ŭi 고급의 ; (*intense*)
kang-ryŏl-han 강렬한 : *a ~ words* kwa-gyŏk-han
mal 과격한 말. —*adv.* (*intensely*) sim-ha-ge 심하게 ;
(*luxuriously*) sa-ch'i-sŭ-rŏp-ge 사치스럽게.

highland *n.* ko-ji 고지, san-gan chi-yŏk 산간 지역.

highly *adv.* no-p'i 높이, mae-u 매우.

highway *n.* kan-sŏn to-ro 간선 도로, kong-ro 공로.

hijack *v.* kong-jung nap-ch'i-ha-da 공중 납치하다.

hike *n.* ① to-bo yŏ-haeng 도보 여행. ② (*increase*) in-
sang 인상. —*v.* kku-rŏ-ol-ri-da 끌어올리다.

hill *n.* ŏn-dŏk 언덕, chak-ŭn san 작은 산.

him *pron.* kŭ-rŭl 그를, kŭ-e-ge 그에게.

himself *pron.* kŭ cha-sin 그 자신. ⌐암사슴.

hind *adj.* twi-jjok-ŭi 뒤쪽의. —*n.* (*doe*) am-sa-sŭm

hinder *adj.* twi-ŭi 뒤의, hu-bang-ŭi 후방의. —*v.* pang-
hindrance *n.* pang-hae 방해. ⌐hae-ha-da 방해하다.

hinge *n.* tol-jjŏ-gwi 돌쩌귀, kyŏng-ch'ŏp 경첩. —*v.*
(*on*) …yŏ-ha-e tal-ryŏ-it-da …여하에 달려있다.

hint *n.* am-si 암시. —*v.* am-si-rŭl chu-da 암시를 주다.

hip *n.* ŏng-dŏng-i 엉덩이, kung-dung-i 궁둥이.

hire *n.* ko-yong 고용 ; im-dae 임대(賃貸) ; sak 삯. —*v.*

(engage) ko-yong-ha-da 고용하다.

his *pron.* kŭ-ŭi 그의. 「nae-da 쉿 소리 내다.

hiss *n.* swit ha-nŭn so-ri 쉿 하는 소리. —*v.* swit so-ri

historian *n.* yŏk-sa-ga 역사가, sa-hak-ja 사학자.

historic *adj.* yŏk-sa-sang yu-myŏng-han 역사상 유명한.

historical *adj.* yŏk-sa-ŭi 역사의, sa-hak-ŭi 사학(史學)의.

history *n.* ① yŏk-sa 역사. ② kyŏng-ryŏk 경력, nae-ryŏk 내력 : *one's personal* ~ i-ryŏk-sŏ 이력서. 「하다.

hit *v.* *(strike)* ch'i-da 치다, myŏng-jung-ha-da 명중

hitch *v.* ① hwaek um-jik-i-da 홱 움직이다. ② *(tie)* mae-da 매다. ③ *(key)* kŏl-da 걸다.

hither *adv.* i-jjok-ŭ-ro 이쪽으로. —*adj.* i-jjok-ŭi 이쪽의.

hitherto *adv.* yŏ-t'ae-gga-ji 여태까지.

hive *n.* pŏl-jip 벌집, pŏl-t'ong 벌통.

hives *n.* tu-dŭ-rŏ-gi 두드러기.

hoard *n.* chŏ-jang 저장. —*v.* chŏ-jang-ha-da 저장하다.

hoarse *adj.* mok-swin 목쉰, mok-swin so-ri-ŭi 목쉰 소리의, *(rough)* kwi-e kŏ-sŭl-ri-nŭn 귀에 거슬리는.

hoary *adj.* *(white)* ha-yan 하얀 ; paek-bal-ŭi 백발의.

hobble *v.* chŏl-rŭm-gŏ-ri-da 절름거리다.

hobby *n.* ① *(taste)* ch'wi-mi 취미, to-rak 도락. ② *(hobbyhorse)* mok-ma 목마.

hockey *n.* ha-k'i 하키 : *ice* ~ a-i-sŭ ha-k'i 아이스 하키.

hoe *n.* kwaeng-i 괭이. —*v.* kwaeng-i-jil-ha-da 괭이질 하다 : ~ *up weeds* chap-ch'o-rŭl p'a-he-ch'i-da 잡초 를 파헤치다. ㄴ

hog *n.* *(pig)* twae-ji 돼지.

hoist *v.* no-p'i ol-ri-da 높이 올리다, *(lift up)* tŭ-rŏ-ol-ri-da 들어올리다. —*n.* *(crane)* ki-jung-gi 기중기.

hold *v.* ① *(keep)* chi-ni-da 지니다. ② *(open)* kae-ch'oe-ha-da 개최하다. ③ *(grasp)* put-jap-da 붙잡다. ④ *(support)* chi-t'aeng-ha-da 지탱하다. —*n.* ① *(grasp)* p'o-ch'ak 포착. ② *(ship)* sŏn-ch'ang 선창.

holder *n.* ① (*person*) po-yu-ja 보유자. ② (*thing*) pat-ch'i-nŭn mul-gŏn 받치는 물건, yong-gi 용기(容器).
hole *n.* ku-mŏng 구멍.
holiday *n.* hyu-il 휴일, ch'uk-je-il 축제일.
holiness *n.* sin-sŏng-ham 신성함.
Holiness Church sŏng-gyo-hoe-p'a 성교회파(聖敎會派).
hollow *n.* u-muk-han kot 우묵한 곳. —*adj.* (*empty*) pin 빈, (*sunken*) o-mok-hi tŭ-rŏ-gan 오목히 들어간. —*v.* (*excavate*) to-ryŏ-nae-da 도려내다.
hollyhock *n.* chŏp-si-ggot 접시꽃.
holy *adj.* sin-sŏng-han 신성한, kŏ-ruk-han 거룩한.
homage *n.* chŏn-gyŏng 존경, kyŏng-ŭi 경의(敬意): *pay* ~ *to* kyŏng-ŭi-rŭl p'yo-ha-da 경의를 표하다.
home *n.* ka-jŏng 가정 ; (*native land*) pon-guk 본국.
homeland *n.* cha-gi na-ra 자기 나라, ko-guk 고국(故國).
homely *adj.* su-su-han 수수한 ; ka-jŏng-jŏk-in 가정적인 ; hŭn-hi it-nŭn 흔히 있는. 「hyang-ŭi 망향의.
homesick *adj.* hyang-su-byŏng-ŭi 향수병의, mang-
homesickness *n.* hyang-su 향수(鄕愁). 「p'ŏn 호움스펀.
homespun *adj.* son-ŭ-ro jjan 손으로 짠. —*n.* ho-um-sŭ-
homework *n.* ① suk-je 숙제. ② ka-nae kong-ŏp 가내
homicide *n.* sa-rin(-bŏm) 살인(범). 「공업.
hone *n.* sut-dol 숫돌. —*v.* sut-dol-ro kal-da 숫돌로 갈다.
honest *adj.* chŏng-jik-han 정직한, sŏng-sil-han 성실한; (*legitimate*) chŏng-dang-han 정당한.
honesty *n.* chŏng-jik 정직, song-sil 성실.
honey *n.* ① kkul 꿀. ② (*darling*) ae-in 애인.
honeycomb *n.* pŏl-jip 벌집. 「신혼 여행.
honeymoon *n.* mil-wŏl 밀월 : ~ *trip* sin-hon yŏ-haeng
hono(u)r *n.* ① myŏng-ye 명예, (*esteem*) kyŏng-ŭi 경의. ② (*pl.*) hun-jang 훈장. ③ (*top grade*) u-dŭng 우등. —*v.* chon-gyŏng-ha-da 존경하다.

honorable *adj.* chon-gyŏng-hal man-han 존경할 만한.

hood *n.* tu-gŏn 두건, tŏp-gae 덮개.

hoof *n.* pal-gup 발굽, mal pal-gup 말 발굽 : *a cloven* ~ kal-ra-jin pal-gup 갈라진 발굽.

hook *n.* kal-go-ri 갈고리, huk 훅, (*for fishing*) nak-si-ba-nŭl 낚시바늘. —*v.* ku-bu-rŏ-ji-da 구부러지다, kal-go-ri-ro kŏl-da 갈고리로 걸다.

hoop *n.* t'e 테, soe-t'e 쇠테 ; (*plaything*) kul-rŏng-soe 굴렁쇠, hu-u-p'ŭ 후우프.

hop *v.* ① kkang-ch'ong-ggang-ch'ong ttwi-da 깡총깡총 뛰다. ② (*jump on one leg*) han-bal-ro ttwi-da 한 발로 뛰다. —*n.* ang-gam-jil 앙감질.

hope *n.* hŭi-mang 희망, so-mang 소망. —*v.* pa-ra-da 바라다, hŭi-mang-ha-da 희망하다. 「희망에 찬.

hopeful *adj.* yu-mang-han 유망한, hŭi-mang-e ch'an

hopeless *adj.* hŭi-mang-i ŏp-nŭn 희망이 없는. 「선.

horizon *n.* chi-p'yŏng-sŏn 지평선, su-p'yŏng-sŏn 수평

horizontal *adj.* su-p'yŏng-ŭi 수평의, (*level*) p'yŏng-p'yŏng-han 평평한 : ~ *bar* ch'ŏl-bong 철봉.

hormone *n.* ho-rŭ-mon 호르몬. 「호른.

horn *n.* ① ppul 뿔. ② (*bugle*) na-p'al 나팔, ho-rŭn

horrible *adj.* kkŭm-jjik-han 끔찍한, mu-sŏ-un 무서운.

horrid *adj.* mu-si-mu-si-han 무시무시한, chin-jŏ-ri-na-nŭn 진저리나는.

horrify *v.* so-rŭm-ggi-ch'i-ge ha-da 소름끼치게 하다.

horror *n.* kong-p'o 공포, chŏn-yul 전율.

horse *n.* mal 말 : ~ *opera* sŏ-bu-gŭk 서부극.

horse chestnut ma-ro-ni-e 마로니에.

horsefly *n.* mal-p'a-ri 말파리, tŭng-e 등에.

horseman *n.* ki-su 기수, sŭng-ma-ja 승마자.

horsepower *n.* ma-ryŏk 마력(馬力).

horse race kyŏng-ma 경마.

horseshoe *n.* p'yŏn-ja 편자, che-ch'ŏl 제철.
horticulture *n.* wŏn-ye 원예.　　　　「mal 긴양말.
hose *n.* ① ho-o-sŭ 호오스. ② (*stockings*) kin-yang-
hospitable *adj.* ① tae-u-ga cho-ŭn 대우가 좋은, (*gen-*
erous) hu-dae-ha-nŭn 후대하는. ② ho-ŭi-jŏk-in 호의
hospital *n.* (chong-hap) pyŏng-wŏn (종합) 병원. ⌊적인.
hospitality *n.* hwan-dae 환대, hu-dae 후대.
host *n.* ① chu-in 주인. ② (*majority*) ta-su 다수.
hostage *n.* in-jil 인질, (*pledge*) chŏ-dang 저당.
hostel *n.* hap-suk-so 합숙소, (*inn*) yŏ-in-suk 여인숙.
hostess *n.* an-ju-in 안주인, yŏ-ju-in 여주인.
hostile *adj.* chŏk-ŭi-e ch'an 적의에 찬, (*opposed*) pan-
dae-ha-nŭn 반대하는, chŏk-ŭi 적의.
hot *adj.* ① (*temperature*) to-un 더운, ttŭ-gŏ-un 뜨거운;
(*taste*) mae-un 매운. ② (*fresh*) kat-na-on 갓나온.
hotel *n.* ho-t'el 호텔, yŏ-gwan 여관.　　　「천장.
hot spring on-ch'ŏn 온천 : *a ~ resort* on-ch'ŏn-jang 온
hound *n.* sa-nyang-gae 사냥개 ; yŏl-jung-ha-nŭn sa-ram
열중하는 사람 : *a jazz ~* chae-jŭ-gwang 재즈광(狂).
hour *n.* si-gan 시간 : (*o'clock*) si 시(時).
house *n.* ① chip 집, ka-ok 가옥. ② (*A~*)ŭi-hoe 의회.
household *n. & adj.* ka-jok(-ŭi) 가족(의).
housekeeper *n.* chu-bu 주부, ka-jŏng-bu 가정부.
housemaid *n.* ha-nyŏ 하녀, sik-mo 식모.
house-rent *n.* chip-se 집세.　　　「jit-go-ri 반짇고리.
housewife *n.* ① chu-bu 주부. ② (*a sewing box*) pan-
hover *v.* ha-nŭl-ŭl nal-da 하늘을 날다 ; (*linger*) sŏ-
sŏng-gŏ-ri-da 서성거리다. —*n.* pae-hoe 배회.
how *adv.* (*in what state*) ŏ-ddŏ-k'e 어떻게 ; (*to what*
extent) ŏ-nŭ chŏng-do 어느 정도 ; (*why*) wae 왜.
—*int.* ya 야, a-i ch'am 아이 참. —*n.* (*means*) pang-
bŏp 방법, pang-sik 방식.

however adv. a-mu-ri ···hae-do 아무리 ···해도. —conj.
(*though*) kŭ-rŏ-na 그러나, kŭ-rŏ-ch'i-man 그렇지만.

howl v. (*of animals*) chit-da 짖다, ul-bu-jit-da 울부
짖다 ; (*of the wind*) mop-si pul-da 몹시 불다.

huddle v. ma-gu kŭl-gŏ-mo-ŭ-da 마구 긁어모으다;
(*curl up*) tung-gŭl-ge ku-bu-ri-da 둥글게 구부리다.
—n. (*confusion*) hon-jap 혼잡, pum-bim 붐빔.

hue n. (*color*) pit-ggal 빛깔, saek-jo 색조.

hug v. kkok kkyŏ-an-da 꼭 껴안다, p'um-da 품다.

huge adj. kŏ-dae-han 거대한, mak-dae-han 막대한.

hull v. kkŏp-jil-ŭl pŏt-gi-da 껍질을 벗기다. —n. ①
(*husk*) kkŏp-jil 껍질. ② (*ship*) sŏn-ch'e 선체(船體).

hum v. wing-wing-gŏ-ri-da 윙윙거리다, k'ot-no-rae-rŭl
pu-rŭ-da 콧노래를 부르다.

human n. in-gan 인간. —adj. in-gan-ŭi 인간의, in-
gan-da-un 인간다운.　　　　　　　　　　「비로운.

humane adj. in-jŏng-it-nŭn 인정있는, cha-bi-ro-un 자

humble adj. (*lowly*) pi-ch'ŏn-han 비천한 ; (*modest*)
kyŏm-son-han 겸손한.　　　　　　　　　　「눅한.

humid adj. ch'uk-ch'uk-han 축축한, nuk-nuk-han 눅

humility n. kyŏm-son 겸손 ; pi-ha 비하(卑下).

humo(u)r n. ① (*mood*) ki-jil 기질 ; ki-bun 기분. ② ik-
sal 익살, yu-u-mŏ 유우머.　　　　　　　　　　「리다.

hump n. hok 혹, yuk-bong 육봉. —v. ku-bu-ri-da 구부

humpback n. kkop-ch'u 꼽추, kop-sa-dŭng-i 곱사등이.

hundred n. paek 백.　　　　　　「mang 간절한 소망.

hunger n. ① kum-ju-rim 굶주림. ② kan-jŏl-han so-

hungry adj. pae-go-p'ŭn 배고픈, kum-ju-rin 굶주린:
go [be] ~ pae-go-p'ŭ-da 배고프다.

hunt n. sa-nyang 사냥, (*search*) ch'u-jŏk 추적. —v.
sa-nyang-ha-da 사냥하다: ~ for ch'at-da 찾다.

hunter n. sa-nyang-gun 사냥군, t'am-gu-ga 탐구가.

hunting *n.* sa-nyang 사냥, su-ryŏp 수렵 ; (*pursuit*)
t'am-gu 탐구, ch'u-gu 추구.

hurdle *n.* pa-ja(-ul) 바자(울), chang-ae-mul 장애물.

hurl *v.* nae-dŏn-ji-da 내던지다, p'aeng-gae-ch'i-da 팽개

hurrah·hurray *int.* man-se 만세, hu-ra 후라. ⌊치다.

hurricane *n.* p'ok-p'ung 폭풍, t'ae-p'ung 태풍.

hurry *v.* sŏ-du-rŭ-da 서두르다. —*n.* (*haste*) sŏ-du-rŭm
서두름, kŭp-sok 급속 : *in a* ~ kŭp-hi 급히.

hurt *v.* (*injure*) hae-ch'i-da 해치다, (*pain*) a-p'ŭ-da
아프다. —*n.* (*wound*) sang-ch'ŏ 상처 ;(*damage*) son-
hae 손해 ; (*pain*) ko-t'ong 고통. 「하다.

husband *n.* nam-p'yŏn 남편. —*v.* chŏl-yak-ha-da 절약

husbandry *n.* ① (*farming*) nong-ŏp 농업, kyŏng-jak
경작. ② (*thrift*) kŏm-yak 검약.

hush *v.* cho-yong-ha-ge ha-da 조용하게 하다, ip-ŭl ta-
mul-ge ha-da 입을 다물게 하다. —*int.* swit 쉿.

husk *n.* kkŏp-jil 껍질, oe-p'i 외피(外皮).

hustle *v.* ttŏ-mil-da 떠밀다 ; nan-p'ok-ha-ge mil-da 난
폭하게 밀다. —*n.* mil-ch'i-gi 밀치기.

hut *n.* o-du-mak-jip 오두막집, im-si mak-sa 임시 막사.

hybrid *n.* chap-jong 잡종, hon-hyŏ-ra 혼혈아. —*adj.*
chap-jong-ŭi 잡종의, hon-hap-ŭi 혼합의.

hydrant *n.* kŭp-su-jŏn 급수전 ; so-hwa-jŏn 소화전.

hydrogen *n.* su-so 수소 : *H*~ *bomb* su-so-p'ok-t'an 수
소폭탄/*heavy* ~ chung-su-so 중수소.

hydroplane *n.* su-sang pi-haeng-gi 수상 비행기.

hygiene *n.* kŏn-gang-bŏp 건강법 ; (*sanitary science*)
wi-saeng-hak 위생학, sŏp-saeng-bŏp 섭생법.

hymn *n.* ch'an-song-ga 찬송가. —*v.* ch'an-song-ha-da
hyphen *n.* ha-i-p'ŭn 하이픈. ⌊찬송하다.

hypocrite *n.* wi-sŏn-ja 위선자. 「병적 흥분.

hysteria *n.* hi-sŭ-t'e-ri 히스테리, pyŏng-jŏk hŭng-bun

I

I *pron.* na-nŭn 나는, nae-ga 내가. 「da 열리다.

ice *n.* ŏ-rŭm 얼음, ping-su 빙수. —*v.* (*freeze*) ŏl-ri-

iceberg *n.* ping-san 빙산, yu-bing 유빙(流氷).

icebox *n.* naeng-jang-go 냉장고, naeng-jang-gwe 냉장

ice cream a-i-sŭ-k'ŭ-rim 아이스크림. 「궤.

icehouse *n.* ŏ-rŭm ch'ang-go 얼음 창고, ping-go 빙고

ice water ŏ-rŭm-mul 얼음물, ping-su 빙수. 「(氷庫).

icicle *n.* ko-dŭ-rŭm 고드름. 「쌀쌀한.

icy *adj.* ŏ-rŭm-ga-t'ŭn 얼음같은, (*cold*) ssal-ssal-han

idea *n.* ① (*conception*) kwan-nyŏm 관념, (*thought*)
sa-sang 사상, (*notion*) saeng-gak 생각. ② (*opinion*)
ŭi-gyŏn 의견. ③ (*plan*) kye-hoek 계획.

ideal *n.* i-sang 이상(理想). —*adj.* i-sang-jŏk-in 이상적
인 ; to-hal na-wi-ŏp-nŭn 더할 나위없는.

identical *adj.* (*exactly alike*) tong-il-han 동일한, ttok-
ga-t'ŭn 똑같은, pa-ro kŭ 바로 그.

identification card sin-bun-jŭng 신분증.

identify *v.* tong-il-si-ha-da 동일시하다, tong-il-ham-ŭl
chŭng-myŏng-ha-da 동일함을 증명하다.

idiom *n.* suk-ŏ 숙어, kwan-yong-ŏ 관용어.

idiot *n.* ch'ŏn-ch'i 천치, paek-ch'i 백치, pa-bo 바보.

idiotic *adj.* paek-ch'i-ga-t'ŭn 백치같은.

idle *adj.* ke-ŭ-rŭn 게으른 ; (*worthless*) mu-ik-han 무
익한 ; (*baseless*) kŭn-gŏ-ŏp-nŭn 근거없는. —*v.* ke-
ŭ-rŭm-p'i-u-da 게으름피우다.

idleness *n.* ke-ŭ-rŭm 게으름, t'ae-man 태만.

idler *n.* ke-ŭ-rŭm-baeng-i 게으름뱅이, kŏn-dal 건달.

idol *n.* u-sang 우상, sung-bae-mul 숭배물.

idolatry *n.* u-sang sung-bae 우상 숭배.

if *conj.* ① (*in case that*) man-il···i-ra-myŏn 만일···이라면. ② (*even if*) ···il-ji-ra-do ···일지라도. ③ (*whether*) in-ji ŏ-ddŏn-ji 인지 어떤지. 「da 점화하다.

ignite *v.* pul-ŭl pu-ch'i-da 불을 붙이다, chŏm-hwa-ha-

ignoble *adj.* ch'ŏn-han 천한, pi-yŏl-han 비열한.

ignominy *n.* (*dishonor*) pul-myŏng-ye 불명예, ch'i-yok 치욕 ; (*misconduct*) ch'u-haeng 추행.

ignorance *n.* mu-sik 무식, mu-ji 무지.

ignorant *adj.* mu-sik-han 무식한. 「른 체하다.

ignore *v.* mu-si-ha-da 무시하다, mo-rŭn ch'e-ha-da 모

ill *adj.* ① (*sick*) pyŏng-dŭn 병든. ② (*bad*) na-bbŭn 나쁜. ③ (*malevolent*) sim-sul-gu-jŭn 심술궂은. —*n.* (*evil*) ak 악, (*misfortune*) pul-haeng 불행.

ill-bred *adj.* pŏ-rŭt-ŏp-si cha-ran 버릇없이 자란.

illegal *adj.* pul-bŏp-ŭi 불법의, pi-hap-bŏp-jŏk-in 비합법적인 : *an* ~ *act* pul-bŏp haeng-wi 불법 행위.

ill-fated *adj.* pul-haeng-han 불행한.

illiteracy *n.* mu-sik 무식, mun-maeng 문맹.

illiterate *adj.* mu-sik-han 무식한, mun-maeng-ŭi 문맹의. —*n.* mun-maeng-ja 문맹자, mu-sik-ja 무식자.

ill-natured *adj.* sim-sul-gu-jŭn 심술궂은.

illness *n.* (*disease*) pyŏng 병, p'yŏn-ch'an-ŭm 편찮음.

ill-treatment *n.* p'u-dae-jŏp 푸대접, hak-dae 학대.

illuminate *v.* pi-ch'u-da 비추다, cho-myŏng-ha-da 조명(照明)하다. 「루미네이션.

illumination *n.* cho-myŏng 조명, il-ru-mi-ne-i-syŏn 일

illusion *n.* hwan-sang 환상, ch'ak-gak 착각.

illustrate *v.* ① (*example*) ye-rŭl tŭ-rŏ sŏl-myŏng-ha-da 예를 들어 설명하다, ye-jŭng-ha-da 예증(例證)하다. ② (*picture*) kŭ-rim-ŭl nŏ-t'a 그림을 넣다.

illustration *n.* ① (*example*) ye-jŭng 예증(例證). ② (*picture*) sap-hwa 삽화, sŏl-myŏng-do 설명도.

illustrious *adj.* ① (*famous*) yu-myŏng-han 유명한.
② (*glorious*) pit-na-nŭn 빛나는.

image *n.* ① yŏng-sang 영상, (*statue*) cho-sang 조상
(影像). ② (*symbol*) sang-jing 상징. ③ (*form*) mo-
yang 모양. —*v.* sang-sang-ha-da 상상하다.

imaginary *adj.* sang-sang-jŏk-in 상상적인.

imagination *n.* sang-sang 상상, sang-sang-ryŏk 상상력.

imagine *v.* sang-sang-ha-da 상상하다, (*think*) saeng-
gak-ha-da 생각하다.   「모방하다.

imitate *v.* hyung-nae-nae-da 흉내내다, mo-bang-ha-da

imitation *n.* mo-bang 모방, hyung-nae 흉내.

immeasurable *adj.* he-a-ril su ŏp-nŭn 헤아릴 수 없는.

immediate *adj.* (*direct*) chik-jŏp-jŏk-in 직접적인 ;
(*instant*) chŭk-sok-ŭi 즉석의.

immediately *adv.* kot 곧, pa-ro 바로, chŭk-si 즉시.

immense *adj.* mak-dae-han 막대한, mu-han-han 무한한.

immigrant *n.* i-min 이민, i-ju-ja 이주자.

immigrate *v.* i-ju-ha-yŏ o-da 이주하여 오다.

imminent *adj.* (*impending*) im-bak-han 임박한, chŏl-
bak-han 절박한.   「룻없는.

immodest *adj.* mu-rye-han 무례한, pŏ-rŭt-ŏp-nŭn 버

immoral *adj.* pu-do-dŏk-han 부도덕한.

immortal *adj.* pul-sa-ŭi 불사의, pul-myŏl-ŭi 불멸의.

immovable *adj.* um-jik-il su ŏp-nŭn 움직일 수 없는.

imp *n.* (*little devil*) kko-ma to-ggae-bi 꼬마 도깨비.

impair *v.* ① (*injure*) hae-ch'i-da 해치다, son-sang-
ha-da 손상하다. ② (*reduce*) chu-ri-da 줄이다.

impart *v.* na-nu-ŏ-ju-da 나누어주다 ; al-ri-da 알리다.

impartial *adj.* kong-p'yŏng-han 공평한, ch'i-u-ch'i-ji
an-ŭn 치우치지 않은.   「han 침착한.

impassive *adj.* mu-gam-gak-han 무감각한; ch'im-ch'ak-

impatient *adj.* ch'am-ŭl-sŏng-ŏp-nŭn 참을성없는, sŏng-gŭp-han 성급한, sŏng-ma-rŭn 성마른. 「규탄하다.

impeach v. t'an-haek-ha-da 탄핵하다, kyu-t'an-ha-da

impediment n. (*obstacle*) pang-hae 방해.

impel v. ch'u-jin-si-k'i-da 추진시키다; (*urge*) chae-ch'ok-ha-da 재촉하다. 「im-bak-han 임박한.

impending adj. kot i-rŏ-nal tŭt-han 곧 일어날 듯한,

imperative adj. myŏng-ryŏng-jŏk-in 명령적인.

imperceptible adj. kam-ji-hal su ŏp-nŭn 감지할 수 없는, nun-e po-i-ji an-nŭn 눈에 보이지 않는.

imperfect adj. pul-wan-jŏn-han 불완전한.

imperial adj. (*of an empire*) che-guk-ŭi 제국의, hwang-je-ŭi 황제의; (*majestic*) tang-dang-han 당당한;

imperialism n. che-guk-ju-ŭi 제국주의.

imperishable adj. pul-myŏl-ŭi 불멸의, pul-hu-ŭi 불후의.

impersonal adj. pi-gae-in-jŏk-in 비개인적인, pi-in-gyŏk-jŏk-in 비인격적인.

impertinent adj. (*insolent*) kŏn-bang-jin 건방진, chŏk-jŏl-ha-ji an-ŭn 적절하지 않은; mu-rye-han 무례한.

impetuous adj. (*violent*) maeng-ryŏl-han 맹렬한, (*rash*) sŏng-gŭp-han 성급한, ch'ung-dong-jŏk-in 충동적인.

impious adj. sin-ang-sim-ŏp-nŭn 신앙심없는; pul-gyŏng-ŭi 불경의; (*wicked*) sa-ak-han 사악한. 「han 엄한.

implacable adj. tal-rae-gi him-dŭn 달래기 힘든; ŏm-

implement n. to-gu 도구, (*instrument*) ki-gu 기구. —v. ① wan-sŏng-ha-da 완성하다, su-haeng-ha-da 수행하다. ② (*satisfy*) man-jok-si-k'i-da 만족시키다.

implicate v. (*entangle*) ŏl-k'i-ge ha-da 얽히게 하다, kwal-lyŏn-si-k'i-da 관련시키다.

implore v. (*entreat*) kan-ch'ŏng-ha-da 간청하다.

imply v. ŭi-mi-ha-da 의미하다; (*hint*) am-si-ha-da 암

impolite adj. pŏ-rŭt-ŏp-nŭn 버릇없는. 「시하다.

import v. (*bring in*) su-ip-ha-da 수입하다. —n. ① su-ip 수입. ② (*meaning*) ŭi-mi 의미. ③ (*importance*) chung-yo-sŏng 중요성.

importance *n.* chung-yo(-sŏng) 중요(성). 「중대한.

important *adj.* chung-yo-han 중요한, chung-dae-han

impose *v.* pu-gwa-ha-da 부과하다, kang-yo-ha-da 강요

impossible *adj.* pul-ga-nŭng-han 불가능한. 「하다.

impotent *adj.* mu-ryŏk-han 무력한. —*n.* hŏ-yak-ja 허약

impractical *adj.* sil-je-jŏk-i a-nin 실제적이 아닌. 「자.

impress *v.* in-sang-ŭl chu-da 인상을 주다.

impression *n.* in-sang 인상, kam-myŏng 감명.

impressive *adj.* in-sang-jŏk-in 인상적인. 「옥하다.

imprison *v.* kam-gŭm-ha-da 감금하다, t'u-ok-ha-da 투

improper *adj.* pu-jŏk-dang-han 부적당한 ; kŭ-rŭt-doen 그릇된, (*indecent*) pŏ-rŭt-ŏp-nŭn 버릇없는.

improve *v.* ① kae-sŏn-ha-da 개선하다, cho-a-ji-da 좋 아지다. ② (*use well*) i-yong-ha-da 이용하다.

improvement *n.* kae-sŏn 개선, kae-ryang 개량.

imprudence *n.* kyŏng-sol 경솔, so-hol 소홀.

imprudent *adj.* (*rash*) kyŏng-sol-han 경솔한, (*indiscreet*) pun-byŏl-ŏp-nŭn 분별없는. 「러운.

impudent *adj.* (*insolent*) ppŏn-bbŏn-sŭ-rŏ-un 뻔뻔스

impulse *n.* ch'ung-dong 충동, (*stimulus*) cha-gŭk 자극, (*a driving force*) ch'u-jin-ryŏk 추진력.

impunity *n.* myŏn-bŏl 면벌(免罰). 「불결한.

impure *adj.* pul-sun-han 불순한, (*dirty*) pul-gyŏl-han

impute *v.* (*attribute*) …ŭi t'a-sŭ-ro tol-ri-da …의 탓으로 돌리다, tto-mat-gi-da 떠맡기다. 「[으로].

in *prep.* …ŭi an-e …의 안에. —*adv.* an-e[ŭ-ro] 안에

inability *n.* mu-nŭng 무능, mu-ryŏk 무력. 「린.

inaccurate *adj.* pu-jŏng-hwak-han 부정확한, t'ŭl-rin 틀

inactive *adj.* hwal-bal-ha-ji an-ŭn 활발하지 않은, (*motionless*) hwal-dong-ha-ji an-ŭn 활동하지 않은.

inadequate *adj.* pu-jŏk-dang-han 부적당한; (*insufficient*) pul-ch'ung-bun-han 불충분한.

inattention *n.* pu-ju-ŭi 부주의, pang-sim 방심.

inaudible *adj.* a-ra-dŭ-rŭl su ŏp-nŭn 알아들을 수 없는.

inaugurate *v.* ch'wi-im-sik-ŭl ha-da 취임식을 하다; (*open*) kae-si-ha-da 개시하다. 「성식.

inauguration *n.* ch'wi-im-sik 취임식, nak-sŏng-sik 낙

incapable *adj.* …hal nŭng-ryŏk-i ŏp-nŭn …할 능력이 없는; mu-nŭng-han 무능한.

incendiary *n.* (*arsonist*) pang-hwa-bŏm 방화범; (*bomb*) so-i-t'an 소이탄. —*adj.* pang-hwa-ŭi 방화의.

incense *n.* hyang 향 : ～ *burner* hyang-ro 향로.

incentive *adj.* cha-gŭk-jŏk 자극적. —*n.* (*stimulus*) cha-gŭk 자극 ; (*motive*) tong-gi 동기.

incessant *adj.* kkŭn-im-ŏp-nŭn 끊임없는, yŏn-sok-jŏk-

inch *n.* in-ch'i 인치(＝2.54cm). 「in 연속적인.

incident *n.* sa-gŏn 사건, sa-byŏn 사변.

inclination *n.* ① (*slope*) kyŏng-sa 경사. ② (*tendency*) kyŏng-hyang 경향. ③ (*liking*) ki-ho 기호.

incline *v.* ki-ul-da 기울다 ; (*be disposed*) ma-ŭm-i ssol-ri-da 마음이 쏠리다. —*n.* kyŏng-sa-myŏn 경사면.

include *v.* p'o-ham-ha-da 포함하다 : *postage* ～d u-song-ryo p'o-ham-ha-yŏ 우송료 포함하여.

incoherent *adj.* cho-ri-ga sŏ-ji an-nŭn 조리가 서지 않는, ap-dwi-ga mat-ji an-nŭn 앞뒤가 맞지 않는.

income *n.* su-ip 수입, so-dŭk 소득.

incomparable *adj.* pi-gyo-ga an-doe-nŭn 비교가 안되는; yu-rye-ŏp-nŭn 유례없는. 「는, mo-sun-doen 모순된.

incompatible *adj.* yang-rip-hal su ŏp-nŭn 양립할 수 없

incomplete *adj.* pul-wan-jŏn-han 불완전한, mi-wan-sŏng-ŭi 미완성의. 「sol-han 경솔한.

inconsiderate *adj.* chi-gak-ŏp-nŭn 지각없는, kyŏng-.

inconsistent *adj.* (*contradictory*) il-ch'i-ha-ji an-nŭn 일치하지 않는, mo-sun-doen 모순된.

inconvenience *n.* pul-p'yŏn 불편, pu-ja-yu 부자유.

inconvenient *adj.* pul-p'yŏn-han 불편한 ; (*causing trouble*) p'ye-ga toe-nŭn 폐가 되는.

incorporate *adj.* pŏp-in-jo-jik-ŭi 법인조직의. —*v.* (*combine*) hap-dong-ha-da 합동하다 ; chu-sik-hoe-sa-ro ha-da 주식회사로 하다.

incorporation *n.* hoe-sa 회사, pŏp-in tan-ch'e 법인 단체.

incorrect *adj.* pu-jŏng-hwak-han 부정확한, t'ŭl-rin 틀린, ol-ch'i an-ŭn 옳지 않은. 「증가.

increase *v.* chŭng-ga-ha-da 증가하다. —*n.* chŭng-ga

incredible *adj.* mit-ŭl su ŏp-nŭn 믿을 수 없는.

incubate *v.* (*hatch*) al-ŭl kka-da 알을 까다.

incubator *n.* pu-hwa-gi 부화기, po-yuk-gi 보육기.

incur *v.* ch'o-rae-ha-da 초래하다, ip-da 입다.

incurable *adj.* ko-ch'il su ŏp-nŭn 고칠 수 없는, pul-ch'i-ŭi 불치의. —*n.* pul-ch'i pyŏng-ja 불치 병자.

indebted *adj.* pu-ch'ae-ga it-nŭn 부채가 있는 ; (*owing gratitude*) ŭn-hye-rŭl ip-ŭn 은혜를 입은.

indecent *adj.* (*ill-bred*) pŏ-rŭt-ŏp-nŭn 버릇없는 ; (*immodest*) ch'u-jap-han 추잡한.

indecisive *adj.* u-mul-jju-mul-ha-nŭn 우물쭈물하는.

indeed *adv.* ch'am-ŭ-ro 참으로, kwa-yŏn 과연.

indefinite *adj.* ① (*not precise*) myŏng-hwak-ha-ji an-nŭn 명확하지 않는. ② (*unlimited*) pu-jŏng-ŭi 부정의.

independent *adj.* tok-rip-han 독립한.

indescribable *adj.* hyŏng-ŏn-hal su ŏp-nŭn 형언할 수

indestructible *adj.* pul-myŏl-ŭi 불멸의. 「없는.

index *n.* saek-in 색인, in-dek-sŭ 인덱스.

India *n.* in-do 인도 : ～ ink mŏk 먹.

indicate *v.* chi-jŏk-ha-da 지적하다, ka-ri-k'i-da 가리키다 ;

(*show*) p'yo-si-ha-da 표시하다.

indict *v.* ko-bal-ha-da 고발하다, ki-so-ha-da 기소하다.

indifferent *adj.* mu-gwan-sim-han 무관심한 ; (*careless*) kae-ŭi-ch'i an-nŭn 개의치 않는.   「지방 고유의.

indigenous *adj.* t'o-ch'ak-ŭi 토착의, chi-bang ko-yu-ui

indigestion *n.* so-hwa pul-ryang 소화 불량.   「격분한.

indignant *adj.* hwa-ga nan 화가 난, kyŏk-bun-han

indigo *n.* nam-saek 남색, jjok-bit 쪽빛, in-di-go 인디고.

indirect *adj.* kan-jŏp-jŏk-in 간접적인 ;(*roundabout*) u-hoe-jŏk-in 우회적인.

indiscreet *adj.* pun-byŏl-ŏp-nŭn 분별없는, mu-mo-han 무모한, (*not prudent*) kyŏng-sol-han 경솔한.

indiscriminate *adj.* ch'a-byŏl-ŏp-nŭn 차별없는, ka-ri-ji an-nŭn 가리지 않는 ; (*random*) nan-jap-han 난잡한.

indispensable *adj.* chŏl-dae p'i-ryo-han 절대 필요한, (*unavoidable*) p'i-hal su ŏp-nŭn 피할 수 없는.

indisputable *adj.* (*unquestionable*) non-ŭi-hal yŏ-ji-ŏp-nŭn 논의할 여지없는, myŏng-baek-han 명백한.

indistinct *adj.* ttu-ryŏt-ha-ji an-ŭn 뚜렷하지 않은, pun-myŏng-ch'i an-ŭn 분명치 않은, hŭi-mi-han 희미한.

individual *adj.* tan-dok-jŏk-in 단독적인, kae-in-jŏk-in 개인적인. —*n.* kae-in 개인, kae-ch'e 개체.

individualism *n.* kae-in-ju-ŭi 개인주의.

indolent *adj.* ke-ŭ-rŭn 게으른, t'ae-man-han 태만한.

indomitable *adj.* kul-ha-ji an-nŭn 굴하지 않는.

indoor *adj.* chip-an-ŭi 집안의, ok-nae-ŭi 옥내의, sil-nae-ŭi 실내의 : ~ *sports* sil-nae-un-dong 실내운동.

indoors *adv.* ok-nae-e-sŏ 옥내에서, sil-nae-e-sŏ 실내에서.

indorse *v.* i-sŏ-ha-da 이서(裏書)하다.

induce *v.* (*exhort*) kwŏn-yu-ha-da 권유하다 ; (*persuade*) sŏl-dŭk-ha-da 설득하다.

induct *v.* (*place*) chik-wi-e an-ch'i-da 직위에 앉히다;

(*introduce*) to·ip·ha·da 도입하다.

induction *n*. ① (*introduction*) kkŭ·rŏ·dŭ·rim 끌어들임, to·ip 도입. ② (*logic*) kwi·nap·pŏp 귀납법.

indulge *v*. ···e ppa·ji·da ···에 빠지다.

industrial *adj*. san·ŏp·ŭi 산업의, kong·ŏp·ŭi 공업의.

industrious *adj*. pu·ji·rŏn·han 부지런한. 「근면.

industry *n*. ① san·ŏp 산업. ② (*diligence*) kŭn·myŏn

inefficient *adj*. mu·nŭng·han 무능한, (*wasteful*) pi·nŭng·ryul·jŏk·in 비능률적인. 「석은.

inept *adj*. pu·jŏk·dang·han 부적당한, ŏ·ri·sŏk·ŭn 어리

inequality *n*. ① (*unfairness*) pul·p'yŏng·dŭng 불평등. ② (*disparity*) pu·dong 부동(不同).

inert *adj*. saeng·gi·ga ŏp·nŭn 생기가 없는 ; (*inactive*) t'a·sŏng·jŏk·in 타성적인 ; tun·han 둔한.

inescapable *adj*. p'i·hal su ŏp·nŭn 피할 수 없는.

inestimable *adj*. p'yŏng·ga·hal su ŏp·nŭn 평가할 수

inevitable *adj*. p'i·hal su ŏp·nŭn 피할 수 없는. 「없는.

inexcusable *adj*. yong·sŏ·hal su ŏp·nŭn 용서할 수 없는, pyŏn·myŏng·hal to·ri·ga ŏp·nŭn 변명할 도리가 없는.

inexhaustible *adj*. ① ta ssŭl su ŏp·nŭn 다 쓸 수 없는, mu·jin·jang·ŭi 무진장의. ② (*indefatigable*) pul·gul·ŭi

inexorable *adj*. ka·hok·han 가혹한. 「불굴의.

inexperienced *adj*. kyŏng·hŏm·ŏp·nŭn 경험없는.

inexplicable *adj*. sŏl·myŏng·hal su ŏp·nŭn 설명할 수 없는 ; (*unaccountable*) pul·ga·hae·han 불가해한.

infamous *adj*. ak·myong·i no·p'ŭn 악명이 높은. 「추문.

infamy *n*. pul·myŏng·ye 불명예, (*disgrace*) ch'u·mun

infant *n*. yu·a 유아, so·a 소아, a·dong 아동.

infantile *adj*. yu·a·ŭi 유아의 : ~ *paralysis* so·a·ma·bi

infantry *n*. po·byŏng 보병(步兵). 「소아마비.

infect *v*. chŏn·yŏm·si·k'i·da 전염시키다.

infection *n*. chŏn·yŏm 전염, chŏn·yŏm·byŏng 전염병.

infer *v.* ch'u-ron-ha-da 추론하다 ; am-si-ha-da 암시하다.

inferior *adj.* ha-wi-ŭi 하위의 ; yŏl-dŭng-han 열등한.
—*n.* a-raet-sa-ram 아랫사람, yŏl-dŭng-ja 열등자.

infernal *adj.* ① (*of hell*) chi-ok-ŭi 지옥의. ② (*hellish*)
chi-dok-han 지독한, kŭk-ak-ŭi 극악의.

infest *v.* tŭl-ggŭl-t'a 들끓다 ; mol-ryŏ-dŭl-da 몰려들다.

infinitive *n.* pu-jŏng-sa 부정사(不定詞).

inflation *n.* p'aeng-ch'ang 팽창, in-p'ŭl-re 인플레.

inflict *v.* (*impose*) kwa-ha-da 과하다 : (*lay on*) chu-da
주다 ; (*cause*) ip-hi-da 입히다.

influence *n.* ① yŏng-hyang 영향. ② yu-ryŏk-ja 유력
자. —*v.* yŏng-hyang-ŭl kki-ch'i-da 영향을 끼치다.

influenza *n.* yu-haeng-sŏng kam-gi 유행성 감기.

inform *v.* al-ri-da 알리다, t'ong-ji-ha-da 통지하다.

informal *adj.* pi-gong-sik-ŭi 비공식의, yak-sik-ŭi 약식의.

information *n.* ① (*news*) so-sik 소식. ② (*report*) po-
go 보고. ③ (*intelligence*) chŏng-bo 정보 : ~ *bureau*
chŏng-bo-bu 정보부. ④ (*knowledge*) chi-sik 지식.

ingratitude *n.* pae-ŭn-mang-dŏk 배은망덕.

ingredient *n.* sŏng-bun 성분, yo-in 요인, yo-so 요소.

inhabit *v.* (*live in*) kŏ-ju-ha-da 거주하다, sal-da 살다.

inhabitant *n.* chu-min 주민, kŏ-ju-ja 거주자.

inhale *v.* (*breathe in*) ppa-ra-dŭ-ri-da 빨아들이다.

inherent *adj.* (*natural*) t'a-go-nan 타고난, ch'ŏn-bu-
ŭi 천부의 ; (*inborn*) ko-yu-ŭi 고유의.

inherit *v.* sang-sok-ha-da 상속하다, i-ŏ-bat-da 이어받다.

inhibit *v.* kŭm-ha-da 금하다, che-ji-ha-da 제지하다.

inhospitable *adj.* pul-ch'in-jŏl-han 불친절한.

iniquity *n.* pu-jŏng 부정 ; (*wickedness*) sa-ak 사악.

initial *adj.* ch'ŏ-ŭm-ŭi 처음의, pal-dan-ŭi 발단의. —*n.*
mŏ-rit-gŭl-ja 머릿글자.　　　　　　　　　　「키다.

initiate *v.* si-jak-ha-da 시작하다 ; ka-ip-si-k'i-da 가입시

initiative *adj.* ch'ŏ-ŭm-ŭi 처음의. —*n.* ① (*lead*) sol-sŏn 솔선. ② (*first step*) che-il-bo 제일보. ③ (*leadership*) chu-do-gwŏn 주도권.

inject *v.* ① chu-sa-ha-da 주사하다. ② (*interject*) mal-ch'am-gyŏn-ha-da 말참견하다. 「(灌腸).

injection *n.* chu-sa 주사, chu-ip 주입, kwan-jang 관장

injure *v.* hae-ch'i-da 해치다 ; (*hurt*) ta-ch'i-da 다치다.

injury *n.* (*harm*) sang-hae 상해, (*damage*) son-hae 손해 ; kwŏl-li-ch'im-hae 권리침해.

injustice *n.* (*unfairness*) pu-jŏng 부정.

ink *n.* ing-k'ŭ 잉크 : *India* ~ mŏk 먹.

inkstone *n.* pyŏ-ru 벼루.

inlaid *adj.* a-ro-sae-gin 아로새긴, sang-gam-ŭi 상감(象嵌)의.

inland *n. & adj.* nae-ryuk(-ŭi) 내륙(의), kuk-nae(-ŭi) 국내(의).

inlet *n.* ① hu-mi 후미. ② (*entrance*) ip-gu 입구.

inmate *n.* tong-gŏ-in 동거인, tong-suk-in 동숙인.

inn *n.* yŏ-in-suk 여인숙, yŏ-gwan 여관. 「부의.

inner *adj.* an-jjok-ŭi 안쪽의, (*interior*) nae-bu-ŭi 내

innocent *adj.* ch'ŏn-jin nan-man-han 천진 난만한, (*pure*) sun-gyŏl-han 순결한, kyŏl-baek-han 결백한.

innovate *v.* hyŏk-sin-ha-da 혁신하다. 「han 무수한.

innumerable *adj.* sel su ŏp-nŭn 셀 수 없는, mu-su-

innutrition *n.* yŏng-yang pu-jok 영양 부족.

inoculate *v.* (*vaccinate*) ye-bang-jŏp-jong-ŭl ha-da 예방접종을 하다 ; (*imbue*) chu-ip-ha-da 주입하다.

inoculation *n.* chŏp-jong 접종(接種), chong-du 종두.

inquest *n.* sim-ri 심리 ; (*jury*) pae-sim 배심.

inquire *v.* mut-da 묻다 ; cho-sa-ha-da 조사하다. 「탐구.

inquiry *n.* chil-mun 질문 ; (*investigation*) t'am-gu

inquisitive *adj.* ho-gi-sim-i kang-han 호기심이 강한.

insane *adj.* (*mad*) mi-ch'in 미친.

inscribe *v.* sae-gi-da 새기다 ; ki-ip-ha-da 기입하다.

inscription *n.* pi-mun 비문(碑文).

insect *n.* kon-ch'ung 곤충, pŏl-re 벌레.

insecticide *n.* sal-ch'ung-je 살충제. 「전」한.

insecure *adj.* pu-ran-jŏng〔pu-ran-jŏn〕-han 불안정〔불안

insensible *adj.* (*having no feelings*) mu-gam-gak-han 무감각한, in-sa-bul-sŏng-ŭi 인사불성의.

inseparable *adj.* na-nul su ŏp-nŭn 나눌 수 없는.

insert *v.* kki-wŏ-nŏ-t'a 끼워넣다, (*put into*) sap-ip-ha-da 삽입하다 ; (*publish*) ke-jae-ha-da 게재하다.

inside *n.* an-jjok 안쪽, nae-bu 내부. —*adj.* & *prep.* an-ŭi 안의. —*adv.* an-jjok-ŭ-ro 안쪽으로, an-e 안에.

insight *n.* t'ong-ch'al-ryŏk 통찰력, an-sik 안식(眼識).

insignia *n.* hun-jang 훈장, (*signs*) p'yo-ji 표지.

insignificant *adj.* (*meaningless*) mu-ŭi-mi-han 무의미한, (*trivial*) tae-su-rop-ji an-ŭn 대수롭지 않은.

insincere *adj.* sŏng-ŭi-ŏp-nŭn 성의없는, pul-sŏng-sil-han 불성실한 ; (*hypocritical*) wi-sŏn-jŏk-in 위선적인.

insist *v.* chu-jang-ha-da 주장하다 ; cho-rŭ-da 조르다.

insolent *adj.* kŏ-man-han 거만한, kyo-man-han 교만한.

insoluble *adj.* hae-gyŏl-hal su ŏp-nŭn 해결할 수 없는.

inspect *v.* cho-sa-ha-da 조사하다, kŏm-yŏl-ha-da 검열하다 ; si-ch'al-ha-da 시찰하다.

inspection *n.* kŏm-sa 검사 ; si-ch'al 시찰.

inspector *n.* (*of factory*) kam-dok-gwan 감독관, (*of school*) chang-hak-gwan 장학관, kŏm-sa-gwan 검사관.

inspire *v.* ko-ch'wi-ha-da 고취하다 ; (*encourage*) ko-mu-ha-da 고무하다 ; yŏng-gam-ŭl chu-da 영감을 주다.

install *v.* ① ch'wi-im-si-k'i-da 취임시키다, im-myŏng-ha-da 임명하다. ② (*set up*) sŏl-ch'i-ha-da 설치하다.

instal(l)ment *n.* pun-nap(-gŭm) 분납(금) : *monthly ~*

wŏl-bu 월부. 「기.

instance *n.* (*case*) kyŏng-u 경우 ; (*example*) po-gi 보

instant *n.* chŭk-si 즉시, sun-gan 순간.

instantaneous *adj.* sun-gan-ŭi 순간의, chŭk-sŏk-ŭi 즉

instantly *adv.* kot 곧, chŭk-gak 즉각. ㄴ석의.

instead *adv.* tae-sin-ŭ-ro 대신으로. 「기에 찬.

instinct *n.* pon-nŭng 본능. —*adj.* hwal-gi-e ch'an 활

instinctively *adv.* pon-nŭng-jŏk-ŭ-ro 본능적으로.

institute *v.* (*establish*) sŏl-rip-ha-da 설립하다. —*n.*
(*society*) hak-hoe 학회, hyŏp-hoe 협회.

institution *n.* ① (*establishment*) sŏl-rip 설립. ② (*system*) che-do 제도. ③ (*custom*) sŭp-gwan 습관. ④
(*society*) hak-hoe 학회, hyŏp-hoe 협회.

instruct *v.* (*teach*) ka-rŭ-ch'i-da 가르치다 ; (*direct*)
chi-si-ha-da 지시하다 ; (*inform*) al-ri-da 알리다.

instruction *n.* ① ka-rŭ-ch'im 가르침. ② (*knowledge*)
chi-sik 지식. ③ (*order*) hul-lyŏng 훈령.

instructor *n.* kyo-sa 교사, kang-sa 강사.

instrument *n.* ki-gu 기구 ; (*means*) su-dan 수단.

insufficient *adj.* pul-ch'ung-bun-han 불충분한, (*inadequate*) pu-jŏk-dang-han 부적당한. 「립시키다.

insulate *v.* kyŏk-ri-ha-da 격리하다, ko-rip-si-k'i-da 고

insult *v.* mo-yok-ha-da 모욕하다. —*n.* (*insolence*) mo-yok 모욕 ; (*impoliteness*) mu-rye 무례.

insurance *n.* po-hŏm 보험, po-hŏm-ryo 보험료.

insure *v.* po-hŏm-e nŏ-t'a 보험에 넣다 ; po-jŭng-ha-da
보증하다 ; (*protect*) an-jŏn-ha-ge ha-da 안전하게 하다.

insurrection *n.* p'ok-dong 폭동, pal-lan 반란.

integrity *n.* ① (*sincerity*) sŏng-sil 성실 ; (*uprightness*) ko-gyŏl 고결. ② (*completeness*) wan-jŏn 완전.

intellect *n.* ① chi-sŏng 지성, chi-ryŏk 지력, i-ji 이지
(理智). ② chi-sik-in 지식인, chi-sŏng-in 지성인.

intelligence *n.* ① (*sagacity*) chi-hye 지혜, i-hae-ryŏk 이해력. ② (*information*) chŏng-bo 정보.

intelligent *adj.* chi-jŏk-in 지적인, i-ji-jŏk-in 이지적인; (*acute*) ch'ong-myŏng-han 총명한.

intemperance *n.* pu-jŏl-je 부절제, p'ok-ŭm 폭음.

intend *v.* …hal chak-jŏng-i-da …할 작정이다.

intendant *n.* kam-dok-gwan 감독관, kwal-li-ja 관리자.

intense *adj.* kyŏk-ryŏl-han 격렬한, (*fervent*) yŏl-ryŏl-han 열렬한; kin-jang-doen 긴장된.

intent *n.* ŭi-ji 의지, ŭi-hyang 의향. —*adj.* (*absorbed*) yŏl-jung-ha-nŭn 열중하는, mol-du-ha-nŭn 몰두하는.

intention *n.* ŭi-do 의도, ŭi-ji 의지, ŭi-hyang 의향.

intentionally *adv.* il-bu-rŏ 일부러, ko-ŭi-ro 고의로.

interact *n.* mak-gan-gŭk 막간극, mak-gan 막간.

intercept *v.* ka-ro-mak-da 가로막다, ka-ro-ch'ae-da 가

interchange *v.* kyo-hwan-ha-da 교환하다. ⌞로채다.

intercourse *n.* kyo-je 교제, kyo-ryu 교류; sŏng-gyo 성교(性交): *social* ~ sa-gyo 사교.

interest *n.* ① hŭng-mi 흥미. ② (*money*) i-ja 이자.

interesting *adj.* chae-mi-it-nŭn 재미있는. ⌞정하다.

interfere *v.* kan-sŏp-ha-da 간섭하다; cho-jŏng-ha-da 조

interior *n.* nae-bu 내부. —*adj.* nae-bu-ŭi 내부의.

intermarriage *n.* kuk-je kyŏl-hon 국제 결혼.

intermission *n.* (*pause*) chung-dan 중단, chung-ji 중지; (*between acts*) mak-gan 막간.

internal *adj.* nae-bu-ŭi 내부의, kuk-nae-ŭi 국내의.

international *adj.* kuk-je-jŏk-in 국제적인.

interplanetary *adj.* hok-sŏng-gan-ŭi 혹성간의, ch'ŏn-ch'e-gan-ŭi 천체간의. ⌜gyŏn-ha-da 말참견하다.

interpose *v.* sap-ip-ha-da 삽입하다; (*put in*) mal-ch'am-

interpret *v.* hae-sŏk-ha-da 해석하다, t'ong-yŏk-ha-da 통역하다.

interpretation *n.* ① (*exposition*) hae-sŏk 해석, hae-sŏl 해설. ② (*translation*) t'ong-yŏk 통역.

interpreter *n.* hae-sŏl-ja 해설자 ; t'ong-yŏk-ja 통역자.

interrogation *n.* chil-mun 질문 ; sim-mun 심문.

interrupt *v.* ka-ro-mak-da 가로막다, pang-hae-ha-da 방해하다 ; (*stop*) chung-dan-ha-da 중단하다.

interruption *n.* pang-hae 방해 ; chung-dan 중단.

interval *n.* kan-gyŏk 간격 ; (*break*) hyu-sik ki-gan 휴식 기간 ; (*between acts*) mak-gan 막간.

interview *n.* ① (*meeting*) myŏn-jŏp 면접. ② (*with pressmen*) hoe-gyŏn 회견, in-t'ŏ-byu-u 인터뷰우. ③ (*with rulers of countries*) al-hyŏn 알현.

intimate *adj.* ch'in-mil-han 친밀한, ka-gga-un 가까운. —*n.* ch'in-u 친우. —*v.* (*hint*) am-si-ha-da 암시하다.

intimidate *v.* ŭ-rŭ-da 으르다, wi-hyŏp-ha-da 위협하다.

into *prep.* an-ŭ-ro 안으로, an-e 안에.

intolerable *adj.* ch'am-ŭl su ŏp-nŭn 참을 수 없는.

intonation *n.* ŏ-jo 어조, ŏk-yang 억양.

intoxicate —*v.* ch'wi-ha-ge ha-da 취하게 하다 ; to-ch'wi〔hung-bun〕-ha-da 도취〔흥분〕하다.

intricate *adj.* twi-ŏl-k'in 뒤얽힌, pok-jap-han 복잡한.

intrigue *n.* ŭm-mo 음모 ; mil-t'ong 밀통. —*v.* ŭm-mo-ha-da 음모하다 ; mil-t'ong-ha-da 밀통하다.

intrinsic *adj.* (*essential*) pon-jil-jŏk-in 본질적인, pol-lae-ŭi 본래의, (*inherent*) ko-yu-ŭi 고유의.

introduce *v.* ① so-gae-ha-da 소개하다. ② (*bring in*) i-ggŭ-rŏ-dŭ-ri-da 이끌어들이다.

introduction *n.* ① so-gae 소개. ② (*in a book*) sŏ-mun 서문, mŏ-ri-mal 머리말. ③ (*primer*) ip-mun 입문.

intrude *v.* ch'im-ip-ha-da 침입하다, mil-go tŭ-rŏ-ga-da 밀고 들어가다 ; pang-hae-ha-da 방해하다.

intuition *n.* chik-gak 직각, chik-gwan 직관.

invade *v.* ch'yŏ-dŭ-rŏ-o-da 쳐들어오다, ch'im-ip-ha-da 침입하다, (*violate*) ch'im-hae-ha-da 침해하다.

invalid *n.* hwan-ja 환자. —*adj.* ① (*feeble*) hŏ-yak-han 허약한. ② (*of no force*) mu-hyo-ŭi 무효의.

invalidate *v.* mu-hyo-ro ha-da 무효로 하다.

invaluable *adj.* a-ju kwi-jung-han 아주 귀중한.

invariable *adj.* (*unchangeable*) pul-byŏn-ŭi 불변의 ; (*constant*) il-jŏng-han 일정한.

invasion *n.* ch'im-ip 침입, ch'im-hae 침해.

invent *v.* pal-myŏng-ha-da 발명하다 ; kku-myŏ-nae-da 꾸며내다 ; (*make up*) nal-jo-ha-da 날조하다.

invention *n.* pal-myŏng(-p'um) 발명(품).

inventor *n.* pal-myŏng-ga 발명가, ko-an-ja 고안자.

inventory *n.* chae-san mok-rok 재산 목록 ; (*a stock list*) chae-go-p'um mok-rok 재고품 목록.

inverse *adj.* pan-dae-ŭi 반대의, yŏk-ŭi 역(逆)의.

invest *v.* ① (*funds*) t'u-ja-ha-da 투자하다. ② (*clothes*) ip-hi-da 입히다. ③ (*endow*) chu-da 주다. 「구하다.

investigate *v.* cho-sa-ha-da 조사하다, yŏn-gu-ha-da 연

investigation *n.* cho-sa 조사, yŏn-gu 연구.

investment *n.* t'u-ja 투자 ; (*encirclement*) p'o-wi 포위.

invigorate *v.* wŏn-gi-rŭl tot-gu-da 원기를 돋구다.

invincible *adj.* chŏng-bok-hal su ŏp-nŭn 정복할 수 없는, mu-jŏk-ŭi 무적의, pul-p'ae-ŭi 불패(不敗)의.

invisible *adj.* po-i-ji an-nŭn 보이지 않는. 「대장.

invitation *n.* ch'o-dae 초대 : ～ *card* ch'o-dae-jang 초

invite *v.* ch'o-dae-ha-da 초대하다 ; kkoe-da 꾀다.

invocation *n.* ki-wŏn 기원 ; (*spell*) chu-mun 주문(呪文).

invoice *n.* song-jang 송장(送狀).

involuntary *adj.* mu-ŭi-sik-jung-ŭi 무의식중의 ; (*unwished for*) pon-ŭi a-nin 본의 아닌.

involve *v.* p'o-ham-si-k'i-da 포함시키다, kkŭ-rŏ-nŏ-t'a

끌어넣다 ; (*imply*) ttŭt-ha-da 뜻하다. 「적인.

inward *adj*. nae-bu-ŭi 내부의 ; (*mental*) sim-jŏk-in 심

iris *n*. ① (*plant*) put-ggot 붓꽃, ch'ang-p'o 창포. ②
(*eye*) hong-ch'ae 홍채.

irksome *adj*. sŏng-ga-sin 성가신, kwi-ch'an-ŭn 귀찮은.

iron *n*. ① soe 쇠, ch'ŏl 철. ② (*flatiron*) ta-ri-mi 다
리미. —*adj*. ① ch'ŏl-ŭi 철의. ② kyŏn-go-han 견고한.

ironic(al) *adj*. pin-jŏng-dae-nŭn 빈정대는, pi-ggo-nŭn

ironing *n*. ta-ri-mi-jil 다리미질. 「비꼬는.

ironmonger *n*. ch'ŏl-mul-sang 철물상.

irregular *adj*. pul-gyu-ch'ik-jŏk-in 불규칙적인, (*uneven*)
ko-rŭ-ji an-ŭn 고르지 않은, pyŏn-ch'ik-ŭi 변칙의.

irrelevant *adj*. pu-jŏk-dang-han 부적당한.

irresistible *adj*. chŏ-hang-hal su ŏp-nŭn 저항할 수 없
는 ; (*overmastering*) i-gyŏ-nael su ŏp-nŭn 이겨낼 수
없는 ; kyŏn-dil su ŏp-nŭn 견딜 수 없는.

irresolute *adj*. kyŏl-dan-ryŏk-ŏp-nŭn 결단력없는, (*hesi-
tating*) u-yu-bu-dan-han 우유부단한.

irresponsible *adj*. mu-ch'aek-im-han 무책임한.

irrigate *v*. mul-ŭl tae-da 물을 대다, ch'uk-i-da 축이다,
(*water*) kwan-gae-ha-da 관개(灌漑)하다.

irrigation *n*. mul-daem 물댐, kwan-gae 관개.

irritable *adj*. hwa chal nae-nŭn 화 잘 내는, sŏng-ma-
rŭn 성마른, ae-rŭl t'ae-u-nŭn 애를 태우는.

irritate *v*. (*provoke*) yak-ol-ri-da 약올리다, an-dal-na-
ge ha-da 안달나게 하다, cha-gŭk-ha-da 자극하다.

island *n*. sŏm 섬 : *Namhae I~* nam-hae-sŏm 남해섬.

isolate *v*. ko-rip-si-k'i-da 고립시키다, kyŏk-ri-ha-da 격
리하다 ; (*insulate*) chŏ-ryŏn-ha-da 절연하다.

issue *n*. ① (*flowing out*) yu-ch'ul 유출(流出). ② (*exit*)
ch'ul-gu 출구. ③ (*outcome*) kyŏl-gwa 결과. ④ (*subject
debated*) non-jŏm 논점. ⑤ (*publication*) pal-haeng

발행. —v. ① (make public) kong-p'o-ha-da 공포하
다. ② (publish) kan-haeng-ha-da 간행하다. ③ (result)
i-rŏ-na-da 일어나다.

it pron. kŭ-gŏ-sŭn 그것은, kŭ-gŏ-si 그것이, kŭ-gŏ-sŭl
그것을.

itch n. ka-ryŏ-um 가려움 ; (disease) om 옴. —v. ka-
ryŏ-wŏ-ha-da 가려워하다.

item n. cho-hang 조항, hang-mok 항목.   「반복하다.

iterate v. toe-p'u-ri-ha-da 되풀이하다, pan-bok-ha-da

itinerary n. (plan of travel) yŏ-haeng il-jŏng 여행
일정, yŏ-haeng an-nae 여행 안내, (route) yŏ-ro 여
로, (record of travel) yŏ-haeng il-gi 여행 일기.

itinerate v. sun-hoe-ha-da 순회하다.

itself pron. kŭ cha-sin 그 자신, kŭ cha-ch'e 그 자체.

ivory n. sang-a 상아 ; artificial ∼ in-jo sang-a 인조 상
아/∼ tower sang-a-t'ap 상아탑.   「담쟁이로 덮다.

ivy n. tam-jaeng-i 담쟁이. —v. tam-jaeng-i-ro tŏp-da

◄══ **J** ══►

jab v. jji-rŭ-da 찌르다 ; chwi-ŏ-bak-da 쥐어박다.

jack n. (tool) chaek 잭, (man) nam-ja 남자, (crew)

jacket n. cha-k'et 자켓.   ⌊sŏn-wŏn 선원.

jade n. pi-ch'wi 비취, ok 옥.

jail n. (prison) kyo-do-so 교도소, kam-ok 감옥.

jailer · jailor n. kan-su 간수(看守).

jam n. ① chaem 잼. ② (crowdedness) hon-jap 혼잡. ③
(machinery) ko-jang 고장. —v. ① (press) ssu-
syŏ-nŏ-t'a 쑤셔넣다. ② (machinery) kŏl-ri-da 걸리다.

jangle v. ttaeng-gŭ-rang so-ri-na-da 땡그랑 소리나다.

janitor n. (doorkeeper) mun-ji-gi 문지기, (guard)
su-wi 수위, kwal-li-in 관리인.

January *n.* chŏng-wŏl 정월, il-wŏl 일월.

Japan *n.* il-bon 일본(日本).

Japanese *n.* ① (*people*) il-bon-sa-ram 일본사람. ② (*lang.*) il-bon-mal 일본말. —*adj.* il-bon-ŭi 일본의.

jar *n.* tok 독, tan-ji 단지, hang-a-ri 항아리. 「설수설.

jargon *n.* hŏ-t'ŭn-so-ri 허튼소리, hoeng-sŏl-su-sŏl 횡

jarring *n.* chin-dong 진동. —*adj.* ppi-gŏk-gŏ-ri-nŭn 삐격거리는.

jaundice *n.* hwang-dal 황달.

jaunty *adj.* kyŏng-k'wae-han 경쾌한 ; hwal-gi-it-nŭn 활기있는 ; (*smart*) mal-ssuk-han 말쑥한.

javelin *n.* (*dart*) t'u-ch'ang 투창(投槍).

jaw *n.* t'ŏk 턱 : *Hold your ~!* tak-ch'yŏ 닥쳐 !

jazz *n.* chae-jŭ 재즈 : ~ *band* chae-jŭ-baen-dŭ 재즈밴드.

jealous *adj.* chil-t'u-sim-man-ŭn 질투심많은, si-gi-ha-nŭn 시기하는, t'u-gi-ha-nŭn 투기하는.

jealousy *n.* chil-t'u 질투, kang-jja 강짜.

jeer *v.* cho-rong-ha-da 조롱하다 ; pi-ut-da 비웃다.

jelly *n.* han-ch'ŏn 한천, u-mu 우무 ; chel-ri 젤리.

jellyfish *n.* hae-p'a-ri 해파리.

jeopardize *v.* wi-t'ae-rop-ge ha-da 위태롭게 하다.

jerk *n.* pi-t'ŭl-gi 비틀기 ; kŭn-yuk-ŭi kyŏng-ryŏn 근육의 경련. —*v.* hwaek chap-a-dang-gi-da 홱 잡아당기다.

jest *n.* & *v.* nong-dam(-ha-da) 농담(하다).

Jesus *n.* ye-su 예수, ye-su kŭ-ri-sŭ-do 예수 그리스도.

jet *v.* (*shoot*) ppŭm-ŏ-nae-da 뿜어내다, pun-ch'ul-ha-da 분출하다. —*n.* ① pun-ch'ul 분출. ② hŭk-ok 흑옥

jet plane che-t'ŭ-gi 제트기. 「(黑玉).

jetty *n.* (*breakwater*) pang-p'a-je 방파제 ; (*pier*) pu-du 부두, sŏn-ch'ang 선창. 「자.

Jew *n.* yu-t'ae-in 유태인 ; yu-t'ae-gyo sin-ja 유태교 신

jewel *n.* po-sŏk 보석, po-ok 보옥. 「보석 세공인.

jewel(l)er *n.* po-sŏk-sang 보석상, po-sŏk se-gong-in

jingle v. ttal-rang-ddal-rang ul-ri-da 딸랑딸랑 울리다.

jinx n. pul-gil-han kŏt 불길한 것, ching-k'ŭ-sŭ 징크스.

job n. ① (*work*) il 일, sak-il 삯일. ② (*employment*) chik-ŏp 직업. ③ (*post*) chi-wi 지위.

jocund adj. myŏng-rang-han 명랑한, chŭl-gŏ-un 즐거운.

join v. ka-ip-ha-da 가입하다, (*unite*) kyŏl-hap-ha-da 결합하다, (*connect*) yŏn-gyŏl-ha-da 연결하다.

joint n. ① (*of the body*) kwan-jŏl 관절. ② (*seam*) i-ŭn cha-ri 이은 자리. ③ (*connection*) chŏp-hap 접합. —adj. (*common*) kong-dong-ŭi 공동의.

joke n. nong-dam 농담. —v. nong-dam-ha-da 농담하다.

jolly adj. chŭl-gŏ-un 즐거운. —adv. mae-u 매우.

jolt v. tŏl-k'ŏng-gŏ-ri-da 덜컹거리다.

jostle v. ① (*push roughly*) pu-dit-ch'i-da 부딪치다. ② (*elbow*) mi-rŏ-jŏ-ch'i-da 밀어젖히다.

jot v. (*down*) kan-dan-ha-ge chŏk-ŏ-du-da 간단하게 적어두다. —n. cho-gŭm 조금, yak-gan 약간.

journal n. ① (*diary*) il-gi 일기, il-ji 일지. ② (*daily newspaper*) il-gan-sin-mun 일간신문. ③ (*periodical*) (chŏng-gi kan-haeng) chap-ji (정기 간행) 잡지.

journalist n. ki-ja 기자, chŏ-ŏ-nŏl-ri-sŭ-t'ŭ 저어널리스트.

journey n. yŏ-haeng 여행, yŏ-jŏng 여정(旅程). —v. yŏ-haeng-ha-da 여행하다. 「희

joy n. ki-bbŭm 기쁨, chŭl-gŏ-um 즐거움, hwan-hŭi 환

joyful adj. ki-bbŭn 기쁜, chŭl-gŏ-un 즐거운.

judge n. chae-p'an-gwan 재판관, p'an-sa 판사. —v. p'an-gyŏl-ha-da 판결하다.

judg(e)ment n. ① chae-p'an 재판. ② (*discrimination*) p'an-dan 판단. ③ (*opinion*) ŭi-gyŏn 의견.

jug n. ① chu-jŏn-ja 주전자, hang-a-ri 항아리, tan-ji 단지. ② cho-ggi 조끼.

juggle n. (*sleight of hand*) yo-sul 요술 ; (*imposture*)

sa-gi 사기. 「sa-git-gun 사겟군.

juggler *n.* ① yo-sul-jang-i 요술장이. ② (*impostor*)

juice *n.* chŭp 즙, chu-u-sŭ 주우스 : *fruit* ~ kwa-jŭp

July *n.* ch'il-wŏl 7월. 「과즙.

jumble *n.* chap-dong-sa-ni 잡동사니 ; hol-lan 혼란.

jump *v.* ttwi-ŏ-o-rŭ-da 뛰어오르다, twi-ŏ-nŏm-da 뛰어넘다. —*n.* (*leap*) to-yak 도약, chŏm-p'ŭ 점프.

junction *n.* chŏp-hap 접합, chŏp-hap-jŏm 접합점.

June *n.* yu-wŏl 6월.

jungle *n.* mil-rim 밀림, chŏng-gŭl 정글.

junior *n.* (*younger*) yŏn-so-ja 연소자 ; pu-ha 부하 ; hu-bae 후배. —*adj.* yŏn-so-han 연소한.

junk *n.* ① chŏng-k'ŭ 정크. ② p'ye-mul 페물.

Jupiter *n.* ① chu-p'i-t'ŏ 주피터. ② mok-song 목성(木星).

jurisdiction *n.* ① sa-bŏp-gwŏn 사법권. ② kwan-hal

jury *n.* pae-sim-wŏn 배심원. 「ku-yŏk 관할 구역.

just *adj.* (*right*) chŏng-dang-han 정당한, kong-jŏng-han 공정한. —*adv.* ① (*exactly*) pa-ro 바로. ② (*hardly*) ka-gga-sŭ-ro 가까스로.

justice *n.* chŏng-ŭi 정의, kong-jŏng 공정.

justify *v.* chŏng-dang-hwa-ha-da 정당화하다, ol-t'a-go ha-da 옳다고 하다. 「ch'ul-ha-da 돌출하다.

jut *v.* (*project*) pul-ruk nae-mil-da 불룩 내밀다, tol-

juvenile *adj.* so-nyŏn-so-nyŏ-ŭi 소년소녀의.

K

---

kangaroo *n.* k'aeng-gŏ-ru-u 캥거루우.

keen *adj.* ① nal-k'a-ro-un 날카로운. ② (*strong*) kang-han 강한. ③ (*eager*) yŏl-mang-ha-nŭn 열망하는.

keep *v.* ① (*guard*) chi-k'i-da 지키다. ② (*raise*) ki-rŭ-da 기르다. ③ (*preserve*) po-jon-ha-da 보존하다.

keeper *n.* ① (*guardian*) kwal·li·in 관리인, kam·si·ja 감시자. ② (*proprietor*) so·yu·ja 소유자.

keeping *n.* yu·ji 유지 ; po·jon 보존, pu·yang 부양.

keepsake *n.* yu·p'um 유품, ki·nyŏm·p'um 기념품.

kennel *n.* kae·jip 개집 ; (*lair*) kul 굴.

kernel *n.* kwa·sil·ŭi in 과실의 인(仁), (*grain*) al-maeng·i 알맹이.

kerosene *n.* tŭng·yu 등유(燈油).

kettle *n.* chu·jŏn·ja 주전자, (*pot*) sot 솥.

key *n.* ① yŏl·soe 열쇠. ② (*clue*) sil·ma·ri 실마리. ③ (*secret*) pi·gyŏl 비결. ④ (*piano*) kŏn 건.

keyhole *n.* yŏl·soe ku·mŏng 열쇠 구멍, ma·gae ku·mŏng 마개 구멍.

key industry ki·gan san·ŏp 기간 산업.

key money kwŏl·li·gŭm 권리금, po·jŭng·gŭm 보증금.

khaki *adj.* k'a·a·k'i·saek·ŭi 카아키색의.

kick *v.* ch'a·da 차다. —*n.* pal·ro ch'a·gi 발로 차기.

kid *n.* ① (*young goat*) sae·ggi yŏm·so 새끼 염소. ② (*child*) a·i 아이. —*v.* nong·dam·ha·da 농담하다.

kidnap *v.* (*abduct*) kkoe·ŏ·nae·da 꾀어내다, yu·goe·ha·da 유괴하다, (*hijack*) nap·ch'i·ha·da 납치하다.

kidney *n.* sin·jang 신장(腎臟), k'ong·p'at 콩팥.

kill *v.* ① (*slay*) chuk·i·da 죽이다. ② (*suppress*) ŏk·nu·rŭ·da 억누르다. ③ (*consume*) so·bi·ha·da 소비하다.

killer *n.* chuk·i·nŭn sa·ram 죽이는 사람.

kiln *n.* ka·ma(·sot) 가마(솥).

kilogram *n.* k'il·ro·gŭ·raem 킬로그램.

Kimchi *n.* (*Korean*) kim·ch'i 김치.

kilometer *n.* k'il·ro·mi·t'ŏ 킬로미터.

kin *n.* (*relatives*) ch'in·ch'ŏk 친척, ch'in·jok 친족, hyŏl·jok·gwan·gye 혈족관계, (*family*) ka·mun 가문.

[ka·ma·(sot)]

kind *n.* (*sort*) chong·ryu 종류, (*character*) sŏng·jil 성질. —*adj.* ch'in·jŏl·han 친절한.

kindergarten *n.* yu-ch'i-wŏn 유치원.

kindle *v.* pul-sa-rŭ-da 불사르다;pal-gge ha-da 밝게 하다.

kindly *adj.* ch'in-jŏl-han 친절한, sang-nyang-han 상냥한. —*adv.* ch'in-jŏl-ha-ge 친절하게, ki-ggŏ-i 기꺼이.

kindness *n.* ch'in-jŏl 친절 ; (*love*) ae-jŏng 애정.

kindred *n.* ① (*blood relationship*) hyŏ-ryŏn 혈연 ; (*clan*) tong-jok 동족. ② (*likeness*) yu-sa 유사. —*adj.* ① hyŏ-ryŏn-ŭi 혈연의. ② yu-sa-han 유사한.

king *n.* wang 왕, kuk-wang 국왕, kun-ju 군주.

kingdom *n.* wang-guk 왕국 ; (*realm*) …kye …계.

kingfisher *n.* mul-ch'ong-sae 물총새. 「당한.

kingly *adj.* wang-ŭi 왕의 ; (*royal*) tang-dang-han 당

kinsfolk *n.* ch'in-ch'ŏk 친척, il-ga 일가.

kiss *n.* ip-mat-ch'u-gi 입맞추기, k'i-sŭ 키스. —*v.* ip-mat-ch'u-da 입맞추다. 「취사장.

kitchen *n.* pu-ŏk 부엌, chu-bang 주방, ch'wi-sa-jang

kite *n.* ① (*toy*) yŏn 연(鳶). ② (*bird*) sol-gae 솔개. ③ (*impostor*) sa-git-gun 사깃군. 「끼.

kitten *n.* ko-yang-i sae-ggi 고양이 새

klaxon *n.* cha-dong-ch'a-ŭi kyŏng-jŏk 자동차의 경적. 「령.

knack *n.* som-ssi 솜씨, yo-ryŏng 요 [yŏn]

knapsack *n.* pae-nang 배낭, ran-do-sel 란도셀. 「건달.

knave *n.* (*rascal*) ak-han 악한(惡漢), (*rogue*) kŏn-dal

knead *v.* pan-juk-ha-da 반죽하다, kae-da 개다.

knee *n.* mu-rŭp 무릎 : *on one's ~s* mu-rŭp-ŭl kkul-k'o 무릎을 꿇고.

kneel *v.* mu-rŭp-ŭl kkul-t'a 무릎을 꿇다. 「jo 흉조.

knell *n.* ① cho-jong 조종(弔鍾). ② (*evil omen*) hyung-

knife *n.* chu-mŏ-ni-k'al 주머니칼, na-i-p'ŭ 나이프.

knight *n.* ki-sa 기사(騎士).

knit v. ① (*yarn*) ttŭ-da 뜨다 ; jja-da 짜다. ② (*joint*) chŏp-hap-ha-da 접합하다.

knitting n. ttŭ-gae-jil 뜨개질, p'yŏn-mul 편물.

knob n. ① son-jap-i 손잡이. ② (*lump*) hok 혹.

knock v. (*strike*) tu-dŭ-ri-da 두드리다. —n. (*stroke*) t'a-gyŏk 타격, (*blow*) ku-t'a 구타 ; no-k'ŭ 노크.

knockout n. nok-a-u-t'ŭ 녹아우트, k'e-i-o-u 케이오우.

knoll n. (*mound*) chak-ŭn san 작은 산.

knot n. ① (*tie*) mae-dŭp 매듭. ② (*nautical mile*) hae-ri 해리(海里). ③ no-t'ŭ 노트. —v. mae-dŭp-jit-da 매듭짓다, (*entangle*) ŏl-k'i-da 얽히다.

know v. ① (*understand*) al-da 알다. ② (*recognize*) in-jŏng-ha-da 인정하다. ③ (*be acquainted with*) …wa ch'in-han sa-i-da …와 친한 사이다. 「결.

know-how n. chi-sik 지식, pang-bŏp 방법, pi-gyŏl 비

knowledge n. (*information*) chi-sik 지식, in-sik 인식 ; i-hae 이해 ; (*learning*) hak-mun 학문.

known adj. al-ryŏ-jyŏ it-nŭn 알려져 있는 : *make* ~ al-ri-da 알리다, pal-p'yo-ha-da 발표하다.

knuckle n. son-ga-rak-ŭi kwan-jŏl 손가락의 관절.

Korea n. han-guk 한국 : tae-han-min-guk 대한민국.

Korean n. & adj. (*people*) han-guk-sa-ram(-ŭi) 한국사람(의) ; (*language*) han-guk-mal(-ŭi) 한국말(의).

Kremlin n. k'ŭ-re-mŭl-rin kung-jŏn 크레믈린 궁전 ; so-ryŏn chŏng-bu 소련 정부.

❧ **L** ❧

label n. ttak-ji 딱지, pu-jŏn 부전, re-t'e-rŭ 레테르. —v. ttak-ji-rŭl pu-ch'i-da 딱지를 붙이다.

labo(u)r n. no-dong 노동, (*toil*) ko-doen il 고된 일. —v. il-ha-da 일하다, no-dong-ha-da 노동하다.

laboratory *n.* sil-hŏm-sil 실험실, yŏn-gu-so 연구소 : *chemical* ～ hwa-hak-yŏn-gu-so 화학연구소.

laborious *adj.* him-dŭ-nŭn 힘드는, ko-doen 고된.

labo(u)r union no-dong-jo-hap 노동조합.

labyrinth *n.* (*maze*) mi-gung 미궁(迷宮), mi-ro 미로.

lace *n.* (*fabric*) re-i-sŭ 레이스, kkŭn 끈.

lack *n.* (*want*) pu-jok 부족, (*deficiency*) kyŏl-p'ip 결핍. ―*v.* pu-jok-ha-da 부족하다, mo-ja-ra-da 모자라다.

lacquer *n.* rae-k'ŏ 래커, ch'il 칠(漆), ot 옻.

lacquer ware ch'il-gi 칠기.   「sŏk 녀석.

lad *n.* chŏl-mŭn-i 젊은이, so-nyŏn 소년, (*chap*) nyŏ-

ladder *n.* ① sa-dak-da-ri 사다다리. ② (*means*) su-dan 수단, pang-bŏp 방법.

lade *v.* (*load*) hwa-mul-ŭl sit-da 화물을 싣다 ; (*burden*) chim-ŭl chi-u-da 짐을 지우다.

laden *adj.* chim-ŭl si-rŭn 짐을 실은.

ladies and gentlemen sin-sa suk-nyŏ 신사 숙녀.

lading *n.* chim-sit-gi 짐싣기, chŏk-jae 적재 : *bill of* ～ sŏn-ha-jŭng-gwŏn 선하증권.   「내다.

ladle *n.* kuk-ja 국자. ―*v.* p'u-da 푸다, p'ŏ-nae-da 퍼

lady *n.* kwi-bu-in 귀부인, suk-nyŏ 숙녀 : *a* ～ *clerk* yŏ-sa-mu-wŏn 여사무원/*a* ～ *killer* saek-gol 색골.

lag *v.* kku-mul-gŏ-ri-da 꾸물거리다, ch'ŏ-ji-da 처지다.

lair *n.* (*den*) tŭl-jim-sŭng-ŭi kul 들짐승의 굴.

laity *n.* (*laymen*) sok-in 속인(俗人) ; p'ut-na-gi 풋나기, a-ma-t'yu-ŏ 아마튜어.

lake *n.* ho-su 호수 ; (*pond*) mot 못, yŏn-mot 연못.

lamb *n.* ① (*young sheep*) ŏ-rin yang 어린 양. ② (*innocent person*) yu-sun-han sa-ram 유순한 사람.

lame *adj.* chŏl-rŭm-ba-ri-ŭi 절름발이의 ; (*imperfect*) pul-wan-jŏn-han 불완전한.   「sŭl-p'ŭm 슬픔.

lament *v.* sŭl-p'ŏ-ha-da 슬퍼하다. ―*n.* pi-t'an 비탄,

lamentation *n.* pi-t'an 비탄, t'ong-gok 통곡.

lamp *n.* tŭng 등, nam-p'o 남포 : *a street* ~ ka-ro-dŭng 가로등/*a safety* ~ an-jŏn-dŭng 안전등.

lamplight *n.* tŭng-bul 등불, raem-p'ŭ-bit 램프빛.

lance *n.* ch'ang 창(槍), chak-sal 작살.

land *n.* ① ttang 땅, t'o-ji 토지. ② (*state*) na-ra 나라. —*v.* sang-ryuk-ha-da 상륙하다 ; (*alight*) ha-ch'a-ha-da 하차하다 ; (*arrive*) to-ch'ak-ha-da 도착하다.

landlady *n.* yŏ-ja-ju-in 여자주인, an-ju-in 안주인.

landlord *n.* ① (*house*) chip-ju-in 집주인 ; ka-jang 가장. ② (*property*) chi-ju 지주.

landmark *n.* ① kyŏng-gye-p'yo 경계표. ② (*outstanding event*) hoek-gi-jŏk sa-gŏn 획기적 사건.

landowner *n.* t'o-ji so-yu-ja 토지 소유자, chi-ju 지주.

landscape *n.* p'ung-gyŏng 풍경, chŏn-mang 전망.

landslide *n.* sa-t'ae 사태, san-sa-t'ae 산사태.

lane *n.* chop-ŭn kil 좁은 길, (*byway*) saet-gil 샛길.

language *n.* mal 말, ŏn-ŏ 언어, kuk-ŏ 국어.

languid *adj.* na-rŭn-han 나른한, no-gon-han 노곤한.

languish *v.* soe-yak-hae-ji-da 쇠약해지다, si-dŭl-da 시 들다.

lantern *n.* ch'o-rong 초롱, k'an-del-ra 칸델라.

lap *v.* (*lick*) hal-t'a 핥다. —*n.* mu-rŭp 무릎.

lapse *v.* ① (*backslide*) t'a-rak-ha-da 타락하다. ② (*pass*) si-gan-i chi-na-da 시간이 지나다.

lard *n.* twae-ji ki-rŭm 돼지 기름, ra-a-dŭ 라아드.

large *adj.* k'ŏ-da-ran 커다란, (*spacious*) nŏl-bŭn 넓은, (*copious*) man-ŭn 많은, (*liberal*) kwan-dae-han 관대한.

lark *n.* (*skylark*) chong-da-ri 종다리, chong-dal-sae 종달새.

lascivious *adj.* ŭm-t'ang-han 음탕한.

lash *n.* ch'ae-jjik 채찍. —*v.* ① mae-jil-ha-da 매질하다. ② (*bind*) tong-yŏ-mae-da 동여매다.

lass *n.* so-nyŏ 소녀, chŏl-mŭn yŏ-ja 젊은 여자.

last v. (*continue*) kye-sok-ha-da 계속하다. —*adj.*
ch'oe-hu-ŭi 최후의 ; (*most recent*) ch'oe-gŭn-ŭi 최근
의. —*adv.* ch'oe-hu-ro 최후로. 「영속하는.

lasting *adj.* o-rae ka-nŭn 오래 가는, yŏng-sok-ha-nŭn

latch *n.* pit-jang 빗장, kŏl-soe 걸쇠.

late *adj.* ① nŭ-jŭn 늦은, chi-gak-han 지각한. ② (*recent*)
ch'oe-gŭn-ŭi 최근의. ③ (*dead*) ko 고(故) : *the* ~
Mr. A ko e-i-ssi 고(故) A씨. —*adv.* nŭt-ge 늦게.

lately *adv.* yo-jŭ-ŭm 요즈음, kŭl-lae 근래.

latent *adj.* cham-bok-han 잠복한, cham-jae-jŏk 잠재
적 : ~ *period* cham-bok-gi 잠복기.

latest *adj.* ch'oe-gŭn-ŭi 최근의, ch'oe-hu-ŭi 최후위.

lathe *n.* sŏn-ban 선반(旋盤), nok-ro 녹로.

Latin *adj.* ra-t'in-ŭi 라틴의, ra-t'in-gye-ŭi 라틴계의.
—*n.* ra-t'in-ŏ 라틴어, ra-t'in-sa-ram 라틴사람.

latitude *n.* ① wi-do 위도, ssi-jul 씨줄. ② (*pl.*) chi-
latrine *n.* (*privy*) pyŏn-so 변소. 」dae 지대.

latter *adj.* hu-ja-ŭi 후자의. —*n.* hu-ja 후자.

lattice *n.* kyŏk-ja 격자(格子), kyŏk-ja-ch'ang 격자창.

laudable *adj.* kya-rŭk-han 갸륵한, ki-t'ŭk-han 기특한.

laugh *v.* ut-da 웃다. —*n.* u-sŭm 웃음.

laughter *n.* u-sŭm 웃음, u-sŭm-so-ri 웃음소리.

launch *v.* ① (*ship*) chin-su-ha-da 진수하다. ② (*start*)
si-jak-ha-da 시작하다. —*n.* chin-su(-dae) 진수(대).

laundress *n.* se-t'ak-ha-nŭn yŏ-ja 세탁하는 여자, se-t'ak-
bu 세탁부.

laundry *n.* ① se-t'ak-so 세탁소. ② se-t'ak-mul 세탁물.

laurel *n.* ① wŏl-gye-su 월계수. ② wŏl-gye-gwan 월
계관. ③ (*honor*) yŏng-ye 영예. ④ (*victory*) sŭng-ri
lava *n.* yong-am 용암(溶岩). 」승리.

lavatory *n.* se-myŏn-so 세면소, hwa-jang-sil 화장실.

laver *n.* kim 김.

lavish *v.* a·ggim·ŏp·si chu·da 아낌없이 주다, (*squander*) nang·bi·ha·da 낭비하다. —*adj.* a·ggim·ŏp·nŭn 아낌 없는 ; (*abundant*) p'ung·bu·han 풍부한.

law *n.* pŏp 법, pŏp·ryul 법률 : *constitutional* ~ hŏn-bŏp 헌법/*martial* ~ kun·bŏp 군법.

lawbreaker *n.* pŏm·bŏp·ja 범법자, choe·in 죄인.

lawful *adj.* hap·bŏp·jŏk·in 합법적인, (*legitimate*) chŏk·ch'ul·ŭi 적출(嫡出)의 : *a* ~ *child* chŏk·ja 적자.

lawless *adj.* mu·bŏp·ŭi 무법의, pul·bŏp·jŏk·in 불법적인.

lawn *n.* chan·di 잔디, chan·di·bat 잔디밭 : ~ *mower* chan·di kkak·nŭn ki·gye 잔디 깎는 기계.

lawyer *n.* pŏp·ryul·ga 법률가 ; pyŏn·ho·sa 변호사.

lax *adj.* nŭ·sŭn·han 느슨한 ; ae·mae·han 애매한.

lay *v.* ① (*produce*) na·t'a 낳다. ② (*put down*) no·t'a 놓다, tu·da 두다. ③ (*prepare*) chun·bi·ha·da 준비하다.

layer *n.* ① not·nŭn sa·ram 놓는 사람 : *a brick* ~ pyŏk·dol ssat·nŭn sa·ram 벽돌 쌓는 사람. ② ch'ŭng 층, kyŏp 겹.

layman *n.* ① sok·in 속인(俗人). ② mun·oe·han 문외한.

layoff *n.* hyu·sik 휴식, il·si·jŏk hae·go 일시적 해고.

lazy *adj.* ke·ŭ·rŭn 게으른, kum·ddŭn 굼뜬, nŭ·rin 느린.

leach *v.* kŏ·rŭ·da 거르다. —*n.* yŏ·gwa·gi 여과기.

lead *v.* i·ggŭl·da 이끌다, in·do·ha·da 인도하다, ap·jang·sŏ ka·da 앞장서 가다. —*n.* ① (*direction*) sŏn·do 선도, (*command*) chi·hwi 지휘. ② (*metal*) nap 납.

leader *n.* sŏn·do·ja 선도자, t'ong·sol·ja 통솔자, chi·do·ja 지도자.

leadership *n.* chi·do 지도, t'ong·sol·ryŏk 통솔력.

leading *n.* sŏn·do 선도. t'ong·sol 통솔. —*adj.* chi·do·jŏk·in 지도적인 ; il·ryu·ŭi 일류의 ; (*chief*) chu·yo·han 주요한 ; yu·ryŏk·han 유력한.

leaf *n.* ① (*of tree*) na·mut·ip 나뭇잎. ② (*of book*)

han chang 한 장, p'e-i-ji 페이지.

leaflet *n.* ppi-ra kwang-go 삐라 광고.

league *n.* (*alliance*) yŏn-maeng 연맹, tong-maeng 동맹 : *L~ of Nations* kuk-je yŏn-maeng 국제 연맹.

leak *n.* sae-nŭn kot 새는 곳. —*v.* sae-da 새다.

lean *adj.* yŏ-win 여윈, me-ma-rŭn 메마른. —*v.* (*incline*) ki-ul-da 기울다, (*rely*) ki-dae-da 기대다.

leap *v.* ttwi-da 뛰다. —*n.* ttwi-gi 뛰기, to-yak 도약.

leap year yun-nyŏn 윤년(閏年). 「듣다.

learn *v.* pae-u-da 배우다 ; al-da 알다 ; (*hear*) tŭt-da

learned *adj.* pak-sik-han 박식한, yu-sik-han 유식한.

learning *n.* hak-mun 학문 ; hak-sŭp 학습.

lease *n.* im-dae(-ch'a) kye-yak 임대(차) 계약. —*v.* im-dae(-ch'a)-ha-da 임대(차)하다.

leash *n.* ka-juk-ggŭn 가죽끈, pat-jul 밧줄.

least *adj.* ch'oe-so-ŭi 최소의. —*adv.* ka-jang chŏk-ge 가장 적게. —*n.* ch'oe-so 최소 : *at ~* chŏk-ŏ-do 적어도.

leather *n.* ka-juk 가죽, p'i-hyŏk 피혁 : *~ belt* ka-juk hyŏk-dae 가죽 혁대.

leave *v.* (*go away*) ttŏ-na-da 떠나다 ; (*quit*) kŭ-man-tu-da 그만두다 ; nae-bŏ-ryŏ tu-da 내버려 두다. —*n.* ① (*permission*) hŏ-ga 허가. ② hyu-ga 휴가.

leaven *n.* hyo-mo 효모(酵母), nu-ruk 누룩. —*v.* pal-hyo-si-k'i-da 발효시키다.

lectern *n.* song-sŏ-dae 성서대, tok-gyŏng-dae 독경대.

lecture *n.* kang-ŭi 강의, (*speech*) kang-yŏn 강연 ; hun-gye 훈계. —*v.* kang-ŭi-ha-da 강의하다.

lecturer *n.* kang-sa 강사, yŏn-sa 연사.

ledge *n.* ① sŏn-ban 선반, si-rŏng 시렁. ② (*reef*) am-ch'o 암초. ③ (*mineral vein*) kwang-maek 광맥.

ledger *n.* chang-bu 장부, tae-jang 대장(台帳).

leek *n.* pu-ch'u 부추.

left *adv.* oen-p'yŏn-ŭ-ro 왼편으로. —*adj.* oen-jjok-ŭi 왼쪽의. —*n.* oen-p'yŏn 왼편.   「서투른.

left-handed *adj.* oen-son-jap-i-ŭi 왼손잡이의 ; sŏ-t'u-rŭn

leftover *n. & adj.* na-mŏ-ji(-ŭi) 나머지(의).

left wing chwa-ik 좌익, chwa-p'a 좌파.

leg *n.* ① ta-ri 다리. ② (*prop*) pŏ-t'im-dae 버팀대.

legacy *n.* yu-san 유산(遺産), yu-jŭng 유증.

legal *adj.* ① pŏp-ryul-sang-ŭi 법률상의. ② (*lawful*) hap-bŏp-jŏk-in 합법적인, chŏng-dang-han 정당한.

legation *n.* kong-sa-gwan 공사관(公使館).

legend *n.* ① chŏn-sŏl 전설. ② pŏm-rye 범례(凡例).

legible *adj.* (*of handwriting*) il-ggi swi-un 읽기 쉬운: ～ *writing* il-ggi swi-un p'il-jŏk 읽기 쉬운 필적.

legion *n.* ① kun-dan 군단. ②(*great number*) ta-su 다

legislation *n.* (*enacting of laws*) ip-bŏp 입법.   「수.

legislator *n.* ip-bŏp-ja 입법자, pŏp-ryul-je-jŏng-ja 법률

legislature *n.* ip-bŏp-bu 입법부.   「제정자.

legitimate *adj.* (*lawful*) hap-bŏp-jŏk-in 합법적인 ; (*reasonable*) hap-ri-jŏk-in 합리적인 ; (*regular*) chŏng-t'ong-ŭi 정통의 : *a ～ child* chŏk-ja 적자(嫡子).

leisure *n.* yŏ-ga 여가, t'ŭm 틈, (*ease*) an-il 안일.

leisurely *adj.* nŭ-rit-han 느릿한 ; ch'im-ch'ak-han 침착한. —*adv.* yu-yu-hi 유유히.   「담황색.

lemon *n.* re-mon 레몬 ; (*pale yellow*) tam-hwang-saek

lemonade *n.* re-mon-su 레몬수, ra-mu-ne 라무네.

lend *v.* pil-ryŏ-ju-da 빌려주다 ; (*add*) ch'ŏm-ga-ha-da 첨가하다 ; (*furnish*) che-gong-ha-da 제공하다.   「거리.

length *n.* ki-ri 길이 ; (*time*) tong-an 동안 ; (*space*) kŏ-ri

lenient *adj.* a-ryang-it-nŭn 아량있는, nŏ-gŭ-rŏ-un 너그러운, (*merciful*) in-jŏng-gip'ŭn 인정깊은.

lens *n.* ren-jŭ 렌즈, su-jŏng-ch'e 수정체.

Lent *n.* sa-sun-jŏl 사순절(四旬節).

leopard *n.* p'yo-bŏm 표범.　　　「hwan-ja 문둥병 환자.
leper *n.* na-byŏng hwan-ja 나병 환자, mun-dung-byŏng
leprosy *n.* na-byŏng 나병.　　　「ge 보다 적게.
less *adj.* po-da chŏk-ŭn 보다 적은. —*adv.* po-da chŏk-
lessen *v.* (*make less*) kam-ha-da 감하다.
lesson *n.* (*school subject*) kyo-gwa 교과, hak-gwa 학
　과 ; su-ŏp 수업 ; (*precept*) kyo-hun 교훈.
lest *conj.* …ha-ji an-k'e …하지 않게.
let *v.* (*allow*) hŏ-rak-ha-da 허락하다. —*v.* ① (*allow
to*) …ha-ge ha-da …하게 하다. ② (*lend*) pil-ryŏ-ju-
da 빌려주다 : *house to* ~ set-jip 셋집.
lethargic *adj.* hon-su-sang-t'ae-ŭi 혼수상태의.
letter *n.* ① (*written message*) p'yŏn-ji 편지. ② (*alphabet*) mun-ja 문자. ③ (*learning*) hak-mun 학문.
　④ (*pl.*) (*literature*) mun-hak 문학.
letter box (*mailbox*) u-ch'e-t'ong 우체통.
lettuce *n.* sang-ch'i 상치, re-t'ŏ-su 레터스.
level *adj.* p'yŏng-p'yŏng-han 평평한, ko-rŭn 고른. —*n.*
　① su-p'yŏng 수평. ② (*standard*) su-jun 수준.
lever *n.* chi-ret-dae 지렛대, re-bŏ 레버.
levy *n.* ching-se 징세. —*v.* (*a tax*) pu-gwa-ha-da 부
　과하다, (*collect*) ching-su-ha-da 징수하다.
lewd *adj.* ŭm-t'ang-han 음탕한, ch'u-jap-han 추잡한.
liable *adj.* ch'aek-im-i it-nŭn 책임이 있는.
liaison *n.* yŏl-lak 연락, sŏp-oe 섭외 : ~ *officer* yŏl-
lak-jang-gyo 연락장교.　　　　　　　　「풍장이.
liar *n.* kŏ-jit-mal-jang-i 거짓말장이, ho-p'ung-jang-i 허
liberal *adj.* tae-bŏm-han 대범한, cha-yu-ju-ŭi-ŭi 자유
주의의. —*n.* cha-yu-ju-ŭi-ja 자유주의자.
liberate *v.* cha-yu-rop-ge ha-da 자유롭게 하다, hae-
bang-ha-da 해방하다, sŏk-bang-ha-da 석방하다.
liberty *n.* cha-yu 자유, hae-bang 해방.

librarian *n.* to-sŏ-gwan-wŏn 도서관원 ; sa-sŏ 사서.

library *n.* ① to-sŏ-gwan 도서관, (*study*) sŏ-jae 서재.
② chang-sŏ 장서. ③ ch'ong-sŏ 총서, mun-go 문고.

libretto *n.* ka-sa-jip 가사집, ka-sa 가사(歌詞).

licence · license *n.* ① hŏ-ga 허가, in-ga 인가. ② myŏn-
hŏ-jang 면허장, hŏ-ga-jŭng 허가증.

lick *v.* ① hal-t'a 핥다. ② (*beat*) ttae-ri-da 때리다.

lid *n.* ttu-ggŏng 뚜껑 ; (*eyelid*) nun-gga-p'ul 눈까풀.

lie *n.* kŏ-jit-mal 거짓말. —*v.* ① kŏ-jit-mal-ha-da 거짓
말하다. ② (*recline*) nup-da 눕다. ③ (*exist*) chon-jae-
ha-da 존재하다, (*be situated*) wi-ch'i-ha-da 위치하다.

lieutenant *n.* ① (*1st*) chung-wi 중위, (*2nd*) so-wi
소위, (*s.g., navy*) tae-wi 대위, (*j.g., navy*) chung-
wi 중위. ② (*deputy*) pu-gwan 부관.

lieutenant colonel chung-ryŏng 중령.

lieutenant commander hae-gun so-ryŏng 해군 소령.

lieutenant general chung-jang 중장.

life *n.* ① saeng-myŏng 생명. ② (*span of*) il-saeng 일
생. ③ (*biography*) chŏn-gi 전기(傳記). ④ (*way of
living*) saeng-gye 생계. ⑤ (*energy*) hwal-gi 활기.

lifeboat *n.* ku-jo-sŏn 구조선, ku-myŏng-jŏng 구명정.

life insurance saeng-myŏng po-hŏm 생명 보험.

lifelong *adj.* p'il-saeng-ŭi 필생의.

life preserver ku-myŏng-gu 구명구(具).

life sentence mu-gi ching-yŏk 무기 징역. 「일생.

lifetime *n.* saeng-ae 생애 ; p'yŏng-saeng 평생, il-saeng

lifework *n.* p'il-saeng-ŭi sa-ŏp 필생의 사업.

lift *v.* tŭ-rŏ-ol-ri-da 들어올리다, no-p'i-da 높이다 ; kŏt-
hi-da 걷히다. —*n.* ① tŭ-ro-ol-ri-gi 들어올리기. ②
sŭng-jin 승진. ③ (*elevator*) sŭng-gang-gi 승강기.

light *n.* ① pit 빛. ② (*lamp*) pul 불. —*v.* ① pul-ŭl
k'yŏ-da 불을 켜다. ② (*fire*) pul-p'i-u-da 불피우다.

  —*adj.* ka-byŏ-un 가벼운.   「가볍게 하다.
lighten *v.* ① pi-ch'u-da 비추다. ② ka-byŏp-ge ha-da
lighter *n.* ① (*cigarette*) ra-it'ŏ 라이터. ② (*barge*)
lighthouse *n.* tŭng-dae 등대.   └kŏ-rut-bae 거룻배.
lightly *adv.* ka-byŏp-ge 가볍게, (*easily*) swip-ge 쉽게.
lightning *n.* pŏn-gaet-bul 번갯불. —*adj.* kŭp-sok-han
급속한, chŏn-gwang-sŏk-hwa-ŭi 전광석화의.
like *v.* chǒ-a-ha-da 좋아하다. —*prep.* …wa ka-ch'i …
와 같이, ch'ŏ-rŏm 처럼. —*adj.* tal-mŭn 닮은.
likely *adj.* kŭ-rŏl-dŭt-han 그럴듯한, i-ssŭm-jik-han 있
음직한. —*adv.* a-ma 아마, ta-bun-hi 다분히.
liken *v.* (*compare*) pi-yu-ha-da 비유하다, pi-gi-da 비기
likeness *n.* pi-sŭt-ham 비슷함, yu-sa 유사.   └다.
likewise *adv.* ma-ch'an-ga-ji-ro 마찬가지로.
liking *n.* (*fancy*) ki-ho 기호, cho-a-ham 좋아함 : *Is it
your* ∼? Ma-ŭm-e tŭ-sip-ni-gga? 마음에 드십니까?
lilac *n.* cha-jŏng-hyang 자정향, ra-il-rak 라일락.
lily *n.* na-ri 나리, paek-hap 백합 : ∼ *of the valley* ŭn-
bang-ul-ggot 은방울꽃/*water* ∼ su-ryŏn 수련.
limb *n.* ① (*branch*) k'ŭn ka-ji 큰 가지. ② (*body*) son-
bal 손발, su-jok 수족, (*wing*) nal-gae 날개.
lime *n.* sŏk-hoe 석회 : *caustic* ∼ saeng-sŏk-hoe 생석회.
limelight *n.* (*footlight*) kak-gwang 각광(脚光).
limestone *n.* sŏk-hoe-sŏk 석회석.   「pŏm-wi 범위.
limit *v.* che-han-ha-da 제한하다. —*n.* che-han 제한 ;
limitation *n.* che-han 제한, (*bounds*) han-gye 한계.
limp *v.* chŏl-rŭm-gŏ-ri-da 절름거리다, chŏl-dduk-gŏ-ri-
da 절뚝거리다. —*adj.* (*flexible*) na-gŭt-na-gŭt-han
나긋나긋한. —*n.* chŏl-rŭm-ba-ri 절름발이.   「행.
line *n.* ① sŏn 선. ② (*row*) chul 줄, yŏl 열(列), haeng
linen *n.* a-ma-p'o 아마포, rin-ne-rŭ 린네르.
liner *n.* chŏng-gi hang-gong-gi 정기 항공기.

linger v. u-mul-jju-mul-ha-da 우물쭈물하다, pin-dung-gŏ-ri-da 빈둥거리다, chil-jil kkŭl-da 질질 끌다.

lingering adj. kku-mul-gŏ-ri-nŭn 꾸물거리는.

linguist n. ŏn-ŏ-hak-ja 언어학자, ŏ-hak-ja 어학자.

liniment n. pa-rŭ-nŭn yak 바르는 약.

lining n. ① (of dresses) an 안, an-gam 안감. ② (contents) nae-yong 내용, al-maeng-i 알맹이.

link v. yŏn-gyŏl-ha-da 연결하다. —n. (loop) ko-ri 고리.

lion n. sa-ja 사자, ra-i-on 라이온.

lip n. ip-sul 입술, ip 입. —adj. (insincere) mal-bbun-in 말뿐인.

lipstick n. ip-sul-yŏn-ji 입술연지, rip-sŭ-t'ik 립스틱.

liquid n. aek-ch'e 액체. —adj. aek-ch'e-ŭi 액체의.

liquor n. al-k'o-ol ŭm-ryo 알코올 음료, sul 술.

lisp v. hyŏ-jja-rae-gi so-ri-rŭl ha-da 혀짜래기 소리를 하다. —n. hyŏ-jja-rae-gi so-ri 혀짜래기 소리.

list n. (table) p'yo 표, (roll) myŏng-bu 명부. —v. myŏng-bu-e chŏk-da 명부에 적다.

listen v. tŭt-da 듣다, kwi-rŭl ki-u-ri-da 귀를 기울이다.

literal adj. mun-ja kŭ-dae-ro-ŭi 문자 그대로의 ; (accurate) ; chŏng-hwak-han 정확한.

literary adj. mun-hak-ŭi 문학의, mun-ŏ-jŏk-in 문어적인 : ~ works mun-hak-jak-p'um 문학작품.

literate adj. il-ggo ssŭl su it-nŭn 읽고 쓸 수 있는, (learned) kyo-yang-i it-nŭn 교양이 있는.

literature n. ① mun-hak 문학, mun-ye 문예. ② chŏ-sul 저술. ③ (documents) mun-hŏn 문헌. 「석판화.

lithograph n. sŏk-p'an-in-swae 석판인쇄, sŏk-p'an-hwa

litre · liter n. ri-t'ŏ 리터. 「dong-sa-ni 잡동사니.

litter n. ① (stretcher) tŭl-gŏt 들것. ② (mess) chap-

little adj. (size) chak-ŭn 작은, (amount) chŏk-ŭn 적은 ; ŏ-rin 어린. —n. cho-gŭm 조금, so-ryang 소량.

live v. sal-da 살다, saeng-hwal-ha-da 생활하다. —adj. sa-ra-it-nŭn 살아있는, hwal-gi-it-nŭn 활기있는.

livelihood n. saeng-gye 생계, sal-rim 살림.

lively adj. hwal-bal-han 활발한 ; (vivid) saeng-saeng-han 생생한. —adv. ki-un-ch'a-ge 기운차게.

liver n. kan-jang 간장, kan 간 : ~ oil kan-bu 간유.

livestock n. ka-ch'uk 가축.

living adj. sa-ra-it-nŭn 살아있는. —n. saeng-gye 생계.

lizard n. to-ma-baem 도마뱀.

load n. ① (on a cart) chim 짐. ② (burden) pu-dam 부담. —v. chim-ŭl sit-da 짐을 싣다.

loaf n. (bread) ppang cho-gak 빵 조각. —v. (spend time idly) nol-go chi-nae-da 놀고 지내다.

loan n. tae-bu 대부(貸付), kong-ch'ae 공채, ch'a-gwan 차관. —v. tae-bu-ha-da 대부하다.

loath adj. si-rŭn 싫은, yŏk-gyŏ-un 역겨운. 「실.

lobby n. ro-bi 로비 ; hyu-ge-sil 휴게실 ; tae-gi-sil 대기

lobe n. (of the ear) kwit-bul 귓불.

lobster n. pa-da-ga-jae 바다가재, k'ŭn sae-u 큰 새우.

local adj. chi-bang-ŭi 지방의 : ~ color chi-bang-saek 지방색/a ~ paper chi-bang-sin-mun 지방신문.

locate v. (be situated) cha-ri-jap-da 자리잡다, (find out) wi-ch'i-rŭl a-ra-nae-da 위치를 알아내다.

location n. (position) wi-ch'i 위치 ; ya-oe ch'wal-yŏng-jang 야외 촬영장, ro-k'e-i-syŏn 로케이션.

lock n. ① cha-mul-soe 자물쇠. ② (water) su-mun 수문. —v. cha-mul-soe-rŭl ch'ae-u-da 자물쇠를 채우다, cham-gŭ-da 잠그다.

locker n. ① ro-k'ŏ 로커. ② (cabinet to be locked) ch'an-jang 찬장.

locomotive n. ki-gwan-ch'a 기관차.

locust n. me-ddu-gi 메뚜기 ; (cicada) mae-mi 매미.

lodge *v.* muk-da 묵다, suk-bak-ha-da 숙박하다. *—n.* (*hut*) o-du-mak-jip 오두막집, su-wi-sil 수위실.

lodger *n.* suk-bak-in 숙박인, ha-suk-in 하숙인.

lodging house ha-suk-jip 하숙집.

loft *n.* ko-mi-ta-rak-bang 고미다락방, wi-ch'ŭng 위층.

lofty *adj.* ① mae-u no-p'ŭn 매우 높은. ② (*noble*) ko-sang-han 고상한. ③ (*arrogant*) kŏ-man-han 거만한.

log *n.* ① t'ong-na-mu 통나무. ② (*diary*) hang-hae-il-ji 항해일지 : ~ *cabin* t'ong-na-mu-jip 통나무집.

logic *n.* nol-li-hak 논리학.

loin *n.* hŏ-ri 허리, yo-bu 요부(腰部). 「어정거리다.

loiter *v.* pin-dung-gŏ-ri-da 빈둥거리다, ŏ-jŏng-gŏ-ri-da

loll *v.* (*hang*) ch'uk nu-rŏ-ji-da 축 늘어지다.

lone *adj.* ① ko-dok-han 고독한, ssŭl-ssŭl-han 쓸쓸한. ② oe-jin 외진. ③ (*unmarried*) tok-sin-ŭi 독신의.

loneliness *n.* ko-dok 고독, ssŭl-ssŭl-ham 쓸쓸함.

lonely *adj.* ① oe-ro-un 외로운. ② oe-ddan 외딴.

lonesome *adj.* ssŭl-ssŭl-han 쓸쓸한, oe-ro-un 외로운.

long *adj.* kin 긴, o-raen 오랜. *—adv.* kil-ge 길게, o-rae 오래. *—v.* (*yearn*) tong-gyŏng-ha-da 동경하다; yŏl-mang-ha-da 열망하다.

longevity *n.* chang-su 장수(長壽), su-myŏng 수명.

longing *n.* kal-mang 갈망, yŏl-mang 열망.

longitude *n.* kyŏng-do 경도(經度), kyŏng-sŏn 경선.

long-run *adj.* chang-gi hŭng-haeng-ŭi 장기 흥행의.

look *v.* pa-ra-bo-da 바라보다, (*stare*) yu-sim-hi po-da 유심히 보다 ; (*face*) hyang-ha-da 향하다. *—n.* ① (*glance*) il-gyŏn 일견. ② (*aspect*) yong-mo 용모.

looking glass kŏ-ul 거울, ch'e-gyŏng 체경.

lookout *n.* (*watch*) mang-bo-gi 망보기, kam-si 감시.

loom *n.* pe-t'ŭl 베틀, chik-jo-gi 직조기. *—v.* ŏ-ryŏm-p'u-si na-t'a-na-da 어렴풋이 나타나다.

loop *n.* ko-ri 고리 ; t'e 테 ; ol-ga-mi 올가미.

loophole *n.* (*outlet*) to-mang-gil 도망길.

loose *adj.* (*slack*) hŏl-gŏ-wŏ-jin 헐거워진, (*not tight*) tan-jŏng-ch'i mot-han 단정치 못한. —*v.* (*slacken*) nŭt-ch'u-da 늦추다, p'u-rŏ-ju-da 풀어주다.

loosen *v.* (*untie*) p'ul-da 풀다, nŭ-sŭn-ha-ge ha-da 느슨하게 하다, no-a-ju-da 놓아주다. 「리품」

loot *n.* (*booty*) yak-t'al-p'um 약탈품 ; chŏl-li-p'um 전

lop *v.* chal-ra-nae-da 잘라내다, (*hew*) ch'i-da 치다.

lord *n.* (*ruler*) kun-ju 군주 ; (*master*) chu-in 주인 ; kwi-jok 귀족 ; (*savior*) chu 주(主).

lordly *adj.* tang-dang-han 당당한, sung-go-han 숭고한.

lordship *n.* ① t'ong-ch'i-gwŏn 통치권, chi-bae-ryŏk 지배력. ② (*domain*) yŏng-ji 영지(領地).

lose *v.* il-t'a 잃다 ; (*be defeated*) chi-da 지다 ; (*miss*) no-ch'i-da 놓치다 ; (*waste*) hŏ-bi-ha-da 허비하다.

loser *n.* pun-sil-ja 분실자, p'ae-ja 패자.

loss *n.* pun-sil 분실, son-sil 손실 ; mol-rak 몰락. 「명의.

lost *adj.* i-rŭn 잃은, haeng-bang-bul-myŏng-ŭi 행방불

lot *n.* ① ch'u-ch'ŏm 추첨. ② (*destiny*) un-myŏng 운명. ③ (*house*) pu-ji 부지. ④ (*plenty*) man-ŭm 많음.

lotion *n.* se-je 세제(洗劑) ; hwa-jang-su 화장수.

lottery *n.* che-bi 제비, pok-gwŏn 복권.

lotus *n.* yŏn 연(蓮). 「ggŭ-rŏ-un 시끄러운.

loud *adj.* ① so-ri-ga k'ŭn 소리가 큰. ② (*noisy*) si-

loudspeaker *n.* hwak-sŏng-gi 확성기.

lounge *n.* ① (*stroll*) man-bo 만보(漫步). ② (*social hall*) sa-gyo-sil 사교실, ra-un-ji 라운지.

louse *n.* ① i 이(虱). ② ki-saeng-ch'ung 기생충.

lousy *adj.* tŏ-rŏ-un 더러운 ; ya-bi-han 야비한.

lov(e)able *adj.* sa-rang-sŭ-rŏ-un 사랑스러운.

love *n.* ① sa-rang 사랑, ae-jŏng 애정 ; cho-a-ham 좋아

함. ② (*sweetheart*) yŏn-in 연인, ae-in 애인. —*v.* sa-rang-ha-da 사랑하다.   「멋진.

lovely *adj.* ye-bbŭn 예쁜, kwi-yŏ-un 귀여운 ; mŏt-jin

lover *n.* ① ae-in 애인, yŏn-in 연인. ② (*devotee*) ae-ho-ga 애호가, ch'an-mi-ja 찬미자.

low *adj.* na-jŭn 낮은 ; kap-ssan 값싼 ; (*mean*) pi-ch'ŏn-han 비천한. —*adv.* nat-ge 낮게, ssa-ge 싸게.

lower *v.* nat-ch'u-da 낮추다, nae-ri-da 내리다, ttŏ-rŏ-ddŭ-ri-da 떨어드리다. —*adj.* chŏ-gŭp-han 저급한.

lowly *adj.* pi-ch'ŏn-han 비천한, (*shabby*) ch'o-ra-han 초라한 ; (*humble*) kup-sil-gŏ-ri-nŭn 굽실거리는.

loyal *adj.* ch'ung-sŏng-sŭ-rŏn 충성스런, sŏng-sil-han 성실한. —*n.* ch'ung-sin 충신 ; ae-guk-ja 애국자.

lubricant *n.* yun-hwal-yu 윤활유, yun-hwal-je 윤활제.

lubricate *v.* ki-rŭm-ŭl ch'i-da 기름을 치다.   「한.

lucid *adj.* (*clear*) mal-gŭn 맑은, t'u-myŏng-han 투명

luck *n.* un 운, haeng-un 행운, yo-haeng 요행.

luckily *adv.* ta-haeng-hi 다행히, un-jo-k'e 운좋게.

lucky *adj.* un-jo-ŭn 운좋은, haeng-un-ŭi 행운의.

lucrative *adj.* ton-i pŏl-ri-nŭn 돈이 벌리는.

ludicrous *adj.* ik-sal-sŭ-rŏn 익살스런, (*absurd*) pa-bo-ga-t'ŭn 바보같은, ssuk-sŭ-rŏ-un 쑥스러운.   「물.

luggage *n.* su-ha-mul 수하물, yŏ-haeng-ha-mul 여행하

lukewarm *adj.* mi-ji-gŭn-han 미지근한, mi-on-jŏk-in 미온적인, ma-ji-mot-hae-ha-nŭn 마지못해하는.

lull *v.* (*soothe*) tal-rae-da 달래다 ; chae-u-da 재우다. —*n.* cham-jam-ham 잠잠함, ttŭm-ham 뜸함.

lullaby *n.* (*cradle song*) cha-jang-ga 자장가.

lumber *n.* ① chae-mok 재목. ② (*rubbish*) ssŭ-re-gi 쓰레기. —*v.* k'ung-k'ung kŏt-da 쿵쿵 걷다.

luminous *adj.* pit-na-nŭn 빛나는 ; (*clear*) myŏng-

lump *n.* tŏng-ŏ-ri 덩어리, hok 혹. ⌊baek-han 명백한.

lunar *adj.* tal-ŭi 달의 : ~ *calendar* ŭm-ryŏk 음력.
lunatic *n.* mi-ch'in sa-ram 미친 사람. —*adj.* (*insane*)
　mi-ch'in 미친 : *a* ~ *asylum* chŏng-sin pyŏng-wŏn
lunch *n.* chŏm-sim 점심, to-si-rak 도시락. ⌊정신 병원.
lung *n.* p'ye 폐(肺), hŏ-p'a 허파. 「물.
lure *v.* yu-hok-ha-da 유혹하다. —*n.* yu-hok-mul 유혹
lurk *v.* sum-da 숨다, cham-jŏk-ha-da 잠적하다.
lust *n.* (*carnal desire*) saek-yok 색욕, sŏng-jŏng 성정.
lusty *adj.* ① (*strong*) t'ŭn-t'ŭn-han 튼튼한. ② (*vig-
　orous*) hwal-bal-han 활발한. 「産)의.
luxuriant *adj.* mu-sŏng-han 무성한 ; ta-san-ŭi 다산(多
luxurious *adj.* sa-ch'i-sŭ-rŏ-un 사치스러운, ho-sa-sŭ-
luxury *n.* sa-ch'i 사치, ho-sa 호사. ⌊rŏn 호사스런.
lye *n.* chaet-mul 잿물, al-k'al-ri aek 알칼리 액(液).
lynch *n. & v.* rin-ch'i(-rŭl ka-ha-da) 린치(를 가하다).
lyre *n.* su-gŭm 수금(竪琴), ra-i-ŏ 라이어.
lyric *n.* sŏ-jŏng-si 서정시. —*adj.* sŏ-jŏng-si-jŏk-in 서
　정시적인.

─◄ **M** ►─

machine *n.* ki-gye 기계, ki-gu 기구.
machine gun ki-gwan-ch'ong 기관총.
machinery *n.* ki-gye 기계, ki-gye chang-ch'i 기계 장치.
mackerel *n.* ko-dŭng-ŏ 고등어.
macrocosm *n.* tae-u-ju 대우주, tae-se-gye 대세계.
mad *adj.* mi-ch'in 미친 ; (*furious*) maeng-ryŏl-han 맹
　렬한 ; (*angry*) hwa-ga nan 화가 난.
madam *n.* ma-dam 마담, (*lady*) pu-in 부인.
made *adj.* (*artificially produced*) man-dŭn 만든,
　…che …제(製) : ~ *in Korea* han-guk-je 한국제/~
　in U.S.A. mi-guk-je 미국제.

madman *n.* mi-ch'in sa-ram 미친 사람, kwang-in 광인.

maestro *n.* tae-ŭm-ak-ga 대음악가, kŏ-jang 거장(巨匠).

magazine *n.* ① (*periodical*) chap-ji 잡지, chŏng-gi kan-haeng-mul 정기 간행물. ② (*army*) t'an-yak-go 탄

maggot *n.* ① ku-dŏ-gi 구더기. ② pyŏn-dŏk 변덕. ⌞약고.

magic *n.* ma-bŏp 마법, yo-sul 요술 ; ma-ryŏk 마력. —*adj.* ma-bŏp-ŭi 마법의, yo-sul-ŭi 요술의.

magician *n.* ma-sul-sa 마술사, ma-bŏp-sa 마법사.

magistrate *n.* haeng-jŏng-jang-gwan 행정장관, (*justice of the peace*) ch'i-an p'an-sa 치안 판사.

magnanimous *adj.* to-ryang-i k'ŭn 도량이 큰, a-ryang-it-nŭn 아량있는 ; (*noble*) ko-gyŏl-han 고결한.

magnet *n.* cha-sŏk 자석(磁石), chi-nam-ch'ŏl 지남철.

magnetic *adj.* ① cha-sŏk-ŭi 자석의, cha-gi-ŭi 자기의. ② (*attractive*) mae-ryŏk-it-nŭn 매력있는.

magnificent *adj.* chang-ŏm-han 장엄한 ; (*stately*) tang-dang-han 당당한, (*splendid*) hul-ryung-han 훌륭한.

magnify *v.* hwak-dae-ha-da 확대하다 ; (*exaggerate*) kwa-jang-ha-da 과장하다, ch'an-mi-ha-da 찬미하다.

magnitude *n.* k'ŭ-gi 크기, pang-dae 방대 ; chung-yo-ham 중요함, wi-dae-ham 위대함. ⌜ryŏn 백목련.

magnolia *n.* mok-ryŏn 목련 : *a white* ~ paek-mok-

magpie *n.* kka-ch'i 까치. ⌜하녀

maid *n.* so-nyŏ 소녀, a-ga-ssi 아가씨 ; (*servant*) ha-nyŏ

maiden *n.* so-nyŏ 소녀, ch'ŏ-nyŏ 처녀.

maidservant *n.* ha-nyŏ 하녀. ⌜하다.

mail *n.* u-p'yŏn-mul 우편물. —*v.* u-song-ha-da 우송.

mailbox *n.* u-ch'e-t'ong 우체통, u-p'yŏn-ham 우편함.

maim *v.* pyŏng-sin-ŭl man-dŭl-da 병신을 만들다.

main *adj.* chung-yo-han 중요한 ; (*leading*) yu-ryŏk-han 유력한. —*n.* ① (*might*) him 힘. ② (*principal pipe*) pon-gwan 본관(本管).

mainland *n*. pon-t'o 본토, tae-ryuk 대륙.

mainly *adv*. chu-ro 주로, tae-gae 대개, o-ro-ji 오로지.

maintain *v*. yu-ji-ha-da 유지하다 ; (*assert*) chu-jang-ha-da 주장하다 ; (*support*) pu-yang-ha-da 부양하다.

maize *n*. ok-su-su 옥수수. 「it-nŭn 위엄있는.

majestic *adj*. chang-ŏm-han 장엄한, (*stately*) wi-ŏm-

majesty *n*. ① chon-ŏm 존엄. ② (*sovereignty*) chu-gwŏn 주권. ③ (*title of emperor*) (*M*∼) p'ye-ha 폐하.

major *n*. (*army*) yuk-gun so-ryŏng 육군 소령. —*adj*. k'ŭn p'yŏn-ŭi 큰 편의, chu-yo-han 주요한. —*v*. (*specialize*) chŏn-gong-ha-da 전공하다.

major general yuk-gun so-jang 육군 소장.

majority *n*. tae-da-su 대다수, kwa-ban-su 과반수.

make *v*. ① man-dŭl-da 만들다. ② (*compel*) …ha-ge ha-da …하게 하다, …i toe-da …이 되다. ③ (*gain*) hoek-dŭk-ha-da 획득하다. —*n*. ku-jo 구조.

make-believe *n*. ① ku-sil 구실, p'ing-gye 핑계. ② …ch'e-ha-nŭn sa-ram …체하는 사람. 「i-k'ŏ 메이커.

maker *n*. che-jak-ja 제작자, che-jo-ŏp-ja 제조업자, me-

makeshift *n*. im-si pyŏn-t'ong 임시 변통 ; mi-bong-ch'aek 미봉책. 「*struction*) cho-rip 조립.

make-up *n*. ① hwa-jang 화장, pun-jang 분장. ② (*con-*

malady *n*. chil-byŏng 질병, pyŏng 병.

malaria *n*. hak-jil 학질, mal-ra-ri-a 말라리아.

male *n*. & *adj*. ① nam-sŏng(-ŭi) 남성(의). ② (*of animals*) su-k'ŏt(-ŭi) 수컷(의) : *a* ∼ *dog* su-k'ae 수캐.

malice *n*. ak-ŭi 악의(惡意) ; wŏn-han 원한. 「악의있는.

malicious *adj*. sim-sul-gu-jŭn 심술궂은, ak-ŭi-it-nŭn

maltreat *v*. hak-dae-ha-da 학대하다, naeng-dae-ha-da

mamma *n*. ŏm-ma 엄마. 「냉대하다.

mammal *n*. p'o-yu tong-mul 포유 동물.

man *n*. ① sa-ram 사람. ② (*male*) nam-ja 남자.

manage *v.* kwal-li-ha-da 관리하다 ; (*handle*) ta-ru-da 다루다 ; kyŏng-yŏng-ha-da 경영하다.

management *n.* kwal-li 관리 ;ch'wi-gŭp 취급.

manager *n.* chi-bae-in 지배인, kyŏng-yŏng-ja 경영자,

Manchuria *n.* man-ju 만주.   ⌊kam-dok 감독.

mandate *n.* ① myŏng-ryŏng 명령. ② wi-t'ak 위탁 ; (*trusteeship*) sin-t'ak-t'ong-ch'i 신탁통치.

mandolin(e) *n.* man-dol-rin 만돌린.

mane *n.* (*horse, lion etc.*) kal-gi 갈기.

maneuver · manoeuvre *n.* ki-dong-yŏn-sŭp 기동연습. —*v.* yŏn-sŭp-ha-da 연습하다.

manful *adj.* ssik-ssik-han 씩씩한, tan-ho-han 단호한.

manger *n.* yŏ-mul-t'ong 여물통, ku-yu 구유.

mangle *v.* nan-do-jil-ha-da 난도질하다.

manhole *n.* maen-ho-ul 맨호울, cham-ip-gu 잠입구.

manhood *n.* in-gyŏk 인격 ; sŏng-nyŏn 성년 ; (*manliness*) nam-ja-da-um 남자다움.   ⌈광(狂).

mania *n.* yŏl-gwang 열광, yŏl-jung 열중, ···kwang ···

maniac *adj.* mi-ch'in 미친. —*n.* mi-ch'i-gwang-i 미치 광이, yŏl-gwang-ja 열광자.   ⌈gi 손톱다듬기.

manicure *n.* mae-ni-k'yu-ŏ 매니큐어 ; son-t'op-da-dŭm-

manifest *adj.* myŏng-baek-han 명백한. —*v.* myŏng-si-ha-da 명시하다 ; na-t'a-na-da 나타나다. —*n.* chŏk-ha-mok-rok 적하목록.   ⌈myŏn-ŭi 다방면의.

manifold *adj.* yŏ-rŏ ka-ji-ŭi 여러 가지의, ta-bang-

manipulate *v.* kyo-myo-ha-ge ta-ru-da 교묘하게 다루다.

mankind *n.* il-lyu 인류 ; (*male*) nam-sŏng 남성.

manlike *adj.* (*manly*) nam-ja-da-un 남자다운.   ⌈한.

manly *adj.* nam-ja-da-un 남자다운, ssik-ssik-han 씩씩

manner *n.* pang-bŏp 방법 ; ye-jŏl 예절 ; t'ae-do 태도.

mansion *n.* tae-jŏ-t'aek 대저택.   ⌈마재비.

mantis *n.* (*insect*) sa-ma-gwi 사마귀, pŏ-ma-jae-bi 버

mantle *n.* (*cloak*) mang-t'o 망토 ; (*covering*) mak막. —*v.* tŏp-da 덮다, kam-ch'u-da 감추다.

manual *adj.* son-ŭi 손의. —*n.* (*small book*) so-ch'aek-ja 소책자, (*handbook*) p'yŏl-lam 편람.

manufacture *n.* & *v.* che-jo(-ha-da) 제조(하다).

manufacturer *n.* che-jo-ŏp-ja 제조업자 ; kong-jang-ju공장주.

manure *n.* pi-ryo 비료, kŏ-rŭm 거름. ㄴ공장주.

manuscript *n.* wŏn-go 원고(原稿), sa-bon 사본.

many *adj.* man-ŭn 많은, ta-su-ŭi 다수의.

map *n.* ① chi-do 지도(地圖). ② ch'ŏn-ch'e-do 천체도.

maple *n.* tan-p'ung(-na-mu) 단풍(나무). 「손하다.

mar *v.* mang-ch'yŏ-no-t'a 망쳐놓다, hwe-son-ha-da 훼

marathon *n.* (*race*) ma-ra-t'on 마라톤.

marble *n.* ① tae-ri-sŏk 대리석. ② kong-gi-dol 공기돌.

March *n.* sam-wŏl 3월.

march *n.* haeng-jin 행진, chin-jŏn 전전 ; (*music*) haeng-jin-gok 행진곡. —*v.* haeng-jin-ha-da 행진하다.

mare *n.* (*female horse*) am-mal 암말.

margin *n.* ① (*edge*) ka-jang-ja-ri 가장자리. ② (*limit*) han-gye 한계. ③ (*commerce*) i-mun 이문.

marine *adj.* pa-da-ŭi 바다의 ; (*of the navy*) hae-gun-ŭi 해군의 : ~ *insurance* hae-sang-bo-hŏm 해상보험 / ~ *force* hae-byŏng-dae 해병대. —*n.* sŏn-bak 선박.

Marine Corps hae-byŏng-dae 해병대.

marine products hae-san-mul 해산물.

mariner *n.* (*seaman*) sŏn-wŏn 선원, su-bu 수부.

marital *adj.* nam-p'yŏn-ŭi 남편의, pu-bu-gan-ŭi 부부간

maritime *adj.* pa-da-ŭi 바다의, hae-un-ŭi 해운의 ㄴ의.

mark *n.* ① (*trace*) p'yo-jŏk 표적, cha-guk 자국. ② (*pl.*) ki-ho 기호 ; (*point*) chŏm-su 점수. —*v.* p'yo-ha-da 표하다, ma-a-k'ŭ-rŭl ha-da 마아크를 하다.

market *n.* si-jang 시장(市場), chang 장 : *black* ~ am-si-jang 암시장/*fish* ~ ŏ-mul-si-jang 어물시장/*fruit* ~ ch'ŏng-gwa-si-jang 청과시장.

market place si-jang 시장(市場), chang-t'ŏ 장터.

market price *n.* si-se 시세, sit-ga 싯가.

marking *n.* ① (*mark*) p'yŏ 표. ② (*pattern*) mu-nŭi 무늬. —*adj.* (*prominent*) t'ŭk-ch'ul-han 특출한.

marksman *n.* ① sa-su 사수, sa-gyŏk-su 사격수. ② (*sharpshooter*) chŏ-gyŏk-pyŏng 저격병.

marmot *n.* ma-a-mŏt 마아못, mo-rŭ-mo-t'ŭ 모르모트.

marriage *n.* kyŏl-hon 결혼, (*wedding*) kyŏl-hon-sik 결혼식 ; (*close union*) hap-ch'e 합체.

marrow *n.* ① kol-su 골수, ppyŏ-gol 뼈골. ② (*essence*) chŏng-su 정수 ; (*vitality*) hwal-ryŏk 활력.

marry *v.* kyŏl-hon-ha-da 결혼하다, kyŏl-hon-si-k'i-da 결혼시키다 ; (*for man*) chang-ga-dŭl-da 장가들다 ; (*for woman*) si-jip-ga-da 시집가다.

marsh *n.* (*swamp*) nŭp 늪, (*bog*) sŭp-ji 습지.

marshal *n.* yuk-gun wŏn-su 육군 원수(元帥): *provost* ~ hŏn-byŏng-sa-ryŏng-gwan 헌병사령관.

martial *adj.* ① kun-sa-ŭi 군사의, chŏn-jaeng-ŭi 전쟁의 : ~ *law* kye-ŏm-ryŏng 계엄령/~ *rule* kun-jŏng 군정(軍政). ② (*brave*) yong-gam-han 용감한.

martyr *n.* sun-gyo-ja 순교자, (*victim*) hŭi-saeng-ja 희생자. —*v.* (*persecute*) pak-hae-ha-da 박해하다.

marvel *n.* kyŏng-t'an 경탄, nol-raem 놀램.

marvel(l)ous *adj.* nol-ra-un 놀라운, ki-i-han 기이한, mŏt-jin 멋진.

mascot *n.* ma-sŭ-k'o-t'ŭ 마스코트.

masculine *adj.* nam-sŏng-ŭi 남성의, (*manly*) nam-sŏng-da-un 남성다운, nam-ja-ga-t'ŭn 남자같은.

mask *n.* pok-myŏn 복면, ka-myŏn 가

[ka-myŏn]

면. *—v.* ka-myŏn-ŭl ssŭ-da 가면을 쓰다, (*disguise*) ka-jang-ha-da 가장하다, kam-ch'u-da 감추다.

mason *n.* sŏk-gong 석공(石工), sŏk-su 석수(石手).

masquerade *n.* ① (*masked assembly*) ka-jang mu-do-hoe 가장 무도회. ② (*pretence*) kŏt-ch'i-re 겉치레.

mass *n.* ① tŏng-ŏ-ri 덩어리. ② (*large number*) ta-su 다수, (*great quantity*) ta-ryang 다량. ③ (*crowd*) chip-dan 집단. ④ mi-sa 미사. *—v.* mo-ŭ-da 모으다.

massacre *n. & v.* tae-hak-sal(-ha-da) 대학살(하다).

massage *n.* ma-sa-a-ji 마사아지 ; an-ma 안마.

massive *adj.* ① pu-p'i-ga k'ŭn 부피가 큰. ② (*solid*) kŏn-jang-han 건장한. ③ (*imposing*) tang-dang-han 당당한.

mast *n.* tot-dae 돛대, ma-sŭ-t'ŭ 마스트. 「당당한.

master *n.* chu-in 주인, (*employer*) ko-yong-ju 고용주 ; (*teacher*) sŏn-saeng 선생.

masterpiece *n.* kŏl-jak 걸작, myŏng-jak 명작.

mat *n.* (*straw*) tot-ja-ri 돗자리 ; (*bamboo*) tae-ja-ri 대자리, kŏ-jŏk 거적, kkal-gae 깔개.

match *n.* ① sŏng-nyang 성냥. ② (*athletic*) kyŏng-gi 경기. ③ (*rival*) chŏk-su 적수. ④ (*marriage*) kyŏl-hon 결혼. *—v.* (*be equal to*) …e p'il-jŏk-ha-da …에 필적하다 ; (*be a rival to*) sang-dae-ga toe-da 상대가 되다, (*fit*) cho-hwa-ha-da 조화하다.

matchbox *n.* sŏng-nyang-gap 성냥갑.

mate *n.* pae-p'il 배필 ; (*companion*) tong-ryo 동료.

material *adj.* ① mul-jil-ŭi 물질의. ② (*essential*) chung-yo-han 중요한. *—n.* chae-ryo 재료.

maternal *adj.* ŏ-mŏ-ni-ŭi 어머니의, mo-gye-ŭi 모계의.

maternity *n.* (*motherhood*) mo-sŏng 모성 : ~ *hospital* san-gwa pyŏng-wŏn 산과 병원.

mathematics *n.* su-hak 수학(數學). 「티네.

matinee *n.* chu-gan-gong-yŏn 주간공연, ma-t'i-ne 마

matron *n.* ① (*married woman*) ki-hon pu-in 기혼 부
인. ② kan-ho-bu-jang 간호부장, po-mo 보모.

matter *n.* ① (*substance*) mul-jil 물질. ② (*affair*) sa-
gŏn 사건. ③ (*material*) chae-ryo 재료. ④ (*consti-
tuents*) yo-so 요소. —*v.* kwan-gye-ga it-da 관계가
있다, chung-dae-ha-da 중대하다.

mattress *n.* (ch'im-dae-yong) yo (침대용) 요, mae-t'ŭ-
ri-sŭ 매트리스.   「han 성숙한.

mature *adj.* (*things*) ik-ŭn 익은 ; (*people*) sŏng-suk-

mausoleum *n.* nŭng 능(陵), yŏng-myo 영묘(靈廟).

maxim *n.* kyŏk-ŏn 격언, (*proverb*) kŭm-ŏn 금언.

maximum *adj.* ch'oe-dae-han-ŭi 최대한의. —*n.* ch'oe-
go-jŏm 최고점, ch'oe-dae-han 최대한, ch'oe-dae-ryang

May *n.* o-wŏl 5월.   [최대량.

may *aux. v.* … il-ji-do mo-rŭn-da …일지도 모른다 ;
…hae-do cho-t'a …해도 좋다 ; …hal su it-da …할 수
있다 ; wŏn-k'ŏn-dae …ha-gi-rŭl 원컨대 …하기를.

maybe *adv.* a-ma 아마, ŏ-jjŏ-myŏn 어쩌면.

mayor *n.* si-jang 시장(市長).

maze *n.* (*labyrinth*) mi-gung 미궁.

me *pron.* na-e-ge 나에게, na-rŭl 나를.   「목초지.

meadow *n.* p'ul-bat 풀밭, ch'o-wŏn 초원. mok-ch'o-ji

meager·meagre *adj.* (*thin*) ma-rŭn 마른, yŏ-win 여윈,
(*poor*) pin-yak-han 빈약한.   「ru 굵은 가루.

meal *n.* ① (*food*) sik-sa 식사. ② (*corn*) kul-gŭn ka-

mealtime *n.* sik-sa si-gan 식사 시간.

mean *adj.* ① ch'ŏn-han 천한. ② (*average*) p'yŏng-
gyun-ŭi 평균의. ③ (*stingy*) in-saek-han 인색한. —*v.*
ŭi-mi-ha-da 의미하다 ; (*intend*) ye-jŏng-ha-da 예정하
다. —*n.* ① chung-gan 중간. ② (*pl.*) su-dan 수단.

meaning *n.* ttŭt 뜻, ŭi-mi 의미. —*adj.* (*significant*)
ŭi-mi-sim-jang-han 의미심장한.

meantime *n. & adv.* kŭ tong-an(·e) 그 동안(에).

measles *n.* hong-yŏk 홍역, p'ung-jin 풍진.

measure *n.* ch'i-su 치수, ch'ŭk-jŏng 측정 ; (*pl.*) su-dan 수단. —*v.* ch'ŭk-jŏng-ha-da 측정하다.

meat *n.* ko-gi 고기 : *tender* ~ yŏn-han ko-gi 연한 고기.

mechanic *n.* chik-gong 직공, ki-gye-gong 기계공. 「인.

mechanical *adj.* ki-gye-ŭi 기계의, ki-gye-jŏk-in 기계적

mechanism *n.* ki-gu 기구 ; ku-jo 구조 ; ki-gye-jang-ch'i 기계장치, me·k'ŏ·ni·jŭm 메커니즘.

medal *n.* hun-jang 훈장, me-dal 메달. 「르다.

meddle *v.* kan-sŏp-ha-da 간섭하다 ; chu-mu-rŭ-da 주무

medi(a)eval *adj.* chung-se-ŭi 중세의.

mediate *v.* cho-jŏng-ha-da 조정하다 ; (*intermediate*) chung-jae-ha-da 중재하다.

medical *adj.* ŭi-hak-ŭi 의학의, ŭi-sul-ŭi 의술의 : *a* ~ *college* ŭi-gwa tae-hak 의과 대학 /*a* ~ *examination* kŏn-gang chin-dan 건강 진단.

medicine *n.* ① yak 약. ② (*science*) ŭi-hak 의학. 「통의.

mediocre *adj.* p'yŏng-bŏm-han 평범한, po-t'ong-ŭi 보

meditate *v.* ① suk-go-ha-da 숙고하다, muk-sang-ha-da 묵상하다. ② (*plan*) kkoe-ha-da 꾀하다.

Mediterranean *n.* chi-jung-hae 지중해. —*adj.* chi-jung-hae-ŭi 지중해의.

medium *n.* ① chung-gan 중간. ② mae-gae 매개, (*means*) su-dan 수단. —*adj.* chung-ch'i-ŭi 중치의.

medley *n.* chap-dong-sa-ni 잡동사니, hon-hap 혼합.

meek *adj.* (*mild*) pu-dŭ-rŏ-un 부드러운.

meet *v.* man-na-da 만나다 ; ma-ji-ha-da 맞이하다 ; (*join*) hap-ch'i-da 합치다.

meeting *n.* (*assembly*) hoe 회, hoe-hap 회합, mo-im 모임.

megaphone *n.* hwak-sŏng-gi 확성기, me-ga-p'on 메가폰.

melancholy *n. & adj.* u-ul(·han) 우울(한).

mellow *adj.* ik-ŭn 익은, pu-dŭ-rŏ-un 부드러운.
melodious *adj.* kok-jo-ga a-rŭm-da-un 곡조가 아름다운.
melodrama *n.* mel-ro-dŭ-ra-ma 멜로드라마.
melody *n.* (*harmony*) sŏn-yul 선율 ; mel-ro-di 멜로디,
  ka-rak 가락 ; (*tune*) kok-jo 곡조.
melon *n.* mel-ron 멜론, ch'am-oe 참외. 「용해.
melt *v.* nok-da 녹다, nok-i-da 녹이다. —*n.* yong-hae
member *n.* il-wŏn 일원 ; (*of a company*) sa-wŏn 사
  원 ; (*of an association*) hoe-wŏn 회원.
memorable *adj.* ki-ŏk-hal man-han 기억할 만한.
memorandum *n.* me-mo 메모 ; kak-sŏ 각서.
memorial *adj.* ki-nyŏm-ŭi 기념의. —*n.* ki-nyŏm-mul
  기념물 ; (*monument*) ki-nyŏm-bi 기념비.
memory *n.* ki-ŏk 기억, (*recollection*) ch'u-ŏk 추억.
menace *n.* wi-hyŏp 위협. —*v.* wi-hyŏp-ha-da 위협하다.
mend *v.* ko-ch'i-da 고치다, su-sŏn-ha-da 수선하다.
menstruation *n.* wŏl-gyŏng 월경, men-sŭ 멘스.
mental *adj.* chŏng-sin-ŭi 정신의, tu-noe-ŭi 두뇌의.
mention *v.* (*speak of*) …ŭl mal-ha-da …을 말하다.
mercantile *adj.* sang-ŏp-ŭi 상업의, sang-in-ŭi 상인의 :
  a ~ city sang-ŏp to-si 상업 도시.
merchandise *n.* (*goods*) sang-p'um 상품.
merchant *n.* sang-in 상인. —*adj.* sang-ŏp-ŭi 상업의.
merciful *adj.* cha-bi-ro-un 자비로운;ta-haeng-in 다행인.
mercury *n.* ① su-ŭn 수은. ② on-do-gye 온도계. 「행운.
mercy *n.* ① cha-bi 자비, yŏn-min 연민. ② haeng-un
mere *adj.* tan-sun-han 단순한, sun-jŏn-han 순전한.
merely *adv.* tan-sun-hi 단순히, o-jik 오직. 「기.
meridian *n.* ① cha-o-sŏn 자오선. ② chŏn-sŏng-gi 전성
merit *n.* ① (*forte*) chang-jŏm 장점, (*worth*) ka-ch'i
  가치. ② (*exploits*) kong-jŏk 공적.
merry *adj.* k'wae-hwal-han 쾌활한, chŭl-gŏ-un 즐거운.

mesh *n.* ① kŭ-mul-k'o 그물코. ② ol-ga-mi 올가미.

mess *n.* ① ŭm-sik-mul 음식물. ② hon-hap 혼합, twi-juk-bak-juk 뒤죽박죽 ; ~ *hall* sik-dang 식당.

message *n.* so-sik 소식, t'ong-sin 통신, chŏn-gal 전갈, me-si-ji 메시지 ; (*mission*) sa-myŏng 사명.

messenger *n.* sim-bu-rŭm-gun 심부름군 ; (*envoy*) sa-ja 사자(使者) ; (*herald*) sŏn-gu-ja 선구자.

Messiah *n.* ku-se-ju 구세주, me-si-a 메시아.

messy *adj.* ŏ-ji-rŏ-un 어지러운, chi-jŏ-bun-han 지저분한.

metabolism *n.* sin-jin tae-sa 신진 대사.

metal *n.* kŭm-sok 금속, soe-bu-ch'i 쇠붙이. 「속성의.

metallic *adj.* kŭm-sok-ŭi 금속의, kŭm-sok-sŏng-ŭi 금

meteor *n.* (*shooting star*) yu-sŏng 유성(流星).

meteorology *n.* ki-sang 기상, ki-sang-hak 기상학.

meter · metre *n.* ① (*measure*) mi-t'ŏ 미터 ; (*instrument*) kye-ryang-gi 계량기. ② un-yul 운율.

method *n.* pang-bŏp 방법 ; (*order*) sun-sŏ 순서.

Methodist Church kam-ri-gyo-hoe 감리교회.

metropolis *n.* su-do 수도(首都). 「min 수도의 주민.

metropolitan *adj.* su-do-ŭi 수도의. —*n.* su-do-ŭi chu-

mew *v.* (*cat*) ya-ong-ha-go ul-da 야옹하고 울다.

microbe *n.* mi-saeng-mul 미생물 ; se-gyun 세균.

microfilm *n.* ch'uk-sa p'il-rŭm 축사(縮寫) 필름.

microphone *n.* hwak-sŏng-gi 확성기, ma-i-k'ŭ 마이크.

microscope *n.* hyŏn-mi-gyŏng 현미경.

mid *adj.* chung-ang-ŭi 중앙의, chung-gan-ŭi 중간의.

midday *n.* (*noon*) chŏng-o 정오, han-nat 한낮.

middle *n.* ka-un-de 가운데, chung-ang 중앙. —*adj.* chung-ang-ŭi 중앙의, han-ga-un-de-ŭi 한가운데의.

middle-aged *adj.* chung-nyŏn-ŭi 중년의.

middle-class *adj.* chung-ryu-ŭi 중류의, chung-san-gye-gŭp-ŭi 중산계급의.

midnight *n.* han-bam-jung 한밤중, ya-ban 야반.

midst *n.* han-ga-un-de 한가운데, pok-p'an 복판.

midsummer *n.* han-yŏ-rŭm 한여름.　　　「중도의.

midway *adv.* chung-gan-e 중간에. —*adj.* chung-do-ŭi

midwife *n.* cho-san-wŏn 조산원, san-p'a 산파.

midwinter *n.* & *adj.* han-gyŏ-ŭl(-ŭi) 한겨울(의).

might *n.* (*power*) him 힘, nŭng-ryŏk 능력 : *M ~ is right.* Him-ŭn chŏng-ŭi-da 힘은 정의다.

mighty *adj.* (*powerful*) kut-sen 굳센 ; kŏ-dae-han 거대한 ; (*wonderful*) koeng-jang-han 굉장한.　「하다.

migrate *v.* om-gyŏ sal-da 옮겨 살다, i-ju-ha-da 이주

mild *adj.* (*gentle*) chŏm-jan-ŭn 점잖은, (*warm*) on-

mildew *n.* kom-p'ang-i 곰팡이.　　　[hwa-han 온화한.

mile *n.* ma-il 마일 (1, 609. 3m).　　　「획기적 사건.

milestone *n.* i-jŏng-p'yo 이정표 ; hoek-gi-jŏk sa-gŏn

militant *adj.* ho-jŏn-jŏk-in 호전적인, t'u-jaeng-jŏk-in

militarism *n.* kun-guk-ju-ŭi 군국주의.　　[투쟁적인.

military *adj.* kun-ŭi 군의 : *~ attache* tae-sa-gwan-so-sok mu-gwan 대사관소속 무관/*~ academy* yuk-gun sa-gwan-hak-gyo 육군 사관학교.　　　「gun 의용군.

militia *n.* (*citizen army*) min-byŏng 민병, ŭi-yong-

milk *n.* u-yu 우유, chŏt 젖, mil-k'ŭ 밀크.

Milky Way ŭn-ha-su 은하수.　　　　　　「아.

mill *n.* pang-at-gan 방앗간 : *water ~* mul-bang-a 물방

miller *n.* ① pang-at-gan chu-in 방앗간 주인. ② che-bun-ŏp-ja 제분업자.

millet *n.* ki-jang 기장 : *African ~* su-su 수수.

million *n.* & *adj.* paek-man(-ŭi) 백만(의).

million(n)aire *n.* paek-man-jang-ja 백만장자.

millstone *n.* maet-dol 맷돌, yŏn-ja-mae 연자매.

mimeograph *n.* tŭng-sa-p'an 등사판, pok-sa-p'an 복사판. —*v.* tŭng-sa[pok-sa]-ha-da 등사[복사]하다.

mimic v. hyung-nae-nae-da 흉내내다. —*adj.* hyung-nae-nae-nŭn 흉내내는. 「ko·gi 다진 고기.

mince v. chal·ge ssŏl·da 잘게 썰다 : ∼*d meat* ta·jin

mind n. ma·ŭm 마음, saeng·gak 생각 ; (*intent*) ŭi·hyang 의향. —v. (*heed*) cho·sim·ha·da 조심하다.

mindful adj. chu·ŭi·gi·p'ŭn 주의깊은. 「ŭn 어리석은.

mindless adj. mu·sim·han 무심한, (*stupid*) ŏ·ri·sŏk·

mine pron. na·ŭi kŏt 나의 것. —n. kwang·san 광산 ; chi·roe 지뢰 : *a coal* ∼ t'an·gwang 탄광.

miner n. kwang·bu 광부, kaeng·bu 갱부.

mineral n. kwang·mul 광물. —adj. kwang·mul·ŭi 광물의 : ∼ *right* ch'ae·gul·gwŏn 채굴권.

mingle v. ① (*mix*) sŏk·da 섞다, (*unite*) hap·ch'i·da 합치다. ② (*participate*) ch'am·ga·ha·da 참가하다.

miniature n. se·mil·hwa 세밀화, ch'uk·do 축도, mi·ni·ŏ·ch'ŏ 미니어처. —adj. so·gyu·mo·ŭi 소규모의.

minimize v. ch'oe·so·ro ŏ·rim·jap·da 최소로 어림잡다.

minimum n. ch'oe·so·han·do 최소한도. —adj. (*smallest possible*) ch'oe·so·han·do·ŭi 최소한도의.

minimum wage ch'oe·jŏ im·gŭm 최저 임금.

mining industry kwang·ŏp 광업.

minister n. ① (*government*) chang·gwan 장관. ② (*church*) mok·sa 목사. ③ (*envoy*) kong·sa 공사(公使) : *the Prime M*∼ kuk·mu·ch'ong·ri 국무총리.

ministry n. ① (*cabinet*) nae·gak 내각. ② (*of the church*) sŏng·jik 성직. ③ (*suffix*) …pu …부(部) : *the M*∼ *of Education* mun·gyo·bu 문교부.

minor adj. (*lesser*) so·su·ŭi 소수의, (*inferior*) ha·ch'an·ŭn 하찮은. —n. mi·sŏng·nyŏn·ja 미성년자.

minority n. ① so·su 소수. ② (*legal infancy*) mi·sŏng·nyŏn 미성년. ③ (*faction*) so·su·p'a 소수파.

mint n. ① (*plant*) pak·ha 박하. ② (*coining money*)

cho-p'ye-guk 조폐국. —v. (coin) chu-jo-ha-da 주조
하다, man-dŭ-rŏ-nae-da 만들어내다.
minus adj. ma-i-nŏ-sŭ-ŭi 마이너스의, pu-ŭi 부(負)의.
—prep. …ŭl ppaen …을 뺀. —n. (minus sign) ma-
i-nŏ-sŭ ki-ho 마이너스 기호, pu-ho 부호(負號).
minute adj. mi-se-han 미세한, (detailed) sang-se-
han 상세한. —n. ① pun 분(分). ② sun-gan 순간.
minute hand pun-ch'im 분침, chang-ch'im 장침.
minutes n. (record of proceedings) ŭi-sa-rok 의사록.
minx n. mal-gwal-ryang-i 말괄량이, wal-p'ae 왈패.
miracle n. (supernatural event) ki-jŏk 기적.
miraculous adj. ki-jŏk-jŏk-in 기적적인.
mire n. (mud) chin-hŭk 진흙, chin-ch'ang 진창.
mirror n. ① kŏ-ul 거울. ② (pattern) mo-bŏm 모범.
—v. (reflect) pan-yŏng-ha-da 반영하다.
mirth n. (gaiety) yu-k'wae 유쾌 ; hwal-lak 환락.
misapply v. o-yong-ha-da 오용하다.
miscarriage n. (failure) sil-su 실수, sil-ch'aek 실책.
miscellaneous adj. chap-jong-ŭi 잡종의.   「손해.
mischief n. ① chang-nan 장난. ② (damage) son-hae
mischievous adj. (annoying) mal-ssŏng-bu-ri-nŭn 말
썽부리는, (harmful) hae-ro-un 해로운.
misconception n. o-hae 오해, o-in 오인, (false opinion)
chal-mot-doen saeng-gak 잘못된 생각.
misconduct n. pi-haeng 비행. —v. sil-su-ha-da 실수하다.
misdeed n. na-bbŭn chit 나쁜 짓, ak-haeng 악행.
miser n. ku-du-soe 구두쇠, no-rang-i 노랑이, su-jŏn-no
수전노.   「행한, ka-yŏp-sŭn 가엾은.
miserable adj. pi-ch'am-han 비참한, pul-haeng-han 불
misery n. pul-haeng 불행, (poverty) pin-gon 빈곤.
misfortune n. pu-run 불운, (adversity) yŏk-gyŏng
역경, (calamity) chae-nan 재난.

mishap n. (*unhappiness*) pu-run 불운, (*disaster*) chae-nan 재난 ; (*accident*) ch'am-sa 참사.

misjudge v. o-p'an-ha-da 오판(誤判)하다.

mislay v. (*lose*) tu-go i-jŏ-bŏ-ri-da 두고 잊어버리다, ŏng-ddung-han ko-se tu-da 엉뚱한 곳에 두다.

mislead v. chal-mot in-do-ha-da 잘못 인도하다, kŭ-rŭ-ch'i-da 그르치다 ; (*dazzle*) hyŏn-hok-si-k'i-da 현혹시키다.

misplace v. chal-mot tu-da 잘못 두다.

misprint n. o-sik 오식, mi-sŭ-p'ŭ-rin-t'ŭ 미스프린트.

miss v. no-ch'i-da 놓치다, …i ŏp-sŏ-sŏ sŏ-un-ha-da …이 없어서 서운하다. —n. ① (*failure*) sil-ch'aek 실책. ② (*omission*) t'al-rak 탈락.

Miss n. yang 양 : ~ *Kim* kim-yang 김양.

missile n. & adj. na-ra-ga-nŭn mu-gi(-ŭi) 날아가는 무기(의), mi-sa-il(-ŭi) 미사일(의).

missing adj. op-so-jin 없어진, haeng-bang-bul-myŏng-ŭi 행방불명의.

mission n. ① (*commission*) sa-myŏng 사명. ② (*delegation*) sa-jŏl 사절(使節). ③ (*evangelism*) chŏn-do 전도 : ~ *school* chŏn-do-hak-gyo 전도학교.

missionary n. ① sŏn-gyo-sa 선교사. ② sŏn-jŏn-ja 선전자. ③ sa-jŏl 사절.

mist n. an-gae 안개, (*haze*) nol 놀.

mistake n. chal-mot 잘못, sil-su 실수. —v. t'ŭl-ri-da 틀리다, chal-mot saeng-gak-ha-da 잘못 생각하다.

mistaken adj. t'ŭl-rin 틀린, kŭ-rŭt-doen 그릇된.

mistress n. an-ju-in 안주인, chu-bu 주부.

mistrust v. (*suspect*) ŭi-sim-ha-da 의심하다. —n. (*distrust*) pul-sin 불신 ; (*suspicion*) ŭi-hok 의혹.

misty adj. an-gae kkin 안개 낀, hŭi-mi-han 희미한.

misunderstand v. o-hae-ha-da 오해하다.

mitigate v. wan-hwa-ha-da 완화하다, nŭt-ch'u-da 늦추다.

mix *v.* sŏk-da 섞다, hon-hap-ha-da 혼합하다.

mixer *n.* hon-hap-ha-nŭn sa-ram 혼합하는 사람 ; hon-hap-gi 혼합기, mik-sŏ 믹서.

mixture *n.* hon-hap 혼합, hon-hap-mul 혼합물.

moan *n. & v.* sin-ŭm(-ha-da) 신음(하다).

mob *n.* (*rioter*) p'ok-do 폭도, (*crowd*) kun-jung 군중.

mobile *adj.* (*movable*) um-jik-i-gi swi-un 움직이기 쉬운, (*fickle*) pyŏn-dŏk-sŭ-rŏ-un 변덕스러운.

mock *v.* (*ridicule*) cho-rong-ha-da 조롱하다, (*imitate*) hyung-nae-nae-da 흉내내다. —*n.* cho-rong 조롱, hyung-nae 흉내. —*adj.* ka-jja-ŭi 가짜의. 「흉내.

mockery *n.* cho-rong 조롱 ; si-nyung 시늉, hyung-nae

mockingbird *n.* ip-nae-sae 입내새, aeng-mu-sae 앵무새.

mode *n.* pang-bŏp 방법, yang-sik 양식 ; yu-haeng 유행.

model *n.* (*pattern*) mo-bŏm 모범 ; (*ideal*) p'yo-bon 표본. —*v.* pon-ddŭ-da 본뜨다.

moderate *adj.* on-gŏn-han 온건한, (*medium*) chŏk-dang-han 적당한. —*n.* on-gŏn-p'a 온건파.

moderation *n.* (*temperance*) chŏl-je 절제 ; (*mildness*) on-gŏn 온건 ; (*medium*) al-ma-jŭm 알맞음.

moderator *n.*(*chairman*) sa-hoe-ja 사회자, ŭi-jang 의장.

modern *adj.* hyŏn-dae-ŭi 현대의, sin-sik-ŭi 신식의. —*n.* hyŏn-dae-in 현대인. 「근대화.

modernization *n.* hyŏn-dae-hwa 현대화, kŭn-dae-hwa

modest *adj.* (*humble*) kyŏm-son-han 겸손한, yam-jŏn-han 얌전한 ; (*shy*) su-jup-ŭn 수줍은.

modesty *n.* kyŏm-son 겸손 ; (*decency*) chŏng-suk 정숙.

modifier *n.* su-jŏng-ja 수정자 ; su-sik-ŏ 수식어.

modify *v.* (*change*) pyŏn-gyŏng-ha-da 변경하다, su-jŏng-ha-da 수정하다 ; su-sik-ha-da 수식하다.

modulate *v.* cho-jŏl-ha-da 조절하다. 「물젖은.

moist *adj.* ch'uk-ch'uk-han 축축한 ; nun-mul-jŏ-jun 눈

moisture *n.* sŭp-gi 습기, mul-gi 물기.

molasses *n.* tang-mil 당밀(糖蜜).

mole *n.* ① (*on face*) sa-ma-gwi 사마귀, chu-gŭn-ggae 주근깨. ② (*animal*) tu-dŏ-ji 두더지.　　　　「하다.

molest *v.* koe-rop-hi-da 괴롭히다, pang-hae-ha-da 방해

moment *n.* sun-gan 순간 ; (*occasion*) ki-hoe 기회, kyŏng-u 경우 ; (*element*) yo-so 요소.　　　　「덧없는.

momentary *adj.* sun-sik-gan-ŭi 순식간의 ; tŏt-ŏp-nŭn

monarch *n.* kun-ju 군주, che-wang 제왕.

monarchy *n.* kun-ju-guk 군주국 ; kun-ju chŏng-ch'i 군

monastery *n.* su-do-wŏn 수도원.　　　　　L주 정치.

Monday *n.* wŏ-ryo-il 월요일.

money *n.* ton 돈, kŭm-jŏn 금전, (*wealth*) pu 부(富).

money changer hwan-jŏn-sang 환전상(換錢商).

money order hwan 환(換), (*postal order*) u-p'yŏn-hwan 우편환.

monitor *n.* (*in a school*) pan-jang 반장 ; (*adviser*) ch'ung-go-ja 충고자, mo-ni-t'ŏ 모니터.

monk *n.* su-do-sŭng 수도승 ; sŭng-ryŏ 승려.

monkey *n.* wŏn-sung-i 원숭이.

monolog(ue) *n.* tok-baek 독백 ; i-rin-gŭk 일인극(一人劇).

monoplane *n.* tan-yŏp pi-haeng-gi 단엽 비행기.

monopolize *v.* tok-jŏm-ha-da 독점하다.

monopoly *n.* tok-jŏm 독점, chŏn-mae 전매.　　「노레일.

monorail *n.* tan-gwe-ch'ŏl-do 단궤철도, mo-no-re-il 모

monotonous *adj.* tan-jo-ro-un 단조로운, pyŏn-hwa-ga ŏp-nŭn 변화가 없는 ; chi-ru-han 지루한.　　　「철.

monsoon *n.* kye-jŏl-p'ung 계절풍 ; chang-ma-ch'ŏl 장마

monster *n.* koe-mul 괴물, kŏ-in 거인.

monstrous *adj.* ki-goe-han 기괴한, mu-si-mu-si-han 무시무시한, (*huge*) ŏm-ch'ŏng-nan 엄청난.　　　「아지.

montage *n.* hon-sŏng-hwa 혼성화, mong-t'a-a-ji 몽타

month *n.* tal 달, wŏl 월 : *this* ∼ i-dal 이달/ *last* ∼ chi-nan-dal 지난달/*next* ∼ nae-dal 내달.

monthly *adj.* mae-dal-ŭi 매달의 : *a* ∼ *salary* wŏl-gŭp 월급. —*n.* wŏl-gan chap-ji 월간 잡지.

monument *n.* ki-nyŏm-bi 기념비, myo-bi 묘비 ; ki-nyŏm-mul 기념물 : *natural* ∼ ch'ŏn-yŏn ki-nyŏm-mul 천연 기념물. 「불멸의.

monumental *adj.* ki-nyŏm-bi-ŭi 기념비의, pul-myŏl-ŭi

mood *n.* ki-bun 기분, sim-jŏng 심정 ; p'ung-jo 풍조.

moon *n.* tal 달 : *a full* ∼ po-rŭm-dal 보름달, man-wŏl 만월/*a new* ∼ ch'o-sŭng-dal 초승달/*an old* ∼ kŭ-mŭm-dal 그믐달 / *a half* ∼ pan-dal 반달.

moonlight *n.* tal-bit 달빛 : *a* ∼ *ramble* tal-bam-ŭi san-ch'aek 달밤의 산책. 「bak-ha-da 정박하다.

moor *n.* hwang-mu-ji 황무지. —*v.* (*anchor*) chŏng-

moot *n.* t'o-ron-hoe 토론회, t'o-ŭi 토의.

mop *n.* cha-ru kŏl-re 자루 걸레, mop 몹.

moral *adj.* yul-li-jŏk-in 윤리적인, to-dŏk-jŏk-in 도덕 적인. —*n.* ① kyo-hun 교훈. ② yul-li 윤리. 「풍기.

morale *n.* (*military*) sa-gi 사기 ; (*civilian*) p'ung-gi

moralist *n.* to-dŏk-ga 도덕가, to-hak-ja 도학자, mo-ral-ri-sŭ-t'ŭ 모랄리스트. 「상도덕.

morality *n.* to-dŏk 도덕 : *commercial* ∼ sang-do-dŏk

morbid *adj.* pyŏng-jŏk-in 병적인, pyŏng-ŭi 병의.

more *adj.* tŏ man-ŭn 더 많은. —*adv.* tŏ man-i 더 많 이. —*n.* tŏ man-ŭn kŏt 더 많은 것.

moreover *adv.* kŭ wi-e 그 위에, ke-da-ga 게다가.

morning *n.* a-ch'im 아침, (*before noon*) o-jŏn 오전.

morphine *n.* mo-rŭ-p'in 모르핀.

morsel *n.* han ip 한 입, (*a bite*) han cho-gak 한 조각.

mortal *adj.* ① chuk-ŭl un-myŏng-ŭi 죽을 운명의. ② (*human*) in-gan-ŭi 인간의. —*n.* in-gan 인간.

mortar n. ① (*utensil*) chŏl-gu 절구. ② (*gun*) pak-gyŏk-p'o 박격포. ③ (*for building*) mo-rŭ-t'a-rŭ 모르타르.

mortgage n. chŏ-dang 저당(抵當).

mortify v. ŏk-je-ha-da 억제하다.

mortuary n. si-ch'e im-si an-ch'i-so 시체 임시 안치소.

mosquito n. mo-gi 모기.

mosquito net mo-gi-jang 모기장.

[chŏl-gu]

moss n. i-ggi 이끼 : *stones covered with* ~ i-ggi kkin tol 이끼 낀 돌.

most adj. ka-jang man-ŭn 가장 많은. —n. ch'oe-dae-[ryang 최대량.

mostly adv. tae-gae 대개, tae-bu-bun 대부분.

mote n. (*particle*) t'i-ggŭl 티끌, mŏn-ji 먼지.

motel n. (*motorists' hotel*) cha-dong-ch'a yŏ-haeng-ja suk-bak-so 자동차 여행자 숙박소. [re 좀벌레.

moth n. ① na-bang 나방. ② (*clothes moth*) chom-bŏl-

mother n. ŏ-mŏ-ni 어머니, mo-ch'in 모친. —v. (*bring up*) po-yuk-ha-da 보육하다.

mother country mo-guk 모국(母國), pon-guk 본국.

mother-in-law n. ① (*for woman*) si-ŏ-mŏ-ni 시어머니. ② (*for man*) chang-mo 장모.

mother-of-pearl n. chin-ju-mo 진주모, cha-gae 자개.

motif n. chu-je 주제, (*theme*) t'e-e-ma 테에마.

motion n. ① un-dong 운동. ② (*gesture*) mom-jit 몸짓. ③ (*proposal*) tong-ŭi 동의. ④ un-jŏn 운전.

motive n. tong-gi 동기, mo-t'i-bŭ 모티브. [모우터.

motor n. (*prime mover*) pal-dong-gi 발동기, mo-u-t'ŏ

motorboat n. mo-u-t'ŏ-bo-u-t'ŭ 모우터보우트.

motorcade n. cha-dong-ch'a haeng-ryŏl 자동차 행렬.

motorcar n. cha-dong-ch'a 자동차. [gŏ 자동 자전거.

motorcycle n. o-o-t'o-ba-i 오오토바이, cha-dong cha-jŏn-

motor pool (*motor park*) chu-ch'a-jang 주차장.

motto *n.* p'yo-ŏ 표어, ch'ŏ-se-hun 처세훈, mo-t'o 모토.

mo(u)ld *n.* ① t'ŭl 틀, kŏ-p'u-jip 거푸집. ② (*mildew*) kom-p'ang-i 곰팡이. ③ (*fertile soil*) ok-t'o 옥토.

mound *n.* ŏn-dŏk 언덕, (*raised bank*) tuk 둑.

mount *v.* o-rŭ-da 오르다. —*n.* san 산.

mountain *n.* san 산 : ~ *range* san-maek 산맥.

mountaineer *n.* tŭng-san-ga 등산가. —*v.* tŭng-san-ha-

mountainous *adj.* san-i man-ŭn 산이 많은. ∟da 등산하다.

mourn *v.* (*lament*) sŭl-p'ŏ-ha-da 슬퍼하다.

mourner *n.* cho-gaek 조객, ae-do-ja 애도자(哀悼者) : *the chief* ~ sang-ju 상주.

mourning *n.* ae-do 애도, sang 상(喪), sang-bok 상복 : ~ *badge* sang-jang 상장 /~ *card* pu-go 부고.

mouse *n.* saeng-jwi 생쥐 : ~ *trap* chwi-dŏt 쥐덫.

m(o)ustache *n.* k'ot-su-yŏm 콧수염. 「동성으로.

mouth *n.* ip 입 : *with one* ~ i-gu-dong-sŏng-ŭ-ro 이구

move *v.* ① um-jik-i-da 움직이다. ② (*touch*) kam-dong-si-k'i-da 감동시키다. ③ (*propose*) che-ŭi-ha-da 제의 하다. ④ (*remove*) i-sa-ha-da 이사하다.

movement *n.* ① un-dong 운동, tong-jak 동작 ; i-dong 이동 ; (*operation*) un-jŏn 운전. ② (*pl.*) t'ae-do 태도.

movie *n.* (*motion picture*) yŏng-hwa 영화.

moving *adj.* um-jik-i-nŭn 움직이는 ; (*touching*) kam-dong-si-k'i-nŭn 감동시키는 : ~ *picture* hwal-dong-sa-jin 활동사진, yŏng-hwa 영화.

mow *v.* pe-da 베다, kŏ-du-ŏ-dŭ-ri-da 거두어들이다. —*n.* kok-sik-dŏ-mi 곡식더미.

mower *n.* ① (*machine*) p'ul-be-nŭn ki-gye 풀베는 기계. ② (*person*) p'ul-be-nŭn sa-ram 풀베는 사람.

Mr. *n.* ssi 씨, kun 군, nim 님.

Mrs. *n.* …ssi pu-in …씨 부인, …yŏ-sa …여사(女史).

much *adj.* man-ŭn 많은. —*adv.* man-i 많이.

muck *n.* (*manure*) kŏ-rŭm 거름, t'oe-bi 퇴비.

mud *n.* chin-hŭk 진흙, (*mire*) chin-ch'ang 진창.

muddle *v.* hol-lan-si-k'i-da 혼란시키다. —*n.* hol-lan 혼란, ŏng-mang-jin-ch'ang 영망진창.

muddy *adj.* chin-hŭk t'u-sŏng-i-ŭi 진흙 투성이의.

muffle *v.* (*wrap up*) ssa-da 싸다, tŏp-da 덮다.

muffler *n.* ① (*neck scarf*) mok-do-ri 목도리, mŏ-p'ŭl-rŏ 머플러. ② so-ŭm chang-ch'i 소음 장치.

mug *n.* k'ŭn ch'at-jan 큰 찻잔, cho-ggi 조끼.

mulatto *n.* hŭk-baek hon-hyŏl-a 흑백 혼혈아.

mulberry *n.* ppong-na-mu 뽕나무 ; (*berry*) o-di 오디.

mule *n.* no-sae 노새; ko-jip-jang-i 고집장이. 「ho 대부호.

multimillionaire *n.* ch'ŏn-man-jang-ja 천만장자, tae-bu-

multiplication *n.* kop-sem 곱셈 ; chŭng-sik 증식.

multiply *v.* chŭng-ga-ha-da 증가하다, pŏn-sik-si-k'i-da 번식시키다 ; kop-sem-ha-da 곱셈하다.

multipurpose dam ta-mok-jŏk-daem 다목적댐.

multitude *n.* ① (*large number*) ta-su 다수. ② (*great crowd*) kun-jung 군중. 「da 우물거리다.

mumble *v.* chung-ŏl-gŏ-ri-da 중얼거리다, u-mul-gŏ-ri-

mummy *n.* ① mi-i-ra 미이라. ② (*mamma*) ŏm-ma 엄

munch *v.* wa-sak-wa-sak mŏk-da 와삭와삭 먹다. 「마.

municipal *adj.* si-ŭi 시(市)의 : ~ *office* si-ch'ŏng 시청.

munition *n.* ① kun-su-p'um 군수품. ② t'an-yak 탄약.

murder *n.* sa-rin 살인, sal-hae 살해. —*v.* sal-hae-ha-da 살해하다, chuk-i-da 죽이다.

murderer *n.* sa-rin-ja 살인자, ha-su-in 하수인.

murmur *n.* sok-sak-im 속삭임, chol-jol so-ri 졸졸 소리 ; (*grumble*) pul-p'yŏng 불평. —*v.* sok-sak-i-da 속삭이다, (*complain*) t'u-dŏl-gŏ-ri-da 투덜거리다. 「완력.

muscle *n.* kŭn-yuk 근육 ; (*bodily strength*) wal-lyŏk

muse v. saeng-gak-e cham-gi-da 생각에 잠기다.

museum n. pak-mul-gwan 박물관.

mushroom n. ① (*toadstool*) pŏ-sŏt 버섯. ② (*upstart*) pyŏ-rak-bu-ja 벼락부자.   「악곡.

music n. ŭm-ak 음악 ; (*musical composition*) ak-gok

musical adj. ŭm-ak-ŭi 음악의, (*melodious*) ŭm-ak-jŏk-in 음악적인. —n. (*musicale*) ŭm-ak-hoe 음악회.

musician n. ŭm-ak-ga 음악가, ak-sa 악사.

musk n. ① sa-hyang 사향. ② sa-hyang no-ru 사향 노루.

muslin n. mo-sŭl-rin 모슬린, ok-yang-mok 옥양목.

muss n. twi-juk-bak-juk 뒤죽박죽, so-dong 소동.

must aux. v. …hae-ya han-da …해야 한다 ; …ham-e t'ŭl-rim-op-da …함에 틀림없다. —n. kom-p'ang-i 곰팡이.

mustard n. kyŏ-ja 겨자(芥子), kat 갓.

muster v. pul-rŏ-mo-ŭ-da 불러모으다, so-jip-ha-da 소집하다. —n. so-jip 소집, chŏm-ho 점호.

mute adj. so-ri-ŏp-nŭn 소리없는, pŏng-ŏ-ri-ŭi 벙어리의.

mutilate v. chŏl-dan-ha-da 절단하다, hwe-son-ha-da 훼손하다, pul-gu-ro man-dŭl-da 불구로 만들다.

mutiny n. (*rebellion*) p'ok-dong 폭동. —v. p'ok-dong-ŭl i-rŭ-k'i-da 폭동을 일으키다 ; chŏ-hang-ha-da 저항하다.

mutter v. chung-ŏl-gŏ-ri-da 중얼거리다, t'u-dŏl-gŏ-ri-da 투덜거리다. —n. sok-sak-im 속삭임, pul-p'yŏng 불평.

mutton n. yang-go-gi 양고기.

mutual adj. sŏ-ro-ŭi 서로의, sang-ho-ŭi 상호의.

muzzle n. ① ip-ma-gae 입마개, chae-gal 재갈. ② (*snout*) chu-dung-i 주둥이. ③ (*gun*) ch'ong-gu 총구.

my pron. na-ŭi 나의. —int. M~!=Oh, m~! chŏ-rŏn! 저런 ! ŏ-mŏ-na 어머나 ! i-gŏt ch'am! 이것 참 !

myself pron. na cha-sin 나 자신.

mystery n. sin-bi 신비, i-sang-han kŏt 이상한 것.

myth *n.* sin-hwa 신화, (*legend*) chŏn-sŏl 전설 ; yet-nal i-ya-gi 옛날 이야기.

──◦ N ◦──

nail *v.* mo-sŭl pak-da 못을 박다. —*n.* ① (*instrument*) mot 못. ② (*finger*) son-t'op 손톱 ; (*toe*) pal-t'op 발톱 : ~ *clippers* son-t'op-gga-ggi 손톱깎이.

naive *adj.* sun-jin-han 순진한, u-jik-han 우직한.

naked *adj.* pŏl-gŏ-bŏ-sŭn 벌거벗은, na-ch'e-ŭi 나체의 ; (*exposed*) no-ch'ul-doen 노출된.

name *n.* i-rŭm 이름, sŏng-myŏng 성명. —*v.* i-rŭm-jit-da 이름짓다, (*appoint*) chi-myŏng-ha-da 지명하다.

namely *adv.* chŭk 즉, ta-si mal-ha-myŏn 다시 말하면.

name plate mun-p'ae 문패, myŏng-ch'al 명찰.

nap *v.* chol-da 졸다. —*n.* ① (*of wool*) po-p'ul 보풀. ② (*short sleep*) nat-jam 낮잠, sŏn-jam 선잠.

nape *n.* mok-dŏl-mi 목덜미.

napkin *n.* naep-k'in 냅킨.

narcissus *n.* ① su-sŏn-hwa 수선화. ② (*N~*) na-rŭ-si-so-sŭ 나르시소스.   「취제.

narcotic *adj.* ma-ch'wi-ŭi 마취의. —*n.* ma-ch'wi-je 마취제

narrate *v.* mal-ha-da 말하다, chin-sul-ha-da 진술하다.

narration *n.* i-ya-gi 이야기, tam-hwa 담화, sŏ-sul 서술, (*gram.*) hwa-bŏp 화법(話法).   「기체의.

narrative *n.* i-ya-gi 이야기. —*adj.* i-ya-gi-ch'e-ŭi 이야

narrator *n.* i-ya-gi-ha-nŭn sa-ram 이야기하는 사람, na-re-i-t'ŏ 나레이터.

narrow *adj.* chop-ŭn 좁은, p'yŏn-hyŏp-han 편협한.

narrow-minded *adj.* ma-ŭm-i chop-ŭn 마음이 좁은.

nasty *adj.* (*dirty*) tŏ-rŏ-un 더러운, pul-gyŏl-han 불결한 ; (*malicious*) sim-sul-gu-jŭn 심술궂은.

nation *n.* ① kuk-min 국민. ② (*state*) kuk-ga 국가. ③ (*race*) min-jok 민족.

national *adj.* kuk-min-ŭi 국민의, kuk-ga-ŭi 국가의 : ～ *flag* kuk-gi 국기/～ *anthem* kuk-ga 국가(國歌)/ ～ *defence* kuk-bang 국방.

nationalism *n.* kuk-ga-ju-ŭi 국가주의, min-jok-ju-ŭi 민족주의, (*patriotism*) ae-guk-sim 애국심.

nationality *n.* kuk-jŏk 국적, kuk-min-sŏng 국민성.

nationalization *n.* kuk-min-hwa 국민화, kuk-yu-hwa 국유화, kuk-yŏng 국영(國營).

nation-wide *adj.* chŏn-guk-jŏk-in 전국적인.

native *adj.* ① (*inborn*) t'a-go-nan 타고난. ② (*aboriginal*) t'o-ch'ak-ŭi 토착의. ③ pol-lae-ŭi 본래의 : ～ *country* ko-guk 고국/～ *place* ko-hyang 고향.

natural *adj.* cha-yŏn-ŭi 자연의, cha-yŏn kŭ-dae-ro-ŭi 자연 그대로의, (*innate*) t'a-go-nan 타고난.

naturalization *n.* kwi-hwa 귀화(歸化).

naturally *adv.* cha-yŏn-hi 자연히, ch'ŏn-sŏng-jŏk-ŭ-ro 천성적으로, tang-yŏn-hi 당연히.

nature *n.* ① cha-yŏn 자연. ② (*character*) ch'ŏn-sŏng 천성, sŏng-jil 성질. ③ (*sort*) chong-ryu 종류.

naught·nought *n.* (*zero*) yŏng 영, mu 무(無).

naughty *adj.* (*mischievous*) chang-nan-ggu-rŏ-gi-ŭi 장난꾸러기의 ; pŏ-rŭt-ŏp-nŭn 버릇없는.

nauseous *adj.* me-sŭ-ggŏ-un 메스꺼운, si-rŭn 싫은.

naval *adj.* hae-gun-ŭi 해군의 : ～ *forces* hae-gun 해군/ N～ *Academy* hae-gun-sa-gwan-hak-gyo 해군사관학교.

navigate *v.* hang-hae-ha-da 항해하다 ; (*steer*) cho-jong-ha-da 조종하다, chin-haeng-si-k'i-da 진행시키다.

navigation *n.* hang-hae 항해 : *aerial* ～ hang-gong-sul 항공술/～ *company* ki-sŏn-hoe-sa 기선회사.

navy *n.* hae-gun 해군, hae-gun kun-in 해군 군인.

near *adj.* ka-gga-un 가까운. —*adv.* ka-gga-i 가까이. —*prep.* ···ŭi ka-gga-i-e ···의 가까이에, ···ŭi kŭn-ch'ŏ-e ···의 근처에.

near-by *adj.* ka-gga-un 가까운, ka-gga-i-ŭi 가까이의: *a ~ village* pa-ro i-ut ma-ŭl 바로 이웃 마을.

Near East kŭn-dong 근동(近東).

nearly *adv.* kŏ-ŭi 거의, ha-ma-t'ŏ-myŏn 하마터면.

nearsighted *adj.* kŭn-si-ŭi 근시(近視)의.

neat *adj.* cho-ch'ol-han 조촐한, san-ddŭt-han 산뜻한.

necessary *adj.* p'i-ryo-han 필요한, (*inevitable*) p'i-hal su ŏp-nŭn 피할 수 없는, p'i-ryŏn-jŏk-in 필연적인.

necessity *n.* p'i-ryo 필요; p'il-su-p'um 필수품.

neck *n.* mok 목, mok-dŏl-mi 목덜미.   「치프.

neckerchief *n.* mok-do-ri 목도리, ne-k'ŏ-ch'i-p'ŭ 네커

necklace *n.* mok-gŏ-ri 목걸이.

necktie *n.* nek-t'a-i 넥타이.

need *n.* ① p'i-ryo 필요; yo-gu 요구. ② (*poverty*) pin-gon 빈곤. —*v.* ① (*want*) p'i-ryo-ha-da 필요하다. ② (*be needy*) kon-gung-e ppa-jyŏ-it-da 곤궁에 빠져있다.

needle *n.* pa-nŭl 바늘, cha-ch'im 자침(磁針).

needlewoman *n.* ch'im-mo 침모, pa-nŭ-jil-ha-nŭn yŏ-ja

needlework *n.* pa-nŭ-jil 바느질.   [바느질하는 여자.

needy *adj.* saeng-hwal-i ttak-han 생활이 딱한.

negative *n.* ① pu-jŏng 부정(否定); (*refusal*) kŏ-bu 거부. ② (*film*) wŏn-p'an 원판. —*adj.* pu-jŏng-jŏk-in 부정적인; so-gŭk-jŏk-in 소극적인.

neglect *v.* so-hol-hi-ha-da 소홀히하다; mu-si-ha-da 무시하다. —*n.* t'ae-man 태만; (*disregard*) mu-si 무시.

negligee *n.* sil-nae-bok 실내복, ne-gŭl-ri-je 네글리제.

negligence *n.* t'ae-man 태만, pang-sim 방심.

negotiate *v.* ① (*bargain*) tam-p'an-ha-da 담판하다. ② (*arrange*) hyŏp-jŏng-ha-da 협정하다. ③ (*convert* *into cash*) ton-ŭ-ro pa-ggu-da 돈으로 바꾸다.

negotiation *n.* tam-p'an 담판 ; (*parley*) kyo-sŏp 교섭.

Negro *n.* hŭk-in 흑인, ni-gŭ-ro 니그로.

neigh *v.* (*whinny*) mal-i ul-da 말이 울다. —*n.* mal u-rŭm-so-ri 말 울음소리. 「tong-p'o 동포.

neighbo(u)r *n.* i-ut(-sa-ram) 이웃사람, (*fellowman*)

neighbo(u)rhood *n.* kŭn-ch'ŏ 근처, i-ut 이웃 ; i-ut-sa-ram-dŭl 이웃사람들. 「…도 아니다.

neither ~ **nor** …do a-ni-go …do a-ni-da …도 아니고

neon *n.* ne-on 네온 : ~ *signs* ne-on-sa-in 네온사인.

nephew *n.* cho-k'a 조카, saeng-jil 생질.

nerve *n.* sin-gyŏng 신경 ; (*vigor*)ki-ryŏk 기력 ; (*courage*) yong-gi 용기 ; (*pl.*) sin-gyŏng kwa-min 신경 과민.

nerveless *adj.* mu-gi-ryŏk-han 무기력한.

nerve war sin-gyong-jŏn 신경전, sŏn-jŏn-jŏn 선전전.

nervous *adj.* sin-gyŏng-ŭi 신경의, sin-gyŏng-jil-ŭi 신경질의.

nervousness *n.* sin-gyŏng-jil 신경질, sin-gyŏng-gwa-min 신경과민.

nest *n.* ① sae-dung-u-ri 새둥우리, sae-jip 새집. ② po-gŭm-ja-ri 보금자리. ③ (*retreat*) p'i-nan-ch'ŏ 피난처. —*v.* po-gŭm-ja-ri-rŭl chit-da 보금자리를 짓다.

nestle *v.* kit-dŭ-ri-da 깃들이다, ki-bun cho-k'e nup-da [an-da] 기분 좋게 눕다[앉다].

net *n.* ① kŭ-mul 그물. ② (*snare*) ham-jŏng 함정. —*adj.* (*business*) sun-i-ik-ŭi 순이익의.

nettle *n.* sswae-gi-p'ul 쐐기풀.

network *n.* ① kŭ-mul se-gong 그물 세공, kŭ-mul-k'o 그물코. ② (*broadcasting*) pang-song-mang 방송망.

neurosis *n.* sin-gyŏng-jŭng 신경증, no-i-ro-je 노이로제.

neuter *adj.* chung-sŏng-ŭi 중성의, chung-rip-ŭi 중립의 : *a* ~ *gender* chung-sŏng 중성(中性).

neutral *adj.* chung-rip-ŭi 중립의, pul-p'yon-bu-dang-ŭi 불편부당의 : *a ~ zone* chung-rip-ji-dae 중립지대.

neutron *n.* chung-sŏng-ja 중성자.

never *adv.* kyŏl-k'o …a-ni-da 결코 …아니다.

nevertheless *conj.* kŭ-rŏm-e-do pul-gu-ha-go 그럼에도 불구하고, ku-rŏ-ch'i-man 그렇지만.

new *adj.* sae-ro-un 새로운, sin-sik-ŭi 신식의 ; (*recently appointed*) sin-im-ŭi 신임(新任)의.

newly *adv.* sae-ro-i 새로이, (*recently*) yo-sa-i 요사이.

news *n.* nyu-u-sŭ 뉴우스, ki-sa 기사, so-mun 소문.

newspaper *n.* sin-mun 신문 : *daily ~* il-gan-sin-mun 일간신문/~ *report* sin-mun-bo-do 신문보도.

newsreel *n.* (*news film*) si-sa yŏng-hwa 시사 영화.

New Year sae-hae 새해 : *New Year's Day* sŏl-nal 설날, chŏng-wŏl ch'o-ha-ru 정월 초하루.

next *adj.* ta-ŭm-ŭi 다음의. —*adv.* ta-ŭm-e 다음에. —*prep.* …e ka-jang ka-gga-un …에 가장 가까운.

nibble *v.* ① cho-gŭm-ssik kal-ga-mŏk-da 조금씩 갉아먹다. ② (*carp*) hŭm-jap-da 흠잡다. 「고운.

nice *adj.* cho-ŭn 좋은, kkae-ggŭt-han 깨끗한 ; ko-un

nice-looking *adj.* kwi-yŏ-un 귀여운, ko-un 고운.

nickel *n.* ni-k'el 니켈, paek-t'ong 백통(白銅).

nickname *n.* pyŏl-myŏng 별명 ; ae-ch'ing 애칭.

nicotine *n.* ni-k'o-t'in 니코틴 : ~ *poisoning* ni-k'o-t'in chung-dok 니코틴 중독.

niece *n.* cho-k'a-ddal 조카딸, chil-nyŏ 질녀.

night *n.* pam 밤, ya-gan 야간, chŏ-nyŏk 저녁.

night duty ya-gŭn 야근, suk-jik 숙직.

nightgown *n.* cham-ot 잠옷. 「kong-p'o-gam 공포감.

nightmare *n.* ak-mong 악몽, ka-wi-nul-rim 가위눌림.

nimble *adj.* min-ch'ŏp-han 민첩한, (*clever*) chae-ch'i-it-nŭn 재치있는, nun-ch'i-ga ppa-rŭn 눈치가 빠른.

nine *n.* & *adj.* a-hop(-ŭi) 아홉(의), ku(-ŭi) 9(의).

ninefold *adj.* & *adv.* a-hop-bae-ŭi[ro] 아홉배의[로].

nineteen *n.* yŏl a-hop 열 아홉, sip-gu 19.

ninety *n.* a-hŭn 아흔, ku-sip 90. 「tta-da 따다.

nip *v.* kko-jip-da 꼬집다; (*bite*) mul-da 물다; (*cut*)

nipple *n.* chŏt-ggok-ji 젖꼭지, yu-do 유두(乳頭).

nitrogen *n.* chil-so 질소.

no *adj.* mu-ŭi 무(無)의, ha-na-do ŏp-nŭn 하나도 없는.
—*adv.* ① cho-gŭm-do …a-ni-da 조금도 …아니다. ②
a-ni-o 아니오. —*n.* pu-jŏng 부정, kŏ-jŏl 거절.

noble *adj.* ko-sang-han 고상한, ko-gyŏl-han 고결한;
kwi-jok-ŭi 귀족의; (*grand*) tang-dang-han 당당한.

nobleman *n.* (*peer*) kwi-jok 귀족.

nobody *pron.* a-mu-do a-ni-da 아무도 … 아니다. —*n.*
ha-ch'an-ŭn sa-ram 하찮은 사람.

nocturn(e) *n.* ① ya-gok 야곡, ya-sang-gok 야상곡; nok-
t'ŏ-ŏn 녹터언. ② ya-gyŏng-hwa 야경화(夜景畵).

nod *v.* kkŭ-dŏk-i-da 끄덕이다, chol-da 졸다. —*n.* kkŭ-
dŏk-im 끄덕임, su-gŭng 수궁; cho-rŭm 졸음.

noise *n.* (*clamor*) so-ŭm 소음, pŏp-sŏk 법석.

noisy *adj.* ① si-ggŭ-rŏ-un 시끄러운, ttŏ-dŭl-ssŏk-han
떠들썩한. ② (*showy*) ya-han 야한.

nomad(e) *n.* yu-mok-min 유목민, pang-rang-ja 방랑자.

nominal *adj.* myŏng-ŭi-sang-ŭi 명의상의; (*gram.*)
myŏng-sa-ŭi 명사(名詞)의. 「지정하다.

nominate *v.* chi-myŏng-ha-da 지명하다, chi-jŏng-ha-da

nonalignment *n.* pi-dong-maeng 비동맹.

none *pron.* (*no person*) a-mu-do …an-t'a 아무도 …않다.

nonsense *n.* mu-ŭi-mi 무의미; hŏt'ŭn so-ri 허튼 소리,
nŏn-sen-sŭ 넌센스. —*int.* pa-bo-ga-ch'i 바보같이.

nonstop *adj.* chik-haeng-ŭi 직행의; mu-ch'ak-ryuk-ŭi
무착륙의: *a ~ flight* mu-ch'ak-ryuk pi-haeng 무착

륙 비행. —*adv.* chik-haeng-ŭ-ro 직행으로.

noodles *n.* kuk-su 국수. 「ch'ŏ 은신처.

nook *n.* ① ku-sŏk 구석 ; oe-ddan-got 외딴곳. ② ŭn-sin-

noon *n.* (*midday*) chŏng-o 정오, tae-nat 대낮.

noose *n.* ① (*slipknot*) mae-dŭp 매듭. ② (*snare*) ol-ga-mi 올가미. ③ (*bond*) yu-dae 유대.

nor *conj.* …do tto-han …a-ni-da …도 또한 …아니다.

normal *adj.* ① chŏng-sang-ŭi 정상의, chŏng-gyu-ŭi 정규의. ② (*average*) p'yŏng-gyun-ŭi 평균의.

normal school sa-bŏm hak-gyo 사범 학교. 「(의).

north *n. & adj.* puk(-ŭi) 북(의), puk-jjok(-ŭi) 북쪽

northeast *n.* tong-buk 동북, tong-buk-bu 동북부.

northern *adj.* puk-ŭi 북의, puk-jjok-ŭi 북쪽의.

North Pole puk-gŭk 북극(北極).

northwest *n.* sŏ-buk 서북, sŏ-buk-bu 서북부.

nose *n.* k'o 코 ; (*sense of smell*) hu-gak 후각.

nostril *n.* k'ot-gu-mŏng 콧구멍.

not *adv.* …a-ni-da …아니다, …an-t'a …않다.

notable *adj.* chu-mok-hal man-han 주목할 만한, tu-dŭ-rŏ-jin 두드러진. —*n.* myŏng-sa 명사(名士).

notary *n.* kong-jŭng-in 공증인(公證人).

note *n.* ① (*mark*) pu-ho 부호. ② (*memo*) me-mo 메모. ③ (*annotation*) chu-hae 주해. ④ (*short letter*) tan-sin 단신. ⑤ (*score*) ak-bo 악보. —*v.* ① (*see*) chu-mok-ha-da 주목하다. ② (*write*) ki-rok-ha-da 기록하다.

notebook *n.* ① kong-ch'aek 공책, p'il-gi-jang 필기장, no-u-t'ŭ 노우트. ② su-ch'ŏp 수첩, pi-mang-rok 비망

notepaper *n.* p'yŏn-ji-ji 편지지. 「록.

nothing *pron.* ① (*not anything*) a-mu-gŏt-do …a-ni-da 아무것도 …아니다. ② mu 무(無). ③ (*trifle*) po-jal-gŏt-ŏp-nŭn kŏt 보잘것없는 것. —*adv.* cho-gŭm-do …an-t'a 조금도 …않다.

notice *n.* (*information*) t'ong-ji 통지, (*warning*) ye-go 예고;(*observation*) chu-mok 주목. —*v.*(*perceive*) a-ra-ch'ae-da 알아채다 ; chu-mok-ha-da 주목하다.

notify *v.* (*inform*) t'ong-ji-ha-da 통지하다, t'ong-go-ha-da 통고하다, kong-go-ha-da 공고하다.

notion *n.* ① (*idea*) kae-nyŏm 개념. ② (*intention*) ŭi-hyang 의향. ③ (*opinion*) kyŏn-hae 견해.

notorious *adj.* so-mun-nan 소문난, ak-myŏng-no-p'ŭn 악명높은, chu-ji-ŭi 주지의.

noun *n.* (*gram.*) myŏng-sa 명사(名詞).

nourish *v.* ① ki-rŭ-da 기르다. ② ma-ŭm-e p'um-da 마음에 품다.

novel *n.* so-sŏl 소설. —*adj.* (*new*) sae-ro-un 새로운, (*strange*) sin-gi-han 신기한, ki-bal-han 기발한.

novelette *n.* tan[chŭng]-p'yŏn so-sŏl 단[중]편 소설.

novelist *n.* so-sŏl-ga 소설가. 「je-p'um 신제품.

novelty *n.* sin-gi-ham 신기함, chin-gi-ham 진기함, sin-

November *n.* sip-il-wŏl 11월.

novice *n.* p'ut-na-gi 풋나기, ch'o-sim-ja 초심자(初心者) ; (*new convert*) sae sin-ja 새 신자.

now *adv.* i-je 이제, chi-gŭm 지금. —*n.* chi-gŭm 지금, hyŏn-jae 현재. —*conj.* …han i-sang …한 이상.

nowadays *adv.* o-nŭl-nal-e-nŭn 오늘날에는, yo-jŭm-e-nŭn 요즘에는. —*n.* hyŏn-jae 현재, o-nŭl-nal 오늘날.

nowhere *adv.* a-mu-de-do …ŏp-da 아무데도 …없다.

nuance *n.* mi-myo-han ch'a-i 미묘한 차이 ; saek-jo 색조(色調), nwi-ang-sŭ 뉘앙스.

nuclear *adj.* haek-ŭi 핵의 ; wŏn-ja-haek-ŭi 원자핵의.

nucleus *n.* haek 핵, haek-sim 핵심 ; wŏn-ja-haek 원자핵.

nude *adj.* na-ch'e-ŭi 나체의, pŏl-gŏ-bŏ-sŭn 벌거벗은.

nudge *v.* p'al-ggum-ch'i-ro jji-rŭ-da 팔꿈치로 찌르다.

nuisance *n.* sŏng-ga-sin il 성가신 일, tu-t'ong-gŏ-ri 두

통거리, p'ye 폐(弊).

nullify v. mu-hyo-ro ha-da 무효로 하다, pye-gi-ha-da 폐기하다, (*cancel*) ch'wi-so-ha-da 취소하다.

numb adj. kam-gak-ŭl i-rŭn 감각을 잃은.

number n. ① (*figure*) sut-ja 숫자. ② (*series*) pŏn-ho 번호, pŏn-ji 번지, (*suffix*) pŏn 번.　　「의.

numerous adj. man-ŭn su-ŭi 많은 수의, ta-su-ŭi 다수

nun n. su-nyŏ 수녀, yŏ-sŭng 여승.

nuptial adj. kyŏl-hon-ŭi 결혼의, hol-lye-ŭi 혼례의 : *a ~ ceremony* kyŏl-hon-sik 결혼식, hol-lye 혼례.

nurse n. ① yu-mo 유모. ② kan-ho-wŏn 간호원. —v. ① (*hospital*) kan-ho-ha-da 간호하다. ② (*give suck*) chŏ-jŭl mŏk-i-da 젖을 먹이다.

nursery n. ŏ-rin-i pang 어린이 방, yuk-a-sil 육아실.

nursery rhyme cha-jang-ga 자장가 ; tong-yo 동요.

nut n. (*chestnut, walnut, filbert, etc.*) kyŏn-gwa 견과 (堅果) ; na-mu yŏl-mae 나무 열매.　　「물.

nutrition n. yŏng-yang 영양, (*food*) ŭm-sik-mul 음식

nylon n. na-il-ron 나일론.　　　　　　　　「미소녀.

nymph n. nim-p'ŭ 님프, yo-jŏng 요정(妖精) ; mi-so-nyŏ

———❰◗◗◗❱———

oaf n. ki-hyŏng-a 기형아, (*idiot*) paek-ch'i 백치.

oak n. ch'am-na-mu 참나무, ttŏk-gal-na-mu 떡갈나무.

oar n. no 노.

oat n. kwi-ri 귀리.　　　　　　　　「yak-ha-da 서약하다.

oath n. maeng-se 맹세, sŏ-yak 서약 : *make an ~* sŏ-

oatmeal n. o-u-t'ŭ-mil 오우트밀.　　　　　　「고한.

obdurate adj. ko-jip-i sen 고집이 센, wan-go-han 완

obedience n. pok-jong 복종, sun-jong 순종.

obedient adj. pok-jong-ha-nŭn 복종하는, sun-song-ha-nŭn 순종하는, (*filial*) hyo-sŏng-sŭ-rŏ-un 효성스러운.

obey *v.* pok-jong-ha-da 복종하다, tta-rŭ-da 따르다.

obituary *n.* pu-go 부고, sa-mang ki-sa 사망 기사. —*adj.* sa-mang-ŭi 사망의.

object *n.* ① (*aim*) mok-jŏk 목적. ② (*thing*) mul-ch'e 물체. ③ (*gram.*) mok-jŏk-ŏ 목적어. —*v.* pan-dae-ha-da 반대하다, hang-ŭi-ha-da 항의하다.

objection *n.* pan-dae 반대, hang-ŭi 항의.

objective *adj.* kaek-gwan-jŏk-in 객관적인. —*n.* (*aim*) mok-jŏk 목적 ; (*gram.*) mok-jŏk-ŏ 목적어.

objector *n.* pan-dae-ja 반대자.

obligation *n.* ① (*duty*) ŭi-mu 의무. ② (*debt*) ch'ae-mu 채무. ③ (*debt of gratitude*) ŭn-hye 은혜.

oblige *v.* ① ŭi-mu-rŭl chi-u-da 의무를 지우다. ② (*favor*) ŭn-hye-rŭl pe-p'ul-da 은혜를 베풀다.

oblivion *n.* mang-gak 망각 ; kŏn-mang 건망(健忘).

oblong *n.* chang-bang-hyŏng 장방형.

obscene *adj.* ŭm-t'ang-han 음탕한, ch'u-jap-han 추잡한.

obscure *adj.* ae-mae-han 애매한 ; (*dim*) hŭ-rin 흐린, (*unknown*) mu-myŏng-ŭi 무명의.

observance *n.* ① chun-su 준수. ② ŭi-sik 의식(儀式).

observation *n.* (*notice*) kwan-ch'al 관찰, kwan-ch'ŭk 관측 ; (*experiment*) sil-hŏm kwan-ch'al 실험 관찰.

observatory *n.* ① (*astron.*) ch'ŏn-mun-dae 천문대. ② (*meteor.*) ch'ŭk-hu-so 측후소.

observe *v.* ① kwan-ch'al-ha-da 관찰하다. ② (*obey*) chun-su-ha-da 준수하다. ③ (*remark*) mal-ha-da 말하다, chin-sul-ha-da 진술하다.

observer *n.* kwan-ch'ŭk-ja 관측자, chun-su-ja 준수자 ; (*witness*) ip-hoe-in 입회인, ŏp-jŏ-ŏ-bŏ 엎저어버.

obstacle *n.* chang-ae 장애, pang-hae 방해.

obstetrics *n.* san-gwa-hak 산과학(産科學).

obstinate *adj.* ko-jip-sen 고집센, wan-go-han 완고한.

obstruct *v.* pang-hae-ha-da 방해하다.

obstruction pang-hae 방해, chi-jang 지장.

obtain *v.* ŏt-da 얻다, son-e nŏ-t'a 손에 넣다.

obvious *adj.* myŏng-baek-han 명백한, ppan-han 빤한.

occasion *n.* ki-hoe 기회 ; (*case*) kyŏng-u 경우.

occasionally *adv.* ttae-ddae-ro 때때로, ka-ggŭm 가끔.

Occident *n.* sŏ-yang 서양, sŏ-gu 서구.

occidental *adj.* sŏ-yang-ŭi 서양의, ku-mi-ŭi 구미의.

occupant *n.* ① (*inhabitant*) kŏ-ju-ja 거주자. ② (*occupier*) chŏm-yu-ja 점유자, chŏm-gŏ-ja 점거자.

occupation *n.* ① (*work*) chik-ŏp 직업. ② (*military*) chŏm-ryŏng 점령, chŏm-gŏ 점거.

occupational disease chik-ŏp-byŏng 직업병.

occupy *v.* ① chŏm-ryŏng-ha-da 점령하다. ② chong-sa-ha-da 종사하다.

occur *v.* i-rŏ-na-da 일어나다 ; saeng-gi-da 생기다.

occurrence *n.* pal-saeng 발생, (*accident*) sa-gŏn 사건.

ocean *n.* tae-yang 대양 : *Atlantic O~* tae-sŏ-yang 대서양/*Pacific O~* t'ae-p'yŏng-yang 태평양.

o'clock *n.* …si …시(時).

octave *n.* ok-t'a-bŭ 옥타브, che-p'al-ŭm 제8음.

October *n.* si-wŏl 10월.

octopus *n.* mun-ŏ 문어, nak-ji 낙지.

oculist *n.* an-gwa ŭi-sa 안과(眼科) 의사.

odd *adj.* ① (*strange*) i-sang-han 이상한. ② (*extra*) yŏ-bun-ŭi 여분의. ③ (*not even*) ki-su-ŭi 기수(奇數)의.

odds *n.* (*inequalities*) pul-p'yŏng-dŭng 불평등.

odious *adj.* si-rŭn 싫은, (*hateful*) mi-un 미운.

odo(u)r *n.* hyang-gi 향기, naem-sae 냄새. 「…로 된」

of *prep.* ① (*poss.*) …ŭi …의. ② (*made of*) …ro toen

off *adv.* ttŏ-rŏ-jyŏ 떨어져, mŏl-li 멀리.

offence · offense *n.* ① pŏm-joe 범죄. ② (*attack*) kong-
gyŏk 공격. ③ (*foul*) pan-ch'ik 반칙.

offend *v.* ① no-ha-ge ha-da 노하게 하다. ② (*transgress*)
pŏm-ha-da 범하다, ŏ-gi-da 어기다.

offensive *adj.* ① si-rŭn 싫은, (*unpleasant*) pul-k'wae-
han 불쾌한. ② (*attack*) kong-gyŏk-jŏk 공격적.

offer *v.* che-ch'ul-ha-da 제출하다 ; che-ŭi-ha-da 제의하
다 ; (*show*) p'yo-si-ha-da 표시하다. —*n.* che-an 제안,
sin-ch'ŏng 신청.   「mul 제물.

offering *n.* (*church*) hŏn-gŭm 헌금 ; (*to a diety*) che-

office *n.* ① (*room*) sa-mu-sil 사무실. ② (*section*) …kwa
…과, …pu …부, …ch'ŏng …청, …kuk …국.

office boy sa-hwan 사환, kŭp-sa 급사.

officer *n.* ① (*civil*) kwal-li 관리, kong-mu-wŏn 공무
원. ② (*army*) chang-gyo 장교.

official *adj.* (*formal*) kong-sik-ŭi 공식의 ; (*public*)
kong-mu-sang-ŭi 공무상의. —*n.* kwal-li 관리, kong-
mu-wŏn 공무원, chik-wŏn 직원.

off limits ch'u-rip kŭm-ji(-gu-yŏk) 출입 금지(구역).

often *adv.* ka-ggŭm 가끔, chong-jong 종종, cha-ju 자

oil *n. & v.* ki-rŭm(-ŭl ch'i-da) 기름(을 치다).   「주.

oily *adj.* ① ki-rŭm-ŭl pa-rŭn 기름을 바른, ki-rŭm t'u-
sŏng-i-ŭi 기름 투성이의. ② ku-byŏn-i cho-ŭn 구변이 좋

ointment *n.* yŏn-go 연고.   「은.

old *adj.* (*person*) nŭl-gŭn 늙은 ; (*thing*) nal-gŭn 낡은.

older brother (*boy*) hyŏng-nim 형님 ; (*girl*) o-bba
오빠.

older sister (*girl*) ŏn-ni 언니 ; (*boy*) nu-nim 누님.

old-fashioned *adj.* ku-sik-ŭi 구식의, ko-p'ung-ŭi 고풍

Old Testament ku-yak sŏng-sŏ 구약 성서.   「의.

olive *n.* ol-ri-bŭ 올리브, kam-ram 감람(橄欖).

Olympics *n.* (=*Olympic games*) ol-rim-p'ik kyŏng-gi 올림픽 경기.

omen *n.* (*foreboding*) chŏn-jo 전조, ching-jo 징조 : *good* ~ kil-jo 길조/*bad* ~ hyung-jo 흉조.

omission *n.* saeng-ryak 생략, nu-rak 누락.

omit *v.* ① saeng-ryak-ha-da 생략하다, ppa-ddŭ-ri-da 빠드리다. ② (*neglect*) ke-ŭl-ri-ha-da 게을리하다.

omnibus *n.* hap-sŭng cha-dong-ch'a 합승 자동차.

on *prep.* …wi-e …위에, …e kwan-ha-yŏ …에 관하여.

once *adv.* han pŏn 한 번 ; (*formerly*) il-jji-gi 일찌기.

one *adj.* ha-na-ŭi 하나의. —*n.* ha-na 하나, il 일.

oneself *pron.* cha-gi cha-sin-i 자기 자신이, sŭ-sŭ-ro 스스로, cha-gi cha-sin-ŭl[e] 자기 자신을[에].

one-sided *adj.* han-jjok-ŭ-ro ki-un 한쪽으로 기운.

one-way *adj.* il-bang-t'ong-haeng-ŭi 일방통행의 : *a* ~ *ticket* p'yŏn-do ch'a-p'yo 편도 차표.

onion *n.* yang-p'a 양파, p'a 파.

onlooker *n.* ku-gyŏng-gun 구경군, mok-gyŏk-ja 목격자.

only *adj.* yu-il-han 유일한. —*adv.* ta-man 다만.

onset *n.* sŭp-gyŏk 습격, kong-gyŏk 공격. 「향상하는.

onward *adv.* a-p'ŭ-ro 앞으로. —*adj.* hyang-sang-ha-nŭn

opal *n.* tan-baek-sŏk 단백석, o-p'al 오팔.

open *v.* yŏl-da 열다. —*adj.* yŏl-rin 열린.

opening *n.* ① (*beginning*) si-jak 시작. ② (*meeting*) kae-hoe 개회. ③ (*open space*) ku-mŏng 구멍.

openwork *n.* (*sculpture*) to-rim-jil se-gong 도림질 세공.

opera *n.* ka-gŭk 가극, o-p'e-ra 오페라.

opera house o-p'e-ra kŭk-jang 오페라 극장.

operate *v.* ① (*mech.*) un-jŏn-ha-da 운전하다. ② (*surg.*) su-sul-ha-da 수술하다.

operation *n.* ① (*surg.*) su-sul 수술. ② (*milit.*) chak-jŏn 작전. ③ (*function*) chak-yong 작용. ④ (*mech.*) un-jŏn 운전. ⑤ (*management*) kyŏng-yŏng 경영.

operator *n.* un-jŏn-ja 운전자, ki-sa 기사 : *telegraph* ~ chŏn-sin ki-sa 전신 기사/*telephone* ~ chŏn-hwa kyo-hwan-su 전화 교환수. 「소신.

opinion *n.* ŭi-gyŏn 의견, kyŏn-hae 견해, (*pl.*) so-sin

opium *n.* a-p'yŏn 아편.

opponent *n.* pan-dae-ja 반대자, chŏk-su 적수 ; kyŏng-jaeng-ja 경쟁자. —*adj.* chŏk-dae-ha-nŭn 적대하는.

opportunist *n.* ki-hoe-ju-ŭi-ja 기회주의자.

opportunity *n.* ki-hoe 기회, ho-gi 호기(好機).

oppose *v.* pan-dae-ha-da 반대하다, chŏ-hang-ha-da 저항하다, (*hinder*) pang-hae-ha-da 방해하다.

opposite *adj.* chŏng-ban-dae-ŭi 정반대의 ; chŏ-jjok-ŭi 저쪽의 ; (*front*) ma-jŭn-p'yŏn-ŭi 맞은편의.

opposition *n.* ① pan-dae 반대. ② ya-dang 야당.

oppress *v.* ap-bak-ha-da 압박하다, hak-dae-ha-da 학대

optical *adj.* nŭn-ŭi 눈의, si-gak-ŭi 시각의. 「하다.

optimism *n.* nak-ch'ŏn-ju-ŭi 낙천주의.

or *conj.* tto-nŭn 또는, hok-ŭn 혹은.

oracle *n.* sin-t'ak 신탁, t'ak-sŏn 탁선(託宣).

oral *adj.* (*spoken*) ku-du-ŭi 구두의. —*n.* (*oral exam.*) ku-du si-hŏm 구두 시험. 「bi-ch'ŭi 오렌지빛의.

orange *n.* kyul 귤, o-ren-ji 오렌지. —*adj.* o-ren-ji-

orator *n.* yŏn-sŏl-ja 연설자, pyŏn-sa 변사. 「눈구멍.

orbit *n.* ① kwe-do 궤도. ② (*eye socket*) nun-gu-mŏng

orchard *n.* kwa-su-wŏn 과수원, kwa-su 과수(果樹).

orchestra *n.* kwan-hyŏn-ak-dan 관현악단, o-k'e-sŭ-t'ŭ-ra 오케스트라.

orchid *n.* nan 난(蘭), nan-ch'o 난초.

ordain *v.* ① (*appoint*) im-myŏng-ha-da 임명하다. ② (*estab.*) che-jŏng-ha-da 제정하다. ③ (*order*) myŏng-ha-da 명하다 ; (*destine*) un-myŏng-ji-u-da 운명지우다.

order *n.* ① (*command*) myŏng-ryŏng 명령. ② (*se-*

quence) sun-sŏ 순서. ③ (*commission to supply*) chu-mun 주문. ④ (*decoration*) hun-jang 훈장. —*v.* ① (*command*) myŏng-ryŏng-ha-da 명령하다. ② (*goods*) chu-mun-ha-da 주문하다.

orderly *adj.* tan-jŏng-han 단정한. —*n.* (*messenger*) chŏl-lyŏng 전령, yŏl-lak-byŏng 연락병.

ordinance *n.* ① pŏp-ryŏng 법령. ② (*rite*) ŭi-sik 의식.

ordinary *adj.* po-t'ong-ŭi 보통의, p'yŏng-bŏm-han 평범한. —*n.* ① po-t'ong-il 보통일. ② chŏng-sik 정식(定

ordnance *n.* p'o 포, (*weapons*) pyŏng-gi 병기. ⌊(食.

ore *n.* kwang-sŏk 광석, wŏn-gwang 원광.

organ *n.* ① (*music*) o-ru-gan 오르간. ② (*of body*) ki-gwan 기관(器官). ③ (*agent*) ki-gwan 기관(機關).

organization *n.* (*system*) cho-jik 조직, tan-ch'e 단체; (*outfit*) ki-gu 기구. ⌈립하다.

organize *v.* cho-jik-ha-da 조직하다 ; ch'ang-rip-ha-da 창

orgie·orgy *n.* pŏp-sŏk 법석, puk-sae 북새.

orient *n.* tong-yang 동양. —*adj.* tong-yang-ŭi 동양의.

oriental *adj.* tong-yang-ŭi 동양의. —*n.* tong-yang-in 동양인, a-si-a-in 아시아인.

origin *n.* kŭn-wŏn 근원, pal-dan 발단.

original *adj.* ch'oe-ch'o-ŭi 최초의 ; tok-ch'ang-jŏk-in 독창적인. —*n.* wŏn-mun 원문, wŏn-hyŏng 원형.

originality *n.* tok-ch'ang-sŏng 독창성, ch'ang-ŭi-ryŏk 창의력 ; ch'am-sin 참신, sin-gi 신기(新奇).

ornament *n.* chang-sik 장식. —*v.* kku-mi-da 꾸미다.

orphan *n.* ko-a 고아. —*adj.* pu-mo-ŏp-nŭn 부모없는.

orphanage *n.* ko-a-wŏn 고아원.

orthodox *adj.* chŏng-t'ong-ŭi 정통의, pon-sik-ŭi 본식의.

ostensible *adj.* p'yo-myŏn-sang-ŭi 표면상의, oe-yang-

ostrich *n.* t'a-jo 타조. ⌊man-ŭi 외양만의.

other *adj.* ta-rŭn 다른, ttan 딴, kŭ-ba-ggŭi 그밖의.

otherwise *adj.* kŭ-rŏ-ch'i an-ŭ-myŏn 그렇지 않으면.

ought *aux. v.* …ha-yŏ-ya han-da …하여야 한다, …ha-nŭn kŏ-si tang-yŏn-ha-da …하는 것이 당연하다.

ounce *n.* on-sŭ 온스.

our *pron.* u-ri-ŭi 우리의, u-ri-dŭl-ŭi 우리들의.

ours *pron.* u-ri kŏt 우리 것, u-ri-dŭl-ŭi kŏt 우리들의 것.

out *adv.* pa-gge 밖에, pa-ggŭ-ro 밖으로. —*adj.* pa-ggŭi 밖의. —*prep.* …e-sŏ …에서. —*n.* pak 밖.

outbreak *n.* tol-bal 돌발, pal-bal 발발.

outcast *n.* pu-rang-ja 부랑자 ; pang-rang-ja 방랑자.

outcome *n.* kyŏl-gwa 결과 ; sŏng-gwa 성과.

outcry *n.* ko-ham 고함, a-u-sŏng 아우성.

outdoors *adv.* chip pa-gge-sŏ 집 밖에서, ok-oe-e-sŏ 옥외에서. —*n.* ok-oe 옥외, mun-bak 문밖 ; se-sang 세상.

outfit *n.* chang-bi 장비, ch'ae-bi 채비, yong-p'um 용품.

outing *n.* so-p'ung 소풍, na-dŭ-ri 나들이.

outline *n.* yun-gwak 윤곽. —*v.* yun-gwak-ŭl kŭ-ri-da 윤곽을 그리다. 「ya 시야.

outlook *n.* kyŏng-ch'i 경치, chŏn-mang 전망; (*view*) si-

out-of-date *adj.* si-dae-e twi-jin 시대에 뒤진.

outpost *n.* chŏn-ch'o 전초(前哨).

output *n.* saeng-san-go 생산고 ; ch'ul-ryŏk 출력(出力).

outrage *n.* p'ok-haeng 폭행, mo-yok 모욕.

outright *adj.* sol-jik-han 솔직한 ; ttok-ba-rŭn 똑바른. —*adv.* t'ŏ-no-k'o 터놓고 ; chŭk-sŏk-e-sŏ 즉석에서.

outside *n.* oe-bu 외부, pa-ggat 바깥. —*prep.* …ŭi pa-ggŭi …의 밖의. —*adv.* chip pa-ggŭ-ro 집 밖으로. —*adj.* pa-ggŭi 밖의, oe-bu-ŭi 외부의. 「한.

outstanding *adj.* ttu-ryŏt-han 뚜렷한, hyŏn-jŏ-han 현저

outward *adj.* oe-bu-ŭi 외부의, oe-myŏn-jŏk-in 외면적인.

oval *adj.* t'a-wŏn-hyŏng-ŭi 타원형의.

oven *n.* sot 솥, ka-ma 가마(釜), hwa-dŏk 화덕.

over *prep.* …ŭi wi-e …의 위에. —*adv.* to-ch'ŏ-e 도처에, kkŭt-na-go 끝나고.

overall *adj.* chŏn-ch'e-ŭi 전체의.

overalls *n.* chak-ŏp-bok 작업복, kŏt-ot 겉옷.

overcast *v.* ku-rŭm-ŭ-ro ka-ri-da 구름으로 가리다.

overcoat *n.* oe-t'u 외투.

overcome *v.* i-gi-da 이기다, kŭk-bok-ha-da 극복하다.

overcrowded *adj.* ch'o-man-wŏn-ŭi 초만원의, hon-jap-han 혼잡한.

overflow *v.* nŏm-ch'i-da 넘치다, pŏm-ram-ha-da 범람하다. —*n.* ① hong-su 홍수. ② (*excess*) kwa-ing 과잉.

overgrow *v.* ① cha-ra-sŏ twi-dŏp-da 자라서 뒤덮다, mu-sŏng-ha-da 무성하다. ② nŏ-mu k'ŏ-ji-da 너무 커지다.

overhang *v.* …ŭi wi-e kŏl-ch'i-da …의 위에 걸치다.

overhead *adv.* mŏ-ri wi-e 머리 위에 ; ha-nŭl-e 하늘에. —*adj.* mŏ-ri wi-ŭi 머리 위의. 「듣다.

overhear *v.* yŏt-dŭt-da 엿듣다, mol-rae tŭt-da 몰래

overlook *v.* pa-ra-bo-da 바라보다, nae-ryŏ-da-bo-da 내려다보다 ; nun-gam-a-ju-da 눈감아주다.

oversea(s) *adv.* hae-oe-ro 해외로, hae-oe-e-sŏ 해외에서. —*adj.* hae-oe-ŭi 해외의, hae-oe-ro ka-nŭn 해외로 가는.

oversee *v.* kam-dok-ha-da 감독하다.

overshoe *n.* tŏt-sin 덧신, o-u-bŏ-syu-u-jŭ 오우버슈우즈.

overtake *v.* tta-ra-jap-da 따라잡다 ; ch'u-wŏl-ha-da 추

overturn *v.* twi-jip-ŏ-no-t'a 뒤집어놓다. 「월하다.

overwhelm *v.* ap-do-ha-da 압도하다, twi-ŏp-da 뒤엎다, wi-ch'uk-si-k'i-da 위축시키다. 「과로.

overwork *v.* kwa-ro-si-k'i-da 과로시키다. —*n.* kwa-ro

owe *v.* pi-jŭl chi-da 빚을 지다, him-ip-da 힘입다.

owing to … ttae-mun-e … 때문에.

owl *n.* ol-bbae-mi 올빼미, pu-ŏng-i 부엉이.

own *adj.* cha-gi cha-sin-ŭi 자기 자신의. —*v.* ① so-yu-ha-da 소유하다. ② cha-baek-ha-da 자백하다.

owner *n.* im-ja 임자, so-yu-ja 소유자.

ox *n.* hwang-so 황소 ; su-so 수소.

oxcart *n.* u-ch'a 우차(牛車), tal-gu-ji 달구지.

oxygen *n.* san-so 산소 : ～ *breathing apparatus* san-so ho-hŭp-gi 산소 호흡기.

oyster *n.* kul 굴 ; *raw* ～ saeng-gul 생굴.

──❧ **P** ❧──

pace *n.* kŏ-rŭm 걸음, po-jo 보조(步調), kŏt-nŭn sok-do 걷는 속도. —*v.* kŏ-rŭm-ŭ-ro chae-da 걸음으로 재다.

pacific *adj.* p'yŏng-on-han 평온한, t'ae-p'yong-han 태 **Pacific Ocean** t'ae-p'yŏng-yang 태평양. 「평한.

pack *n.* chim 짐, (*bundle*) ta-bal 다발, (*gang*) han p'ae 한 패. —*v.* p'o-jang-ha-da 포장하다. 「포장.

package *n.* (*parcel*) so-p'o 소포, chim 짐 ; p'o-jang

packet *n.* so-ha-mul 소하물, (*bundle*) ta-bal 다발.

packing *n.* p'o-jang 포장 :～ *charge* p'o-jang-ryo 포장료.

pad *v.* sok-ŭl ch'ae-u-da 속을 채우다. —*n.* mit-bat-ch'im 밑받침, tŏt-dae-nŭn mul-gŏn 덧대는 물건.

padded clothes som-ot 솜옷.

padding *n.* sim-nŏ-k'i 심넣기 ; sim 심.

paddle *n.* no 노. —*v.* no-ro chŏt-da 노로 젓다.

paddyfield *n.* (*rice field*) non 논.

padlock *n.* maeng-ggong-i cha-mul-soe 맹공이 자물쇠.

pagan *n.* (*heathen*) i-gyo-do 이교도. 「사환.

page *n.* ① p'e-i-ji 페이지, myŏn 면. ② (*boy*) sa-hwan

pageant *n.* ya-oe-gŭk 야외극, mi-gwan 미관(美觀) ; (*parade*) ho-hwa haeng-jin 호화 행진. 「층탑.

pagoda *n.* t'ap 탑 : *a five-storeyed* ～ o-ch'ŭng-t'ap 오

pail *n.* mul-t'ong 물통.

pain *n.* ① ko-t'ong 고통, a-p'ŭm 아픔. ② kŭn-sim 근심.

painful *adj.* ① a-p'ŭn 아픈, koe-ro-un 괴로운. ② (*toilsome*) him-i tŭ-nŭn 힘이 드는.

painkiller *n.* chin-t'ong-je 진통제.

paint *n.* kŭ-rim-mul-gam 그림물감, p'e-in-t'ŭ 페인트. —*v.* ch'il-ha-da 칠하다, kŭ-ri-da 그리다.

paintbrush *n.* kŭ-rim put 그림 붓, hwa-p'il 화필.

painter *n.* ① hwa-ga 화가. ② ch'il-jang-i 칠장이.

painting *n.* ① kŭ-rim 그림. ② p'e-in-t'ŭ-ch'il 페인트 칠 : *oil* ~ yu-hwa 유화/*water color* ~ su-ch'ae-hwa 수채화.

paintress *n.* yŏ-ryu hwa-ga 여류 화가. ⌐수채화.

pair *n.* han ssang 한 쌍, (*couple*) pu-bu 부부.

pal *n.* ch'in-gu 친구, tong-a-ri 동아리, jjak-p'ae 짝패.

palace *n.* kung-jŏn 궁전, kung-gwŏl 궁궐.

palanquin *n.* ka-ma 가마.

palate *n.* ① ip-ch'ŏn-jang 입천장, ku-gae 구개(口蓋). ② mi-gak 미각.

pale *adj.* (*wan*) ch'ang-baek-han 창백한. —*n.* ul-t'a-ri 울타리.

pallbearer *n.* sang-yŏ-gun 상여군.

palm *n.* ① (*of hand*) son-ba-dak 손바닥. ② (*tree*) ya-ja-su 야자수.

[ka-ma]

palmist *n.* son-gŭm-jang-i 손금장이, su-sang-ga 수상가.

pamphlet *n.* p'am-p'ŭl-ret 팜플렛.

pan *n.* nam-bi 남비 : *frying* ~ p'ŭ-ra-i-p'aen 프라이팬.

pane *n.* p'an-yu-ri 판유리, ch'ang-yu-ri 창유리.

panel *n.* p'ae-nŏl 패널, hwa-p'an 화판.

pang *n.* ko-t'ong 고통 ; pi-t'ong 비통 ; sang-sim 상심.

panic *n.* ① (*sudden alarm*) tang-hwang 당황 ; kong-p'o 공포. ② (*commerce*) kong-hwang 공황.

panorama *n.* chŏn-gyŏng 전경, p'a-no-ra-ma 파노라마.

pansy *n.* ho-jŏp che-bi-ggot 호접 제비꽃, p'aen-ji 팬지.

pant v. hŏl-ddŏk-gŏ-ri-da 헐떡거리다. —n. hŏl-ddŏk-gŏ-rim 헐떡거림 ; ko-dong 고동, tong-gye 동계(動悸).

panther n. p'yo-bŏm 표범, p'yu-u-ma 퓨우마.

pantry n. sik-ryo-p'um-sil 식료품실, sik-gi-sil 식기실.

pants n. pa-ji 바지, p'aen-ch'ŭ 팬츠.

papa n. (dad, daddy) a-bba 아빠. ⌜non-mun 논문.

paper n. ① chong-i 종이 ; sin-mun-ji 신문지. ② (essay)

paper file chong-i kko-ji 종이 꽂이.

paper mill che-ji kong-jang 제지 공장.

papeterie n. (stationary case) mun-gap 문갑(文匣), sŏ-ryu-ham 서류함.

parachute n. nak-ha-san 낙하산, p'a-ra-swi-t'ŭ 파라쉬트.

parade n. haeng-ryŏl 행렬, yŏl-byŏng-sik 열병식, p'ŏ-re-i-dŭ 퍼레이드. —v. haeng-ryŏl-ha-da 행렬하다.

paradise n. nak-wŏn 낙원 ; (Budd.) kŭk-rak 극락.

paragraph n. tal-lak 단락, chŏl 절(節), hang 항.

parallel adj. p'yŏng-haeng-ŭi 평행의. —n. (latitude) wi-do-sŏn 위도선 : 38th P~ sam-p'al·sŏn 삼팔선.

paralysis n. ma-bi 마비, chung-p'ung 중풍.

paramount adj. ch'oe-go-ŭi 최고의, chi-sang-ŭi 지상 (至上)의. —n. ch'oe-go kwŏn-wi-ja 최고 권위자.

parapet n. ① nan-gan 난간. ② hyung-jang 흉장(胸墻).

paraphrase n. swip-ge pa-ggu-ŏ ssŭ-gi 쉽게 바꾸어 쓰기, ŭi-yŏk 의역(意譯). —v. pa-ggu-ŏ ssŭ-da[mal-ha-da] 바꾸어 쓰다[말하다].

parasite n. ① (insect) ki-saeng-ch'ung 기생충. ② (tree) kyŏ-u-sa-ri 겨우살이. ③ (person) sik-gaek 식객.

parasol n. yang-san 양산, p'a-ra-sol 파라솔.

parcel n. (post) so-p'o 소포, so-ha-mul 소하물.

parch v. ① (roast) pok-da 볶다, kup-da 굽다. ② (dry up) pa-ssak mal-ri-da 바싹 말리다.

pardon n. & v. yong-sŏ(-ha-da) 용서(하다) : I beg your

~. Choe-song-hap-ni-da. 죄송합니다.

pare v. (*cut*) kkak-da 깎다, chal-ra-nae-da 잘라내다, (*strip*) kkŏp-jil-ŭl pŏt-gi-da 껍질을 벗기다.

parent n. ŏ-bŏ-i 어버이, yang-ch'in 양친.

parenthesis n. ① kwal-ho 괄호. ② sap-ip-gu 삽입구.

parish n. kyo-gu 교구(教區). 「ch'a-jang 주차장.

park n. ① kong-wŏn 공원. ② (*for motorcars*) chu-

parliament n. kuk-hoe 국회, ŭi-hoe 의회.

parlo(u)r n. kaek-sil 객실, kŏ-sil 거실, ŭng-jŏp-sil 응

parole n. sŏ-yak 서약, maeng-se 맹세.   ㄴ접실.

parrot n. aeng-mu-sae 앵무새.

parson n. kyo-gu mok-sa 교구 목사, mok-sa 목사.

part n. ① pu-bun 부분, pu 부, p'yŏn 편. ② chi-yŏk 지역. ③ (*role*) yŏk-hal 역할. —v. (*seperate*) na-nu-da 나누다, kal-ra-ji-da 갈라지다. 「han 불공평한.

partial adj. ① pu-bun-jŏk 부분적. ② pul-gong-p'yŏng-

participate v. ch'am-ga-ha-da 참가하다.

participle n. (*gram.*) pun-sa 분사(分詞).

particle n. ip-ja 입자(粒子), mi-bun-ja 미분자.

particular adj. ① (*individual*) kak-gak-ŭi 각각의. ② (*special*) kak-byŏl-han 각별한. ③ (*detailed*) sang-se-han 상세한. —n. (*details*) sa-hang 사항.

parting n. chak-byŏl 작별, (*division*) pun-hal 분할.

partisan n. han p'ae 한 패, to-dang 도당 ; (*guerilla*) yu-gyŏk-dae 유격대, ppal-ch'i-san 빨치산.

partition n. ku-bun 구분, ku-hoek 구획 ; pun-hal 분할.

partly adv. pu-bun-jŏk-ŭ-ro 부분적으로.

partner n. ① tong-mu 동무, jjak-p'ae 짝패, p'a-a-t'ŭ-nŏ 파아트너. ② cho-hap-wŏn 조합원.

partnership n. ① yŏn-hap 연합, hyŏp-ryŏk 협력. ② hap-myŏng-hoe-sa 합명회사, cho-hap 조합.

part-time adj. ŏ-nŭ si-gan-man il-ha-nŭn 어느 시간만

일하는, p'a-a-t'ŭ-t'a-im-ŭi 파아트타임의.

party *n.* ① (*entertainment*) yŏn-hoe 연회, p'a-a-t'i 파아티. ② (*polit.*) chŏng-dang 정당.

pass *n.* hap-gyŏk 합격, p'ae-sŭ 패스 ; (*of admission*) ip-jang-gwŏn 입장권. —*v.* ① t'ong-gwa-ha-da 통과하다, chi-na-da 지나다.. ② (*die*) chuk-da 죽다.

passage *n.* ① (*passing*) t'ong-gwa 통과. ② (*voyage*) hang-hae 항해. ③ (*way*) t'ong-ro 통로.

passenger *n.* sŭng-gaek 승객, yŏ-gaek 여객.

passer-by *n.* chi-na-ga-nŭn sa-ram 지나가는 사람, t'ong-haeng-in 통행인. 「jae-ŭi 현재의.

passing *adj.* chi-na-ga-nŭn 지나가는, (*current*) hyŏn-

passion *n.* chŏng-yŏl 정열(情熱), (*zeal*) yŏl-sim 열심.

passionate *adj.* yŏl-ryŏl-han 열렬한.

passive *adj.* su-dong-jŏk 수동적, p'i-dong-jŏk 피동적: (*gram.*) ～ *voice* su-dong-t'ae 수동태.

Passover *n.* yu-wŏl-jŏl 유월절(逾越節).

passport *n.* yŏ-gwŏn 여권, p'ae-sŭ-p'o-o-t'ŭ 패스포오트.

password *n.* am-ho 암호. 「—*n.* kwa-gŏ 과거.

past *adj.* chi-na-gan 지나간. —*prep.* chi-na-sŏ 지나서.

paste *n.* p'ul 풀(糊). —*v.* p'ul-ch'il-ha-da 풀칠하다.

pasteboard *n.* ma-bun-ji 마분지, p'an-ji 판지(板紙).

pastime *n.* so-il-gŏ-ri 소일거리, ki-bun-jŏn-hwan 기분
「전환.

pastor *n.* (*minister*) mok-sa 목사.

pastry *n.* pan-juk kwa-ja 반죽 과자, saeng-gwa-ja 생과자, p'e-sŭ-t'ŭ-ri 페스트리.

pasture *n.* mok-jang 목장, mok-ch'o(-ji) 목초(지).

pat *n.* t'uk-t'uk-ch'i-gi 툭툭치기. —*v.* ka-byŏp-ge ch'i-da 가볍게 치다 ; ssu-da-dŭm-da 쓰다듬다.

patch *n.* hŏng-gŏp cho-gak 헝겊 조각. —*v.* kip-da 깁다.

patent *n.* chŏn-mae t'ŭk-hŏ 전매 특허. 「부성애.

paternal *adj.* a-bŏ-ji-ŭi 아버지의 : ～ *love* pu-sŏng-ae

path *n.* kil 길, (*footpath*) po-do 보도 ; (*course in life*) in-saeng haeng-ro 인생 행로.

pathetic *adj.* ae-ch'ŏ-ro-un 애처로운 ; kam-sang-jŏk-in 감상적인

pathos *n.* pi-ae 비애, p'a-t'o-sŭ 파토스.

pathway *n.* o-sol-gil 오솔길, chop-ŭn kil 좁은 길.

patience *n.* in-nae 인내, ch'am-ŭl-sŏng 참을성.

patient *adj.* ch'am-ŭl-sŏng-it-nŭn 참을성있는. —*n.* hwan-ja 환자, pyŏng-ja 병자.

patina *n.* p'u-rŭn nok 푸른 녹, nok-ch'ŏng 녹청(綠靑).

patrimony *n.* se-sŭp chae-san 세습 재산.

patriot *n.* ae-guk-ja 애국자, chi-sa 지사(志士).

patriotic *adj.* ae-guk-sim-i kang-han 애국심이 강한.

patriotism *n.* ae-guk-sim 애국심, u-guk-sim 우국심.

patrol *n.* & *v.* sun-ch'al(-ha-da) 순찰(하다).

patrolman *n.* sun-ch'al-dae-wŏn 순찰대원.

patron *n.* ① po-ho-ja 보호자, hu-wŏn-ja 후원자. ② tan-gol son-nim 단골 손님, p'ae-t'ŭ-rŏn 패트런. 「하다.

patronize *v.* hu-wŏn-ha-da 후원하다, po-ho-ha-da 보호

patten *n.* tŏt-na-mak-sin 덧나막신, na-mak-sin 나막신.

pattern *n.* mo-bŏm 모범, (*model*) kyŏn-bon 견본.

pauper *n.* kŭk-bin-ja 극빈자, pin-min 빈민.

pause *n.* mŏm-ch'um 멈춤, chung-dan 중단 ; hyu-sik 휴식. —*v.* mŏm-ch'u-da 멈추다, (*rest*) swi-da 쉬다.

pave *v.* p'o-jang-ha-da 포장(鋪裝)하다.

pavement *n.* p'o-jang 포장, p'o-jang-do-ro 포장도로.

pavilion *n.* ① (*arbor*) chŏng-ja 정자. ② pyŏl-gwan 별관. ③ (*large tent*) k'ŭn ch'ŏn-mak 큰 천막.

paw *n.* ap-bal 앞발. —*v.* ap-bal-ro kŭk-da 앞발로 긁다.

pawn *n.* & *v.* (*pledge*) chŏn-dang (chap-da) 전당 (잡다).

pawnshop *n.* chŏn-dang-p'o 전당포.

pay *n.* chi-bul 지불 ; (*salary*) pong-gŭp 봉급, po-su 보수. —*v.* chi-bul-ha-da 지불하다.

paymaster *n.* hoe-gye-wŏn 회계원, kyŏng-ri-gwa-jang 경리과장, (*mil.*) chae-jŏng-gwan 재정관.

payment *n.* chi-bul 지불, chi-bul-gŭm 지불금.

pea *n.* wan-du-k'ong 완두콩.

peace *n.* p'yŏng-hwa 평화, p'yŏng-on 평온 ; (*reconciliation*) kang-hwa 강화(講和). 「온화한.

peaceful *adj.* p'yŏng-hwa-rŏ-un 평화로운, on-hwa-han

peach *n.* pok-sung-a 복숭아, pok-sung-a-na-mu 복숭아

peacock *n.* kong-jak 공작. 「나무.

peak *n.* kkok-dae-gi 꼭대기, pong-u-ri 봉우리 ; ch'oe-go-jŏm 최고점.

peal *n.* u-rŏng-ch'an so-ri 우렁찬 소리. —*v.* ul-ryŏ-p'ŏ-ji-da 울려퍼지다, p'ŏ-ddŭ-ri-da 퍼뜨리다.

peanut *n.* ttang-k'ong 땅콩, nak-hwa-saeng 낙화생.

peapod *n.* wan-du-ggo-t'u-ri 완두꼬투리.

pear *n.* pae 배(梨), (*plant*) pae-na-mu 배나무.

pearl *n.* chin-ju 진주 : *artificial* ~ in-jo chin-ju 인조 진주/*black* ~ hŭk-jin-ju 흑진주.

peasant *n.* ① nong-bu 농부. ② si-gol-ddŭ-gi 시골뜨기.

peat *n.* t'o-t'an 토탄, i-t'an 이탄(泥炭).

pebble *n.* cha-gal 자갈, cho-yak-dol 조약돌.

peck *v.* jjo-da 쪼다, jjo-a-mŏk-da 쪼아먹다.

peculiar *adj.* tok-t'ŭk-han 독특한, t'ŭk-yu-han 특유한.

pecuniary *adj.* ton-ŭi 돈의, kŭm-jŏn-sang-ŭi 금전상의.

pedagog(ue) *n.* sŏn-saeng 선생 ; hyŏn-hak-ja 현학자.

pedal *n.* pal-p'an 발판 ; p'e-dal 페달.

pedant *n.* a-nŭn ch'e-ha-nŭn sa-ram 아는 체하는 사람.

peddler *n.* (*bell ringer*) haeng-sang-in 행상인, (*hawker*) to-bu-jang-su 도부장수.

pedestal *n.* chu-ch'ut-dae 주춧대 ; tae-jwa 대좌(台座).

pedestrian *n.* po-haeng-ja 보행자. 「t'ong 혈통.

pedigree *n.* (*genealogy*) chok-bo 족보; (*lineage*) hyŏl-

peel *n.* kkŏp-jil 껍질. —*v.* kkŏp-jil-ŭl pŏt-gi-da 껍질을
peep *n.* yŏt-bom 엿봄. —*v.* yŏt-bo-da 엿보다. ⌞벗기다.
peer *v.* cha-se-hi po-da 자세히 보다. —*n.* ① (*equal*)
tong-ryo 동료. ② (*nobleman*) kwi-jok 귀족. 「쌍의.
peerless *adj.* yu-rye-op-nŭn 유례없는, mu-ssang-ŭi 무
peevish *adj.* sŏng-ma-rŭn 성마른 ; pul-p'yŏng-ha-nŭn
peg *n.* na-mu-mot 나무못, mal-dduk 말뚝. ⌞불평하는.
peke *n.* (*Pekinese dog*) pal-ba-ri 발바리.
pen *n.* ① p'en 펜, ch'ŏl-p'il 철필. ② (*writing*) mun-
p'il 문필. ③ (*fold*) u-ri 우리, ul-t'a-ri 울타리.
penalty *n.* ① hyŏng-bŏl 형벌. ② (*fine*) pŏl-gŭm 벌금.
③ (*sport*) p'e-nŏl-t'i 페널티.
penance *n.* (*repentance*) ch'am-hoe 참회, hoe-gae 회개.
pencil *n.* yŏn-p'il 연필 : ~ *sharpener* yŏn-p'il-gga-ggi
연필깎이.
pencil case (yŏn-)p'il-t'ong (연)필통.
pendant *n.* mok-gŏ-ri 목걸이, p'en-dŏn-t'ŭ 펜던트.
pending *adj.* (*undecided*) mi-gyŏl-ŭi 미결의 : *a* ~
question hyŏn-an mun-je 현안 문제.
pendulum *n.* si-gye-ch'u 시계추. 「투시하다.
penetrate *v.* kwan-t'ong-ha-da 관통하다, t'u-si-ha-da
penholder *n.* p'en-dae 펜대, p'en-gŏ-ri 펜걸이.
peninsula *n.* pan-do 반도(半島).
penis *n.* cha-ji 자지, ŭm-gyŏng 음경, p'e-ni-sŭ 페니스.
penitence *n.* nwi-u-ch'im 뉘우침. 「ko-hae-ja 고해자.
penitent *adj.* nwi-u-ch'i-nŭn 뉘우치는. —*n.* (*Cath.*)
penman *n.* sŏ-ga 서가(書家), sŭp-ja kyo-sa 습자 교사.
penmanship *n.* sŭp-ja 습자, sŏ-do 서도 ; (*style of
handwriting*) p'il-jŏk 필적. 「im 펜네임.
pen name p'il-myŏng 필명, a-ho 아호(雅號), p'en-ne-
penniless *adj.* han-p'un-ŏp-nŭn 한푼없는, mu-il-p'un-
ŭi 무일푼의.

penny *n.* p'e-ni 페니.   「給).
pension *n.* (*annuity*) yŏn-gŭm 연금, ŭn-gŭp 은급(恩
pensive *adj.* ① (*thoughtful*) saeng-gak-e cham-gin
    생각에 잠긴. ② (*sad*) ku-sŭl-p'ŭn 구슬픈.
pentagon *n.* ① o-gak-hyŏng 5 각형. ② (*Am.*) kuk-
    bang-sŏng 국방성.
peony *n.* chak-yak 작약.
people *n.* sa-ram-dŭl 사람들 ; kuk-min 국민.
pepper *n.* ① (*black*) hu-ch'u 후추. ② (*red*) ko-ch'u
peppermint *n.* pak-ha 박하.   ⌊고추.
peppery *adj.* (*pungent*) mae-un 매운, a-ral-han 알알한.
perceive *v.* chi-gak-ha-da 지각(知覺)하다 ; i-hae-ha-da
    이해하다 ; (*discern*) sik-byŏl-ha-da 식별하다.
percent *n.* p'ŏ-sen-t'ŭ 퍼센트(%) ; paek-bun-yul 백분율.
percentage *n.* ① (*proportion*) paek-bun-yul 백분율 ;
    pi-yul 비율. ② (*commission*) su-su-ryo 수수료.
perch *v.* ol-ra-an-da 올라앉다. —*n.* ① (*roost*) hwaet-
    dae 횃대. ② no-p'ŭn chi-wi 높은 지위.
percolate *v.* kŏ-rŭ-da 거르다, yŏ-gwa-ha-da 여과하다.
perennial *adj.* sa-ch'ŏl ma-ru-ji an-nŭn 사철 마르지
    않는 ; ta-nyŏn-saeng-ŭi 다년생의.   「완성하다.
perfect *adj.* wan-jŏn-han 완전한. —*v.* wan-sŏng-ha-da
perform *v.* ① (*accomplish*) su-haeng-ha-da 수행하다,
    (*do*) ha-da 하다, i-haeng-ha-da 이행하다. ② (*play*)
    yŏn-ju〔kong-yŏn〕-ha-da 연주〔공연〕하다.
performance *n.* ① i-haeng 이행, sil-haeng 실행. ②
    (*drama*) yŏn-gi 연기 ;(*entertainment*) yŏ-hŭng 여흥.
perfume *n.* hyang-su 향수, pang-hyang 방향(芳香).
perhaps *adv.* a-ma 아마, ŏ-jjŏ-myŏn 어쩌면.
peril *n.* (*danger*) wi-hŏm 위험 ; mo-hŏm 모험. 「지부.
period *n.* ① ki-gan 기간 ; si-dae 시대. ② chong-ji-bu 종
periodical *n.* chŏng-gi kan-haeng-mul 정기 간행물.

periscope *n.* cham-mang-gyŏng 잠망경.

perish *v.* (*die*) chuk-da 죽다 ; (*pass away*) sa-ra-ji-da 사라지다 ; myŏl-mang-ha-da 멸망하다.

permanent *adj.* yŏng-sok-ha-nŭn 영속하는, yŏng-gu-jŏk-in 영구적인, pyŏn-ham-ŏp-nŭn 변함없는.

permanent tooth yŏng-gu-ch'i 영구치(永久齒).

permission *n.* hŏ-ga 허가 ; (*licence*) myŏn-hŏ 면허 : *without* ~ mu-dan-hi 무단히. 「ha-da 허락하다.

permit *n.* (*licence*) hŏ-ga-jŭng 허가증. —*v.* hŏ-rak-

perpendicular *adj.* (*vertical*) su-jik-ŭi 수직의, kka-gga se-un tŭt-han 깎아 세운 듯한. —*n.* su-jik 수직.

perpetual *adj.* yŏng-wŏn-han 영원한 ; (*incessant*) kkŭn-im-ŏp-nŭn 끊임없는 ; chong-sin-ŭi 종신(終身)의.

perplex *v.* ŏ-ri-dung-jŏl-ha-ge ha-da 어리둥절하게 하다.

perplexity *n.* ① tang-hwang 당황, nang-p'ae 낭패. ② (*dilemma*) nan-guk 난국. 「da 괴롭히다.

persecute *v.* ① pak-hae-ha-da 박해하다. ② koe-rop-hi-

perseverance *n.* ch'am-ŭl-sŏng 참을성, in-nae 인내.

persevere *v.* ch'am-da 참다, kyŏn-di-da 견디다.

persimmon *n.* kam 감 : *dried* ~ kot-gam 곶감.

persist *v.* ko-jip-ha-da 고집하다 ; chi-sok-ha-da 지속하다.

person *n.* sa-ram 사람, in-mul 인물 ; in-p'um 인품.

personal *adj.* kae-in-ŭi 개인의, il-sin-sang-ŭi 일신상의.

personality *n.* kae-sŏng 개성, in-gyŏk 인격.

personnel *n.* chik-wŏn 직원 : ~ *office* in-sa-ch'ŏ 인사처.

perspective *n.* chŏn-mang 전망 ; wŏn-gŭn-bŏp 원근법.

perspiration *n.* (*sweat*) ttam 땀, pal-han 발한.

perspire *v.* ttam-nae-da 땀내다, ttam-i na-da 땀이 나다.

persuade *v.* sŏl-bok-si-k'i-da 설복시키다.

persuasion *n.* sŏl-dŭk 설득 ; (*conviction*)hwak-sin 확신.

pertain *v.* ① sok-ha-da 속하다. ② ŏ-ul-ri-da 어울리다.

pertinent *adj.* chŏk-jŏl-han 적절한 ; kwal-lyŏn-doen

관련된. —*n.* (*pl.*) pu-sok-mul 부속물.

perusal *n.* chŏng-dok 정독(精讀), suk-dok 숙독.

pervade *v.* po-gŭp-ha-da 보급하다, ko-ru mi-ch'i-da 고루 미치다, ch'im-t'u-ha-da 침투하다. 「고집의.

perverse *adj.* sim-sul-gu-jŭn 심술궂은, oe-go-jip-ŭi 외

pessimism *n.* yŏm-se-ju-ŭi 염세주의.

pessimist *n.* pi-gwal-lon-ja 비관론자, yŏm-se-ju-ŭi-ja 염세주의자.

pest *n.* ① hae-ch'ung 해충; (*nuisance*) kol-ch'it-gŏ-ri 골칫거리. ② (*plague*) hŭk-sa-byŏng 흑사병, p'e-sŭ-

pesticide *n.* sal-ch'ung-je 살충제. 「t'ŭ 페스트.

pestilence *n.* hŭk-sa-byŏng 흑사병, p'e-sŭ-t'ŭ 페스트.

pestle *n.* chŏl-gut-gong-i 절굿공이, mak-ja 막자.

pet *adj.* kwi-yŏ-un 귀여운. —*n.* ae-wan-dong-mul 애완동물; kwi-yŏm-dong-i 귀염둥이, p'e-t'ŭ 페트. —*v.* kwi-yŏ-wŏ-ha-da 귀여워하다, ch'ong-ae-ha-da 총애하다.

petal *n.* kkot-ip 꽃잎.

petition *n.* (*appeal*) t'an-wŏn 탄원, ch'ŏng-wŏn 청원. —*v.* t'an-wŏn-ha-da 탄원하다. 「솔린.

petrol *n.* (*gasoline*) hwi-bal-yu 휘발유, ka-sol-rin 가

petroleum *n.* sŏk-yu 석유: *crude* ~ wŏn-yu 원유.

petticoat *n.* sok-ch'i-ma 속치마, sŭ-k'ŏ-ŏ-t'ŭ 스커어트.

petty *adj.* chak-ŭn 작은, sa-so-han 사소한.

pew *n.* chwa-sŏk 좌석, kŏl-sang 걸상, cha-ri 자리.

phantasy *n.* kong-sang 공상, hwan-sang 환상.

phantom *n.* ① (*vision*) hwan-yŏng 환영, (*image*) yŏng-sang 영상. ② (*spectre*) yu-ryŏng 유령.

pharmacist *n.* yak-je-sa 약제사.

pharmacy *n.* ① cho-je-bŏp 조제법. ② yak-guk 약국.

phase *n.* ① tan-gye 단계, kuk-myŏn 국면. ② (*aspect*) myŏn 면, sang 상(相).

pheasant *n.* kkwŏng 꿩.

phenomenon *n.* (*of nature*) hyŏn-sang 현상.

philanthropy *n.* pak-ae 박애(博愛), in-ja 인자.

philosopher *n.* ch'ŏl-hak-ja 철학자, hyŏn-in 현인.

philosophy *n.* ch'ŏl-hak 철학, ch'ŏl-ri 철리.

phoenix *n.* pul-sa-jo 불사조 ; pong-hwang-sae 봉황새.

phone *n.* chŏn-hwa(-gi) 전화(기). —*v.* chŏn-hwa-rŭl kŏl-da 전화를 걸다. 「가(音價).

phonetic *adj.* ŭm-sŏng-ŭi 음성의 : ~ *value* ŭm-ga 음

phonograph *n.* ch'uk-ŭm-gi 축음기.

photograph *n.* sa-jin 사진. —*v.* sa-jin-ŭl jjik-da 사진 을 찍다, ch'wal-yŏng-ha-da 촬영하다.

phrase *n.* ku 구, suk-ŏ 숙어, kwan-yong-gu 관용구.

physical *adj.* ① cha-yŏn-ŭi 자연의. ② (*body*) sin-ch'e-ŭi 신체의 : ~ *beauty* yuk-ch'e-mi 육체미/~ *examination* sin-ch'e kŏm-sa 신체 검사/~ *exercise* ch'e-jo 체조. ③ (*choose*) mul-ri-hak-ŭi 물리학의. 「사.

physician *n.* (*internist*) nae-gwa-ŭi 내과의, ŭi-sa 의

physics *n.* (*science*) mul-ri-hak 물리학.

physiology *n.* saeng-ri-hak 생리학. 「피아노 연주자.

pianist *n.* p'i-a-ni-sŭ-t'ŭ 피아니스트, p'i-a-no yŏn-ju-ja

pick *n.* (*pickaxe*) kok-gwaeng-i 곡괭이. —*v.* ① (*poke*) ssu-si-da 쑤시다. ② (*dig into*) p'a-da 파다. ③ (*gather*) mo-ŭ-da 모으다. ④ (*choose*) ko-rŭ-da 고르다.

pickle *n.* chŏ-rin kŏt 절인 것, chang-a-jji 장아찌.

pickpocket *n.* so-mae-ch'i-gi 소매치기.

picnic *n.* so-p'ung 소풍, tŭl-no-ri 들놀이, p'i-k'ŭ-nik 피 크닉 : *go on a* ~ so-p'ung-ga-da 소풍가다.

picture *n.* kŭ-rim 그림 ; sa-jin 사진 ; yŏng-hwa 영화.

pie *n.* p'a-i 파이 : *apple* ~ sa-gwa p'a-i 사과 파이.

piece *n.* han cho-gak 한 조각 ; p'a-p'yŏn 파편.

pier *n.* pu-du 부두, sŏn-ch'ang 선창. 「하다.

pierce *v.* kkwe-ddŭl-t'a 꿰뚫다, kwan-t'ong-ha-da 관통

piety *n.* ① (*godliness*) kyŏng-gŏn 경건. ② ch'ung-jŏl 충절. ③ (*devotion*) sin-sim 신심.

pig *n.* (*swine, hog*) twae-ji 돼지, (*pork*) twae-ji-go-gi 돼지고기.

pigeon *n.* pi-dul-gi 비둘기 : ～ *hole* pi-dul-gi-jang 비둘기장/*carrier* ～ chŏn-sŏ-gu 전서구(傳書鳩).

pigment *n.* ① kŭ-rim mul-gam 그림 물감 ; (*paint*) al-lyo 안료. ② (*biol.*) saek-so 색소.

pigtail *n.* (*queue*) pyŏn-bal 변발(辮髮).

pike *n.* (*spear*) ch'ang 창. ―*v.* ch'ang-ŭ-ro jji-rŭ-da 창으로 찌르다.

pile *n.* ① mu-dŏ-gi 무더기, tae-ryang 대량. ② (*stake*) mal-ddŭk 말뚝. ―*v.* ssa-a-ol-ri-da 쌓아올리다.

pilgrim *n.* sul-lye-ja 순례자, na-gŭ-ne 나그네.

pilgrimage *n.* sul-lye 순례(巡禮).

piling *n.* (*piles*) mal-dduk 말뚝. 「da 약탈하다.

pill *n.* hwan-yak 환약, al-yak 알약. ―*v.* yak-t'al-ha-

pillage *n.* (*plunder*) yak-t'al 약탈, (*booty*) yak-t'al-p'um 약탈품. ―*v.* yak-t'al-ha-da 약탈하다.

pillar *n.* ki-dung 기둥, chu-sŏk 주석(柱石).

pillow *n.* pe-gae 베개 ; mok-ch'im 목침. 「커버.

pillowcase *n.* pe-gaet-it 베갯잇, pe-gae k'ŏ-bŏ 베개

pilot *n.* (*plane*) cho-jong-sa 조종사, p'a-il-rŏt 파일럿 ; (*ship*) su-ro an-nae-in 수로 안내인.

pimp *n.* ttu-jang-i 뚜장이 ; (*pander*) p'o-ju 포주.

pimple *n.* yŏ-dŭ-rŭm 여드름, ppyo-ru-ji 뽀루지. 「전핀.

pin *n.* p'in 핀, ap-p'in 압핀 : *safety* ～ an-jŏn-p'in 안

pincers *n.* mot-bbop-i 못뽑이, (*nippers*) ppen-jji 뻰찌.

pinch *n.* (*with nails*) kko-jip-da 꼬집다, choe-da 죄다.

pine *n.* so-na-mu 소나무. ―*v.* yŏn-mo-ha-da 연모하다 ; (*yearn*) kal-mang-ha-da 갈망하다.

pineapple *n.* p'a-in-ae-p'ŭl 파인애플.

ping-pong *n.* (*table tennis*) t'ak-gu 탁구, p'ing-p'ong 핑퐁 : *a* ~ *table* t'ak-gu-dae 탁구대.

pink *adj.* pun-hong-bi-ch'ŭi 분홍빛의. —*n.* ① (*color*) pun-hong-saek 분홍색. ② (*flower*) p'ae-raeng-i-ggot 패랭이꽃, sŏk-juk 석죽. 「대기.

pinnacle *n.* ① ppyo-jok-t'ap 뾰족탑. ② kkok-dae-gi 꼭

pin-up *n.* in-gi-it-nŭn mi-in sa-jin 인기있는 미인 사진.

pioneer *n.* kae-ch'ŏk-ja 개척자.

pious *adj.* sin-ang-i tu-t'ŏ-un 신앙이 두터운 ; kyŏng-gŏn-han 경건한 ; (*worthy*) kya-rŭk-han 갸룩한.

pipe *n.* ① (*for smoking*) tam-baet-dae 담뱃대. ② (*for liquid, gas*) p'a-i-p'ŭ 파이프, kwan 관(管) : *water* ~ su-do-gwan 수도관. 「*ment*) pun-no 분노.

pique *n.* (*enmity*) chŏk-ŭi 적의, ak-gam 악감, (*resent-*

pirate *n.* ① hae-jŏk 해적. ② p'yo-jŏl-ja 표절자.

piss *v.* o-jum-nu-da 오줌누다, so-byŏn-bo-da 소변보다.

pistil *n.* am-sul 암술.

pistol *n.* kwŏn-ch'ong 권총, p'i-sŭ-t'ol 피스톨.

piston *n.* p'i-sŭ-t'on 피스톤.

pit *n.* ① ku-mŏng 구멍 ; (*pitfall*) ham-jŏng 함정. ② kaeng 갱(坑). ③ u-muk-han kot 우묵한 곳.

pitch *n.* ① (*tar*) song-jin 송진. ② (*throw*) tŏn-ji-gi 던지기. —*v.* tŏn-ji-da 던지다 ; ch'i-da 치다.

pitcher *n.* ① mul-ju-jŏn-ja 물주전자. ② (*baseball*) t'u-su 투수, p'i-ch'ŏ 피쳐.

pitchfork *n.* soe-sŭ-rang 쇠스랑, (*rake*) kal-k'wi 갈퀴.

piteous *adj.* pul-ssang-han 불쌍한, ka-yŏp-sŭn 가엾은.

pity *n.* pul-ssang-hi yŏ-gim 불쌍히 여김, yŏn-min 연민. —*v.* pul-ssang-hi yŏ-gi-da 불쌍히 여기다.

pivot *n.* ch'uk 축(軸), chung-sim-jŏm 중심점.

placard *n.* ① p'ŭl-rae-k'a-a-dŭ 플래카아드. ② pyŏk-bo 벽보. ③ p'o-sŭ-t'ŏ 포스터, ppi-ra 삐라.

place *n.* chang-so 장소. —*v.* tu-da 두다.

placid *adj.* p'yŏng-on-han 평온한; cho-yong-han 조용한.

plague *n.* (*epidemic*) hŭk-sa-byŏng 흑사병.

plain *adj.* ① (*clear*) myŏng-baek-han 명백한. ② (*flat*) p'yŏng-p'yŏng-han 평평한. ③ (*simple*) su-su-han 수수한. —*n.* (*moor*) p'yŏng-ya 평야.

plait *n.* ① chu-rŭm 주름. ② kkon kkŭn 꼰 끈. —*v.* chu-rŭm-jap-da 주름잡다; tta-t'a 땋다.

plan *n.* ① (*drawing*) to-myŏn 도면. ② (*project*) kye-hoek 계획. —*v.* kye-hoek-ha-da 계획하다.

plane *n.* ① (*flat*) p'yŏng-myŏn 평면. ② (*aviation*) pi-haeng-gi 비행기. ③ (*carpenter*) tae-p'ae 대패. —*v.* tae-p'ae-jil-ha-da 대패질하다.

planet *n.* yu-sŏng 유성(遊星), hok-sŏng 혹성.

plank *n.* (*board*) nŏl 널, nŏl-bban-ji 널빤지.

plant *n.* ① (*vegetable*) sik-mul 식물. ② (*mill*) kong-jang 공장. —*v.* sim-da 심다, (*sow*) ppu-ri-da 뿌리다.

plantation *n.* nong-wŏn 농원, chae-bae-ji 재배지.

plaster *n.* ① sŏk-go 석고. ② (*med.*) ko-yak 고약. —*v.* hoe-ch'il-ŭl ha-da 회칠을 하다.

plastic *adj.* p'ŭl-ra-sŭ-t'ik-ŭi 플라스틱의; (*formative*) hyŏng-sŏng-jŏk-in 형성적인; (*pliable*) yu-yŏn-han 유연한. —*n.* hap-sŏng-su-ji che-p'um 합성수지 제품.

plate *n.* ① (*dish*) chŏp-si 접시. ② (*of metal*) p'an 판 : *silver* ~ ŭn-ban 은반(銀盤).

platform *n.* ① (*stage*) yŏn-dan 연단. ② (*station*) p'ŭl-raet-p'o-om 플랫포옴. ③ (*plank*) chŏng-gang 정강.

plausible *adj.* kŭ-rŏl-dŭt-han 그럴듯한.

play *n.* ① un-dong 운동, kyŏng-gi 경기. ② yŏn-gŭk 연극. —*v.* ① nol-da 놀다. ② yon-ju-ha-da 연주하다; (*act*) yŏn-gi-rŭl ha-da 연기를 하다.

playboy *n.* nan-bong-gun 난봉군, pa-ram-dung-i 바람

둥이, p'ŭl-re-i-bo-i 플레이보이.

player *n.* (*of sport*) sŏn-su 선수 ; (*actor*) pae-u 배우; (*of instrument*) yŏn-ju-ja 연주자.

playground *n.* un-dong-jang 운동장, no-ri-t'ŏ 놀이터.

playmate *n.* no-ri ch'in-gu 놀이 친구, so-ggop-dong-mu 소꿉동무. 「노리개.

plaything *n.* (*toy*) chang-nan-gam 장난감, no-ri-gae

playwright *n.* kŭk-jak-ga 극작가.

plaza *n.* ① kwang-jang 광장. ② (*market*) si-jang 시장.

plea *n.* ch'ŏng-wŏn 청원 ; (*in law*) so-song 소송.

plead *v.* ① t'an-wŏn-ha-da 탄원하다. ② chu-jang-ha-da 주장하다 ; pyŏn-ho-ha-da 변호하다. 「쾌한.

pleasant *adj.* ki-bun-jo-ŭn 기분좋은, yu-k'wae-han 유

please *v.* ① chŭl-gŏp-ge ha-da 즐겁게 하다. ② (*in Korean, a suffix*) ⋯chu-sip-si-o ⋯주십시오. 「족한.

pleased *adj.* ki-bbŏ-ha-nŭn 기뻐하는, man-jok-han 만

pleasing *adj.* yu-k'wae-han 유쾌한, chŭl-gŏ-un 즐거운.

pleasure *n.* chŭl-gŏ-um 즐거움, k'wae-rak 쾌락.

pleasure boat yu-ram-sŏn 유람선.

pledge *n.* ① sŏ-yak 서약. ② chŏ-dang-mul 저당물.

plentiful *adj.* p'ung-bu-han 풍부한, nŏk-nŏk-han 넉넉한 : *a* ~ *harvest* p'ung-jak 풍작.

plenty *n.* man-ŭm 많음, p'ung-bu 풍부, ta-ryang 다량.

pleurisy *n.* nŭk-mak-yŏm 늑막염. 「이어.

pliers *n.* chip-ge 집게, ppen-jji 뻰찌, p'ŭl-ra-i-ŏ 플라

plight *n.* kon-gyŏng 곤경, kung-ji 궁지.

plod *v.* ①ttu-bŏk-ddu-bŏk kŏt-da 뚜벅뚜벅 걷다. ②kkŭn-gi-it-ge il(kong-bu)-ha-da 끈기있게 일〔공부〕하다.

plot *n.* ① (*conspiracy*) mo-ryak 모략. ② (*ground*) t'ŏ 터, chi-myŏn 지면. —*v.* ŭm-mo-ha-da 음모하다.

plough · plow *n.* chaeng-gi 쟁기. —*v.* kal-da 갈다.

pluck *v.* (*pull off*) ttŭt-da 뜯다, tta-da 따다.

plug *n.* ma-gae 마개. —*v.* ma-gae-rŭl kki-u-da 마개를
끼우다, t'ŭ-rŏ-mak-da 틀어막다.

plum *n.* o-yat 오얏 : ~ *blossom* mae-hwa 매화.

plumage *n.* kit-t'ŏl 깃털, u-mo 우모(羽毛).

plumb *n.* ch'u 추, (~ *bob*) pun-dong 분동(分銅).

plumber *n.* yŏn-gong 연공(鉛工).

plumb line ch'u-sŏn 추선(錘線), ta-rim-jul 다림줄 ;
(*plumb rule*) mŏk-jul-ch'u 먹줄추.

plump *adj.* sal-jjin 살찐, t'o-sil-t'o-sil-han 토실토실한.

plunder *v.* yak-t'al-ha-da 약탈하다.

plunge *v.* ① jji-rŭ-da 찌르다. ② ttwi-ŏ-dŭ-rŏ-ga-da 뛰
.어들어가다, tol-jin-ha-da 돌진하다. —*n.* ① jji-rŭ-gi
찌르기. ② ttwi-ŏ-dŭ-rŏ-ga-gi 뛰어들어가기.

plural *adj.* pok-su-ŭi 복수의. —*n.* (*gram.*) pok-su 복수.

plus *prep.* tŏ-ha-yŏ 더하여. —*adj.* tŏ-ha-gi-ŭi 더하기의.
—*n.* p'ŭl-rŏ-sŭ ki-ho 플러스 기호. 「재벌.

plutocrat *n.* pu-ho-jŏng-ch'i-ga 부호정치가, chae-bŏl

ply *v.* yŏl-sŏng-ŭl nae-da 열성을 내다, (*wield diligently*)
pu-ji-rŏn-hi nol-ri-da 부지런히 놀리다.

pneumonia *n.* p'ye-ryŏm 폐렴.

pocket *n.* ho-ju-mŏ-ni 호주머니, p'o-k'et 포켓.

pocketbook *n.* chi-gap 지갑 ; su-ch'ŏp 수첩.

pocketmoney *n.* yong-don 용돈.

pockmark *n.* kom-bo 곰보, ma-ma-ja-guk 마마자국.

pod *n.* (*seed vessel*) kkak-ji 깍지, kko-t'u-ri 꼬투리.

poem *n.* si 시(詩) : *a prose* ~ san-mun-si 산문시.

poet *n.* si-in 시인. 「sa-si 서사시.

poetry *n.* si 시 : *lyric* ~ sŏ-jŏng-si 서정시/*epic* ~ sŏ-

poignant *adj.* ① (*bitter*) kyŏk-ryŏl-han 격렬한. ②
(*keen*) ye-ri-han 예리한 ; (*pungent*) sso-nŭn 쏘는.

point *n.* ① (*dot*) chŏm 점. ② (*end*) kkŭt 끝. ③ (*view*)
kyŏn-hae 견해. —*v.* (*with hand*) ka-ri-k'i-da 가리키다.

poison *n.* tok-yak 독약. —*v.* tok-ŭl nŏ-t'a 독을 넣다.
poisonous *adj.* yu-dok-han 유독한, hae-ro-un 해로운.
poke *v.* jji-rŭ-da 찌르다, ssu-si-da 쑤시다, ssu-syŏ i-rŭ-k'i-da 쑤셔 일으키다.
poker *n.* (*for stove*) pu-ji-ggaeng-i 부지깽이 ; (*for brazier*) hwa-jŏt-ga-rak 화젓가락. 「극의.
polar *adj.* kŭk-ji-ŭi 극지의, nam[puk]-gŭk-ŭi 남[북]
pole *n.* ① chang-dae 장대, mak-dae-gi 막대기. ② kŭk 극, (*plus*) yang-gŭk 양극, (*minus*) ŭm-gŭk 음극 : *South P*~ nam-gŭk 남극.
police *n.* kyŏng-ch'al 경찰 : *the chief of* ~ kyŏng-ch'al-sŏ-jang 경찰서장/~ *box* p'a-ch'ul-so 파출소.
policeman *n.* kyŏng-ch'al-gwan 경찰관, sun-gyŏng 순
police station kyŏng-ch'al-sŏ 경찰서. 「경.
policy *n.* chŏng-ch'aek 정책, pang-ch'im 방침.
polish *n.* ① yun 윤, kwang-t'aek 광택. ② yŏn-ma-je 연마제. —*v.* tak-da 닦다, ta-dŭm-da 다듬다.
polite *adj.* kong-son-han 공손한 ; se-ryŏn-doen 세련된.
politeness *n.* kong-son 공손, chŏng-jung 정중.
political *adj.* chŏng-ch'i-ŭi 정치의 : ~ *economy* kyŏng-je-hak 경제학/~ *party* chŏng-dang 정당.
politician *n.* chŏng-ch'i-ga 정치가, chŏng-gaek 정객.
politics *n.* chŏng-ch'i 정치, chŏng-ch'i-hak 정치학.
poll *n.* t'u-p'yo 투표. —*v.* t'u-p'yo-ha-da 투표하다.
pollen *n.* kkot-ga-ru 꽃가루, hwa-bun 화분.
pollution *n.* o-yŏm 오염 : *air* ~ tae-gi o-yŏm 대기 오
pond *n.* mot 못(池), yŏn-mot 연못, nŭp 늪. 「염.
ponder *v.* ki-p'i saeng-gak-ha-da 깊이 생각하다, muk-sang-ha-da 묵상하다, suk-go-ha-da 숙고하다.
pontoon *n.* kŏ-rut-bae 거룻배 : ~ *bridge* pu-gyo 부교 (浮橋).
pony *n.* cho-rang-mal 조랑말, p'o-u-ni 포우니.

pool *n.* ① mul·ung·dŏng·i 물웅덩이. ② p'u·ul 푸울.

poor *adj.* ka·nan·han 가난한; (*pitiable*) ka·yŏp·sŭn 가엾은; (*inferior*) yŏl·dŭng·han 열등한.

pop *n.* ① (*music*) yu·haeng·ga 유행가, tae·jung·ga·yo 대중가요. ② (*dad*) a·bba 아빠. —*v.* p'ŏng·ha·go t'ŏ·ji·da 펑하고 터지다. 「팝코온.

popcorn *n.* t'wi·gim ok·su·su 튀김 옥수수, p'ap·k'o·on

Pope *n.* ro·ma kyo·hwang 로마 교황.

poplar *n.* p'o·p'ŭl·ra 포플라. 「hong·saek 진홍색.

poppy *n.* ① yang·gwi·bi 양귀비. ② (*scarlet*) chin·

popular *adj.* t'ong·sok·jŏk 통속적; in·gi·it·nŭn 인기있는.

popularity *n.* in·gi 인기, p'yŏng·p'an 평판; yu·haeng 유행: *win* ~ in·gi·rŭl ŏt·da 인기를 얻다.

population *n.* in·gu 인구.

porcelain *n.* sa·gi kŭ·rŭt 사기 그릇, cha·gi 자기(瓷器).

porch *n.* hyŏn·gwan 현관, (*Am.*) pe·ran·da 베란다.

pore *n.* t'ŏl·gu·mŏng 털구멍. —*v.* yŏl·jung·ha·da 열중하다; kom·gom·i saeng·gak·ha·da 곰곰이 생각하다.

pork *n.* twae·ji·go·gi 돼지고기. 「리지.

porridge *n.* o·o·t'ŭ·mil chuk 오오트밀 죽, p'o·ri·ji 포

port *n.* ① hang·gu 항구. ② (~ *wine*) p'o·o·t'ŭ·wa·in 포오트와인. ③ (*bearing*) t'ae·do 태도. 「bŭl 포오터블.

portable *adj.* hyu·dae·yong·ŭi 휴대용의. —*n.* p'o·o·t'ŏ·

portal *n.* chŏng·mun 정문(正門), ip·gu 입구.

porter *n.* ① (*gatekeeper*) mun·ji·gi 문지기. ② (*carrier*) chim·gun 짐군, un·ban·in 운반인. 「gŭm 지참금.

portion *n.* ① pu·bun 부분. ② mok 몫. ③ chi·ch'am·

portrait *n.* ch'o·sang·hwa 초상화; sa·jin 사진.

portray *v.* kŭ·ri·da 그리다, myo·sa·ha·da 묘사하다.

pose *n.* cha·se 자세, p'o·u·jŭ 포우즈. 「ch'aek 직책.

position *n.* ① wi·ch'i 위치. ② sin·bun 신분. ③ chik·

positive *adj.* ① (*definite*) myŏng·hwak·han 명확한;

(*active*) chŏk-gŭk-jŏk-in 적극적인. ② (*photo*) yang-hwa-ŭi 양화(陽畵)의. —*n.* yang-hwa 양화.

positively *adv.* chŏk-gŭk-jŏk-ŭ-ro 적극적으로, hwak-sil-hi 확실히.

possess *v.* so-yu-ha-da 소유하다.

possession *n.* so-yu 소유, chŏm-yu 점유 ; chae-san 재산.

possibility *n.* ka-nŭng-sŏng 가능성, ka-mang 가망.

possible *adj.* ka-nŭng-han 가능한.

possibly *adv.* a-ma 아마, ŏ-jjŏ-myŏn 어쩌면.

post *n.* ① (*mail*) u-p'yŏn 우편 : *parcel* ~ so-p'o 소포. ② (*pole*) ki-dung 기둥. ③ (*station*) pu-sŏ 부서(部署). —*v.* u-song-ha-da 우송하다.

postage *n.* u-p'yŏn-yo-gŭm 우편요금 : ~ *due* song-ryo 송료 미달.

postage stamp u-p'yo 우표.

postcard *n.* u-p'yŏn yŏp-sŏ 우편 엽서.

poster *n.* p'o-sŭ-t'ŏ 포스터, pyŏk-bo 벽보.

posterity *n.* cha-son 자손, hu-se 후세. 「유복자.

posthumous *adj.* sa-hu-ŭi 사후의 : *a* ~ *child* yu-bok-ja

postman *n.* u-p'yŏn pae-dal-bu 우편 배달부, u-ch'e-bu 우체부, chip-bae-wŏn 집배원.

postmark *n.* & *v.* so-in(-ŭl jjik-da) 소인(을 찍다).

post office u-ch'e-guk 우체국.

postpone *v.* yŏn-gi-ha-da 연기하다, mi-ru-da 미루다.

postscript *n.* ch'u-sin 추신(追申), hu-gi 후기. 「상태.

posture *n.* ① cha-se 자세, t'ae-do 태도. ② sang-t'ae

postwar *adj.* chŏn-hu-ŭi 전후의 : ~ *days* chŏn-hu 전후.

pot *n.* (*jar*) tan-ji 단지, (*pan*) nam-bi 남비, (*bowl*) sa-bal 사발 : *a flower* ~ hwa-bun 화분(花盆).

potato *n.* kam-ja 감자 : *sweet* ~ ko-gu-ma 고구마.

potential *adj.* ① (*possible*) ka-nŭng-han 가능한. ② (*latent*) cham-jae-jŏk-in 잠재적인.

pottery *n.* to-gi 도기(陶器), chil-gŭ-rŭt 질그릇.

pouch *n.* chak-ŭn chu-mŏ-ni 작은 주머니, ssam-ji 쌈지 :

tobacco ~ tam-bae ssam-ji 담배 쌈지. 「닭.

poultry *n.* (*domestic fowls*) ka-gŭm 가금(家禽), tak

pounce *v.* wa-rak tŏm-byŏ-dŭl-da 와락 덤벼들다.

pound *n.* ① (*weight*) p'a-un-dŭ 파운드. ② ul-t'a-ri 울 타리. —*v.* tu-dŭl-gi-da 두들기다.

pour *v.* ① (*flow*) p'ŏ-but-da 퍼붓다, ssot-da 쏟다, tta-rŭ-da 따르다. ② (*shed*) pal-san-ha-da 발산하다.

poverty *n.* ① ka-nan 가난, pin-gon 빈곤, (*scarcity*) kyŏl-p'ip 결핍. ② (*inferiority*) yŏl-dŭng 열등.

powder *n.* ① (*dust*) ka-ru 가루. ② (*explosive*) hwa-yak 화약 : *toilet* ~ pun 분(粉).

power *n.* him 힘, nŭng-ryŏk 능력 : *electric* ~ chŏl-lyŏk 전력 / *horse*~ ma-ryŏk 마력.

powerful *adj.* kang-ryŏk-han 강력한 : *a* ~ *nation* kang-ryŏk-han min-jok 강력한 민족.

power house pal-jŏn-so 발전소. 「용적인.

practical *adj.* sil-je-jŏk-in 실제적인, si-ryong-jŏk-in 실

practice *n.* ① (*exercise*) yŏn-sŭp 연습. ② (*habit*) sŭp-gwan 습관. ③ (*business*) ŏp-mu 업무.

practise·practice *v.* sil-haeng-ha-da 실행하다 ; yŏn-sŭp-ha-da 연습하다.

practitioner *n.* kae-ŏp-ŭi 개업의, pyŏn-ho-sa 변호사.

pragmatism *n.* si-ryong-ju-ŭi 실용주의.

prairie *n.* tae-ch'o-wŏn 대초원, mok-jang 목장.

praise *n.* ch'an-yang 찬양 ; sung-bae 숭배. —*v.* ch'ing-ch'an-ha-da 칭찬하다, ch'an-yang-ha-da 찬양하다.

prank *n.* chang-nan 장난, nong-dam 농담.

prate *v.* chi-ggŏ-ri-da 지껄이다. —*n.* su-da 수다.

pray *v.* pil-da 빌다, ki-do-ha-da 기도하다. 「도문.

prayer *n.* ① ki-do 기도, ki-wŏn 기원. ② ki-do-mun 기

prayer book ki-do-sŏ 기도서. 「하다.

preach *v.* sŏl-gyo-ha-da 설교하다 ; chŏn-do-ha-da 전도

preacher *n.* chŏn-do-sa 전도사, sŏl-gyo-ja 설교자.

precaution *n.* cho-sim 조심, kyŏng-gye 경계. 「하다.

precede *v.* ap-sŏ-da 앞서다, …e u-sŏn-ha-da …에 우선

precedent *n.* chŏl-lye 전례, kwal-lye 관례 : *without* ~ chŏl-lye-ga ŏp-nŭn 전례가 없는.

preceding *adj.* chŏn-ŭi 전의, ap-sŏn 앞선 ; chŏn-sul-han 전술한 : ~ *year* chŏn-nyŏn 전년. 「hun 교훈.

precept *n.* (*maxim*) kyŏk-ŏn 격언, (*instruction*) kyo-

precinct *n.* ① kyong-nae 경내, ku-nae 구내. ② kwan-hal-gu 관할구, (*Am.*) sŏn-gŏ-gu 선거구.

precious *adj.* ① kwi-jung-han 귀중한, ka-ch'i-it-nŭn 가치있는. ② (*gross*) tae-dan-han 대단한.

precipice *n.* chŏl-byŏk 절벽, nang-ddŏ-rŏ-ji 낭떠러지.

precipitate *v.* ① (*throw down*) ttŏ-rŏ-ddŭ-ri-da 떨어드리다. ② (*urge*) chae-ch'ok-ha-da 재촉하다. 「정밀한.

precise *adj.* chŏng-hwak-han 정확한, chŏng-mil-han

precocious *adj.* ol-doen 올된, cho-suk-han 조숙한.

predecessor *n.* ① (*senior*) chŏn-im-ja 전임자, sŏn-bae 선배. ② (*forefather*) sŏn-jo 선조.

predestination *n.* suk-myŏng 숙명 ; ye-jŏng 예정.

predicate *n.* (*gram.*) sul-bu 술부.

predict *v.* ye-ŏn-ha-da 예언하다, ye-bo-ha-da 예보하다.

pre-election *n.* ye-sŏn 예선, ye-bi sŏn-gŏ 예비 선거.

preface *n.* mŏ-ri-mal 머리말, sŏ-mun 서문.

prefecture *n.* hyŏn 현, to 도(道).

prefer *v.* ① …jjok-ŭl cho-a-ha-da …쪽을 좋아하다. ② (*present*) che-ch'ul-ha-da 제출하다.

prefix *n.* chŏp-du-sa 접두사(接頭辭).

pregnant *adj.* ① im-sin-han 임신한. ② (*filled*) ka-dŭk-ch'an 가득찬, ch'ung-man-han 충만한.

prejudice *n.* p'yŏn-gyŏn 편견, sŏn-ip-gwan 선입관. 「의.

preliminary *adj.* ① ye-bi-jŏk 예비적. ② sŏ-mun-ŭi 서문

prelude *n.* sŏ-mak 서막, (*overture*) sŏ-gok 서곡. 「이른.
premature *adj.* cho-suk-han 조숙한, nŏ-mu i-rŭn 너무
premier *n.* kuk-mu-ch'ong-ri 국무총리, su-sang 수상.
premium *n.* ① p'ŭ-ri-mi-ŏm 프리미엄. ② sang-yŏ-gŭm 상여금(賞與金). ③ po-hŏm-ryo 보험료.
preoccupy *v.* ma-ŭm-ŭl ppae-at-da 마음을 빼앗다.
preparation *n.* chun-bi 준비, ma-ryŏn 마련.
prepare *v.* chun-bi-ha-da 준비하다, ma-ryŏn-ha-da 마
preposition *n.* (*gram.*) chŏn-ch'i-sa 전치사. 「련하다.
prerogative *n.* (*privilege*) t'ŭk-gwŏn 특권.
Presbyterian *n.* chang-ro-gyo hoe-wŏn 장로교 회원.
 —*adj.* chang-ro-gyo-hoe-ŭi 장로교회의 : ～ *Church* chang-ro-gyo-hoe 장로교회.
prescribe *v.* (*med.*) ch'ŏ-bang-ha-da 처방하다; (*ordain*) kyu-jŏng-ha-da 규정하다.
prescription *n.* ① kyu-jŏng 규정. ② (*med.*) ch'ŏ-bang 처방 : ～ *slip* ch'ŏ-bang-jŏn 처방전.
presence *n.* ① (*being*) chon-jae 존재. ② (*attendance*) ch'ul-sŏk 출석. ③ (*bearing*) t'ae-do 태도.
present *v.* chŭng-jŏng-ha-da 증정하다, sŏn-sa-ha-da 선사하다. —*adj.* ch'ul-sŏk-han 출석한; (*current*) hyŏn-jae-ŭi 현재의. —*n.* sŏn-mul 선물.
presently *adv.* i-nae 이내, kot 곧; hyŏn-jae 현재.
preserve *v.* po-jon-ha-da 보존하다. 「(主宰)하다.
preside *v.* sa-hoe-ha-da 사회하다, chu-jae-ha-da 주재
president *n.* tae-t'ong-ryŏng 대통령; (*of company*) sa-jang 사장; (*of bank*) ch'ong-jae 총재.
press *v.* ① nu-rŭ-da 누르다. ② (*urge*) ch'ok-gu-ha-da 촉구하다. —*n.* (*newspapers*) sin-mun 신문.
pressing *adj.* (*urgent*) kin-gŭp-han 긴급한.
pressure *n.* ap-ryŏk 압력, ap-bak 압박 : *atmospheric* ～ ki-ap 기압.

prestige *n.* ① (*power*) wi-ryŏk 위력, wi-sin 위신. ② (*fame*) myŏng-sŏng 명성. ③ (*credit*) sin-mang 신망.

presume *v.* ① ch'u-ch'ŭk-ha-da 추측하다, chim-jak-ha-da 짐작하다. ② i-yong-ha-da 이용하다.

pretend *v.* …ch'e-ha-da …체하다. 「변명.

pretext *n.* p'ing-gye 핑계, ku-sil 구실, pyŏn-myŏng

pretty *adj.* ko-un 고운, ŏ-yŏ-bbŭn 어여쁜, (*fine*) hul-ryung-han 훌륭한. —*adv.* (*fairly*) kkwae 꽤.

prevail *v.* ① u-se-ha-da 우세하다. ② yu-haeng-ha-da

prevent *v.* pang-ji-ha-da 방지하다. 「유행하다.

prevention *n.* ① ye-bang 예방, pang-ji 방지. ② (*hindering*) pang-hae 방해.

previous *adj.* i-jŏn-ŭi 이전의, mŏn-jŏ-ŭi 먼저의.

prey *v.* chap-a-mŏk-da 잡아먹다. —*n.* mŏk-i 먹이.

price *n.* ① kap 값, ka-gyŏk 가격. ② (*reward*) po-sang

price index mul-ga chi-su 물가 지수. 「보상.

priceless *adj.* mop-si kwi-jung-han 몹시 귀중한.

price tag chŏng-ga-p'yo 정가표, chŏng-ch'al 정찰.

prick *v.* jji-rŭ-da 찌르다 ; ko-t'ong-ŭl chu-da 고통을 주다. —*n.* jji-rŭ-gi 찌르기, ka-si 가시. 「다.

prickle *n.* ka-si 가시, pa-nŭl 바늘. —*v.* jji-rŭ-da 찌르

pride *n.* cha-bu-sim 자부심, cha-rang 자랑, kŭng-ji 긍지. —*v.* cha-rang-ha-da 자랑하다.

priest *n.* (*monk*) sŭng-ryŏ 승려, su-do-ja 수도자 ; (*minister*) mok-sa 목사, sa-je 사제.

primary *adj.* pol-lae-ŭi 본래의, ch'o-bo-ŭi 초보의 : ~ *school* kuk-min-hak-gyo 국민학교.

prime *adj.* ch'ŏt-jjae-ŭi 첫째의 ; chu-yo-han 주요한 ; pol-lae-ŭi 본래의 : ~ *minister* su-sang 수상.

primer *n.* ip-mun-(sŏ) 입문(서). 「시인.

primitive *adj.* wŏn-si-ŭi 원시의 : ~ *man* wŏn-si-in 원

primrose *n.* aeng-ch'o 앵초, tal-ma-ji-ggot 달맞이꽃.

prince *n.* ① wang-ja 왕자. ② (*duke*) kong-jak 공작.
princess *n.* ① kong-ju 공주. ② wang-bi 왕비.
principal *adj.* chung-yo-han 중요한 ; che-il-ŭi 제일의.
  —*n.* ① u-du-mŏ-ri 우두머리. ② kyo-jang 교장.
principle *n.* wŏn-ch'ik 원칙 ; (*doctrine*) chu-ŭi 주의.
print *n.* ① (*mark*) cha-guk 자국. ② (*printing*) in-
  swae 인쇄. —*v.* in-swae-ha-da 인쇄하다.
printer *n.* in-swae-ŏp-ja 인쇄업자 ; in-swae-gi 인쇄기.
printing *n.* in-swae 인쇄.
prior *adj.* ① (*former*) a-p'ŭi 앞의, i-jŏn-ŭi 이전의. ②
  (*more important*) po-da chung-yo-han 보다 중요한.
priority *n.* u-sŏn-gwŏn 우선권, sang-wi 상위(上位).
prism *n.* p'ŭ-ri-jŭm 프리즘.
prison *n.* kam-ok 감옥, kyo-do-so 교도소.
prisoner *n.* choe-su 죄수 : ~ *of war* p'o-ro 포로.「생활.
privacy *n.* sa-jŏk cha-yu 사적 자유, sa-saeng-hwal 사
private *adj.* sa-jŏk-in 사적인, pi-mil-ŭi 비밀의. —*n.*
  pyŏng-sa 병사(兵士), pyŏng-jol 병졸.
privilege *n.* t'ŭk-gwŏn 특권, t'ŭk-jŏn 특전 ; ŭn-jŏn 은
  전. —*v.* t'ŭk-gwŏn-ŭl chu-da 특권을 주다.
privy *adj.* sum-ŭn 숨은, pi-mil-ŭi 비밀의. —*n.*(*latrine*)
  pyŏn-so 변소.
prize *n.* ① (*reward*) sang 상. ② (*booty*) chŏl-li-p'um
  전리품. —*v.* so-jung-hi ha-da 소중히 하다.
pro *n.* chik-ŏp sŏn-su 직업 선수, p'ŭ-ro 프로.
probable *adj.* ① (*likely*) i-ssŭm-jik-han 있음직한, kŭ-
  rŏl-ssa-han 그럴싸한. ② yu-mang-han 유망한.
probably *adv.* a-ma 아마, sip-jung-p'al-gu 십중팔구.
problem *n.* mun-je 문제 ; nan-mun 난문.
procedure *n.* sun-sŏ 순서, chŏl-ch'a 절차.   「하다.
proceed *v.* na-a-ga-da 나아가다, chin-haeng-ha-da 진행
proceedings *n.* ŭi-sa-rok 의사록, hoe-ŭi-rok 회의록.

process *n.* chin-haeng 진행, kwa-jŏng 과정 ; (*method*)
pang-bŏp 방법. —*v.* ka-gong-ha-da 가공하다.

procession *n.* haeng-ryŏl 행렬, haeng-jin 행진.

proclaim *v.* kong-p'yo-ha-da 공표하다, sŏn-ŏn-ha-da
선언하다. 「myŏng 성명.

proclamation *n.* ① sŏn-ŏn 선언, p'o-go 포고. ② sŏng-

procurator *n.* so-song tae-ri-in 소송 대리인.

procure *v.* son-e nŏ-t'a 손에 넣다, ŏt-da 얻다.

prodigal *adj.* ① (*wasteful*) nang-bi-ha-nŭn 낭비하는.
② (*dissipated*) pang-t'ang-han 방탕한.

prodigious *adj.* kŏ-dae-han 거대한; i-sang-han 이상한.

prodigy *n.* ① kyŏng-i 경이(驚異). ② ch'ŏn-jae 천재.

produce *v.* saeng-san[san-ch'ul]-ha-da 생산[산출]하다.

producer *n.* saeng-san-ja 생산자, che-jak-ja 제작자,
p'ŭ-ro-dyu-u-sŏ 프로듀우서. 「성과.

product *n.* san-mul 산물, che-p'um 제품 ; song-gwa

production *n.* ① saeng-san 생산. ② yŏn-ch'ul 연출.

productive *adj.* saeng-san-jŏk-in 생산적인.

profane *adj.* (*irreverent*) mo-dok-jŏk-in 모독적인.

profanity *n.* mo-dok 모독. 「백하다.

profess *v.* kong-ŏn-ha-da 공언하다 ; ko-baek-ha-da 고

profession *n.* ① chik-ŏp 직업. ② kong-ŏn 공언(公言).

professor *n.* kyo-su 교수 : *assistant* ～ cho-gyo-su 조교
수/*associate* ～ pu-gyo-su 부교수. 「하다.

proffer *v.* che-gong-ha-da 제공하다 ; che-ŭi-ha-da 제의

proficient *adj.* ik-suk-han 익숙한, nŭng-ran-han 능란한.

profile *n.* ① (*of person's face*) yŏp mo-sŭp 옆 모습,
p'ŭ-ro-u-p'il 프로우필. ② (*outline*) yun-gwak 윤곽.

profit *n.* i-ik 이익, i-dŭk 이득. 「있는.

profitable *adj.* yu-ri-han 유리한, i-mun-i it-nŭn 이문이

profiteer *n.* pu-dang i-dŭk-ja 부당 이득자.

profound *adj.* ki-p'ŭn 깊은, sim-wŏn-han 심원한;(*very*

learned) hae-bak-han 해박한.

profuse *adj.* (*generous*) t'ong-i k'ŭn 통이 큰 ; nang-bi-ha-nŭn 낭비하는;(*abundant*) p'ung-bu-han 풍부한.

progeny *n.* cha-son 자손 ; (*outcome*) so-san 소산.

program(me) *n.* p'ŭ-ro-gŭ-raem 프로그램 ; (*schedule*) ye-jŏng-p'yo 예정표.   「da 나아가다.

progress *n.* pal-dal 발달, chin-bo 진보. —*v.* na-a-ga-

progressive *adj.* chin-bo-jŏk-in 진보적인.

prohibit *v.* kŭm-ha-da 금하다;pang-hae-ha-da 방해하다.

prohibition *n.* kŭm-ji 금지, kŭm-ji-ryŏng 금지령.

project *n.* kye-hoek 계획 ; sŏl-gye 설계. —*v.* ① (*on screen*) yŏng-sa-ha-da 영사하다. ② (*jut out*) tol-ch'ul-ha-da 돌출하다.   「han 장황한.

prolix *adj.* (*tedious*) chi-ru-han 지루한, chang-hwang-

prolog(ue) *n.* mŏ-ri-mal 머리말, sŏ-ŏn 서언 ; sŏ-gok 서

prolong *v.* yŏn-jang-ha-da 연장하다.   ⌊곡.

promenade *n.* san-ch'aek-gil 산책길, san-ch'aek 산책.

prominent *adj.* t'wi-ŏ-na-on 튀어나온 ; (*distinguished*) chŏ-myŏng-han 저명한, t'ak-wŏl-han 탁월한.

promise *n.* & *v.* yak-sok(-ha-da) 약속(하다).

promising *adj.* (*hopeful*) yu-mang-han 유망한.

promote *v.* ① (*raise*) sŭng-jin-si-k'i-da 승진시키다. ② (*further*) ch'ok-jin-si-k'i-da 촉진시키다.

promotion *n.* sŭng-jin 승진, chin-gŭp 진급.

prompt *adj.* ppa-rŭn 빠른 ; chŭk-sŏk-ŭi 즉석의. —*v.* ch'ok-jin-ha-da 촉진하다, cha-gŭk-ha-da 자극하다.

prone *adj.* …ha-gi swi-un …하기 쉬운, ŏp-dŭ-rin 엎드

pronoun *n.* (*gram.*) tae-myŏng-sa 대명사.   ⌊린.

pronounce *v.* pa-rŭm-ha-da 발음하다.

pronunciation *n.* pa-rŭm 발음.

proof *n.* ① (*evidence*) chŭng-gŏ 증거. ② (*of book*) kyo-jŏng(-swae) 교정(쇄).

prop *n.* (*support*) pŏ-t'im-mok 버팀목.

propaganda *n.* sŏn-jŏn 선전(宣傳). 「da 보급시키다.

propagate *v.* pŏn-sik-si-k'i-da 번식시키다, po-gŭp-si-k'i-

propel *v.* ch'u-jin-ha-da 추진하다, a-p'ŭ-ro mil-da 앞으

propeller *n.* p'ŭ-ro-p'el-rŏ 프로펠러. 「로 밀다.

proper *adj.* chŏk-dang-han 적당한; tok-t'ŭk-han 독특한.

properly *adv.* chŏk-dang-hi 적당히.

property *n.* chae-san 재산, so-yu-mul 소유물.

prophecy *n.* ye-ŏn 예언, ye-ŏn-sŏ 예언서. 「다.

prophesy *v.* ye-ŏn-ha-da 예언하다, ye-bo-ha-da 예보하

prophet *n.* ye-ŏn-ja 예언자, sŏn-ji-ja 선지자.

proportion *n.* ① (*ratio*) pi-yul 비율 ; (*share*) mok 몫.
② (*balance*) kyun-hyŏng 균형.

proposal *n.* sin-ch'ŏng 신청, che-ŭi 제의; (*plan*)an 안.

propose *v.* ① che-ŭi-ha-da 제의하다. ② (*woo*) ku-hon-
ha-da 구혼하다. 「kye-hoek 계획.

proposition *n.* ① (*assertion*) chu-jang 주장. ② (*plan*)

proprietor *n.* so-yu-ja 소유자 ; chi-ju 지주(地主).

propriety *n.* ① chŏk-dang 적당. ② (*decency*) ye-jŏl 예

prose *n.* san-mun(-ch'e) 산문(체). 「절.

prosecute *v.* ① (*carry out*) su-haeng-ha-da 수행하다,
chong-sa-ha-da 종사하다. ② (*sue*) ki-so-ha-da 기소

prosecutor *n.* kŏm-sa 검사(檢事). 「하다.

prospect *n.* ① (*scene*) cho-mang 조망. ② (*expectation*)
ye-sang 예상. —*v.* ① (*promise*) yu-mang-ha-da 유
망하다. ② (*explore*) tap-sa-ha-da 답사하다.

prosper *v.* ① pŏn-ch'ang[pŏn-yŏng]-ha-da 번창[번영]
하다. ② (*succeed*) sŏng-gong-ha-da 성공하다.

prosperity *n.* pŏn-ch'ang 번창 ; sŏng-gong 성공.

prosperous *adj.* pŏn-ch'ang-han 번창한.

prostitute *n.* ch'ang-nyŏ 창녀, mae-ch'un-bu 매춘부.

prostrate *adj.* ŏp-dŭ-rin 엎드린, kul-bok-han 굴복한.

protagonist *n.* (*leading actor*) chu-yŏk 주역.

protect *v.* po-ho-ha-da 보호하다, (*defend*) mak-da 막

protection *n.* po-ho 보호, pang-ŏ 방어. 「다.

protector *n.* po-ho-ja 보호자, ong-ho-ja 옹호자.

protectory *n.* so-nyŏn-wŏn 소년원, po-yuk-wŏn 보육원.

protein *n.* tan-baek-jil 단백질.

protest *v.* hang-ŭi-ha-da 항의하다. —*n.* hang-ŭi 항의.

Protestant *n.* sin-gyo-do 신교도.

prototype *n.* wŏn-hyŏng 원형, (*pattern*) p'yo-jun 표준.

protract *v.* (*lengthen*) o-rae kkŭl-da 오래 끌다, (*extend*) yŏn-jang-ha-da 연장하다.

proud *adj.* ① cha-rang-ha-nŭn 자랑하는. ② (*haughty*) kŏ-man-han 거만한. ③ (*grand*) tang-dang-han 당당한.

prove *v.* chŭng-myŏng-ha-da 증명하다.

proverb *n.* sok-dam 속담, (*wise saying*) kŭm-ŏn 금언.

provide *v.* (*supply*) kong-gŭp-ha-da 공급하다 ; (*prepare*) chun-bi-ha-da 준비하다.

provided *conj.* man-yak …i-ra-myŏn 만약 …이라면, …i-ra-nŭn cho-gŏn-ŭ-ro …이라는 조건으로.

providence *n.* sŏp-ri 섭리, sin-ŭi 신의(神意).

province *n.* to 도(道) ; (*state*) chu 주 ; chi-bang 지방.

provision *n.* ① chun-bi 준비, kong-gŭp 공급. ② (*supplies of food*) sik-ryang 식량.

provisional *adj.* im-si-ŭi 임시의. 「노하게 하다.

provoke *v.* cha-gŭk-ha-da 자극하다 ; no-ha-ge ha-da

prowess *n.* yong-gam 용감 ; (*excellence*) t'ak-wŏl 탁월.

prowl *v.* (*wander*) pae-hoe-ha-da 배회하다, to-ra-da-ni-da 돌아다니다, sŏ-sŏng-gŏ-ri-da 서성거리다.

prudence *n.* sin-jung 신중, cho-sim 조심. 「별있는.

prudent *adj.* sin-jung-han 신중한, pun-byŏl-it-nŭn 분

pry *v.* yŏt-bo-da 엿보다, sal-p'i-da 살피다.

psalm *n.* ch'an-song-ga 찬송가, sŏng-ga 성가.

psychology *n.* sim-ri-hak 심리학.

psychosis *n.* chŏng-sin-byŏng 정신병.

puberty *n.* (*sexual maturity*) sa-ch'un-gi 사춘기.

public *adj.* kong-jung-ŭi 공중(公衆)의.

publication *n.* ① pal-p'yo 발표. ② ch'ul-p'an 출판.

publish *v.* ① (*books*) ch'ul-p'an-ha-da 출판하다. ② pal-p'yo-ha-da 발표하다.   「행자.

publisher *n.* ch'ul-p'an-ŏp-ja 출판업자, pal-haeng-ja 발

publishing *n.* ch'ul-p'an 출판.

pucker *n.* chu-rŭm 주름. —*v.* chu-rŭm-sal-ji-ge ha-da 주름살지게 하다.

pudding *n.* p'u-ding 푸딩.

puddle *n.* mul ung-dŏng-i 물 웅덩이.   「훅 내불다.

puff *n.* huk nae-bul-gi 훅 내불기. —*v.* huk nae-bul-da

pull *v.* kkŭl-da 끌다, tang-gi-da 당기다.

pulley *n.* hwal-ch'a 활차(滑車), to-rŭ-rae 도르래.

pulp *n.* ① p'ŏl-p'ŭ 펄프. ② (*fruit*)kwa-yuk 과육(果肉).

pulpit *n.* sŏl-gyo-dan 설교단.

pulsate *v.* ttwi-da 뛰다 ; chin-dong-ha-da 진동하다.

pulse *n.* maek-bak 맥박, ko-dong 고동.

pump *n.* p'ŏm-p'ŭ 펌프 : *fire* ～ so-bang-p'ŏm-p'ŭ 소방 펌프. —*v.* p'ŏm-p'ŭ-jil-ha-da 펌프질하다.

pumpkin *n.* ho-bak 호박.

punch *v.* ① (*a hole*) ttul-t'a 뚫다. ② (*hit*) t'a-gyŏk-ŭl chu-da 타격을 주다. —*n.* p'ŏn-ch'i 펀치.

punctual *adj.* si-gan-ŭl ŏm-su-ha-nŭn 시간을 엄수하는.

punctuality *n.* si-gan ŏm-su 시간 엄수.

punctuation *n.* ku-du-jŏm 구두점, ku-du-bŏp 구두법.

puncture *n.* ppang-ggu 빵꾸.

punish *v.* pŏl-ju-da 벌주다, ch'ŏ-bŏl-ha-da 처벌하다.

punishment *n.* hyŏng-bŏl 형벌, ch'ŏ-bŏl 처벌.

pupa *n.* pŏn-de-gi 번데기.

pupil *n.* saeng-do 생도 ; che-ja 제자(弟子).

puppet *n.* ① (*doll*) in-hyŏng 인형. ② (*marionette*) kkok-duk-gak-si 꼭둑각시 ; kŏe-roe 괴뢰.

puppy *n.* (*young dog*) kang-a-ji 강아지. ⌜ip 구입.

purchase *v.* sa-da 사다, ku-ip-ha-da 구입하다. —*n.* ku-

pure *adj.* sun-su-han 순수한, sun-gyŏl-han 순결한.

purely *adv.* sun-su-ha-ge 순수하게.

purge *v.* ① (*cleanse*) kkae-ggŭ-si ha-da 깨끗이 하다. ② (*expel*) suk-ch'ŏng-ha-da 숙청하다.

purify *v.* kkae-ggŭ-si[mal-gge] ha-da 깨끗이[맑게] 하 다, chŏng-hwa-ha-da 정화하다.

Puritan *n.* ch'ŏng-gyo-do 청교도.

purity *n.* sun-su 순수, sun-gyŏl 순결, kyŏl-baek 결백.

purple *n. & adj.* cha-jut-bit(-ŭi) 자주빛(의).

purpose *n.* (*aim*) mok-jŏk 목적, (*intention*) ŭi-do 의 도 ; (*effect*) hyo-gwa 효과.

purposely *adv.* il-bu-rŏ 일부러, ko-ŭi-ro 고의로.

purr *v.* kŭ-rŭ-rŏng-gŏ-ri-da 그르렁거리다.

purse *n.* chi-gap 지갑. ⌜행하다.

pursue *v.* ch'u-jŏk-ha-da 추적하다 ; su-haeng-ha-da 수

pursuit *n.* ① ch'u-jŏk 추적 ; su-haeng 수행. ② (*occu-pus* *n.* ko-rŭm 고름. ⌊*pation*) chik-ŏp 직업.

push *n.* mil-gi 밀기, ap-ryŏk 압력. —*v.* mil-da 밀다.

push-over *n.* a-ju swi-un il 아주 쉬운 일.

puss *n.* ① (*cat*) ko-yang-i 고양이. ② so-nyŏ 소녀.

pussyfoot *v.* sal-gŭm-sal-gŭm kŏt-da 살금살금 걷다.

put *v.* ① (*place*) nŏ-t'a 놓다. ② (*cause*) …si-k'i-da …시키다. ③ (*express*) p'yo-hyŏn-ha-da 표현하다. ④ (*entrust*) mat-gi-da 맡기다.

puzzle *n.* su-su-gge-ggi 수수께끼, k'wi-jŭ 퀴즈. —*v.* tang-hwang-ha-da 당황하다.

pyramid *n.* kŭm-ja-t'ap 금자탑 ; p'i-ra-mit 피라밑.

❧ Q ❧

quack *n.* tol-p'a-ri ŭi-sa 돌팔이 의사 ; (*imposter*) sa-git-gun 사깃군.

quadrangle *n.* sa-gak-hyŏng 사각형, sa-byŏn-hyŏng 사변형.

quadruped *n.* ne-bal chim-sŭng 네발 짐승.

quail *n.* me-ch'u-ra-gi 메추라기.

quaint *adj.* ki-myo-han 기묘한, chin-gi-han 진기한.

quake *v.* hŭn-dŭl-ri-da 혼들리다 ; ttŏl-da 떨다.

Quaker *n.* k'we-i-k'ŏ kyo-do 퀘이커 교도.

qualification *n.* ① cha-gyŏk 자격 : *a medical ~* ŭi-sa myŏn-hŏ-jang 의사 면허장. ② (*adaptation*) chŏk-ŭng 적응. ③ (*faculty*) nŭng-ryŏk 능력.

qualify *v.* ① cha-gyŏk-ŭl chu-da 자격을 주다. ② (*gram.*) (*modify*) su-sik-ha-da 수식하다.

quality *n.* p'um-jil 품질, t'ŭk-sŏng 특성.

quantity *n.* (*amount*) yang 양(量), (*numbers*) su-ryang 수량, (*pl.*) ta-su 다수, ta-ryang 다량.

quarantine *n.* (*medical inspection*) kŏm-yŏk 검역.

quarrel *n. & v.* mal-da-t'um(-ha-da) 말다툼(하다).

quarrelsome *adj.* si-bi[ta-t'u-gi]-rŭl cho-a-ha-nŭn 시비[다투기]를 좋아하는, si-bi-jo-ŭi 시비조의.

quarry *v.* tol-ŭl ttŏ-nae-da 돌을 떠내다. —*n.* ① ch'ae-sŏk-jang 채석장. ② (*source*) ch'ul-ch'ŏ 출처.

quarter *n.* ① (1/4) sa-bun-ŭi il 4 분의 1. ② (*district*) chi-bang 지방. ③ (*lodge*) suk-so 숙소.

quarterly *n.* kye-gan chap-ji 계간 잡지.

quartz *n.* sŏk-yŏng 석영(石英).

quay *n.* pu-du 부두, pang-p'a-je 방파제.

queen *n.* yŏ-wang 여왕, wang-bi 왕비 : *a ~ of beauty* mi-ŭi yŏ-wang 미의 여왕.

queer *adj.* i-sang-han 이상한, myo-han 묘한.

quest *n.* t'am-saek 탐색, t'am-gu 탐구.

question *n.* ① chil-mun 질문, ŭi-mun 의문. ② (*problem*) non-jŏm 논점. —*v.* chil-mun-ha-da 질문하다.

question mark mu-rŭm-p'yo 물음표(?).

question(n)aire *n.* chil-mun-sŏ 질문서.

queue *n.* (*pigtail*) pyŏn-bal 변발; (*waiting line*) haeng-ryŏl 행렬. —*v.* yŏl-ŭl chit-da 열을 짓다.

quick *adj.* ppa-rŭn 빠른, min-gam-han 민감한.

quicken *v.* ppal-ra-ji-da 빨라지다; sal-ri-da 살리다.

quick-eyed *adj.* nun-ch'i-bba-rŭn 눈치빠른.

quickly *adv.* ppal-ri 빨리, sin-sok-hi 신속히.

quicksilver *n.* (*mercury*) su-ŭn 수은.

quiet *adj.* (*still*) ko-yo-han 고요한, (*gentle*) on-hwa-han 온화한, (*peaceful*) p'yŏng-hwa-sŭ-rŏn 평화스런. —*n.* ko-yo 고요, p'yŏng-on 평온.

quilt *n.* i-bul 이불, nu-bi i-bul 누비 이불.

quinine *n.* kŭm-gye-rap 금계랍, k'i-ni-ne 키니네.

quit *v.* kŭ-man-du-da 그만두다, ttŏ-na-da 떠나다.

quite *adv.* a-ju 아주, chŏn-hyŏ 전혀. 「da 멀다.

quiver *n.* hwa-sal-t'ong 화살통. —*v.* (*tremble*) ttŏl-

quota *n.* mok 몫, mo-ga-ch'i 모가치, hal-dang-ryang 할당량.

quotation *n.* ① in-yong 인용(引用). ② (*current price*) si-se 시세, si-ga 시가(時價).

quote *v.* in-yong-ha-da 인용하다.

—◆ **R** ◆—

rabbit *n.* chip-t'o-ggi 집토끼, t'o-ggi 토끼.

race *n.* ① (*contest*) kyŏng-ju 경주. ② (*the human*) in-jong 인종. —*v.* kyŏng-ju-ha-da 경주하다.

racial *adj.* in-jong-ŭi 인종의, chong-jok-ŭi 종족의.

rack *n.* kŭ-mul si-rŏng 그물 시렁, sŏn-ban 선반 : *a hat* ~ mo-ja-gŏ-ri 모자걸이.

racket *n.* ① ra-k'et 라켓. ② (*din*) so-dong 소동.

radar *n.* chŏn-p'a t'am-ji-gi 전파 탐지기, re-i-da-a 레이다아 : ~ *fence* re-i-da-a-mang 레이다아망(網).

radiant *adj.* pit-na-nŭn 빛나는 ; (*phys.*) pang-sa-ha-nŭn 방사(放射)하는 : ~ *heat* pang-sa-yŏl 방사열.

radiate *v.* (*send forth*)pang-sa-ha-da 방사(放射)하다 ; (*emit*) pal-san-ha-da 발산하다.

radiator *n.* ra-di-e-i-t'ŏ 라디에이터, pang-yŏl-gi 방열기.

radical *adj.* (*fundamental*) kŭn-bon-jŏk-in 근본적인 ; (*extreme*) kŭp-jin-jŏk-in 급진적인.

radio *n.* ra-di-o 라디오 ; mu-sŏn-jŏn-sin 무선전신.

radioactivity *n.* pang-sa-nŭng 방사능.

radish *n.* mu-u 무우 : *red* ~ hong-dang-mu 홍당무.

radium *n.* ra-di-um 라디움.   「범위

radius *n.* pan-ji-rŭm 반지름, pan-gyŏng 반경, pŏm-wi

raft *n.* ① ttet-mok 뗏목. ② (*abundance*) ta-ryang 다

rafter *n.* sŏ-gga-rae 서까래.   [량.

rag *n.* nŏng-ma 넝마, nu-dŏ-gi 누더기.

rage *n.* kyŏk-bun 격분 ; (*enthusiasm*) yŏ-rŭi 열의. —*v.* sa-nap-ge nal-ddwi-da 사납게 날뛰다 ; (*scold*) ya-dan-ch'i-da 야단치다.

ragged *adj.* nu-dŏ-gi-rŭl ip-ŭn 누더기를 입은 ; hŏp-su-ruk-han 헙수룩한, t'ŏp-su-ruk-han 텁수룩한.

raid *n. & v.* sŭp-gyŏk(-ha-da) 습격(하다) ; (*search*) su-saek(-ha-da) 수색(하다).   「gan 난간

rail *n.* ① sŏl-lo 선로, re-il 레일. ② (*handrail*) nan-

railing *n.* ① nan-gan 난간. ② (*jeers*) cho-rong 조롱.

railroad *n.* ch'ŏl-do 철도, ch'ŏl-ro 철로.

rain *n.* pi 비 : *a drizzling* ~ ka-rang-bi 가랑비/*a fine*

~ i-sŭl-bi 이슬비. —*v.* pi-ga o-da 비가 오다.

rainbow *n.* mu-ji-gae 무지개.

raincoat *n.* pi-ot 비옷, re-in-k'o-u-t'ŭ 레인코우트.

raindrop *n.* pit-bang-ul 빗방울, nak-su-mul 낙수물.

rainfall *n.* kang-u 강우, kang-u-ryang 강우량. 「방수용.

rainproof *adj.* pi-rŭl mak-nŭn 비를 막는, pang-su-yong 「방수용.

rainstorm *n.* pi-ba-ram 비바람, p'ok-p'ung-u 폭풍우.

rainy *adj.* pi-ga o-nŭn 비가 오는 : *a ~ day* pi-o-nŭn
 nal 비오는 날, u-ch'ŏn 우천. 「up) ki-rŭ-da 기르다.

raise *v.* ① i-rŭk'i-da 일으키다, ol-ri-da 올리다. ② (*bring*

raisin *n.* kŏn-p'o-do 건포도.

rake *n.* (*implement*) kal-k'wi 갈
 퀴, soe-sŭ-rang 쇠스랑.

rally *v.* ta-si mo-ŭ-da 다시 모으다.
 —*n.* (*mass meeting*) kun-jung
 tae-hoe 군중 대회.

[kal-k'wi]

ram *n.* su-yang 수양. —*v.* pu-dit-ch'i-da 부딪치다.

ramble *v.* ① kŏ-nil-da 거닐다. ② (*digress*) yŏ-dam-
 ha-da 여담하다. —*n.* san-ch'aek 산책, so-yo 소요.

ramp *n.* pi-t'al-gil 비탈길. 「pang-ŏ-ha-da 방어하다.

rampart *n.* (*bulwark*) sŏng-byŏk 성벽. —*v.* (*defend*)

ranch *n.* nong-jang 농장, mok-jang 목장.

random *adj.* tak-ch'i-nŭn-dae-ro-ŭi 닥치는대로의. —*n.*
 at ~ toe-nŭn-dae-ro 되는대로.

range *n.* ① (*scope*) pŏm-wi 범위. ② (*mount.*) san-
 maek 산맥. ③ (*distance*) kŏ-ri 거리.

rank *n.* ① (*row*) yŏl 열. ② (*station*) chi-wi 지위.

ransack *v.* sat-sa-ch'i twi-ji-da 샅샅이 뒤지다 ; (*plunder*) yak-t'al-ha-da 약탈하다.

ransom *n.* mom-gap 몸값. —*v.* mom-gap-sŭl ch'i-rŭ-
 go toe-ch'at-da 몸값을 치르고 되찾다.

rap *v.* (*tap*) ttok-ddok tu-dŭ-ri-da 똑똑 두드리다.

rape *v.* (*violate*) kang-gan-ha-da 강간하다. ;(*plunder*) yak-t'al-ha-da 약탈하다.

rapid *adj.* (*quick*) ppa-rŭn 빠른 ; (*steep*) ka-p'a-rŭn 가파른 : *a* ~ *slope* ka-p'a-rŭn pi-t'al 가파른 비탈. —*n.* (*swift current*) yŏ-ul 여울.   「하게.

rapidly *adv.* chae-bbal-ri 재빨리, sin-sok-ha-ge 신속

rapt *adj.* nŏk-sŭl ppae-at-gin 넋을 빼앗긴.

rapture *n.* (*ecstasy*) hwan-hŭi 환희, hwang-hol 황홀.

rare *adj.* (*scarce*) tŭ-mun 드문, chin-gi-han 진기한 ; (*thin*) hŭi-bak-han 희박한.

rare book chin-bon 진본.

rarely *adv.* chom-ch'e-ro … an-k'e 좀체로 …않게, tŭ-
rarity *n.* chin-p'um 진품(珍品).   「mul-ge 드물게.

rascal *n.* pul-ryang-bae 불량배, ak-han 악한.

rash *adj.* sŏng-gŭp-han 성급한, kyŏng-sol-han 경솔한. —*n.* (*eruption*) pal-jin 발진, ppyo-ru-ji 뾰루지.

rashly *adv.* kyŏng-sol-ha-ge 경솔하게, mu-mo-ha-ge 무
raspberry *n.* na-mu-ddal-gi 나무딸기.   「모하게.

rasping *adj.* pak-bak kŭk-nŭn 박박 긁는.

rat *n.* chwi 쥐 : *like a drowned* ~ mul-e ppa-jin saeng-jwi-ch'ŏ-rŏm 물에 빠진 생쥐처럼.

rate *n.* ① (*ratio*) pi-yul 비율. ② (*grade*) tŭng-gŭp 등급. ③ (*charge*) yo-gŭm 요금. —*v.* p'yŏng-ga-ha-da 평가하다, ŏ-rim-jap-da 어림잡다.   「째.

rather *adv.* o-hi-ryŏ 오히려, ch'a-ra-ri 차라리, kkwae

ratification *n.* pi-jun 비준(批准), chae-ga 재가.

ratify *v.* (*sanction*) pi-jun-ha-da 비준하다.

ratio *n.* (*proportion*) pi 비(比), pi-yul 비율.

ration *n.* pae-gŭp(-ryang) 배급(량), ha-ru-bun-ŭi sik-ryang 하루분의 식량, (*provision*) yang-sik 양식.

rational *adj.* hap-ri-jŏk-in 합리적인, i-sŏng-jŏk-in 이성
rationalism *n.* hap-ri-ju-ŭi 합리주의.   「적인.

rat poison chwi-yak 쥐약.

rattle *v.* tŏl-gŏk-tŏl-gŏk so-ri-nae-da 덜걱덜걱 소리내다.

ravage *n.* p'a-goe 파괴, (*ruin*) hwang-p'ye 황폐. —*v.* hwang-p'ye-ha-ge ha-da 황폐하게 하다.

raven *n.* (*bird*) kal-ga-ma-gwi 갈가마귀.

ravenous *adj.* (*greedy*) ke-gŏl-sŭ-rŏ-un 게걸스러운.

ravine *n.* (*deep gully*) ki-p'ŭn kye-gok 깊은 계곡; (*gorge*) hyŏp-gok 협곡.

raw *adj.* nal-gŏ-sŭi 날것의, mi-suk-han 미숙한: ~ *materials* wŏl-lyo 원료/*a* ~ *recruit* sin-byŏng 신병.

rawhide *n.* saeng-ga-juk 생가죽. 「sa-ha-da 방사하다.

ray *n.* kwang-sŏn 광선. —*v.* pal-sa-ha-da 발사하다, pang-

rayon *n.* (*artificial silk*) in-jo-gyŏn-sa 인조견사, re-i-

razor *n.* myŏn-do-k'al 면도칼. 　　　　　 ㄴon 레이온.

reach *v.* to-ch'ak-ha-da 도착하다, tang-do-ha-da 당도하다; (*extend*) nae-bbŏt-da 내뻗다.

react *v.* pan-dong-ha-da 반동하다. 「bal 반발.

reaction *n.* pan-dong 반동, pan-jak-yong 반작용, pan-

reactionary *adj.* pan-dong-ŭi 반동의, pan-ŭng-ŭi 반응

read *v.* ik-da 읽다, tok-sŏ-ha-da 독서하다. 　ㄴ의.

reader *n.* tok-ja 독자; (*book*) tok-bon 독본.

readily *adv.* swip-sa-ri 쉽사리; k'wae-hi 쾌히.

reading *n.* il-ggi 읽기, nang-dok 낭독, tok-sŏ 독서.

ready *adj.* chun-bi-ga toen 준비가 된.

ready-made *adj.* ki-sŏng-p'um-ŭi 기성품의, man-dŭ-rŏ no-ŭn 만들어 놓은.

ready money mat-don 맞돈, hyŏn-gŭm 현금.

real *adj.* ① chin-sil-ŭi 진실의; sil-je-ŭi 실제의. ② pu-dong-san-ŭi 부동산의: ~ *estate* pu-dong-san 부동산.

realism *n.* sa-sil-ju-ŭi 사실주의, hyŏn-sil-ju-ŭi 현실주의.

reality *n.* hyŏn-sil-sŏng 현실성; chin-sil 진실.

realization *n.* sil-hyŏn 실현, hyŏn-sil-hwa 현실화.

realize v. sil-hyŏn-ha-da 실현하다;kkae-dat-da 깨닫다.

really adv. ch'am-ŭ-ro 참으로, chŏng-mal-ro 정말로.

realm n. yŏng-yŏk 영역 ; wang-guk 왕국.

reap v. (*cut*) pe-da 베다, su-hwak-ha-da 수확하다, kŏ-du-ŏ-dŭ-ri-da 거두어들이다: ~ *a harves t*nong-jak-mul-ŭl kŏ-du-ŏ-dŭ-ri-da 농작물을 거두어들이다.

reappear v. chae-hyŏn[chae-bal]-ha-da 재현[재발]하다.

rear n. twi 뒤. —*adj.* pae-hu-ŭi 배후의. —v. ① (*bring up*) ki-rŭ-da 기르다. ② (*raise*) ol-ri-da 올리다.

rearrange v. ta-si pa-ro-jap-da 다시 바로잡다.

reason n. (*cause*) i-yu 이유 ; (*rationality*) i-sŏng 이성.

reasonable adj. (*rational*) hap-ri-jŏk-in 합리적인, (*moderate*) al-ma-jŭn 알맞은 ; hap-dang-han 합당한.

reassure v. (*give courage*) an-sim-si-k'i-da 안심시키다.

rebel n. pan-yŏk-ja 반역자. —v. (*revolt*) pan-yŏk-ha-da 반역하다, pae-ban-ha-da 배반하다.

rebellion n. pal-lan 반란, p'ok-dong 폭동.

rebuff n. kŏ-jŏl 거절, t'oe-jja 퇴짜. —v. t'oe-jja-no-t'a 퇴짜놓다, (*check*) chŏ-ji-ha-da 저지하다. 「축하다.

rebuild v. chae-gŏn-ha-da 재건하다, kae-ch'uk-ha-da 개

rebuke v. kku-jit-da 꾸짖다, ching-gye-ha-da 징계하다. —n. pi-nan 비난, kyŏn-ch'aek 견책.

recall n. & v. ① (*call back*) so-hwan(-ha-da) 소환 (하다). ② (*recollect*) sang-gi(-ha-da) 상기(하다).

recapture v. t'al-hwan-ha-da 탈환하다.

recede v. ① mul-rŏ-na-da 물러나다, son-ŭl tte-da 손을 떼다. ② (*return*) pan-hwan-ha-da 반환하다.

receipt n. yŏng-su-jŭng 영수증.

receive v. pat-da 받다, yŏng-su-ha-da 영수하다.

receiver n. ① (*recipient*) su-ryŏng-in 수령인. ② (*of telephone*) su-hwa-gi 수화기.

recent adj. ch'oe-gŭn-ŭi 최근의, yo-jŭm-ŭi 요즘의 ;

(*new*) sae-ro-un 새로운.

reception *n.* (*welcoming*) chŏp-dae 접대 ; (*party*) hwan-yŏng-hoe 환영회, ri-sep-syŏn 리셉션.

receptivity *n.* kam-su-sŏng 감수성, i-hae-ryŏk 이해력.

recess *n.* swi-nŭn si-gan 쉬는 시간, hyu-hoe 휴회.

recipe *n.* ch'ŏ-bang 처방, cho-ri-bŏp 조리법. 「器).

recipient *n.* ① su-ryŏng-ja 수령자. ② yong-gi 용기(容

reciprocal *adj.* (*mutual*) sang-ho-ŭi 상호의 ;(*compensatory*) po-sang-jŏk-in 보상적(補償的)인. 「창회.

recital *n.* (*mus.*) tok-ju-hoe 독주회, tok-ch'ang-hoe 독

recitation *n.* nang-dok 낭독, am-song 암송.

recite *v.* oe-da 외다, nang-dok-ha-da 낭독하다, (*narrate*) i-ya-gi-ha-da 이야기하다.

reckless *adj.* mu-mo-han 무모한, pun-byŏl-ŏp-nŭn 분별 없는 : *a ~ fellow* tang-dol-han nom 당돌한 놈.

reckon *v.* (*count*) kye-san-ha-da 계산하다, sem-ha-da 셈하다. ch'u-jŏng-ha-da 추정하다.

reclaim *v.* ① (*bring back*) to-ro ch'at-da 도로 찾다 ; ② (*reform*) kae-sŏn-ha-da 개선하다.

recline *v.* ki-dae-da 기대다, ŭi-ji-ha-da 의지하다. 「다.

recognize *v.* a-ra-bo-da 알아보다, in-jŏng-ha-da 인정하

recoil *v.* twi-ro mul-rŏ-na-da 뒤로 물러나다 ; um-jjil-ha-da 움찔하다. 「da 다시 모으다.

recollect *v.* ① hoe-sang-ha-da 회상하다. ② ta-si mo-ŭ-

recollection *n.* hoe-sang 회상, ch'u-ŏk 추억.

recommend *v.* ch'u-ch'ŏn-ha-da 추천하다, (*advise*) kwŏn-go-ha-da 권고하다. 「ch'ŏn-sŏ 추천서.

recommendation *n.* ch'u-ch'ŏn 추천 : *letter of ~* ch'u-

recompense *v.* po-dap-ha-da 보답하다, po-sang-ha-da 보상하다. —*n.* po-su 보수, po-sang 보상.

reconcile *v.* hwa-hae-si-k'i-da 화해시키다, chung-jae-ha-da 중재하다, (*adjust*) cho-jŏng-ha-da 조정하다.

reconnaissance *n.* chŏng-ch'al 정찰.
reconsider *v.* chae-go-ha-da 재고하다. 「부흥하다.
reconstruct *v.* chae-gŏn-ha-da 재건하다, pu-hŭng-ha-da
record *n.* ① (*written note*) ki-rok 기록. ② (*phonograph*) re-k'o-o-dŭ 레코오드, ŭm-ban 음반. ③ (*personal history*) kyŏng-ryŏk 경력. —*v.* ki-rok-ha-da 기록하다.
recount *n.* cha-se-hi mal-ha-da 자세히 말하다.
recover *v.* hoe-bok-ha-da 회복하다, toe-ch'at-da 되찾다.
recovery *n.* hoe-bok 회복 ; pok-gu 복구.
recreation *n.* ki-bun chŏn-hwan 기분 전환 ; o-rak 오락, re-k'ŭ-ri-e-i-syŏn 레크리에이션.
recruit *n.* sin-byŏng 신병(新兵). —*v.* sin-byŏng-ŭl mo-jip-ha-da 신병을 모집하다.
rectangle *n.* chik-sa-gak-hyŏng 직사각형.
rectify *v.* ko-ch'i-da 고치다, kae-jŏng-ha-da 개정하다.
rector *n.* ① (*clergyman*) kyo-gu mok-sa 교구 목사, su-do-wŏn-jang 수도원장. ② (*college*) hak-jang 학장.
recuperate *v.* hoe-bok-doe-da 회복되다, nat-da 낫다.
recur *v.* toe-do-ra-ga-da 되돌아가다 ; hoe-sang-ha-da 회상하다 ; chae-bal-ha-da 재발하다.
red *adj.* ppal-gan 빨간 : *R~ China* chung-gong 중공/ *R~ Cross* chŏk-sip-ja 적십자. —*n.* chŏk-saek 적색.
redeem *v.* toe-sa-da 되사다 ; sok-joe-ha-da 속죄하다.
redemption *n.* (*from sin*) sok-joe 속죄.
reduce *v.* chul-da 줄다, kam-so-ha-da 감소하다.
reduction *n.* ch'uk-so 축소 ; (*discount*) ha-rin 할인.
redundant *adj.* yŏ-bun-ŭi 여분의, kwa-da-han 과다한.
reed *n.* kal-dae 갈대.
reef *n.* am-ch'o 암초.
reel *n.* (*spool*) ŏl-re 얼레, sil-gam-gae 실감개. —*v.* kam-da 감다.

[ŏl-re]

re-elect *v.* chae-sŏn-ha-da 재선하다. 「da 재건하다.

re-establish *v.* pu-hŭng-ha-da 부흥하다, chae-gŏn-ha-

re-examine *v.* chae-gŏm-t'o-ha-da 재검토하다.

refectory *n.* sik-dang 식당 ; ta-sil 다실.

refer *v.* ① cho-hoe-ha-da 조회하다. ② (*attribute*) …e tol-ri-da …에 돌리다. ③ ch'am-jo-ha-da 참조하다.

referee *n.* sim-p'an 심판, re-p'ŏ-ri 레퍼리.

reference *n.* ch'am-go 참고 ; (*inquiry*) cho-hoe 조회 ; (*testimonial*) chŭng-myŏng-sŏ 증명서.

referendum *n.* kuk-min t'u-p'yo 국민 투표.

refine *v.* ① se-ryŏn-ha-da 세련하다. ② (*purify*) chŏng-je-ha-da 정제하다, mal-gge-ha-da 맑게하다.

refined *adj.* se-ryŏn-doen 세련된, chŏng-je-doen 정제된.

refinement *n.* se-ryŏn 세련 ; ki-p'um 기품 ; u-a 우아.

reflect *v.* pan-sa-ha-da 반사하다 ; pi-ch'u-da 비추다.

reflection *n.* pan-sa 반사, pan-yŏng 반영 ; pan-sŏng 반성. 「—n. kae-ryang 개량.

reform *v.* kae-hyŏk[kae-ryang]-ha-da 개혁[개량]하다.

reformation *n.* kae-hyŏk 개혁, kae-sŏn 개선. 「화원.

reformatory *n.* so-nyŏn-wŏn 소년원, kam-hwa-wŏn 감

refrain *v.* sam-ga-da 삼가다, cha-je-ha-da 자제하다.

refresh *v.* hwal-gi-ddi-ge ha-da 활기띠게 하다 ; (*renew*) sae-rop-ge ha-da 새롭게 하다.

refreshment *n.* ① wŏn-gi-hoe-bok 원기회복 ; hyu-yang 휴양. ② (*pl.*) (*light meal*) ŭm-sik-mul 음식물.

refrigerate *v.* naeng-gak-si-k'i-da 냉각시키다, naeng-dong[naeng-jang]-ha-da 냉동[냉장]하다.

refrigerator *n.* naeng-jang-go 냉장고.

refuge *n.* p'i-nan-ch'ŏ 피난처, tae-p'i-so 대피소.

refugee *n.* ① p'i-nan-min 피난민. ② mang-myŏng-ja

refusal *n.* kŏ-jŏl 거절, sa-t'oe 사퇴. 「망명자.

refuse *v.* kŏ-jŏl-ha-da 거절하다, kŏ-bu-ha-da 거부하다.

—*n.* (*rubbish*) ssŭ-re-gi 쓰레기, p'ye-mul 폐물.

refute *v.* (*disprove*) pan-bak-ha-da 반박하다.

regain *v.* toe-ch'at-da 되찾다; (*recover*) hoe-bok-ha-da 회복하다; pok-gwi-ha-da 복귀하다.

regard *v.* yŏ-gi-da 여기다; (*respect*) chon-jung-ha-da 존중하다; (*heed*) chu-ŭi-ha-da 주의하다. —*n.* (*consideration*) ko-ryŏ 고려; chon-gyŏng 존경.

regarding *prep.* …e kwan-ha-yŏ …에 관하여.

regatta *n.* (*boat, etc.*) kyŏng-jo 경조.

regenerate *v.* chae-saeng-si-k'i-da 재생시키다.

regime *n.* (*system*) che-do 제도; (*political system*) chŏng-ch'e 정체. 「gu-dan 야구단.

regiment *n.* ① (*army*) yŏn-dae 연대. ② (*Am.*) ya-

region *n.* chi-bang 지방, yŏng-yŏk 영역.

register *v.* tŭng-gi-ha-da 등기하다, tŭng-rok-ha-da 등록하다. —*n.* tŭng-gi 등기, tŭng-rok 등록.

registrar *n.* ho-jŏk-gye-won 호적계원; (*of school*) kyo-mu-ch'ŏ-jang 교무처장.

registration *n.* ki-jae 기재, tŭng-rok 등록.

registry office ho-jŏk tŭng-gi-so 호적 등기소.

regret *v.* yu-gam-ŭ-ro saeng-gak-ha-da 유감으로 생각하다. —*n.* (*remorse*) yu-gam 유감; hu-hoe 후회.

regular *adj.* kyu-ch'ik-jŏk-in 규칙적인, chŏng-gi-jŏk-in 정기적인. —*n.* (*pl.*) chŏng-gyu-byŏng 정규병.

regulate *v.* kyu-jŏng-ha-da 규정하다; (*moderate*) cho-jŏl-ha-da 조절하다, (*control*) tan-sok-ha-da 단속하다.

regulation *n.* kyu-ch'ik 규칙, kyu-yul 규율.

rehabilitate *v.* pok-gu-si-k'i-da 복구시키다.

rehabilitation *n.* pok-gu 복구, pu-hŭng 부흥.

rehearsal *n.* yŏn-sŭp 연습, ri-hŏ-sŏl 리허설.

rehearse *v.* yŏn-sŭp-ha-da 연습하다, si-yŏn-ha-da 시연 (試演)하다; (*recite*) am-song-ha-da 암송하다.

reign *n.* t'ong-ch'i 통치. —*v.* t'ong-ch'i-ha-da 통치하다.
rein *n.* ko-bbi 고삐 ; (*pl.*) kyŏn-je 견제.
reindeer *n.* sul-lok 순록(馴鹿), mal-sa-sŭm 말사슴.
reinforce *v.* po-gang-ha-da 보강하다.
reiterate *n.* pan-bok-ha-da 반복하다.
reject *v.* kŏ-jŏl-ha-da 거절하다, kŏ-bu-ha-da 거부하다 ; (*refuse to grant*) kak-ha-ha-da 각하하다.
rejection *n.* kŏ-jŏl 거절, pu-gyŏl 부결, ki-gak 기각.
rejoice *v.* ki-bbŏ-ha-da 기뻐하다.
relapse *v.* ① toe-do-ra-ga-da 되돌아가다. ② t'a-rak-ha-da 타락하다. —*n.* chae-bal 재발 ; t'a-rak 타락.
relate *v.* ① chin-sul-ha-da 진술하다, i-ya-gi-ha-da 이야기하다. ② (*connect*) kwal-lyŏn-si-k'i-da 관련시키다.
relation *n.* ① (*connection*) kwan-gye 관계. ② (*kinsman*) ch'in-ch'ŏk 친척. ③ chin-sul 진술.
relationship *n.* (ch'in-ch'ŏk) kwan-gye (친척) 관계.
relative *n.* ch'in-ch'ŏk 친척 ; (*gram.*) kwan-gye-sa 관계사. —*adj.* (*comparative*) sang-dae-jŏk-in 상대적인.
relax *v.* (*loosen*) nŭt-ch'u-da 늦추다. 「중계.
relay *v.* chung-gye-ha-da 중계하다. —*n.* chung-gye
release *v.* p'u-rŏ-no-t'a 풀어놓다, sŏk-bang-ha-da 석방하다 ; (*remit*) myŏn-je-ha-da 면제하다. 「지다.
relent *v.* sun-hae-ji-da 순해지다. nu-gŭ-rŏ-ji-da 누그러
relevant *adj.* chŏk-jŏl-han 적절한. 「han 확실한.
reliable *adj.* mit-ŭl su it-nŭn 믿을 수 있는 ; hwak-sil-
relic *n.* yu-mul 유물, yu-jŏk 유적 ; (*pl.*) yu-gol 유골.
relief *n.* ① ku-je 구제. ② (*removal*) che-gŏ 제거. ③ (*comfort*) wi-an 위안. ④ yang-gak 양각(陽刻).
relieve *v.* ku-je-ha-da 구제하다 ; (*make less*) tŏ-rŏ-ju-da 덜어주다 ; p'yŏn-an-ha-ge ha-da 편안하게 하다.
religion *n.* chong-gyo 종교. 「ki-p'ŭn 신앙심이 깊은.
religious *adj.* chong-gyo-jŏk-in 종교적인 ; sin-ang-sim-i

relinquish v. (*give up*) p'o-gi-ha-da 포기하다, pŏ-ri-da 버리다 : (*loosen*) no-t'a 놓다.

relish n. (*taste*) mat 맛, (*flavor*) p'ung-mi 풍미 ; (*liking*) ki-ho 기호, —v. mat-bo-da 맛보다, (*enjoy*) chŭl-gi-da 즐기다.

reluctant adj. (*unwilling*) si-rŏ-ha-nŭn 싫어하는.

rely v. ŭi-ji-ha-da 의지하다. mit-da 믿다.

remain v. mŏ-mu-rŭ-da 머무르다 ; nam-da 남다.

remainder n. ① na-mŏ-ji 나머지. ② chal-lyu-ja 잔류자. ③ (*relics*) yu-jŏk 유적.

remand home im-si su-yong-so 임시 수용소.

remark v. ① chu-mok-ha-da 주목하다. ② (*speak*) mal-ha-da 말하다. —n. pa-rŏn 발언 ; pi-p'yŏng 비평.

remarkable adj. hyŏn-jŏ-han 현저한. 「재혼.

remarry v. chae-hon-ha-da 재혼하다. —n. chae-hon

remedy n. (*med.*) ŭi-yak 의약 ; (*cure*) yo-bŏp 요법. —v. ko-ch'i-da 고치다. 「da 상기하다.

remember v. (*recall*) ki-ŏk-ha-da 기억하다, sang-gi-ha-

remembrance n. (*memory*) ki-ŏk 기억 ; (*souvenir*) ki-nyŏm-p'um 기념품. 「u-ch'i-da 깨우치다.

remind v. saeng-gak-na-ge ha-da 생각나게 하다, kkae-

reminiscence n. hoe-sang 회상, (*pl.*) hoe-go-dam 회고담.

remission n. yong-sŏ 용서, sa-myŏn 사면.

remit v. ① (*send*) song-gŭm-ha-da 송금하다. ② (*abate*) wan-hwa-ha-da 완화하다. ③ (*pardon*) yong-sŏ-ha-da 용서하다. 「ic ～ chŏn-sin-hwan 전신환.

remittance n. (*of money*) song-gŭm 송금 : *telegraph-*

remnant n. na-mŏ-ji 나머지 ; (*relic*) yu-mul 유물.

remonstrate v. ch'ung-go-ha-da 충고하다, kan-ha-da 간(諫)하다 ; (*protest*) hang-ŭi-ha-da 항의하다.

remorse n. hu-hoe 후회, nwi-u-ch'im 뉘우침.

remote adj. (*distant*) mŏn 먼, mŏn-go-sŭi 먼곳의.

removal *n.* (*transfer*) i·dong 이동, i·sa 이사 ; (*dismissal*) hae·im 해임, che·gŏ 제거.

remove *v.* om·gi·da 옮기다 ; ch'i·u·da 치우다.

Renaissance *n.* mun·ye·bu·hŭng 문예부흥.

render *v.* ① (*give back*) tol·ryŏ·ju·da 돌려주다. ② (*make*) ···toe·ge ha·da ···되게 하다. ③ (*submit*) che·ch'ul·ha·da 제출하다. ④ pŏn·yŏk·ha·da 번역하다.

rendezvous *n.* rang·de·bu 랑데부 ; hoe·hap chang·so 회합 장소 ; mil·hoe chang·so 밀회 장소.

renew *v.* sae·rop·ge ha·da 새롭게 하다 ; hoe·bok·ha·da 회복하다, pok·gu·si·k'i·da 복구시키다.

renounce *v.* p'o·gi·ha·da 포기하다 ; pu·in·ha·da 부인하다.

renown *n.* myŏng·sŏng 명성, yu·myŏng 유명.

rent *n.* ① (*house*) chip·se 집세 ; (*land*) chi·dae 지대 (地代) ; im·dae·ryo 임대료. ② (*gap*) kal·ra·jin t'ŭm 갈라진 틈. —*v.* (*to somebody*) pil·ryŏ·ju·da 빌려주다, (*from somebody*) pil·ri·da 빌리다.

reorganize *v.* chae·p'yŏn·sŏng·ha·da 재편성하다.

repair *v.* (*mend*) su·sŏn·ha·da 수선하다, kyo·jŏng·ha·da 교정하다 ; (*restore*) hoe·bok·ha·da 회복하다.

reparation *n.* pae·sang 배상, (*pl.*) pae·sang·gŭm 배상금.

repast *n.* (*meal*) sik·sa 식사.

repatriate *v.* pon·guk·ŭ·ro song·hwan·ha·da 본국으로 송환하다. —*n.* kwi·hwan tong·p'o 귀환 동포.

repay *v.* kap·da 갚다, po·dap·ha·da 보답하다.

repeal *n.* (*annul*) p'ye·ji·ha·da 폐지하다, ch'wi·so·ha·da 취소하다. —*n.* p'ye·ji 폐지, ch'wi·so 취소.

repeat *n. & v.* toe·p'u·ri(·ha·da) 되풀이(하다).

repel *v.* kyŏk·t'oe·ha·da 격퇴하다. 「da 후회하다.

repent *v.* (*regret*) nwi·u·ch'i·da 뉘우치다, hu·hoe·ha-

repetition *n.* toe·p'u·ri 되풀이, pan·bok 반복.

replace *v.* che·ja·ri·e kat·da tu·da 제자리에 갖다 두다 ;

(*repay*) tol-ryŏ-ju-da 돌려주다.

replacement *n.* kyo-dae 교대 ; (*substitute*) tae-ch'i 대치, kyo-ch'e-ja〔mul〕 교체자〔물〕.

replay *n. & v.* chae-si-hap(-ha-da) 재시합(하다).

replenish *n.* po-ch'ung-ha-da 보충하다.

reply *n. & v.* tae-dap(-ha-da) 대답(하다).

report *n. & v.* po-go(-ha-da) 보고(하다).

report card sŏng-jŏk-p'yo 성적표, t'ong-sin-bu 통신부.

reporter *n.* po-go-ja 보고자 ; (*jour.*) ki-ja 기자.

repose *v.* ① hyu-sik-ha-da 휴식하다 ; cha-da 자다. ② (*rely*) ŭi-ji-ha-da 의지하다. —*n.* hyu-sik 휴식 ; cham 잠.

reprehend *v.* kku-jit-da 꾸짖다, pi-nan-ha-da 비난하다.

represent *v.* ① sŏl-myŏng-ha-da 설명하다, myo-sa-ha-da 묘사하다. ② (*stand for*) tae-p'yo-ha-da 대표하다.

representative *n.* tae-p'yo-ja 대표자, tae-ri-in 대리인.

repress *v.* ŏk-nu-rŭ-da 억누르다, chin-ap-ha-da 진압하다.

reprieve *n.* chip-haeng-yu-ye 집행유예.

reprimand *v.* (*censure*) ching-gye-ha-da 징계하다.

reprint *n. & v.* chae-p'an(-ha-da) 재판(再版)(하다).

reproach *v.* kku-jit-da 꾸짖다, pi-nan-ha-da 비난하다.

reproduce *v.* pok-sa-ha-da 복사하다, chae-saeng-ha-da 재생하다.   「pok-je 복제.

reproduction *n.* chae-saeng 재생, chae-hyŏn 재현 ;

reproof *n.* (*censure*) kyŏn-ch'aek 견책.

reprove *v.* pi-nan-ha-da 비난하다 ; kku-jit-da 꾸짖다.

reptile *n.* (*crawling animal*) p'a-ch'ung-ryu 파충류.

republic *n.* kong-hwa-guk 공화국.   「da 거부하다.

repudiate *v.* in-yŏn-ŭl kkŭn-t'a 인연을 끊다 ; kŏ-bu-ha-

repulse *v.* ① kyŏk-t'oe-ha-da 격퇴하다, mul-ri-ch'i-da 물리치다. ② (*refute*) non-bak-ha-da 논박하다.

reputation *n.* p'yŏng-p'an 평판, myŏng-sŏng 명성.

request *n.* yo-mang 요망, yo-gu 요구. —*v.* kan-ch'ŏng-ha-da 간청하다, yo-gu-ha-da 요구하다.

require *v.* p'i-ryo-ro ha-da 필요로 하다 ; yo-gu-ha-da 요구하다. 「p'il-su-p'um 필수품.

requisite *adj.* p'i-ryo-han 필요한, p'il-su-ŭi 필수의. —*n.*

requite *v.* ① (*reward*) po-dap-ha-da 보답하다. ② (*avenge*) po-bok-ha-da 보복하다. 「다.

rescue *v.* ku-ch'ul-ha-da 구출하다, ku-jo-ha-da 구조하

research *n.* (*investigation*) cho-sa-yŏn-gu 조사연구. —*v.* cho-sa-yŏn-gu-ha-da 조사연구하다.

resemblance *n.* yu-sa(-jŏm) 유사(점), tal-mŭm 닮음.

resemble *v.* pi-sŭt-ha-da 비슷하다, tam-da 닮다.

resent *v.* pun-gae-ha-da 분개하다, wŏn-mang-ha-da 원망하다. 「ryu 보류.

reservation *n.* (*of hotel room, etc.*) ye-yak 예약 ; po-

reserve *v.* (*keep*) po-jon-ha-da 보존하다 ; (*retain*) po-ryu-ha-da 보류하다 ; ye-yak-ha-da 예약하다.

residence *n.* chu-t'aek 주택 ; chu-so 주소.

resident *n.* ① kŏ-ju-ja 거주자. ② kŏ-ryu-min 거류민.

resign *v.* ① tan-nyŏm-ha-da 단념하다. ② sa-jik-ha-da 사

resignation *n.* sa-jik 사직, sa-p'yo 사표. 「직하다.

resist *v.* chŏ-hang-ha-da 저항하다, (*repel*) mul-ri-ch'i-da 물리치다 ; (*withstand*) kyŏn-di-da 견디다.

resistance *n.* chŏ-hang 저항, hang-jaeng 항쟁.

resolute *adj.* tan-ho-han 단호한, hwak-go-han 확고한.

resolution *n.* kyŏ-rŭi 결의, kyŏl-sim 결심.

resolve *v.* ① (*decide*) kyŏl-sim-ha-da 결심하다. ② (*solve*) hae-gyŏl-ha-da 해결하다.

resort *n.* yu-hŭng-ji 유흥지 ; hyu-yang-ji 휴양지. —*v.* cha-ju ta-ni-da 자주 다니다.

resound *v.* (*echo*) ul-ri-da 울리다.

resource *n.* ① cha-wŏn 자원(資源) ; cha-gŭm 자금. ② (*means*) su-dan 수단, pang-p'yŏn 방편.

respect v. ① chon-gyŏng-ha-da 존경하다. ② (*regard*) ko-ryŏ-ha-da 고려하다. —n. chon-jung 존중.

respectable adj. chon-gyŏng-hal man-han 존경할 만한.

respectful adj. (*polite*) kong-son-han 공손한, chŏng-jung-han 정중한. 「ro 따로따로.

respectively adj. kak-gak 각각, kak-ja 각자 ; tta-ro-dda-

respiration n. ho-hŭp 호흡, sum 숨 : *artificial* ~ in-gong-ho-hŭp 인공호흡.

respire v. sum-swi-da 숨쉬다, ho-hŭp-ha-da 호흡하다.

respite n. & v. yu-ye(-ha-da) 유예(하다).

respond v. tae-dap-ha-da 대답하다, ŭng-ha-da 응하다.

respondent n. (*defendant*) p'i-go 피고. —adj. tae-dap-ha-nŭn 대답하는, ŭng-dap-ha-nŭn 응답하는.

response n. ŭng-dap 응답 ; (*reaction*) pan-ŭng 반응.

responsibility n. ch'aek-im 책임 ; chik-ch'aek 직책.

responsible adj. ch'aek-im-it-nŭn 책임있는.

rest v. swi-da 쉬다 ; ki-dae-da 기대다. —n. ① (*repose*) hyu-sik 휴식. ② (*remainder*) na-mŏ-ji 나머지.

restaurant n. yo-jŏng 요정 ; ŭm-sik-jŏm 음식점, re-sŭ-t'o-rang 레스토랑. 「한.

restless adj. tŭl-ddŏ-it-nŭn 들떠있는, pu-ran-han 불안

restoration n. hoe-bok 회복 ; su-bok 수복. 「복하다.

restore v. hoe-bok-si-k'i-da 회복시키다 ; su-bok-ha-da 수

restrain v. ① (*hold back*) ŏk-je-ha-da 억제하다. ② (*check*) kŭm-ji-ha-da 금지하다. 「하다.

restrict v. che-han-ha-da 제한하다 ; sok-bak-ha-da 속박

result n. kyŏl-gwa 결과, sŏng-jŏk 성적. —v. (*follow*) kyŏl-gwa-ro i-rŏ-na-da 결과로 일어나다.

resume v. ① (*begin again*) chae-gae-ha-da 재개하다. ② (*reoccupy*) ta-si ch'a-ji-ha-da 다시 차지하다.

resumption n. chae-gae 재개, hoe-bok 회복.

resurrection n. pu-hwal 부활, chae-saeng 재생.

retail *n.* & *v.* so-mae(-ha-da) 소매(하다).

retain *v.* ① po-ryu-ha-da 보류하다, po-yu-ha-da 보유
하다. ② (*keep in mind*) ki-ŏk-ha-da 기억하다.

retaliate *v.* po-bok-ha-da 보복하다. 「방해하다.

retard *v.* (*delay*) nŭt-ch'u-da 늦추다 ; pang-hae-ha-da

reticent *adj.* mal-i ŏp-nŭn 말이 없는.

retire *v.* mul-rŏ-ga-da 물러가다, t'oe-gŏ-ha-da 퇴거하다;
(*from office*) t'oe-jik-ha-da 퇴직하다.

retirement *n.* t'oe-gŏ 퇴거 ; (*seclusion*) ŭn-t'oe 은퇴.

retort *v.* mal-dae-ggu-ha-da 말대꾸하다. —*n.* pan-bak

retouch *n.* & *v.* su-jŏng(-ha-da) 수정(하다). 「반박.

retrace *v.* toe-do-ra-ga-da 되돌아가다, hoe-go-ha-da 회고
하다. 「*draw*) um-ch'ŭ-ri-da 움츠리다.

retract *v.* ① (*recant*) ch'wi-so-ha-da 취소하다. ② (*with-

retreat *n.* & *v.* hu-t'oe(-ha-da) 후퇴(하다).

retrieve *v.* (*recover*) hoe-bok-ha-da 회복하다.

retroactive *adj.* so-gŭp-ha-nŭn 소급하는 ; pan-jak-yong-
ha-nŭn 반작용하는. 「상.

retrospect *v.* hoe-go-ha-da 회고하다. —*n.* hoe-sang 회

return *v.* to-ra-o-da 돌아오다 ; pan-hwan-ha-da 반환하다.
—*n.* ① pok-gwi 복귀. ② (*profit*) su-ik 수익.

reunion *n.* chae-hoe 재회(再會), yung-hwa 융화.

reunite *v.* ta-si kyŏl-hap-si-k'i-da 다시 결합시키다 ; hwa-
hae-si-k'i-da 화해시키다. 「ro-ha-da 폭로하다.

reveal *v.* na-t'a-nae-da 나타내다, po-i-da 보이다 ; p'ok-

revel *v.* ma-si-go hŭng-ch'ŏng-gŏ-ri-da 마시고 흥청거리
다, chŭl-gŏ-wŏ-ha-da 즐거워하다. —*n.* (*carousal*)
sul-jan-ch'i 술잔치. 「p'ok-ro 폭로.

revelation *n.* ① (*of God*) kye-si 계시. ② (*disclosure*)

revenge *n.* & *v.* pok-su(-ha-da) 복수(하다).

revenue *n.* (*annual income*) se-ip 세입 ; (*income*) su-
ip 수입 : ~ *stamp* su-ip-in-ji 수입인지.

revere v. sung-bae-ha-da 숭배하다.

reverence n. chon-gyŏng 존경, sung-bae 숭배.

reverend adj. chong-gyŏng-hal man-han 존경할 만한.

reverie·revery n. (*deep musing*) myŏng-sang 명상 ; (*daydream*) paek-il-mong 백일몽, hwan-sang 환상.

reverse v. kŏ-ggu-ro ha-da 거꾸로 하다, yŏk-dong-si-k'i-da 역동시키다. —n. yŏk 역(逆), pan-dae 반대.

revert v. (*return*) toe-do-ra-ga-da 되돌아가다.

review v. ① (*book*) p'yŏng-ron-ha-da 평론하다. ② (*lessons*) pok-sŭp-ha-da 복습하다. ③ (*troops*) yŏl-byŏng-ha-da 열병하다. —n. pok-sŭp 복습.

revile v. yok-ha-da 욕하다, yok-sŏl-ha-da 욕설하다.

revise v. kyo-jŏng-ha-da 교정하다.

revision n. kyo-jŏng 교정 ; (*book*) kae-jŏng-p'an 개정판.

revival n. pu-hwal 부활, chae-saeng 재생.

revive v. so-saeng-ha-da 소생하다, pu-hwal-ha-da 부활하다 ; pu-hŭng-ha-da 부흥하다. 「pal-lan 반란.

revolt v. pan-yŏk-ha-da 반역하다. —n. (*rebellion*)

revolution n. hyŏk-myŏng 혁명, hoe-jŏn 회전 : *the Industrial R~* san-ŏp hyŏk-myŏng 산업 혁명.

revolve v. tol-da 돌다, hoe-jŏn-ha-da 회전하다.

revolver n. yŏn-bal kwŏn-ch'ong 연발 권총.

reward n. ① po-su 보수, sang 상(賞). ② hyŏn-sang-gŭm 현상금. —v. po-su-rŭl chu-da 보수를 주다.

rewrite v. ta-si ssŭ-da 다시 쓰다, ko-ch'yŏ ssŭ-da 고

rheumatism n. ryu-mŏ-t'i-jŭm 류머티즘. 「쳐 쓰다.

rhythm n. yul-dong 율동, ŭm-yul 음율, ri-dŭm 리듬.

rib n. kal-bit-dae 갈빗대, nŭk-gol 늑골.

ribbon n. ri-bŏn 리번, tti 띠.

rice n. ssal 쌀, (*cooked*) pap 밥, (*cooked, polite form*) chin-ji 진지 ; (*unshelled*) pyŏ 벼.

rich adj. ton-man-ŭn 돈많은 ; p'ung-bu-han 풍부한 ;

(*color*) chi-t'ŭn 짙은.

riches *n.* chae-san 재산, chae-mul 재물, pu 부(富).

rick *n.* (*stack*) chip-ga-ri 짚가리. 「곱사등.

rickets *n.* ku-ru-byŏng 구루병(佝僂病), kop-sa-dŭng

rid *v.* (*free*) myŏn-ha-ge ha-da 면하게 하다, che-gŏ-ha-da 제거하다 : *get* ~ *of* pŏ-sŏ-na-da 벗어나다.

riddle *n.* su-su-gge-ggi 수수께끼, nan-mun 난문.

ride *v.* t'a-da 타다. —*n.* sŭng-ch'a 승차; sŭng-ma 승마.

ridge *n.* (*of mountain*) san-ma-ru 산마루, san-dŭng-sŏng-i 산등성이 ; (*of roof*) yong-ma-ru 용마루.

ridicule *n.* cho-rong 조롱. —*v.* cho-rong-ha-da 조롱하다.

ridiculous *adj.* u-sŭ-ggwang-sŭ-rŏ-un 우스꽝스러운.

rifle *n.* so-ch'ong 소총, ra-i-p'ŭl ch'ong 라이플 총.

rift *n.* kal-ra-jin t'ŭm 갈라진 틈. —*v.* jjo-gae-da 쪼개다.

rig *v.* chang-bi[ch'ae-bi]-ha-da 장비[채비]하다.

right *adj.* ① o-rŭn 옳은, chŏng-dang-han 정당한. ② o-rŭn-jjok-ŭi 오른쪽의. —*n.* kwŏl-li 권리. 「게.

rightly *adv.* pa-rŭ-ge 바르게, kong-jŏng-ha-ge 공정하

right-wing *n.* u-ik 우익(右翼), po-su-p'a 보수파.

rigid *adj.* kut-ŭn 굳은, (*strict*) ŏm-gyŏk-han 엄격한.

rigo(u)r *n.* ŏm-gyŏk 엄격 ; hok-dok-ham 혹독함.

rim *n.* ka-jang-ja-ri 가장자리, t'e 테.

rind *n.* (*skin, bark, peel*) kkŏp-jil 껍질.

ring *n.* (*circle*) ko-ri 고리 ; (*finger*) pan-ji 반지 ; (*ear*) kwi-go-ri 귀고리. —*v.* ul-ri-da 울리다.

rink *n.* sŭ-k'e-i-t'ŭ-jang 스케이트장.

rinse *v.* heng-gu-da 헹구다, ssit-da 씻다.

riot *n.* p'ok-dong 폭동, so-dong 소동. —*v.* p'ok-dong-ŭl i-rŭ-k'i-da 폭동을 일으키다.

rip *v.* jjit-da 찢다. —*n.* (*rent*) jjae-jin t'ŭm 째진 틈.

ripe *adj.* ik-ŭn 익은, wŏn-suk-han 원숙한.

ripen *v.* ik-da 익다, ik'-hi-da 익히다.

ripple *n*. chan-mul-gyŏl 잔물결.

rise *v*. ol-ra-ga-da 올라가다 ; i-rŏ-na-da 일어나다 ; (*sun*) ttŭ-da 뜨다. —*n*. sang-sŭng 상승, o-rŭm 오름.

risk *n*. wi-hŏm 위험. —*v*. (*venture*) nae-gŏl-da 내걸다 : ~ *one's life* mok-sum-ŭl kŏl-da 목숨을 걸다.

rite *n*. ŭi-sik 의식 ; kwan-sŭp 관습.

rival *n*. kyŏng-jaeng-ja 경쟁자 ; chŏk-su 적수. —*v*. kyŏng-jaeng-ha-da 경쟁하다, kyŏ-ru-da 겨루다.

river *n*. kang 강, nae 내.

rivulet *n*. si-nae 시내, sil-gae-ch'ŏn 실개천, kae-ul 개울.

road *n*. ① kil 길, chil-lo 진로. ② (*way*) pang-bŏp 방법.

ròadside *n*. kil-ga 길가, no-byŏn 노변.   「하다.

roam *v*. to-ra-da-ni-da 돌아다니다, pae-hoe-ha-da 배회

roar *v*. pu-rŭ-jit-da 부르짖다. —*n*. ① (*of animals*) ŭ-rŭ-rŏng-gŏ-rim 으르렁거림. ② (*of inanimate nature*) no-ho 노호. ③ (*of cannon*) p'o-sŏng 포성.

roast *n*. ku-un-go-gi 구운고기. —*v*. kup-da 굽다. —*adj*. ku-un 구운 : ~ *beef* pul-go-gi 불고기.

rob *v*. kang-t'al-ha-da 강탈하다, hum-ch'i-da 훔치다.

robber *n*. (*bandit*) kang-do 강도, to-duk 도둑.

robbery *n*. kang-t'al 강탈, yak-t'al 약탈.

robe *n*. ka-un 가운 ; (*pl*.) ye-bok 예복, pŏp-bok 법복.

robot *n*. ro-bot 로봇, in-jo in-gan 인조 인간.

robust *adj*. kang-gŏn-han 강건한, t'ŭn-t'ŭn-han 튼튼한.

rock *n*. pa-wi 바위. —*v*. hŭn-dŭl-da 흔들다.

rocket *n*. ① ro-k'et 로켓. ② (*beacon*) pong-hwa 봉화.

rod *n*. chang-dae 장대, (*stick*) mak-dae-gi 막대기.

rogue *n*. ak-han 악한(惡漢), kkang-p'ae 깡패.

roll *n*. ① (*of paper*) tu-ru-ma-ri 두루마리. ② (*list of names*) myŏng-bu 명부. ③ (*of ship*) yo-dong 요동. —*v*. ① kul-ri-da 굴리다. ② u-rŭ-rŭ ul-ri-da 우르르

roller *n*. ro-ul-rŏ 로울러.   「울리다.

romantic *adj.* nang-man-jŏk-in 낭만적인.   「괄량이.

romp *v.* ttwi-nol-da 뛰놀다. —*n.* mal-gwal-ryang-i 말

roof *n.* ① chi-bung 지붕. ② (*summit*) kkok-dae-gi 꼭
대기 : *live under the same* ~ tong-gŏ-ha-da 동거하다.

rook *n.* (*crow*) ttang-gga-ma-gwi 땅까마귀.

room *n.* ① (*chamber*) pang 방. ② (*space*) yŏ-ji 여지.

roommate *n.* han-bang ch'in-gu 한방 친구, tong-suk-

roost *n.* hwae 홰, po-gŭm-ja-ri 보금자리. ⌊ja 동숙자.

rooster *n.* su-t'ak 수탉.   「wŏn 근원.

root *n.* ① ppu-ri 뿌리, ki-ch'o 기초. ② (*cause*) kŭn-

rope *n.* pat-jul 밧줄, sae-ggi 새끼.

rosary *n.* (*Cath.*)(*beads*) ro-ja-ri-o 로자리오 ; (*Budd.*)
(*beads*) yŏm-ju 염주.   「무궁화.

rose *n.* chang-mi 장미 : ~ *of Sharon* mu-gung-hwa

rostrum *n.* yŏn-dan 연단, sŏl-gyo-dan 설교단.

rosy *adj.* ① chang-mi-bi-ch'ŭi 장미빛의, pal-gŭ-re-han
밝그레한. ② (*promising*) yu-mang-han 유망한.

rot *v.* ssŏk-da 썩다, pu-p'ae-ha-da 부패하다.

rotary *adj.* hoe-jŏn-ha-nŭn 회전하는.

rotate *v.* ① tol-da 돌다. ② kyo-dae-ha-da 교대하다.

rotation *n.* hoe-jŏn 회전, cha-jŏn 자전 ; sun-hwan 순
환 ; (*change in turn*) kyo-dae 교대.

rotten *adj.* ssŏk-ŭn 썩은, pu-p'ae-han 부패한.

rouge *n.* yŏn-ji 연지, ru-u-jŭ 루우즈.

rough *adj.* ① kŏ-ch'in 거친 ;(*uneven*) ul-t'ung-bul-t'ung-
-han 울퉁불퉁한. ② (*rude*) pŏ-rŭt-ŏp-nŭn 버릇없는.

round *adj.* tung-gŭn 둥근. —*prep.* chu-wi-e 주위에.
—*adv.* to-ra-sŏ 돌아서. —*n.* il-hoe-jŏn 일회전.

roundabout *adj.* to-ra-sŏ ka-nŭn 돌아서 가는.

roundup *n.* kŏm-gŏ 검거, ch'e-p'o 체포.

rouse *v.* kkae-u-da 깨우다 ; cha-gŭk-ha-da 자극하다.

route *n.* kil 길, (*line*) hang-ro 항로, no-sŏn 노선.

routine *n.* il-gwa 일과 ; ki-gye-jŏk chŏl-ch'a 기계적 절차.

rove *v.* (*wander about*) pae-hoe-ha-da 배회하다.

row *n.* ① (*line*) chul 줄, yŏl 열(列). ② (*disturbance*) pŏp-sŏk 법석. —*v.* no-jŏt-da 노젓다.

royal *adj.* kuk-wang-ŭi 국왕의 ; wi-ŏm-it-nŭn 위엄있는.

royalty *n.* ① wang-gwŏn 왕권. ② (*to owner*) sa-yong-ryo 사용료. ③ (*on a book*) in-se 인세(印稅).

rub *v.* pi-bi-da 비비다. —*n.* ma-ch'al 마찰.

rubber *n.* ko-mu 고무, chi-u-gae 지우개.

rubbish *n.* ssŭ-re-gi 쓰레기 ; chap-dong-sa-ni 잡동사니.

ruby *n.* hong-ok 홍옥, ru-u-bi 루우비.

rucksack *n.* pae-nang 배낭, ruk-jak 룩작. 「방향타.

rudder *n.* (*boat*) k'i 키, (*airplane*) pang-hyang-t'a

ruddy *adj.* pul-gŭ-re-han 불그레한 ; hong-an-ŭi 홍안의: ～ *cheeks* hong-an 홍안(紅顏).

rude *adj.* mu-rye-han 무례한, (*uneducated*) kyo-yang-ŏp-nŭn 교양없는 ; (*rough*) nan-p'ok-han 난폭한.

rue *v.* nwi-u-ch'i-da 뉘우치다, hu-hoe-ha-da 후회하다.

ruffian *n.* ak-dang 악당, kkang-p'ae 깡패.

ruffle *v.* hŭ-t'ŭ-rŏ-ddŭ-ri-da 흐트러뜨리다.

rug *n.* yang-t'an-ja 양탄자, ma-ru kkal-gae 마루 깔개.

rugged *adj.* ul-t'ung-bul-t'ung-han 울퉁불퉁한.

ruin *n.* ① (*destruction*) p'a-myŏl 파멸. ② (*impairment*) hwe-son 훼손. ③ (*remains*) p'ye-hŏ 폐허. —*v.* p'a-goe-ha-da 파괴하다, mang-ch'i-da 망치다.

rule *n.* ① kyu-ch'ik 규칙. ② (*control*) chi-bae 지배. —*v.* chi-bae-ha-da 지배하다 ; p'an-gyŏl-ha-da 판결하다.

ruler *n.* ① chi-bae-ja 지배자, t'ong-ch'i-ja 통치자. ② (*measure*) cha 자. 「dŏk so-ri 덜거덕 소리.

rumble *v.* u-rŭ-rŭ ul-ri-da 우르르 울리다. —*n.* tŏl-gŏ-

rumo(u)r *n.* so-mun 소문, p'ung-mun 풍문.

run *v.* ① tal-ri-da 달리다. ② (*flee*) to-mang-ga-da 도

망가다. ③ (*manage*) kyŏng-yŏng-ha-da 경영하다.

rural *adj.* si-gol-ŭi 시골의, chŏn-wŏn-ŭi 전원의 : ～
life chŏn-wŏn-saeng-hwal 전원생활.

ruse *n.* (*trick*) mo-ryak 모략, ch'aek-ryak 책략.

rush *n.* tol-jin 돌진, pun-mang 분망 : ～ *hour* hon-jap-
han si-gan 혼잡한 시간, rŏ-si-a-wŏ 러시아워. —*v.*
tol-jin-ha-da 돌진하다 ; tal-ryŏ-dŭl-da 달려들다.

rust *n.* nok 녹. —*v.* nok-sŭl-da 녹슬다.

rustic *adj.* si-gol-ddŭ-gi-ŭi 시골뜨기의. 「리가 나다.

rustle *v.* sal-rang-sal-rang so-ri-ga na-da 살랑살랑 소

rusty *adj.* nok-sŭ-rŭn 녹슬은 ; (*old*) nal-gŭn 낡은.

rut *n.* (*wheel track*) pa-k'wi cha-guk 바퀴 자국.

ruthless *adj.* mu-ja-bi-han 무자비한, in-jŏng-ŏp-nŭn
인정없는, (*cruel*) chan-in-han 잔인한.

rye *n.* ho-mil 호밀, ssal-bo-ri 쌀보리.

———◆≪ **S** ≫◆———

Sabbath *n.* an-sik-il 안식일.

saber · sabre *n.* kun-do 군도, sa-a-bŭ-rŭ 사아브르.

sabotage *n.* t'ae-ŏp 태업(怠業), sa-bo-t'a-a-ji 사보타아지.

saccharin *n.* sa-k'a-rin 사카린.

sack *n.* cha-ru 자루, pu-dae 부대, pong-ji 봉지.

sack dress cha-ru-ot 자루옷, saek-dŭ-re-sŭ 색드레스.

sacrament *n.* sŏng-rye 성례, sŏng-sa 성사(聖事).

sacred *adj.* sin-sŏng-han 신성한, kŏ-ruk-han 거룩한 ;
(*sin-e-ge*) pa-ch'in (신에게) 바친. 「하다.

sacrifice *n.* hŭi-saeng 희생. —*v.* hŭi-saeng-ha-da 희생

sad *adj.* sŭl-p'ŭn 슬픈, pi-ch'am-han 비참한.

saddle *n.* an-jang 안장, kil-ma 길마. —*v.* an-jang-ŭl
no-t'a 안장을 놓다. 「pi-t'an 비탄.

sadness *n.* sŭl-p'ŭm 슬픔, pi-ae 비애 ; (*mournfulness*)

safe *adj.* an-jŏn-han 안전한. —*n.* kŭm-go 금고.
safe-conduct *n.* an-jŏn t'ong-haeng-gwŏn〔jŭng〕 안전
safeguard *n.* po-ho 보호, ho-wi 호위.   〔통행권〔증〕.
safely *adv.* an-jŏn-ha-ge 안전하게, mu-sa-hi 무사히.
safety *n.* an-jŏn 안전 : ~ belt ku-myŏng-dae 구명대.
safety pin an-jŏn-p'in 안전핀.   「영리한.
sagacious *adj.* ch'ong-myŏng-han 총명한, yŏng-ri-han
sage *adj.* sŭl-gi-ro-un 슬기로운. —*n.* (*wise man*) hyŏn-
in 현인(賢人), sŏng-in 성인.
sail *n.* tot 돛. —*v.* (*navigate*) hang-hae-ha-da 항해
하다 ; (*airplane*) cho-jong-ha-da 조종하다.
sailing *n.* ch'ul-bŏm 출범, hang-hae 항해.
sailing boat tot-bae 돛배, pŏm-sŏn 범선.
sailor *n.* (*seaman*) sŏn-wŏn 선원 ; su-byŏng 수병.
saint *n.* sŏng-in 성인(聖人), sŏng-ja 성자.
sake *n.* mok-jŏk 목적 ; i-yu 이유 ; (*interest*) i-ik 이익 :
for the ~ of …ŭl wi-ha-yŏ …을 위하여.
salad *n.* sael-rŏ-dŭ 샐러드, saeng-ch'ae-yo-ri 생채요리.
salary *n.* pong-gŭp 봉급, kŭp-ryo 급료 : get a high ~
wŏl-gŭp-ŭl man-i pat-da 월급을 많이 받다.
sale *n.* p'an-mae 판매 : bargain ~ ssa-gu-ryŏ p'an-
mae 싸구려 판매, yŏm-ga p'an-mae 염가 판매.
salesman·saleswoman *n.* p'an-mae-wŏn 판매원, chŏm-
wŏn 점원 ; (*Am.*) oe-p'an-wŏn 외판원.
salient *adj.* hyŏn-jŏ-han 현저한, (*projecting*) tol-ch'ul-
saliva *n.* ch'im 침, t'a-aek 타액.   〔han 돌출한.
salmon *n.* yŏn-ŏ 연어.
saloon *n.* ① (*hall*) tae-ch'ŏng 대청. ② tam-hwa-sil 담
화실. ③ (*barroom*) sul-jip 술집.
salt *n.* so-gŭm 소금 ; the ~ of the earth se-sang-ŭi so-
gŭm 세상의 소금. —*v.* so-gŭm-ŭl ch'i-da 소금을 치다.
saltation *n.* (*leaping*) ttwi-gi 뛰기, to-yak 도약.

salty *adj.* jjan 짠, jjap-jjal-han 짭짤한.
salutation *n.* in-sa 인사, kyong-rye 경례 : *return one's* ~ tap-rye-ha-da 답례하다. 「rye 경례.
salute *v.* in-sa-ha-da 인사하다. —*n.* chŏl 절, kyŏng-
salvage *v.* (*salve*) ku-jo-ha-da 구조하다. —*n.* hae-nan-gu-jo 해난구조. 「gun 구세군.
salvation *n.* (*rescue*) ku-je 구제 : *S*~ *Army* ku-se-
salve *n.* ko-yak 고약. —*v.* ① ko-yak-ŭl pa-rŭ-da 고약 을 바르다. ② (*soothe*) tal-rae-da 달래다.
salvo *n.* ① il-je sa-gyŏk 일제 사격. ② ye-p'o 예포.
same *adj.* ka-t'ŭn 같은, tong-il-han 동일한.
sample *n.* kyŏn-bon 견본, p'yo-bon 표본.
sanatorium *n.* ① yo-yang-so 요양소. ② p'i-sŏ-ji 피서지.
sanctify *v.* sin-sŏng-hwa-ha-da 신성화하다.
sanction *n.* ① (*approval*) in-ga 인가 ; (*consent*) ch'an-sŏng 찬성. ② (*penalty*) che-jae 제재.
sanctuary *n.* sŏng-yŏk 성역, kŏ-ruk-han kot 거룩한 곳.
sand *n.* mo-rae 모래, (*pl.*) mo-rae-t'ŏp 모래톱.
sandbag *n.* mo-rae pu-dae 모래 부대, sa-nang 사낭.
sand bar mo-rae-t'op 모래톱, sa-ju 사주(砂洲).
sandstorm *n.* mo-rae p'ok-p'ung 모래 폭풍.
sandwich *n.* saen-dŭ-wi-ch'i 샌드위치.
sandy *adj.* mo-rae-ŭi 모래의, mo-rae-bi-ch'ŭi 모래빛의.
sane *adj.* (*sound*) che-jŏng-sin-ŭi 제정신의.
sanguine *adj.* ta-hyŏl-jil-ŭi 다혈질의, p'i-ŭi 피의.
sanitary *adj.* wi-saeng-ŭi 위생의 ; *a* ~ *inspector* wi-saeng kŏm-sa-gwan 위생 검사관.
sanitation *n.* kong-jung wi-saeng 공중 위생. 「미치다.
sanity *n.* che-jŏng-sin 제정신 : *lose one's* ~ mi-ch'i-da
Santa Claus san-t'a-k'ŭl-ro-o-sŭ ha-ra-bŏ-ji 산타클로오 스 할아버지. 「ryŏk 활력.
sap *n.* (*of trees*) su-aek 수액(樹液) ; (*vigor*) hwal-

sapling n. ① (*tree*) ŏ-rin-na-mu 어린나무. ② (*youth*) p'ut-na-gi 풋나기, ae-song-i 애송이.

sapphire n. sa-p'a-i-ŏ 사파이어, ch'ŏng-ok 청옥(靑玉).

sarcastic adj. pi-ggo-nŭn 비꼬는, pin-jŏng-dae-nŭn 빈 정대는, (*mocking*) nol-ri-nŭn 놀리는.

sardine n. chŏng-ŏ-ri 정어리.

sarira n. (*Sans.*) (*Buddha*'s *bone*) sa-ri 사리(舍利).

sash n. ① chang-sik-ddi 장식띠, (*shoulder strap*) kyŏn-jang 견장(肩章). ② (*of window*) sae-si 새시.

Satan n. ak-ma 악마, sa-t'an 사탄.

satchel n. hak-saeng ka-bang 학생 가방, chak-ŭn ka-bang 작은 가방.

satellite n. wi-sŏng 위성.

satellite communication wi-sŏng t'ong-sin 위성 통신.

satin n. kong-dan 공단, su-ja 수자.

satire n. p'ung-ja 풍자, pin-jŏng-daem 빈정댐.

satisfaction n. man-jok 만족, hŭp-jok 흡족.

satisfactory adj. ① man-jok-han 만족한, ch'ung-bun-han 충분한. ② (*adequate*) chŏk-jŏl-han 적절한.

satisfy v. man-jok-si-k'i-da 만족시키다.

saturate v. p'uk chŏk-si-da 푹 적시다, tam-gŭ-da 담그다.

Saturday n. t'o-yo-il 토요일.

sauce n. sŏ-yang kan-jang 서양 간장, so-o-sŭ 소오스.

saucepan n. sŭ-t'yu-u nam-bi 스튜우 남비.

saucer n. pat-ch'im chŏp-si 받침 접시.

saucy adj. ① (*pert*) kŏn-bang-jin 건방진 ; yŏm-ch'i-ŏp-nŭn 염치없는. ② (*smart*) nal-ssin-han 날씬한.

sausage n. so-si-ji 소시지, sun-dae 순대.

savage adj. ya-man-ŭi 야만의. —n. ya-man-in 야만인.

save v. ① ku-ha-da 구하다. ② (*hoard*) chŏ-ch'uk-ha-da 저축하다. —prep. ···ŭl che-oe-ha-go ···을 제외하고.

savings n. chŏ-gŭm 저금, chŏ-ch'uk 저축.

savings bank chŏ-ch'uk ŭn-haeng 저축 은행.

savio(u)r *n.* (*Jesus Christ*) ku-se-ju 구세주, kŭ-ri-sŭ-do 그리스도 ; (*rescuer*) ku-jo-ja 구조자.

savo(u)r *n.* mat 맛, p'ung-mi 풍미, hyang-gi 향기.

saw *n.* t'op 톱. —*v.* t'op-jil-ha-da 톱질하다. 「제재용 톱.

sawmill *n.* ① che-jae-so 제재소. ② che-jae-yong t'op

say *v.* mal-ha-da 말하다 ; i-rŭl-t'e-myŏn 이를테면 ; i-bwa 이봐, cham-ggan-man 잠깐만.

saying *n.* mal 말 ; (*proverb*) sok-dam 속담.

scab *n.* sang-ch'ŏ-ŭi ttak-ji 상처의 딱지 ; om 옴.

scabbard *n.* (*sheath*) k'al-jip 칼집.

scabby *adj.* ttak-ji-t'u-sŏng-i-ŭi 딱지투성이의, tŏ-rŏ-un

scabies *n.* om 옴. [더러운 ; in-saek-han 인색한.

scaffold *n.* ① pal-p'an 발판. ② kyo-su-dae 교수대.

scald *v.* te-ge ha-da 데게 하다, te-ch'i-da 데치다.

scale *n.* ① (*of fish*) pi-nŭl 비늘. ② (*map*) ch'ŏk-do 척도 ; kyu-mo 규모. ③ (*weighing machine*) chŏl-ul

scamper *v.* kŭp-hi tal-ri-da 급히 달리다. [저울.

scan *v.* cha-se-hi cho-sa-ha-da 자세히 조사하다.

scandal *n.* (*disgrace*) ch'u-mun 추문, ch'ang-p'i 창피, sŭ-k'aen-dŭl 스캔들. 「han 인색한.

scanty *adj.* mo-ja-ra-nŭn 모자라는 ; (*sparing*) in-saek-

scar *n.* hyung-t'ŏ 흉터, hŭm 흠 ; hŭn-jŏk 흔적.

scarce *adj.* pu-jok-han 부족한, (*rare*) tŭ-mun 드문.

scarcely *adv.* kan-sin-hi 간신히 ; ka-gga-sŭ-ro 가까스로 ; kŏ-ŭi …ŏp-da 거의 …없다.

scarcity *n.* pu-jok 부족 ; sik-ryang-nan 식량난.

scare *v.* nol-ra-ge ha-da 놀라게 하다. —*n.* kong-p'o 공

scarecrow *n.* hŏ-su-a-bi 허수아비. [포.

scarf *n.* mok-do-ri 목도리, sŭ-k'a-a-p'ŭ 스카아프.

scarlet *n.* chin-hong-saek 진홍색. 「하다.

scatter *v.* hŭt-bbu-ri-da 흩뿌리다, pun-san-ha-da 분산

scene *n.* ① kwang-gyŏng 광경. ② (*theatre*) mu-dae 무

대. ③ (*movie*) chang-myŏn 장면.
scenery *n.* kyŏng-ch'i 경치, p'ung-gyŏng 풍경.
scent *n.* naem-sae 냄새, (*perfume*) hyang-su 향수.
sceptical *adj.* ŭi-sim-man-ŭn 의심많은.
schedule *n.* si-gan-p'yŏ 시간표, ye-jŏng-p'yo 예정표.
scheme *n.* ① (*plan*) kye-hoek 계획. ② (*intrigue*) ŭm-mo 음모. ③ (*system*) ch'e-gye 체계.   「do 학도.
scholar *n.* (*learned man*) hak-ja 학자 ; (*student*) hak-
scholarship *n.* ① (*learning*) hak-mun 학문, hak-sik 학식. ② (*grant*) chang-hak-gŭm 장학금.
school *n.* ① hak-gyo 학교, su-ŏp 수업 : *primary* ～ kuk-min-hak-gyo 국민학교/*middle* ～ chung-hak-gyo 중학교/*high* ～ ko-dŭng-hak-gyo 고등학교/*a graduate* ～ tae-hak-wŏn 대학원. ② (*doctrinal faction*)
schoolboy *n.* nam-hak-saeng 남학생.   [hak-p'a 학파.
schoolfellow *n.* tong-ch'ang 동창, hak-u 학우.
schoolgirl *n.* yŏ-hak-saeng 여학생.   「sa 교장 관사.
schoolhouse *n.* ① kyo-sa 교사(校舍). ② kyo-jang kwan-
school inspector *n.* chang-hak-sa〔gwan〕 장학사〔관〕.
schoolmaster *n.* kyo-wŏn 교원 ; kyo-jang 교장.
schoolmate *n.* tong-ch'ang 동창, hak-u 학우.
schoolroom *n.* (*classroom*) kyo-sil 교실.
science *n.* kwa-hak 과학, hak-sul 학술, …hak …학 (學) : *political* ～ chŏng-ch'i-hak 정치학. 「과학 소설.
science fiction *n.* (kong-sang) kwa-hak so-sŏl (공상)
scientific *adj.* kwa-hak-jŏk-in 과학적인, kwa-hak-ŭi
scientist *n.* kwa-hak-ja 과학자.   [과학의.
scissors *n.* ka-wi 가위.
scoff *n.* & *v.* (*jeer*) cho-rong(-ha-da) 조롱(하다).
scold *v.* kku-jit-da 꾸짖다, ya-dan-ch'i-da 야단치다.
scoop *n.* kuk-ja 국자, pu-sap 부삽.
scope *n.* (*range*) pŏm-wi 범위 ; (*room*) yŏ-ji 여지.

scorch *v.* kŭ-sŭl-ri-da 그슬리다, te-da 데다.

score *n.* tŭk-jŏm 득점 ; (*pl.*) ta-su 다수. —*v.* tŭk-jŏm-ha-da 득점하다, ki-rok-ha-da 기록하다.

scorn *n.* & *v.* myŏl-si(-ha-da) 멸시(하다).

scorpion *n.* chŏn-gal 전갈.

scoundrel *n.* ak-dang 악당, ak-han 악한.「샅샅이 뒤지다.

scour *v.* kal-go tak-da 갈고 닦다, sat-sa-ch'i twi-ji-da

scout *n.* chŏng-ch'al-byŏng 정찰병 ; so-nyŏn〔so-nyŏ〕 tan-wŏn 소년〔소녀〕단원. —*v.* sŭ-k'a-u-t'ŭ-ha-da 스카

scowl *v.* jji-p'u-ri-da 찌푸리다.   〔우트하다.

scramble *v.* ① (*climb*) ki-ŏ-o-rŭ-da 기어오르다. ② (*struggle*) ta-t'u-ŏ ppae-at-da 다투어 빼앗다.

scrap *n.* cho-gak 조각, sŭ-k'ŭ-raep 스크랩.

scrape *v.* mun-ji-rŭ-da 문지르다, kŭk-da 긁다.

scratch *n.* kŭl-ggi 긁기. —*v.* kŭk-da 긁다.

scream *n.* a-u-sŏng 아우성, pi-myŏng 비명. —*v.* a-u-sŏng-ch'i-da 아우성치다.

screen *n.* ① pyŏng-p'ung 병풍, kan-mak-i 간막이. ② (*movie*) yŏng-sa-mak 영사막, sŭ-k'ŭ-ri-in 스크리인.

screw *n.* na-sa 나사, sŭ-k'ŭ-ru-u 스크루우.

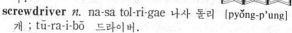

[pyŏng-p'ung]

screwdriver *n.* na-sa tol-ri-gae 나사 돌리 개 ; tŭ-ra-i-bŏ 드라이버.

scribble *n.* nan-p'il 난필. —*v.* kal-gyŏ ssŭ-da 갈겨 쓰다.

scribe *n.* tae-so 대서(代書), p'il-gi-ja 필기자, sŏ-gi 서기 ; (*Judaism*) yul-bŏp-hak-ja 율법학자.

script *n.* ① ssŭn kŭl-ja 쓴 글자, p'il-gi-ch'e hwal-ja 필기체 활자. ② (*play*) kak-bon 각본, tae-bon 대본, sŭ-k'ŭ-rip-t'ŭ 스크립트.

scripture *n.* sŏng-gyŏng 성경, (*sacred books*) kyŏng-jŏn 경전.

scroll *n.* ① tu-ru-ma-ri 두루마리. ② mok-rok 목록.
scrub *n.* tŏm-bul 덤불. —*v.* puk-buk mun-ji-rŭ-da 북
북 문지르다, puk-buk tak-da 북북 닦다. 「한.
scrupulous *adj.* sin-jung-han 신중한, se-sim-han 세심
scrutiny *n.* ① myŏn-mil-han cho-sa 면밀한 조사 ; ŭm-
mi 음미. ② t'u-p'yo chae-gŏm-sa 투표 재검사.
sculptor *n.* cho-gak-ga 조각가.
sculpture *n.* cho-gak 조각, cho-gak-sul 조각술.
scurry *v.* chong-jong-gŏ-rŭm-ŭ-ro tal-ri-da 종종걸음으
scythe *n.* (*sickle*) k'ŭn nat 큰 낫. 「로 달리다.
sea *n.* pa-da 바다 : *the East S~* tong-hae 동해.
sea bathing hae-su-yok 해수욕.
seacoast *n.* pa-dat-ga 바닷가, hae-an 해안, hae-byŏn 해
sea gull kal-mae-gi 갈매기. 「변.
seal *n.* ① (*animal*) pa-da-p'yo-bŏm 바다표범. ② (*mark*)
to-jang 도장, pong-in 봉인. —*v.* na-rin-ha-da 날인하
다 ; pong-in-ha-da 봉인하다.
seam *n.* sol-gi 솔기. —*v.* kkwe-mae-da 꿰매다.
seaman *n.* sŏn-wŏn 선원, su-byŏng 수병. 「재봉사.
seamstress *n.* ch'im-mo 침모 ; yŏ-ja chae-bong-sa 여자
search *v.* ch'at-da 찾다, su-saek-ha-da 수색하다. —*n.*
su-saek 수색, t'am-saek 탐색. 「어치라이트.
searchlight *n.* t'am-jo-dŭng 탐조등, sŏ-ŏ-ch'i-ra-i-t'ŭ 서
seashore *n.* hae-byŏn 해변, hae-an 해안, pa-dat-ga 바
seasickness *n.* paet-mŏl-mi 뱃멀미. 「닷가.
season *n.* ① kye-jŏl 계절. ② (*right time*) ho-gi 호기.
—*v.* (*flavor*) kan-ŭl mat-ch'u-da 간을 맞추다.
seat *n.* cha-ri 자리. —*v.* an-ch'i-da 앉히다 : *Please ~
yourself.* Pu-di an-jŭ-se-yo. 부디 앉으세요.
seaweed *n.* hae-ch'o 해초 : *brown ~* mi-yŏk 미역.
seclude *v.* (*separate*) tte-ŏ-no-t'a 떼어놓다; (*withdraw*)
ŭn-t'oe-si-k'i-da 은퇴시키다.

second *adj.* tul-jjae-ŭi 둘째의. —*n.* (*time*) ch'o 초(秒).
secondary *adj.* che i-wi-ŭi 제 2위의, pu-ch'a-jŏk 부차적.
second-hand *adj.* muk-ŭn 묵은, chung-go-ŭi 중고의.
　—*n.* ① chung-go-p'um 중고품. ② (*clock*) ch'o-ch'im
secrecy *n.* pi-mil 비밀, ŭn-mil 은밀.　　　　　⌊초침.
secret *n.* pi-mil 비밀. —*adj.* pi-mil-ŭi 비밀의.
secretary *n.* pi-sŏ 비서, sŏ-gi 서기, pi-sŏ-gwan 비서관;
　(*Am. gov.*) chang-gwan 장관: *the S~ of State*
　kuk-mu-jang-gwan 국무장관.
secretion *n.* ① pun-bi(-mul) 분비(물). ② ŭn-nik 은닉.
sect *n.* kyo-p'a 교파; tang-p'a 당파; hak-p'a 학파.
section *n.* ku-bun 구분; (*area*) chi-gu 지구; (*office*)
　kwa[pu] 과[부]. —*v.* ku-bun[ku-hoek]-ha-da 구분
　[구획]하다: *a personnel ~* in-sa-gwa 인사과.
secular *adj.* se-sok-jŏk 세속적, hyŏn-se-ŭi 현세의.
secure *v.* (*make safe*) an-jŏn-ha-ge ha-da 안전하게 하
　다; (*obtain*) hoek-dŭk-ha-da 획득하다. —*adj.* an-jŏn-
　han 안전한, (*sure*) hwak-sil-han 확실한.
security *n.* an-jŏn 안전, po-jŭng 보증: *S~ Council(U.
　N.)* an-jŏn-bo-jang i-sa-hoe 안전보장 이사회.
seduce *v.* yu-hok-ha-da 유혹하다, kkoe-da 꾀다.
see *v.* ① po-da 보다. ② (*meet*) man-na-da 만나다. ③
　(*understand*) i-hae-ha-da 이해하다. ④ (*escort*) pae-
　ung-ha-da 배웅하다. ⑤ (*attend*) tol-bo-da 돌보다.
seed *n.* ssi 씨, yŏl-mae 열매, chong-ja 종자.
seeing *n.* po-gi 보기, si-gak 시각(視覺): *S~ is be-
　lieving.* Paek-mun-i pu-ryŏ-il-gyŏn. 백문이 불여일견.
seek *v.* ch'at-da 찾다, (*ask for*) ku-ha-da 구하다.
seem *v.* (*appear*) …ch'ŏ-rŏm po-i-da …처럼 보이다.
seeming *adv. & adj.* oe-gwan-sang(-ŭi) 외관상(의).
　—*n.* oe-gwan 외관, oe-yang 외양.
seesaw *n.* si-i-so-o 시이소오, nŏl-ddwi-gi 널뛰기.

segment *n.* kkŭn·ŭn cho-gak 끊은 조각 ; pun-jŏl 분절.

segregate *v.* kyŏk-ri-ha-da 격리하다.

seize *v.* ① (*grasp*) chap-da 잡다. ② (*understand*) p'a-ak-ha-da 파악하다. ③ (*arrest*) ch'e-p'o-ha-da 체

seizure *n.* ap-ryu 압류, kang-t'al 강탈. ⌐포하다.

seldom *adj.* tŭ-mul-ge 드물게, kan-hok 간혹, chom-ch'ŏ-rŏm …an-nŭn 좀처럼 …않는.

select *v.* ko-rŭ-da 고르다, sŏn-t'aek-ha-da 선택하다. —*adj.* ch'u-ryŏ-naen 추려낸.

self *n.* cha-gi 자기, cha-a 자아(自我).

self-centred *adj.* cha-gi chung-sim-ŭi 자기 중심의.

self-confident *adj.* cha-sin-it-nŭn 자신있는.

self-education *n.* tok-hak 독학, ko-hak 고학.

self-indulgence *n.* oe-go-jip 외고집, pang-jong 방종.

self-interest *n.* sa-ri 사리, sa-yok 사욕.

selfish *adj.* i-gi-jŏk 이기적, i-gi-ju-ŭi-jŏk-in 이기주의적인.

self-satisfaction *n.* cha-gi man-jok 자기 만족.

sell *v.* p'al-da 팔다, (*be sold*) p'al-ri-da 팔리다.

seller *n.* p'a-nŭn sa-ram 파는 사람, p'an-mae-in 판매

semblance *n.* yu-sa 유사 ; oe-gwan 외관. ⌐인.

semester *n.* hak-gi 학기(學期).

seminar *n.* yŏn-gu-ban 연구반, se-mi-na-a 세미나아.

seminary *n.* (*a divinity school*) sin-hak-gyo 신학교 ; hak-wŏn 학원 ; yang-sŏng-so 양성소.

senate *n.* ① wŏl-lo-wŏn 원로원. ② sang-wŏn 상원.

senator *n.* sang-wŏn ŭi-wŏn 상원 의원.

send *v.* po-nae-da 보내다, pu-ch'i-da 부치다.

sender *n.* ① po-nae-nŭn sa-ram 보내는 사람, pal-song-in 발송인. ② song-sin-gi 송신기.

senior *adj.* son-wi-ŭi 손위의, yŏn-sang-ŭi 연상의. —*n.* (*elder*) yŏn-jang-ja 연장자, sŏn-bae 선배.

sensation *n.* ① kam-gak 감각. ② k'ŭn hwa-je 큰 화제,

sen-se-i-syŏn 센세이션.

sense *n.* ① kam-gak 감각 ; (*five senses*) o-gwan 오관; pun-byŏl 분별. ② (*meaning*) ttŭt 뜻.

senseless *adj.* mu-gam-gak-ŭi 무감각의. 「식한.

sensible *adj.* pun-byŏl-it-nŭn 분별있는 ; ŭi-sik-han 의

sensitive *adj.* min-gam-han 민감한, sin-gyŏng-gwa-min-ŭi 신경과민의. 「음란한.

sensual *adj.* kwan-nŭng-jŏk-in 관능적인, ŭm-ran-han

sentence *n.* ① mun-jang 문장. ② (*for crime*) sŏn-go 선고, ŏn-do 언도. —*v.* sŏn-go-ha-da 선고하다.

sentiment *n.* kam-jŏng 감정, chŏng-sŏ 정서.

sentimental *adj.* kam-sang-jŏk-in 감상적인.

sentry *n.* po-ch'o 보초, p'a-su-byŏng 파수병. 「수도.

Seoul *n.* sŏ-ul 서울 ; tae-han-min-guk su-do 대한민국

separate *v.* tte-ŏ-no-t'a 떼어놓다, pul-li-ha-da 분리하다. —*adj.* pul-li-doen 분리된.

separation *n.* pul-li 분리, pul-lyu 분류(分類).

September *n.* ku-wŏl 구월.

sequel *n.* kye-sok 계속 ; sok-p'yŏn 속편, hu-p'yŏn 후편.

sequence *n.* yŏn-sok 연속 ; sun-sŏ 순서.

serenade *n.* so-ya-gok 소야곡, se-re-na-dŭ 세레나드.

serene *adj.* ch'ŏng-myŏng-han 청명한, hwa-ch'ang-han 화창한 ; (*tranquil*) ch'im-ch'ak-han 침착한.

serf *n.* nong-no 농노(農奴) ; no-ye 노예.

serge *n.* sa-a-ji 사아지, se-ru 세루. 「sa 중사.

sergeant *n.* ha-sa-gwan 하사관, sang-sa 상사, chung-

serial *adj.* yŏn-sok-jŏk-in 연속적인 : ∼ *number* il-lyŏn pŏn-ho 일련 번호 : kun-bŏn 군번(軍番).

sericulture *n.* yang-jam-ŏp 양잠업(養蠶業).

series *n.* yŏn-sok 연속 ; ch'ong-sŏ 총서.

serious *adj.* (*grave*) chin-ji-han 진지한 ; (*critical*) chung-dae-han 중대한: *a* ∼ *illness* chung-byŏng 중병.

seriously *adv.* sim-gak-ha-ge 심각하게, chin-ji-ha-ge 진지하게.

sermon *n.* sŏl-gyo 설교, hun-gye 훈계.

serpent *n.* (*snake*) paem 뱀.

servant *n.* ha-in 하인, chong 종 : *a man* ~ ha-in 하인, mŏ-sŭm 머슴/*a maid* ~ ha-nyŏ 하녀.

serve *v.* sŏm-gi-da 섬기다, si-jung-ŭl tŭl-da 시중을 들다.

service *n.* ① (*employ*) ko-yong 고용, pong-sa 봉사. ② (*devotion to God*) ye-bae 예배. ③ (*official duty*) kŭn-mu 근무. ④ (*conscription*) pyŏng-yŏk 병역. ⑤ (*treatment in hotels*) chŏp-dae 접대.

serviceable *adj.* (*useful*) ssŭl-mo-it-nŭn 쓸모있는, p'yŏl-li-han 편리한 ; (*obliging*) ch'in-jŏl-han 친절한.

service station chu-yu-so 주유소.

session *n.* (*cong.*) kae-hoe 개회 ; hoe-gi 회기.

set *v.* ① (*put*) tu-da 두다. ② (*start*) ch'ak-su-ha-da 착수하다. ③ (*impose*) pu-gwa-ha-da 부과하다. *—adj.* (*fixed*) ko-jŏng-doen 고정된. *—n.* han cho 한 조(組).

setback *n.* pang-hae 방해 ; yŏk-ryu 역류(逆流).

setting *n.* (*plays*) mu-dae chang-ch'i 무대 장치.

settle *v.* cha-ri-jap-da 자리잡다 ; (*decide*) kyŏl-jŏng-ha-da 결정하다 ; (*solve*) hae-gyŏl-ha-da 해결하다.

settlement *n.* chŏng-ch'ak 정착(定着) ; (*conclusion*) hae-gyŏl 해결 ; (*colony*) kŏ-ryu-ji 거류지.

settler *n.* kae-ch'ŏk-min 개척민, i-ju-min 이주민.

seven *n. & adj.* il-gop(-ŭi) 일곱(의), ch'il 7.

seventeen *n.* yŏl-il-gop 열일곱, sip-ch'il 17.

Seventh-Day Adventists an-sik-gyo 안식교. 70(의).

seventy *n. & adj.* il-hŭn(-ŭi) 일흔(의), ch'il-sip(-ui) 칠십(의).

sever *v.* kkŭn-t'a 끊다, chŏl-dan-ha-da 절단하다.

several *adj.* myŏt-myŏ-ch'ŭi 몇몇의. *—n.* myŏt kae 몇개.

severe *adj.* ŏm-gyŏk-han 엄격한, sim-han 심한.

severity *n.* ŏm-gyŏk 엄격 ; hok-dok 혹독.

sew *v.* pa-nŭ-jil-ha-da 바느질하다, chae-bong-ha-da 재

sewage *n.* si-gung-ch'ang 시궁창. ⌐봉하다.

sewer *n.* ① (*ditch*) ha-su-do 하수도. ② (*butler*) u-du-mŏ-ri kŭp-sa 우두머리 급사. ③ (*seamstress*) chae-bong-sa 재봉사, ch'im-mo 침모.

sewing *n.* pa-nŭ-jil 바느질, chae-bong 재봉 : ~ *machine* chae-bong-t'ŭl 재봉틀. ⌐sŏng 남성.

sex *n.* sŏng 성(性), sŏng-byŏl 성별 : *the male* ~ nam-

sexual *adj.* nam-nyŏ-ŭi 남녀의, sŏng-jŏk-in 성적인 : ~ *appetite* sŏng-yok 성욕/~ *disease* sŏng-byŏng 성병.

shabby *adj.* ch'o-ra-han 초라한, kkoe-joe-han 꾀죄한.

shack *n.* p'an-ja-jip 판자집, t'ong-na-mu-jip 통나무집.

shackle *n.* su-gap 수갑, soe-go-rang 쇠고랑.

shade *n.* kŭ-nŭl 그늘 ; (*blind*) ch'a-yang 차양.

shadow *n.* kŭ-rim-ja 그림자. ⌐su-sang-han 수상한.

shady *adj.* kŭ-nŭl-jin 그늘진 ; (*of dubious character*)

shaft *n.* hwa-sal-dae 화살대, kul-dae 굴대.

shaggy *adj.* t'ŏl-i man-ŭn 털이 많은. ⌐수하다.

shake *v.* hŭn-dŭl-da 흔들다 ; (*hands*) ak-su-ha-da 악

shall *aux.v.* …il(hal) kŏ-si-da …일〔할〕 것이다.

shallow *adj.* ya-t'ŭn 얕은 ; ch'ŏn-bak-han 천박한 : *a* ~ *mind* ch'ŏn-bak-han ma-ŭm 천박한 마음.

sham *n. & adj.* sok-im-su(-ŭi) 속임수(의), ka-jja(-ŭi) 가짜(의) : *a* ~ *exam* mo-ŭi si-hŏm 모의 시험.

Shamanism *n.* mu-gyo 무교, sya-mŏn-gyo 샤면교.

shamble *n.* to-sal-jang 도살장, su-ra-jang 수라장.

shame *n.* pu-ggŭ-rŏ-um 부끄러움, su-ch'i 수치.

shamefaced *adj.* su-jup-ŏ-ha-nŭn 수줍어하는, am-ddin

shameful *adj.* su-ch'i-sŭ-rŏ-un 수치스러운. ⌐암면.

shameless *adj.* yŏm-ch'i-ŏp-nŭn 염치없는.

shampoo *v.* mŏ-ri-rŭl kam-da 머리를 감다. —*n.* syaem-p'u-u 샘푸우.

shank *n.* ① (*shin*) chŏng-gang-i 정강이. ② (*handle*) cha-ru 자루, son-jap-i 손잡이.

shape *n.* mo-yang 모양. —*v.* hyŏng-sŏng-ha-da 형성하다.

share *n.* ① mok 몫. ② (*stock*) chu-sik 주식. —*v.* ① pae-dang-ha-da 배당하다. ② ka-ch'i-ha-da 같이하다.

sharecropper *n.* so-jak-in 소작인.

shark *n.* ① sang-ŏ 상어. ② yok-sim-jang-i 욕심장이.

sharp *adj.* nal-k'a-ro-un 날카로운. —*adv.* nal-k'a-rop-ge 날카롭게 : *Look* ~! Cho-sim-ha-yŏ-ra! 조심하여라!

sharpen *v.* nal-k'a-rop-ge ha-da 날카롭게 하다 ; kal-da 갈다 ; kkak-da 깎다.

shatter *v.* pu-su-da 부수다 ; kkŏk-da 꺾다 : ~ *one's hopes* hŭi-mang-ŭl kkŏk-da 희망을 꺾다.

shave *v.* myŏn-do-ha-da 면도하다. —*n.* myŏn-do 면도.

shawl *n.* syo-ol 쇼올, ŏ-ggae-gŏ-ri 어깨걸이.

she *pron.* kŭ-nyŏ-nŭn〔ga〕 그녀는〔가〕.

sheaf *n.* ta-bal 다발, mu-ggŭm 묶음.   「wi 큰 가위.

shear *v.* pe-da 베다, cha-rŭ-da 자르다. —*n.* k'ŭn ka-

sheath *n.* k'al-jip 칼집, (*cover*) chip 집.

shed *v.* (*drop off*) t'ŏl-da 털다 ; (*tears*) hŭl-ri-da 흘리다. —*n.* (*hut*) o-du-mak 오두막, hŏt-gan 헛간.

sheen *n.* kwang-ch'ae 광채, (*lustre*) yun 윤.

sheep *n.* yang 양, myŏn-yang 면양.

sheer *adj.* sun-jŏn-han 순전한 ; (*steep*) ka-p'a-rŭn 가파른: *a* ~ *cliff* ka-p'a-rŭn pyŏ-rang 가파른 벼랑.

sheet *n.* hot-i-bul 홑이불, si-i-t'ŭ 시이트 ; (*piece of paper*) chong-i han chang 종이 한 장.

shelf *n.* sŏn-ban 선반, si-rŏng 시렁.

shell *n.* ① kkŏp-jil 껍질. ② (*gun*) p'o-t'an 포탄. ③ cho-

shellfire *n.* p'o-hwa 포화(砲火).   「gae 조개

shelter *n.* tae-p'i-so 대피소, p'i-nan-ch'ŏ 피난처. —*v.* p'i-nan-ha-da 피난하다 ; sum-gi-da 숨기다.

shelve v. sŏn-ban-e ŏn-da 선반에 얹다 ; po-ryu-ha-da 보류하다 ; (*ignore*) muk-sal-ha-da 묵살하다.

shepherd n. yang-ch'i-nŭn sa-ram 양치는 사람.

sheriff n. (*Am.*) kun po-an-gwan 군(郡) 보안관 ; chu chang-gwan 주(州) 장관.

shield v. po-ho-ha-da 보호하다. —n. pang-p'ae 방패.

shiftless adj. sok-su-mu-ch'aek-ŭi 속수무책의.

shimmer n. ka-mul-gŏ-ri-nŭn pit 가물거리는 빛. —v. ka-mul-gŏ-ri-da 가물거리다. 「기어오르다.

shin n. chŏng-gang-i 정강이. —v. (*climb*) ki-ŏ-o-rŭ-da

shine v. ① pit-na-da 빛나다, pan-jjak-i-da 반짝이다. ② (*polish*) tak-da 닦다. —n. haet-bit 햇빛, il-gwang 일광.

ship n. pae 배. —v. su-song-ha-da 수송하다 : *sailing* ~ pŏm-sŏn 범선. 「주.

shipowner n. sŏn-bak so-yu-ja 선박 소유자, sŏn-ju 선

shipping company hae-un-hoe-sa 해운회사.

shipwreck n. nan-p'a 난파(難破) ; nan-p'a-sŏn 난파선.

shipyard n. cho-sŏn-so 조선소.

shirk v. (*evade*) p'i-ha-da 피하다, hoe-p'i-ha-da 회피

shirt n. wa-i-syŏ-ŏ-ch'ŭ 와이셔어츠. 「하다.

shiver v. ttŏl-da 떨다. —n. chŏn-yul 전율.

shoal n. yŏ-ul 여울 ; (*crowd*) tte 떼, mu-ri 무리.

shock n. ch'ung-gyŏk 충격, syo-k'ŭ 쇼크.

shoe n. ku-du 구두, tan-hwa 단화, (*Korean*) sin 신 : *rubber* ~s ko-mu-sin 고무신.

shoebrush n. ku-dut-sol 구둣솔.

shoehorn n. ku-dut-ju-gŏk 구둣주걱.

shoelace n. (*shoestring*) ku-du-ggŭn 구두끈.

shoemaker n. ku-du ko-ch'i-nŭn sa-ram 구두 고치는 사람, che-hwa-gong 제화공.

shoe polish ku-du-yak 구두약.

shoeshine n. ku-du-dak-ggi 구두닦기.

shoot *n.* sa-gyŏk 사격. —*v.* sso-da 쏘다.

shooting *n.* sa-gyŏk 사격, (*hunting*) sa-nyang 사냥.

shop *n.* ka-ge 가게, sang-jŏm 상점 ; (*workshop*) kong-jang 공장 ; chak-ŏp-jang 작업장.

shopkeeper *n.* ka-ge chu-in 가게 주인, (*retailer*) so-mae sang-in 소매 상인. 「주인.

shopman *n.* ① chŏm-wŏn 점원. ② ka-ge chu-in 가게

shopping *n.* chang-bo-gi 장보기, mul-gŏn sa-gi 물건 사기, syo-p'ing 쇼핑.

shore *n.* mul[kang]-ga 물[강]가, hae-an 해안.

short *adj.* jjal-bŭn 짧은 ; pu-jok-han 부족한 ; (*blunt*) mu-dduk-dduk-han 무뚝뚝한. —*n.* (*pl.*) pan-ba-ji 반 「바지.

shortage *n.* pu-jok 부족, kyŏl-p'ip 결핍.

shorten *v.* jjal-gge ha-da 짧게 하다, chul-da 줄다.

shorthand *n.* sok-gi-sul 속기술.

shorts *n.* jjal-bŭn pa-ji 짧은 바지, pan-ba-ji 반바지.

short-sighted *adj.* kŭn-si-ŭi 근시(近視)의.

shot *n.* ① t'an-hwan 탄환, p'o-t'an 포탄. ② (*shooting*) sa-gyŏk 사격. ③ (*marksman*) sa-su 사수.

shoulder *n.* ŏ-ggae 어깨. —*v.* me-da 메다.

shout *n.* ko-ham 고함. —*v.* oe-ch'i-da 외치다.

shove *v.* ttŏ-mil-da 떠밀다, mi-rŏ-nŏ-t'a 밀어넣다.

shovel *n.* sap 삽, pu-sap 부삽, ka-rae 가래.

show *v.* po-i-da 보이다, ka-ri-k'i-da 가리키다. —*n.* kwa-si 과시 ; ku-gyŏng-gŏ-ri 구경거리.

shower *n.* so-na-gi 소나기 ; (*bath*) sya-u-ŏ 샤우어.

showy *adj.* tu-dŭ-rŏ-jin 두드러진 ; ya-han 야한.

shred *n.* han cho-gak 한 조각, p'a-p'yŏn 파편 ; (*bit*) yak-gan 약간. —*v.* chal-ge jji-t'a 잘게 찢다.

shrewd *adj.* pin-t'ŭm-ŏp-nŭn 빈틈없는.

shriek *n.* nal-k'a-ro-un so-ri 날카로운 소리, pi-myŏng 비명. —*v.* pi-myŏng-ŭl ol-ri-da 비명을 올리다.

shrill *adj.* jjae-nŭn tŭt-han 째는 듯한. —*v.* nal-k'a-ro-un so-ri-rŭl nae-da 날카로운 소리를 내다. 「이.

shrimp *n.* ① sae-u 새우. ② (*dwarf*) nan-jang-i 난장

shrine *n.* sa-dang 사당, myo 묘(廟) ; sŏng-dang 성당.

shrink *v.* o-gŭ-ra-dŭl-da 오그라들다.

shroud *n* su-ŭi 수의(壽衣). —*v.* (*cover*) tŏ-p'ŏ ssŭi-u-da 덮어 씌우다, ssa-da 싸다.

shrub *n.* kwan-mok 관목, tŏm-bul 덤불.

shrug *v.* ŏ-ggae-rŭl ŭ-ssŭk-ha-da 어깨를 으쓱하다.

shudder *v.* mom-sŏ-ri-ch'i-da 몸서리치다.

shuffle *v.* ① pal-ŭl kkŭl-go ka-da 발을 끌고 가다. ② (*cards*) sŏk-da 섞다. ③ ŏl-bŏ-mu-ri-da 얼버무리다.

shun *v.* p'i-ha-da 피하다, pi-ggi-da 비끼다 : ~ *danger* wi-hŏm-ŭl p'i-ha-da 위험을 피하다.

shut *v.* tat-da 닫다, cham-gŭ-da 잠그다.

shutter *n.* tŏt-mun 덧문, syŏ-t'ŏ 셔터. 「왕복 열차.

shuttle *n.* ① (*loon*) puk 북. ② wang-bok yŏl-ch'a

shy *adj.* su-jup-ŭn 수줍은, am-ddin 암띤.

sick *adj.* ① pyŏng-dŭn 병든 ; (*nauseating*) me-sŭ-ggŏ-un 메스꺼운. ② (*longing*) kŭ-ri-wŏ-ha-nŭn 그리워하는.

sickle *n.* chak-ŭn nat 작은 낫.

sickness *n.* pyŏng 병(病) ; yok-ji-gi 욕지기.

side *n.* jjok 쪽, myŏn 면 ; (*flank*) yŏp-gu-ri 옆구리.

sideboard *n.* ch'an-jang 찬장, sal-gang 살강.

sidewalk *n.* po-do 보도, in-do 인도.

sideways *adv.* yŏ-p'ŭ-ro 옆으로, pi-sŭ-dŭm-hi 비스듬히.

siege *n.* p'o-wi kong-gyŏk 포위 공격.

sieve *n.* ① ch'e 체. ② (*person*) ip-i ka-byŏ-un sa-ram 입이 가벼운 사람. —*v.* ch'e-jil-ha-da 체질하다.

sift *v.* ch'e-ro ch'i-da 체로 치다, ko-rŭ-da 고르다.

sigh *n.* han-sum 한숨. —*v.* han-sum-ŭl swi-da 한숨을 쉬다, t'an-sik-ha-da 탄식하다.

sight *n.* ① si-ryŏk 시력. ② kwang-gyŏng 광경, kyŏng-ch'i 경치. —*v.* a-ra-bo-da 알아보다.

sightseeing *n.* ku-gyŏng 구경, kwan-gwang 관광.

sign *n.* (*token*) ching-jo 징조 ; (*signal*) sin-ho 신호 ; (*symbol*) pu-ho 부호. —*v.* sŏ-myŏng-ha-da 서명하다.

signal *n.* & *v.* sin-ho(-ha-da) 신호(하다).

signal fire pong-hwa 봉화.   「주제 음악.

signature *n.* sŏ-myŏng 서명 : ～ *tune* chu-je ŭm-ak

signboard *n.* kan-p'an 간판, ke-si-p'an 게시판.

signet *n.* mak-do-jang 막도장, (*seal*) in-jang 인장.

significant *adj.* chung-yo-han 중요한.

signify *v.* ŭi-mi-ha-da 의미하다 ; na-t'a-nae-da 나타내다.

silence *n.* ch'im-muk 침묵, chŏng-jŏk 정적.

silent *adj.* ko-yo-han 고요한, mal-ŏp-nŭn 말없는.

silently *adv.* cho-yong-hi 조용히, cham-ja-k'o 잠자코.

silk *n.* pi-dan 비단 ; (*Korean*) myŏng-ju 명주.

silkworm *n.* nu-e 누에.

sill *n.* mun-ji-bang 문지방, ch'ang-t'ŏk 창턱.

silly *adj.* ŏ-ri-sŏk-ŭn 어리석은 : *Don't be* ～! Ŏ-ri-sŏk-ŭn chit ma-ra! 어리석은 짓 마라 !

silver *n.* ŭn 은 : ～ *screen* ŭn-mak 은막.

silvery *adj.* ŭn-bi-ch'ŭi 은빛의 : ～ *hair* ŭn-bal 은발.

similar *adj.* tal-mŭn 닮은, yu-sa-han 유사한.

simple *adj.* kan-dan-han 간단한, tan-sun-han 단순한 ; (*plain*) so-bak-han 소박한 : ～ *manner* kku-mim-ŏp-nŭn t'ae-do 꾸밈없는 태도.

simplicity *n.* kan-dan 간단 ; tan-sun 단순 ; sun-jin 순진.

simplify *v.* kan-dan-ha-ge ha-da 간단하게 하다.

simply *adv.* kan-dan-hi 간단히 ; (*plainly*) so-bak-ha-ge 소박하게 ; (*only*) ta-man 다만.

simultaneous *adj.* tong-si-jŏk-in 동시적인.

sin *n.* choe 죄 ; kwa-sil 과실, (*offense*) wi-ban 위반.

since *conj.* ① (*because*) ···ttae-mun-e ···때문에. ②
(*time*) ···i-hu ···이후. —*prep.* ···i-rae ···이래.

sincere *adj.* chin-sil-han 진실한, sŏng-sil-han 성실한.

sincerely *adv.* sŏng-sil-ha-ge 성실하게, chin-jŏng-ŭ-ro

sinew *n.* kŏn 건(腱) ; (*pl.*) kŭn-yuk 근육. ㄴ진정으로.

sinful *adj.* choe-man-ŭn 죄많은.

sing *v.* ① no-rae-ha-da 노래하다, (*chirp*) chi-jŏ-gwi-da
지저귀다, ul-da 울다. ② (*ring*) wing-wing-gŏ-ri-da
윙윙거리다. ③ (*praise*) ye-ch'an-ha-da 예찬하다.

singe *v.* kŭ-ŭl-da 그을다, chi-ji-da 지지다.

singer *n.* ka-su 가수, sŏng-ak-ga 성악가.

singing *n.* no-rae-bu-rŭ-gi 노래부르기, ch'ang-ga 창가.

single *adj.* tan-il-ŭi 단일의, tan ha-na-ŭi 단 하나의 ;
(*unmarried*) tok-sin-ŭi 독신의. —*n.* han kae 한 개.

singular *adj.* koe-sang-han 괴상한. —*n.* tan-su 단수.

sinister *adj.* pul-gil-han 불길한, chae-su-ŏp-nŭn 재수
없는 ; ak-ŭi-rŭl p'um-ŭn 악의(惡意)를 품은.

sink *n.* sŏl-gŏ-ji-t'ong 설겆이통 ; (*drain*) su-ch'ae 수채,
ha-su-gu 하수구. —*v.* ka-ra-an-da 가라앉다.

sip *v.* hol-jjak-hol-jjak ma-si-da 홀짝홀짝 마시다, ppal-
da 빨다. —*n.* han mo-gŭm 한 모금.

siphon *n.* sa-i-p'ŏn 사이펀.

sir *n.* (*Korean polite title*) nim 님 ; sŏn-saeng 선생.

siren *n.* sa-i-ren 사이렌, ho-jŏk 호적(號笛).

sister *n.* yŏ-ja hyŏng-je 여자 형제, cha-mae 자매(姉
妹) ; (*boy's older sister*) nu-nim 누님, (*boy's younger sister*) nu-i tong-saeng 누이 동생 ; (*girl's younger sister*) tong-saeng 동생, (*girl's older sister*)
ŏn-ni 언니.

sister-in-law *n.* ① of a man (*elder brother's wife*)
hyŏng-su 형수, (*younger brother's wife*) kye-su
계수, (*wife's older sister*) ch'ŏ-hyŏng 처형, (*wife's*

younger sister) ch'ŏ-je 처제. ② of a woman (*elder brother's wife*) ol-k'e 올케, (*younger brother's wife*) a-u-nim 아우님, (*husband's sister*) si-nu-i 시누이.

sit *v.* an-da 앉다 : ～ *down* an-da 앉다/～ *for* ch'i-rŭ-da 치르다/～ *on*[*upon*] …ŭl cho-sa-ha-da …을 조사하다/～ *up* i-rŏ-na an-da 일어나 앉다.

situation *n.* ch'ŏ-ji 처지 ; (*place*) chang-so 장소.

six *n.* yŏ-sŏt 여섯, yuk 6. —*adj.* yŏ-sŏt-sŭi 여섯의.

sixteen *n. & adj.* yŏl-yŏ-sŏt(-ŭi) 열여섯(의), sip-yuk 16(의).

sixty *n.* ye-sun 예순, yuk-sip 60.

size *n.* k'ŭ-gi 크기, ch'i-su 치수.

skate *n.* sŭ-k'e-i-t'ŭ 스케이트. —*v.* sŭ-k'e-i-t'ŭ-rŭl t'a-da 스케이트를 타다, ŏ-rŭm-ŭl chi-ch'i-da 얼음을 지치다.

skating *n.* ŏ-rŭm chi-ch'i-gi 얼음 지치기, sŭ-k'e-i-t'ing 스케이팅, sŭ-k'e-i-t'ŭ 스케이트.

skeleton *n.* ① hae-gol 해골. ② kol-gyŏk 골격.

sketch *n.* (*rough drawing*) sŭ-k'e-ch'i 스케치 ; (*outline*) kae-yo 개요 ; ch'o-an 초안.

ski *n. & v.* sŭ-k'i-i(-rŭl t'a-da) 스키이(를 타다).

skil(l)ful *adj.* nŭng-suk-han 능숙한, som-ssi-it-nŭn 솜씨있는.

skill *n.* suk-ryŏn 숙련, som-ssi 솜씨.

skim *v.* sŭ-ch'yŏ chi-na-ga-da 스쳐 지나가다, (*read hastily*) tae-ch'ung il-dda 대충 읽다.

skin *n.* kkŏp-jil 껍질, (*animal*) ka-juk 가죽 ; (*human*) p'i-bu 피부.

skip *v.* kkang-ch'ung-ggang-ch'ung ttwi-da 깡충깡충 뛰다 ; (*leave out*) ppa-ddŭ-ri-da 빠뜨리다.

skirmish *n.* so-ch'ung-dol 소충돌. —*v.* chak-ŭn ch'ung-dol-ŭl ha-da 작은 충돌을 하다.

skirt *n.* ① cha-rak 자락. ② sŭ-k'ŏ-ŏ-t'ŭ 스커어트, ch'i-ma 치마. ③ (*border*) pyŏn-du-ri 변두리, ka-jang-ja-ri 가장자리.

skull *n.* tu-gae-gol 두개골.

sky *n.* ha-nŭl 하늘 ; (*weather*) nal-ssi 날씨.

skylark *n.* chong-dal-sae 종달새, chong-da-ri 종다리.

skylight *n.* ch'ŏn-ch'ang 천창(天窓).

skyscraper *n.* ma-ch'ŏl-lu 마천루, ko-ch'ŭng 고층.

slab *n.* p'yŏng-p'an 평판, sŏk-p'an 석판 ; sŭl-raep 슬 랩 : *a ~ of marble* tae-ri-sŏk-p'an 대리석판.

slack *adj.* nŭ-sŭn-han 느슨한, nŭ-rin 느린.

slacken *v.* nŭ-sŭn-hae-ji-da 느슨해지다, nŭt-ch'u-da 늦 추다 ; (*neglect*) ke-ŭl-ri-ha-da 게을리하다.

slacks *n.* pa-ji 바지, sŭl-raek-sŭ 슬랙스. 「때리다.

slam *v.* ① (*bang*)k'wang tat-da 쾅 닫다. ② ttae-ri-da

slander *n.* & *v.* chung-sang(-ha-da) 중상(中傷)(하다).

slang *n.* sok-ŏ 속어, sŭl-raeng 슬랭.

slant *n.* pi-t'al 비탈, kyŏng-sa 경사. —*v.* ki-u-ri-da 기 울이다. —*adj.* ki-u-rŏ-jin 기울어진.

slap *n.* ch'al-ssak tu-dŭl-gim 찰싹 두들김. —*v.* ch'al-ssak ch'i-da 찰싹 치다. —*adv.* ch'al-ssak 찰싹.

slash *v.* ① (*hack violently*) ki-p'i pe-da 깊이 베다, nan-dol-jil-ha-da 난도질하다. ② (*lash*) mae-jil-ha-da 매질하다. —*n.* ① il-gyŏk 일격. ② k'ŭn sang-ch'ŏ 큰 상처.

slate *n.* sŏk-p'an 석판, sŭl-re-i-t'ŭ 슬레이트.

slaughter *n.* to-sal 도살, (*carnage*) sal-ryuk 살륙.

slave *n.* no-ye 노예. 「ri-nŭn 침을 흘리는.

slavery *n.* no-ye che-do 노예 제도. —*adj.* ch'im-ŭl hŭl-

slay *v.* chuk-i-da 죽이다, sal-hae-ha-da 살해하다.

sled *n.* ssŏl-mae 썰매. —*v.* ssŏl-mae-rŭl t'a-da 썰매를 타다. 「nŭn 광택이 나는.

sleek *adj.* mae-ggŭ-rŏ-un 매끄러운, kwang-t'aek-i na-

sleep *n.* cham 잠, su-myŏn 수면. —*v.* cha-da 자다.

sleeping car ch'im-dae-ch'a 침대차. 「듯한.

sleepy *adj.* chol-ri-nŭn 졸리는, cha-nŭn tŭt-han 자는

sleet *n.* chin-nun-ggae-bi 진눈깨비.

sleeve *n.* so-mae 소매, so-maet-ja-rak 소맷자락.

sleigh *n.* ssŏl-mae 썰매. —*v.* ssŏl-mae-rŭl t'a-da 썰매를 타다, ssŏl-mae-ro na-rŭ-da 썰매로 나르다.

slender *adj.* hol-jjuk-han 홀쭉한, pin-yak-han 빈약한: *a ~ income* pin-yak-han su-ip 빈약한 수입.

slice *n.* yal-bŭn cho-gak 얇은 조각. —*v.* yal-gge ssŏl-da 얇게 썰다.

slicker *n.* pi-ot 비옷, re-in-k'o-u-t'ŭ 레인코우트.

slide *v.* mi-ggŭ-rŏ-ji-da 미끄러지다. —*n.* hwal-ju 활주, sŭl-ra-i-dŭ 슬라이드.

slight *adj.* yak-gan-ŭi 약간의, kŭn-so-han 근소한. —*v.* kyŏng-si-ha-da 경시하다. —*n.* kyŏng-myŏl 경멸.

slightly *adv.* cho-gŭm 조금, ka-nyal-p'ŭ-ge 가냘프게.

slim *adj.* ka-nŭ-da-ran 가느다란, ho-ri-ho-ri-han 호리[호리한.

slime *n.* chin-hŭk 진흙.

sling *n.* t'u-sŏk-gi 투석기. —*v.* tŏn-ji-da 던지다.

slink *v.* sal-myŏ-si to-mang-ch'i-da 살며시 도망치다.

slip *v.* mi-ggŭ-rŏ-ji-da 미끄러지다. —*n.* sil-su 실수.

slipper *n.* sŭl-ri-p'ŏ 슬리퍼.

slippery *adj.* mi-ggŭ-rŏ-un 미끄러운.

slit *n.* kal-ra-jin t'ŭm 갈라진 틈, t'ŭm-sae 틈새.

slogan *n.* p'yo-ŏ 표어, sŭl-ro-u-gŏn 슬로우건.

slope *n.* pi-t'al 비탈, kyŏng-sa 경사. —*v.* kyŏng-sa-ji-da 경사지다, pi-t'al-ji-da 비탈지다.

sloth *n.* ke-ŭ-rŭm 게으름, t'ae-man 태만, na-t'ae 나태.

slow *adj.* nŭ-rin 느린, tŏ-din 더딘. —*v.* sok-ryŏk-ŭl nŭt-ch'u-da 속력을 늦추다.

slowly *adv.* ch'ŏn-ch'ŏn-hi 천천히, nŭ-rit-nŭ-rit 느릿느릿.

slug *n.* ① (*animal*) min-dal-p'aeng-i 민달팽이. ② (*idler*) nŭ-ri-gwang-i 느리광이.

sluggard *n.* (*idler*) ke-ŭ-rŭm-baeng-i 게으름뱅이 ; nom-p'ang-i 놈팡이, (*lounger*) kŏn-dal 건달.

sluggish *adj.* nŭ-rin 느린, ke-ŭ-rŭn 게으른.

slum *n.* pin-min-gul 빈민굴, pin-min-ga 빈민가.

slumber *n.* sŏn-jam 선잠, su-myŏn 수면. —*v.* kku-bŏk-ggu-bŏk chol-da 꾸벅꾸벅 졸다.

slump *n.* p'ok-rak 폭락; pu-jin-sang-t'ae 부진상태.

sly *adj.* kyo-hwal-han 교활한, ŏng-k'ŭm-han 엉큼한; mol-rae 몰래 : *on the* ~ ŭn-mil-hi 은밀히.

smack *n.* ① (*taste*) mat 맛, p'ung-mi 풍미. ② (*loud kiss*) jjok-ha-nŭn k'i-sŭ 쪽하는 키스. —*v.* ip-ma-sŭl ta-si-da 입맛을 다시다.

small *adj.* (*not large*) chak-ŭn 작은, (*little*) chŏk-ŭn 적은 ; (*trivial*) po-jal-gŏt-ŏp-nŭn 보잘것없는.

smallpox *n.* ma-ma 마마, ch'ŏn-yŏn-du 천연두.

smart *adj.* chae-ch'i-it-nŭn 재치있는 ; mŏt-jin 멋진.

smash *v.* pun-swae-ha-da 분쇄하다, tu-dŭl-gyŏ p'ae-da 두들겨 패다. 「히다. —*n.* ŏl-ruk 얼룩.

smear *v.* ch'il-ha-da 칠하다 ; (*stain*) tŏ-rŏp-hi-da 더럽

smell *n.* naem-sae 냄새. —*v.* naem-sae mat-da 냄새 맡다, naem-sae-ga na-da 냄새가 나다.

smelt *v.* che-ryŏn-ha-da 제련하다, (*fuse*) yong-hae-ha-da 용해하다. 「gŭt ut-da 생긋 웃다.

smile *n.* mi-so 미소. —*v.* mi-so-ha-da 미소하다, saeng-
smiling *adj.* mi-so-ha-nŭn 미소하는.

smith *n.* (*blacksmith*) tae-jang-jang-i 대장장이.

smoke *n.* yŏn-gi 연기. —*v.* yŏn-gi-nae-da 연기내다; (*cigarette*) tam-bae p'i-u-da 담배 피우다.

smoker *n.* tam-bae p'i-nŭn sa-ram 담배 피는 사람, hŭp-yŏn-ga 흡연가.

smoking *n.* hŭp-yŏn 흡연 : *No* ~. Kŭm-yŏn 금연.

smooth *adj.* mae-ggŭ-rŏ-un 매끄러운, sun-t'an-han 순탄한 : *a* ~ *road* p'yŏng-p'yŏng-han kil 평평한 길. —*v.* mae-ggŭ-rŏp-ge ha-da 매끄럽게 하다.

smother *v.* sum-ŭl mak-da 숨을 막다, chil-sik-si-k'i-da 질식시키다. 「nŭn 뻐기는.

smug *adj.* chal-nan ch'e-ha-nŭn 잘난 체하는, ppŏ-gi-

smuggle *v.* mil-su-ip[ch'ul]-ha-da 밀수입[출]하다.

smuggler *n.* mil-su-ja 밀수자, mil-su-sŏn 밀수선 : *a ring of* ~*s* mil-su-dan 밀수단.

snack *n.* kan-dan-han sik-sa 간단한 식사.

snail *n.* tal-p'aeng-i 달팽이.

snake *n.* paem 뱀.

snap *v.* (*break*) t'ak kkŏk-da 탁 꺾다 ; (*dog*) tŏp-sŏk mul-da 덥석 물다. —*n.* ① choem-soe 쬠쇠, kŏl-soe 걸쇠. ② (*picture*) sŭ-naep sa-jin 스냅 사진.

snappy *adj.* ki-un-ch'an 기운찬, p'al-p'al-han 팔팔한 : *Make it* ~*!* Ŏ-sŏ hae-ra! 어서 해라!

snare *n.* tŏt 덫, ol-ga-mi 올가미.

snarl *v.* ŭ-rŭ-rŏng-gŏ-ri-da 으르렁거리다 ; hol-lan 혼란.

snatch *v.* chap-a-ch'ae-da 잡아채다, tal-ryŏ-dŭl-da 달려들다. —*n.* kang-t'al 강탈 ; (*a short period*) cham-ggan 잠깐 ; (*fragments*) tan-p'yŏn 단편.

sneak *v.* (*slink*) sal-gŭm-sal-gŭm ta-ni-da 살금살금 다니다 ; (*cringe*) kup-sil-gŏ-ri-da 굽실거리다.

sneer *v.* pi-ut-da 비웃다, kyŏng-myŏl-ha-da 경멸하다. —*n.* naeng-so 냉소.

sneeze *n.* chae-ch'ae-gi 재채기. —*v.* ① chae-ch'ae-gi-ha-da 재채기하다. ② (*despise*) kkal-bo-da 깔보다.

sniff *v.* k'o-rŭl k'ŭng-k'ŭng-gŏ-ri-da 코를 콩콩거리다, naem-sae-rŭl mat-da 냄새를 맡다.

snip *n.* cho-gak 조각. —*v.* cha-rŭ-da 자르다. 「속물.

snob *n.* sa-i-bi sin-sa 사이비 신사;(*worldling*) sok-mul

snore *n.* k'o-go-nŭn so-ri 코고는 소리. —*v.* k'o-rŭl kol-da 코를 골다.

snout *n.* ① k'o 코. ② (*muzzle*) chu-dung-i 주둥이.

snow *n.* nun 눈. —*v.* nun-i o-da 눈이 오다.

snowball *n.* nun-mung-ch'i 눈뭉치, nun-dŏng-i 눈덩이.

snowdrift *n.* nun-dŏ-mi 눈더미.

snowfall *n.* kang-sŏl 강설, kang-sŏl-ryang 강설량.

snowflake *n.* nun-song-i 눈송이.

snowman *n.* nun-sa-ram 눈사람.

snowplough·snowplow *n.* che-sŏl-gi 제설기(除雪機).

snowslide *n.* (*avalanche*) nun-sa-t'ae 눈사태.

snowstorm *n.* nun-bo-ra 눈보라.

snowy *adj.* nun-i man-ŭn 눈이 많은, sae-ha-yan 새하얀.

snuff *v.* k'o-ro tŭ-ri-ma-si-da 코로 들이마시다. —*n.* k'o-dam-bae 코담배. 「다.

snuffle *n.* k'ot-so-ri 콧소리. —*v.* k'o-ga me-da 코가 메

snug *adj.* a-nŭk-han 아늑한, al-lak-han 안락한.

so *adv.* kŭ-rŏ-k'e 그렇게. —*conj.* kŭ-rŏ-mŭ-ro 그러프 로. —*pron.* kŭ-wa ka-t'ŭn kŏt 그와 같은 것.

soak *n.* tam-gŭ-da 담그다, chŏk-si-da 적시다; (*permeate*) sŭ-myŏ-dŭl-da 스며들다. 「누.

soap *n.* pi-nu 비누: *toilet* ~ hwa-jang pi-nu 화장 비

soapsuds *n.* pi-nu kŏ-p'um 비누거품, pi-nut-mul 비눗물.

soar *v.* no-p'i nal-da 높이 날다; ch'i-sot-da 치솟다.

sob *n.* hŭ-nŭ-ggim 흐느낌. —*v.* hŭ-nŭ-ggyŏ ul-da 흐느 껴 울다, mok-me-ŏ ul-da 목메어 울다.

sober *adj.* chin-ji-han 진지한, kŭn-sil-han 근실한, ch'wi-ha-ji an-ŭn 취하지 않은.

so-called *adj.* i-rŭn-ba 이른바, so-wi 소위.

sociable *adj.* sa-gyo-jŏk-in 사교적인, sa-gŭn-sa-gŭn-han 사근사근한, pu-ch'im-sŏng-it-nŭn 붙임성있는.

social *adj.* sa-hoe-ŭi 사회의, sa-gyo-jŏk-in 사교적인.

society *n.* sa-hoe 사회; (*institution*) hak-hoe 학회.

sociology *n.* sa-hoe-hak 사회학.

sock *n.* jjal-bŭn yang-mal 짧은 양말.

socket *n.* (kki·u·nŭn) ku·mŏng (끼우는) 구멍, so·k'et 소켓.

sod *n.* chan·di 잔디, tte 떼.

soda *n.* t'an·san·su 탄산수, so·o·da 소오다.

soever *adv.* pi·rok …il·ji·ra·do 비록 …일지라도.

sofa *n.* kin al·lak·ŭi·ja 긴 안락의자, so·p'a 소파.

soft *adj.* pu·dŭ·rŏ·un 부드러운, on·hwa·han 온화한.

soften *v.* pu·dŭ·rŏp·ge ha·da 부드럽게 하다.

softly *adv.* pu·dŭ·rŏp·ge 부드럽게.

soil *n. n.* ① hŭk 흙, t'o·ji 토지. ② (*dirt*) o·mul 오물. —*v.* tŏ·rŏp·hi·da 더럽히다.

sojourn *v.* ch'e·ryu·ha·da 체류하다. —*n.* ch'e·ryu 체류, ch'e·jae 체재.

solace *n.* wi·ro 위로, wi·an 위안. —*v.* wi·ro·ha·da 위로하다, wi·an·i toe·da 위안이 되다.

solar *adj.* t'ae·yang·ŭi 태양의 : ~ *calendar* yang·ryŏk 양력(陽曆)/~ *eclipse* il·sik 일식.

soldier *n.* kun·in 군인, sa·byŏng 사병.

sole *n.* ① (*one and only*) tan ha·na 단 하나. ② (*of shoes*) ch'ang 창. ③ (*of foot*) pal·ba·dak 발바닥.

solely *adv.* o·jik 오직, ta·man 다만, hon·ja·sŏ 혼자서.

solemn *adj.* ŏm·suk·han 엄숙한, chang·ŏm·han 장엄한.

solicit *v.* ① (*entreat*) kan·ch'ŏng·ha·da 간청하다. ② (*ask earnestly*) cho·rŭ·da 조르다.

solid *adj.* ko·ch'e·ŭi 고체의 ; tan·dan·han 단단한 ; kyŏng·go·han 견고한. —*n.* ko·ch'e 고체.

solidarity *n.* tan·gyŏl 단결, yŏn·dae·ch'aek·im 연대책임.

solidify *v.* (*make solid*) kut·hi·da 굳히다, ko·ch'e·hwa·ha·da 고체화하다.

solitary *adj.* ko·dok·han 고독한, oe·ro·un 외로운.

solitude *n.* ① ko·dok 고독. ② oe·ddan kot 외딴 곳.

solo *n.* (*vocal*) tok·ch'ang 독창, (*inst.*) tok·ju 독주.

solstice *n.* (*winter*) tong·ji 동지, (*summer*) ha·ji 하지.

solution *n.* ① hae·gyŏl 해결. ② yong·hae 용해.

solve *v.* hae-gyŏl-ha-da 해결하다.

somber·sombre *adj.* ch'im-ch'im-han 침침한.

some *adj.* ŏ-ddŏn 어떤, yak-gan-ŭi 약간의. —*pron.* 약간, ta-so 다소, ŏ-ddŏn kŏt 어떤 것.

somebody *n. & pron.* ŏ-ddŏn sa-ram 어떤 사람 ; (*person of some note*) sang-dang-han in-mul 상당한 인물.

somehow *adj.* ŏ-ddŏ-k'e-dŭn 어떻게든.

somersault *n.* chae-ju-nŏm-gi 재주넘기, (*handspring*) kong-jung-je-bi 공중제비.

something *pron.* ŏ-ddŏn kŏt 어떤 것, (*thing of some value*) sang-dang-han kŏt 상당한 것.

sometime *adj.* ŏn-jen-ga 언젠가, ŏn-je-go 언제고.

sometimes *adv.* ttae-ddae-ro 때때로, i-dda-gŭm 이따금.

somewhat *adv.* ŏl-ma-gan 얼마간, ta-so 다소.

somewhere *adv.* ŏ-di-ron-ga 어디론가, ŏ-din-ji 어딘지.

son *n.* a-dŭl 아들, cha-son 자손.　　　　「리.

song *n.* ① no-rae 노래. ② (*birds*) u-nŭn so-ri 우는 소

son-in-law *n.* sa-wi 사위 ; (*adopted son*) yang-ja 양자.

sonnet *n.* sip-sa-haeng-si 14행시(行詩), so-ne-t'ŭ 소네트.

soon *adv.* kot 곧, i-nae 이내, ppal-ri 빨리.

soot *n.* kŏm-daeng 검댕, mae-yŏn 매연.　　　　「키다.

soothe *v.* tal-rae-da 달래다, chin-jŏng-si-k'i-da 진정시

sophisticated *adj.* yak-sak-bba-rŭn 약삭빠른, ki-gyo-e ch'i-u-ch'in 기교에 치우친, sok-im-su-ŭi 속임수의.

soprano *n.* so-p'ŭ-ra-no 소프라노.

sorcerer *n.* ma-sul-sa 마술사, ma-bŏp-sa 마법사.

sorceress *n.* mu-dang 무당.

sordid *adj.* (*dirty*) tŏ-rŏ-un 더러운, nu-ch'u-han 누추한 ; t'am-yok-sŭ-rŏ-un 탐욕스러운.

sore *adj.* ① (*painful to the touch*) a-p'ŭn 아픈, ssŭ-ra-rin 쓰라린. ② (*sorrowful*) sŭl-p'ŭn 슬픈.

sorrow *n.* sŭl-p'ŭm 슬픔. —*v.* sŭl-p'ŏ-ha-da 슬퍼하다.

sorry adj. sŏp-sŏp-han 섭섭한, (feeling regret) yu-gam-su-rŏn 유감스런 : I am ~. ① (my fault) Mi-an-hap-ni-da. 미안합니다. ② (not my fault) An-dwae-ssŭm-ni-da. 안됐읍니다.

sort n. chong-ryu 종류. — v. pul-lyu-ha-da 분류하다.

soul n. ① yŏng-hon 영혼, chŏng-sin 정신. ② (person) sa-ram 사람. 「so-ri-ga na-da 소리가 나다.

sound adj. kŏn-jŏn-han 건전한. —n. so-ri 소리. —v.

soundproof adj. pang-ŭm-jang-ch'i-ga toen 방음장치가 된, pang-ŭm-ŭi 방음의.

soup n. kuk 국, su-u-p'ŭ 수우프.

sour adj. (acid) sin 신, si-k'ŭm-han 시큼한.

source n. kŭn-wŏn 근원, ch'ul-ch'ŏ 출처.

south n. nam-jjok 남쪽. —adj. nam-jjok-ŭi 남쪽의.

southeast n. tong-nam 동남, tong-nam-bu 동남부.

southern adj. nam-jjok-ŭi 남쪽의. 「jjok-ŭi 남쪽의.

southward adv. nam-jjok-ŭ-ro 남쪽으로. —adj. nam-

souvenir n. ki-nyŏm-p'um 기념품 ; sŏn-mul 선물.

sovereign n. chu-gwŏn-ja 주권자, kun-ju 군주.

sow v. ssi-rŭl ppu-ri-da 씨를 뿌리다, p'ŏ-ddŭ-ri-da 퍼뜨리다. —n. (a female hog) am-t'wae-ji 암퇘지.

soy n. (sauce) kan-jang 간장.

soy(a)bean n. k'ong 콩 ; ~ paste toen-jang 된장.

space n. (interval) kan-gyŏk 간격 ; (celestial) kong-gan 공간 ; (universe) u-ju 우주.

spacious adj. nŏl-bŭn 넓은, kwang-dae-han 광대한.

spade n. sap 삽, ka-rae 가래.

span n. han ppyŏm 한 뼘 ; (short distance) jjal-bŭn kŏ-ri 짧은 거리. —v. son-ga-rak-ŭ-ro chae-da 손가락으로 재다, (extend) …e mi-ch'i-da …에 미치다.

spangle n. pŏn-jjŏk-gŏ-ri-nŭn chang-sik 번쩍거리는 장식. —v. pŏn-jjŏk-i-da 번쩍이다.

Spanish *n.* sŭ-p'e-in-ŏ 스페인어 ; (*people*) sŭ-p'e-in-sa-ram 스페인사람. —*adj.* sŭ-p'e-in-ŭi 스페인의.

spank *v.* ch'al-ssak ttae-ri-da 찰싹 때리다.

spare *adj.* (*scanty*) pu-jok-han 부족한 ; (*reserved*) ye-bi-ŭi 예비의. —*v.* a-ggyŏ ssŭ-da 아껴 쓰다.

spark *n.* pul-ggot 불꽃, pul-ddong 불똥.

sparkle *n.* pul-t'i 불티, sŏm-gwang 섬광. —*v.* (*glitter*) pŏn-jjŏk-gŏ-ri-da 번쩍거리다.

sparrow *n.* ch'am-sae 참새.

sparse *adj.* (*thin*) sŏng-gin 성긴, tŭ-mun-dŭ-mun-han 드문드문한.

spasm *n.* kyŏng-ryŏn 경련, pal-jak 발작.

speak *v.* mal-ha-da 말하다, (*converse*) i-ya-gi-ha-da 이야기하다 ; (*speech*) yŏn-sŏl-ha-da 연설하다.

speaker *n.* ① yŏn-sa 연사, pyŏn-sa 변사. ② hwak-sŏng-gi 확성기.

spear *n.* ch'ang 창.

special *adj.* t'ŭk-byŏl-han 특별한.

specialist *n.* chŏn-mun-ga 전문가 ; chŏn-mun-ŭi 전문의(醫).

specialize *v.* chŏn-mun-ŭ-ro yŏn-gu-ha-da 전문으로 연구하다, chŏn-gong-ha-da 전공하다.

specially *adv.* t'ŭk-byŏl-hi 특별히, t'ŭk-hi 특히.

species *n.* chong 종(種), chong-ryu 종류.

specific *adj.* t'ŭk-jong-ŭi 특종의 ; (*explicit*) myŏng-hwak-han 명확한. —*n.* t'ŭk-hyo-yak 특효약.

specify *v.* cha-se-hi ki-ip-ha-da 자세히 기입하다.

specimen *n.* kyŏh-bon 견본, p'yo-bon 표본.

speck *n.* ŏl-ruk 얼룩, pan-jŏm 반점 ; o-jŏm 오점.

speckle *n.* chak-ŭn pan-jŏm 작은 반점.

spectacle *n.* ① kwang-gyŏng 광경. ② an-gyŏng 안경.

spectacled *adj.* an-gyŏng-ŭl kkin 안경을 낀.

spectator *n.* ku-gyŏng-gun 구경군, kwan-gaek 관객.

spectroscope *n.* pun-gwang-gi 분광기.

speculate *v.* sa-saek-ha-da 사색하다 ; (*gamble in*

stocks) t'u·gi·ha·da 투기하다.

speculation *n.* ① (*meditation*) sa·saek 사색, suk·go 숙고. ② (*stockjobbing*) t'u·gi 투기.

speech *n.* (*address*) yŏn·sŏl 연설 ; (*language*) ŏn·ŏ 언어, mal 말 ; (*gram.*) hwa·bŏp 화법. 「sok 신속.

speed *n.* sok·do 속도, sok·ryŏk 속력. (*swiftness*) sin-

spell *n.* ① chu·mun 주문(呪文). ② (*short period*) cham·si 잠시. —*v.* ch'ŏl·ja·ha·da 철자하다.

spelling *n.* ch'ŏl·ja(-bŏp) 철자(법). 「다.

spend *v.* so·bi·ha·da 소비하다 ; (*time*) po·nae·da 보내

spendthrift *n.* nang·bi·ga 낭비가 ; pang·t'ang·a 방탕아.

sphere *n.* ① (*globe*) ku·ch'e 구체(球體), ku·hyŏng 구형. ② (*scope*) pŏm·wi 범위, pun·ya 분야.

spice *n.* yang·nyŏm 양념, hyang·ryo 향료.

spider *n.* ① kŏ·mi 거미. ② sam·ba·ri 삼발이. 「파이크.

spike *n.* (*nail*) mot 못 ; (*for shoes*) su·p'a·i·k'ŭ 스

spill *v.* ŏp·ji·rŭ·da 엎지르다, hŭl·ri·da 흘리다.

spin *v.* (*yarn*) chat·da 잣다, pang·jŏk·ha·da 방적하다 ; (*a top*) tol·ri·da 돌리다. —*n.* hoe·jŏn 회전.

spinach *n.* si·gŭm·ch'i 시금치.

spinal *adj.* ch'ŏk·ch'u·ŭi 척추의.

spindle *n.* puk 북.

spine *n.* ch'ŏk·ch'u 척추.

spinning wheel mul·re 물레.

spinster *n.* (*old maid*) no·ch'ŏ·nyŏ 노처녀, o·ul·dŭ·mi·sŭ 오울드미스. [mul·re]

spire *n.* ppyo·jok·t'ap 뾰족탑, ch'ŏm·t'ap 첨탑.

spirit *n.* ① (*soul*) chŏng·sin 정신 ; (*ghost*) mang·ryŏng 망령 ; (*vigor*) ki·un 기운. ② al·k'o·ol 알코올. —*v.* (*animate*) hwal·gi·rŭl tti·ge ha·da 활기를 띠게 하다.

spiritual *adj.* chŏng·sin·jŏk·in 정신적인, yŏng·jŏk·in 영적인. —*n.* yŏng·ga 영가(靈歌).

spit *v.* ch'im-ŭl paet-da 침을 뱉다. —*n.* ch'im 침.

spite *n.* ak-ŭi 악의, wŏn-han 원한. —*v.* (*vex*) koe-rop-hi-da 괴롭히다, hak-dae-ha-da 학대하다.

spiteful *adj.* sim-sul-gu-jŭn 심술궂은, ang-sim-gi-p'ŭn 앙심깊은.

spittoon *n.* t'a-gu 타구(唾具).

splash *v.* (*spatter*) t'wi-gi-da 튀기다.

spleen *n.* pi-jang 비장(脾臟) ; (*ill humor*) ul-hwa 울화.

splendid *adj.* (*fine*) hul-ryung-han 훌륭한, (*grand*) tang-dang-han 당당한, koeng-jang-han 굉장한.

splendo(u)r *n.* kwang-ch'ae 광채, pit-nam 빛남.

splice *v.* it-da 잇다, kyŏp-ch'yŏ it-da 겹처 잇다.

splinter *n.* na-mu cho-gak 나무 조각, t'o-mak 토막 ; (*thorn*) ka-si 가시. —*v.* jjo-gae-da 쪼개다.

split *v.* jjo-gae-da 쪼개다, jjit-da 찢다. —*n.* ① kal-ra-jin t'ŭm 갈라진 틈. ② (*rupture*) pul-hwa 불화.

spoil *n.* yak-t'al-p'um 약탈품. —*v.* (*ruin*) mang-ch'i-da 망치다 ; (*damage*) son-sang-ha-da 손상하다.

spokesman *n.* tae-byŏn-in[ja] 대변인[자].

sponge *n.* hae-myŏn 해면, sŭ-p'ŏn-ji 스펀지.

spongy *adj.* hae-myŏn mo-yang-ŭi 해면 모양의 ; p'ok-sin-p'ok-sin-han 폭신폭신한.

sponsor *n.* (*supporter*) hu-wŏn-ja 후원자 ; (*promoter*) pal-gi-in 발기인 ; kwang-go-ju 광고주. —*v.* ① hu-wŏn-ha-da 후원하다. ② kwang-go-rŭl ha-da 광고를 하다.

spontaneous *adj.* (*voluntary*) cha-bal-jŏk-in 자발적인, (*natural*) cha-yŏn-jŏk-in 자연적인.

spool *n.* sil-p'ae 실패, sil-gam-gae 실감개.

spoon *n.* sut-ga-rak 숟가락. sŭ-p'u-un 스푸운.

sporadic *adj.* ka-ggŭm i-rŏ-na-nŭn 가끔 일어나는.

sport *n.* un-dong 운동 ; (*pastime*) no-ri 놀이 ; (*jest*) nong-dam 농담.

sportsman *n.* un-dong-ga 운동가.

sportsmanship *n.* un-dong-ga chŏng-sin 운동가 정신,

sŭ-p'o-ch'ŭ-maen-sip 스포츠맨십.

spot *n.* (*place*) chi-jŏm 지점 ; (*dot*) ŏl-ruk 얼룩. —*v.*
tŏ-rŏ-wŏ-ji-da 더러워지다. 「nŭn 흠이 없는.

spotless *adj.* ŏl-ruk-i ŏp-nŭn 얼룩이 없는, hŭm-i ŏp-

spouse *n.* pae-u-ja 배우자, (*pl.*) pu-bu 부부.

spout *v.* nae-bbum-da 내뿜다. —*n.* chu-dung-i 주둥이.

sprain *n.* chŏp-jil-rim 접질림. —*v.* ppi-da 삐다.

sprawl *v.* son-bal-ŭl jjuk ppŏt-da 손발을 쭉 뻗다 ;
(*scramble*) ki-ŏ-da-ni-da 기어다니다.

spray *n.* ① (*from water*) mul-bo-ra 물보라. ② (*small
branch*) chak-ŭn ka-ji 작은 가지. —*v.* mul-bo-ra-rŭl
nal-ri-da 물보라를 날리다, ppum-da 뿜다.

spread *v.* ppu-ri-da 뿌리다, p'ŏ-ddŭ-ri-da 퍼뜨리다.

sprig *n.* chan-ga-ji 잔가지, ŏ-rin ka-ji 어린 가지.

sprightly *adj.* (*gay*) k'wae-hwal-han 쾌활한.

spring *n.* ① (*fountain*) saem 샘. ② (*season*) pom
봄. ③ (*wire*) sŭ-p'ŭ-ring 스프링. —*v.* ttwi-da 뛰다.

sprinkle *v.* ppu-ri-da 뿌리다, kki-ŏn-da 끼얹다.

sprout *v.* ssak-i na-da 싹이 나다. —*n.* ssak 싹 ; (*bean
sprouts*) k'ong-na-mul 콩나물.

spur *n.* pak-ch'a 박차. —*v.* (*urge*) pak-ch'a-rŭl ka-
ha-da 박차를 가하다, ko-mu-ha-da 고무하다.

spurn *v.* jjo-ch'a-bŏ-ri-da 쫓아버리다. —*n.* kŏ-jŏl 거절.

sputter *v.* ch'im-ŭl t'wi-gi-da 침을 튀기다.

spy *n.* kan-ch'ŏp 간첩, sŭ-p'a-i 스파이. —*v.* chŏng-
t'am-ha-da 정탐하다, ch'a-ja-nae-da 찾아내다.

spyglass *n.* chak-ŭn mang-wŏn-gyŏng 작은 망원경.

squad *n.* pan 반(班), pun-dae 분대. 「대.

squadron *n.* pi-haeng chung-dae 비행 중대 ; ham-dae 함

square *n.* ne-mo-ggol 네모꼴, chŏng-bang-hyŏng 정방
형 ; (*open space*) kwang-jang 광장.

squash *n.* sŏ-yang ho-bak 서양 호박. —*v.* jji-gŭ-rŏ-ddŭ-ri-da 찌그러뜨리다.

squat *v.* ung-k'ŭ-ri-go an-da 웅크리고 앉다.

squawk *v.* kkak-ggak ul-da 꽥꽥 울다.

squeak *v.* ppi-gŏk-bbi-gŏk so-ri nae-da 삐꺽삐꺽 소리 내다 ; (*peach*) ko-ja-jil-ha-da 고자질하다.

squeal *n.* a-u-sŏng 아우성. —*v.* kkik-ggik-gŏ-ri-da 끽 끽거리다 ; pul-p'yŏng-ha-da 불평하다.

squeeze *v.* jja-da 짜다, kkwak choe-da 꽉 죄다.

squint *n.* sa-p'al-nun 사팔눈, kyŏt-nun-jil 곁눈질. —*v.* kyŏt-nun-jil-ha-da 곁눈질하다. 「주.

squire *n.* chi-bang myŏng-sa 지방 명사, tae-ji-ju 대지

squirm *v.* kkum-t'ŭl-gŏ-ri-da 꿈틀거리다.

squirrel *n.* ta-ram-jwi 다람쥐. 「출하다.

squirt *v.* ppum-ŏ-nae-da 뿜어내다, pun-ch'ul-ha-da 분

stab *v.* jji-rŭ-da 찌르다, (*pierce*) kkwe-da 꿰다.

stability *n.* an-jŏng 안정, kyŏn-go 견고.

stable *adj.* kyŏn-go-han 견고한 ; an-jŏng-doen 안정된. —*n.* ma-gut-gan 마굿간, oe-yang-gan 외양간.

stack *n.* nat-ga-ri 낟가리, tŏ-mi 더미.

stadium *n.* kyŏng-gi-jang 경기장, sŭ-t'a-di-um 스타디움.

staff *n.* ① (*pole*) mak-dae-gi 막대기, chang-dae 장대. ② pu-wŏn 부원, chik-wŏn 직원. ③ (*army*) ch'am-mo 참모 : *chief of* ~ ch'am-mo-ch'ong-jang 참모총장.

stag *n.* su-sa-sŭm 수사슴.

stage *n.* ① mu-dae 무대, sŭ-t'e-i-ji 스테이지, pal-p'an 발판. ② (*period*) si-gi 시기 ; tan-gye 단계. 「설이다.

stagger *v.* pi-t'ŭl-gŏ-ri-da 비틀거리다 ; mang-sŏ-ri-da 망

stagnant *adj.* koe-ŏ-it-nŭn 괴어있는 ; (*slump*) pul-gyŏng-gi-ŭi 불경기의. 「doen 고정된.

staid *adj.* ch'im-ch'ak-han 침착한 ; (*fixed*) ko-jŏng-

stain *v.* tŏ-rŏp-hi-da 더럽히다. —*n.* ① (*spot*) ŏl-ruk 얼룩, tŏ-rŏm 더럼. ② (*blot*) o-jŏm 오점.

stainless *adj.* nok-sŭl-ji an-nŭn 녹슬지 않는, ŏl-ruk-ji-ji an-ŭn 얼룩지지 않은.

stair *n.* sa-da-ri 사다리, kye-dan 계단.

staircase *n.* kye-dan 계단, ch'ŭng-gye 층계. 「판돈.

stake *n.* ① (*post*) mal-dduk 말뚝. ② (*wager*) p'an-don

stale *adj.* sang-han 상한, (*flat*) kim-bba-jin 김빠진; (*trite*) k'ye-k'ye-muk-ŭn 케케묵은.

stalk *n.* chul-gi 줄기. —*v.* sal-gŭm-sal-gŭm ka-da 살금살금 가다; (*stride*) hwal-bo-ha-da 활보하다.

stall *n.* ① (*stable*) ma-gut-gan 마굿간. ② (*stand*) mae-jŏm 매점. —*v.* (*bogged down*) o-do-ga-do mot-ha-da 오도가도 못하다, chŏ-ji-ha-da 저지하다.

stalwart *adj.* t'ŭn-t'ŭn-han 튼튼한, kŏn-jang-han 건장한.

stamen *n.* (*of flower*) su-sul 수술. 「한.

stammer *v.* mal-ŭl tŏ-dŭm-da 말을 더듬다.

stamp *n.* (*postage*) u-p'yo 우표, in-ji 인지; (*seal*) to-jang 도장. —*v.* (*impress*) jjik-da 찍다; (*feet*) pal-ŭl ku-rŭ-da 발을 구르다, kŏt-da 걷다.

stand *n.* (*position*) ip-jang 입장; (*support*) tae 대(臺). —*v.* ① sŏ-da 서다. ② (*endure*) ch'am-da 참다.

standard *n.* ① p'yo-jun 표준. ② (*flag*) kun-gi 군기.

standing *n.* (*standing place*) sŏn chang-so 선 장소; (*rank*) chi-wi 지위, myŏng-mang 명망.

staple *n.* chu-san-mul 주산물, (*raw material*) wŏl-lyo 원료. —*adj.* (*principal*) chu-yo-han 주요한.

star *n.* ① pyŏl 별; (*destiny*) un-myŏng 운명. ② (*popular actor, actress*) sŭ-t'a-a 스타아.

starch *n.* nok-mal 녹말, (*paste*) p'ul 풀. —*v.* p'ul-ŭl mŏk-i-da 풀을 먹이다. 「다. —*n.* ŭng-si 응시.

stare *v.* no-ryŏ-bo-da 노려보다, ppan-hi po-da 빤히 보

starry *adj.* pyŏl-ŭi 별의; pyŏl-i pan-jjak-i-nŭn 별이 반짝이는; pyŏl-bit pal-gŭn 별빛 밝은.

start *n.* ① si-jak 시작, (*in races*) ch'ul-bal 출발. ②
(*shock*) kkam-jjak nol-ram 깜짝 놀람. —*v.* si-jak-ha-
da 시작하다, ch'ul-bal-ha-da 출발하다.

starting point ch'ul-bal-jŏm 출발점.

startle *v.* kkam-jjak nol-ra-ge ha-da 깜짝 놀라게 하다.

starvation *n.* kum-ju-rim 굶주림, ki-a 기아.

starve *v.* kum-ju-ri-da 굶주리다 ; kal-mang-ha-da 갈망
하다 : ～ *to death* kul-mŏ chuk-da 굶어 죽다.

state *n.* (*body politic*) kuk-ga 국가 ; (*a province*)
chu 주(州) : (*condition*) sang-t'ae 상태. —*v.* (*express
formally*) chin-sul-ha-da 진술하다. 「있는.

stately *adj.* tang-dang-han 당당한, wi-ŏm-it-nŭn 위엄

statement *n.* chin-sul 진술 ; sŏng-myŏng 성명.

stateroom *n.* t'ŭk-dŭng-sil 특등실, chŏn-yong-sil 전용

statesman *n.* chŏng-ch'i-ga 정치가. 「실.

station *n.* (*of a railway*) chŏng-gŏ-jang 정거장 ; (*position*) wi-ch'i 위치 ; (*rank*) sin-bun 신분. —*v.* chu-
dun-ha-da 주둔하다, pae-ch'i-ha-da 배치하다.

stationary *adj.* um-jik-i-ji an-nŭn 움직이지 않는, chŏng-
ji-doen 정지된 ; sang-bi-ŭi 상비(常備)의.

stationery *n.* p'yŏn-ji-ji 편지지, mun-bang-gu 문방구.

statistical *adj.* t'ong-gye-ŭi 통계의.

statistics *n.* ① t'ong-gye(-p'yo) 통계(표). ② (*science*)
t'ong-gye-hak 통계학. 「상.

statue *n.* cho-sang 조상(彫像) : *bronze* ～ tong-sang 동

stature *n.* sin-jang 신장(身長), k'i 키.

status *n.* (*rank*) sin-bun 신분 ; (*condition*) sang-t'ae

statute *n.* pŏp-ryŏng 법령, pŏp-gyu 법규. 「상태.

stay *v.* mŏ-mu-rŭ-da 머무르다, (*stop*) mŏm-ch'u-da 멈추
다. —*n.* ch'e-ryu 체류 ; chŏng-ji 정지. 「대신하여.

stead *n.* tae-sin 대신 : *in* ～ *of* …ŭl tae-sin-ha-yŏ …을

steadfast *adj.* hwak-go-han 확고한, pul-byŏn-ŭi 불변의.

steady *adj.* (*firm*) tan-dan-han 단단한, (*faithful*)
ch'ak-sil-han 착실한, han-gyŏl-ga-t'ŭn 한결같은.

steak *n.* sŭ-t'e-i-k'ŭ 스테이크, pul-go-gi 불고기.

steal *adj.* hum-ch'i-da 훔치다. —*n.* chŏl-do 절도.

steam *n.* chŭng-gi 증기, kim 김. —*v.* jji-da 찌다.

steam engine chŭng-gi ki-gwan 증기 기관.

steamer *n.* ① ki-sŏn 기선. ② si-ru 시루.

steamship *n.* ki-sŏn 기선, sang-sŏn 상선.

steed *n.* (*for horse riding*) mal 말, kun-ma 군마.

steel *n.* kang-ch'ŏl 강철, kang 강(鋼).

steelyard *n.* tae-jŏ-ul 대저울.

steep *adj.* hŏm-han 험한, ka-p'a-rŭn 가파른: *a ~
mountain* ka-p'a-rŭn san 가파른 산.

steeple *n.* ppyo-jok-t'ap 뾰족탑, ch'ŏm-t'ap 첨탑.

steer *v.* ① cho-jong-ha-da 조종하다 ; (*direct*) tol-ri-da
돌리다. ② (*conduct oneself*) ch'ŏ-sin-ha-da 처신하다.

stem *n.* (*of plants*) chul-gi 줄기. —*v.* (*stop*) mak-a-
nae-da 막아내다, (*resist*) chŏ-hang-ha-da 저항하다.

stenographer *n.* sok-gi-sa 속기사.

stenography *n.* sok-gi 속기, sok-gi-sul 속기술.

step *v.* (*walk*) kŏt-da 걷다 ; na-a-ga-da 나아가다 ;
(*tread*) pap-da 밟다. —*n.* kŏ-rŭm-sae 걸음새.

stepbrother *n.* i-bok-hyŏng-je 이복형제.

stepchild *n.* ŭi-but-ja-sik 의붓자식.

stepdaughter *n.* ŭi-but-ddal 의붓딸.

stepfather *n.* ŭi-but-a-bŏ-ji 의붓아버지, kye-bu 계부.

stepmother *n.* ŭi-but-ŏ-mŏ-ni 의붓어머니, kye-mo 계모.

sterile *adj.* (*barren*) me-ma-rŭn 메마른 ; pu-rim-ŭi 불
임의 ; (*unable to produce*) pul-mo-ŭi 불모의.

stern *adj.* ŏm-gyŏk-han 엄격한. —*v.* (*of a ship*) ko-
mul 고물, sŏn-mi 선미(船尾).

steward *n.* (*of ship*) sŏn-sil-gye 선실계 ; (*in hotels*) po-i 보이, chŏp-dae-wŏn 접대원.

stewardess *n.* sŭ-t'yu-ŏ-di-sŭ 스튜어디스.

stick *n.* chi-p'ang-i 지팡이. —*v.* (*to*) put-da 붙다 ; (*into*) jji-rŭ-da 찌르다 ; (*catch*) kŏl-ri-da 걸리다.

sticking plaster pan-ch'ang-go 반창고.

sticky *adj.* kkŭn-jŏk-ggŭn-jŏk-han 끈적끈적한.

stiff *adj.* (*hard*) kut-ŭn 굳은, ttak-ddak-han 딱딱한, ppŏt-bbŏt-han 뻣뻣한 ; (*dense*) kŏl-jjuk-han 걸쭉한.

stifle *v.* ① chil-sik-si-k'i-da 질식시키다. ② (*put out*) kkŭ-da 끄다. ③ (*repress*) ŏk-nu-rŭ-da 억누르다.

stigma *n.* (*stain*) o-myŏng 오명 ; ch'i-yok 치욕.

stile *n.* ti-dim-p'an 디딤판.

still *adj.* ko-yo-han 고요한, chŏng-ji-han 정지한. —*adv.* tŏ-uk 더욱, sang-gŭm 상금 ; a-jik-do 아직도.

stillness *n.* ko-yo 고요, ch'im-muk 침묵.

stimulant *n.* hŭng-bun-je 흥분제 ; (*pl.*) sul 술.

stimulate *v.* (*excite*) cha-gŭk-ha-da 자극하다, (*animate*) hwal-gi-ddi-ge ha-da 활기띠게 하다.

sting *n.* jjil-rin sang-ch'ŏ 찔린 상처, (*pain*) sim-han ko-t'ong 심한 고통. —*v.* (*prick*) jji-rŭ-da 찌르다 ; sso-da 쏘다.

stingy *adj.* ① in-saek-han 인색한 : ~ *man* ku-du-soe 구두쇠. ② sso-nŭn 쏘는.

stink *v.* ak-ch'wi-rŭl ppum-da 악취를 뿜다. —*n.* ak-ch'wi 악취 ; ku-rin-nae 구린내.

stint *v.* (*grudge*) chu-gi si-rŏ-ha-da 주기 싫어하다.

stipend *n.* pong-gŭp 봉급, (*salary*) kŭp-ryo 급료.

stipulate *v.* (*require*) kyu-jŏng-ha-da 규정하다, yak-jŏng-ha-da 약정하다, (*specify*) myŏng-gi-ha-da 명기하다

stir *v.* hwi-jŏt-da 휘젓다 ; um-jik-i-da 움직이다. [다.

stitch *v.* (*sew*) kkwe-mae-da 꿰매다.

stock *n.* (*goods for business*) chae-go-p'um 재고품 ;

(lineage) hyŏl-t'ong 혈통, ka-mun 가문.

stocking *n.* yang-mal 양말, *(Korean)* pŏ-sŏn 버선.

stomach *n.* wi 위, *(belly)* pae 배.

stone *n.* tol 돌, tol-meng-i 돌멩이, sŏk-jae 석재.

stone coal *(anthracite)* mu-yŏn-t'an 무연탄.

stonemason *n.* sŏk-su 석수, sŏk-gong 석공.

stonework *n.* sŏk-jo-mul 석조물 ; tol-se-gong 돌세공.

stony *adj.* tol-ŭi 돌의, tol-i man-ŭn 돌이 많은 ; *(merciless)* naeng-hok-han 냉혹한 ; *(motionless)* um-jik-i-ji an-nŭn 움직이지 않는.

stool *n.* kŏl-sang 걸상 ; *(commode)* pyŏn-gi 변기.

stoop *v.* kku-bu-ri-da 꾸부리다. —*n.* sae-u-dŭng 새우등.

stop *n.* *(pause)*chung-ji 중지 ; *(stopping place)* chŏng-gŏ-jang 정거장. —*v.* mŏm-ch'u-da 멈추다.

store *n.* sang-jŏm 상점. —*v.* chŏ-jang-ha-da 저장하다.

storehouse *n.* ch'ang-go 창고, kwang 광.

stor(e)y *n.* ch'ŭng 층, kye-ch'ŭng 계층 : *a house of one* ~ tan-ch'ŭng-jip 단층집/*the first* ~ il-ch'ŭng

stork *n.* hwang-sae 황새. ⌐1층.

storm *n.* p'ok-p'ung-u 폭풍우 ; so-dong 소동 : *a* ~ *warning* p'ok-p'ung chu-ŭi-bo 폭풍 주의보. —*v.* *(weather)* sa-na-wa-ji-da 사나와지다.

stormy *adj.* p'ok-p'ung-u-ŭi 폭풍우의.

story *n.* ① *(tale)* i-ya-gi 이야기, sŏl-hwa 설화. ② *(plot)* chul-gŏ-ri 줄거리. ③ *(report)* so-mun 소문.

stout *adj.* kŏn-gang-han 건강한, kang-in-han 강인한.

stove *n.* nal-lo 난로 : *cooking* ~ hwa-dŏk 화덕/*electric* ~ chŏn-gi nal-lo 전기 난로.

stovepipe *n.* sŭ-t'o-o-bŭ-ŭi yŏn-t'ong 스토오브의 연통.

stowaway *n.* mil-hang-ja 밀항자.

straight *adj.* *(erect)* ttok-ba-rŭn 똑바른, *(upright)* su-jik-ŭi 수직의. —*n.* chik-sŏn 직선. —*adv.* ttok-ba-ro 똑바로, (*honestly*) sol-jik-ha-ge 솔직하게.

strain *n.* (*tension*) kin-jang 긴장 ; (*overwork*) kwa-ro
과로. —*v.* kin-jang-si-k'i-da 긴장시키다 ; kwa-ro-si-
k'i-da 과로시키다.

strainer *n.* (*sieve*) ch'e 체, yŏ-gwa-gi 여과기.

strait *n.* ① hae-hyŏp 해협. ② (*pl.*) kon-gyŏng 곤경.

strand *v.* chwa-ch'o-ha-da 좌초하다. —*n.* mul-ga 물가.

strange *adj.* i-sang-han 이상한, nat-sŏn 낯선.

stranger *n.* mo-ru-nŭn sa-ram 모르는 사람 ; mun-oe-
han 문외한 ; (*foreigner*) oe-guk-in 외국인.

strangle *v.* mok-jol-ra chuk-i-da 목졸라 죽이다, chil-
sik-si-k'i-da 질식시키다.

strap *n.* ka-juk-ggŭn 가죽끈. —*v.* ka-juk-ggŭn-ŭ-ro
mae-da 가죽끈으로 매다.

stratagem *n.* chŏl-lyak 전략, ch'aek-ryak 책략.

strategy *n.* chŏl-lyak 전략, pyŏng-bŏp 병법.

straw *n.* chip 짚, mil-jip 밀짚 : ~ *bag* 가마니.

strawberry *n.* ttal-gi 딸기, yang-ddal-gi 양딸기.

straw vote pi-gong-sik t'u-p'yo 비공식 투표.

stray *v.* kil-ŭl il-t'a 길을 잃다, (*go wrong*) kil-ŭl chal-
mot tŭl-da 길을 잘못 들다. —*n.* mi-a 미아(迷兒).

streak *n.* ① chul-mu-nŭi 줄무늬. ② ki-jil 기질.

stream *n.* (*current*) hŭ-rŭm 흐름 ; (*small river*) kae-
ul 개울, nae 내. —*v.* hŭ-rŭ-da 흐르다.

streamline *n.* yu-sŏn-hyŏng 유선형(流線型).

street *n.* kŏ-ri 거리 ; ka-ro 가로.

streetcar *n.* (*tramcar*) si-ga chŏn-ch'a 시가 전차.

street lamp ka-ro-dŭng 가로등.

strength *n.* him 힘, se-ryŏk 세력.

strengthen *v.* kang-ha-ge ha-da 강하게 하다.

strenuous *adj.* pun-t'u-jŏk-in 분투적인 : *make ~ effort*
mu-ch'ŏk no-ryŏk-ha-da 무척 노력하다.

stress *n.* ap-bak 압박. —*v.* kang-jo-ha-da 강조하다.

stretch *v.* (*spread*) nŭl-ri-da 늘리다 ; (*reach out*) nae-mil-da 내밀다. —*n.* nŏl-bi 넓이, pŏm-wi 범위.

strew *v.* ppu-ri-da 뿌리다, kki-ŏn-da 끼얹다.

strict *adj.* ŏm-gyŏk-han 엄격한 ; chŏng-mil-han 정밀한.

stride *v.* sŏng-k'ŭm-sŏng-k'ŭm kŏt-da 성큼성큼 걷다.

strife *n.* ssa-um 싸움, pun-t'u 분투 ; ch'ung-dol 충돌.

strike *v.* ttae-ri-da 때리다, tu-dŭ-ri-da 두드리다. —*n.* (*industry*) tong-maeng-p'a-ŏp 동맹파업.

string *n.* kkŭn 끈 : *shoe* ~ ku-du-ggŭn 구두끈.

strip *v.* pŏt-gi-da 벗기다. —*n.* (*of cloth*) cho-gak 조각.

stripe *n.* chul 줄, chul-mu-nŭi 줄무늬 : *the Stars and S*~ sŏng-jo-gi 성조기.

strive *v.* no-ryŏk-ha-da 노력하다, ae-ssŭ-da 애쓰다.

stroke *n.* ① (*of Korean characters*) hoek 획. ② (*illness*) chol-do 졸도. —*v.* ssŭ-da-dŭm-da 쓰다듬다.

stroll *n. & v.* san-ch'aek(-ha-da) 산책(하다).

strong *adj.* (*powerful*) kang-han 강한, (*tough*) t'ŭn-t'ŭn-han 튼튼한, (*robust*) kŏn-gang-han 건강한 ; (*thick*) chin-han 진한.

structure *n.* ku-jo 구조 ; (*building*) kŏn-mul 건물.

struggle *n.* ssa-um 싸움 ; no-ryŏk 노력. —*v.* no-ryŏk-ha-da 노력하다 ; (*fight*) ta-t'u-da 다투다.

strut *v.* ppom-nae-myŏ kŏt-da 뽐내며 걷다. —*n.* ppom-naen kŏ-rŭm-gŏ-ri 뽐낸 걸음걸이.

stub *n.* kŭ-ru-t'ŏ-gi 그루터기, tong-gang 동강.

stubborn *adj.* wan-go-han 완고한, ko-jip-sen 고집센.

stud *n.* ① (*of shirt*) tan-ch'u 단추. ② (*nail head*) mot 못. ③ (*horse*) mal-dde 말떼. 「연구가.

student *n.* hak-saeng 학생 ; (*investigator*) yŏn-gu-ga

studio *n.* sŭ-t'yu-di-o 스튜디오, pang-song-sil 방송실 ; hwa-sil 화실 ; sa-jin-gwan 사진관.

study *n.* ① kong-bu 공부. ② (*room*) sŏ-jae 서재. —*v.* kong-bu-ha-da 공부하다, yŏn-gu-ha-da 연구하다.

stuff *n.* (*material*) chae-ryo 재료 ; mul-ja 물자; (*rubbish*) p'ye-mul 폐물. —*v.* ch'ae-u-da 채우다.

stumble *v.* (kŏl-ryŏ) nŏm-ŏ-ji-da (걸려) 넘어지다 ; pi-t'ŭl-gŏ-ri-da 비틀거리다. —*n.* sil-p'ae 실패.

stump *n.* kŭ-ru-t'ŏ-gi 그루터기, mong-dang yŏn-p'il 몽 당 연필.

stun *v.* ki-jŏl-si-k'i-da 기절시키다.

stupefy *v.* ma-bi-si-k'i-da 마비시키다.

stupendous *adj.* (*amazing*) nol-ral-man-han 놀랄만한, ŏm-ch'ŏng-nan 엄청난, kŏ-dae-han 거대한.

stupid *adj.* ŏ-ri-sŏk-ŭn 어리석은, u-dun-han 우둔한.

sturdy *adj.* sil-han 실한, t'ŭn-t'ŭn-han 튼튼한.

stutter *v.* (*stammer*) mal-ŭl tŏ-dŭm-da 말을 더듬다.

sty *n.* ① (*for pigs*) twae-ji-u-ri 돼지우리. ② (*eye*) da-rae-ggi 다래끼.

style *n.* (*manner*) mo-yang 모양, (*mode*) hyŏng 형; (*of writing*) mun-ch'e 문체.

stylus *n.* ch'ŏl-p'il 철필 ; (*phonograph*) pa-nŭl 바늘.

subdue *v.* (*suppress*) chin-ap-ha-da 진압하다.

subject *n.* ① (*of a country*) sin-ha 신하, paek-sŏng 백성. ② (*theme*) chu-je 주제 ; (*of study*) hak-gwa 학과, kwa-mok 과목 ; (*gram.*) chu-ŏ 주어.

subjugate *v.* pok-jong-si-k'i-da 복종시키다.

subjunctive *n.* (*gram.*) ka-jŏng-bŏp 가정법. 「한.

sublime *adj.* chang-ŏm-han 장엄한, sung-go-han 숭고

submarine *adj.* pa-da-mi-t'ŭi 바다밑의, hae-jŏ-ŭi 해저 의. —*n.* cham-su-ham 잠수함.

submerge *v.* mul-sok-e cham-gŭ-da 물속에 잠그다.

submission *n.* pok-jong 복종, hang-bok 항복.

submit *v.* ① (*present*) che-ch'ul-ha-da 제출하다. ② (*surrender*) kul-bok-ha-da 굴복하다.

subordinate *adj.* chong-sok-ha-nŭn 종속하는 ; ha-wi-ŭi

하위의. —*n.* pu-ha 부하(部下).

subscribe *v.* ① (*pre-engage*) ye-yak-ha-da 예약하다. ② (*contribute*) ki-bu-ha-da 기부하다. ③ (*sign*) sŏ-myŏng-ha-da 서명하다. ④ (*take in*) ku-dok-ha-da 구독하다.

subscription *n.* ye-yak 예약 ; ki-bu 기부 ; sŏ-myŏng 서명 : ～ *edition* ye-yak-p'an 예약판.

subsequent *adj.* kŭ hu-ŭi 그 후의.   「잠잠해지다.

subside *v.* ka-ra-an-da 가라앉다, cham-jam-hae-ji-da

subsidize *v.* po-jo-gŭm-ŭl chu-da 보조금을 주다.

subsidy *n.* po-jo-gŭm 보조금, chang-ryŏ-gŭm 장려금.

subsist *v.* (*continue to live*) saeng-jon-ha-da 생존하다 ; (*maintain*) mŏk-yŏ sal-ri-da 먹여 살리다.

subsistence *n.* saeng-jon 생존, saeng-gye 생계.

substance *n.* ① sil-ch'e 실체. ② mul-jil 물질.

substantial *adj.* (*actual*) sil-jae-ha-nŭn 실재하는, (*solid*) sil-sok-it-nŭn 실속있는, kyŏn-sil-han 견실한.

substitute *n.* (*a person*) tae-ri 대리 ; (*a thing*) tae-yong-p'um 대용품. —*v.* tae-ch'i-ha-da 대치하다.

substitution *n.* tae-ch'i 대치 ; tae-ri 대리.

subtle *adj.* (*delicate*) mi-myo-han 미묘한 ; min-gam-han 민감한 ; (*elaborate*) chŏng-gyo-han 정교한.

subtract *v.* ppae-da 빼다, kam-ha-da 감하다.

subtraction *n.* sak-gam 삭감, (*math.*) kam-bŏp 감법,

suburb *n.* kyo-oe 교외(郊外).   「ppae-gi 빼기.

subversive *adj.* twi-jip-ŏ ŏp-nŭn 뒤집어 엎는.

subway *n.* (*underground passage*) chi-ha-do 지하도 ; (*underground railway*) chi-ha-ch'ŏl 지하철.

succeed *v.* ① sŏng-gong-ha-da 성공하다. ② (*follow*) it-da-ra i-rŏ-na-da 잇달아 일어나다 ; (*be successor to*) sang-sok[kye-sŭng]-ha-da 상속[계승]하다.

success *n.* sŏng-gong 성공, sŏng-ch'wi 성취.

successful *adj.* sŏng-gong-jŏk-in 성공적인.

succession *n.* (*inheritance*) sang-sok 상속, kye-sŭng 계승 ; (*continuation*) yŏn-sok 연속.

successive *adj.* yŏn-sok-jŏk-in 연속적인.

successor *n.* hu-gye-ja 후계자, sang-sok-in 상속인.

succumb *v.* (*yield*) kul-bok-ha-da 굴복하다.

such *adj.* kŭ-rŏ-han 그러한, i-rŏ-han 이러한.

suck *v.* ppal-da 빨다 : chŏ-jŭl mŏk-da 젖을 먹다.

sudatorium *n.* han-jŭng-mak 한증막, chŭng-gi-t'ang 증기탕. 「뜻밖의, to-ryŏn-han 돌연한.

sudden *adj.* kap-jak-sŭ-rŏ-un 갑작스러운, ttŭt-ba-ggŭi

suddenly *adv.* kap-ja-gi 갑자기, to-ryŏn 돌연.

sue *v.* ① ko-so-ha-da 고소하다.② (*beseech*) kan-ch'ŏng-ha-da 간청하다. ③ (*court*) ku-hon-ha-da 구혼하다.

suet *n.* soe-gi-rŭm 쇠기름, yang-gi-rŭm 양기름.

suffer *v.* (*undergo*) kyŏk-da 겪다, (*bear pain*) koe-ro-wa-ha-da 괴로와하다 ; (*tolerate*) ch'am-da 참다.

suffering *n.* (*pain*) ko-t'ong 고통 ; (*loss*) son-hae 손해.

suffice *v.* man-jok-si-k'i-da 만족시키다, ch'ung-bun-ha-da 충분하다, (*be enough*) chok-ha-da 족하다.

sufficient *adj.* ch'ung-bun-han 충분한, man-ŭn 많은.

suffix *n.* (*gram.*) chŏp-mi-ŏ 접미어(接尾語).

suffocate *v.* (*choke*) chil-sik-si-k'i-da 질식시키다, sum-ŭl mak-da 숨을 막다 ; (*extinguish*) kkŭ-da 끄다.

suffrage *n.* t'u-p'yo 투표, sŏn-gŏ-gwŏn 선거권.

sugar *n.* sŏl-t'ang 설탕 : *cube* ~ kak-sŏl-t'ang 각설탕.

sugar cane sa-t'ang-su-su 사탕수수.

suggest *v.* am-si-ha-da 암시하다 ; che-an-ha-da 제안하다.

suggestion *n.* am-si 암시 ; che-ŭi 제의. 「하다.

suicide *n.* cha-sal 자살 : *commit* ~ cha-sal-ha-da 자살

suit *n.* ① (*law*) so-song 소송, ko-so 고소. ② (*clothes*) han pŏl 한 벌. —*v.* chŏk-hap-ha-da 적합하다. 「는.

suitable *adj.* chŏk-dang-han 적당한 ; ŏ-ul-ri-nŭn 어울리

suitor *n.* ① (*for marriage*) ku-hon-ja 구혼자. ② (*law*) so-song-in 소송인. 「da 뽀로통해지다.

sulk *v.* sael-jjuk-ha-da 샐쭉하다, ppyo-ro-t'ong-hae-ji-

sulky *adj.* sael-jjuk-han 샐쭉한, ttung-han 뚱한.

sullen *adj.* si-mu-ruk-han 시무룩한, mu-dduk-dduk-han

sulphur · sulfur *n.* yu-hwang 유황. └무뚝뚝한.

sultry *adj.* mu-dŏ-un 무더운, hu-dŏp-ji-gŭn-han 후덥지 근한 : ~ *weather* mu-dŏ-un nal-ssi 무더운 날씨.

sum *n.* ① (*total amount*) hap-gye 합계. ② (*outline*) kae-yo 개요. ③ (*pl.*) (*calculation*) kye-san 계산.

summarize *v.* yo-yak-ha-da 요약하다.

summary *n.* yo-yak 요약, chŏk-yo 적요(摘要). —*adj.* yo-yak-han 요약한, tae-gang-ŭi 대강의.

summer *n.* yŏ-rŭm 여름, yŏ-rŭm-ch'ŏl 여름철.

summit *n.* chŏng-sang 정상, kkok-dae-gi 꼭대기 : *a ~ talk* chŏng-sang-hoe-dam 정상회담.

summon *v.* so-hwan-ha-da 소환하다, so-jip-ha-da 소집 하다. —*n.* (*a writ*) so-hwan-jang 소환장.

sumptuous *adj.* kap-bi-ssan 값비싼 ; sa-ch'i-han 사치한.

sun *n.* hae 해, t'ae-yang 태양, haet-bit 햇빛.

sunbeam *n.* haet-sal 햇살, t'ae-yang kwang-sŏn 태양

sunburn *v.* haet-byŏ-t'e t'a-da 햇볕에 타다. └광선.

Sunday *n.* i-ryo-il 일요일, kong-il 공일, chu-il 주일.

Sunday best na-dŭ-ri-ot 나들이옷, cho-ŭn ot 좋은 옷.

sundial *n.* hae-si-gye 해시계.

sunflower *n.* hae-ba-ra-gi 해바라기.

sunlight *n.* haet-bit 햇빛, il-gwang 일광.

sunny *adj.* haet-byŏt jjoe-nŭn 햇볕 쬐는, yang-ji-ba-rŭn 양지바른.

sunrise *n.* hae-do-ji 해돋이, sae-byŏk-nyŏk 새벽녘.

sunset *n.* hae-jil-nyŏk 해질녘, hae-gŏ-rŭm 해거름.

sunshade *n.* (*parasol*) yang-san 양산, ch'a-yang 차양.

sunshine *n.* haet-byŏt 햇볕, il-gwang 일광.

sunspot *n.* t'ae-yang-ŭi hŭk-jŏm 태양의 흑점.

sunstroke *n.* il-sa-byŏng 일사병. 「훌륭한.

superb *adj.* ch'oe-go-gŭp-ŭi 최고급의, hul-ryung-han

superficial *adj.* p'yo-myŏn-ŭi 표면의 ; p'i-sang-jŏk-in 피상적인 ; (*shallow*) ch'ŏn-bak-han 천박한.

superfluous *adj.* yŏ-bun-ŭi 여분의, nam-a-do-nŭn 남아도

superintendent *n.* kam-dok(-ja) 감독(자). 「는.

superior *adj.* hul-ryung-han 훌륭한, u-su-han 우수한.
  —*n.* wit-sa-ram 윗사람, sang-gwan 상관, sŏn-bae 선

superiority *n.* u-wŏl 우월, u-wi 우위. 「배.

superlative *adj.* ch'oe-go-ŭi 최고의. —*n.* ch'oe-go 최고.

supermarket *n.* syu-u-p'ŏ-ma-a-k'it 슈우퍼마아킷.

superstition *n.* mi-sin 미신.

supervise *v.* kam-dok〔kwal-li〕-ha-da 감독〔관리〕하다.

supervisor *n.* kam-dok-ja 감독자, kwal-li-in 관리인.

supper *n.* chŏ-nyŏk-sik-sa 저녁식사.

supple *adj.* ① na-gŭt-na-gŭt-han 나긋나긋한, yu-sun-han 유순한. ② (*flexible*) chal hwi-nŭn 잘 휘는.

supplement *n.* pu-rok 부록 ; (*addition*) ch'u-ga 추가.

supplication *n.* t'an-wŏn 탄원, ae-wŏn 애원.

supply *n.* (*supplying*) kong-gŭp 공급 ; (*stock*) chae-go-p'um 재고품 ; (*provisions*) yang-sik 양식. —*v.* kong-gŭp-ha-da 공급하다. 「jo-ha-da 원조하다.

support *n.* chi-ji 지지. —*v.* chi-ji-ha-da 지지하다, wŏn-

supporter *n.* ① (*prop*) chi-ju 지주(支柱). ② (*sustainer*) pu-yang-ja 부양자. ③ pak-dae 박대.

suppose *v.* (*assume*) ka-jŏng-ha-da 가정하다 ; (*think*) saeng-gak-ha-da 생각하다, ch'u-ch'ŭk-ha-da 추측하다.

supposition *n.* ch'u-ch'ŭk 추측, ka-jŏng 가정.

suppress *v.* (*subdue*) chin-ap-ha-da 진압하다 ; (*stop*) kŭm-ha-da 금하다 ; (*conceal*) sum-gi-da 숨기다.

supreme *adj.* ch'oe-go-ŭi 최고의, kŭk-do-ŭi 극도의 : *the S~ Court* tae-bŏp-wŏn 대법원.

sure *adj.* hwak-sil-han 확실한, (*reliable*) mit-ŭl su it-nŭn 믿을 수 있는 ; (*safe*) an-jŏn-han 안전한.

surely *adv.* hwak-sil-hi 확실히 ; (*answer*) a-mu-ryŏm 아무렴 ; mul-ron 물론.

surety *n.* (*sponsor*) po-jŭng-in 보증인, tam-bo 담보.

surf *n.* mil-ryŏ-o-nŭn p'a-do 밀려오는 파도.

surface *n.* p'yo-myŏn 표면, oe-gwan 외관.

surge *n.* kŏ-sen p'a-do 거센 파도. 「군의관.

surgeon *n.* ① oe-gwa ŭi-sa 외과 의사. ② kun-ŭi-gwan

surly *adj.* mu-dduk-dduk-han 무뚝뚝한, ku-jŭn 궂은.

surmise *n. & v.* ch'u-ch'ŭk(-ha-da) 추측(하다).

surmount *v.* nŏm-da 넘다 ; kŭk-bok-ha-da 극복하다.

surname *n.* sŏng 성(姓) ; pyŏl-myŏng 별명.

surpass *v.* …po-da nat-da …보다 낫다, …ŭl nŭng-ga-ha-da …을 능가하다. —*adj.* ttwi-ŏ-nan 뛰어난.

surplus *n.* yŏ-bun 여분, na-mŏ-ji 나머지. 「하다.

surprise *n.* nol-ram 놀람. —*v.* nol-ra-ge ha-da 놀라게

surprising *adj.* nol-ral-man-han 놀랄만한, nun-bu-sin

surrender *n. & v.* hang-bok(-ha-da) 항복(하다). 「눈부신.

surround *v.* tul-rŏ-ssa-da 둘러싸다, e-wŏ-ssa-da 에워싸다 ; p'o-wi-ha-da 포위하다.

surroundings *n.* chu-wi 주위, hwan-gyŏng 환경.

surtax *n.* pu-ga-se 부가세, nu-jin-se 누진세.

survey *v.* ① (*look over*) tul-ro-bo-da 둘러보다. ② (*examine*) cho-sa-ha-da 조사하다. ③ (*measure*) ch'ŭk-ryang-ha-da 측량하다. —*n.* ① kae-gwan 개관. ② ch'ŭk-ryang 측량. 「da 살아 남다.

survive *v.* po-da o-rae sal-da 보다 오래 살다, sa-ra nam-

susceptible *adj.* min-gam-han 민감한, (*liable*) …e kŏl-ri-gi swi-un …에 걸리기 쉬운.

suspect *v.* ŭi-sim-ha-da 의심하다, su-sang-hi yŏ-gi-da 수상히 여기다. —*n.* hyŏm-ŭi-ja 혐의자.

suspend *v.* ① (*hang*) ta-ra-mae-da 달아매다. ② (*from work*) chŏng-jik-si-k'i-da 정직(停職)시키다 ; (*stop temporarily*) chung-ji-ha-da 중지하다. ③ (*delay*) yŏn-gi-ha-da 연기하다.

suspenders *n.* mel-bbang 멜빵. 「pu-ran 불안.

suspense *n.* ① (*pending*) mi-gyŏl 미결. ② (*anxiety*)

suspension *n.* (*hanging up*) mae-dal-gi 매달기 ; (*pending question*) mi-gyŏl 미결 ; (*from office*) chŏng-jik 정직, (*from school*) chŏng-hak 정학.

suspicion *n.* ŭi-sim 의심, hyŏm-ŭi 혐의.

suspicious *adj.* ŭi-sim-man-ŭn 의심많은, ŭi-sim-sŭ-rŏ-un 의심스러운, su-sang-jjŏk-ŭn 수상적은.

sustain *v.* kyŏn-di-da 견디다, yu-ji-ha-da 유지하다.

sustenance *n.* ① saeng-gye 생계. ② (*nourishment*) yŏng-yang-mul 영양물. ③ (*support*) yu-ji 유지.

swagger *v.* hwal-bo-ha-da 활보하다. —*n.* hwal-bo 활보.

swallow *n.* che-bi 제비. —*v.* sam-k'i-da 삼키다.

swallowtail *n.* che-bi kkong-ji 제비 꽁지.

swamp *n.* (*bog*) nŭp 늪, (*marsh*) sŭp-ji 습지.

swan *n.* paek-jo 백조.

swarm *n.* tte 떼. —*v.* mo-yŏ-dŭl-da 모여들다.

sway *v.* hŭn-dŭl-ri-da 흔들리다, hŭn-dŭl-da 흔들다.

swear *v.* ① maeng-se-ha-da 맹세하다. ② (*curse*) yok-ŭl ha-da 욕을 하다. —*n.* ① sŏn-sŏ 선서. ② chŏ-ju 저

sweat *n.* ttam 땀. —*v.* ttam hŭl-ri-da 땀 흘리다. 「주.

sweater *n.* (*jersey*) sŭ-we-t'ŏ 스웨터.

sweep *v.* ssŭl-da 쓸다, ch'ŏng-so-ha-da 청소하다 ; (*remove*) il-so-ha-da 일소하다. —*n.* ch'ŏng-so 청소.

sweet *adj.* tal-k'om-han 달콤한 ; hyang-gi-ro-un 향기로운 ; (*pleasing*) yu-k'wae-han 유쾌한.

sweetheart *n.* (*lover*) ae-in 애인, yŏn-in 연인.
sweetly *adv.* (*fragrantly*) hyang-gi-rop-ge 향기롭게 ;
　sang-nyang-ha-ge 상냥하게, kwi-yŏp-ge 귀엽게.
sweet potato ko-gu-ma 고구마.
swell *v.* pu-p'ul-da 부풀다, k'ŏ-ji-da 커지다.
swelter *v.* mu-dŏp-da 무덥다, tŏ-wi-mŏk-da 더위먹다.
swerve *v.* pit-na-ga-da 빗나가다, pŏ-sŏ-na-da 벗어나다.
swift *adj.* ppa-rŭn 빠른, sin-sok-han 신속한.
swiftly *adv.* ppa-rŭ-ge 빠르게, sin-sok-hi 신속히.
swim *v.* he-ŏm-ch'i-da 헤엄치다 ; (*float*) ttŭ-da 뜨다.
swimming *n.* su-yŏng 수영.
swimming bath sil-nae su-yŏng-jang 실내 수영장.
swindle *v.* sok-i-da 속이다, sa-ch'wi-ha-da 사취하다.
swine *n.* (*pigs*) twae-ji 돼지.
swing *n.* ① chin-dong 진동. ② kŭ-ne 그네. —*v.* hŭn-dŭl-
　da 흔들다 ; (*on swing*) kŭ-ne-rŭl ttwi-da 그네를 뛰다.
swirl *v.* so-yong-do-ri-ch'i-da 소용돌이치다.
switch *n.* sŭ-wi-ch'i 스위치, kae-p'ye-gi 개폐기. —*v.*
　① chŏn-hwan-ha-da 전환하다, pa-ggu-da 바꾸다. ②
　(*whip*) mae-jil-ha-da 매질하다. 「환데
switchboard *n.* pae-jŏn-p'an 배전판 ; kyo-hwan-dae 교
swoon *n.* & *v.* (*faint*) ki-jŏl(-ha-da) 기절(하다).
swoop *v.* nae-ri-dŏp-ch'i-da 내리덮치다. 「검무.
sword *n.* k'al 칼 : ~ *dance* k'al-ch'um 칼춤, kŏm-mu
syllable *n.* ŭm-jŏl 음절, ch'ŏl-ja 철자.
syllabus *n.* kae-yo 개요 ; tae-gang 대강. 「기호.
symbol *n.* (*emblem*) sang-jing 상징 ; (*mark*) ki-ho
symbolize *v.* sang-jing-ha-da 상징하다.
symmetry *n.* kyun-hyŏng 균형, tae-ch'ing 대칭.
sympathetic *adj.* tong-jŏng-ha-nŭn 동정하는 ; (*con-
genial*) ma-ŭm-e tŭ-nŭn 마음에 드는.
sympathize *v.* ① tong-jŏng-ha-da 동정하다. ② (*agree*

with) tong-ŭi-ha-da 동의하다, ch'an-sŏng-ha-da 찬성하다. ③ (*condole*) wi-ro-ha-da 위로하다.

sympathy *n.* tong-jŏng 동정, kong-myŏng 공명(共鳴).

symphony *n.* kyo-hyang-ak 교향악, sim-p'o-ni 심포니.

synonym *n.* tong-ŭi-ŏ 동의어, yu-ŏ 유어(類語).

syntax *n.* ku-mun-ron 구문론, mun-jang-ron 문장론.

syphilis *n.* mae-dok 매독, ch'ang-byŏng 창병.

system *n.* cho-jik 조직, ch'e-gye 체계 ; (*method*) pang-bŏp 방법, pang-sik 방식.   「체계적인.

systematic *adj.* cho-jik-jŏk-in 조직적인, ch'e-gye-jŏk-in

T

table *n.* t'ak-ja 탁자, (*food*) sik-t'ak 식탁.

tablecloth *n.* sik-t'ak-bo 식탁보.

tablespoon *n.* k'ŭn sut-ga-rak 큰 숟가락, t'e-i-bŭl sŭ-p'u-un 테이블 스푸운.   「chŏng-je 정제.

tablet *n.* ① p'yŏng-p'an 평판(平板), p'ae 패. ② (*med.*)

taboo *n.* (*ban*) kŭm-gi 금기, kŭm-je 금제.

tacit *adj.* mu-ŏn-ŭi 무언의 ; cham-jam-han 잠잠한.

taciturn *adj.* ip-i mu-gŏ-un 입이 무거운.

tack *n.* ① nap-jak-mot 납작못, ap-jŏng 압정. ② chu-rŭm 주름.

tackle *n.* to-gu 도구, yŏn-jang 연장 : *fishing ~* nak-si to-gu 낚시 도구. —*v.* tal-ryŏ-dŭl-da 달려들다.

tact *n.* chae-ch'i 재치 ; som-ssi 솜씨.

tactics *n.* ① (*strategy*) chŏn-sul 전술, pyŏng-bŏp 병법. ② (*tricks*) sul-ch'aek 술책, ch'aek-ryak 책략.

tadpole *n.* ol-ch'aeng-i 올챙이.

tag *n.* ① kko-ri-p'yo 꼬리표. ② sul-rae-jap-gi 술래잡기.

tail *n.* kko-ri 꼬리 ; kkŭ-t'ŭ-mŏ-ri 끄트머리.

tailor *n.* chae-bong-sa 재봉사, yang-bok-jŏm 양복점.

taint *n.* (*stain*) o-jŏm 오점, tŏ-rŏ-um 더러움. —*v.* tŏ-rŏp-hi-da 더럽히다.

take *v.* (*seize*) chwi-da 쥐다, (*grasp*) chap-da 잡다 ; (*carry*) ka-ji-go ka-da 가지고 가다 ; (*go on board*) t'a-da 타다 ; (*eat*) mŏk-da 먹다. 「흉내.

take-off *n.* ① to-yak 도약, i-ryuk 이륙. ② hyung-nae

tale *n.* i-ya-gi 이야기, (*rumor*) so-mun 소문.

talent *n.* ① chae-nŭng 재능, su-wan 수완. ② (*person of* ~) in-jae 인재, t'ael-rŏn-t'ŭ 탤런트.

talisman *n.* pu-jŏk 부적, ho-bu 호부(護符).

talk *n.* i-ya-gi 이야기, sang-dam 상담. —*v.* mal-ha-da 말하다, i-ya-gi-ha-da 이야기하다.

talkative *adj.* su-da-sŭ-rŏ-un 수다스러운.

tall *adj.* k'i-ga k'ŭn 키가 큰 ; ŏm-ch'ŏng-nan 엄청난.

tallow *n.* su-ji 수지(獸脂) ; chim-sŭng ki-rŭm 짐승 기름.

talon *n.* (*animal*) pal-t'op 발톱.

tame *adj.* kil-dŭ-rin 길들인. —*v.* kil-dŭ-ri-da 길들이다.

tan *n.* hwang-gal-saek 황갈색, (*pl.*) kal-saek ku-du 갈색 구두. —*v.* (*leather*) mu-du-jil-ha-da 무두질하다 ; (*body*) haet-byŏ-t'e t'ae-u-da 햇볕에 태우다.

tangle *v.* ŏng-k'ŭ-rŏ-ji-da 엉클어지다. 「chŏn-ch'a 전차.

tank *n.* ① t'aeng-k'ŭ 탱크, mul-t'ong 물통. ② (*army*)

tap *v.* ka-byŏp-ge tu-dŭ-ri-da 가볍게 두드리다. —*n.* (*faucet*) chu-dung-i 주둥이, kkok-ji 꼭지.

tape *n.* ① t'e-i-p'ŭ 테이프. ② chul-ja 줄자.

tape measure chul-ja 줄자. 「mŏk-in sim-ji 먹인 심지.

taper *n.* ka-nŭn ch'o 가는 초, ch'o mŏk-in sim-ji 초

tapestry *n.* pyŏk-gŏ-ri yung-dan 벽걸이 융단.

tar *n.* t'a-a-rŭ 타아르. 「nŭ-jŭn 늦은.

tardy *adj.* (*slow*) nŭ-rin 느린, tŏ-din 더딘 ; (*late*) nŭ-

target *n.* p'yo-jŏk 표적, kwa-nyŏk 과녁.

tariff *n.* ① kwan-se 관세, se 세. ② (*a price list*)

yo-gŭm-p'yo 요금표, un-im-p'yo 운임표.

task *n.* (*job*) il 일, (*duty*) chik-mu 직무, (*lesson*)
kwa-ŏp 과업 : *a home* ~ suk-je 숙제.

task force (*mil.*) ki-dong pu-dae 기동 부대.

tassel *n.* sul 술 ; (*plant*) song-i-ggot 송이꽃.

taste *n.* mat 맛, mi-gak 미각 ; (*liking*) ch'wi-mi 취
미, ki-ho 기호. —*v.* mat-bo-da 맛보다.

tatter *n.* nŏng-ma 넝마, nu-dŏ-gi-ot 누더기옷.

taunt *v.* cho-rong-ha-da 조롱하다 ; tta-ji-da 따지다.

tavern *n.* (*public house*) sŏn-sul-jip 선술집, chu-mak
주막 ; (*inn*) yŏ-in-suk 여인숙.

tax *n.* se-gŭm 세금. —*v.* kwa-se-ha-da 과세하다.

taxi *n.* t'aek-si 택시.   「차.

tea *n.* ch'a 차, hong-ch'a 홍차 : *coarse* ~ yŏp-ch'a 엽

teach *v.* ka-rŭ-ch'i-da 가르치다, sŏl-myŏng-ha-da 설명

teacher *n.* sŏn-saeng 선생, kyo-sa 교사.   「하다.

teacup *n.* ch'a-jan 차잔, ch'a-jong 차종.

teakettle *n.* chu-jŏn-ja 주전자.

team *n.* t'i-im 티임, (*group*) p'ae 패.

teapot *n.* ch'a-ju-jŏn-ja 차주전자, ch'a-byong 차병.

tear *n.* ① (*drop*) nun-mul 눈물. ② (*rip*) jjae-jin t'ŭm
쩨진 틈. —*v.* jjit-da 찢다.

tearoom *n.* ta-bang 다방.   「da 성가시게 굴다.

tease *v.* chi-bun-gŏ-ri-da 지분거리다, sŏng-ga-si-ge kul-

technic *n.* su-bŏp 수법, (*pl.*) ki-gyo 기교.

technical *adj.* ki-sul-jŏk-in 기술적인, chŏn-mun-jŏk-in
전문적인 : ~ *terms* chŏn-mun-ŏ 전문어, su-rŏ 술어.

technology *n.* kong-ŏp ki-sul 공업 기술.

tedious *adj.* chi-ru-han 지루한, chi-gyŏ-un 지겨운.

teem *v.* (*abound*) ch'ung-man-ha-da 충만하다.

teen-age *adj.* sip-dae-ŭi 10대의.

teens *n.* sip-dae 10대.

telegram *n.* chŏn-bo 전보. 「전보를 치다.

telegraph *n.* chŏn-sin 전신. —*v.* chŏn-bo-rŭl ch'i-da

telepathy *n.* chŏng-sin kam-ŭng 정신 감응.

telephone *n.* chŏn-hwa 전화 : ~ *booth* kong-jung chŏn-hwa-sil 공중 전화실/~ *directory* chŏn-hwa-bu 전화부/~ *operator* kyo-hwan-su 교환수/*public* ~ kong-jung chŏn-hwa 공중 전화. —*v.* chŏn-hwa-rŭl kŏl-da

telescope *n.* mang-wŏn-gyŏng 망원경. ㄴ전화를 걸다.

television *n.* t'el-ri-bi-jyŏn 텔리비전.

tell *v.* mal-ha-da 말하다, i-ya-gi-ha-da 이야기하다 ; al-ri-da 알리다 : myŏng-ha-da 명하다.

temper *n.* ki-jil 기질, sŏng-mi 성미, (*anger*) no-gi 노

temperament *n.* ch'e-jil 체질, ki-jil 기질. ㄴ기.

temperance *n.* (*moderation*) chŏl-je 절제 ; (*liquor*) chŏl-ju 절주, kŭm-ju 금주. 「화한.

temperate *adj.* chŏl-je-it-nŭn 절제있는, on-hwa-han 온

temperature *n.* on-do 온도 ; ch'e-on 체온.

tempest *n.* tae-p'ok-p'ung-u 대폭풍우.

temple *n.* ① kwan-ja-no-ri 관자놀이. ② (*rel.*) sin-jŏn 신전(神殿), sa-wŏn 사원, chŏl 절. 「世)의.

temporal *adj.* il-si-jŏk-in 일시적인, hyŏn-se-ŭi 현세(現

temporary *adj.* il-si-jŏk-in 일시적인, im-si-ŭi 임시의.

tempt *v.* yu-hok-ha-da 유혹하다, pu-ch'u-gi-da 부추기

temptation *n.* yu-hok 유혹. ㄴ다.

ten *n. & adj.* yŏl(-ŭi) 열(의), sip(-ŭi) 10(의).

tenacious *adj.* wan-gang-han 완강한, wan-go-han 완고한. 「ja 차용자.

tenant *n.* (*farmer*) so-jak-in 소작인 ;(*hirer*) ch'a-yong-

tend *v.* ① …ŭi kyŏng-hyang-i it-da …의 경향이 있다. ② tol-bo-da 돌보다, chi-k'i-da 지키다.

tendency *n.* kyŏng-hyang 경향, sŏng-hyang 성향.

tender *adj.* (*soft*) pu-dŭ-rŏ-un 부드러운, mu-rŭn 무른.

tenderness *n.* pu-dŭ-rŏ-um 부드러움.

tenement *n.* ch'a-yong-ji 차용지, set-jip 셋집.

tennis *n.* chŏng-gu 정구, t'e-ni-sŭ 테니스.

tense *adj.* kin-jang-han 긴장한, p'aeng-p'aeng-han 팽 팽한. —*n.* (*gram.*) si-je 시제(時制).

tent *n.* ch'ŏn-mak 천막, t'en-t'ŭ 텐트.

tenth *adj.* yŏl-bŏn-jjae-ŭi 열번째의.

term *n.* ① (*school*) hak-gi 학기. ② (*period*) ki-han 기한. ③ (*tech.*) yong-ŏ 용어. ④ (*pl.*) cho-gŏn 조 건. —*v.* (*name*) ch'ing-ha-da 칭하다.

terminal *n.* chong-jŏm 종점, chong-ch'ak-yŏk 종착역, t'ŏ-ŏ-mi-nŏl 터어미널. 「종결시키다.

terminate *v.* kkŭt-nae-da 끝내다, chong-gyŏl-si-k'i-da

terrace *n.* (*height*) tae-ji 대지, ko-ji 고지 ; no-dae 노 대(露臺) ; t'e-ra-sŭ 테라스.

terrapin *n.* (*turtle*) sik-yong kŏ-buk 식용 거북.

terrible *adj.* mu-sŏ-un 무서운, ka-gong-hal 가공할.

terrify *v.* (*frighten*) nol-ra-da 놀라다, kŏp-na-ge ha-da 겁나게 하다.

territory *n.* yŏng-t'o 영토 ; chi-yŏk 지역.

terror *n.* kong-p'o 공포, kong-p'o-ŭi ssi 공포의 씨.

test *n. & v.* si-hŏm(-ha-da) 시험(하다).

testament *n.* (*will*) yu-ŏn(-jang) 유언(장) : *the Old [New]* *T*~ ku[sin]-yak sŏng-sŏ 구[신]약 성서.

testify *v.* (*give evidence*) chŭng-ŏn-ha-da 증언하다, ip-jŭng-ha-da 입증하다.

testimony *n.* chŭng-ŏn 증언, chŭng-gŏ 증거.

text *n.* ① wŏn-mun 원문, pon-mun 본문. ② kyo-gwa- 「sŏ 교과서.

textbook *n.* kyo-gwa-sŏ 교과서.

than *conj.* …po-da-do …보다도.

thank *v.* kam-sa-ha-da 감사하다 : *T*~ *you.* Ko-map-sŭp-ni-da 고맙습니다, Kam-sa-hap-ni-da 감사합니다.

thankful *adj.* kam-sa-ha-nŭn 감사하는, ko-ma-wa-ha-nŭn 고마와하는.

thanks *n.* kam-sa 감사, sa-rye 사례.

Thanksgiving Day ch'u-su kam-sa-jŏl 추수 감사절.

that *adj.* kŭ 그, chŏ 저. —*pron.* kŭ-gŏt 그것, chŏ-gŏt 저것. —*adv.* kŭ-rŏ-k'e 그렇게. —*conj.* …ha-da-nŭn[i-ra-nŭn] kŏt …하다는〔이라는〕 것.

thatch *n.* i-ŏng 이엉.

thaw *v.* nok-da 녹다, nok-i-da 녹이다, (*soften*) p'ul-ri-da 풀리다.

the *art.* kŭ 그, chŏ 저.

theatre · theater *n.* kŭk-jang 극장.

theft *n.* to-duk-jil 도둑질, chŏl-do 절도.

their *pron.* kŭ-dŭl-ŭi 그들의.

theirs *pron.* kŭ-dŭl-ŭi kŏt 그들의 것.

them *pron.* kŭ-dŭl-ŭl 그들을, kŭ-dŭl-e-ge 그들에게.

theme *n.* chu-je 주제, non-je 논제, t'e-e-ma 테에마, chu-sŏn-yul 주선율(主旋律) : ～ *song* chu-je-ga 주제가.

themselves *pron.* kŭ-dŭl cha-sin 그들 자신.

then *adv.* kŭ-ddae 그때, kŭ-ri-go-nŭn 그리고는, kŭ ta-ŭm-e 그 다음에, kŭ-rae-sŏ 그래서.

theology *n.* sin-hak 신학.

theoretical *adj.* i-ron-jŏk-in 이론적인.   「의견

theory *n.* i-ron 이론 ; hak-sŏl 학설 ; (*opinion*) ŭi-gyŏn

there *adv.* kŏ-gi-e 거기에, kŏ-gi-sŏ 거기서.

therefore *adv.* kŭ-rŏ-mŭ-ro 그러므로, tta-ra-sŏ 따라서.

thermal *adj.* yŏl-ŭi 열(熱)의, on-do-ŭi 온도의.

thermometer *n.* han-nan-gye 한난계 ; on-do-gye 온도계.

these *pron.* i-gŏt-dŭl 이것들. —*adj.* i-gŏt-dŭl-ŭi 이것들의 : ～ *days* yo-jŭ-ŭm 요즈음.

they *pron.* kŭ-dŭl 그들, ku-dŭl-ŭn 그들은.

thick *adj.* tu-ggŏ-un 두꺼운 ; (*dense*) chin-han 진한.

—*adv.* tu-ggŏp-ge 두껍게, chin-ha-ge 진하게.
thicket *n.* su-p'ul 수풀, chap-mok sup 잡목 숲.
thickness *n.* tu-gge 두께, kul-ggi 굵기 ; (*liquid, color*) nong-do 농도.
thief *v.* to-duk 도둑, chom-do-duk 좀도둑.
thieve *v.* hum-ch'i-da 훔치다. 「가랑이」.
thigh *n.* nŏp-jŏk-da-ri 넓적다리, ka-rang-i
thimble *n.* kol-mu 골무.
thin *adj.* yal-bŭn 얇은 ; (*slender*) yŏ-win 여윈 ; (*sparse*) tŭ-mun-dŭ-mun-han 드문드문한. [kol-mu]
thing *n.* mul-gŏn 물건, mul-ch'e 물체, sa-mul 사물.
think *v.* saeng-gak-ha-da 생각하다.
thinker *n.* sa-sang-ga 사상가. 「째(의).
third *n. & adj.* che sam(-ŭi) 제 3 (의), se-jjae(-ŭi) 세
third-class *adj.* sam-dŭng-ŭi 삼등의 ; sam-ryu-ŭi 삼류의.
thirst *n.* kal-jŭng 갈증, mok-ma-rŭm 목마름. —*v.* mok-ma-rŭ-da 목마르다 ; kal-mang-ha-da 갈망하다.
thirsty *adj.* mok-ma-rŭn 목마른, kal-jŭng-nan 갈증난.
thirteen *n. & adj.* yŏl-set(-ŭi) 열셋(의), sip-sam(-ŭi)
thirty *n.* sŏ-rŭn 서른, sam-sip 30. [13(의).
this *adj.* i 이, kŭm 금(今). —*pron.* i-gŏt 이것.
thistle *n.* ŏng-gŏng-k'wi 엉겅퀴.
thorn *n.* ① ka-si 가시. ② (*pain*) ko-t'ong 고통.
thorough *adj.* wan-jŏn-han 완전한 ; ch'ŏl-jŏ-han 철저한.
thoroughfare *n.* han-gil 한길, tae-ro 대로 : (*notice*) No ~. T'ong-haeng kŭm-ji 통행 금지.
thoroughly *adv.* wan-jŏn-hi 완전히 ; ch'ŏl-jŏ-hi 철저히.
those *pron.* kŭ-gŏt-dŭl 그것들. —*adj.* kŭ-gŏt-dŭl-ŭi 그것들의. 「pul-gu-ha-go …에도 불구하고.
though *adv.* kŭ-rŏ-na 그러나. —*conj.* (*even if*) …e-do
thought *n.* sa-sang 사상, saeng-gak 생각.

thoughtful *adj.* saeng-gak-i ki-p'ŭn 생각이 깊은, saeng-gak-e cham-gin 생각에 잠긴. 「ŏp-nŭn 지각없는.

thoughtless *adj.* pun-byŏl-ŏp-nŭn 분별없는, chi-gak-

thousand *n. & adj.* ch'ŏn(-ŭi) 천(의) : ten ~ man 만.

thrash *v.* (*beat*) ttae-ri-da 때리다, tu-dŭ-ri-da 두드리다.

thrasher *n.* (*machine*) t'al-gok-gi 탈곡기.

thread *n.* sil 실 : *a spool of* ~ sil-pae 실패. —*v.* sil-ŭl kkwe-da 실을 꿰다.

threadbare *adj.* (*worn-out*) nal-ga-bba-jin 낡아빠진.

threat *n.* wi-hyŏp 위협, hyŏp-bak 협박.

threaten *v.* wi-hyŏp-ha-da 위협하다, ŭ-rŭ-da 으르다.

threatening *adj.* (*weather*) hŏm-ak-han 험악한.

three *n. & adj.* set(-ŭi) 셋(의), sam(-ŭi) 3 (의).

threescore *n.* yuk-sip 60, yuk-sip-se 60세.

thresh *v.* (*thrash*) kok-sik-ŭl tu-dŭ-ri-da 곡식을 두드리다, t'a-jak-ha-da 타작하다.

threshold *n.* mun-ji-bang 문지방, mun-gan 문간.

thrice *adv.* (*three times*) se-bŏn 세번, sam-hoe 3 회, se-bae-ro 세배로.

thrift *n.* chŏl-yak 절약, kŏm-yak 검약. 「낭비하는.

thriftless *adj.* chŏl-je-ŏp-nŭn 절제없는. nang-bi-ha-nŭn

thrifty *adj.* ① chŏl-yak-ha-nŭn 절약하는, kŏm-so-han 검소한. ② (*prosper*) pŏn-ch'ang-ha-nŭn 번창하는.

thrill *n.* tŭ-ril 드릴, chŏn-yul 전율, kam-dong 감동.

thrive *v.* (*prosper*) pŏn-ch'ang-ha-da 번창하다.

throat *n.* mok-gu-mŏng 목구멍. 「가슴이 두근거리다.

throb *n.* ko-dong 고동. —*v.* ka-sŭm-i tu-gŭn-gŏ-ri-da

throne *n.* wang-jwa 왕좌, wang-wi 왕위.

throng *n.* kun-jung 군중. —*v.* mo-yŏ-dŭl-da 모여들다.

through *prep. & adv.* …ŭl t'ong-ha-yŏ …을 통하여.

throughout *prep. & adv.* to-ch'ŏ-e 도처에, nae-nae

throw *v.* nae-dŏn-ji-da 내던지다. 「내내.

thrust v. (*push*) mil-da 밀다, mil-ch'i-da 밀치다.

thumb n. ŏm-ji son-ga-rak 엄지 손가락.

thump v. t'ak ttae-ri-da 탁 때리다.

thunder n. ch'ŏn-dung 천둥, pyŏ-rak 벼락, u-roe 우뢰. —v. ch'ŏn-dung-ch'i-da 천둥치다.

thunderbolt n. pyŏ-rak 벼락, nak-roe 낙뢰(落雷).

thundering n. & adj. ch'ŏn-dung(-ch'i-nŭn) 천둥(치는).

thunderous adj. ch'ŏn-dung-ŭi 천둥의, u-roe-ga-t'ŭn 우뢰같은.

thunderstorm n. noe-u 뇌우(雷雨).

Thursday n. mok-yo-il 목요일.

thus adv. i-wa ka-ch'i 이와 같이, tta-ra-sŏ 따라서.

thwart v. (*hinder*) ka-ro-mak-da 가로막다, pang-hae-ha-da 방해하다.

tick n. (*mite*) chin-dŭ-gi 진드기. —v. ttok-ddak so-ri-nae-da 똑딱 소리내다.

ticket n. p'yo 표 ; ip-jang-gwŏn 입장권 : *single* ~ p'yŏn-do sŭng-ch'a-gwŏn 편도 승차권.

tickle v. kan-ji-ri-da 간질이다 ; (*amuse*) ki-bbŭ-ge-ha-da 기쁘게 하다.

tide n. ① cho-su 조수. ② (*tendency*) p'ung-jo 풍조 : *ebb* ~ ssŏl-mul 썰물/*flood* ~ mil-mul 밀물.

tidings n. (*news*) so-sik 소식, ki-byŏl 기별.

tidy adj. chŏng-don-doen 정돈된, mal-ssuk-han 말쑥한.

tie v. mae-da 매다, muk-da 묶다. —n. nek-t'a-i 넥타이.

tiger n. ho-rang-i 호랑이, pŏm 범.

tiger cat sal-gwaeng-i 삵괭이, sŭ-ra-so-ni 스라소니.

tiger lily ch'am-na-ri 참나리.

tight adj. (*firm*)tan-dan-han 단단한 ; (*tense*) p'aeng-p'aeng-han 팽팽한 ; (*close-fitting*) kkok mat-nŭn 꼭 맞는.

tighten v. choe-da 죄다.

tightly adv. tan-dan-hi 단단히 ; kkok mat-ge 꼭 맞게.

tile *n.* (*of roof*) ki-wa 기와, t'a-il 타일.

till *prep.* …kka-ji …까지. —*v.* (*cultivate*) kyŏng-jak-ha-da 경작하다.

timber *n.* chae-mok 재목.

time *n.* si-gan 시간, ttae 때.

timely *adj.* ttae-e al-ma-jŭn 때에 알맞은, chŏk-si-ŭi 적시(適時)의.

[ki-wa]

times *n.* ① si-dae 시대. ② (*arith.*) pae 배(倍).

timid *adj.* kŏp-man-ŭn 겁많은, su-jup-ŭn 수줍은.

tin *n.* chu-sŏk 주석 ; yang-ch'ŏl 양철.

tinge *n.* pit-ggal 빛깔 ; (*trace*) ki-mi 기미.

tingle *v.* ŏ-rŏl-ha-da 얼얼하다, a-ri-da 아리다.

tint *n.* pit-ggal 빛깔. —*v.* mul-gŭ-ri-da 물들이다.

tiny *adj.* chak-ŭn 작은, cho-gŭ-ma-han 조그마한.

tip *n.* ① kkŭ-t'ŭ-mŏ-ri 끄트머리. ② (*money*) t'ip 팁. —*v.* t'ip-ŭl chu-da 팁을 주다.

tipsy *adj.* ŏl-gŭn-han 얼근한 ; (*unsteady*) pi-t'ŭl-gŏ-ri-nŭn 비틀거리는. 「끝으로 걷다.

tiptoe *n.* pal-ggŭt 발끝. —*v.* pal-ggŭt-t'ŭ-ro kŏt-da 발

tire *n.* t'a-i-ŏ 타이어. —*v.* (*fatigue*) p'i-gon-ha-da 피곤하다, (*fore*) sil-jŭng-na-da 싫증나다.

tiresome *adj.* chi-ru-han 지루한 ; sŏng-ga-sin 성가신.

tissue *n.* yal-bŭn chik-mul 얇은 직물 ; (*cell*) cho-jik 조직 ; pak-yŏp-ji 박엽지.

title *n.* che-mok 제목, ch'ing-ho 칭호.

to *prep.* ① (*up to and including*) …kka-ji …까지. ② (*place*) …ŭ-ro …으로. ③ …ŭl wi-ha-yŏ …을 위하여.

toad *n.* tu-ggŏ-bi 두꺼비.

toadstool *n.* pŏ-sŏt 버섯, tok-bŏ-sŏt 독버섯.

toast *n.* ① t'o-u-sŭ-t'ŭ 토우스트. ② ch'uk-bae 축배. —*v.* ① kup-da 굽다. ② ch'uk-bae-rŭl dŭl-da 축배를 들다.

tobacco *n.* tam-bae 담배 ; hŭp-yŏn 흡연.

tobacco pouch tam-bae ssam-ji 담배 쌈지. 「늘날.

today *n.* ① o-nŭl 오늘. ② hyŏn-jae 현재, o-nŭl-nal 오

toddle *n.* a-jang-a-jang kŏt-da 아장아장 걷다.

toe *n.* pal-ga-rak 발가락.

together *adv.* ham- gge 함께, ta ka-ch'i 다 같이.

toil *n.* no-go 노고, (*effort*) ae 애, no-yŏk 노역(勞役).
  —*v.* (*labor*) ae-ssŏ il-ha-da 애써 일하다.

toilet *n.* (*lavatory*) pyŏn-so 변소, hwa-jang-sil 화장실.

toilet paper hyu-ji 휴지.

toilet room hwa-jang-sil 화장실. 「nyŏm-p'um 기념품.

token *n.* p'yo 표, t'o-u-k'ŭn 토우큰 ; (*keepsake*) ki-

tolerable *adj.* ch'am-ŭl su it-nŭn 참을 수 있는 ; wen-
  man-han 웬만한, kwaen-ch'an-ŭn 괜찮은.

tolerance *n.* kwan-yong 관용, a-ryang 아량.

tolerate *v.* ① (*allow*) nŏ-gŭ-rŏp-ge po-a chu-da 너그럽
  게 보아 주다. ② (*endure*) ch'am-da 참다, kyŏn-di-da
  견디다.

toll *n.* (*passage money*) t'ong-haeng-se 통행세.

tomato *n.* t'o-ma-t'o 토마토.

tomb *n.* (*grave*) mu-dŏm 무덤, myo 묘.

tombstone *n.* tol-bi-sŏk 돌비석, myo-bi 묘비.

tomorrow *n.* nae-il 내일 : *the day after* ~ mo-re 모레/
  two days after ~ kŭl-p'i 글피.

ton *n.* t'on 톤.

tone *n.* ① (*sound*) ŭm-jo 음조(音調). ② (*hue*) saek-jo
  색조. —*v.* (*attune*) cho-yul-ha-da 조율(調律)하다.

tongs *n.* pu-jŏt-ga-rak 부젓가락, chip-ge 집게.

tongue *n.* ① hyŏ 혀. ② (*language*) mal 말 : *mother*
  〔~ mo-guk-ŏ 모국어.

tonic *n.* kang-jang-je 강장제.

tonight *n.* & *adv.* o-nŭl-bam(-e) 오늘밤(에).

too *adv.* (*also*) tto-han 또한 ; nŏ-mu 너무.

tool *n.* yŏn-jang 연장, to-gu 도구.

tooth *n.* i 이, i-bbal 이빨.

toothache *n.* ch'i-t'ong 치통.

tooth-brush *n.* ch'it-sol 칫솔.

toothpick *n.* i-ssu-si-gae 이쑤시개.

top *n.* ① (*summit*) kkok-dae-gi 꼭
대기, (*head*) su-sŏk 수석. ②
(*toy*) p'aeng-i 팽이.

[p'aeng-i]

topic *n.* hwa-je 화제, non-je 논제.

topknot *n.* ta-bal 다발 ; sang-t'u 상투.

topple *v.* hŭn-dŭl-gŏ-ri-da 흔들거리다 ; nŏm-ŏ-ji-da 넘어
지다, twi-jip-ŏ-ŏp-da 뒤집어엎다.

torch *n.* ① hwaet-bul 횃불. ② tŭng-bul 등불.

torment *n.* ko-t'ong 고통 ; (*torture*) ka-ch'aek 가책.
—*v.* koe-rop-hi-da 괴롭히다.

torpedo *n.* ŏ-roe 어뢰, su-roe 수뢰.

torpedo boat ŏ-roe-jŏng 어뢰정.

torrent *n.* ① kŭp-ryu 급류. ② (*pl.*) ŏk-su 억수.

torrid *adj.* (*very hot*) mop-si tŏ-un 몹시 더운 ; *the
T~ Zone* yŏl-dae chi-bang 열대 지방.

tortoise *n.* kŏ-buk 거북.

torture *n.* & *v.* ko-mun(-ha-da) 고문(拷問)하다.

toss *v.* ① (*throw*) tŏn-jyŏ-ol-ri-da 던져올리다. ②
(*tossup*) tong-jŏn-dŏn-ji-gi 동전던지기.

total *n.* & *adj.* ch'ong-gye(-ŭi) 총계(의) : *the ~ number*
ch'ong-su 총수. —*v.* hap-gye-ha-da 합계하다.

totalitarianism *n.* chŏn-ch'e-ju-ŭi 전체주의.

totally *adv.* a-ju 아주 ; chŏn-jŏk-ŭ-ro 전적으로.

totem *n.* t'o-t'em 토템. 「da 아장아장 걷다.

totter *v.* pi-t'ŭl-gŏ-ri-da 비틀거리다, a-jang-a-jang kŏt-

touch *v.* (*with hand*) tae-da 대다. man-ji-da 만지다.
—*n.* ① chŏp-ch'ok 접촉. ② (*dash*) p'il-ch'i 필치.

touching *adj.* kam-dong-si-k'i-nŭn 감동시키는 ; (*pitiful*)

ae-ch'ŏ-ro-un 애처로운.

tough *adj.* (*hard*) tan-dan-han 단단한, (*strong*) t'ŭn-t'ŭn-han 튼튼한 ; (*sturdy*) wan-gang-han 완강한.

tour *n.* yu-ram 유람, yŏ-haeng 여행. —*v.* yu-ram-ha-da 유람하다, yŏ-haeng-ha-da 여행하다.

tourist *n.* kwan-gwang-gaek 관광객.

tournament *n.* kyŏng-gi 경기, si-hap 시합.

tow *v.* (*pull*) kkŭl-go ka-da 끌고 가다.

toward(s) *prep.* (*direction*) …jjok-ŭ-ro …쪽으로 ; (*about*) jjŭm 쯤, kyŏng 경 ; (*for*) …ŭl wi-ha-yŏ …을 위하여.

towel *n.* su-gŏn 수건, t'a-wŏl 타월.

tower *n.* t'ap 탑. —*v.* u-dduk sot-da 우뚝 솟다.

town *n.* ŭp 읍 ; (*big* ~) to-hoe-ji 도회지.

toy *n.* chang-nan-gam 장난감.

toyshop *n.* chang-nan-gam ka-ge 장난감 가게.

trace *n.* hŭn-jŏk 흔적. —*v.* ch'u-jŏk-ha-da 추적하다.

track *n.* ① pal-ja-guk 발자국. ② (*railway*) ch'ŏl-do 철도. —*v.* twi-rŭl jjot-da 뒤를 쫓다.

tractor *n.* t'ŭ-raek-t'ŏ 트랙터, kyŏn-in-ch'a 견인차.

trade *n.* sang-ŏp 상업, mu-yŏk 무역. —*v.* chang-sa-ha-da 장사하다 ; (*barter*) kyo-hwan-ha-da 교환하다.

trademark *n.* sang-p'yo 상표.

trader *n.* sang-in 상인, mu-yŏk-ŏp-ja 무역업자 ; (*trading vessel*) mu-yŏk-sŏn 무역선.

tradition *n.* chŏn-t'ong 전통, kwan-sŭp 관습.

traffic *n.* ① kyo-t'ong 교통. ② (*trade*) mae-mae 매매, kŏ-rae 거래. —*v.* kŏ-rae-ha-da 거래하다.

tragedy *n.* pi-gŭk 비극 ; ch'am-sa 참사.

tragic *adj.* pi-gŭk-ŭi 비극의, pi-gŭk-jŏk-in 비극적인.

trail *v.* (*drag*) (chil-jil) kkŭl-da (질질) 끌다.

train *n.* ki-ch'a 기차, yŏl-ch'a 열차. —*v.* (*teach*) hul-lyŏn-ha-da 훈련하다.

trainer *n.* hul-lyŏn-ja 훈련자, t'ŭ-re-i-nŏ 트레이너.

training *n.* hul-lyŏn 훈련, yŏn-sŭp 연습 ; tal-lyŏn 단 련 : ~ *school* yang-sŏng-so 양성소.

trait *n.* t'ŭk-saek 특색, t'ŭk-jing 특징.

traitor *n.* pan-yŏk-ja 반역자, pae-ban-ja 배반자.

tram *n.* (*streetcar*) si-ga chŏn-ch'a 시가 전차.

tramp *n.* ① (*vagabond*) pang-rang-ja 방랑자. ② (*trudge*) to-bo yŏ-haeng 도보 여행. —*v.* pap-da 밟다.

trample *v.* chit-bap-da 짓밟다.

trance *n.* mong-hwan 몽환(夢幻) ; hwang-hol 황홀.

tranquil *adj.* cho-yong-han 조용한, p'yŏng-on-han 평 온한, (*calm*) ch'im-ch'ak-han 침착한. 「하다.

transact *v.* ch'ŏ-ri-ha-da 처리하다 ; kŏ-rae-ha-da 거래

transaction *n.* ① (*conducting*) ch'ŏ-ri 처리. ② (*business*) kŏ-rae 거래. ③ (*pl.*) (*proceedings*) ui-sa-rok 의사록. 「nŭng-ga-ha-da 능가하다.

transcend *v.* (*go beyond*) ch'o-wŏl-ha-da 초월하다,

transcribe *v.* pok-sa-ha-da 복사하다, pe-ggi-da 베끼다.

transcript *n.* sa-bon 사본, tŭng-bon 등본.

transfer *n.* i-jŏn 이전(移轉). —*v.* (*convey*) om-gi-da 옮기다 ; (*make over*) yang-do-ha-da 양도하다.

transform *v.* pyŏn-hyŏng-ha-da 변형하다.

transformer *n.* pyŏn-ap-gi 변압기. 「없는.

transient *adj.* sun-gan-jŏk-in 순간적인, tŏt-ŏp-nŭn 덧

transit *n.* t'ong-gwa 통과, t'ong-haeng 통행.

translate *v.* pŏn-yŏk-ha-da 번역하다, hae-sŏk-ha-da 해

translation *n.* pŏn-yŏk 번역. 「석하다.

transmission *n.* chŏn-dal 전달 ; yang-do 양도.

transmit *v.* chŏn-dal-ha-da 전달하다, chŏn-ha-da 전하다.

transmitter *n.* song-sin〔song-hwa〕-gi 송신〔송화〕기.

transparent *adj.* t'u-myŏng-han 투명한. 「식하다.

transplant *v.* om-gyŏ sim-da 옮겨 심다, i-sik-ha-da 이

transport *v.* (*convey*) su-song-ha-da 수송하다.

transportation *n.* su-song 수송, un-song 운송.

trap *n.* tŏt 덫. —*v.* tŏ-ch'ŭ-ro chap-da 덫으로 잡다.

trash *n.* ssŭ-re-gi 쓰레기. jji-ggi 찌끼.

travel *n.* & *v.* yŏ-haeng(-ha-da) 여행(하다).

travel(l)er *n.* yŏ-haeng-ja 여행자, na-gŭ-ne 나그네.

traverse *v.* hoeng-dan-ha-da 횡단하다.

tray *n.* chaeng-ban 쟁반 : *ash* ~ chae-ddŏ-ri 재떨이.

treacherous *adj.* pae-ban-ha-nŭn 배반하는, pae-sin-ha-nŭn 배신하는 ; mit-ŭl su ŏp-nŭn 믿을 수 없는.

treachery *n.* pae-sin 배신, pae-ban 배반.

tread *v.* (*walk*) kŏt-da 걷다, (*trample*) pap-da 밟다.

treason *n.* pan-yŏk 반역, pul-sin 불신. 「hwa 재화.

treasure *n.* po-mul 보물, po-sŏk 보석, (*wealth*) chae-

treasurer *n.* hoe-gye-wŏn 회계원, kŭm-go-gye 금고계.

treasury *n.* kuk-go 국고(國庫) ; po-go 보고.

treat *v.* ① ch'wi-gŭp-ha-da 취급하다 ; tae-jŏp-ha-da 대접하다. ② (*cure*) ch'i-ryo-ha-da 치료하다.

treatise *n.* non-mun 논문. 「료.

treatment *n.* ① tae-u 대우. ② (*medical*) ch'i-ryo 치

treaty *n.* (*agreement*) cho-yak 조약, yak-jŏng 약정.

treble *adj.* se-gop-ŭi 세곱의, se-bae-ŭi 세배의.

tree *n.* na-mu 나무, su-mok 수목.

tremble *v.* ttŏl-da 떨다, ttŏl-ri-da 떨리다.

tremendous *adj.* (*awful*) mu-sŏ-un 무서운 ; (*huge*) koeng-jang-han 굉장한.

tremulous *adj.* ttŏl-ri-nŭn 떨리는, kŏp-man-ŭn 겁많은.

trench *n.* (*mil.*) ch'am-ho 참호 ; (*ditch*) to-rang 도랑.

trend *n.* kyŏng-hyang 경향, ch'u-se 추세.

trespass *v.* (*invade*) ch'im-ip-ha-da 침입하다.

trial *n.* ① (*test*) si-do 시도. ② (*hardship*) si-ryŏn 시련. ③ (*law*) kong-p'an 공판.

triangle *n.* sam-gak-hyŏng 3각형.

tribe *n.* chong-jok 종족, pu-jok 부족.

tribunal *n.* pŏp-jŏng 법정, p'an-sa-sŏk 판사석.

tribute *n.* ① kong-mul 공물. ② ch'an-sa 찬사.

trick *n.* kye-ryak 계략. —*v.* sok-i-da 속이다.

trickle *v.* ttuk-dduk ttŏ-rŏ-ji-da 뚝뚝 떨어지다.「발 자전거.

tricycle *n.* sam-ryun-ch'a 3륜차, se-bal cha-jŏn-gŏ 세

trifle *n.* sa-so-han il 사소한 일, so-ryang 소량. —*v.* nang-bi-ha-da 낭비하다, chang-nan-ha-da 장난하다.

trifling *adj.* si-si-han 시시한, ha-ch'an-ŭn 하찮은.

trigger *n.* pang-a-soe 방아쇠, che-dong-gi 제동기.

trilogy *n.* sam-bu-jak 3부작, sam-bu-gŭk 3부극.

trim *adj.* mal-ssuk-han 말쑥한, chŏng-don-doen 정돈된. —*v.* chal-ra pŏ-ri-da 잘라 버리다, ka-ji-rŏn-hi ha-da 가지런히 하다, ta-dŭm-da 다듬다.

trinity *n.* sam-wi-il-ch'e 3위일체.

trio *n.* (*persons*) sam-in-jo 3인조 ; (*singers or musicians*) sam-jung-ju 3중주.「디다.

trip *n.* yŏ-haeng 여행. —*v.* chal-mot ti-di-da 잘못 디

triple *adj.* se-gyŏp-ŭi 세겹의 ; (*three times*) se-bae-ŭi 세배의.「bu-han 진부한.

trite *adj.* (*stale*) k'ye-k'ye-muk-ŭn 케케묵은, chin-

triumph *n.* sŭng-ri 승리. —*v.* sŭng-ri-ha-da 승리하다, kae-sŏn-ha-da 개선하다.「양양한.

triumphant *adj.* i-gin 이긴, ŭi-gi-yang-yang-han 의기

trivial *adj.* si-si-han 시시한, ha-ch'an-ŭn 하찮은 : *a ~ matters* si-si-han il 시시한 일.

trolley *n.* t'ŭ-rol-ri 트롤리, si-ga chŏn-ch'a 시가 전차.

troop *n.* ① (*band*) tte 떼. ② (*pl.*) kun-dae 군대.

trooper *n.* ki-ma kyŏng-gwan 기마 경관 ; (*parachutist*) nak-ha-san-byŏng 낙하산병.「t'ŭ-ro-p'i 트로피.

trophy *n.* chŏl-li-p'um 전리품 ; u-sŭng-p'ae 우승패,

tropic *n.* ① hoe-gwi-sŏn 회귀선(回歸線). ② yŏl-dae
tropical *adj.* yŏl-dae-ŭi 열대의. └열대.
tropics *n.* yŏl-dae chi-bang 열대 지방. 「리다.
trot *n.* sok-bo 속보. —*v.* sok-bo-ro tal-ri-da 속보로 달
trouble *n.* ① kŏk-jŏng 걱정, kŭn-sim 근심, ko-noe 고뇌.
② (*disease*) pyŏng 병. —*v.* koe-rop-hi-da 괴롭히다.
troublesome *adj.* kka-da-ro-un 까다로운, kwi-ch'an-
ŭn 귀찮은, sŏng-ga-sin 성가신.
trough *n.* yŏ-mul-t'ong 여물통, ku-yu 구유.
trousers *n.* yang-bok pa-ji 양복 바지, chŭ-bong 즈봉.
trousseau *n.* hon-su-gam 혼수감, hon-su ot-ga-ji 혼수
trout *n.* song-ŏ 송어. └옷가지.
trowel *n.* hŭk-son 흙손, mo-jong-sap 모종삽.
truant *n.* ① ke-ŭ-rŭm-baeng-i 게으름뱅이. ② (*absentee*)
mu-dan kyŏl-sŏk-ja 무단 결석자.
truce *n.* hyu-jŏn 휴전 : *a* ~ *line* hyu-jŏn-sŏn 휴전선.
truck *n.* hwa-mul cha-dong-ch'a 화물 자동차, t'ŭ-rŏk
트럭 ; son-su-re 손수레. 「ŭi 실제의.
true *adj.* ch'am-doen 참된, chin-jŏng-ŭi 진정의 ; sil-je-
truly *adv.* chin-sil-ro 진실로 ; (*loyally*) ch'ung-sil-hi
충실히 ; (*correctly*) chŏng-hwak-hi 정확히.
trump *n.* t'ŭ-rŏm-p'ŭ 트럼프, ŭ-ddŭm-p'ae 으뜸패.
trumpet *n.* na-p'al 나팔, t'ŭ-rŏm-p'et 트럼펫. —*v.* na-
p'al-ŭl pul-da 나팔을 불다. 「기.
trunk *n.* ① t'ŭ-rŏng-k'ŭ 트렁크. ② (*tree*) chul-gi 줄
trust *n.* (*belief*) sin-yong 신용 ; (*responsibility*) sin-
t'ak 신탁. —*v.* mit-da 믿다, sin-yong-ha-da 신용하다.
trustee *n.* ① po-gwan-in 보관인, su-t'ak-ja 수탁자. ②
(*univ.*) p'yŏng-ŭi-wŏn 평의원, i-sa 이사.
trustful *adj.* mit-nŭn 믿는, sil-loe-ha-nŭn 신뢰하는.
truth *n.* chil-li 진리, chin-sil-sŏng 진실성, sa-sil 사실.
truthful *adj.* sŏng-sil-han 성실한, ch'am-doen 참된.

try *v.* ① si-do-ha-da 시도하다, (*endeavor*) no-ryŏk-ha-da 노력하다. ② (*law*) chae-p'an-ha-da 재판하다.

tub *n.* t'ong 통 : *bath* ~ mok-yok-t'ong 목욕통.

tube *n.* kwan 관, t'yu-u-bŭ 튜우브.

tuberculosis *n.* p'ye-byŏng 폐병, kyŏl-haek 결핵.

tuck *v.* kŏt-ŏ ol-ri-da 걷어 올리다, ch'aeng-gyŏ nŏ-t'a 챙겨 넣다.

Tuesday *n.* hwa-yo-il 화요일.

tuft *n.* song-i 송이, tŏm-bul 덤불.

tug *n.* (*boat*) ye-in-sŏn 예인선. —*v.* (*drag*) tang-gi-da 당기다, kku-rŏ-dang-gi-da 끌어당기다.

tuition *n.* su-ŏp 수업, su-ŏp-ryo 수업료.

tulip *n.* t'yu-ul-rip 튜울립. 「떨어지다.

tumble *v.* nŏm-ŏ-ji-da 넘어지다, kul-rŏ ttŏ-rŏ-ji-da 굴러

tumbler *n.* ① k'ŏp 컵. ② (*acrobat*) kok-ye-sa 곡예사.

tumo(u)r *n.* chong-gi 종기, chong-yang 종양.

tumult *n.* so-dong 소동, so-ran 소란, tong-ran 동란.

tuna *n.* ta-rang-ŏ 다랑어.

tune *n.* (*melody*) kok-jo 곡조, (*tone*) ka-rak 가락. —*v.* kok-jo-rŭl mat-ch'u-da 곡조를 맞추다.

tunic *n.* kun-bok chŏ-go-ri 군복 저고리. 「을 파다.

tunnel *n.* t'ŏ-nŏl 터널, kul 굴. —*v.* kul-ŭl p'a-da 굴

turbulent *adj.* si-ggŭ-rŏ-un 시끄러운 ; (*violent*) sa-na-

turf *n.* chan-di 잔디, chan-di-bat 잔디밭. 「un 사나운.

turkey *n.* ch'il-myŏn-jo 칠면조.

turmoil *n.* so-ran 소란, so-dong 소동, hol-lan 혼란.

turn *v.* ① hoe-jŏn-ha-da 회전하다, to-ra-sŏ-da 돌아서다. ② (*curve*) ku-bu-rŏ-ji-da 구부러지다. ③ (*change*) pyŏn-ha-da 변하다. —*n.* ① hoe-jŏn 회전. ② kul-gok 굴곡. ③ pyŏn-hwa 변화. ④ (*order*) ch'a-rye 차례.

turning point chŏn-hwan-jŏm 전환점, pun-gi-jŏm 분

turnip *n.* sun-mu 순무. 「기점.

turpentine *n.* t'e-re-bin-yu 테레빈유(油).

turret *n.* chak-ŭn t'ap 작은 탑 ; (*gun*) p'o-t'ap 포탑.
turtle *n.* pa-da-gŏ-buk 바다거북.
tusk *n.* ŏm-ni 엄니 ; ppŏ-dŭ-rŏng-ni 뻐드렁니.
tussle *n.* tŭ-jap-i 드잡이, nan-t'u 난투.
tutor *n.* ka-jŏng-gyo-sa 가정교사, kang-sa 강사.
tweezers *n.* chok-jip-ge 족집게, p'in-set 핀셋.
twelve *n.* yŏl-dul 열둘, sip-i 12.
twenty *n.* su-mul 스물, i-sip 20.
twice *adv.* tu-bae-ro 두배로, tu-bŏn 두번, i-hoe 2회.
twig *n.* chan-ga-ji 잔가지, ka-nŭn ka-ji 가는 가지.
twilight *n.* hwang-hon 황혼, ttang-gŏ-mi 땅거미.
twin *n.* ssang-dong-i 쌍동이, ssang-saeng-a 쌍생아.
twine *n.* no-ggŭn 노끈, kkon sil 꼰 실. 「깜박이다.
twinkle *v.* pan-jjak-gŏ-ri-da 반짝거리다, kkam-bak-i-da
twirl *v.* ping-bing tol-ri-da 빙빙 돌리다.
twist *v.* kko-da 꼬다, (*distort*) pi-t'ŭl-da 비틀다.
twitch *v.* (*pull at*)chap-a-ggŭl-da 잡아끌다.
twitter *v.* ① chi-jŏ-gwi-da 지저귀다. ② (*excited*) hŭng-bun-ha-yŏ mom-ŭl ttŏl-da 흥분하여 몸을 떨다.
two *n.* tul 둘, i 2. —*adj.* tu-gae-ŭi 두개의.
type *n.* ① (*sort*) hyŏng 형, yu-hyŏng 유형. ② (*printing*) hwal-ja 활자. —*v.* t'a-i-p'ŭ-ra-i-t'ŏ-ro ch'i-da 타이프라이터로 치다. 「라이터.
typewriter *n.* t'a-ja-gi 타자기, t'a-i-p'ŭ-ra-i-t'ŏ 타이프
typhoid *n.* chang-t'i-p'u-sŭ 장티푸스.
typhoon *n.* t'ae-p'ung 태풍.
typhus *n.* pal-jin-t'i-p'u-sŭ 발진티푸스. 「in 대표적인.
typical *adj.* chŏn-hyŏng-jŏk-in 전형적인, tae-p'yo-jŏk-
typist *n.* t'a-ja-su 타자수, t'a-i-p'i-sŭ-t'ŭ 타이피스트.
tyranny *n.* ① p'o-hak 포학. ② p'ok-jŏng 폭정 ; chŏn-je chŏng-ch'i 전제 정치.
tyrant *n.* p'ok-gun 폭군, chŏn-je kun-ju 전제 군주.

⟨ U ⟩

udder *n.* (*cow*) chŏt-t'ong 젖통, yu-bang 유방.

ugly *adj.* ch'u-ak-han 추악한, mot saeng-gin 못 생긴.

ulcer *n.* kwe-yang 궤양, chong-gi 종기.

ultimate *adj.* ch'oe-hu-ŭi 최후의, kung-gŭk-ŭi 궁극의; (*fundamental*) kŭn-bon-jŏk-in 근본적인.

ultimatum *n.* ch'oe-hu t'ong-ch'ŏp 최후 통첩.

umbrella *n.* (*for rain*) u-san 우산, pak-jwi-u-san 박쥐우산, (*for sunlight*) yang-san 양산.

umpire *n.* sim-p'an(-gwan) 심판(관).

unable *adj.* hal su ŏp-nŭn 할 수 없는. 「없는.

unaccountable *adj.* sŏl-myŏng-hal su ŏp-nŭn 설명할 수

unacquainted *adj.* nat-sŏn 낯선, saeng-so-han 생소한.

unaffected *adj.* kku-mim-ŏp-nŭn 꾸밈없는.

unanimous *adj.* man-jang-il-ch'i-ŭi 만장일치의.

unarm *v.* mu-jang-hae-je-ha-da 무장해제하다.

unavoidable *adj.* p'i-hal su ŏp-nŭn 피할 수 없는, p'i-ch'i-mot-hal 피치못할, pul-ga-p'i-han 불가피한.

unaware *adj.* al-ji mot-ha-nŭn 알지 못하는.

unbearable *adj.* kyŏn-dil su ŏp-nŭn 견딜 수 없는.

unbelievable *adj.* mit-ŭl su ŏp-nŭn 믿을 수 없는.

unceasing *adj.* kkŭn-im-ŏp-nun 끊임없는, pu-dan-ŭi

uncertain *adj.* pul-hwak-sil-han 불확실한. 「부단의.

uncle *n.* a-jŏ-ssi 아저씨, (*sup.*) paek-bu 백부, (*inf.*) suk-bu 숙부.

unclean *adj.* tŏ-rŏ-un 더러운, pul-gyŏl-han 불결한.

uncomfortable *adj.* pul-yu-k'wae-han 불유쾌한, pul-k'wae-han 불쾌한; pul-p'yŏn-han 불편한.

uncommon *adj.* pi-bŏm-han 비범한, chin-gi-han 진기한.

unconscious *adj.* mu-ŭi-sik-ŭi 무의식의.

uncouth *adj.* t'u-bak-han 투박한, kŏ-ch'in 거친.

uncover *v.* pŏt-gi-da 벗기다 ; (*disclose*) p'ok-ro-ha-da 폭로하다, tŭ-rŏ-nae-da 드러내다.

under *prep. & adv.* a-rae-e 아래에, mi-t'e 밑에.

underclothes *n.* sok-ot 속옷, nae-ŭi 내의.

underdeveloped *adj.* chŏ-gae-bal-ŭi 저개발의.

undergo *v.* (*experience*) kyŏk-da 겪다. (*suffer*) tang-ha-da 당하다 ; (*endure*) kyŏn-di-da 견디다.

undergraduate *n.* tae-hak chae-hak-saeng 대학 재학생.

underground *adj.* chi-ha-ŭi 지하의. —*n.* (*Am.*) (*subway*) chi-ha-ch'ŏl 지하철. 「래에.

underneath *adv.* a-rae-ro 아래로. —*prep.* a-rae-e 아

understand *v.* i-hae-ha-da 이해하다, al-da 알다.

undertake *v.* mat-da 맡다 ; ch'ak-su-ha-da 착수하다.

undertaker *n.* ① (*of funerals*) chang-ŭi-sa 장의사. ② (*contractor*) to-gŭp-ja 도급자, ch'ŏng-bu-in 청부인.

underwear *n.* sok-ot 속옷, nae-ŭi 내의.

undo *v.* wŏn-sang-dae-ro ha-da 원상대로 하다.

undoubted *adj.* ŭi-sim-ŏp-nŭn 의심없는, hwak-sil-han

undress *v.* o-sŭl pŏt-da 옷을 벗다. 「확실한.

undue *adj.* pu-dang-han 부당한, kwa-do-ŭi 과도의.

uneasy *adj.* pu-ran-han 불안한. p'yŏn-ch'an-ŭn 편찮은.

unemployment *n.* si-rŏp 실업, sil-jik 실직.

unequal *adj.* pul-gong-p'yong-han 불공평한.

uneven *adj.* ko-rŭ-ji an-ŭn 고르지 않은.

unexpected *adj.* ye-gi-ch'i an-ŭn 예기치 않은, ttŭt-ba-ggŭi 뜻밖의, ŭi-oe-ŭi 의외의. 「히.

unexpectedly *adv.* ttŭt-ba-gge 뜻밖에. to-ryŏn-hi 돌연

unfair *adj.* pul-gong-p'yŏng-han 불공평한.

unfaithful *adj.* sŏng-sil-ch'i mot-han 성실치 못한, pul-sil-han 불실한, pu-jŏng-han 부정(不貞)한.

unfavorable *adj.* pul-ri-han 불리한: ~ *balance of trade*

mu-yŏk yŏk-jo 무역 역조.　　　　　　「적임이 아닌.

unfit *adj.* pu-jŏk-dang-han 부적당한, chŏk-im-i a-nin

unfold *v.* p'yŏ-da 펴다, yŏl-da 열다.

unforeseen *adj.* ye-ch'ŭk-mot-han 예측못한.

unfortunate *adj.* pu-run-han 불운한, pul-haeng-han
불행한. —*n.* pul-haeng-han sa-ram 불행한 사람.

unfrequented *adj.* in-jŏk-i tŭ-mun 인적이 드문.

unfriendly *adj.* u-ae-ŏp-nŭn 우애없는, pak-jŏng-han
박정한, pul-ch'in-jŏl-han 불친절한.

unfurl *v.* (*spread*) p'yŏ-da 펴다, p'ŏl-rŏk-i-da 펄럭이다.

ungrateful *adj.* ŭn-hye-rŭl mo-rŭ-nŭn 은혜를 모르는 ;
(*unrewarding*) po-ram-ŏp-nŭn 보람없는.

unhappy *adj.* pul-haeng-han 불행한.

unheard *adj.* tŭl-ri-ji an-nŭn 들리지 않는 ; al-ryŏ-ji-ji
an-nŭn 알려지지 않는.

unidentified *adj.* sin-wŏn-mi-sang-ŭi 신원미상의, mi-
hwak-in-ŭi 미확인의.

uniform *adj.* han-mo-yang-ŭi 한모양의, han-gyŏl-ga-
t'ŭn 한결같은. —*n.* che-bok 제복.　　　　　　「하다.

unify *v.* t'ong-il-ha-da 통일하다, t'ong-hap-ha-da 통합

unilateral *adj.* il-bang-jŏk-in 일방적인.

unimportant *adj.* chung-yo-ha-ji an-ŭn 중요하지 않은.

union *n.* ① kyŏl-hap 결합. ② (*trade* ~) cho-hap 조
합. ③ (*marriage*) kyŏl-hon 결혼. ④ (*league*) yŏn-
hap 연합. ⑤ (*concord*) il-ch'i 일치.

unique *adj.* yu-il-han 유일한, tok-t'ŭk-han 독특한.

unison *n.* ① cho-hwa 조화. ② (*mus.*) che-ch'ang 제창.

unit *n.* ① tan-wi 단위. ② (*mil.*) pu-dae 부대.

unite *v.* kyŏl-hap-ha-da 결합하다, hap-ch'i-da 합치다.

United Nations kuk-je yŏn-hap 국제 연합.

universal *adj.* u-ju-ŭi 우주의 ; po-p'yŏn-jŏk-in 보편적인.

universe *n.* u-ju 우주, chŏn-se-gye 전세계.

university *n.* chong-hap tae-hak-gyo 종합 대학교.

unjust *adj.* ol-ch'i an-ŭn 옳지 않은, pu-jŏng-han 부정한 ; (*unfair*) pul-gong-p'yŏng-han 불공평한.

unkind *adj.* pul-ch'in-jŏl-han 불친절한.

unknown *adj.* al-ryŏ-ji-ji an-ŭn 알려지지 않은.

unlatch *v.* kŏl-soe-rŭl pŏt-gi-da 걸쇠를 벗기다.

unlawful *adj.* pul-bŏp-ŭi 불법의, wi-bŏp-ŭi 위법의.

unlearned *adj.* mu-sik-han 무식한.

unless *conj.* …i a-ni-myŏn …이 아니면.

unlike *adj.* kat-ji an-ŭn 같지 않은, ta-rŭn 다른. — *prep.* …tap-ji an-k'e …답지 않게.

unload *v.* (chim-ŭl) pu-ri-da (짐을) 부리다. 「나쁜.

unlucky *adj.* pu-run-han 불운한, un-i na-bbŭn 운이

unmanly *adj.* nam-ja-dap-ji an-ŭn 남자답지 않은.

unnatural *adj.* pu-ja-yŏn-han 부자연한, ki-goe-han 기

unnecessary *adj.* pul-p'i-ryo-han 불필요한. 「괴한.

unnoticed *adj.* nam-ŭi nun-e ttŭi-ji an-nŭn 남의 눈에 띄지 않는. 「it-nŭn 비어있는.

unoccupied *adj.* im-ja-ŏp-nŭn 임자없는 ; (*vacant*) pi-ŏ-

unofficial *adj.* pi-gong-sik-ŭi 비공식의.

unpack *v.* chim-ŭl p'ul-da 짐을 풀다. 「ŭi 미불의.

unpaid *adj.* chi-bul-ha-ji an-ŭn 지불하지 않은, mi-bul-

unpardonable *adj.* yong-sŏ-hal su ŏp-nŭn 용서할 수 없는.

unpleasant *adj.* pul-yu-k'wae-han 불유쾌한.

unprecedented *adj.* chŏl-lye-ŏp-nŭn 전례없는.

unquestionable *adj.* ŭi-sim-hal yŏ-ji ŏp-nŭn 의심할 여지 없는, hwak-sil-han 확실한.

unravel *v.* p'ul-da 풀다, kkŭ-rŭ-da 끄르다.

unreasonable *adj.* pul-hap-ri-han 불합리한 ; pu-dang-han 부당한 ; t'ŏ-mu-ni-ŏp-nŭn 터무니없는.

unroll *v.* p'ul-da 풀다, p'yŏl-ch'i-da 펼치다.

unseen *adj.* po-i-ji an-nŭn 보이지 않는.

unselfish *adj.* sa-sim-i ŏp-nŭn 사심이 없는.

unskilled *adj.* mi-suk-han 미숙한. 「p'ae-han 실패한.

unsuccessful *adj.* sŏng-gong mot-han 성공 못한, sil-

untie *v.* kkŭ-rŭ-da 끄르다, p'ul-da 풀다.

until *prep.* ···kka-ji ···까지.

untimely *adj.* ttae a-nin 때 아닌, ch'ŏl a-nin 철 아닌.

untrue *adj.* hŏ-wi-ŭi 허위의.

unusual *adj.* i-sang-han 이상한 ; tŭ-mun 드문.

unwelcome *adj.* hwan-yŏng-bat-ji mot-ha-nŭn 환영받
지 못하는, tal-gap-ji an-ŭn 달갑지 않은.

unwilling *adj.* ma-ŭm nae-k'i-ji an-nŭn 마음 내키지
않는, si-rŏ-ha-nŭn 싫어하는. 「한.

unwise *adj.* ŏ-ri-sŏk-ŭn 어리석은, ch'ŏn-bak-han 천박

unworthy *adj.* ka-ch'i-ŏp-nŭn 가치없는.

up *adv. & prep.* ···wi-e ···위에 ; ···ŭi wi-ro···의 위로.

uphill *adj.* ol-ra-ga-nŭn 올라가는, o-rŭ-mak-ŭi 오르막의.

uphold *v.* (*support*) chi-ji-ha-da 지지하다.

upon *prep.* ···wi-e ···위에.

upper *adj.* wi-jjok-ŭi 위쪽의, sang-wi-ŭi 상위의.

upright *adj.* ttok-ba-rŭn 똑바른 ; chŏng-jik-han 정직한.

uprising *n.* p'ok-dong 폭동 ; pal-lan 반란.

uproar *n.* k'ŭn so-dong 큰 소동 ; so-ŭm 소음.

uproot *v.* ppu-ri ppop-da 뿌리 뽑다 ; kŭn-jŏl-ha-da 근절
하다, mo-ra-nae-da 몰아내다. 「복.

upset *v.* twi-jip-ŏ ŏp-da 뒤집어 엎다. —*n.* chŏn-bok 전

upside-down *adj.* twi-jip-ŏ-jin 뒤집어진 ; chŏn-do-doen
전도된 ; ŏng-mang-in 영망인.

upstairs *adj.* wi-ch'ŭng-ŭi 위층의, i-ch'ŭng-ŭi 2층의.
—*n.* wi-ch'ŭng 위층, i-ch'ŭng 2층. 「대적인.

up-to-date *adj.* ch'oe-sin-ŭi 최신의, hyŏn-dae-jŏk-in 현

upward *adj.* wi-ro hyang-han 위로 향한.

upwards *adv.* wi-rŭl hyang-ha-yŏ 위를 향하여, wi-jjok-ŭ-ro 위쪽으로.

urban *adj.* to-si-ŭi 도시의, to-hoe-p'ung-ŭi 도회풍의.

urge *v.* kwŏn-go-ha-da 권고하다, (*push*) chae-ch'ok-ha-da 재촉하다, kyŏk-ryŏ-ha-da 격려하다.

urgent *adj.* kin-gŭp-han 긴급한, chŏl-bak-han 절박한.

urn *n.* (*vase*) hang-a-ri 항아리, tan-ji 단지, tok 독.

us *pron.* (*accus.*) u-ri-rŭl 우리를, (*dat.*) u-ri-e-ge 우리에게.
「다, sa-yong-ha-da 사용하다.

use *n.* sa-yong 사용, yong-bŏp 용법. —*v.* ssŭ-da 쓰

useful *adj.* yu-yong-han 유용한, ssŭl-mo-it-nŭn 쓸모

useless *adj.* ssŭl-mo-ŏp-nŭn 쓸모없는. 「있는.

usher *n.* an-nae-in 안내인, mun-ji-gi 문지기.

usual *adj.* po-t'ong-ŭi 보통의, p'yong-so-ŭi 평소의.

usually *adv.* po-t'ong 보통, tae-gae 대개.

utensil *n.* kŭ-rŭt 그릇, ki-gu 기구 ; pu-ŏk ki-gu 부엌 기구 : *farming* ~s nong-gi-gu 농기구.

utilize *v.* i-yong-ha-da 이용하다.

utmost *adj.* kŭk-do-ŭi 극도의, ch'oe-go-do-ŭi 최고도의.

Utopia *n.* i-sang-hyang 이상향, yu-t'o-p'i-a 유토피아.

utter *adj.* wan-jŏn-han 완전한 ; (*total*) chŏn-jŏk-in 전적인. —*v.* (*speak*) pa-rŏn-ha-da 발언하다.

utterance *n.* pa-rŏn 발언, mal-ssi 말씨.

utterly *adv.* a-ju 아주, wan-jŏn-hi 완전히.

V

vacancy *n.* kong-hŏ 공허 ; (*vacant post*) kong-sŏk 공석, (*blank*) pin-t'ŭm 빈틈.

vacant *adj.* pin 빈 : *a* ~ *house* pin-jip 빈집.

vacate *v.* pi-u-da 비우다 ; mul-rŏ-na-da 물러나다.

vacation *n.* hyu-ga 휴가, pang-hak 방학.

vaccinate *v.* chong-du-rŭl no-t'a 종두를 놓다.

vaccination *n.* chong-du 종두, u-du 우두.

vacuum *n.* chin-gong 진공(眞空).

vagabond *n.* pang-rang-ja 방랑자. 「모호한.

vague *adj.* mak-yŏn-han 막연한 ; (*obscure*) mo-ho-han

vain *adj.* hŏt-doen 헛된, kong-hŏ-han 공허한.

vainly *adv.* kong-yŏn-hi 공연히, hŏt-doe-i 헛되이.

valiant *adj.* ssik-ssik-han 씩씩한, yong-gam-han 용감한.

valid *adj.* yu-hyo-han 유효한 ; hwak-sil-han 확실한.

valley *n.* kol-jja-gi 골짜기, kye-gok 계곡.

valor *n.* yong-gi 용기, yong-maeng 용맹. 「귀중품.

valuable *adj.* kwi-jung-han 귀중한. —*n.* kwi-jung-p'um

value *n.* ka-ch'i 가치. —*v.* ① chon-jung-ha-da 존중하
다. ② (*appraise*) p'yŏng-ga-ha-da 평가하다.

valve *n.* p'an 판(瓣) : *safety* ~ an-jŏn-p'an 안전판.

vamp *n.* yo-bu 요부, t'ang-nyŏ 탕녀.

vampire *n.* ① (*bloodsucker*) hŭp-hyŏl-gwi 흡혈귀. ②
(*enchantress*) yo-bu 요부(妖婦).

vane *n.* pa-ram-gae-bi 바람개비, p'ung-hyang-gye 풍향
계, p'ung-sin-gi 풍신기.

vanguard *n.* chŏn-wi 전위(前衛), sŏn-bong 선봉.

vanish *v.* sa-ra-ji-da 사라지다, ŏp-sŏ-ji-da 없어지다.

vanity *n.* hŏ-yŏng 허영, kong-hŏ 공허.

vanquish *v.* chŏng-bok-ha-da 정복하다, i-gyŏ-nae-da 이

vantage *n.* yu-ri 유리(有利), i-dŭk 이득. 「겨내다.

vapid *adj.* kim ppa-jin 김 빠진, hŭng-mi-op-nŭn 흥미

vaporize *v.* chŭng-bal-si-k'i-da 증발시키다. 「없는.

vapo(u)r *n.* chŭng-gi 증기, kim 김. 「채로운.

varied *adj.* yŏ-rŏ ka-ji-ŭi 여러 가지의, ta-ch'ae-ro-un 다

variety *n.* pyŏn-hwa 변화 ; ta-yang(-sŏng) 다양(성).

various *adj.* yŏ-rŏ ka-ji-ŭi 여러 가지의.

vary *v.* (*change*) pyŏn-gyŏng-ha-da 변경하다 ; (*diver-sify*) ta-ch'ae-rop-ge ha-da 다채롭게 하다.

vase *n.* pyŏng 병, hang-a-ri 항아리, tan-ji 단지 ; (*for flower*) kkot-byŏng 꽃병.

vassal *n.* (*subject*) sin-ha 신하, (*servant*) ha-in 하인.

vast *adj.* nŏl-bŭn 넓은, kwang-dae-han 광대한.

vault *n.* ① tung-gŭn ch'ŏn-jang 둥근 천장. ② (*cellar*) chi-ha-sil 지하실. —*v.* (*jump*) ttwi-da 뛰다.

vegetable *n.* ya-ch'ae 야채, ch'ae-so 채소.

vegetation *n.* sik-mul 식물, ch'o-mok 초목.

vehicle *n.* ch'a-ryang 차량, t'al kŏt 탈 것.

veil *v.* kam-ch'u-da 감추다, tŏp-da 덮다. —*n.* pe-il 베일, nŏ-ul 너울, chang-mak 장막.

vein *n.* hyŏl-gwan 혈관, chŏng-maek 정맥.

velocity *n.* (*speed*) sok-ryŏk 속력, sok-do 속도.

velvet *n.* u-dan 우단, pil-ro-o-do 빌로오도, pel-bet 벨벳.

venerable *adj.* ① chon-gyŏng-hal man-han 존경할 만한. ② (*ancient*) yu-sŏ-gi-p'ŭn 유서깊은.

venerate *v.* (*respect*) chon-gyŏng-ha-da 존경하다.

vengeance *n.* pok-su 복수, ang-ga-p'ŭm 앙갚음.

venom *n.* ① tok 독, tok-aek 독액. ② (*spite*) wŏn-han 원한.

vent *n.* ku-mŏng 구멍, pae-ch'ul-gu 배출구.

ventilate *v.* hwan-gi-ha-da 환기하다.

ventilation *n.* hwan-gi 환기, t'ong-p'ung 통풍.

venture *n.* mo-hŏm 모험. —*v.* wi-hŏm-ŭl mu-rŭp-ssŭ-da 위험을 무릅쓰다, kam-haeng-ha-da 감행하다.

veranda(h) *n.* pe-ran-da 베란다 ; t'oet-ma-ru 툇마루.

verb *n.* (*gram.*) tong-sa 동사.

verbal *adj.* mal-ŭi 말의, ŏn-ŏ-ŭi 언어의 ; *a ~ explana tion* ku-du-sŏl-myŏng 구두설명.

verdict *n.* (*law*) p'yŏng-gyŏl 평결 ; p'an-dan 판단.

verge *n.* pyŏn-du-ri 변두리, ka-jang-ja-ri 가장자리.

verify *v.* hwak-in-ha-da 확인하다, (*prove*) chŭng myŏng[ip-jŭng]-ha-da 증명[입증]하다.

vernacular *n.* ① kuk-ŏ 국어. ② sa-t'u-ri 사투리.
—*adj.* (*native*) pon-guk-ŭi 본국의.
vernal equinox ch'un-bun 춘분(春分).
verse *n.* sit-gwi 싯귀(詩句), un-mun 운문.
versed *adj.* (*skilled*) chŏng-t'ong-han 정통한.
very *adj.* ch'am-da-un 참다운, pa-ro kŭ 바로 그. —
adv. tae-dan-hi 대단히, mae-u 매우.
vessel *n.* ① kŭ-rŭt 그릇. ② (*ship*) pae 배.
vest *n.* (*waistcoat*) cho-ggi 조끼.
veteran *n.* no-ryŏn-ga 노련가. —*adj.* no-ryŏn-han 노
련한. 「다.
veto *n.* kŏ-bu-gwŏn 거부권. —*v.* kŏ-bu-ha-da 거부하
vex *v.* (*provoke*) sŏng-na-ge ha-da 성나게 하다, (*annoy*) sŏng-ga-si-ge kul-da 성가시게 굴다.
vexation *n.* sok-sang-ham 속상함 ; ae-t'am 애탐.
via *prep.* (*by way of*) …ŭl kŏ-ch'yŏ-sŏ …을 거쳐서,
…kyŏng-yu-ha-yŏ …경유하여.
vibrate *v.* chin-dong-ha-da 진동하다, ttŏl-ri-da 떨리다.
vibration *n.* chin-dong 진동, tong-yo 동요.
vicar *n.* (kyo-gu) mok-sa (교구) 목사.
vice *n.* ① ak-dŏk 악덕. ② (*tool*) kkŏk-soe 꺾쇠.
vice-president *n.* pu-t'ong-ryŏng 부통령.
vicinity *n.* pu-gŭn 부근, kŭn-ch'ŏ 근처.
vicious *adj.* ak-dŏk-ŭi 악덕의, sa-ak-han 사악한.
vicissitude *n.* pyŏn-hwa 변화, hŭng-mang 흥망.
victim *n.* hŭi-saeng-ja 희생자, su-nan-ja 수난자.
victor *n.* sŭng-ri-ja 승리자, chŏng-bok-ja 정복자.
victorious *adj.* sŭng-ri-ŭi 승리의, i-gin 이긴.
victory *n.* sŭng-ri 승리, u-sŭng 우승.
vie *v.* kyŏ-ru-da 겨루다, kyŏng-jaeng-ha-da 경쟁하다.
view *n.* ① (*scene*) kyŏng-ch'i 경치. ② (*opinion*) ŭi-gyŏn 의견. —*v.* kwan-ch'al-ha-da 관찰하다.

vigil *n.* pam-sae-um 밤새움, ch'ŏ-rya 철야.

vigorous *adj.* chŏng-ryŏk wang-sŏng-han 정력 왕성한, (*lively*) ki-un-ch'an 기운찬.

vigo(u)r *n.* hwal-ryŏk 활력, wŏn-gi 원기.

vile *adj.* (*base*) pi-yŏl-han 비열한 ; ch'ŏn-han 천한.

villa *n.* pyŏl-jang 별장, pyŏl-jŏ 별저(別邸).

village *n.* ma-ŭl 마을, ch'ol-lak 촌락.

villager *n.* ma-ŭl sa-ram 마을 사람, ch'on-min 촌민.

villain *n.* ak-han 악한, ak-dang 악당.   「호하다.

vindicate *v.* pyŏn-ho-ha-da 변호하다, ong-ho-ha-da 옹

vine *n.* tŏng-gul 덩굴 ; p'o-do-na-mu 포도나무.

vinegar *n.* ch'o 초, sik-ch'o 식초.

vineyard *n.* p'o-do-wŏn[bat] 포도원[밭].

viola *n.* pi-ol-ra 비올라.

violate *v.* ① wi-ban-ha-da 위반하다, ŏ-gi-da 어기다 ;
② (*profane*) tŏ-rŏp-hi-da 더럽히다.

violence *n.* p'ok-haeng 폭행, p'ok-ryŏk 폭력.

violent *adj.* ① maeng-ryŏl-han 맹렬한, nan-p'ok-han
난폭한. ② (*unnatural*) pu-ja-yŏn-han 부자연한.

violet *n.* o-rang-k'ae-ggot 오랑캐꽃, che-bi-ggot 제비꽃.

violin *n.* pa-i-ŏl-rin 바이얼린 ; che-gŭm 제금(提琴).

viper *n.* tok-sa 독사, sal-mu-sa 살무사.

virgin *n.* ch'ŏ-nyŏ 처녀. —*adj.* sun-gyŏl-han 순결한 ;
(*untrodden*) chŏn-in mi-dap-ŭi 전인 미답의 : ∼ *gold*
sun-gŭm 순금/ ∼ *paper* paek-ji 백지.

virtual *adj.* sa-sil[sil-je]-sang-ŭi 사실[실제]상의.

virtue *n.* (*goodness*) tŏk 덕(德) ; (*chastity*) chŏng-jo
정조 ; (*merit*) mi-dŏk 미덕.

virtuous *adj.* tŏk-i no-p'ŭn 덕이 높은, ko-gyŏl-han 고
결한, (*chaste*) chŏng-suk-han 정숙한.

visible *adj.* nun-e po-i-nŭn 눈에 보이는.

vision *n* si-gak 시각 ; (∼ *for future*) mi-rae-sang 미

래상 ; (*imagination*) hwan-yŏng 환영.

visit *n. & v.* pang-mun(-ha-da) 방문(하다).

visitor *n.* pang-mun-gaek 방문객, son-nim 손님.

visor *n.* (*peak of cap*) mo-ja-ŭi ch'aeng 모자의 챙.

visual *adj.* si-gak-ŭi 시각의, nun-e po-i-nŭn 눈에 보이는.

vital *adj.* ① (*of life*) saeng-myŏng-ŭi 생명의. ② (*fatal*) ch'i-myŏng-jŏk-in 치명적인.

vitality *n.* saeng-myŏng-ryŏk 생명력, hwal-gi 활기.

vivid *adj.* (*lively*) saeng-saeng-han 생생한 ; (*clear*) sŏn-myŏng-han 선명한.

vocabulary *n.* ŏ-hwi 어휘, yong-ŏ 용어.

vocal *adj.* mok-so-ri-ŭi 목소리의 : ~ *cords* sŏng-dae 성대.

vocalist *n.* sŏng-ak-ga 성악가, ka-su 가수.

vocation *n.* ch'ŏn-jik 천직, chik-ŏp 직업.

vogue *n.* (*fashion*) yu-haeng 유행 ; in-gi 인기.

voice *n.* mok-so-ri 목소리, ŭm-sŏng 음성.

void *adj.* (*empty*) kong-hŏ-han 공허한 ; (*not binding*) mu-hyo-ŭi 무효의. —*n.* kong-gan 공간.

volcano *n.* hwa-san 화산.

volley *n.* ① il-je sa-gyŏk 일제 사격. ② (*tennis*) pal-ri

volleyball *n.* pae-gu 배구.　　　　　　　　　　└발리

voltage *n.* chŏn-ap 전압, chŏn-ap-ryang 전압량.

volume *n.* ① (*quantity*) yang 양, (*bulk, size*) pu-p'i 부피, k'ŭ-gi 크기. ② (*book*) kwŏn 권.

voluntary *adj.* cha-bal-jŏk-in 자발적인.　　┌원하다.

volunteer *n.* chi-wŏn-ja 지원자. —*v.* chi-wŏn-ha-da 지

vomit *v.* (*spew*) t'o-ha-da 토하다, ke-u-da 게우다, nae-bbum-da 내뿜다. —*n.* ku-t'o 구토.

vote *n. & v.* t'u-p'yo(-ha-da) 투표(하다).

voter *n.* t'u-p'yo-ja 투표자, yu-gwŏn-ja 유권자.

vouch *v.* (*guarantee*) po-jŭng-ha-da 보증하다 ; (*assert*) tan-ŏn-ha-da 단언하다.

vow *n. & v.* maeng-se(-ha-da) 맹세(하다).

vowel *n.* mo-ŭm 모음 ; mo-ŭm-ja 모음자.

voyage *n. & v.* hang-hae(-ha-da) 항해(하다).

vulgar *adj.* (*base*) pi-ch'ŏn-han 비천한, chŏ-sok-han 저속한. —*n.* (*common people*) sŏ-min 서민.

vulgarity *n.* ya-bi 야비 ; ch'ŏn-bak 천박.

vulture *n.* tok-su-ri 독수리 ; (*a greedy person*) yok-sim-jang-i 욕심장이.

—≪ W ≫—

waddle *v.* a-jang-a-jang kŏt-da 아장아장 걷다.

wade *v.* mul-sok-ŭl kŏ-rŏ-ga-da 물속을 걸어가다.

waft *v.* ttŏ-dol-da 떠돌다 ; pu-dong-ha-da 부동(浮動)하다.

wag *v.* hŭn-dŭl-da 흔들다.

wage *n.* im-gŭm 임금(賃金) : *a* ~ *raise* im-gŭm in-sang 임금 인상. —*v.* (*carry on*) haeng-ha-da 행하다.

wageworking *n.* im-gŭm no-dong 임금 노동.

wag(g)on *n.* su-re 수레, chim-ma-ch'a 짐마차.

wag(g)oner *n.* ma-ch'a-gun 마차군. 「부짖음.

wail *v.* t'ong-gok-ha-da 통곡하다. —*n.* ul-bu-ji-jŭm 울

waist *n.* hŏ-ri 허리, yo-bu 요부(腰部).

waistcoat *n.* cho-ggi 조끼. 「da 시중들다.

wait *v.* ① ki-da-ri-da 기다리다. ② (*serve*) si-jung-dŭl-

waiter *n.* kŭp-sa 급사, we-i-t'ŏ 웨이터.

waiting room tae-hap-sil 대합실.

waitress *n.* yŏ-gŭp 여급, we-i-t'ŭ-re-sŭ 웨이트레스.

wake *v.* kkae-da 깨다, kkae-u-da 깨우다.

waken *v.* kkae-u-da 깨우다, i-rŭ-k'i-da 일으키다.

walk *n.* kŏ-rŭm 걸음, po-haeng 보행 ; (*stroll*) san-ch'aek 산책 ; (*path*) po-do 보도. —*v.* kŏ-rŏ-ga-da 걸어가다.

wall *n.* pyŏk 벽, tam 담 ; (*pl.*) sŏng-byŏk 성벽.

wallet *n.* chi-gap 지갑, ton-ju-mŏ-ni 돈주머니.

walnut *n.* ho-du 호두, ho-du-na-mu 호두나무.

wan *adj.* ch'ang-baek-han 창백한 ; na-yak-han 나약한.

wand *n.* mak-dae-gi 막대기, chi-p'ang-i 지팡이.

wander *v.* he-mae-da 헤매다, kil-ŭl il-t'a 길을 잃다.

wane *v.* i-ul-da 이울다, soe-t'oe-ha-da 쇠퇴하다. —*n.* i-ji-rŏ-jim 이지러짐, soe-t'oe 쇠퇴.

want *n.* p'i-ryo 필요 ; (*lack*) kyŏl-p'ip 결핍. —*v.* ① wŏn-ha-da 원하다. ② (*need*) p'i-ryo-ha-da 필요하다.

wanton *adj.* pyŏn-dŏk-sŭ-rŏ-un 변덕스러운 ; (*lewd*) ŭm-t'ang-han 음탕한. —*n.* pa-ram-dung-i 바람둥이.

war *n.* chŏn-jaeng 전쟁, t'u-jaeng 투쟁. 「저귐.

warble *v.* chi-jŏ-gwi-da 지저귀다. —*n.* chi-jŏ-gwim 지

ward *n.* ① (*in hosp.*) pyŏng-sil 병실, pyŏng-dong 병동. ② (*guard*) kam-si 감시, kam-dok 감독.

wardrobe *n.* ot-jang 옷장, yang-bok-jang 양복장.

ware *n.* ① (*pl.*) sang-p'um 상품. ② ki-mul 기물: *silver* ~ ŭn-je-p'um 은제품. 「도매 상점.

warehouse *n.* ① ch'ang-go 창고. ② to-mae sang-jŏm

warfare *n.* chŏn-jaeng 전쟁, chŏn-t'u 전투.

warm *adj.* tta-ddŭt-han 따뜻한, tŏ-un 더운. —*v.* tta-ddŭt-ha-ge ha-da 따뜻하게 하다, te-u-da 데우다.

warm-hearted *adj.* tong-jŏng-sim-man-ŭn 동정심많은, ch'in-jŏl-han 친절한.

warmth *n.* tta-ddŭt-ham 따뜻함, on-gi 온기 (溫氣).

warn *v.* kyŏng-go-ha-da 경고하다, t'a-i-rŭ-da 타이르다.

warning *n.* kyŏng-go 경고, hun-gye 훈계.

warp *v.* hwi-da 휘다, twi-t'ŭl-da 뒤틀다.

warrant *n. & v.* po-jŭng(-ha-da) 보증(하다).

warrant officer (*mil.*) chun-wi 준위 (准尉).

warrior *n.* kun-in 군인, chŏn-sa 전사, yong-sa 용사.

warship *n.* kun-ham 군함.

wary *adj.* cho-sim-sŏng-it-nŭn 조심성있는, (*cautious*) sin-jung-han 신중한.

wash *n.* se-t'ak 세탁. —*v.* ① (*self*) ssit-da 씻다. ② (*clothes*) se-t'ak-ha-da 세탁하다.

washerman *n.* se-t'ak-ŏp-ja 세탁업자.

washerwoman *n.* se-t'ak-bu 세탁부.

washing *n.* ppal-rae·빨래·~ *machine* se-t'ak-gi 세탁기.

washroom *n.* yok-sil 욕실(浴室), pyŏn-so 변소.

washstand *n.* se-myŏn-dae 세면대.

wasp *n.* mal-bŏl 말벌, na-na-ni-bŏl 나나니벌.

waste *adj.* hwang-p'ye-han 황폐한. —*v.* nang-bi-ha-da 낭비하다.—*n.* ① nang-bi 낭비. ② hwang-mu-ji 황무지.

watch *n.* ① hoe-jung-si-gye 회중시계. ② (*look out*) kam-si 감시. —*v.* chi-k'yŏ-bo-da 지켜보다.

watchful *adj.* cho-sim-ha-nŭn 조심하는.

watchman *n.* kam-si-in 감시인, p'a-su-gun 파수군.

watchtower *n.* mang-ru 망루, kam-si-t'ap 감시탑.

water *n.* mul 물. —*v.* kŭp-su-ha-da 급수하다.

water colo(u)r su-ch'ae-hwa 수채화.

water dropper (*for inkstone*) yŏn-jŏk 연적(硯滴).

waterfall *n.* p'ok-p'o 폭포.

water gate su-mun 수문.

water lily su-ryŏn 수련.

watermelon *n.* su-bak 수박.

[yŏn-jŏk]

water mill mul-bang-a 물방아, mul-re-bang-a 물레방아.   「pang-su-bok 방수복.

waterproof *adj.* pang-su-ŭi 방수의. —*n.* (*clothes*)

wave *n.* mul-gyŏl 물결, p'a-do 파도. —*v.* mul-gyŏl-ch'i-da 물결치다 p'ŏl-rŏk-i-da 펄럭이다.

wax *n.* mil 밀, mil-ch'o 밀초. 「tom) sŭp-gwan 습관.

way *n.* ① kil 길. ② (*method*) pang-bŏp 방법. ③ (*cus-*

waylay v. sum-ŏ ki-da-ri-da 숨어 기다리다, cham-bok-ha-da 잠복하다 ; yo-gyŏk-ha-da 요격하다.

wayside n. kil-ga 길가, no-byŏn 노변. —*adj.* kil-ga-ŭi 길가의, no-byŏn-ŭi 노변의.

wayward *adj.* pyŏn-dŏk-sŭ-rŏ-un 변덕스러운 ; sun-jong-ch'i an-nŭn 순종치 않는.

we *pron.* u-ri-ga〔nŭn〕 우리가〔는〕.

weak *adj.* ka-nyal-p'ŭn 가냘픈, yak-han 약한.

weaken v. yak-ha-ge ha-da 약하게 하다.

weakness n. hŏ-yak 허약, pak-yak 박약.

wealth n. chae-san 재산 ; pu 부(富) ; p'ung-jok 풍족.

weathy *adj.* chae-san-i man-ŭn 재산이 많은, pu-yu-han 부유한 : *a ~ person* pu-ja 부자. 「키다.

wean v. chŏ-jul tte-da 젖을 떼다, i-yu-si-k'i-da 이유시

weapon n. mu-gi 무기, pyŏng-gi 병기.

wear v. ① (*clothes*) ip-da 입다. ② hae-ŏ-ji-da 해어지다.

weary *adj.* chi-ch'in 지친, sil-jŭng-i nan 싫증이 난. —v. chi-ch'i-da 지치다, sil-jŭng-na-da 싫증나다.

weasel n. chok-je-bi 족제비.

weather n. nal-ssi 날씨, il-gi 일기.

weather-beaten *adj.* p'ung-u-e si-dal-rin 풍우에 시달린.

weathercock n. ① pa-ram-gae-bi 바람개비, p'ung-hyang-gye 풍향계. ② pyŏn-dŏk-jang-i 변덕장이.

weather forecast il-gi ye-bo 일기 예보.

weave v. ① jja-da 짜다, ttŭ-da 뜨다. ② yŏk-da 엮다.

web n. ① kŏ-mi-jul 거미줄. ② p'i-ryuk 피륙.

wed v. kyŏl-hon-ha-da 결혼하다.

wedding n. kyŏl-hon 결혼, hol-lye 혼례.

wedding card kyŏl-hon ch'ŏng-ch'ŏp-jang 결혼 청첩장.

wedding ring kyŏl-hon-ban-ji 결혼반지.

wedge n. ① sswae-gi 쐐기. ② hwe-bang 훼방.

Wednesday n. su-yo-il 수요일.

weed *n*. chap-ch'o 잡초. —*v*. p'ul-ŭl ppop-da 풀을 뽑다.

week *n*. chu 주(週), chu-gan 주간.

weekend *n*. chu-mal 주말. 「gan-ji 주간지.

weekly *adv. & adj*. mae-ju-(ŭi) 매주(의). —*n*. chu-

weep *v*. ul-da 울다, sŭl-p'ŏ-ha-da 슬퍼하다.

weeping willow su-yang-bŏ-dŭl 수양버들.

weigh *v*. ① mu-ge-rŭl tal-da 무게를 달다. ② (*consider*) chung-yo-si-ha-da 중요시하다.

weight *n*. ① mu-ge 무게. ② chung-yo-sŏng 중요성.

weir *n*. ① tuk 둑 ; taem 댐. ② ŏ-sal 어살.

weird *n*. (*fate*) un-myŏng 운명 ; (*omen*) chŏn-jo 전조. —*adj*. mu-si-mu-si-han 무시무시한.

welcome *n. & v*. hwan-yŏng(-ha-da) 환영(하다).

weld *v*. yong-jŏp-ha-da 용접하다.

welfare *n*. hu-saeng 후생, pok-ji 복지.

well *n*. u-mul 우물. —*adv*. hul-ryung-hi 훌륭히. —*v*. so-sa-na-o-da 솟아나오다.

well-being *n*. an-nyŏng 안녕, pok-ji 복지, pok-ri 복리.

well-born *adj*. chip-an-i cho-ŭn 집안이 좋은, myŏng-mun t'ae-saeng-ŭi 명문 태생의.

well-bred *adj* pon-de it-ge cha-ran 본데 있게 자란 ; ye-jŏl-ba-rŭn 예절바른.

well-disposed *adj*. ma-ŭm-ssi ko-un 마음씨 고운.

wellknown *adj*. yu-myŏng-han 유명한.

west *n*. sŏ-jjok 서쪽, sŏ-bu 서부. —*adj*. sŏ-jjok-ŭi 서쪽의. —*adv*. sŏ-jjok-ŭ-ro 서쪽으로.

western *adj*. sŏ-jjok-ŭi 서쪽의, sŏ-yang-ŭi 서양의.

westward *adj. & adv*. sŏ-bang-ŭi[ŭ-ro] 서방의[으로].

wet *adj*. chŏ-jŭn 젖은. —*v*. chŏk-si-da 적시다.

whale *n*. ko-rae 고래.

wharf *n*. pu-du 부두, (*quay*) sŏn-ch'ang 선창.

what *adj*. ŏ-ddŏn 어떤. —*pron*. mu-ŏt 무엇.

whatever *adj.* ŏ-nŭ …i-ra-do 어느 …이라도. —*pron.* ŏ-nŭ kŏ-si-ra-do 어느 것이라도.

wheat *n.* mil 밀, so-maek 소맥.

wheel *n.* pa-k'wi 바퀴. ch'a-ryun 차륜.

wheeze *v.* ssi-gŭn-gŏ-ri-da 씨근거리다.

when *adv.* ŏn-je 언제, …hal ttae …할 때. —*conj.* ttae-e 때에. —*n.* (*time*) ttae 때 ; kyong-u 경우.

whence *adv.* ŏ-di-e-sŏ 어디에서, ŏ-jjae-sŏ 어째서.

whenever *adv.* ŏn-je-na 언제나.

where *adv.* ŏ-di-sŏ 어디서, ŏ-di-e 어디에, ŏ-di-ro 어디로.

whereabouts *adv.* ŏ-di-jjŭm-e 어디쯤에. —*n.* haeng-bang 행방. ⌐

wherever *adv.* ŏ-di-dŭn-ji 어디든지. ⌐bang 행방.

whether *conj.* …in-ji ŏ-ddŏn-ji …인지 어떤지.

whetstone *n.* (*grindstone*) sut-dol 숫돌.

which *adj.* & *pron.* ŏ-nŭ (kŏt) 어느 (것).

whichever *adj.* ŏ-nŭ kŏ-si-dŭn-ji 어느 것이든지.

whiffle *v.* na-p'ul-gŏ-ri-da 나풀거리다.

while *n.* tong-an 동안, cham-si tong-an 잠시 동안. —*conj.* …ha-nŭn tong-an-e …하는 동안에.

whim *n.* (*caprice*) pyŏn-dŏk 변덕.

whimper *v.* hŭ-nŭ-ggyŏ ul-da 흐느껴 울다. ⌐별난.

whimsical *adj.* pyŏn-dŏk-sŭ-rŏ-un 변덕스러운, pyŏl-nan

whine *v.* ① sŭl-p'i ul-da 슬피 울다. ② (*dog*) kking-gging-gŏ-ri-da 낑낑거리다.

whinny *v.* (*neigh*) (mal-i) ul-da (말이) 울다.

whip *n.* ch'ae-jjik 채찍. —*v.* mae-jil-ha-da 매질하다.

whirl *v.* ping-bing tol-da 빙빙 돌다. —*n.* hoe-jŏn 회전.

whirlpool *n.* so-yong-do-ri 소용돌이.

whirlwind *n.* hoe-o-ri-ba-ram 회오리바람.

whiskers *n.* ① ku-re-na-rut 구레나룻. ② su-yŏm 수염.

whisper *n.* sok-sak-im 속삭임, kwi-et-mal 귀엣말. —*v.* sok-sak-i-da 속삭이다.

whistle *n.* ho-gak 호각 ; hwi-p'a-ram 휘파람, hwi-sŭl 휘슬. —*v.* (*mouth*) hwi-p'a-ram-ŭl pul-da 휘파람을 불다 ; ki-jŏk-ŭl ul-ri-da 기적을 울리다.

white *adj.* hŭin 흰, (*pale*) ch'ang-baek-han 창백한. —*n.* hŭin-saek 흰색 ; hŭin-ot 흰옷.

who *pron.* nu-gu 누구, ŏ-ddŏn sa-ram 어떤 사람.

whoever *pron.* nu-gu-dŭn-ji 누구든지.

whole *n.* & *adj.* chŏn-ch'e(-ŭi) 전체(의).

wholesale *adj.* to-mae-ha-nŭn 도매하는. —*n.* to-mae 「도매.

wholesome *adj.* (*healthy*) kŏn-gang-e cho-ŭn 건강에 좋은, kŏn-jŏn-han 건전한.

wholly *adv.* chŏn-hyŏ 전혀, wan-jŏn-hi 완전히.

whom *pron.* nu-gu-rŭl 누구를 : *for* ~? nu-gu-rŭl wi-ha-yŏ 누구를 위하여? / *from* ~? nu-gu-e-ge-sŏ 누구에게서? /*to* ~? nu-gu-e-ge 누구에게?

whooping cough paek-il-hae 백일해.

whose *pron.* nu-gu-ŭi 누구의, ŏ-nŭ pun-ŭi 어느 분의.

why *adv.* wae 왜. —*int.* ŏ-ma 어마.

wick *n.* (*candle or oil lamp*) sim-ji 심지.

wicked *adj.* na-bbŭn 나쁜, (*evil*) sa-ak-han 사악한.

wickedness *n.* sa-ak 사악, sim-sul 심술.

wicket *n.* chak-ŭn mun 작은 문, jjok-mun 쪽문.

wide *adj.* nŏl-bŭn 넓은. —*adv.* nŏl-gge 넓게.

widen *v.* nŏl-p'i-da 넓히다. 「리 퍼진.

widespread *adj.* po-gŭp-doen 보급된, nŏl-ri p'ŏ-jin 널

widow *n.* kwa-bu 과부, mi-mang-in 미망인.

widower *n.* ho-ra-bi 홀아비.

width *n.* nŏl-bi 넓이, p'ok 폭(幅).

wield *v.* hwi-du-rŭ-da 휘두르다, chi-bae-ha-da 지배하다.

wife *n.* ① (*own*) a-nae 아내, ma-nu-ra 마누라, chip-sa-ram 집사람. ② (*another's*) pu-in 부인.

wig *n.* ka-bal 가발(假髮).

wild *adj.* ① ya-saeng-ŭi 야생의. ② (*savage*) mi-gae-han 미개한. ③ (*furious*) nan-p'ok-han 난폭한. —*n.* (*desert*) hwang-mu-ji 황무지.

wild boar san-dwae-ji 산돼지, met-dwae-ji 멧돼지.

wildcat *n.* sal-k'waeng-i 삵쾡이.

wilderness *n.* hwang-mu-ji 황무지, kwang-ya 광야.

wile *n.* kan-gye 간계(奸計).

wilful *adj.* ko-ŭi-ŭi 고의의, kye-hoek-jŏk-in 계획적인.

will *aux. v.* ⋯hal kŏ-si-da ⋯할 것이다, ⋯hal chak-jŏng-i-da ⋯할 작정이다. —*n.* ① ŭi-sa 의사, ŭi-ji 의지. ② (*testament*) yu-ŏn(-jang) 유언(장). —*v.* (*bequeath*) yu-ŏn-ha-da 유언하다.

willing *adj.* ki-ggŏ-i ⋯ha-nŭn 기꺼이 ⋯하는.

willingly *adv.* ki-ggŏ-i 기꺼이, chŭl-gŏ-i 즐거이.

willow *n.* pŏ-dŭl 버들.

wilt *v.* si-dŭl-da 시들다, i-ul-da 이울다.

wily *adj.* kyo-hwal-han 교활한.

win *v.* (*races*) i-gi-da 이기다, (*gain*) ŏt-da 얻다.

wince *v.* chu-ch'um-ha-da 주춤하다, chil-ri-da 질리다.

wind *n.* pa-ram 바람. —*v.* kam-da 감다.

winding *adj.* kku-bul-ggu-bul-han 구불구불한, kup-i-ch'i-nŭn 굽이치는. —*n.* kul-gok 굴곡.

windmill *n.* p'ung-ch'a 풍차(風車).

window *n.* ch'ang 창, ch'ang-mun 창문.

windowpane *n.* ch'ang-yu-ri 창유리.

windpipe *n.* ki-gwan-ji 기관지, sum-t'ong 숨통.

windshield *n.* (*motorcar*) pang-p'ung yu-ri 방풍 유리.

windy *adj.* pa-ram-bu-nŭn 바람부는 : ～ *weather* pa-ram-bu-nŭn nal-ssi 바람부는 날씨.

wine *n.* sul 술, (*from grapes*) p'o-do-ju 포도주.

wing *n.* (*of bird*) nal-gae 날개 ; (*of political party*) ik 익(翼) : *the left* ～ chwa-ik 좌익.

wink *n.* nun-ŭl kkam-bak-gŏ-rim 눈을 깜박거림. —*v.* kkam-bak-gŏ-ri-da 깜박거리다, nun-jit-ha-da 눈짓하다.

winner *n.* sŭng-ri-ja 승리자.

winnow *v.* k'i-jil-ha-da 키질하다.

winter *n.* kyŏ-ul 겨울, tong-gye 동계(冬季).

wipe *v.* ssi-sŏ-nae-da 씻어내다, tak-da 닦다.

wire *n.* ① ch'ŏl-sa 철사. ② (*teleg.*) chŏn-bo 전보. —*v.* chŏn-bo-rŭl ch'i-da 전보를 치다.

wireless *n.* & *adj.* mu-sŏn chŏn-sin(-ŭi) 무선 전신의.

wisdom *n.* chi-hye 지혜 ; (*learning*) chi-sik 지식.

wise *adj.* hyŏn-myŏng-han 현명한, ŏ-jin 어진.

wisecrack *n.* ik-sal 익살, u-sŭ-gaet-so-ri 우스갯소리.

wise guy kŏn-bang-jin sa-na-i 건방진 사나이.

wish *n.* so-wŏn 소원, so-mang 소망. —*v.* (*desire*) hŭi-mang-ha-da 희망하다, pa-ra-da 바라다.

wisteria *n.* tŭng-na-mu 등나무.

wistful *adj.* t'am-nae-nŭn tŭt-han 탐내는 듯한 ; saeng-gak-e cham-gi-nŭn 생각에 잠기는.

wit *n.* ki-ji 기지, chae-ch'i 재치 ; chae-sa 재사(才士).

witch *n.* mu-dang 무당, ma-sul-jang-i 마술쟁이.

witchcraft *n.* ma-bŏp 마법, ma-sul 마술.

with *prep.* …wa ham-gge …와 함께, …ro …로.

withdraw *v.* mul-rŏ-na-da 물러나다, ch'ŏl-su-ha-da 철수하다, (*mil.*) ch'ŏl-byŏng-ha-da 철병하다.

wither *v.* si-dŭl-da 시들다, i-ul-da 이울다.

withhold *v.* po-ryu-ha-da 보류하다. 「—*n.* nae-bu 내부.

within *adv.* an-e 안에, sok-e 속에 ; chip an-e 집 안에.

without *prep.* ŏp-si 없이, …ŭi pa-gge-sŏ …의 밖에서. —*adv.* pa-ggŭn 밖은. —*n.* oe-bu 외부.

withstand *v.* chŏ-hang-ha-da 저항하다, (*endure*) kyŏn-di-ŏ-nae-da 견디어내다.

witness *n.* chŭng-gŏ 증거 ; (*person*) chŭng-in 증인.

—*v.* mok-gyŏk-ha-da 목격하다, ip-jŭng-ha-da 입증하다.

witty *adj.* chae-ch'i-it-nŭn 제치있는.

wizard *n.* yo-sul-jang-i 요술장이, ma-bŏp-sa 마법사.

woe *n.* ① (*grief*) pi-t'ong 비통. ② (*calamity*) ; chae-lang 재앙.

wolf *n.* i-ri 이리, nŭk-dae 늑대.

woman *n.* yŏ-ja 여자, pu-in 부인. 「(닭게).

womanly *adj. & adv.* yŏ-sŏng-da-un〔dap-ge〕 여성다운

womb *n.* cha-gung 자궁, t'ae-nae 태내(胎內).

wonder *n.* nol-ra-um 놀라움, kyŏng-i 경이. —*v.* kyŏng-t'an-ha-da 경탄하다.

wonderful *adj.* nol-ral-man-han 놀랄만한 ; (*remarkable*) kŭn-sa-han 근사한, hul-ryung-han 훌륭한.

wondrous *adj.* nol-ral-man-han 놀랄만한 ; pul-ga-sa-ŭi-han 불가사의한.

woo *v.* ku-ae-ha-da 구애하다, ku-hon-ha-da 구혼하다.

wood *n.* sup 숲 ; na-mu 나무, (*timber*) mok-jae 목재.

woodcutter *n.* na-mut-gun 나뭇군.

wooden *adj.* na-mu-ŭi 나무의, mok-jae-ŭi 목재의.

woodland *n.* sam-rim-ji-dae 삼림지대.

woodpecker *n.* (*bird*) ttak-da-gu-ri 딱다구리.

wool *n.* yang-t'ŏl 양털, yang-mo 양모.

woollen *adj.* yang-mo-ŭi 양모의, mo-jik-ŭi 모직의.

woozy *adj.* mŏng-ch'ŏng-han 멍청한. 「sok 약속.

word *n.* ① mal 말, nat-mal 낱말. ② (*promise*) yak-

work *n.* ① (*labor*) il 일, no-dong 노동. ② che-jak-mul 제작물. ③ (*factory*) kong-jang 공장. —*v.* il-ha-da 일하다, no-dong-ha-da 노동하다.

workaday *adj.* p'yŏng-il-ŭi 평일(平日)의.

worker *n.* il-gun 일군, no-mu-ja 노무자.

workman *n.* no-dong-ja 노동자, chik-gong 직공.

workmanship *n.* som-ssi 솜씨, ki-ryang 기량.

workshop *n.* kong-jang 공장 ; yŏn-gu-hoe 연구회.

world *n.* ① (*phys.*) se-gye 세계. ② (*abs.*) se-sang 세 상 ; se-in 세인(世人). ③ (*sphere*) pun-ya 분야.

worldly *adj.* se-sok-jŏk-in 세속적인.

world-wide *adj.* se-gye-jŏk-in 세계적인.

worm *n.* pŏl-re 벌레 : *earth* ～ chi-rŏng-i 지렁이.

worn-out *adj.* nal-ga-bba-jin 낡아빠진.

worry *v.* ① koe-rop-hi-da 괴롭히다. ② kŏk-jŏng-ha-da 걱정하다. —*n.* kŏk-jŏng 걱정. 「신.

worrying *adj.* kwi-ch'an-ŭn 귀찮은, sŏng-ga-sin 성가

worse *adj.* po-da na-bbŭn 보다 나쁜, ak-hwa-doen 악 화된. —*adv.* po-da na-bbŭ-ge 보다 나쁘게.

worship *n.* sung-bae 숭배 ; chon-gyŏng 존경, ye-bae 예배. —*v.* ye-bae-ha-da 예배하다 ; pil-da 빌다 ; (*others*) sung-bae-ha-da 숭배하다.

worship(p)er *n.* ye-bae-ja 예배자, sung-bae-ja 숭배자.

worst *adj.* ka-jang na-bbŭn 가장 나쁜.

worsted *n.* tŏl-sil 털실. so-mo-sa 소모사.

worth *n. & adj.* ka-ch'i(-it-nŭn) 가치(있는).

worthless *adj.* ka-ch'i-ŏp-nŭn 가치없는, mu-ik-han 무

worthy *adj.* ka-ch'i-it-nŭn 가치있는. 「익한.

wound *n. & v.* pu-sang(-ha-da) 부상(하다).

wrangle *n.* ŏn-jaeng 언쟁. —*v.* mal-da-t'um-ha-da 말 다툼하다, ta-t'u-da 다투다.

wrap *v.* ssa-da 싸다, tu-rŭ-da 두르다, mal-da 말다.

wrath *n.* (*rage*) kyŏk-bun 격분, pun-no 분노.

wreath *n.* hwa-hwan 화환, hwa-gwan 화관.

wreck *n.* ① (*shipwreck*) nan-p'a-sŏn 난파선. ② (*ruin*) p'a-goe 파괴. —*v.* ① nan-p'a-ha-da 난파하다. ② (*destroy*) p'a-goe-ha-da 파괴하다.

wren *n.* kul-dduk-sae 굴뚝새.

wrench *n.* su-p'ae-nŏ 스패너, ren-ch'i 렌치. —*v.* pi-t'ŭl-da 비틀다, pi-ggo-da 비꼬다.

wrest *v.* ① pi-t'ŭl-da 비틀다. ② ppae-at-da 빼앗다.

wrestle *v.* ssi-rŭm-ha-da 씨름하다. —*n.* ssi-rŭm 씨름.

wrestling *n.* re-sŭl-ring 레슬링, ssi-rŭm 씨름.

wretch *n.* pul-ssang-han sa-ram 불쌍한 사람 ; (*scoundrel*) pi-yŏl-han in-gan 비열한 인간.

wretched *adj.* pul-ssang-han 불쌍한.

wriggle *v.* kkum-t'ŭl-gŏ-ri-da 꿈틀거리다. —*n.* kkum-t'ŭl-gŏ-rim 꿈틀거림, mom-bu-rim 몸부림.

wring *v.* jja-nae-da 짜내다 ; pi-t'ŭl-da 비틀다.

wrinkl e*n.* chu-rŭm 주름, ku-gim-sal 구김살. —*v.* chu-rŭm-jap-da 주름잡다.

wrist *n.* son-mok 손목, p'al-mok 팔목.

wristwatch *n.* p'al-mok si-gye 팔목 시계.

writ *n.* yŏng-jang 영장(令狀) ; (*document*) sŏ-ryu 서류 : *a* ~ *of summon* so-hwan-jang 소환장.

write *v.* ssŭ-da 쓰다, ki-rok-ha-da 기록하다.

writer *n.* chŏ-ja 저자, chak-ga 작가, mun-p'il-ga 문필가.

writhe *v.* mom-bu-rim-ch'i-da 몸부림치다.

writings *n.* chŏ-jak 저작 ; (*lit. prod.*) chak-p'um 작품.

wrong *adj.* na-bbŭn 나쁜, t'ŭl-rin 틀린. —*adv.* na-bbŭ-ge 나쁘게. —*n.* pu-dang 부당, chal-mot 잘못. —*v.* pu-jŏng-ŭl chŏ-ji-rŭ-da 부정을 저지르다.

wrongdoer *n.* pi-haeng-ja 비행자(非行者).

wry *adj.* twi-t'ŭl-rin 뒤틀린 ; jji-p'u-rin 찌푸린.

—❈❈❈ **X** ❈❈❈—

Xmas *n.* (*Christmas*) k'ŭ-ri-sŭ-ma-sŭ 크리스마스, sŏng-t'an-jŏl 성탄절.

x-ray *n.* roen-t'ŭ-gen sŏn 뢴트겐 선, ek-sŭ-re-i 엑스레이.

xylophone *n.* mok-gŭm 목금(木琴), sil-ro-p'on 실로폰.

──◄ **Y** ►──

yacht *n.* yo-t'ŭ 요트, k'wae-sok-jŏng 쾌속정.

yachtsman *n.* yo-t'ŭ sŏn-su 요트 선수.

Yalu *the* ~ ap-rok-gang 압록강(鴨綠江).

yam *n.* (*sweet potato*) ko-gu-ma 고구마.

yank *v.* hwak chap-a-dang-gi-da 확 잡아당기다.

yard *n.* ① ma-dang 마당. ② (*measure*) ya-a-dŭ 야아드.

yardstick *n.* ya-a-dŭ cha 야아드 자(尺).

yarn *n.* ① pang-sa 방사(紡糸) : *cotton* ~ myŏn-sa 면사/*woolen* ~ t'ŏl-sil 털실. ② (*tale*) i-ya-gi 이야기.

yawn *n. & v.* ha-p'um(-ha-da) 하품(하다).

yea *int.* ye 예, (*yes*) kŭ-rŏ-so 그렇소.

year *n.* ① hae 해. ② (*in comp.*) nyŏn 년 : *last* ~ chak-nyŏn 작년/*next* ~ nae-nyŏn 내년/*this* ~ kŭm-nyŏn 금년. ③ (*pl.*) yŏn-ryŏng 연령.

yearbook *n.* yŏn-gam 연감, yŏn-bo 연보.

yearlong *adj.* il-nyŏn tong-an-ŭi 1년 동안의.

yearly *adj.* hae-ma-da-ŭi 해마다의. —*adv.* hae-ma-da 해마다. —*n.* yŏn-gan-ji 연간지(年刊誌). 「동경하다.

yearn *v.* kŭ-ri-wŏ-ha-da 그리워하다, tong-gyŏng-ha-da

yearning *n.* tong-gyŏng 동경, yŏl-mang 열망. —*adj.* tong-gyŏng〔yŏl-mang〕-ha-nŭn 동경〔열망〕하는.

yeast *n.* nu-ruk 누룩, hyo-mo 효모(酵母).

yell *n.* ko-ham 고함. —*v.* oe-ch'i-da 외치다.

yellow *adj.* no-ran 노란. —*n.* hwang-saek 황색.

yelp *v.* nal-k'a-rop-ge oe-ch'i-da 날카롭게 외치다 ; chi-jŏ-dae-da 짖어대다. —*n.* chit-nŭn so-ri 짖는 소리.

yes *adv.* ye 예, kŭ-rŏ-sŭp-ni-da 그렇습니다.

yes man kup-sil-dae-nŭn sa-ram 굽실대는 사람. 「저께.

yesterday *n.* ŏ-je 어제 : *the day before* ~ kŭ-jŏ-gge 그

yet *adv.* a-jik 아직, yŏ-jŏn-hi 여전히. —*conj.* kŭ-rŏm-e-do pul-gu-ha-go 그럼에도 불구하고.

yield *v.* ① (*produce*) san-ch'ul-ha-da 산출하다. ② (*surrender*) kul-bok-ha-da 굴복하다. —*n.* (*crop*) su-hwak 수확.

YMCA *n.* ki-dok-gyo ch'ŏng-nyŏn-hoe 기독교 청년회.

yoke *n.* ① mŏng-e 멍에. ② (*clothes*) yo-u-k'ŭ 요우크. —*v.* mŏng-e-rŭl me-u-da 멍에를 메우다.

yolk *n.* no-rŭn-ja-wi 노른자위.

yonder *adj.* chŏ-jjok-ŭi 저쪽의. —*adv.* chŏ-jjok-e 저쪽에.

you *pron.* tang-sin(-dŭl) 당신(들), (*to inf.*) cha-ne (-dŭl) 자네(들), nŏ-hŭi(-dŭl) 너희(들).

young *adj.* chŏl-mŭn 젊은, ŏ-rin 어린.

youngster *n.* a-i 아이, chŏl-mŭn-i 젊은이.

your *pron.* tang-sin(-dŭl)-ŭi 당신(들)의, (*to inf.*) cha-ne(-dŭl)-ŭi 자네(들)의, nŏ(-hŭi-dŭl)-ŭi 너(희들)의.

yours *pron.* tang-sin(-dŭl)-ŭi kŏt 당신(들)의 것, (*to inf.*) cha-ne(-dŭl)-ŭi kŏt 자네(들)의 것, nŏ-hŭi(-dŭl)-ŭi kŏt 너희(들)의 것.

yourself *pron.* tang-sin cha-sin 당신 자신.

youth *n.* ch'ŏng-ch'un 청춘, chŏl-mŭm 젊음.

youthful *adj.* chŏl-mŭn 젊은 ; pal-ral-han 발랄한.

yow *int.* a-yu 아유, e-gŭ-mŏ-ni 에그머니 .

yule *n.* k'ŭ-ri-sŭ-ma-sŭ kye-jŏl 크리스마스 계절.

YWCA *n.* ki-dok-gyo yŏ-ja ch'ŏng-nyŏn-hoe 기독교 여자 청년회.

---◀━ **Z** ▶━---

zeal *n.* yŏl-sim 열심, yŏl-jung 열중.

zealous *adj.* yŏl-jung-ha-nŭn 열중하는, yŏl-sŏng-jŏk-in

zealously *adv.* yŏl-sim-hi 열심히. 「열성적인.

zebra *n.* ŏl-ruk-mal 얼룩말.

zenith *n.* chŏng-jŏm 정점 ; chŏl-jŏng 절정.

zero *n.* yŏng 영(零), che-ro 제로.

zest *n.* (*relish*) p'ung-mi 풍미, mat 맛.

zigzag *adj.* chi-gŭ-jae-gŭ-ŭi 지그재그의, kal-ji-ja hyŏng-ŭi 갈지자 형의.

zinc *n.* a-yŏn 아연(亞鉛), ham-sŏk 함석.

Zionism *n.* si-on-ju-ŭi 시온주의.

zipper *n.* chi-p'ŏ 지퍼, (*slide fastener*) cha-k'ŭ 자크.

zodiac *n.* sip-i-gung 십이궁(十二宮), hwang-do-dae 황도 대(黃道帶).

zone *n.* chi-dae 지대, (*in comp.*) tae 대(帶) : *safety* ～ an-jŏn chi-dae 안전 지대.

zoo *n.* tong-mul-wŏn 동물원.

zoological *adj.* tong-mul-hak-ŭi 동물학의 : ～ *garden*(s) tong-mul-wŏn 동물원.

zoology *n.* tong-mul-hak 동물학.

zoom *n.* ① pung so-ri-nae-da 붕 소리내다. ② kŭp-sang-sŭng-ha-da 급상승하다.

zyme *n.* (*ferment*) hyo-so 효소.

HANGŬL WRITING MODELS

Perpendicular strokes are written from top to bottom; horizontals from left to right. (Read these charts left and down.)

Letter	Stroke order			Letter	Stroke order			Letter	Stroke order		
ㄱ k(g)	ㄱ			아 a	ㅇ / ㅇㅣ / 아			애 yae	ㅇ / ㅇㅣ / 아 / 야 / 애		
ㄴ n	ㄴ			야 ya	ㅇ / ㅇㅣ / 아 / 야			에 e	ㅇ / ㅇ- / 어 / 에		
ㄷ t(d)	⌐ / ㄷ			어 ŏ	ㅇ / ㅇ- / 어			예 ye	ㅇ / ㅇ- / 여 / 예		
ㄹ r(l)	ㄱ / ㄱ / ㄹ			여 yŏ	ㅇ / ㅇ- / ㅇ- / 여			외 oe	ㅇ / ㅇ / ㅗ / 외		
ㅁ m	ㅣ / ㄲ / ㅁ			오 o	ㅇ / ㅇ / ㅗ			위 wi	ㅇ / ㅇ / 우 / 위		
ㅂ p(b)	ㅣ / ㅐ / ㅂ / ㅂ			요 yo	ㅇ / ㅇ / ㅛ / 요			의 ŭi	ㅇ / ㅇ / 의		
ㅅ s	ノ / ㅅ			우 u	ㅇ / ㅇ / 우			와 wa	ㅇ / ㅇ / ㅗ / 외 / 와		
ㅇ -ng	ㅇ			유 yu	ㅇ / ㅇ / 우 / 유			워 wŏ	ㅇ / ㅇ / 우 / 우 / 워		
ㅈ ch(j)	ㄱ / ㅈ			으 ŭ	ㅇ / ㅇ			왜 wae	ㅇ / ㅇ / ㅗ / 외 / 와 / 왜		
ㅊ ch'	` / ㄱ / ㅊ			이 i	ㅇ / 이			웨 we	ㅇ / ㅇ / 우 / 우 / 워 / 웨		
ㅋ k'	ㄱ / ㅋ			애 ae	ㅇ / ㅇㅣ / 아 / 애						
ㅌ t'	ㅡ / =ㅌ / ㅌ										
ㅍ p'	ㅡ / ㅍ / ㅍ										
ㅎ h	` / ㅗ / ㅎ										
ㄲ kk(gg)	ㄱ / ㄲ										
ㄸ tt(dd)	ㄷㄷ / ㄸ										
ㅃ pp(bb)	ㅣ / ㅐ / ㅂ / ㅂ / ㅃ / ㅃ										
ㅆ ss	ノ / ㅅ / ㅆ / ㅆ										
ㅉ jj	ㄱ / ㅈ / ㅉ / ㅉ										